# CHILTON'S

# NISSAN / INFINITI
# REPAIR MANUAL
# 1988-1992

## Complete service information for all models—cars and light trucks

D0073655

| | |
|---|---|
| **Sr. Vice President** | Ronald A. Hoxter |
| **Publisher and Editor-In-Chief** | Kerry A. Freeman, S.A.E. |
| **Managing Editors** | Peter M. Conti, Jr. □ W. Calvin Settle, Jr., S.A.E. |
| **Assistant Managing Editor** | Nick D'Andrea |
| **Senior Editors** | Richard J. Rivele, S.A.E. □ Ron Webb |
| **Director of Manufacturing** | Mike D'Imperio |
| **Manager of Manufacturing** | John F. Butler |

**CHILTON** BOOK COMPANY

*ONE OF THE DIVERSIFIED PUBLISHING COMPANIES,
A PART OF CAPITAL CITIES/ABC, INC.*

Manufactured in USA
© 1992 Chilton Book Company
Chilton Way Radnor, Pa. 19089
ISBN 0–8019–8322–3
ISSN No. 1060–4413

1234567890    1098765432

PUBLIC LIBRARY
EAST ORANGE, NEW JERSEY

629
C538
NIS-I
cop.1

## SAFETY NOTICE

Proper service and repair procedures are vital to the safe, reliable operation of all motor vehicles, as well as the personal safety of those performing service or repairs. This manual outlines procedures for servicing and repairing vehicles using safe, effective methods. The procedures contain many NOTES and CAUTIONS which should be followed along with standard safety procedures to eliminate the possibility of personal injury or improper service which could damage the vehicle or compromise its safety.

It is important to note that repair procedures and techniques, tools and parts for servicing motor vehicles, as well as the skill and experience of the individual performing the work vary widely. It is not possible to anticipate all of the hazards that may result. Standard and accepted safety precautions and equipment should be used when handling toxic or flammable fluids and safety goggles or other protection should be used during cutting, grinding, chiseling, prying or any other process that can cause material removal or projectiles. Similar protection against the high voltages generated in all electronic ignition systems should be employed during service procedures.

Some procedures require the use of tools or test equipment specially designed for a specific purpose. Before substituting another tool or procedure, you must be completely satisfied that neither your personal safety, nor the performance of the vehicle will be endangered.

## PART NUMBERS

Part numbers listed in this reference are not recommendations by Chilton for any product by brand name. They are references that can be used with interchange manuals and aftermarket supplier catalogs to locate each brand supplier's discrete part number.

Although information in this manual is based on industry sources and is complete as possible at the time of publication, the possibility exists that some car manufacturers made later changes which could not be included here. While striving for total accuracy, Chilton Book Company cannot assume responsibility for any errors, changes or omissions that may occur in the compilation of this data.

No part of this publication may be reproduced, transmitted or stored in any form or by any means, electronic or mechanical, including photocopy, recording, or by information storage or retrieval system without prior written permission from the publisher.

19.95
11/15/95
RJ

# Contents

DA

# Nissan

### 200SX • 240SX • 300ZX • MAXIMA • PULSAR
### SENTRA • STANZA—ALL MODELS

# SERIAL NUMBER IDENTIFICATION

## Vehicle Identification Plate

The vehicle identification plate is attached to the hood ledge or the firewall. The VIN plate is mounted on the front of the left strut housing on the 1988 300ZX and on the radiator core on 1990–92 300ZX. The identification plate gives the vehicle type, model, engine displacement in cc, SAE horsepower rating, wheelbase, engine number and chassis number.

VIN location

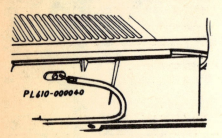

| DATSUN | TYPE | HLS30 |
|---|---|---|
| ENGINE CAPACITY | | 2,393 cc |
| MAX. HP at RPM | | 151 HP at 5,600 rpm |
| WHEEL BASE | | 2,305 mm |
| ENGINE NO. | | L24- ☐☐☐☐☐☐ |
| CAR NO. | | HLS30- ☐☐☐☐☐ |

**NISSAN MOTOR CO., LTD.**
YOKOHAMA JAPAN

Vehicle identification plate

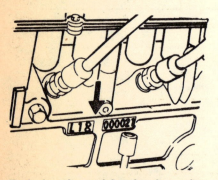

PL610-000040

Chassis number location

Typical engine serial and code number location

L18 000021

## Engine Number

On most vehicles, the engine number is stamped on the right side top edge of the cylinder block. On the 200SX, the number is stamped on the left rear edge of the block, next to the bell housing, looking from driver side seat. On 240SX, the number is stamped on the block just below the valve cover looking from the driver's seat. On the 300ZX, the number is stamped on the right rear edge of the right cylinder bank, looking from driver side seat. On

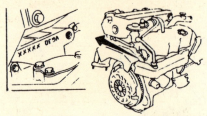

Typical engine serial and code number location

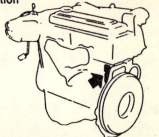

Engine indentification number location— most engines

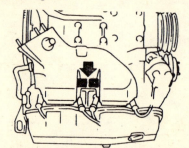

Engine serial number location on 240SX and 1990–92 Stanza

UNIT NUMBER

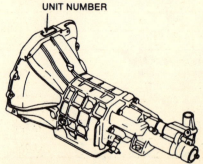

Location of the manual transmission serial number

the Maxima, the number can be found on the driver's side edge of the front cylinder bank, looking from driver's seat. On the 1990–92 Stanza, the number is stamped on the cylinder block just below the valve cover looking down at the front of the engine. The engine serial number is preceded by the engine model code.

## Chassis Number

The chassis number is on the firewall under the hood on all models. On the 240SX, the chassis number plate is affixed to the firewall next to the wiper

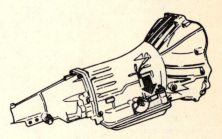

Location of the automatic transmission serial number

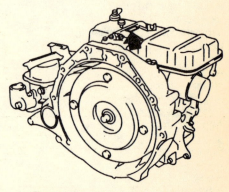

Transaxle serial number location automatic

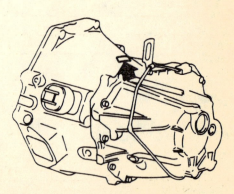

Transaxle serial number location manual

motor on the passenger's side of the engine compartment. All vehicles also have the chassis number (vehicle identification number) on a plate attached to the top of the instrument panel on the driver's side, visible through the windshield. The chassis serial number is preceded by the model designation. All models have an Emission Control information label affixed to the firewall or on the underside of the hood.

## Transmission/ Transaxle Number

The transmission/transaxle identification number tag is attached to the upper area or side area of the unit.

# SPECIFICATIONS

## ENGINE IDENTIFICATION

| Year | Model | Engine Displacement cu. in. (cc/liter) | Engine Series Identification | No. of Cylinders | Engine Type |
|---|---|---|---|---|---|
| 1988 | 200SX | 120.4 (1974/2.0) | CA20E | 4 | SOHC |
| | | 180.6 (2960/3.0) | VG30E | 6 | SOHC |
| | 300ZX | 180.6 (2960/3.0) | VG30E | 6 | SOHC |
| | | 180.6 (2960/3.0) | VG30ET (Turbo) | 6 | SOHC |
| | Maxima | 180.6 (2690/3.0) | VG30E | 6 | SOHC |
| | Pulsar | 97.4 (1597/1.6) | E16i | 4 | SOHC |
| | | 110.3 (1809/1.8) | CA18DE | 4 | DOHC |
| | Sentra | 97.4 (1597/1.6) | E16i | 4 | SOHC |
| | Stanza | 120.4 (1974/2.0) | CA20E | 4 | SOHC |
| 1989 | 240SX | 145.8 (2389/2.4) | KA24E | 4 | SOHC |
| | 300ZX | 180.6 (2960/3.0) | VG30E | 6 | SOHC |
| | | 180.6 (2960/3.0) | VG30ET (Turbo) | 6 | SOHC |
| | Maxima | 180.6 (2690/3.0) | VG30E | 6 | SOHC |
| | Pulsar | 97.5 (1597/1.6) | GA16i | 4 | SOHC |
| | | 110.3 (1809/1.8) | CA18DE | 4 | DOHC |
| | Sentra | 97.5 (1597/1.6) | GA16i | 4 | SOHC |
| | Stanza | 120.4 (1974/2.0) | CA20E | 4 | SOHC |
| 1990 | 240SX | 145.8 (2389/2.4) | KA24E | 4 | SOHC |
| | 300ZX | 180.6 (2960/3.0) | VG30DE | 6 | DOHC |
| | | 180.6 (2960/3.0) | VG30DETT (Twin Turbo) | 6 | DOHC |
| | Maxima | 180.6 (2960/3.0) | VG30E | 6 | SOHC |
| | Pulsar | 97.5 (1597/1.6) | GA16i | 4 | SOHC |
| | Sentra | 97.5 (1597/1.6) | GA16i | 4 | SOHC |
| | Stanza | 145.8 (2389/2.4) | KA24E | 4 | SOHC |
| 1991-92 | 240SX | 145.8 (2389/2.4) | KA24DE | 4 | DOHC |
| | 300ZX | 180.6 (2960/3.0) | VG30DE | 6 | DOHC |
| | | 180.6 (2960/3.0) | VG30DETT (Twin Turbo) | 6 | DOHC |
| | Maxima | 180.6 (2960/3.0) | VG30E | 6 | SOHC |
| | Sentra | 97.5 (1597/1.6) | GA16DE | 4 | DOHC |
| | | 122 (1998/2.0) | SR20DE | 4 | DOHC |
| | Stanza | 145.8 (2389/2.4) | KA24E | 4 | SOHC |

SOHC—Single overhead camshaft
DOHC—Double overhead camshaft

## GENERAL ENGINE SPECIFICATIONS

| Year | Model | Engine Displacement cu. in. (cc) | Fuel System Type | Net Horsepower @ rpm | Net Torque @ rpm (ft. lbs.) | Bore × Stroke (in.) | Compression Ratio | Oil Pressure @ rpm |
|------|-------|------|------|------|------|------|------|------|
| 1988 | 200SX | 120.4 (1974) | EFI | 99 @ 5200 | 116 @ 2800 | 3.33 × 3.46 | 8.5:1 | 60.5 @ 3200 |
| | | 180.6 (2960) | EFI | 165 @ 5200 | 168 @ 3600 | 3.43 × 3.27 | 9.0:1 | 59 @ 3200 |
| | 300ZX | 180.6 (2960) | EFI | 165 @ 5200 | 174 @ 3600 | 3.43 × 3.27 | 9.0:1 | 59 @ 3200 |
| | | 180.6 (2690) ① | EFI | 205 @ 5200 | 227 @ 3600 | 3.43 × 3.27 | 8.3:1 | 58.5 @ 3200 |
| | Maxima | 180.6 (2960) | EFI | 157 @ 5200 | 168 @ 3600 | 3.43 × 3.27 | 9.0:1 | 59 @ 3200 |
| | Pulsar | 97.4 (1597) | EFI | 70 @ 5000 | 94 @ 2800 | 2.99 × 3.46 | 9.4:1 | 64 @ 3200 |
| | | 110.3 (1809) | EFI | 125 @ 6400 | 115 @ 4800 | 3.27 × 3.29 | 10.0:1 | 67 @ 2000 |
| | Sentra | 97.4 (1597) | EFI | 70 @ 5000 | 94 @ 2800 | 2.99 × 3.46 | 9.4:1 | 64 @ 3000 |
| | Stanza | 120.4 (1974) | EFI | 97 @ 5200 | 114 @ 2800 | 3.33 × 3.46 | 8.5:1 | 58 @ 3000 |
| 1989 | 240SX | 145.8 (2389) | EFI | 140 @ 5600 | 152 @ 4400 | 3.50 × 3.78 | 9.1:1 | 65 @ 3000 |
| | 300ZX | 180.6 (2960) | EFI | 165 @ 5200 | 174 @ 4000 | 3.43 × 3.27 | 9.0:1 | 59 @ 3200 |
| | | 180.6 (2960) ① | EFI | 205 @ 5200 | 227 @ 3600 | 3.43 × 3.27 | 8.3:1 | 58 @ 3200 |
| | Maxima | 180.6 (2690) | EFI | 160 @ 5200 | 182 @ 2800 | 3.43 × 3.27 | 9.0:1 | 59 @ 3200 |
| | Pulsar | 97.5 (1597) | EFI | 90 @ 6000 | 96 @ 3200 | 2.99 × 3.46 | 9.4:1 | 64 @ 3000 |
| | | 110.3 (1809) | EFI | 96 @ 3200 | 115 @ 4800 | 3.27 × 3.29 | 9.5:1 | 67 @ 2000 |
| | Sentra | 97.5 (1597) | EFI | 90 @ 6000 | 96 @ 3200 | 2.99 × 3.47 | 9.4:1 | 64 @ 3000 |
| | Stanza | 120.4 (1974) | EFI | 94 @ 5400 | 114 @ 2800 | 3.33 × 3.47 | 8.5:1 | 61 @ 3200 |
| 1990 | 240SX | 145.8 (2389) | EFI | 140 @ 5600 | 152 @ 4400 | 3.50 × 3.78 | 8.6:1 | 60–70 @ 3000 |
| | 300ZX | 180.6 (2960) | EFI | 222 @ 6400 | 198 @ 4800 | 3.43 × 3.27 | 10.5:1 | 51–65 @ 3000 |
| | | 180.6 (2960) ② | EFI | ③ | 283 @ 3600 | 3.43 × 3.27 | 8.1:1 | 51–65 @ 3000 |
| | Maxima | 180.6 (2960) | EFI | 160 @ 5200 | 181 @ 2800 | 3.43 × 3.27 | 9.0:1 | 53–65 @ 3200 |
| | Pulsar | 97.5 (1597) | EFI | 90 @ 6000 | 96 @ 3200 | 2.99 × 3.47 | 9.4:1 | 57–71 @ 3000 |
| | Sentra | 97.5 (1597) | EFI | 90 @ 6000 | 96 @ 3200 | 2.99 × 3.47 | 9.4:1 | 57–71 @ 3000 |
| | Stanza | 145.8 (2389) | EFI | 138 @ 5600 | 148 @ 3200 | 3.50 × 3.78 | 8.6:1 | 60–70 @ 3000 |
| 1991–92 | 240SX | 145.8 (2389) | EFI | 155 @ 5600 | 160 @ 4400 | 3.50 × 3.78 | 8.6:1 | 60–70 @ 3000 |
| | 300ZX | 180.6 (2960) | EFI | 222 @ 6400 | 198 @ 4800 | 3.43 × 3.27 | 10.5:1 | 51–65 @ 3000 |
| | | 180.6 (2960) ② | EFI | ③ | 283 @ 3600 | 3.43 × 3.27 | 8.5:1 | 51–65 @ 3000 |
| | Maxima | 180.6 (2960) | EFI | 160 @ 5200 | 181 @ 2800 | 3.43 × 3.27 | 9.0:1 | 53–65 @ 3200 |
| | Sentra | 97.5 (1597) | EFI | 110 @ 6000 | 108 @ 4000 | 2.99 × 3.46 | 9.5:1 | 50–64 @ 3000 |
| | | 122 (1998) | EFI | 140 @ 6400 | 132 @ 4800 | 3.39 × 3.39 | 9.5:1 | 46–57 @ 3200 |
| | Stanza | 145.8 (2389) | EFI | 138 @ 5600 | 148 @ 4400 | 3.50 × 3.78 | 8.6:1 | 60–70 @ 3000 |

EFI: Electronic Fuel Injection
① Turbo
② Twin Turbo
③ MT: 300 @ 6400
   AT: 280 @ 6400

## ENGINE TUNE-UP SPECIFICATIONS

| Year | Model | Engine Displacement cu. in. (cc) | Spark Plugs Type | Gap (in.) | Ignition Timing (deg.) ⑬ MT | AT | Compression Pressure (psi) | Fuel Pump (psi) | Idle Speed (rpm) MT | AT | Valve Clearance In. | Ex. |
|---|---|---|---|---|---|---|---|---|---|---|---|---|
| 1988 | 200SX | 120.4 (1974) | ② | 0.039–0.043 | 15B | 15B ④ | 171 | 36⑥ | 750 | 750 ④ | Hyd. | Hyd. |
| | | 180.6 (2690) | BCPR6ES-11 | 0.039–0.043 | 20B | 20B | 173 | 37④ ⑦ | 700 | 700 | Hyd. | Hyd. |
| | 300ZX | 180.6 (2960) | BCPR6ES-11 | 0.039–0.043 | 15B | 20B | 173 | 37⑦ | 700 ④ | 700 ④ | Hyd. | Hyd. |
| | | 180.6 (2690) ① | BCPR6E-11 | 0.039–0.043 | 10B | 15B | 169 | 44⑦ | 700 | 650 ④ | Hyd. | Hyd. |
| | Maxima | 180.6 (2960) | BCPR6ES-11 | 0.039–0.043 | 15B | 20B | 173 | 30⑤ | 750 | 700 ④ | Hyd. | Hyd. |
| | Pulsar | 97.4 (1597) | BPR6ES-11 | 0.039–0.043 | 7B | 7B | 181 | 14⑤ | 800 | 700 ④ | Hyd. | Hyd. |
| | | 110.3 (1809) | PFR6A-11 | 0.039–0.043 | 15B | 15B | 199 | 36⑧ | 800 | 700 ④ | Hyd. | Hyd. |
| | Sentra | 97.4 (1597) | BPR6ES-11 | 0.039–0.043 | 7B | 7B | 181 | 14⑨ | 800 | 700 ④ | 0.011 | 0.011 |
| | Stanza | 120.4 (1974) | ② | 0.039–0.043 | 15B | 15B | 171 | 43.4 | 750 | 700 | Hyd. | Hyd. |
| 1989 | 240SX | 145.8 (2389) | ZFR5D-11 | 0.039–0.043 | 15B | 15B | 192 | 33⑧ | 750 | 750 | Hyd. | Hyd. |
| | 300ZX | 180.6 (2690) | BCPR6ES-11 | 0.039–0.043 | 15B | 20B | 173 | 37⑦ | 700 | 700 ④⑩ | Hyd. | Hyd. |
| | | 180.6 (2960) ① | BCPR6ES-11 | 0.039–0.043 | 10B | 15B | 169 | 44⑦ | 700 | 650 | Hyd. | Hyd. |
| | Maxima | 180.6 (2960) | BKR6ES-11 | 0.039–0.043 | 15B | 15B | 181 | 36⑧ | 750 | 700 | Hyd. | Hyd. |
| | Pulsar | 97.5 (1597) | BCPR5ES-11 | 0.039–0.043 | 7B | 7B ⑪ | 181 ⑪ | 43⑤ | 800 ③ | 750 ③ | Hyd. | Hyd. |
| | | 110.3 (1809) | PFR6A-11 | ⑫ | 15B | 15B | 199 | 36⑧ | 800 | 700 ④ | Hyd. | Hyd. |
| | Sentra | 97.5 (1597) | BCPR5ES-11 | 0.039–0.043 | 7B | 7B | 181 | 43⑤ | 800 ⑪ | 700 ④⑪ | Hyd. | Hyd. |
| | Stanza | 120.4 (1974) | BCPR5ES-11 | 0.039–0.043 | 15B | 15B | 171 | 37⑧ | 750 | 700 ④ | Hyd. | Hyd. |
| 1990 | 240SX | 145.8 (2389) | ZFRSE-11 | 0.039–0.043 | 15B | 15B | 175 | ⑮ | 750 | 750 | Hyd. | Hyd. |
| | 300ZX | 180.6 (2960) | PFR6B-11 | 0.039–0.043 | 15B | 15B | 186 | ⑮ | 770 | 750 | Hyd. | Hyd. |
| | | 180.6 (2960) ① | PFR5B-11B | 0.039–0.043 | 15B | 15B | 186 | ⑮ | 770 | 750 | Hyd. | Hyd. |
| | Maxima | 180.6 (2960) | BKR6ES-11 | 0.039–0.043 | 15B | 15B | 173 | ⑮ | 750 | 700 | Hyd. | Hyd. |
| | Pulsar | 97.5 (1597) | BCPRSES-11 | 0.039–0.043 | 7B ⑪ | 7B ⑪ | 181 | ⑮ | 800 ③ | 900 ③ | Hyd. | Hyd. |
| | Sentra | 97.5 (1597) | BCPRSES-11 | 0.039–0.043 | 7B ⑪ | 7B ⑪ | 181 | ⑮ | 800 ⑯ | 900 ⑯ | Hyd. | Hyd. |
| | Stanza | 145.8 (2389) | ZFRSF-11 | 0.039–0.043 | 15B | 15B | 175 | ⑮ | 700 | 700 | Hyd. | Hyd. |

## ENGINE TUNE-UP SPECIFICATIONS

| Year | Model | Engine Displacement cu. in. (cc) | Spark Plugs Type | Gap (in.) | Ignition Timing (deg.) ⑬ MT | AT | Compression Pressure (psi) | Fuel Pump (psi) | Idle Speed (rpm) MT | AT | Valve Clearance In. | Ex. |
|------|-------|------|------|------|------|------|------|------|------|------|------|------|
| 1991 | 240SX | 145.8 (2359) | BKRSE-11 | 0.039–0.043 | 20B | 20B | 175 | ⑮ | 750 | 750 | 0.012–0.015 | 0.013–0.016 |
| | 300ZX | 180.6 (2960) | PFR6B-11 | 0.039–0.043 | 15B | 15B | 186 | ⑮ | 700 | 770 | Hyd. | Hyd. |
| | | 180.6 (2960) ① | PFR5B-11B | 0.039–0.043 | 15B | 15B | 186 | ⑮ | 700 | 750 | Hyd. | Hyd. |
| | Maxima | 180.6 (2960) | BKRGES-11 | 0.039–0.043 | 15B | 15B | 173 | ⑮ | 750 | 700 | Hyd. | Hyd. |
| | Sentra | 97.5 (1597) | BKR5E | 0.039–0.043 | 10B | 10B | 192 | ⑮ | 800 | 800 | 0.015 | 0.016 |
| | | 122 (1998) | BKR6E | 0.031–0.035 | 15B | 15B | 178 | ⑮ | 800 | 800 | Hyd. | Hyd. |
| | Stanza | 145.8 (2389) | ZFR5E-11 | 0.039–0.043 | 15B | 15B | 175 | ⑮ | 750 | 750 | Hyd. | Hyd. |
| 1992 | SEE UNDERHOOD SPECIFICATIONS STICKER | | | | | | | | | | | |

**NOTE:** The Underhood Specifications sticker often reflects tune-up specification changes made in production. Sticker figures must be used if they disagree with those in this chart

MT—Manual transmission
AT—Automatic transmission
NA—Not adjustable
B—Before Top Dead Center
Hyd.—Hydraulic valve lash adjusters
① Turbocharged model
② Intake side: BCPR6ES-11
   Exhaust side: BCPRSES-11
③ Idle speed is computer controlled; not adjustable
④ In drive position
⑤ At idle speed

⑥ Fuel pressure is measured at idle speed between the fuel filter and injector body
⑦ The moment the gas pedal is fully depressed
⑧ Fuel pressure is measured at idle speed between the fuel filter and fuel pipe with the vacuum hose connected at the pressure regulator
⑨ 4WD model—36.6 psi at idle speed
⑩ 600 rpm at high altitudes
⑪ With throttle sensor harness connected With throttle sensor harness disconnected—7° BTDC ±5°

⑫ Spark plug gap not adjustable
⑬ Ignition timing tolerance: ±2°
⑭ Idle speed tolerance: ±50 rpm
⑮ Fuel pressure is measured at idle speed between the fuel filter and fuel pipe (engine) side
   36.3 psi—with pressure regulator vacuum hose connected
   43.4 psi—with pressure regulator vacuum hose disconnected
⑯ Hot

## FIRING ORDERS

**NOTE: To avoid confusion, always replace spark plug wires one at a time.**

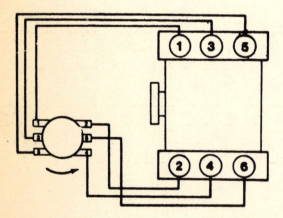

VG30E and VG30ET Series Engines
Engine Firing Order: 1–2–3–4–5–6
Distributor Rotation: Counterclockwise

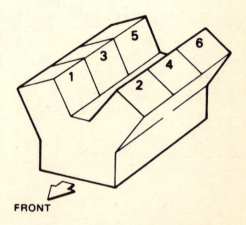

VG30DE and VG30DETT Series Engines
Engine Firing Order: 1–2–3–4–5–6
Distributorless Ignition System

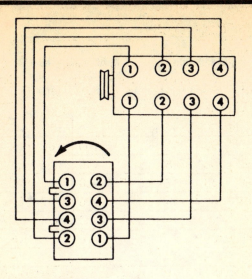

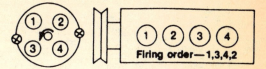

CA20E Engine
Engine Firing Order: 1–3–4–2
Distributor Rotation: Counterclockwise

E16I, KA24E, SR20DE, GA16I and GA16DE Engines
Engine Firing Order: 1–3–4–2
Distributor Rotation: Counterclockwise

## CAPACITIES

| Year | Model | Engine Displacement cu. in. (cc) | Engine Crankcase (qts.) with Filter | Engine Crankcase (qts.) without Filter | Transmission (pts.) 4-Spd | Transmission (pts.) 5-Spd | Transmission (pts.) Auto.■ | Drive Axle (pts.) | Fuel Tank (gal.) | Cooling System (qts.) |
|------|-------|------|------|------|------|------|------|------|------|------|
| 1988 | 200SX | 120.4 (1974) | 3.9 | 3.4 | — | 4.25 | 14.8 | ① | 14 | 9.1 |
|  |  | 180.6 (2690) | 4.5 | 4.0 | — | 4.25 | 14.8 | 2.75 | 14 | 9.6 |
|  | 300ZX | 180.6 (2960) | 4.25 | 3.9 | — | 4.25 | 14.8 | 2.75 | 19 | 11.1② |
|  | Maxima | 180.6 (2960) | 4.5 | 4.1 | — | 10.0 | 14.5 | — | 15.9 | 9.75 |
|  | Pulsar | 97.4 (1597) | 3.4 | 2.9 | — | 5.75 | 13.2 | — | 13.25 | ③ |
|  |  | 110.3 (1809) | 3.7 | 3.3 | — | 10.0 | 14.4 | — | 13.25 | ⑥ |
|  | Sentra | 97.4 (1597) | 3.4 | 3.0 | 5.7 | 5.9 | 13.2 | ⑦ | 13.25⑧ | ③ |
|  | Stanza | 120.4 (1974) | 3.75 | 3.25 | — | 10.0 | 14.4 | ⑦ | 15.9⑤ | 7.75⑨ |
| 1989 | 240SX | 145.8 (2389) | 3.75 | 3.4 | — | 5.1 | 17.5 | 2.75 | 15.9 | 7.1⑪ |
|  | 300ZX | 180.6 (2960) | 4.25 | 3.8 | — | 4.25⑫ | 14.8 | 2.75 | 19 | 11.1⑬ |
|  | Maxima | 180.6 (2960) | 4.5 | 4.1 | — | 10.0 | 15.5 | — | 15.9 | 8.75 |
|  | Pulsar | 97.4 (1597) | 3.4 | 3.0 | — | 5.75 | 6.6 | — | 13.25 | ⑭ |
|  |  | 110.3 (1809) | 3.75 | 3.25 | — | 10.0 | 7.25 | — | 13.25 | 5.9 |
|  | Sentra | 97.5 (1597) | 3.4 | 3.0 | 5.75 | 5.9 | 13.25 | ⑦ | 13.25⑧ | ⑩ |
|  | Stanza | 120.4 (1974) | 3.75 | 3.25 | — | 10.0 | 7.25 | — | 15.9 | 7.75 |
| 1990 | 240SX | 145.8 (2389) | 3.75 | 3.4 | — | 5.1 | 17.5 | 2.75 | 15.9 | 7.1⑪ |
|  | 300ZX | 180.6 (2960) | 4.4 | 3.9 | — | 5.9 | 16.2 | 3.1 | 19 | 10.6 |
|  |  | 180.6 (2960) ③ | 4.4 | 3.9 | — | 5.9 | 16.2 | 3.1 | 19 | 10.6 |
|  | Maxima | 180.6 (2960) | 4.5 | 4.1 | — | 10.0 | 15.5 | — | 15.9 | 8.75 |
|  | Pulsar | 97.5 (1597) | 3.4 | 3.0 | — | 5.9 | 13.2 | — | 13.25 | ⑭ |
|  | Sentra | 97.5 (1597) | 3.4 | 3.0 | 5.75 | 5.9 | 13.2 | ⑦ | 13.25⑧ | ⑩ |
|  | Stanza | 145.8 (2389) | 3.75 | 3.25 | — | 10.0 | 15.8 | — | 16.4 | 7.9 |

## CAPACITIES

| Year | Model | Engine Displacement cu. in. (cc) | Engine Crankcase (qts.) with Filter | without Filter | Transmission (pts.) 4-Spd | 5-Spd | Auto.■ | Drive Axle (pts.) | Fuel Tank (gal.) | Cooling System (qts.) |
|------|-------|----------------------------------|-------------------------------------|----------------|---------------------------|-------|--------|-------------------|------------------|------------------------|
| 1991–92 | 240SX | 145.8 (2389) | 3.75 | 3.4 | — | 5.1 | 17.5 | 2.75 | 15.9 | 7.1⑪ |
| | 300ZX | 180.6 (2960) | 4.1 | 3.7 | — | 5.9 | 16.2 | 3.1 | 19 | 10.6 |
| | | 180.6 (2960) ③ | 4.1 | 3.7 | — | 5.9 | 16.2 | 3.1 | 19 | 10.6 |
| | Maxima | 180.6 (2960) | 4.1 | 3.7 | — | 10.0 | 15.5 | — | 18.5 | 8.7 |
| | Sentra | 97.5 (1597) | 3.4 | 3.0 | — | 6.2 | 15.0 | — | 13.2 | 5.5 |
| | | 122 (1998) | 3.7 | 3.4 | — | 7.5 | 15.0 | — | 13.2 | 6.2 |
| | Stanza | 145.8 (2389) | 3.7 | 3.2 | — | 10.0 | 15.8 | — | 16.4 | 7.9 |

■ Figure is for drain and refill
— Not applicable
① Solid rear axle—2.1
  IRS—2.75
② Turbo—11.5
③ Twin turbo engine
④ 4WD—12.4
⑤ 4WD—13.25
⑥ MT—5.9; AT—6.1

⑦ Rear differential carrier on 4WD—2.1
  Transfer case on 4WD—2.2
⑧ 4WD—12.4
⑨ Station wagon with heater 7.1
  and without heater 6.1
⑩ MT—5.75
  2WD w/AT—5.75
  4WD w/AT—6.25
⑪ Reservoir Capacity—.75

⑫ Turbo—5.1
⑬ Turbo—11.6
⑭ MT—5.75
  AT—6.25

## CAMSHAFT SPECIFICATIONS

All measurements given in inches.

| Year | Engine Displacement cu. in. (cc) | Journal Diameter 1 | 2 | 3 | 4 | 5 | Lobe Lift In. | Ex. | Bearing Clearance | Camshaft End Play |
|------|----------------------------------|---------------------|---|---|---|---|---------------|-----|-------------------|-------------------|
| 1988 | CA20E 120.4 (1974) | 1.8085–1.8092 | 1.8085–1.8092 | 1.8085–1.8092 | 1.8085–1.8092 | 1.8077–1.8055 | 0.335 | 0.374 | 0.0040 ① | 0.0028–0.0055 |
| | V-Series 180.6 (2960) | 1.8866–1.8874 ② | 1.8472–1.8480 | 1.8472–1.8480 | 1.8472–1.8480 | 1.6701–1.6709 | NA | NA | 0.0018–0.0035 | 0.0012–0.0024 |
| | E16i 97.4 (1597) | 1.6515–1.6522 | 1.6498–1.6505 | 1.0515–1.6522 | 1.6498–1.6505 | 1.6515–1.6522 | NA | NA | 0.0014–0.0030 | 0.0059–0.0114 |
| | CA18DE 110.3 (1809) | 1.0998–1.1006 | 1.0998–1.1006 | 1.0998–1.1006 | 1.0998–1.1006 | 1.0998–1.1006 | 0.335 | 0.335 | 0.0018–0.0035 | 0.0028–0.0059 |
| 1989 | CA20E 120.4 (1974) | 1.8085–1.8092 | 1.8085–1.8092 | 1.8085–1.8092 | 1.8085–1.8092 | 1.8077–1.8055 | 0.335 | 0.374 | 0.0040 ① | 0.0028–0.0055 |
| | KA24E 145.8 (2389) | 1.2967–1.2974 | 1.2967–1.2974 | 1.2967–1.2974 | 1.2967–1.2974 | 1.2967–1.2974 | 0.409 | 0.409 | 0.0018–0.0035 | 0.0028–0.0059 |
| | V-Series 180.6 (2960) | 1.8866–1.8874 ② | 1.8472–1.8480 | 1.8472–1.8480 | 1.8472–1.8480 | 1.6701–1.6709 | NA | NA | 0.0018–0.0035 | 0.0012–0.0024 |
| | GA16i 97.5 (1597) | 1.6510–1.6518 | 1.6510–1.6518 | 1.6510–1.6518 | 1.6510–1.6518 | 1.6510–1.6518 | NA | NA | 0.0018–0.0035 | 0.0012–0.0059 |
| | CA18DE 110.3 (1809) | 1.0998–1.1006 | 1.0998–1.1006 | 1.0998–1.1006 | 1.0998–1.1006 | 1.0998–1.1006 | 0.335 | 0.335 | 0.0018–0.0035 | 0.0028–0.0059 |

## CAMSHAFT SPECIFICATIONS

All measurements given in inches.

| Year | Engine Displacement cu. in. (cc) | Journal Diameter 1 | 2 | 3 | 4 | 5 | Lobe Lift In. | Ex. | Bearing Clearance | Camshaft End Play |
|---|---|---|---|---|---|---|---|---|---|---|
| **1990** | GA16i 97.5 (1597) | 1.6510–1.6518 | 1.6510–1.6518 | 1.6510–1.6518 | 1.6510–1.6518 | 1.6510–1.6518 | NA | NA | 0.0018–0.0035 | 0.0012–0.0051 |
| | KA24E 145.8 (2389) | 1.2967–1.2974 | 1.2967–1.2974 | 1.2967–1.2974 | 1.2967–1.2974 | 1.2967–1.2974 | 0.409 | 0.409 | 0.0018–0.0035 | 0.0028–0.0059 |
| | VG30DE 180.6 (2960) | 1.0998–1.1006 | 1.0998–1.1006 | 1.0998–1.1006 | 1.0998–1.1006 | 1.0998–1.1006 | NA | NA | 0.0018–0.0035 | 0.0018–0.0035 |
| | VG30DETT 180.6 (2960) | 1.0998–1.1006 | 1.0998–1.1006 | 1.0998–1.1006 | 1.0998–1.1006 | 1.0998–1.1006 | NA | NA | 0.0018–0.0035 | 0.0018–0.0035 |
| | VG30E 180.6 (2960) | 1.8866–1.8874 ② | 1.8472–1.8480 | 1.8472–1.8480 | 1.8472–1.8480 | 1.6732–1.6742 | NA | NA | 0.0024–0.0041 | 0.0012–0.0024 |
| **1991–92** | KA24DE 145.8 (2389) | 1.0998–1.1006 | 0.9423–0.9431 | 0.9423–0.9431 | 0.9423–0.9431 | 0.9423–0.9431 | NA | NA | 0.0018–0.0035 | 0.0028–0.0059 |
| | VG30DE 180.6 (2960) | 1.0998–1.1006 | 1.0998–1.1006 | 1.0998–1.1006 | 1.0998–1.1006 | 1.0998–1.1006 | NA | NA | 0.0018–0.0034 | 0.0012–0.0031 |
| | VG30DETT 180.6 (2960) | 1.0998–1.1006 | 1.0998–1.1006 | 1.0998–1.1006 | 1.0998–1.1006 | 1.0998–1.1006 | NA | NA | 0.0018–0.0034 | 0.0012–0.0031 |
| | VG30E 180.6 (2960) | 1.8866–1.8874 ② | 1.8472–1.8480 | 1.8472–1.8480 | 1.8472–1.8480 | 1.6701–1.6709 | NA | NA | 0.0018–0.0035 | 0.0012–0.0024 |
| | GA16DE 97.5 (1597) | 1.0998–1.1006 | 0.9423–0.9431 | 0.9423–0.9431 | 0.9423–0.9431 | 0.9423–0.9431 | NA | NA | 0.0018–0.0034 | 0.0045–0.0074 |
| | SR20DE 122.0 (1998) | 1.0998–1.1006 | 1.0998–1.1006 | 1.0998–1.1006 | 1.0998–1.1006 | 1.0998–1.1006 | 0.394 | 0.362 | 0.0018–0.0034 | 0.0022–0.0055 |
| | KA24E 145.8 (2389) | 1.2967–1.2974 | 1.2967–1.2974 | 1.2967–1.2974 | 1.2967–1.2974 | 1.2967–1.2974 | 0.409 | 0.409 | 0.0018–0.0035 | 0.0028–0.0059 |

NA Not available
① Clearance limit
② Front of engine, left hand camshaft only

## CRANKSHAFT AND CONNECTING ROD SPECIFICATIONS

All measurements are given in inches.

| Year | Engine Displacement cu. in. (cc) | Crankshaft Main Brg. Journal Dia. | Main Brg. Oil Clearance | Shaft End-play | Thrust on No. | Connecting Rod Journal Diameter | Oil Clearance | Side Clearance |
|---|---|---|---|---|---|---|---|---|
| **1988** | CA20E 120.4 (1974) | 2.0847–2.0852 | 0.0016–0.0024 | 0.0120 | 3 | 1.7701–1.7706 | 0.0008–0.0024 | 0.0080–0.0120 |
| | V-Series 180.6 (2960) | 2.4790–2.4793 | 0.0011–0.0022 | 0.0020–0.0067 | 4 | 1.9760–1.9675 | 0.0006–0.0021 | 0.0079–0.0138 |
| | E16i 97.4 (1597) | 1.9661–1.9671 | ① | 0.0020–0.0065 | 3 | 1.5733–1.5738 | 0.0004–0.0017 | 0.0040–0.0146 |
| | CA18DE 110.3 (1809) | 2.0847–2.0856 | 0.0008–0.0019 | 0.0020–0.0091 | 3 | 1.7698–1.7706 | 0.0007–0.0018 | 0.0079–0.0138 |

## CRANKSHAFT AND CONNECTING ROD SPECIFICATIONS

All measurements are given in inches.

| Year | Engine Displacement cu. in. (cc) | Crankshaft | | | | Connecting Rod | | |
| --- | --- | --- | --- | --- | --- | --- | --- | --- |
| | | Main Brg. Journal Dia. | Main Brg. Oil Clearance | Shaft End-play | Thrust on No. | Journal Diameter | Oil Clearance | Side Clearance |
| 1989 | CA20 120.4 (1974) | 2.0847–2.0852 | 0.0008–0.0019 | 0.0020–0.0071 | 3 | 1.7701–1.7706 | 0.0004–0.0014 | 0.0080–0.0120 |
| | KAE24 145.8 (2389) | 2.3609–2.3612 | 0.0008–0.0019 | 0.0020–0.0071 | 3 | 1.9672–1.9675 | 0.0004–0.0017 | 0.0080–0.0160 |
| | V-Series 180.6 (2960) | 2.4790–2.4793 | 0.0011–0.0022 | 0.0020–0.0067 | 4 | 1.9667–1.9675 | 0.0006–0.0021 | 0.0079–0.0138 |
| | GA16i 97.5 (1597) | 1.9668–1.9671 | 0.0008–0.0017 | 0.0024–0.0071 | 3 | 1.5731–1.5738 | 0.0004–0.0014 | 0.0079–0.0185 |
| | CA18DE 110.3 (1809) | 2.0847–2.0856 | 0.0008–0.0019 | 0.0020–0.0071 | 3 | 1.7698–1.7706 | 0.0007–0.0018 | 0.0079–0.0138 |
| 1990 | GA16i 97.5 (1597) | 1.9668–1.9671 | 0.0008–0.0017 | 0.0024–0.0071 | 3 | 1.5731–1.5738 | 0.0004–0.0014 | 0.0079–0.0185 |
| | KA24E 145.8 (2389) | 2.3609–2.3612 | 0.0008–0.0019 | 0.0020–0.0071 | 3 | 1.7701–1.7706 | 0.0004–0.0014 | 0.0080–0.0120 |
| | VG30DE 180.6 (2960) | 2.4790–2.4793 | 0.0011–0.0022 | 0.0020–0.0071 | 4 | 1.9672–1.9675 | 0.0011–0.0019 | 0.0079–0.0138 |
| | VG30DETT 180.6 (2960) | 2.4790–2.4793 | 0.0011–0.0022 | 0.0020–0.0071 | 4 | 1.9672–1.9675 | 0.0011–0.0019 | 0.0079–0.0138 |
| | VG30E 180.6 (2960) | 2.4790–2.4793 | 0.0011–0.0022 | 0.0020–0.0067 | 4 | 1.9667–1.9675 | 0.0006–0.0021 | 0.0079–0.0138 |
| 1991–92 | KA24DE 145.8 (2389) | 2.3609–2.3612 | 2.3609–2.3612 | 2.3609–2.3612 | 3 | 1.9672–1.9675 | 0.0004–0.0014 | 0.0080–0.0160 |
| | VG30DE 180.6 (2960) | 2.4790–2.4793 | 2.4790–2.4793 | 2.4790–2.4793 | 4 | 1.9672–1.9675 | 0.0011–0.0019 | 0.0079–0.0138 |
| | VG30DETT 180.6 (2960) | 2.4790–2.4793 | 2.4790–2.4793 | 2.4790–2.4793 | 4 | 1.9672–1.9675 | 0.0011–0.0019 | 0.0079–0.0138 |
| | VG30E 180.6 (2960) | 2.4790–2.4793 | 2.4790–2.4793 | 2.4790–2.4793 | 4 | 1.9667–1.9675 | 0.0006–0.0021 | 0.0079–0.0138 |
| | GA16DE 97.5 (1597) | 1.9668–1.9671 | 1.9668–1.9671 | 1.9668–1.9671 | 3 | 1.5735–1.5738 | 0.0004–0.0014 | 0.0079–0.0185 |
| | SR20DE 122 (1998) | 2.1643–2.1646 | 2.1643–2.1646 | 2.1643–2.1646 | 3 | 1.8885–1.8887 | 0.0008–0.0018 | 0.0079–0.0138 |
| | KA24E 145.8 (2389) | 2.3609–2.3612 | 2.3609–2.3612 | 2.3609–2.3612 | 3 | 1.8491–1.9675 | 0.0004–0.0014 | 0.0080–0.0160 |

① No. 1, 3 & 5—0.0012–0.0022
No. 2 & 4—0.0012–0.0036

## VALVE SPECIFICATIONS

| Year | Engine Displacement cu. in. (cc) | Seat Angle (deg.) | Face Angle (deg.) | Spring Test Pressure (lbs.) | Spring Installed Height (in.) | Stem-to-Guide Clearance (in.) | | Stem Diameter (in.) | |
| --- | --- | --- | --- | --- | --- | --- | --- | --- | --- |
| | | | | | | Intake | Exhaust | Intake | Exhaust |
| 1988 | CA20E 120.4 (1974) | 45° | 45°30′ | 129.9 ③ | 1.959 ④ | 0.0008–0.0021 | 0.0016–0.0029 | 0.2742–0.2748 | 0.2734–0.2740 |
| | V-Series 180.6 (2960) | 45° | 45°30′ | 118 @ 1.18 ② | 1.575 ① | 0.0008–0.0021 | 0.0016–0.0029 | 0.2742–0.2748 | 0.3136–0.3138 |
| | E16i 97.4 (1597) | 45° | 45°30′ | — | 1.543 | 0.0008–0.0020 | 0.0018–0.0030 | 0.2744–0.2750 | 0.2734–0.2740 |

## VALVE SPECIFICATIONS

| Year | Engine Displacement cu. in. (cc) | Seat Angle (deg.) | Face Angle (deg.) | Spring Test Pressure (lbs.) | Spring Installed Height (in.) | Stem-to-Guide Clearance (in.) | | Stem Diameter (in.) | |
|---|---|---|---|---|---|---|---|---|---|
| | | | | | | Intake | Exhaust | Intake | Exhaust |
| **1988** | CA18DE 110.3 (1809) | 45° | 45°30' | ⑤ | ⑥ | 0.0008– 0.0021 | 0.0016– 0.0029 | 0.2348– 0.2354 | 0.2341– 0.2346 |
| **1989** | CAE20 120.4 (1974) | 45° | 45°30' | ⑦ | ⑧ | 0.0008– 0.0021 | 0.0016– 0.0029 | 0.2742– 0.2748 | 0.2734– 0.2740 |
| | KAE24 145.8 (2389) | 45° | 45°30' | ⑨ | ⑩ | 0.0008– 0.0021 | 0.0016– 0.0028 | 0.2742– 0.2748 | 0.3129– 0.3134 |
| | V-Series 180.6 (2960) | 45° | 45°30' | 117.7 @ 1.181 ⑪ | 2.016 ⑤ | 0.0008– 0.0021 | 0.0016– 0.0029 | 0.2742– 0.2748 | 0.3136– 0.3138 ⑬ |
| | GA16i 97.5 (1597) | 45° | 45°30' | ⑫ | 1.634 ⑬ | 0.0008– 0.0020 | 0.0008– 0.0020 | 0.2348– 0.2354 | 0.2582– 0.2587 |
| | CA18DE 110.3 (1809) | 45° | 45°30' | ⑭ | ⑥ | 0.0008– 0.0020 | 0.0008– 0.0020 | 0.2348– 0.2354 | 0.2582– 0.2587 |
| **1990** | GA16i 97.5 (1597) | 45° | 45°15' 45°45' | ⑫ | ⑬ | 0.0008– 0.0020 | 0.0012– 0.0022 | 0.2348– 0.2354 | 0.2582– 0.2587 |
| | KA24E 145.8 (2389) | 45° | 45° | ⑨ | ⑩ | 0.0008– 0.0021 | 0.0016– 0.0028 | 0.2742– 0.2748 | 0.3129– 0.3134 |
| | VG30DE 180.6 (2960) | 45°15' 45°45' | 45° | ⑮ | ⑥ | 0.0008– 0.0021 | 0.0016– 0.0028 | 0.2348– 0.2354 | 0.2341– 0.2346 |
| | VG30DETT 180.6 (2960) | 45°15' 45°45' | 45° | ⑮ | ⑥ | 0.0008– 0.0021 | 0.0016– 0.0028 | 0.2348– 0.2354 | 0.2341– 0.2346 |
| | VG30E 180.6 (2960) | 45°15' 45°45' | 45° | ⑯ | ⑰ | 0.0008– 0.0021 | 0.0016– 0.0029 | 0.2742– 0.2748 | 0.3136– 0.3138 |
| **1991–92** | KA24DE 145.8 (2389) | 45°15' 45°45' | 45° | 123 @ 1.024 | ⑱ | 0.0008– 0.0021 | 0.0016– 0.0029 | 0.2742– 0.2748 | 0.2734– 0.2740 |
| | VG30DE 180.6 (2960) | 45°15' 45°45' | 45° | 120 @ 1.043 | ⑥ | 0.0008– 0.0021 | 0.0016– 0.0029 | 0.2348– 0.2354 | 0.2341– 0.2346 |
| | VG30DETT 180.6 (2960) | 45°15' 45°45' | 45° | 120 @ 1.043 | ⑥ | 0.0008– 0.0021 | 0.0016– 0.0029 | 0.2348– 0.2354 | 0.2341– 0.2346 |
| | VG30E 180.6 (2960) | 45°15' 45°45' | 45° | ⑲ | ⑰ | 0.0008– 0.0021 | 0.0016– 0.0029 | 0.2742– 0.2748 | 0.3136– 0.3138 |
| | GA16DE 97.5 (1597) | 45°15' 45°45' | 45° | NA | ⑳ | 0.0008– 0.0020 | 0.0016– 0.0028 | 0.2152– 0.2157 | 0.2144– 0.2150 |
| | SR20DE 122 (1998) | 45°15' 45°45' | 45° | 130 @ 1.181 | ㉑ | 0.0008– 0.0021 | 0.0016– 0.0029 | 0.2348– 0.2354 | 0.2341– 0.2346 |
| | KA24E 145.8 (2389) | 45°30' 45°30' | 45° | ⑨ | ⑩ | 0.0008– 0.0021 | 0.0016– 0.0028 | 0.2742– 0.2748 | 0.3129– 0.3134 |

① Outer; Inner—1.378
② Outer; Inner—57 @ 0.98
③ Outer; Inner—56 @ 0.965
④ Outer; Inner—1.736
⑤ 0.650 in. @ 121 lbs. of load
⑥ 1.697 in. free height
⑦ Outer—129.9 @ 2.32
   Inner—66.6 @ 1.19
⑧ Free height:
   Outer—1.959
   Inner—1.736
⑨ Intake:
   Outer—135.8 @ 1.480
   Inner—63.9 @ 1.283
  Exhaust:
   Outer—144 @ 1.343
   Inner—73.9 @ 1.146

⑩ Free height:
   Intake—outer, 2.261, inner; 2.100
   Exhaust—outer; 1.343, inner; 1.887
⑪ Outer; Inner—57.3 @ 0.9840
   Maxima; 300ZX—0.3128–0.3134
⑫ Intake—110.0 @ 1.331
   Exhaust—122.6 @ 1.346
⑬ Free height:
   Intake—2.071
   Exhaust—2.154
⑭ 162 @ 2.9
⑮ 26.5 @ 1.043
⑯ 25 @ 0.984
⑰ Free height:
   Outer—2.016
   Inner—1.736
⑱ 1.756—Free height

⑲ Outer—117 lbs. @ 1.181
   Inner—57 lbs. @ 0.984
⑳ Free height:
   Intake—2.071
   Exhaust—2.154
㉑ 1.9433—Free height

## PISTON AND RING SPECIFICATIONS
All measurements are given in inches.

| Year | Engine Displacement cu. in. (cc) | Piston Clearance | Ring Gap | | | Ring Side Clearance | | |
|---|---|---|---|---|---|---|---|---|
| | | | Top Compression | Bottom Compression | Oil Control | Top Compression | Bottom Compression | Oil Control |
| 1988 | CA20E 120.4 (1974) | 0.0010–0.0018 | 0.0098–0.0201 | 0.0059–0.0122 | 0.0079–0.0299 | 0.0016–0.0029 | 0.0012–0.0025 | — |
| | V-Series 180.6 (1960) | 0.0010–0.0018 | 0.0083–0.0173 ④ | 0.0071–0.0173 | 0.0079–0.0299 | 0.0016–0.0029 | 0.0012–0.0025 | 0.0006–0.0075 |
| | E16i 97.4 (1597) | 0.0009–0.0017 | ① | ② | 0.0079–0.0236 | 0.0016–0.0029 | 0.0012–0.0025 | ③ |
| | CA18DE 110.3 (1809) | 0.0006–0.0014 | 0.0087–0.0154 | 0.0075–0.0177 | 0.0079–0.0299 | 0.0016–0.0029 | 0.0012–0.0025 | 0.0010–0.0033 |
| 1989 | CA20E 120.4 (1974) | 0.0010–0.0018 | 0.0098–0.0201 | 0.0059–0.0122 | 0.0079–0.0299 | 0.0016–0.0029 | 0.0012–0.0025 | — |
| | KA24E 145.8 (2389) | 0.0008–0.0016 | 0.0110–0.0169 | ⑤ | 0.0079–0.0236 | 0.0016–0.0031 | 0.0012–0.0028 | 0.0026–0.0053 |
| | V-Series 180.6 (2960) | 0.0010–0.0018 | 0.0083–0.0173 ④ | 0.0071–0.0173 | 0.0079–0.0299 | 0.0016–0.0029 | 0.0012–0.0025 | 0.0006–0.0075 |
| | GA16i 97.5 (1597) | 0.0006–0.0014 | 0.0079–0.0138 | 0.0146–0.0205 | 0.0079–0.0236 | 0.0016–0.0031 | 0.0012–0.0028 | |
| | CA18DE 110.3 (1809) | 0.0010–0.0018 | 0.0098–0.0201 | 0.0059–0.0122 | 0.0079–0.0299 | 0.0016–0.0029 | 0.0012–0.0025 | — |
| 1990 | GA16i 97.5 (1597) | 0.0006–0.0014 | 0.0079–0.0138 | 0.0146–0.0205 | 0.0079–0.0236 | 0.0016–0.0031 | 0.0012–0.0028 | — |
| | KA24E 145.8 (2389) | 0.0008–0.0016 | 0.0110–0.0169 | ⑤ | 0.0079–0.0236 | 0.0016–0.0031 | 0.0012–0.0028 | — |
| | VG30DE 180.6 (2960) | 0.0006–0.0014 | 0.0083–0.0157 | 0.0197–0.0299 | 0.0079–0.0299 | 0.0016–0.0029 | 0.0012–0.0025 | — |
| | VG30DETT 180.6 (2960) | 0.0010–0.0018 | 0.0083–0.0157 | 0.0197–0.0299 | 0.0079–0.0299 | 0.0016–0.0029 | 0.0012–0.0025 | — |
| | VG30E 180.6 (2960) | 0.0006–0.0014 | 0.0083–0.0173 | 0.0071–0.0173 | 0.0079–0.0299 | 0.0016–0.0029 | 0.0012–0.0025 | — |
| 1991–92 | KA24DE 145.8 (2389) | 0.0008–0.0016 | 0.0110–0.0205 | 0.0177–0.0272 | 0.0079–0.0272 | 0.0016–0.0031 | 0.0012–0.0028 | — |
| | VG30DE 180.6 (2960) | 0.0006–0.0010 | 0.0083–0.0157 | 0.0197–0.0299 | 0.0079–0.0299 | 0.0016–0.0029 | 0.0012–0.0025 | 0.0006–0.0075 |
| | VG30DETT 180.6 (2960) | 0.0010–0.0018 | 0.0083–0.0157 | 0.0197–0.0299 | 0.0079–0.0299 | 0.0016–0.0029 | 0.0012–0.0025 | 0.0006–0.0075 |
| | VG30E 180.6 (2960) | 0.0006–0.0014 | 0.0083–0.0173 | 0.0071–0.0173 | 0.0079–0.0299 | 0.0016–0.0029 | 0.0012–0.0025 | 0.0006–0.0075 |
| | GA16DE 97.5 (1597) | 0.0006–0.0014 | 0.0079–0.0138 | 0.0146–0.0205 | 0.0079–0.0236 | 0.0016–0.0031 | 0.0012–0.0028 | — |
| | SR20DE 122 (1998) | 0.0004–0.0012 | 0.0079–0.0118 | 0.0138–0.0197 | 0.0079–0.0236 | 0.0018–0.0031 | 0.0012–0.0026 | — |
| | KA24E 145.8 (2389) | 0.0008–0.0016 | 0.0110–0.0205 | ⑤ | 0.0079–0.0272 | 0.0016–0.0031 | 0.0012–0.0028 | — |

① Type 1: 0.0055–0.0102
   Type 2: 0.0079–0.0118
② Type 1: 0.0110–0.0146
   Type 2: 0.0059–0.0098
③ Type 1: 0.0026–0.0055
   Type 2: 0.0002–0.0069
④ Turbocharged engine
   0.0083–0.0122
⑤ For rings punched with R or T—0.0177–0.0236
   For rings punched with N—0.0217–0.0276

## TORQUE SPECIFICATIONS
All readings in ft. lbs.

| Year | Engine Displacement cu. in. (cc) | Cylinder Head Bolts | Main Bearing Bolts | Rod Bearing Bolts | Crankshaft Pulley Bolts | Flywheel Bolts | Manifold Intake | Manifold Exhaust | Spark Plugs |
|---|---|---|---|---|---|---|---|---|---|
| **1988** | CA20E 120.4 (1974) | ③ | 33–40 | 24–27 | 90–98 | 72–80 | 14–19 | 14–22 | 14–22 |
| | V-Series 180.6 (2960) | 40–47 ① | 67–74 | ④ | 90–98 | 72–80 | ② | 13–16 | 14–22 |
| | E16i 97.4 (1597) | ⑤ | 36–43 | 23–27 | 80–94 | 58–65 ⑥ | 12–15 | 12–15 | 14–22 |
| | CA18DE 110.3 (1809) | ⑦ | 33–40 | ④ | 105–112 | 61–69 | 14–19 | 27–35 | 14–22 |
| **1989** | CA20E 120.4 (1974) | ③ | 33–40 | 24–27 | 90–98 | 72–80 | 14–19 | 14–22 | 14–22 |
| | KA24E 145.8 (2389) | ⑧ | 34–38 | ④ | 87–116 | ⑬ | 12–15 | 14–22 | |
| | V-Series 180.6 (2960) | ① | 67–74 | ④ | 90–98 | 72–80 ⑨ | ② | 13–16 | 14–22 |
| | GA16i 97.5 (1597) | ① | 34–38 | ⑩ | 132–152 | 69–76 | 12–15 | 12–15 | 14–22 |
| | CA18DE 110.3 (1809) | ⑦ | 33–40 | ⑪ | 105–112 | 61–69 | 12–15 | 12–15 | 14–22 |
| **1990** | GA16i 97.5 (1597) | ① | 34–38 | ⑩ | 98–112 | ⑮ | 12–15 | 12–15 | 14–22 |
| | KA24E 145.8 (2389) | ⑧ | 34–38 | ④ | 87–116 | ⑫ | 12–15 | 12–15 | 14–22 |
| | VG30DE 180.6 (2960) | ① | 64–74 | ④ | 159–174 | 61–69 | ⑭ | 17–20 | 14–22 |
| | VG30DETT 180.6 (2960) | ① | 64–74 | ④ | 159–174 | 61–69 | ⑭ | 20–23 | 14–22 |
| | VG30E 180.6 (2960) | ① | 67–74 | ④ | 90–98 | 61–69 ⑬ | ⑭ | 13–16 | 14–22 |
| **1991–92** | KA24DE 145.8 (2389) | ① | 34–38 | ④ | 105–112 | ⑫ | 12–14 | 27–35 | 14–22 |
| | VG30DE 180.6 (2960) | ① | 64–74 | ④ | 159–174 | 61–69 | ⑭ | 17–20 | 14–22 |
| | VG30DETT 180.6 (2960) | ① | 64–74 | ④ | 159–174 | 61–69 | ⑭ | 20–23 | 14–22 |
| | VG30E 180.6 (2960) | ① | 67–74 | ④ | 90–98 | 61–69 | ⑭ | 13–16 | 14–22 |
| | GA16DE 97.5 (1597) | ① | 34–38 | ⑩ | 98–112 | ⑮ | 12–15 | 16–21 | 14–22 |

## TORQUE SPECIFICATIONS
All readings in ft. lbs.

| Year | Engine Displacement cu. in. (cc) | Cylinder Head Bolts | Main Bearing Bolts | Rod Bearing Bolts | Crankshaft Pulley Bolts | Flywheel Bolts | Manifold | | Spark Plugs |
|---|---|---|---|---|---|---|---|---|---|
| | | | | | | | Intake | Exhaust | |
| 1991–92 | SR20DE 122 (1998) | ① | 54–61 | ⑪ | 105–112 | 61–69 | 13–15 | 27–35 | 14–22 |
| | KA24E 145.8 (2389) | ⑧ | 34–38 | ④ | 87–116 | ⑫ | 12–15 | 12–15 | 14–22 |

① See text
② Intake bolt: 12–14 ft. lbs.
Intake nut: 17–20 ft. lbs.
③ Tighten in 2 steps:
  1st—22 ft. lbs.
  2nd—58 ft. lbs.
Then loosen all bolts completely
Final torque is in 2 steps:
  1st—22 ft. lbs.
  2nd—54–61 ft. lbs.
(If angle torquing, tighten bolt 8 to 83–88 degrees and all other bolts to 75–80 degrees clockwise.)
NOTE: No. 8 bolt is the longest bolt.
④ Tighten in 2 steps:
  1st—10–12 ft. lbs.
  2nd—28–33 ft. lbs.
(If angle torquing, tighten bolts to 60–65 degrees clockwise.)
⑤ Tighten in 2 steps:
  1st—22 ft. lbs.
  2nd—51 ft. lbs.
Then loosen all bolts completely.

Final torque in 2 steps:
  1st—22 ft. lbs.
  2nd—51–54 ft. lbs.
⑥ A/T Drive Plate: 69–76 ft. lbs.
⑦ Tighten in 2 steps:
  1st—22 ft. lbs.
  2nd—76 ft. lbs.
Then loosen all bolts completely.
Final torque in 2 steps:
  1st—22 ft. lbs.
  2nd—76 ft. lbs.
(If angle torquing, tighten all bolts to 85–90 degrees clockwise.)
⑧ Tighten in 2 steps:
  1st—22 ft. lbs.
  2nd—58 ft. lbs.
Then loosen all bolts completely.
Final torque is in 2 steps:
  1st—22 ft. lbs.
  2nd—54–61 ft. lbs.
(If angle torquing in 2nd step, turn all bolts 80 to 85 degrees clockwise with an angle torque wrench.)

⑨ 300ZX Maxima—61 to 69
⑩ Tighten in 2 steps:
  1st—10 to 12 ft. lbs.
  2nd—17–21 ft. lbs.
(If angle torquing in 2nd step, turn all nuts 35–40 degrees with an angle torque wrench.)
⑪ Tighten in 2 steps:
  1st—10–12 ft. lbs.
  2nd—30–33 ft. lbs.
(If angle torquing in 2nd step, turn all nuts 60 to 65 degrees with an angle torque wrench.)
⑫ M/T flywheel—105–112
A/T driveplate—69–76
⑬ Flywheel (M/T) or driveplate (A/T)
⑭ Tighten intake nut in two steps:
  1st—2.2–3.6 ft. lbs.
  2nd—17–20 ft. lbs.
Tighten intake bolt in two steps:
  1st—2.2–3.6 ft. lbs.
  2nd—12–14 ft. lbs.
⑮ M/T flywheel—61–69
A/T driveplate—69–76

## BRAKE SPECIFICATIONS
All measurements in inches unless noted.

| Year | Model | Lug Nut Torque (ft. lbs.) | Master Cylinder Bore | Brake Disc | | Standard Brake Drum Diameter | Minimum Lining Thickness | |
|---|---|---|---|---|---|---|---|---|
| | | | | Minimum Thickness | Maximum Runout | | Front | Rear |
| 1988 | 200SX | 87–108 | 0.938 | 0.630 ① | 0.0028 ② | — | 0.080 | 0.080 |
| | 300ZX | 72–87 | 0.938 | 0.787 ③ | 0.0028 ② | — | 0.080 | 0.080 |
| | Maxima | 72–87 | 1.000 | 0.787 ① | 0.0028 ② | — | 0.079 | 0.079 |
| | Pulsar | 72–87 | ④ | ⑤ | 0.0028 | 8.000 | 0.079 | 0.059 |
| | Sentra | 72–87 | ⑧ | ⑤ | 0.0028 | 8.000 ⑥ | 0.079 | 0.059 |
| | Stanza | 72–87 | ④ | 0.787 | 0.0028 | 9.000 ⑦ | 0.079 | 0.059 |

## BRAKE SPECIFICATIONS
All measurements in inches unless noted.

| Year | Model | Lug Nut Torque (ft. lbs.) | Master Cylinder Bore | Brake Disc Minimum Thickness | Brake Disc Maximum Runout | Standard Brake Drum Diameter | Lining Thickness Front | Lining Thickness Rear |
|------|-------|------|------|------|------|------|------|------|
| 1989 | 240SX | 72–87 | 0.875 | 0.709 ⑨ | 0.0028 ⑥ | — | 0.079 | 0.079 |
| | 300ZX | 72–87 | 0.937 | 0.787 ⑯ | 0.0028 ⑥ | — | 0.079 | 0.079 |
| | Maxima | 72–87 | 1.000 | 0.787 ① | 0.0028 ⑥ | 9.06 | 0.079 | 0.059 |
| | Pulsar | 72–87 | ⑩ | ⑪ | 0.0028 | 8.05 | 0.079 | 0.059 |
| | Sentra | 72–87 | ⑫ | ⑤ | 0.0028 | 8.05 ⑬ | 0.079 | 0.059 |
| | Stanza | 72–87 | 1.000 | 0.787 | 0.0028 | 9.06 | 0.079 | 0.059 |
| 1990 | 240SX | 72–87 | ⑭ | ⑮ | 0.0028 | — | 0.079 | 0.059 |
| | 300ZX | 72–87 | ⑯ | ⑰ | 0.0028 | — | 0.079 | 0.079 |
| | 300ZX Twin Turbo | 72–87 | — | ⑱ | 0.0028 | — | 0.079 | 0.079 |
| | Maxima | 72–87 | ⑲ | ⑳ | 0.0028 | 9.000 | 0.079 | ㉑ |
| | Pulsar | 72–87 | ⑩ | 0.394 | 0.0028 | 8.000 | 0.079 | 0.059 |
| | Sentra | 72–87 | ⑫ | ㉒ | 0.0028 | ㉓ | 0.079 | 0.059 |
| | Stanza | 72–87 | ㉔ | ㉕ | 0.0028 | 9.000 | 0.079 | ㉑ |
| 1991–92 | 240SX | 72–87 | ⑭ | ⑮ | 0.0028 | — | 0.079 | 0.059 |
| | 300ZX | 72–87 | ⑯ | ⑰ | 0.0028 | — | 0.079 | 0.079 |
| | 300ZX Twin Turbo | 72–87 | — | ⑱ | 0.0028 | — | 0.079 | 0.079 |
| | Maxima | 72–87 | ⑲ | ⑳ | 0.0028 | 9.000 | 0.079 | ㉑ |
| | Sentra | 72–87 | ⑫ | ㉒ | 0.0028 | ㉓ | 0.079 | 0.059 |
| | Stanza | 72–87 | ㉔ | ㉕ | 0.0028 | 9.000 | 0.079 | ㉑ |

**NOTE:** Minimum lining thickness is as recommended by the manufacturer. Due to variation in state inspection regulations, the minimum allowable thickness may be different than recommended.

—Not applicable

① Front disc on V6 models—0.787
   Rear disc on all models—0.354
② Rear disc—0.0028
③ Front disc on Turbo—0.945
   rear disc on all models—0.709
④ Pulsar
   with CA16DE—1.000
   with E16i—0.9380
   with CA18DE—1.000
   Sentra
   with gasoline engine—0.938
   Stanza
   All except 2WD wagon—1.000
   2WD wagon—0.9380
⑤ Pulsar
   with CA16DE—0.630
   with E16i—0.394
   with CA18DE—0.630
   Sentra
   Gasoline engine except wagon 0.394
   Gasoline engine wagon—0.630
   4WD wagon—0.630

⑥ 4WD—9.000
⑦ Wagon—9.000
⑧ 2WD wagon—0.938
   4WD wagon—1.000
⑨ Front; Rear—0.079
⑩ Pulsar
   with CA18DE
     large—1.000
     small—0.812
   With GA16i
     large—0.937
     Small—0.750
⑪ Pulsar
   with CA18DE 0.630
   with GA16i 0.394
⑫ Sentra 2WD and 4WD
     large—1.000
     small—0.812
⑬ 4WD—9.06
⑭ With ABS—0.937
   without ABS—0.575
⑮ Front disc:
   with ABS—0.709
   without ABS—0.787
   Rear disc: 0.315

⑯ With ABS—0.941
   without ABS—0.937
⑰ Front disc—0.945
   Rear disc—0.630
⑱ Front disc—1.102
   Rear disc—0.630
⑲ GXE, SE (w/o ABS),
   GXE (with ABS)—0.937
   SE with ABS—1.000
⑳ Front disc—0.787
   Rear disc—0.354
㉑ Rear drum—0.059
   Rear disc—0.079
㉒ 2WD except wagon—0.394
   2WD wagon and all 4WD—0.630
㉓ 2WD—8.000
   4WD—9.000
㉔ With ABS—1.000
   without ABS—0.937
㉕ Front—0.787
   Rear—0.354

## WHEEL ALIGNMENT

| Year | Model | Caster Range (deg.) | Caster Preferred Setting (deg.) | Camber Range (deg.) | Camber Preferred Setting (deg.) | Toe-in (in.) | Steering Axis Inclination (deg.) |
|---|---|---|---|---|---|---|---|
| **1988** | 200SX (Front) | 2³⁄₄P–4¹⁄₄P | — | ³⁄₈N–1¹⁄₁₆P | — | ¹⁄₆₄P–¹⁄₁₀P | 12³⁄₄ |
| | (Rear) | — | — | 1¹⁄₄N–¹⁄₄P | — | ⁵⁄₆₄P–0 | — |
| | 300ZX (Front) | 5¹³⁄₁₆P–7⁵⁄₁₆P | — | ⁹⁄₁₆N–¹⁵⁄₁₆P | — | ¹⁄₃₂P–¹⁄₈P | 13¹¹⁄₁₆ |
| | (Rear) | — | — | 1¹⁵⁄₁₆N–⁷⁄₁₆N | — | ① | — |
| | Maxima (Front) | 1¹⁄₄P–2³⁄₄P | — | ⁷⁄₁₆N–¹⁄₁₆P | — | ¹⁄₁₆P–¹⁄₄P | 14¹⁄₂ |
| | (Rear) | — | — | 1³⁄₁₆N–⁵⁄₁₆P | — | ³⁄₃₂P–¹⁄₄P | — |
| | Pulsar (Front) | 1³⁄₁₆P–2¹¹⁄₁₆P | — | 1¹⁄₄N–¹⁄₄P | — | ② | 14¹³⁄₁₆ |
| | (Rear) | — | — | 2N–¹⁄₂N | — | ① | — |
| | Sentra 2WD (Front—Cpe) | ⁷⁄₈P–2³⁄₈P | — | 1¹⁄₁₆N–⁷⁄₁₆P | — | ③ | 14³⁄₄ |
| | (Rear Cpe) | — | — | 1¹⁵⁄₁₆N–⁷⁄₁₆N | — | ¹⁄₃₂P–¹⁄₈P | — |
| | (Front exc Cpe) | ³⁄₄P–2¹⁄₄P | — | ¹⁵⁄₁₆N–⁹⁄₁₆P | — | ③ | 14¹⁄₂ |
| | (Rear exc Cpe) | — | — | 1⁷⁄₈N–³⁄₈N | — | 0–³⁄₁₆P | — |
| | Sentra 4WD (Front) | ¹⁄₈P–1⁵⁄₈P | — | ⁷⁄₈N–⁵⁄₈P | — | ④ | 13¹⁵⁄₁₆ |
| | (Rear) | — | — | ⁷⁄₈N–⁵⁄₈P | — | 0–³⁄₁₆P | — |
| | Stanza (Front) | 1¹⁄₄P–2³⁄₄P | — | ⁷⁄₁₆N–1¹⁄₁₆P | — | ¹⁄₃₂P–¹⁄₈P | 14⁵⁄₈ |
| | (Rear) | — | — | 1³⁄₁₆N–⁵⁄₁₆P | — | ³⁄₃₂P–¹⁄₄P | — |
| | Stanza Wagon (Front 2WD) | ³⁄₄P–2¹⁄₄P | — | ¹⁄₄N–1¹⁄₄P | — | ¹⁄₁₆P–⁹⁄₆₄P | 12 |
| | (Rear 2WD) | — | — | 1N–1P | — | ⑤ | — |
| | (Front 4WD) | ⁹⁄₁₆P–2¹⁄₁₆P | — | ¹⁄₂N–1¹⁄₁₆P | — | ¹⁄₆₄P–¹⁄₁₆P | 11³⁄₄ |
| | (Rear 4WD) | — | — | 0–1¹⁄₂P | — | ⑥ | — |
| **1989** | 240SX (Front) | 6P–7¹⁄₂P | — | 1¹⁄₂N–0 | — | 0–³⁄₁₆P | 13¹⁄₄ |
| | (Rear) | — | — | 2N–¹⁄₂N | — | ¹⁄₁₆–³⁄₃₂ | — |
| | 300ZX (Front) | 5¹³⁄₁₆P | — | ⁹⁄₁₆N–¹⁵⁄₁₆P | — | ¹⁄₃₂–¹⁄₈ | 13⁷⁄₁₆ |
| | (Rear) | — | — | 1¹⁵⁄₁₆N–⁷⁄₁₆N | — | ¹⁄₁₆–³⁄₃₂ | — |
| | Maxima (Front) | ¹⁄₂P–2P | — | 1N–¹⁄₂P | — | ¹⁄₃₂–¹⁄₈ | 14³⁄₈ |
| | (Rear) | — | — | 1⁵⁄₁₆N–³⁄₁₆ | — | ¹⁄₃₂–¹⁄₈P | — |
| | Pulsar (Front) | 1³⁄₁₆P–2¹¹⁄₁₆P | — | 1¹⁄₄N–¹⁄₄P | — | ⑦ | 14¹³⁄₁₆ |
| | (Rear) | — | — | 2N–¹⁄₂N | — | ¹⁄₁₆–³⁄₃₂ | — |
| | Sentra 2WD (Front—Cpe) | ⁷⁄₈P–2³⁄₈P | — | 1¹⁄₁₆N–⁷⁄₁₆P | — | ¹⁄₃₂–¹⁄₁₆ ⑧ | 14³⁄₄ |
| | (Rear Cpe) | — | — | 1¹⁵⁄₁₆N–⁷⁄₁₆N | — | ¹⁄₃₂P–¹⁄₈P ⑨ | — |
| | (Front exc Cpe) | ³⁄₄P–2¹⁄₄P | — | ¹⁵⁄₁₆N–⁹⁄₁₆P | — | ¹⁄₃₂–¹⁄₁₆ ⑧ | 14¹⁄₂ |
| | (Rear exc Cpe) | — | — | 1⁷⁄₈N–³⁄₈N | — | 0–³⁄₁₆P | — |
| | Sentra 4WD (Front) | ¹⁄₈P–1⁵⁄₈P | — | ⁷⁄₈N–⁵⁄₈P | — | ③ | 13¹⁵⁄₁₆ |
| | (Rear) | — | — | ⁷⁄₈N–⁵⁄₈P | — | 0–³⁄₁₆ | — |
| | Stanza (Front) | 1⁵⁄₁₆P–2¹³⁄₁₆P | — | ⁷⁄₁₆N–1¹⁄₁₆P | — | ¹⁄₁₆–⁵⁄₃₂ | 14⁵⁄₈ |
| | (Rear) | — | — | 1³⁄₁₆N–⁵⁄₁₆P | — | ³⁄₃₂–⁵⁄₁₆ ⑤ | — |

## WHEEL ALIGNMENT

| Year | Model | Caster Range (deg.) | Preferred Setting (deg.) | Camber Range (deg.) | Preferred Setting (deg.) | Toe-in (in.) | Steering Axis Inclination (deg.) |
|---|---|---|---|---|---|---|---|
| **1990** | 240SX (Front) | 6P–7½P | — | 1½N–0 | — | 1/32–3/32 | 13¼ |
| | (Rear) | — | — | 1⅝N–⅝N | — | 1/32–3/16 | — |
| | 300ZX (Front) | 9P–10½P | — | 1 9/16N–1/16N | — | 0–3/32 | 12 15/16 |
| | (Rear) | — | — | 1⅝N–⅝N | — | 1/64–3/16 | — |
| | Maxima (Front) | ½P–2P | — | 1N–½P | — | 1/32–⅛ | 14⅜ |
| | (Rear) | — | — | 1 5/16N–3/16P | — | 0–5/32P | — |
| | Pulsar (Front) | 1 3/16P–2 11/16P | — | 1¼N–¼P | — | ⑦ | 14 13/16 |
| | (Rear) | — | — | 2N–½N | — | ① | — |
| | Sentra 2WD (Front—Cpe) | ⅞P–2⅜P | — | 1 1/16N–7/16N | — | ③ | 14¾ |
| | (Rear Cpe) | — | — | 2N–½N | — | ① | — |
| | (Front exc Cpe) | ¾P–2¼P | — | 15/16N–9/16P | — | ⑧ | 14½ |
| | (Rear exc Cpe) | — | — | 1⅞N–⅜N | — | 0–3/16 | — |
| | Sentra 4WD (Front) | ⅛P–1⅝P | — | ⅞N–⅝P | — | ③ | 13 15/16 |
| | (Rear) | — | — | ⅞N–⅝P | — | 0–3/16 | — |
| | Stanza (Front) | ⅝P–2 1/16P | — | ½N–1P | — | 1/16–⅛ | 14½ |
| | (Rear) | — | — | 1 7/16N–3/16 | — | 0–5/16 | — |
| **1991–92** | 240SX (Front) | 6P–7½P | — | 1½N–0 | — | 1/32–3/32 | 13¼ |
| | (Rear) | — | — | 1⅝N–⅝N | — | 1/64–3/16 | — |
| | 300ZX (Front) | 9P–10½P | — | 1 9/16N–1/16N | — | 0–3/32 | 12 15/16 |
| | (Rear) | — | — | 1⅝N–⅝N | — | 1/64–3/16 | — |
| | Maxima (Front) | ½P–2P | — | 1N–½P | — | 1/32–⅛ | 14⅜ |
| | (Rear) | — | — | 1 5/16N–3/16P | — | 0–5/32P | — |
| | Sentra 2WD (Front—Cpe) | ⅞P–2⅜P | — | 1 1/16N–7/16N | — | ③ | 14¾ |
| | (Rear Cpe) | — | — | 2N–½N | — | ① | — |
| | (Front exc Cpe) | ¾P–2¼P | — | 15/16N–9/16P | — | ⑧ | 14½ |
| | (Rear exc Cpe) | — | — | 1⅞N–⅜N | — | 0–3/16 | — |
| | Sentra 4WD (Front) | ⅛P–1⅝P | — | ⅞N–⅝P | — | ③ | 13 15/16 |
| | (Rear) | — | — | ⅞N–⅝P | — | 0–3/16 | — |
| | Stanza (Front) | ⅝P–2 1/16P | — | ½N–1P | — | 1/16–⅛ | 14½ |
| | (Rear) | — | — | 1 7/16N–3/16 | — | 0–5/16 | — |

N—Negative
P—Positive
① 1/16 Toe Out—3/32 Toe In
② 1/16 Toe Out—1/16 Toe In
③ 1/32 Toe Out—1/16 Toe In
④ 1/32 Toe Out—1/32 Toe In
⑤ 3/32 Toe Out—5/16 Toe In
⑥ 5/32 Toe Out—0
⑦ 1/16 Toe Out—1/16 Toe In
⑧ 1/32 Toe Out—1/16 Toe In
⑨ 1/32 Toe Out—⅛ Toe In

# ENGINE MECHANICAL

NOTE: Disconnecting the negative battery cable on some vehicles may interfere with the functions of the on board computer systems and may require the computer to undergo a relearning process, once the negative battery cable is reconnected.

## Engine Assembly

### REMOVAL & INSTALLATION

#### 200SX, 240SX and 1988–89 300ZX

1. Mark the hood hinge relationship and remove the hood.
2. Release the fuel system pressure and disconnect the negative battery cable.
3. Drain the cooling system and transmission fluid.
4. Remove the radiator after disconnecting the automatic transmission coolant tubes, if equipped.
5. Remove the air cleaner.
6. Remove the fan and pulley.
7. Disconnect or remove following:
   Water temperature gauge wire
   Oil pressure sending unit wire
   Ignition distributor primary wire
   Starter motor connections
   Fuel hose
   Alternator leads
   Heater hoses
   Throttle and choke connections
   Engine ground cable and all wiring harnesses
   Any interfering engine accessory

— CAUTION —

*On vehicles with air conditioning, it is necessary to remove the compressor and the condenser from their mounts. Do not attempt to disconnect any of the air conditioner hoses.*

8. Disconnect the power brake booster hose from the engine.
9. Remove the clutch operating cylinder and return spring, if equipped.
10. Disconnect the speedometer cable from the transmission. Disconnect the back up light switch and any other wiring or attachments to the transmission.
11. Disconnect the column shift linkage. Remove the floor shift lever.
12. Raise and safely support the vehicle. Detach the exhaust pipe from the exhaust manifold. Remove the front section of the exhaust system. On 300ZX, remove the right side exhaust manifold and exhaust connecting tube section.
13. Mark the relationship of the flanges and disconnect the driveshaft.
14. Suppport the transmission with a jack. Remove the rear cross member, if required.
15. Attach a hoist to the lifting hooks on the engine at either end of the cylinder head. Support the engine with a suitable jack.
16. Unbolt the front engine mount brackets from the block. Tilt and remove the engine by lowering the jack under the transmission and raising the hoist.

**To install:**

17. Lower the engine into the vehicle and align the block with with the front mount brackets. On the 200SX (V6) and 300ZX, torque the engine gusset bolts in 6 stages to 22–29 ft. lbs. (29–39 Nm). When installing the engine on automatic transmission equipped 200SX (4 cyl.), adjust the rear mounting insulator to 0.451–0.569 in. (11.1–14.5mm). Torque the engine mount bolts to 33–43 ft. lbs. (44–59 Nm), 32–41 ft. lbs. (43–55 Nm) on 240SX and 33–44 ft. lbs. (45–60 Nm) on 300ZX.

NOTE: Never loosen the front engine mount insulator cover nuts on a 200SX (4 cyl.); if removed, the insulator will malfunction due to oil loss.

18. Install the rear cross member, if removed.
19. Connect the driveshaft. Make sure the driveshaft flanges are aligned properly.
20. On 300ZX, install the right exhaust manifold and connecting tube section. On the other models, install the front exhaust section and connect the exhaust pipe to the manifold.

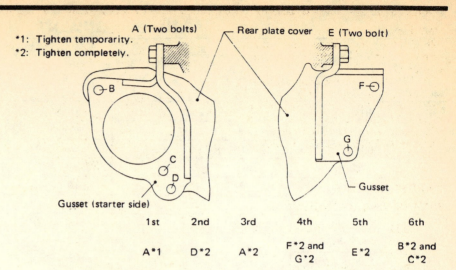

*1: Tighten temporarity.
*2: Tighten completely.

| | 1st | 2nd | 3rd | 4th | 5th | 6th |
|---|---|---|---|---|---|---|
| | A *1 | D *2 | A *2 | F *2 and G *2 | E *2 | B *2 and C *2 |

On 1988–89 300ZX torque the engine gussets in 6 stages to 22–29 ft. lbs.

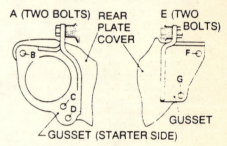

Torquing the 200SX (V6) engine gussets

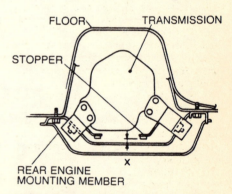

Adjust the rear mount stopper clearance (X) to 13mm ± 1.5mm—200SX (4cyl.) with automatic transmission

21. Install the floor shift lever and connect the column shift linkage.
22. Connect the back-up light switch and any other wiring to the transmission. Connect the speedometer cable.
23. Install the clutch return spring and operating cylinder, if removed.
24. Connect the power brake booster hose to the engine.
25. Connect all engine hoses and electrical wires. Install any removed engine accessory.
26. Install the fan and pulley.

27. Install the air cleaner.
28. Install the radiator and connect the transmission cooling lines, if equipped.
29. Fill the transmission and cooling system to the proper levels.
30. Install the hood and connect the negative battery cable.
31. Make all the necessary engine adjustments. Road test the vehicle for proper operation.

## 1990–92 300ZX
### WITH MANUAL TRANSMISSION

1. Mark the hood hinge relationship and remove the hood.
2. Release the fuel system pressure, disconnect the negative battery cable and raise and safely support the vehicle.
3. Remove the undercover.
4. Drain the coolant from both sides of the block and from the radiator.
5. Drain the oil pan.
6. Disconnect and label all engine vacuum hoses, fuel piping, harnesses and connectors.
7. Disconnect and remove the front exhaust tube sections.
8. Mark the relationship of the flanges and disconnect the driveshaft.
9. Remove the radiator.
10. Remove the drive belts.
11. Remove the cooling fan and coupling.
12. Remove the power steering pump, alternator, starter and clutch operating cylinder.
13. Discharge the air conditioning system and remove the compressor from the engine. Disconnect the air conditioning tube clamps.
14. Disconnect the steering column lower joint from the steering rack.
15. Remove the tension rod retaining bolts on both sides.
16. Loosen the transverse link bolts on both sides.
17. Support the rear suspension member using the proper equipment.
18. Install engine slingers to the block and connect a suitable lifting device to the slingers. Tension the lifting device slightly.
19. Remove the rear suspension member retaining bolts and center nut.
20. Remove the engine mount bracket bolts from both sides and slowly lower the transmission jack. Lift the engine from the vehicle.
**To install:**
21. Lower the engine into the vehicle and slowly raise the transmission jack. Install the engine mount bracket bolts. Torque the bolts to 30–38 ft. lbs. (40–42 Nm).
22. Install the rear suspension bolts and center nut. Torque the bolts to

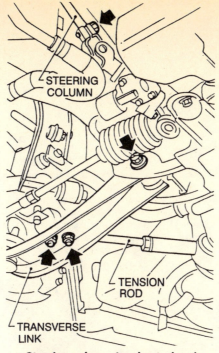

**Steering column, tension rod and transverse link attachment points**

38–48 ft. lbs. (51–65 Nm) and the center nut to 26–33 ft. lbs. (35–45 Nm).
23. Remove the jack and disconnect the engine hoist.
24. Torque the transverse link bolts to 80–94 ft. lbs. (108–127 Nm).
25. Install the tension rod retaining bolts and torque them to 80–94 ft. lbs. (108–127 Nm).
26. Connect the steering column lower joint to the steering rack. Torque the lower joint bolt to 17–22 ft. lbs. (24–29 Nm).
27. Connect the air conditioning tube clamps and mount the air conditioning compressor on the engine.
28. Install the clutch operating cylinder, starter, alternator and power steering pump.
29. Install the cooling fan and coupling.
30. Install the drive belts.
31. Install the radiator.
32. Install the driveshaft. Make sure the flanges are aligned properly. On non-turbo models, torque the flange bolts to 29–33 ft. lbs. (39–45 Nm) and 40–47 ft. lbs. (54–64 Nm) on turbocharged models.
33. Connect and install the front exhaust tube sections.
34. Connect the engine connectors, harnesses, fuel piping and vacuum hoses.
35. Install the undercover.
36. Fill the transmission and cooling system to the proper levels.
37. Install the hood and connect the negative battery cable.

38. Make all the necessary engine adjustments. Charge the air conditioning system.

### WITH AUTOMATIC TRANSMISSION

1. Mark the hood hinge relationship and remove the hood.
2. Relieve the fuel system pressure, disconnect the negative battery cable and raise and support the vehicle safely.
3. Remove the undercover.
4. Drain the coolant from both sides of the block and from the radiator.
5. Drain the oil pan.
6. Disconnect and label all engine vacuum hoses, fuel piping, harnesses and connectors.
7. Disconnect and remove the front exhaust tube sections.
8. Mark the relationship of the flanges and disconnect the driveshaft.
9. Remove the radiator.
10. Remove the drive belts.
11. Remove the cooling fan and coupling.
12. Remove the power steering pump, alternator, starter and clutch operating cylinder.
13. Remove the transmission.
14. Connect an engine hoist to the engine lifting brackets and tension the hoist.
15. Remove the engine mount bracket bolts and slowly lift the engine from the vehicle.

**To install:**
16. Lower the engine into the vehicle and install the engine mount bracket bolts. Torque the bolts to 30–38 ft. lbs. (40–42 Nm).
17. Install the clutch operating cylinder, starter, alternator and power steering pump.
18. Install the cooling fan and coupling.
19. Install the drive belts.
20. Install the radiator.
21. Install the driveshaft. Make sure the flanges are aligned properly. On non-turbo models, torque the flange bolts to 29–33 ft. lbs. (39–45 Nm) and 40–47 ft. lbs. (54–64 Nm) on turbocharged models.
22. Connect and install the front exhaust tube sections.
23. Connect the engine connectors, harnesses, fuel piping and vacuum hoses.
24. Install the undercover.
25. Fill the transmission and cooling system to the proper levels.
26. Install the hood and connect the negative battery cable.
27. Make all the necessary engine adjustments. Charge the air conditioning system. Road test the vehicle for proper operation.

### Maxima, Pulsar, Sentra and Stanza

It is recommended that the engine and transaxle be removed as a unit. If need be, the units may be separated after removal.

**NOTE: On the 1989–92 Sentra (GA16i and GA16DE engines), the engine cannot be removed separately from the tranaxle. Remove the engine and the transaxle as a unit. If equipped with 4WD, remove the engine, transaxle and transfer case together.**

1. Mark the hood hinge relationship and remove the hood.
2. Release the fuel system pressure, disconnect the negative battery cable and raise and support the vehicle safely.
3. Drain the cooling system and the oil pan.
4. Remove the air cleaner and disconnect the throttle cable.
5. Disconnect or remove the following:
    Drive belts
    Ignition wire from the coil to the distributor
    Ignition coil ground wire and the engine ground cable
    Block connector from the distributor
    Fusible links
    Engine harness connectors
    Fuel and fuel return hoses
    Upper and lower radiator hoses
    Heater inlet and outlet hoses
    Engine vacuum hoses
    Carbon canister hoses and the air pump air cleaner hose
    Any interfering engine accessory: power steering pump, air conditioning compressor or alternator
    Driveshaft from transfer for 4WD vehicles. Make sure to matchmark flanges
6. Remove the air pump air cleaner.
7. Remove the carbon canister.
8. Remove the auxiliary fan, washer tank, grille and radiator (with fan assembly).
9. Remove the clutch cylinder from the clutch housing for manual transaxles.
10. Remove both buffer rods without altering the length of the rods. Disconnect the speedometer cable.
11. Remove the spring pins from the transaxle gear selector rods.
12. Install engine slingers to the block and connect a suitable lifting device to the slingers. Do not tension the lifting device at this point.
13. Disconnect the exhaust pipe at both the manifold connection and the clamp holding the pipe to the engine.
14. On the Sentra, Pulsar and 1988–89 Stanza, remove the lower ball joint.

15. Drain the transaxle gear oil.
16. Disconnect the right and left side halfshafts from their side flanges and remove the bolt holding the radius link support.

**NOTE: When drawing out the halfshafts on the Sentra, Stanza and Pulsar, it is necessary to loosen the strut head bolts.**

17. Lower the shifter and selector rods and remove the bolts from the motor mount brackets. Remove the nuts holding the front and rear motor mounts to the frame. On the Sentra, Stanza and Pulsar, disconnect the clutch and accelerator wires and remove the speedometer cable with its pinion from the transaxle.
18. Lift the engine/transaxle assembly up and away from the vehicle.

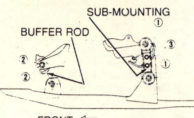

On Stanza Wagon (2WD), tighten the buffer rod and sub-mounting bolts in the order shown

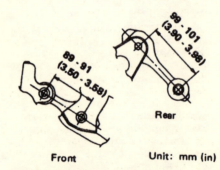

Front and rear buffer rod length adjustment on 1988–90 Pulsar (E16i and GA16i), Maxima and Sentra

**To install:**
19. Lower the engine transaxle assembly into the vehicle. When lowering the engine onto the frame, make sure to keep it as level as possible.
20. Check the clearance between the frame and clutch housing and make sure the engine mount bolts are seated in the groove of the mounting bracket.
21. After installing the motor mounts, adjust and install the buffer rods. On the 1988–90 Pulsar with E16i and GA16i engines, 1989–92 Maxima and 1989–92 Sentra: front should be 3.50–3.58 in. (89–91mm),

and the rear, 3.90–3.98 in. (99–101mm).
22. On the Stanza Wagon (2WD), tighten the engine mount bolts first, then apply a load to the mounting insulators before tightening the buffer rod and sub-mounting bolts.
23. On the Sentra, Stanza and Pulsar, connect the clutch and accelerator wires and remove the speedometer cable with its pinion from the transaxle.
24. Raise the shifter and selector rods to their normal operating positions.
25. Connect the halfshafts.
26. On the Sentra, Pulsar and 1988–89 Stanza, connect the lower ball joint.
27. Connect the exhaust pipe to the manifold connection and the clamp holding the pipe to the engine.
28. Disconnect the lifting device and remove the engine slingers.
29. Insert the spring pins into the transaxle gear selector rods.
30. Connect the speedometer cable.
31. Mount the clutch cylinder onto the clutch housing.
32. Install the auxiliary fan, washer tank, grille and radiator (with fan assembly).
33. Install the carbon canister.
34. Install the air pump air cleaner.
35. Install or connect all hoses, belts, harnesses, connectors and components that were necessary to remove the engine.
36. Connect the throttle cable and install the air cleaner.
37. Fill the transaxle and cooling system to the proper levels.
38. Install the hood and connect the negative battery cable.
39. Make all the necessary engine adjustments. Charge the air conditioning system. Road test the vehicle for proper operation.

## Cylinder Head

### REMOVAL & INSTALLATION

**NOTE: To prevent distortion or warping of the cylinder head, allow the engine to cool completely before removing the head bolts.**

### CA18DE Engine

1. Crank the engine until the No. 1 piston is at TDC of the compression stroke. Relieve the fuel system pressure and disconnect the negative battery cable . Drain the cooling system, remove the air cleaner assembly and raise and safely support the vehicle.
2. Loosen the alternator and remove all drive belts. Remove the alternator.
3. Disconnect the air duct at the throttle chamber.

4. Tag and disconnect all lines, electrical harnesses, hoses and wires which may interfere with cylinder head removal.

5. Remove the ornament cover.

6. Disconnect the oxygen sensor wire.

7. Remove the 2 exhaust heat shield covers.

8. Unbolt the exhaust manifold and wire the entire assembly aside.

9. Disconnect the EGR tube at the passage cover and then remove the passage cover and gasket.

10. Disconnect and remove the crank angle sensor from the upper front cover.

**NOTE: Put an aligning mark on crank angle sensor and timing belt cover.**

11. Remove the support stay from under the intake manifold assembly.

12. Unbolt the intake manifold and remove it along with the collector and throttle chamber.

13. Remove the fuel injectors as an assembly.

14. Remove the upper and lower front covers.

**NOTE: Remove engine mount bracket but support engine under oil pan with wooden blocks.**

15. Remove the timing belt and camshaft sprockets.

**NOTE: When the timing belt has been removed, never rotate the crankshaft and camshaft separately because the valves will hit the top of the pistons.**

16. Remove the camshaft cover.

17. Remove the breather separator.

18. Gradually loosen the cylinder head bolts in several stages, in the proper sequence.

19. Carefully remove the cylinder head from the block, pulling the head up evenly from both ends. If the head seems stuck, do not pry it off. Tap lightly around the lower perimeter of the head with a rubber mallet to help break the joint.

**To install:**

20. Thoroughly clean both the cylinder block and head mating surfaces. Avoid scratching either.

21. Lay the cylinder head gasket onto the block and lower the head onto the gasket.

22. When installing the bolts tighten the 2 center bolts temporarily to 15 ft. lbs. (20 Nm) and install the head bolts loosely. After the breather separator, camshaft cover, timing belt, camshaft sprockets and front cover have been installed, torque all the head bolts in the proper sequence as follows. Tighten all bolts to 22 ft. lbs. (29 Nm). Re-

LOOSENING ORDER

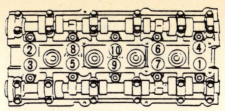

**Cylinder head loosening sequence— CA18DE engine**

Tightening order

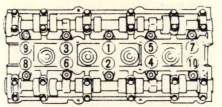

**Cylinder head tightening sequence— CA18DE engine**

tighten all bolts to 76 ft. lbs. (103 Nm). Loosen all bolts completely and then re-tighten them once again to 22 ft. lbs. (29 Nm). Tighten all bolts to a final torque of 76 ft. lbs. (103 Nm) or 85–95 degrees if using an angle torque wrench.

**NOTE: Newer models use cupped washers on the cylinder head bolts, always make sure the flat side of the washer is facing downward before tightening the cylinder head bolts.**

23. Install the fuel injector assembly. Use new O-rings and insulators as required.

24. Install the intake manifold assembly and intake manifold stay.

25. Install the crank angle sensor. Make sure the sensor and upper front matchmarks are aligned properly.

26. Install the passage cover and gasket. Connect the EGR tube to the passage cover.

27. Install the exhaust manifold.

28. Install the exhaust manifold heat shield covers.

29. Install the ornament cover.

30. Connect all lines, electrical harnesses, hoses and wires.

31. Connect the air duct to the throttle chamber.

32. Install the alternator and drive belts.

33. Install the air cleaner assembly.

34. Fill the cooling system to the proper level and connect the negative battery cable.

35. Make all the necessary engine adjustments. Road test the vehicle for proper operation.

### CA20E Engine

1. Relieve the fuel system pressure,

disconnect the negative battery cable and drain the cooling system.

2. Remove the air intake pipe.

3. Remove the cooling fan and radiator shroud.

4. Remove the alternator drive belt, power steering pump drive belt and the air conditioner compressor drive belt, if equipped.

5. Position the No. 1 cylinder at TDC of the compression stroke and remove the upper and lower timing belt covers.

6. Loosen the timing belt tensioner and return spring, then remove the timing belt.

**NOTE: When the timing belt has been removed, do not rotate the crankshaft and the camshaft separately, because the valves will hit the tops of the pistons.**

7. Remove the exhaust manifold.

8. Remove the camshaft pulley.

9. Remove the water pump pulley.

10. Remove the crankshaft pulley.

11. Remove the alternator adjusting bracket.

12. Remove the water pump.

13. Remove the oil pump.

14. Loosen the cylinder head bolts in sequence and in several steps.

15. Remove the cylinder head and manifolds as an assembly.

**To install:**

16. Clean the cylider head gasket surfaces.

17. Lay the cylinder head gasket onto the block and lower the head onto the gasket.

18. Install the cylinder head bolts.

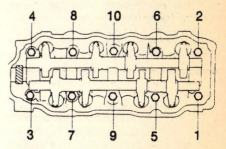

**Cylinder head bolt loosening sequence— CA20E engine**

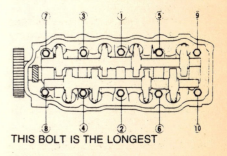

THIS BOLT IS THE LONGEST

**Cylinder head bolt tightening sequence— CA20E engine**

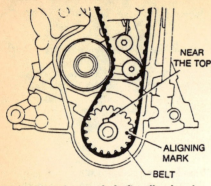

**Make sure the crankshaft pulley key is near the top—C series engine**

When installing the bolts, tighten the two center bolts temporarily to 15 ft. lbs. and install the head bolts loosely. They will be torqued after the timing belt and front cover are installed.

19. Install the oil pump.
20. Install the water pump.
21. Install the alternator adjusting bracket.
22. Install the crankshaft, water pump and camshaft pulleys.
23. Install the exhaust manifold.

**NOTE: Before installing the timing belt, be certain the crankshaft pulley key is near the top and that the camshaft knock pin or sprocket aligning mark is at the top.**

24. Install the timing belt and timing belt covers. After the timing belt and covers have been installed, torque all the head bolts in the torque sequence provided in this section. Tighten all bolts to 22 ft. lbs. (29 Nm). Re-tighten all bolts to 58 ft. lbs. (78 Nm). Loosen all bolts completely and then re-tighten them once again to 22 ft. lbs. (29 Nm). Tighten all bolts to a final torque of 54–61 ft. lbs. (74–83 Nm) or if using an angle torque wrench, give all bolts a final turn to 75–80 degrees except bolt No. 8 which is 83–88 degrees. No. 8 bolt is longer.

**NOTE: Newer models use cupped washers on the cylinder head bolts, always make sure that the flat side of the washer is facing downward before tightening the cylinder head bolts.**

25. Install the drive belts.
26. Install the cooling fan and radiator shroud.
27. Fill the cooling system to the proper level and connect the negative battery cable.
28. Make all the necessary engine adjustments. Road test the vehicle for proper operation.

## E16i Engine

**NOTE: Be sure to use new washers when installing the cylinder head bolts.**

1. Crank the engine until the No. 1 piston is at TDC on its compression stroke. Relieve the fuel system pressure and disconnect the negative battery cable. Drain the cooling system and remove the air cleaner assembly.
2. Remove the alternator.
3. Remove the distributor, with all wires attached.
4. Remove the EAI pipe bracket and EGR tube at the right (EGR valve) side. Disconnect the same pipes on the front side of the manifold.
5. Remove the exhaust manifold cover and the exhaust manifold, taking note that the center manifold nut has a different diameter than the other nuts. Label this nut to ensure proper installation.
6. Remove the air conditioning compressor bracket and power steering pump bracket, if equipped.
7. Disconnect the carburetor throttle linkage, fuel line, and all vacuum and electrical connections.
8. Remove the intake manifold.
9. Remove water pump drive belt and pulley.
10. Remove crankshaft pulley.
11. Remove the rocker (valve) cover.
12. Remove upper and lower dust cover on the camshaft timing belt shroud.
13. Mark the relationship of the camshaft sprocket to the timing belt and the crankshaft sprocket to the timing belt with paint or a grease pencil. This will make setting everything up during reassembly much easier if the engine is disturbed during disassembly.
14. Remove the belt tensioner pulley.
15. Mark an arrow on the timing belt showing direction of engine rotation and slide the belt off the sprockets.
16. Loosen the head bolts in reverse of the tightening sequence and carefully remove the cylinder head from the block, pulling the head up evenly from both ends. If the head seems stuck, do not pry it off. Tap lightly around the lower perimeter of the head with a rubber mallet to help break the seal. Label all head bolts with tape, as they must go back in their original positions.
**To install:**
17. Thoroughly clean both the cylinder block and head mating surfaces. Avoid scratching either.
18. Turn the crankshaft and set the No. 1 cylinder at TDC on its compression stroke. This causes the crankshaft timing sprocket mark to be aligned with the cylinder block cover mark.
19. Align the camshaft sprocket

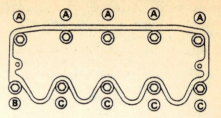

**Cylinder head bolt location on E16i engines**

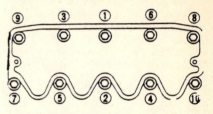

TIGHTEN IN NUMERICAL ORDER

**Cylinder head torque sequence—E series engine**

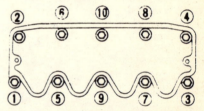

**Loosen the cylinder head bolts, in stages in the order shown—E series engine**

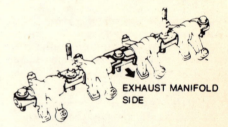

**Make sure the cutout on the E series engine rocker shaft faces the exhaust manifold**

mark with the cylinder head cover mark. This causes the valves for No. 1 cylinder to position at TDC on the compression stroke.
20. Place a new gasket on the cylinder block.

**NOTE: There are 3 different size head bolts used on the E16i engine. Bolt (A) is 3.74 in. (95mm), bolt (B) is 4.33 in. (110mm) and bolt (C) is 3.15 in. (80mm). Measure the length of each bolt prior to installation and make sure they are installed in their proper locations on the head.**

21. Install the cylinder head on the block and tighten the bolts as follows:
   a. Tighten all bolts to 22 ft. lbs. (29 Nm), then retighten them all to 51 ft. lbs. (69 Nm).

b. Loosen all bolts completely, and then retighten them again to 22 ft. lbs. (29 Nm).

c. Tighten all bolts to a final torque of 51–54 ft. lbs. (69–74 Nm); or if an angle wrench is used, turn each bolt until they have achieved the specified number of degrees—bolts 1, 3, 6, 8 and 9: 45–50 degrees; bolt 7: 55–60 degrees and bolts 2, 4, 5 and 10: 40–45 degrees.

22. Install the timing belt.

23. Install the upper and lower dust covers on the camshaft timing belt shroud.

24. Install the rocker arm cover.

25. Install the crankshaft pulley, water pump pulley and drive belt.

26. Install the intake manifold.

27. Connect the throttle linkage, fuel line, and all vacuum and electrical connections.

28. Install the air conditioning compressor bracket and the power steering pump bracket, if equipped.

29. Install the exhaust manifold and exhaust manifold cover. Make sure the center manifold nut, which has a different diameter, is installed in the proper location.

30. Connect the EAI exhaust pipes and tubing.

31. Install the distributor and connect the spark plug wiring.

32. Install the alternator and air cleaner.

33. Fill the cooling system to the proper level and connect the negative battery cable.

34. Make all the necessary engine adjustments. Road test the vehicle for proper operation.

## GA16i Engine

1. Disconnect the negative battery cable, drain the cooling system and relieve the fuel system pressure.

2. Disconnect the exhaust tube from the exhaust manifold.

3. Remove the intake manifold support bracket.

4. Remove the air cleaner assembly.

5. Disconnect the center wire from the distributor cap.

6. Remove the rocker arm cover.

7. Remove the distributor.

8. Remove the spark plugs.

9. Set the No. 1 cylinder at TDC of the compression stroke by rotating the engine until the cut out machined in the rear of the camshaft is horizontally aligned with the cylinder head.

10. Hold the camshaft sprocket stationary with the proper tool and loosen the sprocket bolt. Place highly visible and accurate paint or chalk alignment marks on the camshaft sprocket and the timing chain, then slide the sprocket from the camshaft and lift the timing chain from the sprocket.

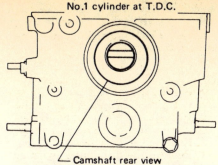

No.1 cylinder at T.D.C.

Camshaft rear view

**When camshaft is aligned as shown, the No. 1 piston is at TDC—GA16i engine**

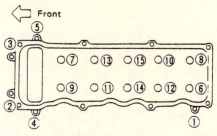

Front

Loosen in numerical order.

**Loosen the cylinder head bolts in several stages in the order shown—GA16i and GA16DE engines**

Remove the sprocket. The timing chain will not fall off the crankshaft sprocket unless the front cover is removed. This is due to the cast portion of the front cover located on the lower side of the crankshaft sprocket which acts a stopper mechanism. For this reason a chain stopper (wedge) is not required to remove the cylinder head.

11. Loosen the cylinder bolts in 2–3 stages to prevent warpage and cracking of the head. One of the cylinder head bolts is longer than the rest. Mark this bolt and make a note of its location.

12. Carefully remove the cylinder head from the block, pulling the head up evenly from both ends. If the head seems stuck, do not pry it off. Tap lightly around the lower perimeter of the head with a rubber mallet to help break the seal. The cylinder head and the intake and exhaust manifolds are removed together. Remove the cylinder head gasket.

**To install:**

13. Thoroughly clean both the cylinder block and head mating surfaces. Avoid scratching either.

14. Turn the crankshaft and set the No. 1 cylinder at TDC on its compression stroke. This is done by aligning the timing pointer with the appropriate timing mark on the pulley. To ensure that the No. 1 piston is at TDC, verify that the knock pin in the front of the camshaft is set at the top.

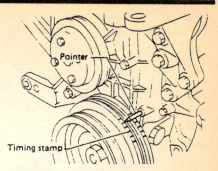

Pointer

Timing stamp

**When the crankshaft pulley marks are aligned as shown, the No. 1 piston is at TDC**

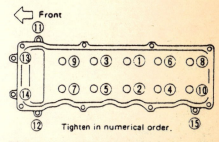

Front

Tighten in numerical order.

**Cylinder head bolt tightening sequence—GA16i and GA16DE engines. Bolt (1) is the longest bolt**

15. Place a new gasket on the block and lower the head onto the gasket.

**NOTE: These engines use 2 different length cylinder head bolts. Bolt (1) is 5.24 in. (133mm) while bolts (2) thru (10) are 4.33 in. (110mm). Do not confuse the location of these bolts.**

16. Coat the threads and the seating surface of the head bolts with clean engine oil and use a new set of washers. Install the cylinder head bolts in their proper locations and tighten as follows:

a. Tighten all the bolts in sequence to 22 ft. lbs. (30 Nm).

b. Tighten all bolts in sequence to 47 ft. lbs.(64 Nm).

c. Loosen all bolts in reverse of the tightening sequence.

d. Tighten all bolts again to 22 ft. lbs. (30 Nm).

e. If an angle torque wrench is not available, torque the bolts in sequence to 43–51 ft. lbs. (58–59 Nm). If using an angle torque wrench for this step, tighten bolt (1) 80–85 degrees clockwise and bolts (6) thru (10) 60–65 degrees clockwise.

f. Finally, tighten bolts (11) thru (15) to 4.6– 6.1 ft. lbs. (6.3–8.3 Nm).

17. Place the timing chain on the camshaft sprocket using the alignment marks. Slide the sprocket and timing chain onto the camshaft and install the center bolt.

18. At this point, check the hydraulic valve lifters for proper operation push-

ing hard on each lifter hard with fingertip pressure. Make sure the rocker arm arm is not on the cam lobe when making this check. If the valve lifter moves more than 0.04 in. (1mm), air may be inside it.

19. Install the spark plugs.
20. Install the distributor.
21. Install the rocker arm cover.
22. Connect the center wire to the distributor cap.
23. Install the air cleaner assembly.
24. Install the intake manifold support bracket.
25. Fill the cooling system to the proper level and connect the negative battery cable.
26. Make all the necessary engine adjustments. If there was air in the lifters, bleed the air by running the engine at 1000 rpm for 10 minutes. Road test the vehicle for proper operation.

### GA16DE Engine

1. Disconnect the negative battery cable, drain the cooling system and relieve the fuel system pressure.
2. Remove all drive belts. Disconnect the exhaust tube from the exhaust manifold.
3. Remove the power steering bracket.
4. Remove the air duct to intake manifold collector.
5. Remove the front right side wheel, splash cover and front undercovers.
6. Remove the front exhaust pipe and engine front mounting bracket.
7. Remove the rocker arm cover.
8. Remove the distributor cap. Remove the spark plugs.
9. Set the No. 1 cylinder at TDC of the compression stroke.
10. Mark and remove the distributor assembly.
11. Remove the cam sprocket cover and gusset. Remove the water pump pulley. Remove the thermostat housing.
12. Remove the chain tensioner, chain guide. Loosen idler sprocket bolt.
13. Remove the camshaft sprocket bolts, camshaft sprocket, camshaft brackets and camshafts. Remove the idler sprocket bolt. These parts should be reassembled in their original position. Bolts should be loosen in 2 or 3 steps.
14. Loosen the cylinder bolts in 2–3 stages to prevent warpage and cracking of the head and note location of all head bolts.
15. Carefully remove the cylinder head from the block, pulling the head up evenly from both ends. If the head seems stuck, do not pry it off. Tap lightly around the lower perimeter of the head with a rubber mallet to help

break the seal. The cylinder head and the intake and exhaust manifolds are removed together. Remove the cylinder head gasket.

**To install:**

16. Thoroughly clean both the cylinder block and head mating surfaces. Avoid scratching either.
17. Coat the threads and the seating surface of the head bolts with clean engine oil and use a new set of washers as necessary. Install the cylinder head assembly (always replace the head gasket). Install head bolts (with washers) in their proper locations and tighten as follows:

    a. Tighten all the bolts in sequence to 22 ft. lbs. (29 Nm).
    b. Tighten all bolts in sequence to 43 ft. lbs.(59 Nm).
    c. Loosen all bolts in reverse of the tightening sequence.
    d. Tighten all bolts again in sequence to 22 ft. lbs. (29 Nm).
    e. Tighten bolts to 50–55 degrss clockwise in sequence or if angle wrench is not available, tighten bolts to 40–46 ft. lbs. in sequence.
    f.Finally, tighten bolts (11) thru (15) to 4.6–6.1 ft. lbs. (6.3–8.3 Nm).
18. Install the upper timing chain assembly.
19. Install all other components in the reverse order of the removal procedure. Refill and check all fluid levels. Road test the vehicle for proper operation.

### KA24E Engine

**NOTE: After completing this procedure, allow the rocker cover to cylinder head rubber plugs to dry for 30 minutes before starting the engine. This will allow the liquid gasket sealer to cure properly.**

1. Release the fuel system pressure.
2. Disconnect the negative battery cable and drain the cooling system.
3. On 240SX, remove the power steering drive belt, power steering pump, idler pulley and power steering brackets.
4. Tag and disconnect all the vacuum hoses, water hoses, fuel tubes and wiring harnesses necessary to gain access to cylinder head.
5. Disconnect the air induction hose from the collector assembly.
6. Detach the accelerator bracket. If necessary mark the position and remove the accelerator cable wire end from the throttle drum.
7. Unbolt the intake manifold collector from the intake manifold.
8. Remove the intake manifold.
9. Unplug the exhaust gas sensor and remove the exhaust cover and exhaust pipe at exhaust manifold connection. Remove the exhaust manifold from the cylinder head.

10. Remove the rocker cover. If cover sticks to the cylinder head, tap it with a rubber hammer. Be careful not to strike the rocker arms when removing the rocker arm cover.

**NOTE: After removing the rocker cover matchmark the timing chain with the camshaft sprocket with paint or equivalent.**

11. Set No. 1 cylinder piston at TDC on its compression stroke. The No. 1 will be at TDC when the timing pointer is aligned with the red timing mark on the crankshaft pulley.
12. Loosen the camshaft sprocket bolt. Do not turn engine when removing the bolt.
13. Support the timing chain with the proper tool.
14. Remove the camshaft sprocket.
15. Remove the front cover-to-cylinder head retaining bolts.

**NOTE: The cylinder head bolts should be loosened in 2–3 steps in the correct order to prevent head warpage or cracking.**

16. Remove the cylinder head bolts in the correct sequence. Lift the cylinder head off the engine block. It may be necessary to tap the head lightly with a rubber mallet to loosen it.

**To install:**

17. Confirm that the No. 1 piston is at TDC on its compression stroke as follows: Align timing mark with the red (0 degree) mark on the crankshaft pulley. Make sure the distributor rotor head is set at No. 1 on the distributor cap. Confirm that the knock pin on the camshaft is set at the top position.
18. Install the cylinder head with a new gasket and torque the head bolts in numerical order using the following 5 step procedure:

    a. Torque all bolts to 22 ft. lbs. (29 Nm).
    b. Torque all bolts to 58 ft. lbs. (78 Nm).
    c. Loosen all bolts completely.
    d. Torque all bolts to 22 ft. lbs. (29 Nm).
    e. Torque all bolts to 54–61 ft. lbs. (74–83 Nm), or if an angle wrench is used, turn all bolts 80–85 degrees clockwise.

**NOTE: Do not rotate crankshaft and camshaft separately, or valves will hit the tops of the pistons.**

19. Remove the tool from the timing chain. Position the timing chain on the camshaft sprocket by aligning each matchmark. Install the camshaft sprocket to the camshaft.
20. Hold the camshaft sprocket stationary, and tighten the sprocket bolt

**On KA24E engine, support the timing chain with a special tool when removing the cylinder head**

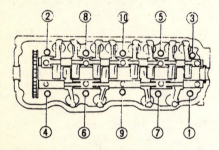

**Cylinder head bolt loosening sequence—KA24E and KA24DE engines**

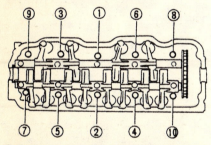

**Cylinder head bolt tightening sequence—KA24E and KA24DE engines**

**When the camshaft knock pin is at the top No. 1 piston is at TDC—KA24E engine**

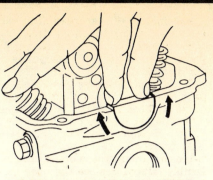

**Rubber plug installation on KA24E engine**

to 87–116 ft. lbs. (118–157 Nm). Install front cover-to-cylinder head retaining bolts. Torque the 6mm bolts to 5–6 ft. lbs. (7–8 Nm) and the 8mm bolts to 12–15 ft. lbs. (16–21 Nm).

21. Install the intake manifold and collector assembly with new gaskets.

22. Install the exhaust manifold with new gaskets.

23. Apply liquid gasket to the rubber plugs and install the rubber plugs in the correct location in the cylinder head. The seating surface of the rubber plugs must be clean and dry. The rubber plugs should be installed within 5 minutes of the sealant application. After the sealant is applied and the rubber plugs are in place, rock the plugs back and forth a few times to distribute the sealant evenly. Wipe the excess sealant from the cylinder head with a clean rag.

24. Install the rocker cover with new gasket.

25. Attach the accelerator bracket and cable if removed.

26. Connect all the vacuum hoses, water hoses, fuel tubes and electrical connections that were removed to gain access to cylinder head.

27. Reconnect the air induction hose to collector assembly.

28. Install the spark plugs and spark plug wires in the correct location.

29. On 240SX, install the power steering brackets, idler pulley, and power steering pump.

30. Install the drive belts.

31. Fill the cooling system and connect the negative battery cable.

32. Make all the necessary engine adjustments. Road test the vehicle for proper operation.

## KA24DE Engine

1. Release the fuel system pressure.

2. Disconnect the negative battery cable and drain the cooling system. Drain the engine oil.

3. Remove all vacuum hoses, fuel lines, wires, electrical connections as necessary.

4. Remove the front exhaust pipe and A.I.V. pipe.

5. Remove the air duct, cooling fan with coupling and radiator shroud.

6. Remove the the fuel injector tube assembly with injectors.

7. Disconnect and mark spark plug wires. Remove the spark plugs.

8. Set No. 1 piston at TDC on compression stroke. Remove the rocker cover assembly.

9. Mark and remove the distributor assembly.

10. Remove the cam sprocket, brackets and camshafts. These parts should be reassembled in their original position. Bolts should be loosened in 2–3 steps.

11. Loosen cylinder head bolts in two or three steps in sequence.

12. Remove the cam sprocket cover. Remove the upper chain tensioner and upper chain guides.

13. Remove the upper timing chain and idler sprocket bolt. Lower timing chain will not disengaged from the crankshaft sprocket.

14. Remove the cylinder head with the intake manifold, collector and exhaust manifold assembly.

**To install:**

15. Check all components for wear. Replace as necessary. Clean all mating surfaces and replace the cylinder head gasket.

16. Install cylinder head. Tighten cylinder head in the following sequence:

    a. Tighten all bolts in sequence to 22 ft. lbs.

    b. Tighten all bolts in sequence to 59 ft. lbs.

    c. Loosen all bolts in sequence completely.

    d. Tighten all bolts in sequence to 18–25 ft. lbs.

    e. Tighten all bolts to 86 to 91 degrees clockwise, or if an angle wrench is not available, tighten all bolts to in sequence to 55–62 ft. lbs.

17. Install upper timing chain assemble in the correct position. Align all timing marks.

18. Install all other components in the reverse order of the removal procedure. Refill and check all fluid levels. Road test the vehicle for proper operation.

## SR20DE Engine

1. Release the fuel pressure. Disconnect the negative battery cable.

2. Raise and safely support the vehicle. Remove the engine undercovers.

3. Remove the front right wheel and engine side cover.

4. Drain the cooling system. Remove the radiator assembly.

5. Remove the air duct to intake manifold.

6. Remove the drive belts and water pump pulley.

**NISSAN**

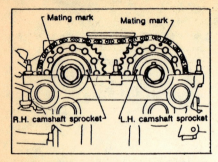

Cam sprocket correct position-SR20DE engine

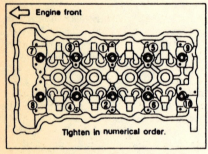

Cylinder head torque sequence—SR20DE engine

7. Remove the alternator and power steering pump.
8. Remove all vacuum hoses, fuel hoses, wires, electrical connections.
9. Remove all spark plugs.
10. Remove the A.I.V. valve and resonator.
11. Remove the rocker cover and oil separator.
12. Remove the intake manifold supports, oil filter bracket and power steering bracket.
13. Set No. 1 at TDC on the compression stroke. Rotate crankshaft until mating marks on camshaft sprockets are in the correct position.
14. Remove the timing chain tensioner.
15. Mark and remove the distributor assembly. Remove the timing chain guide and camshaft sprockets.
16. Remove the camshafts, camshaft brackets, oil tubes and baffle plate. Keep all parts in order for correct installation.
17. Remove the water hose from the cylinder block and water hose from the heater.
18. Remove the starter motor. Remove the water pipe bolt.
19. Remove the cylinder outside bolts. Remove the cylinder head bolts in 2 or 3 steps. Remove the cylinder head completely with manifolds attached.
**To install:**
20. Check all components for wear. Replace as necessary. Clean all mating surfaces and replace the cylinder head gasket.

21. Install cylinder head. Tighten cylinder head in the following sequence:
 a. Tighten all bolts in sequence to 29 ft. lbs.
 b. Tighten all bolts in sequence to 58 ft. lbs.
 c. Loosen all bolts in sequence completely.
 d. Tighten all bolts in sequence to 25–33 ft. lbs.
 e. Tighten all bolts to 90 to 100 degrees clockwise in sequence
 f. Tighten all bolts additional 90 to 100 degrees clockwise in sequence. Do not turn any bolt 180 to 200 degrees clockwise all at once.
22. Install all other components in the reverse order of the removal procedure. Refill and check all fluid levels. Road test the vehicle for proper operation.

### VG30E and VG30ET Engines (200SX and 1988–89 300ZX)

**NOTE: On all models, a special hex head wrench ST10120000 (J24239-01) or equivalent will be needed to remove and install the cylinder head bolts.**

1. Disconnect the negative battery cable.
2. Relieve the fuel system pressure.
3. Remove the timing belt.

**NOTE: Never rotate the crankshaft and camshaft separately after the timing belt has been removed or the valves will hit the tops of the pistons.**

4. Set the No. 1 cylinder at TDC on its compression stroke.
5. Drain the coolant from the cylinder block.
6. Remove the collector cover and collector. Loosen the bolts starting from the ends and work towards the center. On the 200SX, remove the collector together with the throttle chamber, EGR valve and IAA unit.
7. Remove the intake manifold with fuel tube assembly. Loosen the intake manifold bolts starting from the front of the engine and proceed in crisscross pattern.
8. Remove the power steering pump bracket.
9. Remove the exhaust collector bracket.
10. Disconnect the exhaust manifold balance and connecting tubes.
11. Remove the bolts securing the camshaft pulleys and rear timing cover.
12. Discharge the air conditioning system system and remove the compressor and compressor bracket. Remove the rocker covers.
13. Loosen the cylinder head bolts in

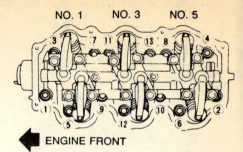

Cylinder head loosening sequence VG30E (200SX)

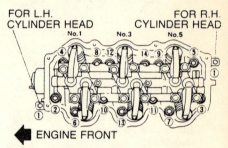

Cylinder head loosening sequence VG30E and VG30ET (Maxima and 300ZX)

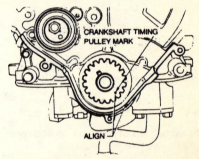

Aligning timing mark and mark oil pump housing—V6 engine

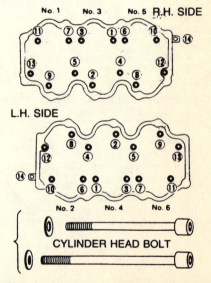

Cylinder head torque sequence—VG30E and VG30ET (Maxima and 300ZX)

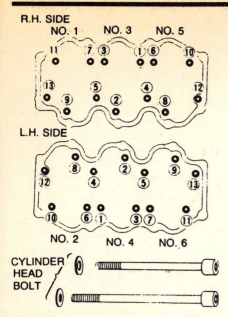

R.H. SIDE
NO. 1   NO. 3   NO. 5

L.H. SIDE

NO. 2   NO. 4   NO. 6

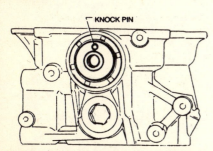

CYLINDER HEAD BOLT

**Cylinder head torque sequence—VG30E (200SX)**

KNOCK PIN

**Knock pin of camshaft facing upward— V6 engine**

the proper sequence. Remove the cylinder head with the exhaust manifolds attached. It may be necessary to tap the head lightly with a rubber mallet to loosen it.

**To install:**

14. Make sure the No. 1 cylinder is set at TDC on its compression stroke as follows:

    a. Align the crankshaft timing mark with the mark on the oil pump housing.

    b. The knock pin in the front end of the camshaft should be facing upward.

**NOTE: Do not rotate crankshaft and camshaft separately because valves will hit the tops of the pistons.**

15. Position the cylinder head and gasket on the block and tighten the cylinder head bolts as follows using the proper sequence:

    a. Tighten all bolts to 22 ft. lbs. (29 Nm).

    b. Tighten all bolts to 43 ft. lbs. (59 Nm).

    c. Loosen all bolts completely.

    d. Tighten all bolts to 22 ft. lbs. (29 Nm).

    e. Tighten all bolts to 40–47 ft. lbs. (54–64 Nm) or if using an angle wrench, turn all bolts 60–65 degrees clockwise.

16. Tighten the rear timing belt cover.

17. Install the camshaft pulley and tighten to 58–65 ft. lbs. (79–88 Nm).

**NOTE: The right hand and left hand camshaft pulleys are different parts. Install them in the correct positions. The right hand pulley has an "R3" identification mark and the left hand pulley has an "L3".**

18. Install the timing belt and adjust the tension.

19. Install the front upper and lower belt covers.

20. Install the rocker covers, compressor bracket and air conditioning compressor.

21. Install the intake manifold and fuel tube and tighten both the nuts and bolts as follows: first to 2–4 ft. lbs. (3–5 Nm), then to 17–20 ft. lbs. (24–27 Nm).

22. Connect the exhaust manifold balance and connecting tubes. Tighten the exhaust manifold connecting tube and tighten to 16–20 ft. lbs. (22–27 Nm).

23. Install the exhaust collector bracket.

24. Install the power steering pump bracket.

25. Install the intake manifold and fuel tube assembly. Make sure to tighten the bolts in 2–3 stages using the proper torque sequence.

26. Install the collector and collector cover. When installing the collector cover, always use a new gasket. On the 200SX and 1988–89 300ZX, tighten the throttle chamber-to-collector bolts in two stages; 6.5–8 ft. lbs. (9–11 Nm) and then to 13–16 ft. lbs. (18–22 Nm).

27. Install and tension the drive belts.

28. Fill the cooling system to the proper level and connect the negative battery cable.

29. Make all the necessary engine adjustments. Charge the air conditioning system.

### VG30E Engine (Maxima)

**NOTE: A special hex head wrench ST10120000 (J24239-01) or equivalent will be needed to remove and install the cylinder head bolts.**

1. Relieve the fuel system pressure and disconnect the negative battery cable.

2. Drain the cooling system. On 1989–92 Maxima, there are 2 cylinder

block drain plugs. The left side drain plug is located beside the oil level gauge and the right side drain plug is located behind the right hand halfshaft boot.

3. Remove the timing belt.

**NOTE: Do not rotate either the crankshaft or camshaft from this point onward, or the valves could be bent by hitting the tops of the pistons.**

4. Disconnect and tag all vacuum and water hoses connected to the intake collector.

5. On 1989–92 Maxima, remove the distributor, ignition wires and disconnect the accelerator and cruise control (ASCD) cables from the intake manifold collector.

6. Remove the collector cover and the collector from the intake manifold. On 1989–92 Maxima, there are upper and lower collector covers. Disconnect and tag all harness connectors and vacuum lines to gain access to the cover retaining bolts on these models.

7. Remove the intake manifold and fuel tube assembly. Loosen the intake manifold bolts starting from the front of the engine and proceed in crisscross pattern towards the center.

8. Remove the exhaust collector bracket.

9. Remove the exhaust manifold covers.

10. Disconnect the exhaust manifold from the exhaust pipe.

11. Remove the camshaft pulleys and the rear timing cover securing bolts. Remove the rocker arm covers.

12. On 1989–92 Maxima, separate the air conditioning compressor and alternator from the their mounting brackets. Remove the mounting brackets. Do not disconnect the refrigerant lines from the compressor or serious injury will result.

13. Remove the cylinder head bolts in the correct sequence. Lift the cylinder head off the engine block with the exhaust manifolds attached. It may be necessary to tap the head lightly with a rubber mallet to loosen it.

**To install:**

14. Make sure the No. 1 cylinder is set at TDC on its compression stroke as follows:

    a. Align the crankshaft timing mark with the mark on the oil pump housing.

    b. The knock pin in the front end of the camshaft should be facing upward.

**NOTE: Do not rotate crankshaft and camshaft separately because valves will hit piston head.**

15. Install the cylinder head with a new gasket. Apply clean engine oil to

the threads and seats of the bolts and install the bolts with washers in the correct position. Note that bolts 4, 5, 12, and 13 are 4.95 in. (127mm) long. The other bolts are 4.13 in. (106mm) long.

16. Torque the bolts in the proper sequence as follows:

a. Torque all bolts, in sequence, to 22 ft. lbs. (29 Nm).

b. Torque all bolts, in sequence, to 43 ft. lbs. (58 Nm).

c. Loosen all bolts completely.

d. Torque all bolts, in sequence, to 22 ft. lbs. (29 Nm).

e. Torque all bolts, in sequence, to 40–47 ft. lbs. (54–64 Nm). If using an angle torque wrench, torque them 60–65 degrees tighter rather than going to 40–47 ft. lbs. (54–64 Nm).

17. On 1989–92 models, install the alternator and air conditioner compressor mounting brackets. Mount the compressor and alternator.

18. Install the rear timing cover bolts. Install the camshaft pulleys. Make sure the pulley marked R3 goes on the right and that marked L3 goes on the left. Align the timing marks if necessary and then install the timing belt and adjust the belt tension.

19. Connect the exhaust manifold to the exhaust pipe.

20. Install the exhaust manifold covers.

21. Install the exhaust collector bracket.

22. Install the intake manifold and fuel tube assembly.

23. Install the intake manifold collector cover.

24. On 1989–92 models, connect the accelerator and cruise control cables to the intake manifold and install the distributor and ignition wires.

25. Connect the vacuum and water hoses to the intake collector.

26. Install and tension the timing belt.

27. Fill the cooling system and connect the negative battery cable.

28. Make all the necessary engine adjustments. Road test the vehicle for proper operation.

## VG30DE and VG30DETT Engines

1. Relieve the fuel system pressure and disconnect the negative battery cable.

2. Drain the cooling system.

3. Remove the intake manifold collector.

4. Remove the injector pipe assembly.

5. Remove the valve covers.

6. Remove the timing belt.

7. Remove the idler pulley and idler pulley stud bolt.

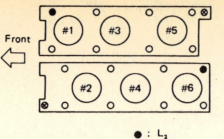

• : L₂
○ : L₁
⊗ : M6 bolt

**Torque the 6mm "X" bolts to 7–9 ft. lbs. (10–12 Nm)**

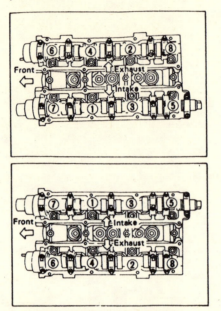

**Cylinder head torque sequence— VG30DE and VG30DETT engines**

8. Remove the intake manifold.

9. Disconnect the exhaust tube from the exhaust manifold.

10. Loosen the cylinder head bolts (in reverse order of installation sequence) in 2–3 stages. Lift the cylinder head off the engine block wih the exhaust manifolds attached It may be necessary to tap the head lightly with a rubber mallet to loosen it.

**To install:**

11. Make sure the No. 1 cylinder is set at TDC on its compression stroke as follows:

a. Align the crankshaft timing mark with the mark on the oil pump housing.

b. Align camshaft sprocket timing mark with the mark on the rear timing belt cover.

12. Install the cylinder head with a new gasket. Apply clean engine oil to the threads and seats of the bolts and install the bolts with washers in the correct position.

13. Torque the bolts in the proper sequence as follows:

a. Torque all bolts, in sequence, to 29 ft. lbs. (39 Nm).

b. Torque all bolts, in sequence, to 90 ft. lbs. (123 Nm).

c. Loosen all bolts completely.

d. Torque all bolts, in sequence, to 25–33 ft. lbs. (34–44 Nm).

e. Torque all bolts, in sequence, to 90 ft. lbs. (123 Nm). If using an angle torque wrench, torque them 60–70 degrees tighter rather than going to 90 ft. lbs. (123 Nm).

f. Torque the 6mm "X" bolts to 7–9 ft. lbs. (10–12 Nm). There is one of these bolts per head.

14. Connect the exhaust tube to the exhaust manifold.

15. Install the intake manifold.

16. Install the idler pulley and stud bolt.

17. Install and tension the timing belt.

18. Install the valve covers. Use sealant on the exhaust side valve cover.

19. Install the injector pipe assembly.

20. Install the intake manifold collector.

21. Fill the cooling system to the proper level and connect the negative battery cable.

22. Make all the necessary engine adjustments. Road test the vehicle for proper operation.

## Valve Lifters

### REMOVAL & INSTALLATION

1. Disconnect the negative battery cable.

2. Remove the cylinder head, if required.

3. Remove the rocker arms and shafts.

4. Withdraw the lifters from the head or from the bore in the rocker. Tag each lifter to the corresponding cylinder head opening or rocker. If the lifter is installed in the rocker, remove the snapring first. Be careful not to bend the snapring during removal.

**NOTE: Do not lay the lifters on their sides because air will be allowed to enter the lifter. When storing lifters, set them straight up. To store lifters on their sides, they must be soaked in a bath of clean engine oil.**

5. Install the lifters in their original locations. Use new lifter snaprings as needed. New lifters should be soaked in a bath of clean engine oil prior to installation to remove the air.

6. Install the rocker arms and shafts.

7. Install the cylinder head and leave the valve cover off.

8. Check the lifters for proper oper-

ation by pushing hard on each lifter with fingertip pressure. If the valve lifter moves more than 0.04 in. (1mm), air may be inside it. Make sure the rocker arm is not on the cam lobe when making this check. If there was air in the lifters, bleed the air by running the engine at 1000 rpm for 10 minutes.

## Valve Lash

Hydraulic valve lifters are used on all engines except on those models listed below. Engines with hydraulic lifters do not require periodic valve adjustment, because the lifter automatically compensates for any required adjustment. Hydraulic valve lifters are best maintained through regular, scheduled engine oil and filter changes.

## ADJUSTMENT

### E16i Engine

1. Run the engine until it reaches normal operating temperature and shut if off.
2. Remove the rocker cover.
3. Bring the No. 1 piston at TDC on the compression stroke. There are at least two ways to do it; bump the engine over with the starter or turn it over by using a wrench on the front pulley attaching bolt. The easiest way to find TDC is to turn the engine over slowly with a wrench, after first removing No. 1 plug, until the piston is at the top of its stroke and the TDC timing mark on the crankshaft pulley

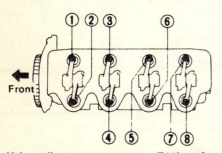

**Valve adjustment sequence—E16i engine**

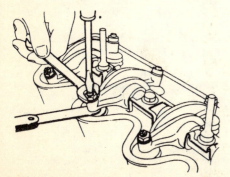

**Adjusting the valves on E series engine**

is in alignment with the timing mark pointer. At this point, the valves for No. 1 should be closed.

**NOTE: Make sure both valves are closed with the valve springs up as high as they will go. An easy way to find the compression stroke is to remove the distributor cap and see toward which spark plug lead the rotor is pointing. If the rotor points to the No. 1 spark plug lead, the No. 1 cylinder is on its compression stroke. When the rotor points to the No. 2 spark plug lead, the No. 2 cylinder is on its compression stroke etc.**

4. With No. 1 piston at TDC of the compression stroke, use a feeler gauge and check the clearance on valves, check valves No. 1, 2, 3 and 6.
5. To adjust the clearance, loosen the locknut and turn the adjuster with a tool while holding the locknut. The correct size feeler gauge should pass with a slight drag between the rocker arm and the valve stem.
6. Turn the crankshaft one full revolution to position the No. 4 piston at TDC of the compression stroke. Adjust valves No. 4, 5, 7 and 8.
7. Replace the valve cover with a new cover gasket or sealing compound.

### GA16DE Engine

1. Run the engine until it reaches normal operating temperature and shut if off.
2. Remove the rocker cover and all spark plugs.

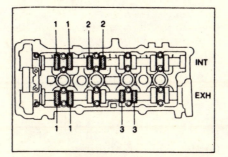

**Valve adjustment step No. 1—GA16DE and KA24DE engines**

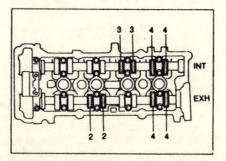

**Valve adjustment step No. 2—GA16DE and KA24DE engines**

3. Set No. 1 cylinder at TDC on compression stroke. Align pointer with TDC mark on crankshaft pulley. Check that the valve lifters on No. 1 cylinder are loose and valve lifters on No. 4 are tight. If not turn crankshaft one revolution 360 degrees and align as above.
4. Check both No. 1 intake and both No. 1 exhaust valves, both No. 2 intake valves and both No. 3 exhaust valves. Using a feeler gauge, measure the clearance between valve lifter and camshaft. Record any valve clearance measurements which are out of specification. Intake Valve clearance (hot) is 0.008–0.019 in. and exhaust valve clearance (hot) is 0.012–0.023 in.
5. Turn crankshaft one revolution 360 degrees and align mark on crankshaft pulley with pointer. Check both No. 2 exhaust valves, both No. 3 intake valves, both No. 4 intake valves and both No. 4 exhaust valves. Using a feeler gauge, measure the clearance between valve lifter and camshaft. Record any valve clearance measurements which are out of specification. Intake valve clearance (hot) is 0.008–0.019 in. and exhaust valve clearance (hot) is 0.012–0.023 in.
6. If all valve clearances are within specification, install all related parts as necessary.
7. If adjusement is necessary, adjust valve clearance while engine is cold by removing adjusting shim. Determine replacement adjusting shim size using formula. Using a micrometer determine thickness of removed shim. Calculate thickness of new adjusting shim so valve clearance comes within specified valves. R = thickness of removed shim, N = thickness of new shim, M = measured valve clearance.

INTAKE: $N = R + (M - 0.0146$ in.$)$
EXHAUST: $N = R + (M - 0.0157$ in.$)$

8. Shims are available in 50 sizes (thickness is stamped on shim-this side always installled down), select new shims with thickness as close as possible to calculate valve.

### KA24DE Engine

1. Run the engine until it reaches normal operating temperature and shut if off.
2. Remove the rocker cover and all spark plugs.
3. Set No. 1 cylinder at TDC on compression stroke. Align pointer with TDC mark on crankshaft pulley. Check that the valve lifters on No. 1 cylinder are loose and valve lifters on No. 4 are tight. If not turn crankshaft one revolution 360 degrees and align as above.
4. Check both No. 1 intake and both

No.1 exhaust valves, both No. 2 intake valves and both No. 3 exhaust valves. Using a feeler gauge, measure the clearance between valve lifter and camshaft. Record any valve clearance measurements which are out of specification. Intake Valve clearance (hot) is 0.012–0.015 in. and exhaust valve clearance (hot) is 0.013–0.016 in.

5. Turn crankshaft one revolution 360 degrees and align mark on crankshaft pulley with pointer. Check both No. 2 exhaust valves, both No. 3 intake valves, both No. 4 intake valves and both No. 4 exhaust valves. Using a feeler gauge, measure the clearance between valve lifter and camshaft. Record any valve clearance measurements which are out of specification. Intake valve clearance (hot) is 0.012–0.015 in. and exhaust valve clearance (hot) is 0.013–0.016 in.

6. If all valve clearances are within specification, install all related parts as necessary.

7. If adjustement is necessary, adjust valve clearance while engine is cold by removing adjusting shim. Determine replacement adjusting shim size using formula. Using a micrometer determine thickness of removed shim. Calculate thickness of new adjusting shim so valve clearance comes within specified valves. R = thickness of removed shim, N = thickness of new shim, M = measured valve clearance.

INTAKE: $N = R + (M - 0.0138 \text{ in.})$
EXHAUST: $N = R + (M - 0.0146 \text{ in.})$

8. Shims are available in 37 sizes (thickness is stamped on shim-this side always installled down), select new shims with thickness as close as possible to calculated value.

## Rocker Arms/Shaft

### REMOVAL & INSTALLATION

NOTE: All rocker shaft removal and installation procedures are given in "Camshaft, Removal and Installation".

## Intake Manifold

### REMOVAL & INSTALLATION

#### Pulsar and Sentra

1. Relieve the fuel system pressure, disconnect the negative battery cable and drain the cooling system.

2. Remove the air cleaner assembly.

3. Disconnect the throttle linkage, electrical connections, fuel and vacuum lines from the throttle body or throttle chamber.

4. The throttle body/throttle cham-

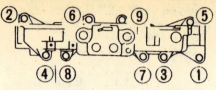

**Intake manifold nut loosening sequence –GA16I, GA16DE and SR20DE engines**

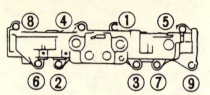

**Intake manifold nut tightening sequence –GA16I, GA16DE and SR20DE engines**

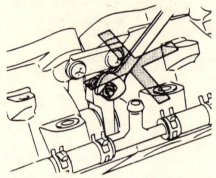

**Never touch this bolt on the CA18DE engine**

ber can be removed from the manifold at this point or can be removed as an assembly with the intake manifold.

5. On all engines, remove the manifold support stays.

6. On CA18DE engine, remove the EGR valve assembly, air regulator and FICD valve from the manifold.

7. Loosen the intake manifold retaining bolts in the the proper sequence and separate the manifold from the cylinder head.

NOTE: Never tighten or loosen the power valve adjusting screw on the CA18DE engine.

8. Remove the intake manifold gasket and clean all the gasket contact surfaces thoroughly with a gasket scraper and suitable solvent. All traces of old gasket material must be removed to ensure proper sealing. Inspect the intake manifold for cracks. Using a metal straight edge, check the surface of the intake manifold for warpage.

**To install:**

9. Lay the new intake manifold gasket onto the cylinder head and position the intake manifold over the mounting studs and onto the gasket. Install the mounting nuts and torque them to specification in the proper sequence.

10. On CA18DE engine, install the EGR valve assembly, air regulator and FICD valve onto the manifold.

11. On all engines, install the manifold support stays.

12. If removed, install the throttle body or throttle chamber.

13. Connect the throttle linkage, electrical connections, fuel and vacuum lines.

14. Install the air cleaner.

15. Fill the cooling system to the proper level and connect the negative battery cable.

16. Road test the vehicle for proper operation.

#### 200SX (4 Cylinder) and 1988–89 Stanza

1. Disconnnect the negative battery cable and drain the cooling system.

2. Remove the air cleaner hoses.

3. Remove the radiator hoses from the manifold.

4. Relieve the fuel pressure. Remove the throttle cable and disconnect the fuel pipe and the fuel return line. Plug the fuel pipe to prevent spilling fuel.

5. Remove all remaining wires, tubes and the EGR and PCV tubes from the rear of the intake manifold. Remove the manifold supports.

6. Unbolt and remove the intake manifold. Remove the manifold with the fuel injectors/injection body, EGR valve, fuel pipes and associated running gear still attached.

7. Remove the intake manifold gasket and clean the gasket surfaces.

**To install:**

8. Install the intake manifold manifold with a new gasket. Tighten the intake manifold bolts in 2–3 stages (working from the center to the ends) to specifications.

9. Install the intake manifold supports. Connect the the fuel pipe, fuel return line and the throttle cable. Reconnect all necessary lines, hoses and or electrical connections.

10. Connect the radiator hoses to the intake manifold. Connect the air cleaner hoses.

11. Fill the cooling system and connect the negative battery cable.

#### 200SX (V6), 1988–89 300ZX and 1988 Maxima

1. Relieve the fuel system pressure, disconnect the negative battery cable and drain the cooling system.

2. Disconnect the valve cover-to-throttle chamber hose at the valve cover.

3. Disconnect the heater housing-to-water inlet tube at the water inlet.

4. Remove the bolt holding the water and fuel tubes to the head.

5. Remove the heater housing-to-thermostat housing tube.

6. Remove the intake collector cover and then remove the collector itself.

7. Disconnect the fuel line and remove the intake manifold bolts. Remove the intake manifold assembly, with the fuel tube assembly still attached, from the vehicle.

**To install:**

8. Install the intake manifold manifold with a new gasket. Tighten the intake manifold bolts in 2–3 stages in the proper sequence to specifications.

9. Connect the fuel line.

10. Install the intake manifold collector with a new gasket. Install the collector cover.

11. Connect the heater-to-thermostat housing tube.

12. Attach the water and fuel tubes to the cylinder head with the mounting bolt.

13. Connect the valve cover-to-throttle chamber hose.

14. Fill the cooling system to the proper level and connect the negative battery cable.

15. Road test the vehicle for proper operation. Make all the necessary engine adjustments.

### 1990–92 300ZX

1. Relieve the fuel system pressure, disconnect the negative battery cable and drain the cooling system.

2. Disconnect the air inlet hoses from both throttle chambers.

3. Disconnect the throttle cable from the accelerator drum located in the middle of the throttle chambers.

4. Disconnect the electrical connectors and vacuum lines from both throttle chambers.

5. Disconnect and tag the electrical wire connectors and vacuum lines from the intake manifold collector.

6. Unbolt and remove the intake manifold collector with the throttle chambers attached. Remove the collector gasket.

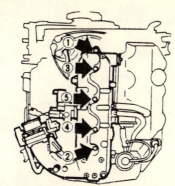

**Intake manifold collector cover bolt removal sequence—200SX (V6), 1988–89 300ZX and 1988 Maxima**

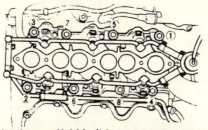

**Intake manifold bolt torque sequence—200SX (V6), 1988–89 300ZX and 1988 Maxima**

7. Disconnect the fuel supply and return lines from the injector assembly. Plug the lines to prevent leakage.

8. Remove the injector assembly from the intake manifold.

9. Remove the intake manifold and gaskets.

**To install:**

10. Install the intake manifold with a

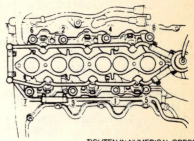

TIGHTEN IN NUMERICAL ORDER.

**Intake manifold bolt removal sequence—200SX (V6), 1988–89 300ZX and 1988 Maxima**

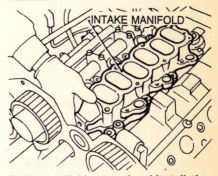

**Intake manifold removal and installation—1990–92 300ZX**

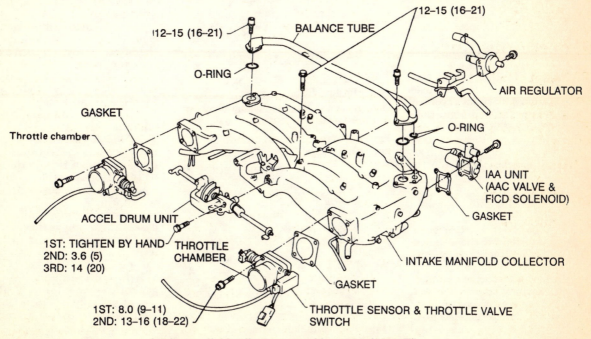

**Intake manifold collector assembly—1990–92 300ZX**

12–15 (16–21)  BALANCE TUBE  12–15 (16–21)

O-RING

GASKET

Throttle chamber

AIR REGULATOR

O-RING

IAA UNIT (AAC VALVE & FICD SOLENOID)

GASKET

ACCEL DRUM UNIT

1ST: TIGHTEN BY HAND
2ND: 3.6 (5)
3RD: 14 (20)

THROTTLE CHAMBER

INTAKE MANIFOLD COLLECTOR

GASKET

1ST: 8.0 (9–11)
2ND: 13–16 (18–22)

THROTTLE SENSOR & THROTTLE VALVE SWITCH

new gasket. Tighten the intake manifold bolts to specification.

11. Install the fuel injectors with new insulators and O-rings.

12. Connect the injector supply and return lines.

13. Install the intake manifold collector with a new gasket. Torque the collector bolts to 12–15 ft. lbs. (16–21 Nm).

14. Connect the vacuum lines and electrical connectors to the collector.

15. Connect the vacuum lines and electrical connectors to the throttle chambers.

16. Connect the throttle cable to the center di

17. Connect the air inlet hoses to the the throttle chambers.

18. Fill the cooling system to the proper level and connect the negative battery cable.

19. Make all the necessary engine adjustments. Road test the vehicle for proper operation.

### 1989–92 Maxima

The 1989–92 Maxima has a slightly different collector/intake manifold assembly than used in 1988 model. The previous single collector is replaced by upper and lower collectors. Each collector has its own bolt removal and installation sequence.

1. Relieve the fuel system pressure, disconnect the negative battery cable and drain the cooling system.

2. Remove the distributor and the ignition wires.

3. Disconnect the Automatic Speed Control Device (ASCD) and accelerator wires from the intake manifold collector.

4. Disconnect the harness connectors for the AAC valve, throttle sensor and idle switch.

5. Disconnect the air cut out valve water hose.

6. Disconnect the PCV valve hoses.

7. Disconnect the vacuum hoses from the vacuum gallery, swirl control valve, master brake cylinder, EGR control valve and EGR flare tube.

8. Loosen the upper collector cover bolts in proper sequence and remove the upper intake manifold collector from the engine. Remove the collector gasket.

9. Disconnect the engine ground harness.

10. Loosen the lower collector bolts, in sequence, and remove the lower intake manifold collector from the engine.

11. Disconnect the harness connectors for all injectors, engine temperature switch and sensor, power valve control solenoid valve, EGR control solenoid valve, EGR. temperature sensor (California only).

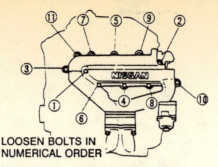

**Upper intake manifold collector bolt loosening sequence—1989–92 Maxima**

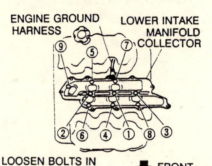

**Lower intake manifold collector bolt loosening sequence—1989–92 Maxima**

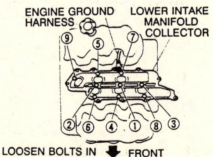

**Intake manifold bolt loosening sequence —1989–92 Maxima**

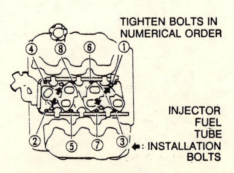

**Intake manifold tightening sequence— 1989–92 Maxima**

12. Disconnect the vacuum gallery hoses.

13. Disconnect the pressure regulator valve vacuum hose, heater hose, fuel feed and return hose.

14. Remove the intake manifold and fuel tube assembly. Loosen intake manifold bolts in numerical order.

**To install:**

15. Install the intake manifold and fuel tube assembly with a new gasket. Tighten the manifold bolts and nuts in 2–3 stages in sequence.

16. Connect the hoses and electrical wires to the intake manifold and fuel tube.

17. Install the upper and lower collector and collector cover with new gaskets. Tighten collector to intake manifold bolts in 2–3 stages by reversing the removal sequence.

18. Connect the vacuum lines, hoses, cables and brackets to the collector cover and collector assembly.

19. Install the distributor and ignition wires.

20. Fill the cooling system to the proper level and connect the negative battrey cable.

21. Make all the necessary engine adjustments. Road test the vehicle for proper operation.

### 240SX and 1990–92 Stanza

1. Relieve the fuel system pressure, disconnect the negative battery cable and drain the cooling system.

2. Remove the air duct between the air flow meter and the throttle body.

3. Disconnect the throttle cable.

4. Disconnect the fuel supply and return lines from the fuel injector assembly. Plug the lines to prevent leakage.

5. Disconnect and tag the electrical connectors and the vacuum hoses to the throttle body and intake manifold/collector assembly.

6. Remove the spark plug wires.

7. Disconnect the EGR valve tube from the exhaust manifold.

8. Remove the intake manifold mounting brackets.

9. Unbolt the intake manifold collector/throttle body from the intake manifold or just remove the mounting bolts and separate the intake manifold from the cylinder head with the collector attached.

10. Using a putty knife, clean the gasket mounting surfaces. Check the intake manifold for cracks and warpage.

**To install:**

11. Install the intake manifold and gasket on the engine. Tighten the mounting bolts 12–15 ft. lbs. (16–20 Nm) from the center working to the end, in 2–3 stages. If the collector was separated from the intake manifold, torque the collector bolts to 12–15 ft.

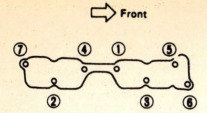

Intake manifold bolt torque sequence—
240SX and 1990–92 Stanza

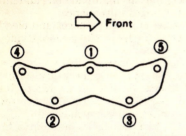

Intake manifold collector bolt torque
sequence—240SX and 1990–92 Stanza

lbs. (16–20 Nm) from the center working to the end.

12. Install intake manifold mounting brackets.

13. Connect the EGR valve tube to the exhaust manifold.

14. Install the spark plug wires.

15. Connect the electrical connectors and the vacuum hoses to the throttle body and intake manifold/collector assembly.

16. Connect the fuel line(s) to the fuel injector assembly.

17. Connect the throttle cable.

18. Connect the air duct between the air flow meter and the throttle body.

19. Fill the cooling system to the proper level and connect the negative battery cable.

20. Make all the necessary engine adjustments. Road test the vehicle for proper operation.

## Exhaust Manifold

### REMOVAL & INSTALLATION

**NOTE: If any fuel system components must be removed, make to relieve the fuel system pressure first. If the engine is equipped with a turbocharger, it may be easier to remove the exhaust manifolds, with the turbo(s) atttached.**

1. Disconnect the negative battery cable. Raise and support the vehicle safely.

2. Remove the undercover and dust covers, if equipped.

3. Remove the air cleaner or collector assembly, if necessary for access.

4. Remove the heat shield(s), if equipped.

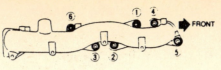

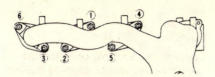

Exhaust manifold torque sequence—
VG30E (200SX and 1988–89 Maxima)

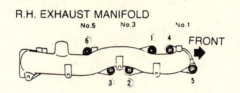

Exhaust manifold torque sequence—
VG30E and VG30ET (1988–89 300ZX)

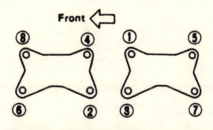

Exhaust manifold torque sequence—
240SX and 1990–92 Stanza

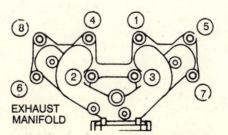

TIGHTEN IN NUMERICAL SEQUENCE

Exhaust manifold torque sequence—
GA16i

5. Disconnect the exhaust pipe from the exhaust manifold or the turbo outlet.

6. Remove or disconnect the temperature sensors, oxygen sensors, air induction pipes, bracketry and other attachments from the manifold.

7. Disconnect the EAI and EGR tubes from their fittings if so equipped.

8. Loosen and remove the exhaust manifold attaching nuts and remove the manifold(s) from the block. Discard the exhaust manifold gaskets and replace with new.

9. Clean the gasket surfaces and check the manifold for cracks and warpage.

**To install:**

10. Install the exhaust manifold with a new gasket. Torque the manifold fasteners from the center outward in several stages to specifications.

11. Connect the EAI and EGR tubes to the connections on the manifold as necessary.

12. Install or connect the temperature sensors, oxygen sensors, air induction pipes, bracketry and other attachments to the manifold.

13. Connect the exhust pipe to the manifold or turbo outlet using a new gasket.

14. Install the heat shields.

15. Install the air cleaner or collector assembly.

16. Install the undercovers and dust covers.

17. Connect the negative battery cable.

## Turbocharger

### REMOVAL & INSTALLATION

**NOTE: If the turbocharger is being replaced, always drain the crankcase and replace the oil and filter to ensure a clean oil supply. This is especially true in cases of complete turbo failure where there is the possibility of metal particles entering the engine's lubricating system and damaging the new turbocharger.**

*1988–89 300ZX Turbo*

1. Disconnect the negative battery cable.

2. Discharge the air conditioning system and remove the compressor and compressor mounting bracket.

3. Disconnect the exhaust front tube.

4. Disconnect the center cable.

5. Remove the heat insulator for the brake master cylinder.

6. Disconnect the air duct and hoses.

7. Disconnect the exhaust manifold

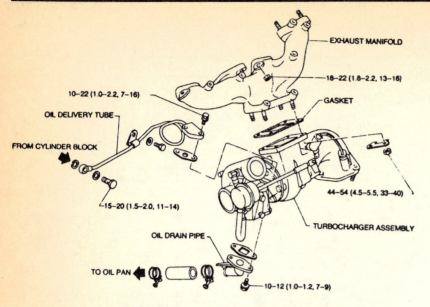

**Turbocharger assembly—1988–89 300ZX**

connecting tube and remove the heat shield plate.

8. Disconnect the oil supply tube and return hose. Plug the ends of the hoses to prevent leakage.

9. Disconnect the water inlet line.

10. Remove the turbocharger from the exhaust manifold.

**To install:**

11. Add 25cc of clean engine oil to the turbocharger oil passages before installing.

12. Mount the turbocharger onto the manifold using new gaskets. Torque the turbocharger-to-manifold nuts to 33–40 ft. lbs. (45–54 Nm).

13. Connect the water inlet tube. Use new metal crush washers on the banjo fitting.

14. Connect the oil supply and return tubes. Use new metal crush washers on the banjo fittings.

15. Install the heat shield plate and connect the exhaust manifold tube.

16. Connect the air duct and hoses.

17. Install the brake master cylinder heat insulator.

18. Connect the center cable.

19. Connect the front exhaust tube.

20. Install the compressor bracket and mount the compressor.

21. Connect the negative battery cable and charge the air conditioning system.

22. Disconnect the coil and crank the engine for 20 seconds to ensure that oil reaches the center bearings. Connect the coil and start the engine, letting it idle for 30 seconds to ensure the proper operation of the turbocharger.

### 1990–92 300ZX Twin Turbo

**RIGHT**

1. Drain the cooling system and the oil pan.

2. Remove the right portion of the cowl top.

3. Remove the battery.

4. Remove the air inlet hose and pipe.

5. Disconnect the lower pipe from the turbo.

6. Remove the Automatic Speed Control Device (ASCD) bracket with wiper motor and solenoid valves.

7. Unplug the exhaust gas harness connector.

8. Disconnect the turbo water hoses and oil supply tube. Plug the ends to prevent leakage.

9. Remove the 2 bolts that attach the pre-catalyst to the turbocharger.

10. Remove the oil pressure switch.

11. Remove the oil filter.

12. Disconnect the oil return tube. Plug the end to prevent leakage.

13. Disconnect the front exhaust tube and pre-catalyst.

14. Disconnect the oil hose from the oil filter bracket. Plug the end to prevent leakage.

15. Disconnect the remaining water tubes from the turbocharger. Plug the ends to prevent leakage.

16. Remove the cotter pin from the wastegate actuating rod.

17. Remove the oil filter bracket.

18. Relieve the tabs on the turbocharger attaching nut locking plates. There are 2 locking plates.

19. Remove the 4 nuts and separate the turbocharger from the exhaust manifold. Clean the gasket surfaces.

**To install:**

20. Mount the turbocharger onto the exhaust manifold with a new gasket. Install the 4 attaching nuts and torque them to 32–40 ft. lbs. (43–54 Nm) in a criss-cross pattern.

21. Once the nuts are torqued, bend the tabs of the locking plates firmly around the flats of each nut.

22. Install the oil filter bracket.

23. Connect the wastegate actuating rod and insert the cotter pin.

24. Connect the water tubes to the turbo. Use new metal crush washers on the banjo fittings.

25. Connect the oil hose to the oil filter bracket.

26. Connect the front exhaust tube and pre-catalyst. Use new gaskets.

27. Connect the oil return tube. Use new metal crush washers on the banjo fitting.

28. Install a new oil filter.

29. Install the oil pressure switch.

30. Attach the pre-catalyst to the turbocharger. Use a new gasket.

31. Connect the oil supply tube and remaining water hoses. Use new metal crush washers on the banjo fittings.

32. Plug in the exhaust gas harness connector.

33. Mount the solenoid valves, wiper motor and Automatic Speed Control Device (ASCD) bracket.

34. Conect the lower pipe to the turbo.

35. Install the air inlet hose and pipe.

36. Install the battery.

37. Install the right portion of the top cowl.

38. Fill the crankcase and cooling system to the proper levels.

39. Start the engine and check for leaks.

**LEFT**

1. Drain the cooling system and the oil pan.

2. Remove the brake master cylinder and brake booster.

3. Remove the air inlet hose and pipe.

4. Disconnect the lower pipe from the turbocharger.

5. Disconnect the water tubes. Plug the the tube ends to prevent leakage.

6. Remove the 2 bolts that attach the pre-catalyst to the turbocharger.

7. Remove the front exhaust tube and pre-catalyst.

8. Disconnect the steering column lower joint from the steering rack.

9. Disconnect the oil return tube and remaining water tubes. Plug the tube ends to prevent leakage.

10. Disconnect the EGR tube and remove the wastegate valve actuator bracket.

11. Remove the exhaust manifold cover.

12. Remove the exhaust manifold attaching nuts. Remove the turbocharger and exhaust manifold together as one unit. Release the tabs on the attaching nut locking plates. There are 2 locking plates. Remove the 4 nuts and separate the turbocharger from the exhaust manifold. Clean the gasket surfaces.

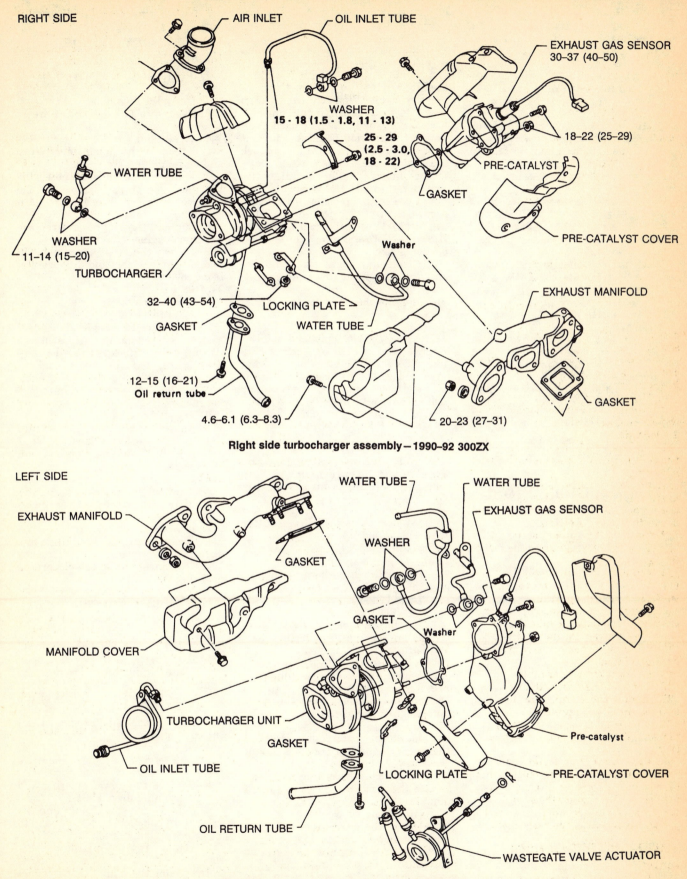

RIGHT SIDE

AIR INLET

OIL INLET TUBE

EXHAUST GAS SENSOR
30–37 (40–50)

WASHER
**15 - 18 (1.5 - 1.8, 11 - 13)**

**25 - 29
(2.5 - 3.0,
18 - 22)**

18–22 (25–29)

PRE-CATALYST

GASKET

PRE-CATALYST COVER

WATER TUBE

Washer

WASHER
11–14 (15–20)

TURBOCHARGER

EXHAUST MANIFOLD

32–40 (43–54)

LOCKING PLATE

GASKET

WATER TUBE

12–15 (16–21)
Oil return tube

GASKET

4.6–6.1 (6.3–8.3)

20–23 (27–31)

**Right side turbocharger assembly – 1990–92 300ZX**

LEFT SIDE

WATER TUBE

WATER TUBE

EXHAUST MANIFOLD

EXHAUST GAS SENSOR

WASHER

GASKET

GASKET

Washer

MANIFOLD COVER

Pre-catalyst

TURBOCHARGER UNIT

GASKET

OIL INLET TUBE

LOCKING PLATE

PRE-CATALYST COVER

OIL RETURN TUBE

WASTEGATE VALVE ACTUATOR

**Left side turbocharger assembly – 1990–92 300ZX**

**1–35**

**To install:**

13. Mount the turbocharger onto the exhaust manifold with a new gasket. Install the 4 attaching nuts and torque them to 32–40 ft. lbs. (43–54 Nm) in a criss-cross pattern.

14. Once the nuts are torqued, bend the tabs of the locking plates firmly around the flats of each nut.

15. Install the exhaust manifold/turbocharger assembly with new gaskets. Torque the exhaust manifold nuts to 20–23 ft. lbs. (27–31 Nm).

16. Install the exhaust manifold cover.

17. Install the wastegate valve actuator bracket and connect the EGR tube.

18. Connect the water tubes and oil return tube. Use new metal crush gaskets on the banjo fittings.

19. Connect the steering column lower joint from the steering rack.

20. Install the front exhaust tube and pre-catalyst.

21. Attach the pre-catalyst to the turbocharger.

22. Connect the remaining water tubes.

23. Connnect the lower pipe to the turbocharger.

24. Install the air inlet hose and pipe.

25. Install the brake booster and master cylinder.

26. Fill the crankcase and cooling system to the proper levels.

27. Start the engine and check for leaks.

## Timing Chain Front Cover

### REMOVAL & INSTALLATION

#### 1989–90 Pulsar and Sentra (GA16I Engine)

1. Disconnect the negative battery cable.

2. Drain the cooling system.

3. Drain the crankcase and remove the oil pan.

4. Remove the power steering belt, if equipped.

5. Remove the air conditioning belt, if equipped.

6. Remove the alternator belt, alternator mounting bracket and alternator.

7. Remove the air cleaner.

8. Connect a suitable lifting device to the front side lifting bracket and tension the hoist to support the engine. Remove the front engine mounting bracket from the block and keep the hoist tensioned to support the weight of the engine.

9. Disconnect the thermo switch connector wire from the thermostat housing and remove the water pump.

10. Loosen the timing chain tensioner mounting bolt and remove the timing chain tensioner and gasket from the front cover.

11. Remove the rocker arm cover and cover gasket.

12. Remove the spark plugs and set the No. 1 piston to TDC of the compression stroke. When the No. 1 piston is at TDC the crankshaft and camshaft keyways will be in the 12 o'clock position or the distributor rotor will point to the No. 1 cylinder. Do not disturb the engine once in this position.

13. Remove crankshaft pulley. Be careful not to lose the Woodruff key.

14. Loosen the retaining bolts and remove the front cover from the cylinder block. There are 6mm and 8mm size bolts. Note and record the location of each size bolt.

15. Clean all the old sealant from the surface of the front cover and the cylinder block.

16. Replace the front cover oil seal.

**To install:**

17. Verify the No. 1 piston is at TDC. Apply a bead of high temperature liquid gasket to both sides of the front cover. Place the front cover onto the cylinder block and install the retaining bolts. Torque the 6mm bolts to 5–6 ft. lbs. (6–8 Nm) and the 8mm bolts to 12–15 ft. lbs. (16–21 Nm).

**NOTE: When installing the front cover, be careful not to damage the cylinder head gasket.**

18. Mount the crankshaft pulley with the Woodruff key. Torque the pulley bolt to 98–112 ft. lbs. (132–152 Nm).

19. Install the spark plugs and connect the spark plug wires.

20. Install the rocker arm cover with a new gasket.

21. Install the timing chain tensioner onto the front cover with a new gasket. Torque the timing chain tensioner bolt to 9–14 ft. lbs. (13–19 Nm).

22. Install the water pump and connect the thermo-switch wire to the thermostat housing. Torque the water pump mounting bolts to 5–6 ft. lbs. (6–8 Nm).

23. Slowly lower the engine and align the holes in the front engine mount bracket with the holes in the block. Install the bracket mounting bolts and torque them to 29–40 ft. lbs. (39–54 Nm).

24. Install the air cleaner.

25. Install the accessories and drive belts and adjust the tension.

26. Fill the crankcase and the cooling system to the proper levels.

27. Connect the negative battery cable.

#### 1991–92 Sentra (GA16DE and SR20DE Engines) 1991–92 240SX (KA24DE Engine)

1. Remove the negative battery cable.

2. Drain the engine oil and coolant.

3. Remove the cylinder head assembly.

4. Raise and support the vehicle safely. Remove the oil pan, oil strainer and baffle plate.

5. Remove the crankshaft pulley using a suitable puller. Removal of the radiator may be necessary to gain clearance.

6. Support the engine and remove the front engine mount.

7. Loosen the front cover bolts in two or three steps and remove the front cover.

**To install:**

8. Clean all mating surfaces of liquid gasket material.

9. Apply a continious bead of liquid gasket to the mating surface of the timing cover. Install the oil pump drive spacer and front cover. Tighten front cover bolts (in steps) to 5–6 ft. lbs. (6–8 Nm). Wipe excess liquid gasket material.

10. Install front engine mount.

11. Install crankshaft pulley and tighten bolt to specifications. Set No. 1 piston at TDC on the compression stroke.

12. Install the oil strainer and baffle. Install the oil pan.

13. Install the cylinder head assembly.

14. Lower the vehicle, connect the negative battery cable, Refill fluid levels, start the engine and check for leaks. Road test the vehicle for proper operation.

#### 240SX (KA24E Engine)

1. Disconnect the negative battery cable.

2. Drain the cooling system and oil pan. To drain the cooling system, open the radiator drain cock and remove the engine block drain plug. The block plug is located on the left side of the block near the engine freeze plugs.

3. Remove the radiator shroud and the cooling fan.

4. Loosen the alternator drive belt adjusting screw and remove the drive belt.

5. Remove the power steering and air conditioning drive belts.

6. Remove the spark plugs and the distributor cap. Set the No. 1 piston to TDC of the compression stroke. Carefully remove the the distributor. Before removal, scribe alignment marks in the timing cover and flat portion of the oil pump/distributor drive spindle.

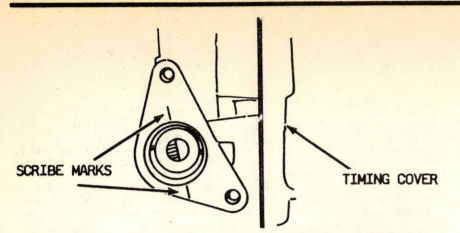

SCRIBE MARKS

TIMING COVER

**Aligning the timing cover and distributor/oil pump drive spindle—KA24E engine**

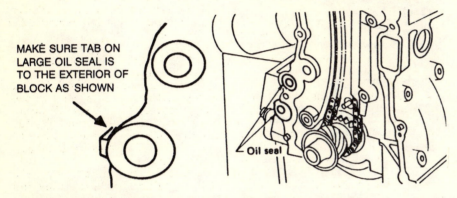

MAKE SURE TAB ON LARGE OIL SEAL IS TO THE EXTERIOR OF BLOCK AS SHOWN

Oil seal

**Cylinder block timing chain cover seals on KA24E engine. Make sure tab on larger seal is positioned as shown**

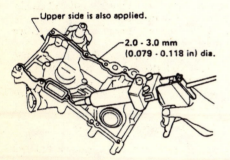

Upper side is also applied.

2.0 - 3.0 mm (0.079 - 0.118 in) dia.

**Applying sealant to front cover—KA24E engine**

This alignment is critical and if not done properly, it could cause difficulty is aligning the distributor and setting the timing.

7. Remove the power steering pump, idler pulley and the power steering brackets.

8. Remove the air conditioning compressor idler pulley.

9. Remove the crankshaft pulley bolt and remove the crankshaft pulley with a 2 jawed puller.

10. Remove the oil pump attaching screws, and withdraw the pump and its drive spindle.

11. Remove the rocker arm cover.

12. Remove the oil pan.

13. Remove the bolts holding the front cover to the front of the cylinder block, the 4 bolts which retain the front of the oil pan to the bottom of the front cover, and the 4 bolts which are screwed down through the front of the cylinder head and into the top of the front cover. Carefully pry the front cover off the front of the engine. Clean all the old sealant from the surface of the front cover and the cylinder block.

14. Replace the crankshaft oil seal and the 2 timing chain cover oil seals in the block. These two seals should be installed in the block and not in the timing cover.

**To install:**

15. Verify the No. 1 piston is at TDC of the compression stroke. Apply a very thin bead of high temperature liquid gasket to both sides of the front cover and to where the cover mates with the cylinder head. Apply a light coating of grease to the crankshaft and timing cover oil seals and carefully bolt the front cover to the front of the engine.

**NOTE: When installing the front cover, be careful not to damage the cylinder head gasket or to disturb the position of the oil seals in the block. Make sure the**

tab on the larger block oil seal is pointing to the exterior of the block.

16. Install new rubber plugs in the cylinder head.

17. Install the oil pan.

18. Install the rocker arm cover.

19. Before installing the oil pump, place the gasket over the shaft and make sure the mark on the drive spindle faces (aligned) with the oil pump hole. Install the oil pump and distributor driving spindle into the front cover with a new gasket.

20. Install the crankshaft pulley and bolt. Torque the pulley bolt to 87–116 ft. lbs. (118–157 Nm).

21. Install the distributor and the spark plugs.

22. Install the compressor idler pulley. Install power steering pump brackets, idler pulley and power steering pump. Install the drive belts and adjust the tension.

23. Install the radiator shroud and the cooling fan.

24. Refill the cooling system and crankcase to the proper levels.

25. Connect the negative battery cable.

26. Start the engine, check/set the ignition timing and check for engine leaks. Road test the vehicle for proper operation.

### 1990–92 Stanza (KA24E Engine)

1. Disconnect the negative battery cable.

2. Raise the front of the vehicle and support safely.

3. Remove the right front wheel.

4. Remove the dust cover and undercover.

5. Drain the oil pan.

6. Set the No. 1 piston at TDC of the compression stroke.

7. Remove the alternator and air conditioning compressor drive belts.

8. Remove the alternator and adjusting bar.

9. Remove the oil separator.

10. Remove the power steering pump pulley, pump stay and mounting bracket.

11. Discharge the air conditioning system and remove the compressor and mounting bracket.

12. Remove the crankshaft pulley and oil pump drive boss.

13. Remove the oil pan.

14. Remove the oil strainer mounting bolt.

15. Remove the bolts that attach the front cover to the head and the block.

16. Remove the rocker cover.

17. Support the engine with a suitable lifting device.

18. Unbolt the right side engine mount bracket from the block and lower the engine.

19. Remove the front cover.
20. Clean all the old sealant from the surface of the front cover and the cylinder block.
21. Replace the crankshaft oil seal and the 2 timing chain cover oil seals in the block. These two seals should be installed in the block and not in the timing cover.

**To install:**

22. Verify the No. 1 piston is at TDC. Apply a very thin bead of high temperature liquid gasket to both sides of the front cover and to where the cover mates with the cylinder head. Apply a light coating of grease to the crankshaft and timing cover oil seals and carefully mount the front cover to the front of the engine.

**NOTE: When installing the front cover, be careful not to damage the cylinder head gasket or to disturb the position of the oil seals in the block. Make sure the tab on the larger block oil seal is pointing to the exterior of the block.**

23. Install new rubber plugs in the cylinder head.
24. Raise the engine and install the right engine mount bracket bolts. Torque the bolts to 58–65 ft. lbs. (78–88 Nm).
25. Install the rocker arm cover.
26. Install the front cover bolts.
27. Install the oil strainer mounting bolt.
28. Install the oil pan.
29. Install the oil pump drive boss and the crankshaft pulley. Torque the pulley bolt to 87–116 ft. lbs. (118–157 Nm).
30. Install the air conditioning compressor bracket and mount the compressor.
31. Install the power steering bracket, pump stay and power steering pump.
32. Install the oil separator.
33. Install the dust cover and undercover.
34. Mount the right front wheel and lower the vehicle.
35. Fill the crankcase to the proper level and charge the air conditioning system.
36. Make all the necessary engine adjustments.

## Front Cover Oil Seal

### REPLACEMENT

1. Disconnect the negative battery cable.
2. Remove the crankshaft pulley.
3. Using a suitable tool, pry the oil seal from the front cover.

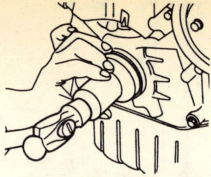

**Timing chain front cover oil seal installation**

**NOTE: When removing the oil seal, be careful not the gouge or scratch the seal bore or crankshaft surfaces.**

4. Wipe the seal bore with a clean rag.
5. Lubricate the lip of the new seal with clean engine oil.
6. Install the seal into the front cover with a suitable seal installer.
7. Install the crankshaft pulley.
8. Connect the negative battery cable.

## Timing Chain and Sprockets

### REMOVAL & INSTALLATION

#### 1989–90 Pulsar and Sentra (GA16i Engine)

1. Disconnect the negative battery cable.
2. Set the No. 1 piston at TDC of the compression stroke.
3. Remove the front cover.
4. If necessary, define the timing marks with chalk or paint to ensure proper alignment.
5. Hold the camshaft sprocket stationary with a spanner wrench or similar tool and remove the camshaft sprocket bolt.
6. Remove the chain guides.
7. Remove the camshaft sprocket.
8. Remove the oil pump spacer.
9. Remove the crankshaft sprocket and timing chain.

**To install:**

10. Verify that the No. 1 piston is at TDC of the compression stroke. The crankshaft keyways should be at the 12 o'clock position.
11. Install the camshaft sprocket, bolt and washer. The alignment mark must face towards the front. When installing the washer, place the non-chamfered side of the washer towards the face of camshaft sprocket. Tighten the bolt just enough to hold the sprocket in place.

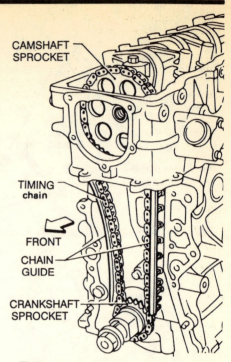

**Timing chain assembly—GA16i engine**

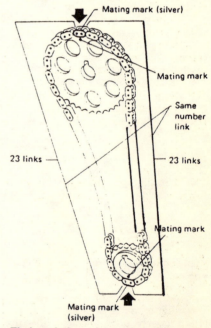

**Timing chain and sprocket alignment marks—GA16i engine**

12. Install the crankshaft sprocket making sure the alignment mark is facing the front.
13. Install the timing chain by aligning the silver links at the 12 o'clock and 6 o'clock positions on the chain with the timing marks on the crankshaft and camshaft sprockets. The number of links between the 2 silver links are the same for the left and the right sides of the chain, so either side

of the chain may be used to align the sprocket timing marks.

14. Torque the camshaft sprocket bolt to 72–94 ft. lbs. (98–128 Nm) once the chain is in place and aligned.

15. Install the chain guides and tenioner. Use a new tensioner gasket and torque the tensioner and chain guide bolts to 9–14 ft. lbs. (13–19 Nm). When installing the chain guide, move the guide in the direction that applies tension to the chain.

16. Install the front cover.

17. Connect the negative battery cable. Road test the vehicle for proper operation.

### 1991–92 Sentra (GA16DE Engine)

1. Disconnect the negative battery cable. Relieve the fuel pressure.

2. Remove the cylinder head assembly.

3. Remove the idle sprocket shaft from the rear side.

4. Remove the upper timing chain assembly.

5. Remove the center member.

6. Remove the oil pan assembly, oil strainer and crankshaft pulley.

7. Support engine and remove the engine front mounting bracket.

8. Remove the front cover. One retaining bolt for the front cover assembly is located on the water pump.

9. Remove the idler sprocket.

10. Remove the lower timing chain assembly, oil pump drive spacer, chain guide, crankshaft sprocket.

**To install:**

11. Confirm that No. 1 piston is set at TDC on compression stroke. Install the chain guide.

12. Install crankshaft sprocket and lower timing chain. Set timing chain

by aligning its mating mark with the one on the crankshaft sprocket. Make sure sprocket's mating mark faces engine front. The number of links between the alignment marks are the same for the left and right side.

13. Install the front cover assembly.

14. Install engine front mounting.

15. Install oil strainer, oil pan assembly and crankshaft pulley.

16. Install center member.

17. Set idler sprocket by aligning the

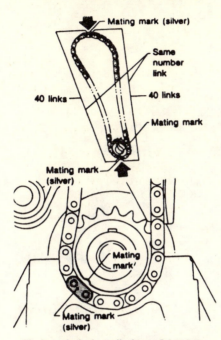

Timing chain installation—GA16DE engine

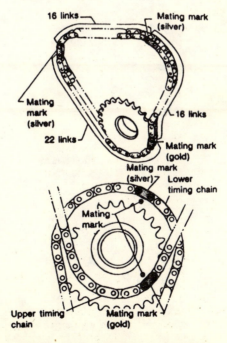

Timing chain installation—GA16DE engine

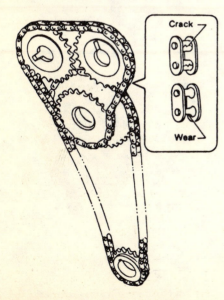

Timing chain assembly—GA16DE engine

mating mark on the larger sprocket with the silver mating mark on the lower timing chain.

18. Install upper timing chain and set it by aligning the mating mark on the smaller sprocket with the silver mating marks on the upper timing chain. Make sure sprocket marks face engine front.

19. Install idler sprocket shaft.

20. Install the cylinder head assembly.

21. Install all remaining components in reverse order of removal.

22. Connect the negative battery cable. Refill all fluid levels. Road test the vehicle for proper operation.

### 1991–92 Sentra (SR20DE Engine)

1. Relieve the fuel system pressure and remove the negative battery cable.

2. Drain the coolant from the radiator and engine block. Remove the radiator.

3. Remove the right front wheel and engine side cover.

4. Remove the drive belts, water pump pulley, alternator and power steering pump.

5. Label and remove the vacuum hoses, fuel hoses and wire harness connectors.

6. Remove the cylinder head.

7. Raise and support the vehicle safely.

8. Remove the oil pan.

9. Remove the crankshaft pulley using a suitable puller.

10. Remove the engine front mount.

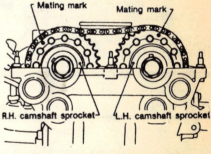

Timing chain installation—SR20DE engine

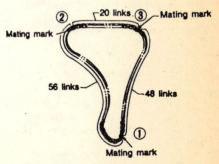

Timing chain installation—SR20DE engine

11. Remove the front cover.

12. Remove the timing chain guides and timing chain. Check the timing chain for excessive wear at the roller links. Replace the chain if necessary.

**To install:**

13. Install the crankshaft sprocket. Position the crankshaft so that No.1 piston is set at TDC (keyway at 12 o'clock, mating mark at 4 o'clock) fit timing chain to crankshaft sprocket so that mating mark is in line with mating mark on crankshaft sprocket. The mating marks on timing chain for the camshaft sprockets should be silver. The mating mark on the timing chain for the crankshaft sprocket should be gold.

14. Install the timing chain and timing chain guides.

15. Install front engine mount.

16. Install the crankshaft pulley and set No.1 piston at TDC on the compression stroke.

17. Install the oil strainer, baffle plate and oil pan.

18. Install the cylinder head, camshafts, oil tubes and baffles. Position the left camshaft key at 12 o'clock and the right camshaft key at 10 o'clock.

19. Install the camshaft sprockets by lining up the mating marks on the timing chain with the mating marks on the camshaft sprockets. Tighten the camshaft bolts to 101–116 ft. lbs. (137–157 Nm).

20. Install the timing chain guide and distributor. Ensure rotor is at 5 o'clock position.

21. Install the chain tensioner. Press the cam stopper down and the press-in sleeve untill the hook can be engaged on the pin. When tensioner is bolted in position the hook will release automatically. Ensure the arrow on the outside faces the front of the engine.

22. Install all other components in reverse order of removal.

23. Connect the negative battery cable. Refill all fluid levels. Road test the vehicle for proper operation.

### 1989–90 240SX and 1990–92 Stanza (KA24E Engine)

1. Disconnect the negative battery cable.

2. Set the No. 1 piston at TDC of the compression stroke.

3. Remove the front cover.

4. If necessary, define the timing marks with chalk or paint to ensure proper alignment.

5. Hold the camshaft sprocket stationary with a spanner wrench or similar tool and remove the camshaft sprocket bolt.

6. Remove chain tensioner.

7. Remove the chain guides.

8. Remove the timing chain.

9. Remove the sprocket oil slinger, oil pump drive gear and crankshaft gear.

**To install:**

10. Install the crankshaft sprocket, oil pump drive gear and oil slinger onto the end of the crankshaft. Make sure the crankshaft sprocket timing marks face toward the front.

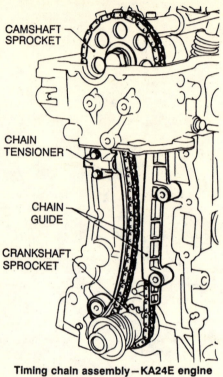

**Timing chain assembly—KA24E engine**

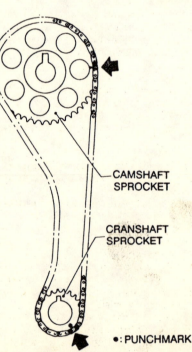

**Timing chain and sprocket alignment marks—KA24E engine**

11. Install the camshaft sprocket, bolt and washer. The alignment mark must face towards the front. Tighten the bolt just enough to hold the sprocket in place.

12. Verify that the No. 1 piston is at TDC of the compression stroke. The crankshaft keyways should be at the 12 o'clock position.

13. Install the timing chain by aligning the marks on the chain with the marks on the crankshaft and camshaft sprockets. Torque the camshaft sprocket bolt to 87–116 ft. lbs. (118–157 Nm) once the timing chain is in place and aligned.

14. Install the chain tensioner and chain guide.

15. Install the front cover.

16. Connect the negative battery cable.

### 1991–92 240SX (KA24DE Engine)

1. Release the fuel system pressure.

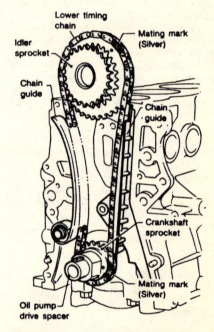

**Timing chain Installation—KA24DE engine**

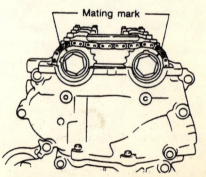

**Timing chain Installation—KA24DE engine**

2. Disconnect the negative battery cable and drain the cooling system. Drain engine oil.

3. Remove the cylinder head assembly.

4. Remove the oil pan.

5. Remove the oil strainer, crankshaft pulley.

6. Remove the front cover assembly.

7. Remove the lower timing chain tensioner, tension arm, lower timing chain guide.

8. Remove the lower timing chain and idler sprocket.

**To install:**

9. Check all components for wear. Replace as necessary. Clean all mating surfaces and replace the cylinder head gasket.

10. Install crankshaft sprocket. Make sure that mating marks of crankshaft sprocket face front of the engine.

11. Rotate crankshaft so that No. 1 piston is set a TDC position.

12. Install idler sprocket and lower timing chain.

13. Install chain tension arm, chain guide and lower timing chain tensioner.

14. Install front cover assembly.

15. Install crankshaft pulley, oil strainer and oil pan.

16. Install the cylinder head assembly.

17. Install all remaining components in reverse order of removal.

18. Connect the negative battery cable. Refill all fluid levels. Road test the vehicle for proper operation.

# Timing Belt Front Cover

## REMOVAL & INSTALLATION

### CA18DE Engine

1. Disconnect the negative battery cable.

2. Drain the cooling system.

3. Remove the upper radiator hose.

4. Remove the right side engine undercover.

5. Remove the power steering and air conditioning compressor drive belts.

6. Remove the water pump pulley.

7. Matchmark the crank angle sensor to the upper front cover and the remove it. Carefully position it aside.

8. Remove the upper front cover.

9. Align the timing marks on the camshaft pulley sprockets and then remove the crankshaft pulley.

**NOTE: The crankshaft pulley may be reached by removing the side cover from inside the right hand wheel opening.**

10. Remove the lower front cover.

**To install:**

11. Install the lower front cover with a new gasket.

12. Install the crankshaft pulley with its washer. Torque the pulley bolt to 105–112 ft. lbs. (145–152 Nm).

13. Install the crank angle sensor so the matchmarks made previously line up and tighten the bolts to 5.1–5.8 ft. lbs. (7–8 Nm).

14. Install the water pump pulley.

15. Install the power steering pump and air conditioning compressor drive belts. Adjust the belt tension.

16. Install the right side undercover.

17. Install the upper radiator hose.

18. Fill the cooling system to the proper level.

19. Connect the negative battery cable.

### CA20E Engine

1. Disconnect the negative battery cable.

2. On 200SX: disconnect the air intake duct, remove the cooling fan and radiator shroud and remove the exhaust side spark plugs.

3. On Stanza: raise and support the front of the vehicle safely, remove the right front wheel, remove the exhaust side spark plugs and remove the dust cover and undercover.

4. Remove the alternator drive belt.

5. Remove the air conditioner compressor drive belt.

6. Remove the crankshaft pulley.

7. Remove the crankshaft damper.

8. Remove the water pump pulley.

9. Remove the upper and lower timing belt covers and gaskets. If the gaskets are in good condition after removal, they can be reused. If they are in way damaged or broken, replace them.

**To install:**

10. Install timing belt cover with new gaskets, as required. Torque the front cover bolts evenly to 2.2–3.6 ft. lbs. (3–5 Nm).

11. Install the water pump pulley. Torque the pulley bolts to 4–7 ft. lbs. (6–10 Nm).

12. Install the crankshaft damper. Torque the bolts to 90–98 ft. lbs. (123–132 Nm).

13. Install the crankshaft pulley. Torque the pulley bolts to 9–10 ft. lbs. 12–14 Nm).

14. Install the drive belts and adjust the drive belt tension.

15. On Stanza: install the undercover and dust cover, install the exhaust side spark plugs, mount the right front wheel and lower the vehicle.

16. On 200SX: install the exhaust side spark plugs, install the radiator shroud and cooling fan and connect the air intake duct.

17. Connect the negative battery cable.

### E16i Engine

1. Disconnect the negative battery cable.

2. Drain the cooling system.

3. Remove the front right side splash cover.

4. Remove the front right side undercover.

5. Remove the air conditioning belt (if so equipped) and alternator belt.

6. Remove the alternator.

7. Remove the power steering belt, if equipped.

8. Remove the water pump pulley.

9. Remove the crankshaft pulley.

**NOTE: The crankshaft pulley is accessible after removing the side cover from the right side wheel house.**

10. Loosen and remove the 8 Torx head bolts securing the timing covers and remove the upper and lower covers.

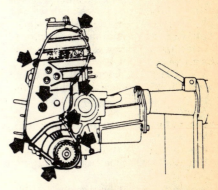

**Front cover removal—E series engine**

**To install:**

11. Install the upper and lower timing belt covers with new gaskets. Tighten the upper cover bolts to 4–5 ft. lbs. (7–8 Nm) and the lower cover bolts to 2–4 ft. lbs. (3–5 Nm).

12. Install the crankshaft pulley. Torque the pulley bolt to 80–94 ft. lbs. (108–127 Nm).

13. Install the water pump pulley. Torque the pulley bolts to 6–8 ft. lbs. (8–11 Nm).

14. Install the power steering belt.

15. Install the alternator.

16. Install the alternator and air conditioning belts.

17. Install the right side engine and splash covers.

18. Fill the cooling system to the proper level and adjust the drive belt tension.

19. Connect the negative battery cable.

### VG30E and VG30ET Engines (1988–89 300ZX)

1. Disconnect the negative battery cable.

2. Drain the cooling system.

3. Remove the engine undercovers.

4. Remove the radiator shroud and fan.

5. Remove the power steering, alternator and air conditioning compressor drive belts.

6. Remove the suction pipe bracket and disconnect the lower coolant hose from the suction pipe.

7. Remove compressor drive belt idler bracket.

8. Set No. 1 cylinder at TDC of the compression stroke.

9. Remove the crankshaft pulley.

10. Remove the front upper and lower belt covers and gaskets.

**To install:**

11. Install the upper and lower timing belt covers with new gaskets. Torque the covers bolts to 2–4 ft. lbs. (3–5 Nm).

12. Install the crankshaft pulley. Torque the pully bolt to 90–98 ft. lbs. (123–132 Nm).

13. Install the compressor drive belt idler bracket.

14. Connect the lower coolant hose to the suction pipe and install the suction pipe bracket.

15. Install and tension the drive belts.

16. Install the radiator fan and shroud.

17. Install the engine undercovers.

18. Fill the cooling system to the proper level.

19. Connect the negative battery.

### VG30DE and VG30DETT Engines (1990–92 300ZX)

1. Disconnect the negative battery cable.

2. Remove the engine undercover.

3. Drain the cooling system.

4. Remove the radiator.

5. Remove the drive belts.

6. Remove the cooling fan and cooling fan coupling.

7. Remove the crankshaft pulley bolt.

8. Remove the starter and lock the flywheel ring gear using a suitable locking device. This is done to prevent the crankshaft gear from turning during removal and installation.

9. Remove the crankshaft pulley using a suitable puller.

10. Remove the water inlet and outlet housings.

11. Remove the timing belt covers and gaskets.

**To install:**

12. Install the timing belt covers with new gaskets. Torque the cover bolts to 2–4 ft. lbs. (3–5 Nm).

13. Install the water inlet and outlet housings with new gaskets.

14. Install the crankshaft pulley.

Torque the pulley bolt to 159–174 ft. lbs. (21–235 Nm).

15. Remove the flywheel locking device and install the starter.

16. Install the cooling fan and cooling fan coupling.

17. Install and tension the drive belts.

18. Install the radiator.

19. Fill the cooling system to the proper level.

20. Connect the negative battery cable.

### VG30E Engine (1988–92 Maxima)

1. Disconnect the negative battery cable.

2. Raise and support the front of the vehicle safely.

3. Remove the engine undercovers.

4. Drain the cooling system.

5. Remove the right front wheel.

6. Remove the engine side cover.

7. On 1988 vehicles, remove the engine coolant reservoir tank, radiator hoses and the Automatic Speed Control Device (ASCD) actuator; remove the lower coolant hose support bracket and disconnect the lower hose from the suction pipe.

8. Remove the alternator, power steering and air conditioning compressor drive belts from the engine. When removing the power steering drive belt, loosen the idler pulley from the right side wheel housing.

9. On 1989–92 vehicles, remove the upper radiator and water inlet hoses; remove the water pump pulley.

10. Remove the idler bracket of the compressor drive belt.

11. Remove the crankshaft pulley with a suitable puller.

12. Remove the upper and lower timing belt covers and gaskets.

**To install:**

13. Install the upper and lower timing belt covers with new gaskets.

14. Install the crankshaft pulley. Torque the pulley bolt to 90–98 ft. lbs. (123–132 Nm).

15. Install the compressor drive belt idler bracket.

16. On 1989–92 vehicles, install the water pump pulley and torque the nuts to 12–15 ft. lbs. (16–21 Nm); install the upper radiator and water inlet hoses.

17. Install the drive belts.

18. On 1988 vehicles, connect the lower coolant hose to the suction pipe and install the hose support bracket; install the Automatic Speed Control Device (ASCD) actuator, radiator hoses and engine coolant reservoir tank.

19. Install the engine side cover.

20. Mount the front right wheel.

21. Install the engine undercovers.

22. Lower the vehicle.

23. Fill the cooling system and connect the negative battery cable.

## OIL SEAL REPLACEMENT

### Except 300ZX

1. Disconnect the negative battery cable.

2. Remove the crankshaft pulley.

3. Using a suitable tool, pry the oil seal from the front cover.

**NOTE: When removing the oil seal, be careful not the gouge or scratch the seal bore or crankshaft surfaces.**

4. Wipe the seal bore with a clean rag.

5. Lubricate the lip of the new seal with clean engine oil.

6. Install the seal into the front cover with a suitable seal installer.

7. Install the crankshaft pulley.

8. Connect the negative battery cable.

### 300ZX

1. Disconnect the negative battery cable.

2. Remove the timing belt.

3. Remove the crankshaft sprocket.

4. Remove the oil pan and oil pump.

5. Using a suitable tool, pry the oil seal from the front cover.

**NOTE: When removing the oil seal, be careful not the gouge or scratch the seal bore or crankshaft surface.**

6. Wipe the seal bore with a clean rag.

7. Lubricate the lip of the new seal with clean engine oil.

8. Install the seal into the front cover with a suitable seal installer.

9. Install the oil pump and oil pan.

10. Install the crankshaft sprocket.

11. Install the timing belt.

12. Connect the negative battery cable.

## Timing Belt and Tensioner

### REMOVAL & INSTALLATION

### CA18DE Engine (1988–89 Pulsar)

1. Disconnect the negative battery cable.

2. Drain the cooling system.

3. Remove the upper radiator hose.

4. Remove the right side engine undercover.

5. Loosen the power steering pump and the air conditioning compressor and then remove the drive belts.

6. Remove the water pump pulley.

7. Matchmark the crank angle sensor to the upper front cover and the remove it. Carefully position it aside.
8. Remove the water pump pulley.
9. Position a floor jack under the engine and raise it just enough to support the engine.
10. Remove the upper engine mount bracket at the right side of the upper front cover.
11. Remove the upper front cover.
12. Align the timing marks on the camshaft pulley sprockets and then remove the crankshaft pulley.

NOTE: The crankshaft pulley may be reached by removing the side cover from inside the right hand wheel opening.

13. Remove the lower front cover.
14. Loosen the tensioner pulley nut to slacken the timing belt and then slide off the belt.
**To install:**

NOTE: Do not bend or twist the timing belt. Never rotate the crankshaft and camshaft separately with the timing belt removed. Make sure the timing belt is free of any oil, water or debris.

15. Install the crankshaft sprocket with the sprocket plates.
16. Before installing the timing belt, ensure that the No. 1 piston is at TDC of the compression stroke. All sprocket timing marks should be aligned with the marks on the case.

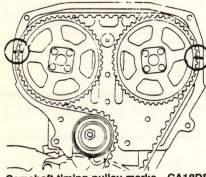

**Camshaft timing pulley marks—CA18DE engine**

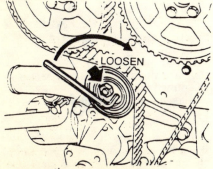

**Loosen the tensioner pulley nut—CA18DE engine**

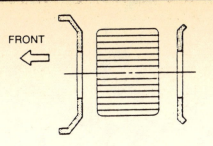

FRONT SPROCKET PLATE    REAR SPROCKET PLATE

**Crankshaft sprocket plate installation—CA18DE engine**

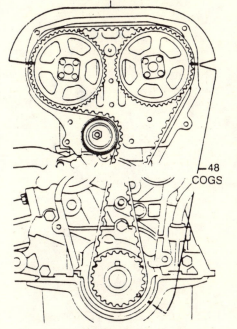

39 COGS
48 COGS

**Timing belt timing mark alignment—CA18DE engine**

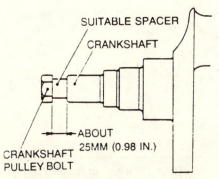

SUITABLE SPACER
CRANKSHAFT
ABOUT 25MM (0.98 IN.)
CRANKSHAFT PULLEY BOLT

**A spacer must be installed between the crankshaft and pulley bolt head before rotating the engine—CA18DE engine**

NOTE: When the timing belt is on and in position, there should be 39 cogs between the timing mark on each of the camshaft sprocket and 48 cogs between the mark on the right camshaft sprocket and the mark on the crankshaft sprocket.

17. Loosen the timing belt tensioner pulley nut.
18. Temporarily install the crankshaft pulley bolt and then rotate the engine two complete revolutions.

NOTE: Fabricate and install a 0.98 in. (25mm) thick spacer between the end of the crankshaft and the head of the crankshaft pulley bolt to prevent bolt damage.

19. Tighten the tensioner pulley bolt to 16–22 ft. lbs. (22–29 Nm).
20. Install the upper and lower front covers with new gaskets.
21. Install the crankshaft pulley with its washer and tighten it to 105–112 ft. lbs. (145–152 Nm).
22. Install the engine mount bracket.
23. Install the water pump pulley. Install the crank angle sensor so the matchmarks made previously line up and tighten the bolts to 5.1–5.8 ft. lbs. (7–8 Nm).
24. Install the water pump pulley.
25. Installl the power steering pump and air conditioning compressor drive belts. Adjust the belt tension.
26. Install the right side undercover.
27. Install the upper radiator hose.
28. Fill the cooling system to the proper level.
29. Connect the negative battery cable.

### CA20E Engine (1988 200SX and 1988–89 Stanza)

1. Disconnect the negative battery cable.
2. On 200SX, disconnect the air intake duct remove the cooling fan and radiator shroud; remove the exhaust side spark plugs.
3. On Stanza, raise and support the front of the vehicle safely. Remove the right front wheel. Remove the exhaust side spark plugs. Remove the dust cover and undercover.
4. Set the No. 1 piston at TDC of the compression stroke. The timing marks will all be aligned.
5. Remove the alternator drive belt.
6. Remove the air conditioner compressor drive belt.
7. Remove the crankshaft pulley.
8. Remove the crankshaft damper.
9. Remove the water pump pulley.
10. Remove the upper and lower timing belt covers and gaskets. If the gaskets are in good condition after remov-

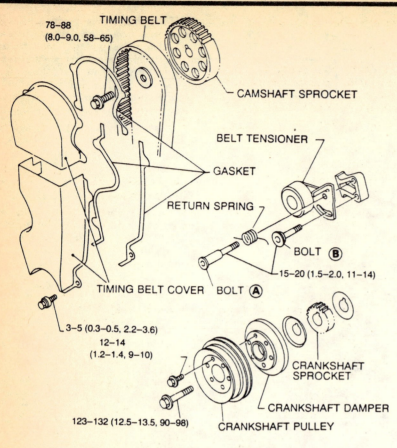

78–88
(8.0–9.0, 58–65)

TIMING BELT

CAMSHAFT SPROCKET

BELT TENSIONER

GASKET

RETURN SPRING

BOLT **B**

15–20 (1.5–2.0, 11–14)

TIMING BELT COVER     BOLT **A**

3–5 (0.3–0.5, 2.2–3.6)
12–14
(1.2–1.4, 9–10)

CRANKSHAFT SPROCKET

CRANKSHAFT DAMPER

123–132 (12.5–13.5, 90–98)     CRANKSHAFT PULLEY

**Timng belt assembly—CA20E engine**

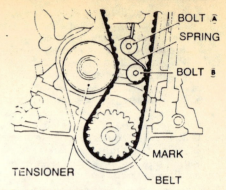

BOLT **A**

SPRING

BOLT **B**

MARK

TENSIONER

BELT

**Setting the tensioner spring—CA20E and CA18DE engines**

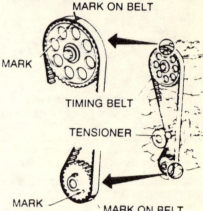

MARK ON BELT

MARK

TIMING BELT

TENSIONER

MARK     MARK ON BELT

**Timing belt installation—CA20E and CA18DE engines**

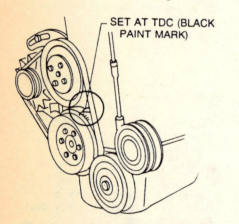

SET AT TDC (BLACK PAINT MARK)

**Setting No. 1 piston to TDC—CA20E engine**

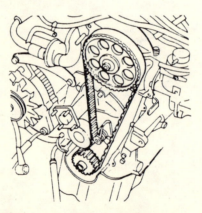

**Timing belt with covers removed—CA20E and CA18DE engines**

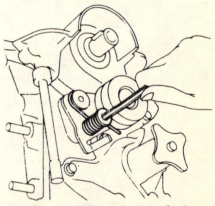

**Installing the belt tensioner and return spring—CA20E and CA18DE engines**

al, they can be reused; if they are damaged or broken, replace them.

11. Loosen the timing belt tensioner and return spring. Remove the timing belt.

12. Carefully inspect the condition of the timing belt. There should be no breaks or cracks anywhere on the belt. Be particularly careful when checking around the bottom of the cog teeth, where they the main belt; cracks often show up here first. Evidence of any wear or damage on the belt calls for replacement.

**To install:**

13. Check to make certain the No. 1 piston is still at TDC on the compression stroke.

14. Install the timing belt tensioner and return spring.

**NOTE: If the coarse stud has been removed, apply Loctite® or another locking thread sealer to the stud threads prior to installation.**

15. Make sure the tensioner mounting bolts are not securely tightened be-

fore installing the timing belt. The tensioner pulley should rotate smoothly.

16. Place the timing belt into position, aligning the lines on the belt with the punch marks on the camshaft and crankshaft pulleys. The arrow on the belt should be pointing toward the front belt covers.

17. Tighten the belt tensioner and assemble the spring. Hook one end of the spring around bolt **B** and then hook the other end over the tensioner bracket pawl. Rotate the crankshaft 2

complete revolutions clockwise, tighten bolt **B** and then bolt **A**.

18. Install timing belt cover with new gaskets, as required. Torque the front cover bolts evenly to 2.2–3.6 ft. lbs. (3–5 Nm).

19. Install the water pump pulley. Torque the pulley bolts to 4–7 ft. lbs. (6–10 Nm).

20. Install the crankshaft damper. Torque the bolts to 90–98 ft. lbs. (123–132 Nm).

21. Install the crankshaft pulley. Torque the pulley bolts to 9–10 ft. lbs. 12–14 Nm).

22. Install the drive belts and adjust the drive belt tension.

23. On Stanza, install the undercover and dust cover. Install the exhaust side spark plugs. Mount the right front wheel and lower the vehicle.

24. On 200SX, install the exhaust side spark plugs. Install the radiator shroud and cooling fan. Connect the air intake duct.

25. Connect the negative battery cable.

### E16i Engine (1988 Pulsar and Sentra)

1. Disconnect the negative battery cable. Raise and safely support the vehicle.

2. Drain the cooling system.

3. Remove the front right side splash cover.

4. Remove the front right side undercover.

5. Remove the air conditioning belt and alternator belt.

6. Remove the power steering belt (if equipped).

7. Set the No. 1 piston to TDC of the compression stroke.

8. Remove the water pump pulley.

9. Remove the crankshaft pulley.

**NOTE: The crankshaft pulley is accessible after removing the side cover from the right side wheel house.**

10. Position a floor jack under the engine and raise it just enough to support the engine. Unbolt the right side engine mounting bracket from the block.

11. Loosen and remove the 8 Torx head bolts securing the timing covers and remove the upper and lower covers.

12. Mark the relationship of the camshaft sprocket to the timing belt and the crankshaft sprocket to the timing belt with paint or a grease pencil. This will make setting everything up during reassembly much easier if the engine is disturbed during disassembly.

13. Loosen the timing belt tensioner locknut and rotate the tensioner clockwise. Retighten the locknut.

14. Mark a rotational, direction arrow on the timing belt and then remove the belt.

**NOTE: After removing the timing belt, do not rotate the crankshaft or camshaft separately or the valves will hit the pistons.**

15. Remove the belt tensioner and its return spring.

**To install:**

16. Check that the timing marks on the camshaft sprocket and upper front cover and on the crankshaft sprocket and lower front cover are in alignment. This will ensure that the No. 1 piston is at TDC of its compression stroke.

17. Install the timing belt tensioner and return spring temporarily.

18. Rotate the tensioner about 70–80 degrees clockwise and then tighten the locknut.

19. Install the timing belt.

20. Loosen the tensioner locknut so the tensioner pushes on the timing belt and then turn the camshaft sprocket about 20 degrees clockwise (2 cogs).

**NOTE: All spark plugs must be removed before turning the camshaft sprocket.**

21. Prevent the the tensioner from spinning and tighten the locknut to 12–15 ft. lbs. (16–21 Nm).

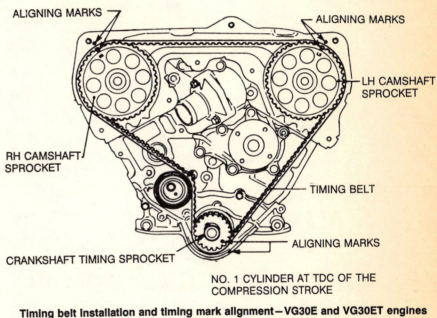

Timing belt installation and timing mark alignment—VG30E and VG30ET engines

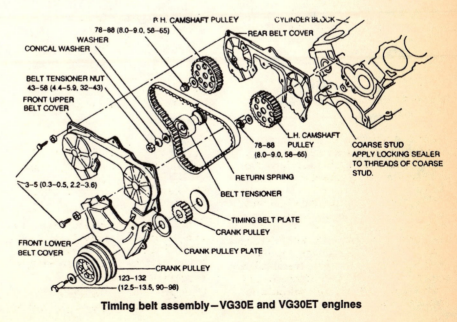

Timing belt assembly—VG30E and VG30ET engines

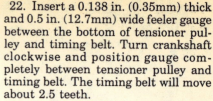

22. Install the upper and lower timing belt covers with new gaskets. Tighten the upper cover bolts to 4–5 ft. lbs. (7–8 Nm) and the lower cover bolts to 2–4 ft. lbs. (3–5 Nm).

23. Attach the right side engine mounting bracket.

24. Install the crankshaft pulley. Torque the pulley bolt to 80–94 ft. lbs. (108–127 Nm).

25. Install the water pump pulley. Torque the pulley bolts to 6–8 ft. lbs. (8–11 Nm).

26. Install the power steering belt.

27. Install the alternator and air conditioning belts.

28. Install the right side engine and splash covers.

29. Fill the cooling system to the proper level and adjust the drive belt tension.

30. Connect the negative battery cable.

### VG30E and VG30ET Engines (1988–89 300ZX)

1. Disconnect the negative battery cable.

2. Drain the cooling system.

3. Remove the engine undercovers.

4. Remove the radiator shroud and fan.

5. Remove the power steering, alternator and air conditioning compressor drive belts.

6. Remove the suction pipe bracket and disconnect the lower coolant hose from the suction pipe.

7. Remove the spark plugs.

8. Set No. 1 cylinder at TDC of the compression stroke.

9. Remove the compressor drive belt idler bracket.

10. Remove the crankshaft pulley.

11. Remove the front upper and lower belt covers and gaskets.

12. Using chalk or paint, mark the relationship of the timing belt to the camshaft and the camshaft sprockets. Also mark the timing belt's direction of rotation. Align the punch mark on the left hand camshaft pulley with the mark on the upper rear timing belt cover. Align the punchmark on the crankshaft with the notch on the oil pump housing. Temporarily install the crankshaft pulley bolt to allow for crankshaft rotation.

13. Loosen the timing belt tensioner and return spring then remove the timing belt. Check that the tensioner spring turns smoothly and check the tensioner spring for wear.

**To install:**

14. Before installing the timing belt confirm that No. 1 cylinder is at TDC on its compression stroke. Install tensioner and tensioner spring. If stud is removed apply locking sealant to threads before installing.

15. Swing the tensioner fully clockwise with hexagon wrench and temporarily tighten locknut.

16. Point the arrow on the timing belt toward the front belt cover. Align the white lines on the timing belt with the punch marks on all 3 pulleys.

**NOTE: There are 133 total timing belt teeth. If timing belt is installed correctly, there will be 40 teeth between left hand and right hand camshaft sprocket timing marks. There will be 43 teeth between left hand camshaft sprocket and crankshaft sprocket timing marks.**

17. Loosen tensioner locknut, keeping tensioner steady with an Allen wrench.

18. Swing tensioner 70–80 degrees clockwise with the Allen wrench and temporarily tighten locknut.

19. Install the spark plugs. Turn crankshaft clockwise 2–3 times, then slowly set No. 1 cylinder at TDC on its compression stroke.

20. Push middle of timing belt between righthand camshaft sprocket and tensioner pulley with a force of 22 ft. lbs.

21. Loosen tensioner locknut, keeping tensioner steady with the Allen wrench.

LH camshaft sprocket timing belt alignment marks—1988–92 VG30E and VG30ET engines

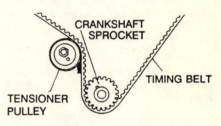

Crankshaft sprocket timing belt alignment marks—1988–92 VG30E and VG30ET engines

22. Insert a 0.138 in. (0.35mm) thick and 0.5 in. (12.7mm) wide feeler gauge between the bottom of tensioner pulley and timing belt. Turn crankshaft clockwise and position gauge completely between tensioner pulley and timing belt. The timing belt will move about 2.5 teeth.

23. Tighten tensioner locknut, keeping tensioner steady with the Allen wrench.

24. Turn crankshaft clockwise or counterclockwise and remove the gauge.

25. Rotate the engine 3 times, then set No. 1 at TDC on its compression stroke.

26. Check timing belt deflection on 1988 vehicles only. Timing belt deflection is 13.0–14.5mm at 22 lbs. of pressure. If it is out of specified range, readjust the timing belt by repeatng Steps 14–25.

27. Install the upper and lower timing belt covers and complete the remainder of the installation in reverse of the removal procedure.

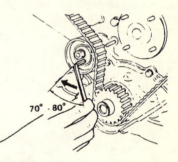

70° - 80°

**Swing the tensioner 70–80 degress clockwise**

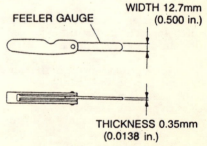

CRANKSHAFT SPROCKET

TIMING BELT

TENSIONER PULLEY

FEELER GAUGE

WIDTH 12.7mm (0.500 in.)

THICKNESS 0.35mm (0.0138 in.)

**Checking timing belt adjustment with a feeler gauge**

### VG30DE and VG30DETT Engines (1990–92 300ZX)

1. Disconnect the negative battery cable.

2. Remove the engine undercover.

3. Drain the cooling system.

4. Remove the radiator.

5. Remove the drive belts.

6. Remove the cooling fan and cooling fan coupling.

7. Remove the crankshaft pulley bolt.

8. Remove the starter and lock the flywheel ring gear using a suitable locking device. This is done to prevent the crankshaft gear from turning during removal and installation.

9. Remove the crankshaft pulley using a suitable puller, then remove the locking device.

10. Remove the water inlet and outlet housings.

11. Remove the timing belt covers and gaskets.

12. Install a suitable 6mm stopper bolt in the tenioner arm of the auto tensioner so the length of the pusher does not change.

13. Set the No. 1 piston at TDC of the compression stroke.

14. Remove the auto-tensioner and the timing belt.

**To install:**

15. Check the auto-tensioner for oil

leaks in the pusher rod and diaphragm. If oil is evident, replace the auto-tensioner assembly.

16. Verify that the No. 1 piston is at TDC of the compression stroke.

17. Align the timing marks on the camshaft and crankshaft sprockets with the timing marks on the rear timing belt cover and the oil pump housing.

18. Remove all the spark plugs.

19. With a feeler gauge, check the clearance between the tensioner arm and the pusher of the auto-tensioner. The clearance should be 0.16 in. (4mm) with a slight drag on the feeler gauge. If the clearance is not as specified, mount the tensioner in a vise and adjust the clearance. When the clearance is set, insert the stopper bolt into the tensioner arm to retain the adjustment.

**NOTE: When adjusting the clearance, do not push the tensioner arm with the stopper bolt fitted, because damage to the threaded portion of the bolt will result.**

20. Mount the auto-tensioner and tighten nuts and bolts by hand.

21. Install the timing belt. Ensure the timing sprockets are free of oil and water. Do not bend or twist the timing belt. Align the white lines on the belt

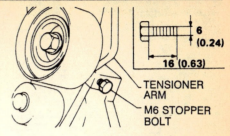

UNIT: IN. (MM)

**Installing suitable stopper bolt into auto-tensioner arm—VG30DE and VG30DETT engines**

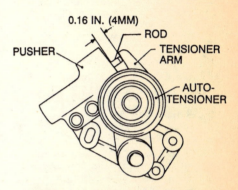

**Checking tensioner arm and pusher clearance—VG30DE and VG30DETT engines**

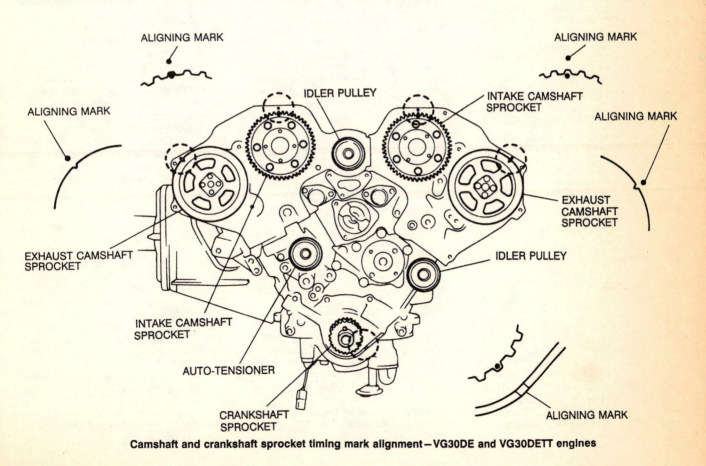

**Camshaft and crankshaft sprocket timing mark alignment—VG30DE and VG30DETT engines**

with the timing marks on the camshaft and crankshaft sprockets. Point the arrow on the belt towards the front.

22. Push the auto-tensioner slightly towards the timing belt to prevent the belt from slipping. At the same time, turn the crankshaft 10 degrees clockwise and torque the tensioner fasteners to 12–15 ft. lbs. (16–21 Nm).

**NOTE: Do not push the tensioner too hard because it will create excessive tension on the belt.**

23. Turn the crankshaft 120 degrees counterclockwise.
24. Turn the crankshaft clockwise and set the No. 1 piston at TDC of the compression stroke.
25. Back off on the auto-tensioner fasteners ½ turn.
26. Using push-pull gauge No. EG1486000 (J-38387) or equivalent, apply approximately 15.2–18.3 lbs. (67.7–81.4 N) of force to the tensioner.
27. Turn the crankshaft 120 degrees clockwise.
28. Turn the crankshaft counterclockwise and set the No. 1 piston at TDC of the compression stroke.
29. Fabricate a 0.35 in. (9mm) wide x 0.10 in. (2mm) deep steel plate. The length of the plate should be slightly longer than the width of the belt.
30. Set the steel plate at positions **A, B, C** and **D** of the timing belt mid-way between the pulleys as shown. Using

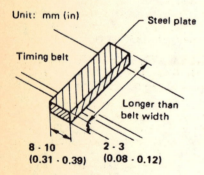

**Fabricate a suitable steel plate as shown**

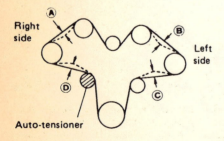

**Set the steel plate at each position on the belt**

the push-pull gauge or equivalent, apply approximately 11 lbs. (49 N) of force to the tensioner and check (and record) the belt deflection at each position with the steel plate in place. The timing belt deflection at each position should be 0.217–0.256 in. (5.5–6.5mm). Another means of determining the belt deflection is to add all deflection readings and divide them by 4. This average deflection should be 0.217–0.256 in. (5.5–6.5mm).

31. If the belt deflection is not as specified, repeat Steps 22–30 until the belt deflection is correct.
32. Once the belt is properly tensioned, torque the auto-tensioner fasteners to 12–15 ft. lbs. (16–21 Nm).
33. Remove the stopper bolt from the tensioner and wait 5 minutes. After 5 minutes, check the clearance between the tensioner arm and the pusher of the auto-tensioner. The clearance should remain at 0.138–0.205 in. (3.5–5.2mm).
34. Make sure the belt is installed and aligned properly on each pulley and timing sprocket. There must be no slippage or misalignment.
35. Install the timing belt covers with new gaskets. Torque the covers bolts to 2–4 ft. lbs. (3–5 Nm).
36. Install the water inlet and outlet housings with new gaskets.
37. Install the crankshaft pulley. Torque the pulley bolt to 159–174 ft. lbs. (21–235 Nm).
38. Remove the flywheel locking device and install the starter.
39. Install the cooling fan and cooling fan coupling.
40. Install and tension the drive belts.
41. Install the radiator.
42. Fill the cooling system to the proper level.
43. Connect the negative battery cable.

## VG30E Engine (1988–92 Maxima)

1. Disconnect the negative battery cable.
2. Raise and support the front of the vehicle safely.
3. Remove the engine undercovers.
4. Drain the cooling system.
5. Remove the front right side wheel.
6. Remove the engine side cover.
7. On 1988 vehicles, remove the engine coolant reservoir tank, radiator hoses and the Automatic Speed Control Device (ASCD) actuator; remove the lower coolant hose support bracket and disconnect the lower hose from the suction pipe.
8. Remove the alternator, power steering and air conditioning compressor drive belts from the engine. When

removing the power steering drive belt, loosen the idler pulley from the right side wheel housing.
9. On 1989–92 vehicles, remove the upper radiator and water inlet hoses; remove the water pump pulley.
10. Remove the idler pulley bracket of the compressor drive belt.
11. Remove the crankshaft pulley with a suitable puller.
12. Remove the upper and lower timing belt covers and gaskets.
13. Rotate the engine with a socket wrench on the crankshaft pulley bolt to align the punch mark on the left hand camshaft pulley with the mark on the upper rear timing belt cover; align the punchmark on the crankshaft with the notch on the oil pump housing; temporarily install the crankshaft pulley bolt to allow for crankshaft rotation.
14. Use a hex wrench to turn the belt tensioner clockwise and tighten the tensioner locknut just enough to hold the tensioner in position. Then, remove the timing belt.

**To install:**

15. Before installing the timing belt confirm that No. 1 cylinder is at TDC on its compression stroke. Install tensioner and tensioner spring. If stud is removed apply locking sealant to threads before installing.
16. Swing tensioner fully clockwise with hexagon wrench and temporarily tighten locknut.
17. Point the arrow on the timing belt toward the front belt cover. Align the white lines on the timing belt with the punch marks on all 3 pulleys.

**NOTE: There are 133 total timing belt teeth. If timing belt is installed correctly there will be 40 teeth between left hand and right hand camshaft sprocket timing marks. There will be 43 teeth between left hand camshaft sprocket and crankshaft sprocket timing marks.**

18. Loosen tensioner locknut, keeping tensioner steady with a hexagon wrench.
19. Swing tensioner 70–80 degrees clockwise with hexagon wrench and temporarily tighten locknut.
20. Turn crankshaft clockwise 2–3 times, then slowly set No. 1 cylinder at TDC of the compression stroke.
21. Push middle of timing belt between righthand camshaft sprocket and tensioner pulley with a force of 22 lbs.
22. Loosen tensioner locknut, keeping tensioner steady with a hexagon wrench.
23. Insert a 0.138 in. (0.35mm) thick and 0.5 in. (12.7mm) wide feeler gauge between the bottom of tensioner pul-

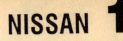

ley and timing belt. Turn crankshaft clockwise and position gauge completely between tensioner pulley and timing belt. The timing belt will move about 2.5 teeth.

24. Tighten tensioner locknut, keeping tensioner steady with a hexagon wrench.

25. Turn crankshaft clockwise or counterclockwise and remove the gauge.

26. Rotate the engine 3 times, then set No. 1 at TDC on its compression stroke.

27. Install the upper and lower timing belt covers with new gaskets.

28. Install the crankshaft pulley. Torque the pulley bolt to 90–98 ft. lbs. (123–132 Nm).

29. Install the compressor drive belt idler bracket.

30. On 1989–92 vehicles, install the water pump pulley and torque the nuts to 12–15 ft. lbs. (16–21 Nm). Install the upper radiator and water inlet hoses.

31. Install the drive belts.

32. On 1988 vehicles, connect the lower coolant hose to the suction pipe and install the hose support bracket; install the Automatic Speed Control Device (ASCD) actuator, radiator hoses and engine coolant reservoir tank.

33. Install the engine side cover.

34. Mount the front right wheel.

35. Install the engine undercovers.

36. Lower the vehicle.

37. Fill the cooling system and connect the negative battery cable.

## Timing Sprockets

### REMOVAL & INSTALLATION

1. Disconect the negative battery cable.

2. Set the No. 1 piston to TDC of the compression stroke.

3. Remove the timing belt covers.

4. Remove the timing belt.

5. Using a suitable spanner wrench and a socket wrench, remove the camshaft pulley bolt and washer.

   a. On CA18DE engine, the sprocket is held to the end of the cmashaft by a plate with 4 bolts.

   b. On E16i engine, the camshaft and jackshaft sprockets are held in place by a plate and 3 bolts. Pull the camshaft sprocket(s) from the camshaft(s). Be careful not to lose the Woodruff key.

   c. On 1990–92 300ZX, remove the front plate, O-ring and spring from the right (intake) camshaft to gain access to the sprocket bolt.

   d. On 1990–92 300ZX, the left camshaft sprocket is held in place by plate and 4 bolts.

6. Using a suitable puller, remove

the crankshaft gear and timing belt plates from the crankshaft. Be careful not to gouge or scratch the surface of the crankshaft when removing the gear.

7. Inspect the timing gear teeth for wear and replace as necessary.
**To install:**

8. Install the crankshaft gear with new Woodruff keys.

9. Install the camshaft sprockets. Torque the sprocket bolts to 58–65 ft. lbs. (78–88 Nm) on CA20, VG30E and VG30ET engines; 90–98 ft. lbs. (123–132 Nm) for right (intake) and 10–14 ft. lbs. (14–19 Nm) for the left (exhaust) on 1990–92 300ZX; 10–14 ft. lbs. (14–19 Nm) on CA18DE engine; 7–9 ft. lbs. (9–12 Nm) on E16i engine.

**NOTE: On VG30E and VG30ET engines, the right hand and left hand camshaft pulleys are different. Install them in their correct positions. The right hand pulley has an R3 identification mark and the left hand pulley has an L3.**

10. Install the timing belt.

11. Install the timing belt covers.

12. Connect the negative battery cable.

## Camshaft

### REMOVAL & INSTALLATION

#### CA18DE Engine (1988–89 Pulsar)

1. Disconnect the negative battery cable and relieve the fuel system pressure.

2. Drain the cooling system and remove the air cleaner assembly.

3. Crank the engine until the No. 1 piston is at TDC on its compression stroke.

4. Remove the drive belts.

5. Remove the alternator.

6. Disconect the air duct at the throttle chamber.

7. Tag and disconnect all lines, hoses and wires which may interfere with removal of the cylinder.

8. Remove the ornament cover.

9. Disconnect the oxygen sensor wire.

10. Remove the 2 exhaust heat shield covers.

11. Unbolt the exhaust manifold and wire the entire assembly aside to gain removal clearance for the cylinder head.

12. Disconnect the EGR tube at the passage cover and then remove the passage cover and its gasket.

13. Disconnect and remove the crank angle sensor from the upper front cover.

**NOTE: Put an aligning mark on crank angle sensor and timing belt cover.**

14. Remove the support stay from under the intake manifold assembly.

15. Unbolt the intake manifold and remove it along with the collector and throttle chamber.

16. Disconnect and remove the fuel injectors as an assembly.

**NOTE: Upper and lower front timing belt cover must be removed. Support engine under oil pan with floor jack or equivalent then remove the upper engine mount bracket at the right side of the front cover.**

17. Remove the timing belt.

18. Remove the camshaft cover and remove the cylinder head.

19. Remove the breather separater.

20. While holding the camshaft sprockets, remove the 4 mounting bolts and then remove the sprockets themselves.

21. Remove the timing belt tensioner pulley. Remove the rear timing belt cover.

22. Loosen the camshaft bearing caps in several stages, in the correct order. Remove the bearing caps, but be sure to keep them in order.

23. Remove the front oil seals and then lift out the camshafts.

24. Check the camshaft runout, endplay, wear and journal clearance.
**To install:**

25. Position the camshafts in the cylinder head so the knock pin on each is on the outboard side.

**NOTE: The exhaust side camshaft has splines to accept the crank angle sensor.**

26. Position the camshaft bearing caps and finger-tighten them. Each cap has an ID mark (E1, E2, I1, I2 etc.) and a directional arrow stamped into its top surface.

27. Coat the new oil seal with engine oil (on the lip) and install it on each camshaft end.

28. Tighten the camshaft bearing cap bolts to 7–9 ft. lbs. (9–12 Nm) in the order shown.

29. Install the cylinder head and cover.

30. Install the rear timing cover and tighten the 4 bolts to 5–6 ft. lbs. (7–8 Nm).

31. Install the timing belt tensioner and tighten it to 16–22 ft. lbs. (22–29 Nm).

32. Install the camshaft sprockets and tighten the bolts to 10–14 ft. lbs. (14–19 Nm) while holding the camshaft in place.

33. Install the cylinder head and related components.

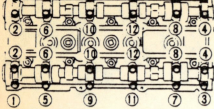

Loosen the camshaft bearing cap bolts in this order—CA18DE engine

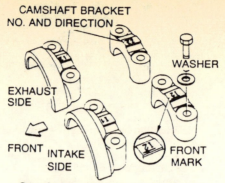

Camshaft bearing cap positioning—CA18DE engine

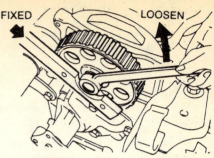

Loosening the camshaft sprocket—C series engine

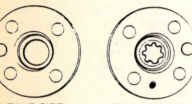

INTAKE SIDE    EXHAUST SIDE

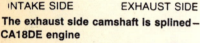

The exhaust side camshaft is splined—CA18DE engine

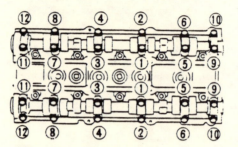

Tighten the camshaft bearing caps in this order—CA18DE engine

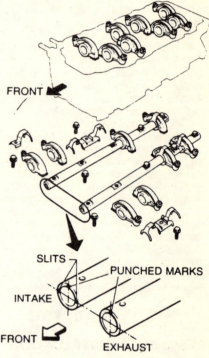

Rocker shaft assembly—C series engine

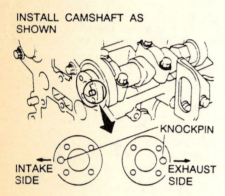

Install the camshaft as shown—CA18DE engine

Timing belt tensioner installation—CA18DE engine

34. Fill the cooling system to the proper level and connect the negative battery cable.

### CA20E Engine (1988 200SX and 1988–89 Stanza)

1. Disconnect the negative battery cable and relieve the fuel system pressure.

2. Set the No. 1 piston to TDC of the compression stroke.

3. Remove the timing belt.

4. Remove the valve rocker cover.

5. Fully loosen all rocker arm adjusting screws (the valve adjusting screws). Loosen the rocker shaft mounting bolts in 2–3 stages and then remove the rocker shafts as an assembly. Keep all components in the correct order for reassembly.

6. Hold the camshaft pulley and re-move the pulley mounting bolt. Remove the pulley. Remove the camshaft thrust plate.

7. Carefully pry the camshaft oil seal out of the front of the cylinder head.

8. Slide the camshaft out the front of the cylinder head, taking extreme care not to score any of the journals.
**To install:**

9. Coat the camshaft with clean engine oil.

10. Carefully slide the camshaft into the cylinder head, coat the end with oil and install a new oil seal. Install the camshaft thrust plate and wedge the camshaft with a small wooden block inserted between one of the cams and the cylinder head. Torque the thrust plate bolt to 58–65 ft. lbs. (78–88 Nm). Remove the wooden block.

11. Lubricate the rocker shafts light-ly with clean engine oil and install them, with the rocker arms, into the head. Both shafts have punch marks on their leading edges, while the intake shaft is also marked with 2 slits on its leading edge.

**NOTE: To prevent the rocker shaft springs from slipping out of the shaft, insert the bracket bolts into the shaft prior to installation.**

12. Tighten the rocker shaft bolts gradually, in 2–3 stages to 13–16 ft. lbs. (18–22 Nm).

13. Install the camshaft pulley and then install the timing belt.

14. Adjust the valves as required and install the cylinder head cover.

15. Connect the negative battery cable.

## E16i Engine (1988 Pulsar)

1. Disconnect the negative battery cable.

2. Remove the timing belt.

3. Remove the rocker shaft along with the rocker arms. Loosen the bolts gradually, in 2–3 stages.

4. Carefully slide the camshaft out the front of the cylinder head.

5. Check the camshaft runout, endplay, wear and journal clearance.

**To install:**

6. Slide the camshaft into the cylinder head carefully and then install a new oil seal. Coat the lip of the new seal with clean engine oil prior to installation.

7. Install the rear timing belt cover.

8. Set the camshaft so the knockpin faces upward and then install the camshaft sprocket so its timing mark aligns with the one on the rear timing cover.

9. Install the timing belt.

10. Coat the rocker shaft and the interior of the rocker arm with engine oil. Install them so the punch mark on the shaft faces forward and the oil holes in the shaft face down. The cut-out in the center retainer on the shaft should face the exhaust manifold side of the engine.

11. Make sure the valve adjusting screws are loose and then tighten the shaft bolts to 13–15 ft. lbs. (18–21 Nm) in several stages, from the center out. The first and last mounting bolts should have a new bolt stopper installed.

12. Adjust the valves and connect the negative battery cable.

## GA16i Engine (1989–90 Pulsar and 1989–90 Sentra)

1. Disconnect the negative battery cable.

2. Remove the timing chain.

3. Remove the cylinder head with manifolds attached.

4. Remove the intake and exhaust manifolds from the cylinder head. Loosen the bolts in 2–3 stages in the proper sequence.

5. Loosen the rocker arm shaft bolts in 2–3 stages and lift the rocker arm/shaft assembly from the cylinder head. The rocker arm shaft is marked with an **F** to indicate that it faces towards the front of the engine. Place a similar mark on the cylinder head for your own reference.

6. Loosen the thrust plate retaining bolt.

7. Withdraw the camshaft and the thrust plate from the front of the cylinder head. The thrust plate is located to the camshaft with a key. Retain this key.

**To install:**

8. Clean all cylinder head, intake

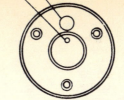

Camshaft positioning — E-Series engines

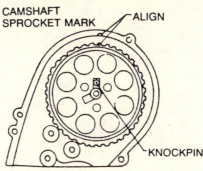

Camshaft sprocket alignment — E-Series engines

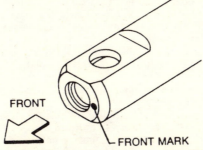

The punch mark on the rocker shaft should face forward — E-Series engines

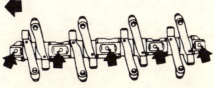

The oil holes must be facing down — E series engine

The center retainer cut-out should face the exhaust manifold — E series engine

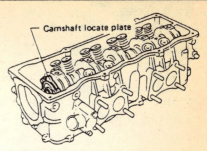

Rocker arm/shaft positioning — GA16i engine

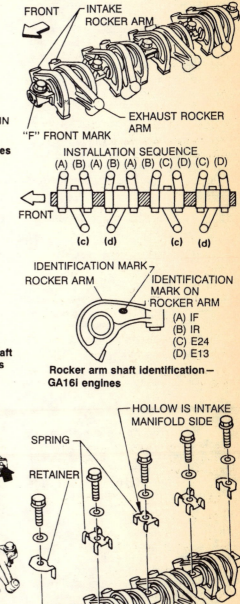

INSTALLATION SEQUENCE
(A) (B) (A) (B) (A) (B) (C) (D) (C) (D)

IDENTIFICATION MARK ON ROCKER ARM
(A) IF
(B) IR
(C) E24
(D) E13

Rocker arm shaft identification — GA16i engines

Rocker arm shaft bolt retainer positioning — GA16i engines

and exhaust manifold gasket surfaces. Lubricate the camshaft and rocker arm/shaft assemblies with a liberal coating of clean engine oil. Then, slide the camshaft and thrust plate into the front of the cylinder head. Don't forget to install the thrust plate key.

9. Install the rocker shafts and rocker arms making sure the **F** on the rocker shaft points toward the front of the engine. Install the rocker shaft retaining bolts, spring clips and washers. The center spring clip has a recess cut into one side. When installing the center clip point this recess toward the intake manifold side of the head. Snug the bolts gradually in 2–3 stages starting from the center and working out. Attach the intake and exhaust manifold to the head with new gaskets.

10. Install the cylinder head and timing chain.

11. After the timing chain is in place, set the No. 1 cylinder to TDC of the compression stroke.

12. Torque the No. 1 and No. 2 rocker shaft bolts to 27–30 ft. lbs. (37–41 Nm). Then, set the No. 4 cylinder to TDC and torque the No. 3 and No. 4 rocker shaft bolts to 27–30 ft. lbs. (37–41 Nm).

13. Connect the negative battery cable.

### GA16DE Engine (1991–92 Sentra)

NOTE: Modify service steps as necessary. This is a complete disassembly repair procedure. Review the complete procedure before starting this repair.

1. Disconnect the negative battery cable, drain the cooling system and relieve the fuel system pressure.
2. Remove all drive belts. Disconnect the exhaust tube from the exhaust manifold.
3. Remove the power steering bracket.
4. Remove the air duct to intake manifold collector.
5. Remove the front right side wheel, splash cover and front undercovers.
6. Remove the front exhaust pipe and engine front mounting bracket.
7. Remove the rocker arm cover.
8. Remove the distributor cap. Remove the spark plugs.
9. Set the No. 1 cylinder at TDC of the compression stroke.
10. Mark and remove the distributor assembly.
11. Remove the cam sprocket cover and gusset. Remove the water pump pulley. Remove the thermostat housing.
12. Remove the chain tensioner, chain guide. Loosen idler sprocket bolt.

13. Remove the camshaft sprocket bolts, camshaft sprockets, camshaft brackets and camshafts. These parts should be reassembled in their original position. Bolts should be loosen in 2 or 3 steps (loosen bolts in the reverse of the tightening order).

**To install:**

14. Install camshafts. Make sure that the camshafts are installed in the correct position. Note identification marks are present on camshafts mark I for intake camshaft and mark E for exhaust camshaft.

15. Install camshafts brackets. Tighten camshafts brackets bolts in two or three steps to 7–9 ft. lbs. in the correct sequence. After completing assembly check valve clearance.

16. Assemble camshaft sprocket with chain. Set timing chain by aligning mating marks with those of camshaft sprockets. Make sure sprockets mating marks face engine front.

17. Install camshaft sprocket bolts. Install upper chain tensioner and chain guide.

18. Install lower chain tensioner (make sure that the gasket is installed properly). Check that no problems occur when engine is rotated. Make sure that No. 1 piston is set to TDC on compression stroke.

19. Install thermostat housing, water pump pulley. Install the distributor assembly.

20. Install cam sprocket cover and rocker cover.

21. Install all remaining components in reverse order of removal.

22. Connect the negative battery cable. Refill all fluid levels. Road test the vehicle for proper operation.

### KA24E Engine (1989–90 240SX and 1989–92 Stanza)

1. Disconnect the negative battery cable.
2. Remove the timing chain.
3. Remove the cylinder head. Do not remove the camshaft sprocket at this time.
4. Loosen the rocker shaft bolt evenly in proper sequence. Start from the outside and work toward the center.
5. Mount a dial indicator to the cylinder head and set the stylus of the indicator on the head of the camshaft sprocket bolt. Zero the indicator and measure the camshaft endplay by moving the camshaft back and forth. Endplay should be within 0.0028–0.0059 in. (0.07–0.15mm).
6. Remove the camshaft brackets and lift the camshaft with sprocket from the cylinder head.

**To install:**

7. Clean all cylinder head, intake and exhaust manifold gasket surfaces.

Lubricate the camshaft and rocker arm/shaft assemblies with a liberal coating of clean engine oil. Lay the camshaft and sprocket into the cylinder head so the knock pin is at the front of the head at the 12 o'clock postion. Install the camshaft brackets. The camshaft bracket directional arrows must face the toward the front of the engine.

8. Install the rocker shaft and rocker arms. Both intake and exhaust rocker shafts are stamped with an **F** mark. This mark must face the front of the engine during installation. Install the rocker arm bolts and spring clips so the cut outs are facing as shown. Torque the rocker arm bolts in the proper sequence to 27–30 ft. lbs. (37–41 Nm).

9. Install the timing chain.

10. Install the cylinder head. Use new rubber plugs when installing the cylinder head.

11. Connect the negative battery cable.

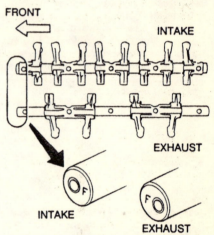

Rocker arm shaft positioning – KA24E engines

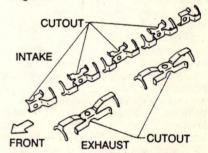

Spring clip installation – KA24E engines

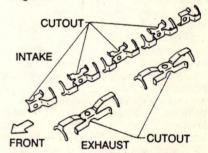

Rocker shaft bolt LOOSENING sequence – KA24E engines. Tighten in reverse of loosening sequence

### KA24DE Engine (1991–92 240SX)

NOTE: Modify service steps as necessary. This is a complete disassembly repair procedure. Review the complete procedure before starting this repair.

1. Release the fuel system pressure.
2. Disconnect the negative battery cable and drain the cooling system. Drain the engine oil.
3. Remove all vacuum hoses, fuel lines, wires, electrical connections as necessary.
4. Remove the front exhaust pipe and A.I.V. pipe.
5. Remove the air duct, cooling fan with coupling and radiator shroud.

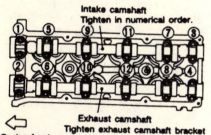

Intake camshaft Tighten in numerical order.

Exhaust camshaft Tighten exhaust camshaft bracket in the same procedure.

Engine front

**Camshaft bracket torque sequence— KA24DE engine**

6. Remove the the fuel injector tube assembly with injectors.
7. Disconnect and mark spark plug wires. Remove the spark plugs.
8. Set No. 1 piston at TDC on compression stroke. Remove the rocker cover assembly.
9. Mark and remove the distributor assembly.
10. Remove the cam sprocket, brackets and camshafts. These parts should be reassembled in their original position. Bolts should be loosened in 2 or 3 steps (loosen all bolts in the reverse of the tightening order).
**To install:**
11. Install camshafts and camshafts brackets. Torque camshaft brackets in two or three steps in sequence. After completing assembly check valve clearance.
12. Install camshaft sprockets.
13. Install chain guide between both camshaft sprockets and distributor assembly.
14. Install all remaining components in reverse order of removal.
15. Connect the negative battery cable. Refill all fluid levels. Road test the vehicle for proper operation.

### SR20DE Engine (1991–92 Sentra)

1. Disconnect the negative battery

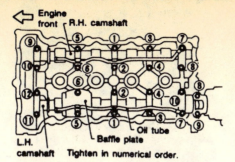

Engine front — R.H. camshaft

L.H. camshaft   Oil tube   Baffle plate   Tighten in numerical order.

**Camshaft bracket torque sequence— SR20DE engine**

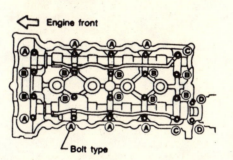

Engine front

Bolt type

**Camshaft bolt location—SR20DE engine**

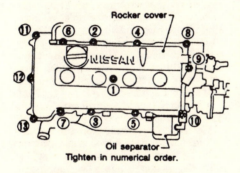

Rocker cover

Oil separator   Tighten in numerical order.

**Rocker cover torque sequence— SR20DE engine**

cable. Remove the rocker cover and oil separator.
2. Rotate the crankshaft until the No.1 piston is at TDC on the compression stroke. Then rotate the crankshaft until the mating marks on the camshaft sprockets line up with the mating marks on the timing chain.
3. Remove the timing chain tensioner.
4. Remove the distributor.
5. Remove the timing chain guide.
6. Remove the camshaft sprockets. Use a wrench to hold the camshaft while loosening the sprocket bolt.
7. Loosen the camshaft bracket bolts in the opposite order of the torquing sequence.
8. Remove the camshaft.
**To install:**
9. Clean the left hand camshaft end bracket and coat the mating surface with liquid gasket. Install the camshafts, camshaft brackets, oil tubes

and baffle plate. Ensure the left camshaft key is at 12 o'clock and the right camshaft key is at 10 o'clock.
10. The procedure for tightening camshaft bolts must be followed exactly to prevent camshaft damage. Tighten bolts as follows:
   a. Tighten right camshaft bolts 9 and 10 (in that order) to 1.5 ft. lbs. (2 Nm) then tighten bolts 1–8 (in that order) to the same specification.
   b. Tighten left camshaft bolts 11 and 12 (in that order) to 1.5 ft. lbs. (2 Nm) then tighten bolts 1–10 (in that order) to the same specification.
   c. Tighten all bolts in sequence to 4.5 ft. lbs. (6 Nm).
   d. Tighten all bolts in sequence to 6.5–8.5 ft. lbs. (9–12 Nm) for type A, B and C bolts, and 13–19 ft. lbs. (18–25 Nm) for type D bolts.
11. Line up the mating marks on the timing chain and camshaft sprockets and install the sprockets. Tighten sprocket bolts to 101–116 ft. lbs. (137–157 Nm).
12. Install the timing chain guide, distributor (ensure that rotor head is at 5 o'clock position) and chain tensioner.
13. Clean the rocker cover and mating surfaces and apply a continious bead of liquid gasket to the mating surface.
14. Install the rocker cover and oil separator. Tighten the rocker cover bolts as follows:
   a. Tighten nuts 1, 10, 11, and 8 in that order to 3 ft. lbs. (4 Nm).
   b. Tighten nuts 1–13 as indicated in the figure to 6–7 ft. lbs. (8–10 Nm).
15. Connect the negative battery cable. Refill all fluid levels. Road test the vehicle for proper operation.

### VG30E and VG30ET Engines (1988–89 300ZX and 1988–92 Maxima)

1. Disconnect the negative battery cable.
2. Drain the cooling system.
3. Remove the timing belt.
4. Remove the collector assembly.
5. Remove the intake manifold.
6. Remove the cylinder head.
7. Remove the rocker shafts with rocker arms. Bolts should be loosened in several steps in the proper sequence.
8. Remove hydraulic valve lifters and lifter guide. Hold hydraulic valve lifters with wire so they will not drop from lifter guide.
9. Using a dial gauge measure the camshaft endplay. If the camshaft endplay exceeds the limit (0.0012–0.0024 in.), select the thickness of a

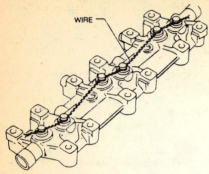

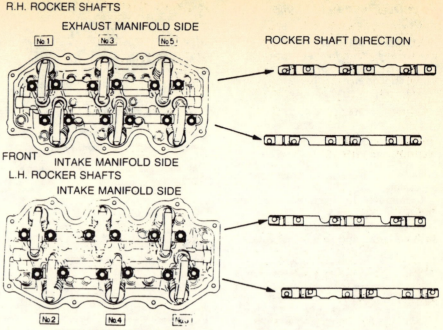

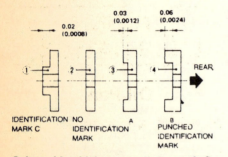

**Holding the V6 valve lifters in place**

**Select shim thickness so that camshaft thickness is within specifications**

R.H. ROCKER SHAFTS
EXHAUST MANIFOLD SIDE
INTAKE MANIFOLD SIDE
L.H. ROCKER SHAFTS
INTAKE MANIFOLD SIDE
EXHAUST MANIFOLD SIDE
ROCKER SHAFT DIRECTION

**Rocker shaft/arm installation procedure—VG30E and VG30ET engines**

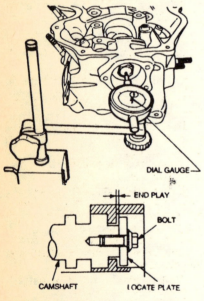

**Using a dial indicator to measure camshaft endplay—V6 engine**

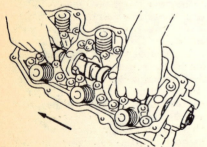

**Remove the V6 camshaft in the direction of the arrow**

cam locate plate so the endplay is within specification. For example, if camshaft end play measures 0.0031 in. (0.08mm) with shim 2 used, then change shim 2 to shim 3 so the camshaft end play is 0.0020 in. (0.05mm).

10. Remove the camshaft front oil seal and slide camshaft out the front of the cylinder head assembly.

**To install:**

11. Install camshaft, locater plates, cylinder head rear cover and front oil seal. Set camshaft knock pin at 12 o'clock position. Install cylinder head with new gasket to engine.

12. Install valve lifter guide assembly. Assemble valve lifters in their original position. After installing them in the correct location remove the wire holding them in lifter guide.

13. Install rocker shafts in correct position with rocker arms. Tighten bolts in 2–3 stages to 13–16 ft. lbs. (18–22 Nm). Before tightening, be sure to set camshaft lobe at the position where lobe is not lifted or the valve closed. Set each cylinder 1 at a time or follow the procedure below. The cylinder head, intake manifold, collector and timing belt must be installed:

   a. Set No. 1 piston at TDC of the compression stroke and tighten rocker shaft bolts for No. 2, No. 4 and No. 6 cylinders.

   b. Set No. 4 piston at TDC of the compression stroke and tighten rocker shaft bolts for No. 1, No. 3 and No. 5 cylinders.

   c. Torque specification for the rocker shaft retaining bolts is 13–16 ft. lbs. (18–22 Nm).

14. Fill the cooling system to the proper level.

15. Connect the negative battery cable.

### VG30DE and VG30DETT Engines (1990–92 300ZX)

1. Disconnect the negative battery cable.

2. Drain the cooling system.

3. Remove the the timing belt.

4. Remove the cylinder head with the exhaust manifold.

5. Separate the exhaust manifold from the cylinder head.

6. Remove the camshaft sprockets. Remove the front plate, O-ring and spring from the right (intake) camshaft to gain access to the sprocket bolt. The left camshaft sprocket is held in place by plate and 4 bolts.

7. Remove the rear timing belt cover.

8. Mount a dial indicator and set the stylus of the indicator on the end of the camshaft. Zero the indicator and measure the camshaft endplay by moving the camshaft back and forth. Endplay should be within 0.0012–0.0031 in. (0.03–0.08mm).

9. Remove the camshaft brackets. Loosen the bolts in the proper sequence gradually in 2–3 stages.

10. Gently pry the camshaft oil seals from the cylinder head.

11. Remove the timing control solenoid valves.

12. Remove the camshafts.

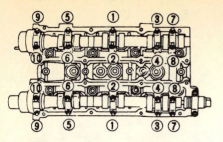

Camshaft bracket torque sequence—
VG30DE and VG30DETT engines

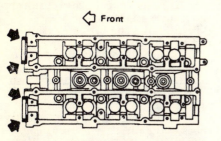

When installing front side camshaft
bracket, apply liquid gasket as shown
—VG30DE and VG30DETT engines

**To install:**

13. Install the camshafts so the knock pins are aligned properly. The exhaust side camshaft (left side) has a spline that accepts the crank angle sensor.

14. Install the timing control solenoid valves. Torque the bracket bolts to 12–18 ft. lbs. (16–25 Nm). Apply liquid gasket to the valve seating surface before installation.

15. Install the camshaft brackets. Torque the bracket bolts in sequence to 7–9 ft. lbs. (9–12 Nm). Tighten the bolts gradually in 2–3 stages. When installing the front camshaft brackets, apply liquid gasket to the bracket seating surface.

16. Coat the lips of the new camshaft seals with clean engine oil and install the seals into the cylinder head.

17. Install the rear timing belt covers. Torque the cover bolts to 5–6 ft. lbs. (6–8 Nm).

18. Install the camshaft sprockets. Torque the right side (intake) sprocket bolt 90–98 ft. lbs. (123–132 Nm) and the left side (exhaust) sprocket retainer bolts to 10–14 ft. lbs. (14–19 Nm). When tightening the sprocket fasteners, make sure to hold the camshafts stationary.

19. Mount the exhaust manifold to the head with new gaskets.

20. Install the cylinder head.

21. Install the timing belt.

22. Fill the cooling system to the proper level.

23. Connect the negative battery cable.

# Piston and Connecting Rod

## POSITIONING

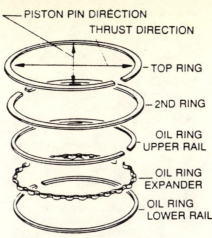

MARK SHOULD BE
FACING UPWARD

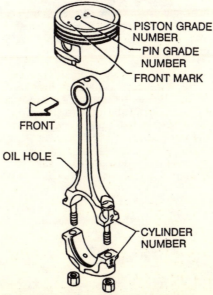

INSTALL TOWARDS ENGINE FRONT

**Piston ring identification and positioning—all engines**

**Piston and connection rod positioning— all engines**

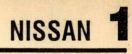

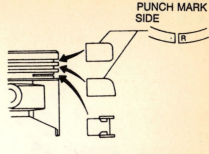

**Piston ring installation—all engines**

# ENGINE LUBRICATION

## Oil Pan

### REMOVAL & INSTALLATION

#### *200SX*

1. Disconnect the negative battery cable.

2. Raise the front of the vehicle and support safely.

3. Drain the oil pan.

4. Remove the power steering bracket from the suspension crossmember.

5. Separate the stabilizer bar from the transverse link.

6. Separate the tension rod from the transverse link.

7. Remove the front engine mounting insulator nuts.

8. Lift the engine.

9. Loosen the oil pan bolts in the proper sequence.

10. Remove the suspension crossmember bolts and remove the screws that secure the power steering oil tubes to the crossmember.

11. Lower the suspension crossmember until there is sufficient clearance to remove the oil pan.

12. Insert a seal cutter between the oil pan and the cylinder block.

13. Tapping the seal cutter with a hammer, slide the cutting tool around the entire edge of the oil pan. Do not drive the seal cutter into the oil pump or rear seal retainer portion or the aluminum mating surface will be deformed.

14. Lower the oil pan from the cylinder block and remove it from the front side of the engine.

**To install:**

15. Carefully scrape the old gasket material away from the pan and cylinder block mounting surfaces.

16. First apply sealant to the oil pump gasket and rear oil seal retainer gasket surfaces. Then, apply a contin-

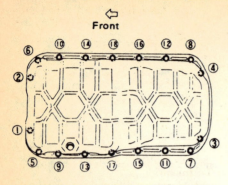

LOOSEN IN NUMERICAL SEQUENCE
FRONT

**Oil pan bolt tightening sequence on 200SX. Loosen in reverse order**

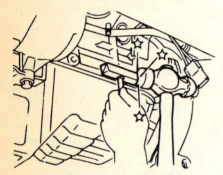

Using a seal cutter on the oil pan

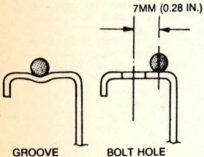

7MM (0.28 IN.)

GROOVE          BOLT HOLE

**Apply sealer on the inside of the bolt holes**

uous bead (3.5–4.5mm) of liquid gasket around the oil pan to the 4 corners of the cylinder block mounting surface. Wait 5 minutes and then install the pan. Tighten the oil pan bolts in sequence to 5–6 ft. lbs. (6–8 Nm).

17. Raise the crossmember from the lowered position. Attach the power steering tubes and install the crossmember bolts.

18. Install the front engine mounting insulator nuts.

19. Connect the tension rod and stabilizer bar to the transverse link.

20. Attach the power steering bracket to the crossmember.

21. Lower the vehicle.

22. Fill the crankcase to the proper level.

23. Connect the negative battery cable. Start the engine and check for leaks.

## 240SX

1. Disconnect the negative battery cable.

2. Raise the front of the vehicle and support safely.

3. Drain the oil pan.

4. Separate the front stabilizer bar from the side member.

5. Position a block of wood between a floor jack and the engine and then raise the engine slightly in its mounts.

6. Remove the oil pan retaining bolts in the proper sequence.

7. Insert a seal cutter between the oil pan and the cylinder block.

8. Tapping the cutter with a hammer, slide it around the entire edge of the oil pan. Do not drive the seal cutter into the oil pump or rear seal retainer portion or the aluminum mating surface will be deformed.

9. Lower the oil pan from the cylinder block and remove it from the front side of the engine.

**To install:**

10. To install, carefully scrape the old gasket material away from the pan and cylinder block mounting surfaces and then apply a continuous bead (3.5–4.5mm) of liquid gasket around the oil pan to the 4 corners of the cylinder block mounting surface. Wait 5 minutes and then install the pan.

11. Install the oil pan and tighten the mounting bolts from the inside, out, to 3.6–5.1 ft. lbs. (5–7 Nm). Wait 30 minutes before refilling the crankcase to allow for the sealant to cure properly.

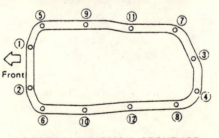

LOOSEN IN NUMERICAL SEQUENCE
FRONT

**Oil pan bolt tightening sequence on 240SX. Loosen bolts in reverse order**

12. Connect the front stabilizer to the side bar.

13. Lower the vehicle.

14. Fill the crankcase to the proper level.

15. Connect the negative battery cable. Start the engine and check for leaks.

## 1988–89 300ZX

1. Disconnect the negative battery cable.

2. Raise the vehicle and support safely.

3. Drain the oil pan.

4. Separate the front stabilizer bar from the suspension crossmember.

5. Remove the steering column shaft from the gear housing.

6. Separate the tension rod retaining nuts from the transverse link.

7. Raise and support the engine.

8. Remove the rear plate cover from the transmission case.

9. Remove the oil pan retaining bolts in the proper sequence.

10. Remove the suspension crossmember retaining bolts.

11. Remove the strut mounting insulator retaining nuts.

12. Remove the screws retaining the refrigerant lines and power steering tubes to the suspension crossmember.

13. Lower the suspension crossmember.

14. Insert a seal cutter between the oil pan and the cylinder block.

15. Tapping the cutter with a hammer, slide it around the entire edge of the oil pan. Do not drive the seal cutter into the oil pump or rear seal retainer portion or the aluminum mating surface will be deformed.

16. Lower the oil pan from the cylinder block and remove it from the front rear of the engine.

**To install:**

17. Carefully scrape the old gasket material away from the pan and cylinder block mounting surfaces and then apply a continuous bead (3.5–4.5mm) of liquid gasket around the oil pan and to the 4 corners of the cylinder block mounting surface. Wait 5 minutes and then install the pan.

18. Install tighten the pan mounting bolts from the inside, out, to 5–6 ft. lbs. (7–8 Nm). Wait 30 minutes before refilling the crankcase to allow for the sealant to cure properly.

19. Raise the crossmember from the lowered postion and attach the power steering and refrigerant lines.

20. Install and tighten the strut mounting insulator nuts.

21. Install the crossmember bolts.

22. Install the rear cover plate to the transmission case.

23. Lower the engine.

24. Connect the tension rod to the transverse link.

25. Connect the steering column shaft to the gear housing.

26. Connnect the front stabilizer bar to the crossmember.

27. Lower the vehicle.

28. Fill the crankcase to the proper level.

29. Connect the negative battery ca-

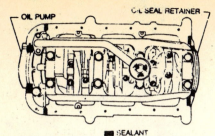

Apply sealant to these areas before installing the oil pan gasket—V6 engine

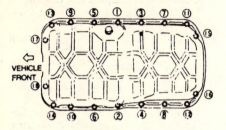

Oil pan bolt tightening sequence on Maxima and 1988–89 300ZX. Loosen bolts in reverse order

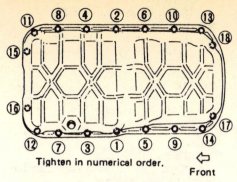

Tighten in numerical order.    ⇦ Front

Oil pan bolt tightening sequence on 1990–92 300ZX. Loosen bolts in reverse order

ble. Start the engine and check for leaks.

### 1990–92 300ZX

1. Disconnect the negative battery cable.
2. Raise the front of the vehicle and support safely.
3. Remove the engine undercover.
4. Drain the oil pan.
5. Remove the oil filter and bracket.
6. Remove the rear engine gussets from both sides.
7. Disconnect the air conditioning tube clamps.
8. Disconnect the lower steering column joint from the steering rack.
9. Remove the tension rod and transverse link bolts from both sides.
10. Support the suspension member with a suitable transmission jack. Install engine lifting slingers, connect a lifting device to the slingers and lift the engine.
11. Remove the suspension member bolts and lower the suspension member.
12. Remove the engine mounting bolts from both sides and slowly lower the transmission jack.
13. Remove the oil pan bolts in the proper sequence.
14. Insert a seal cutter between the oil pan and the cylinder block.
15. Tapping the cutter with a hammer, slide it around the entire edge of the oil pan. Do not drive the seal cutter into the oil pump or rear seal retainer portion or the aluminum mating surface will be deformed.
16. Lower the oil pan from the cylinder block and remove it.

### To install:

17. Carefully scrape the old gasket material away from the pan and cylinder block mounting surfaces and then apply a continuous bead (3.5–4.5mm) of liquid gasket around the oil pan and to the 4 corners of the cylinder block mounting surface. Wait 5 minutes and then install the pan.
18. Install tighten the pan mounting bolts from the inside, out, to 4–6 ft. lbs. (6–8 Nm). Wait 30 minutes before refilling the crankcase to allow for the sealant to cure properly.
19. Slowly raise the transmission jack, then install the engine mounting bolts.
20. Raise the suspension member and install the mounting bolts.
21. Lower the engine, disconnect the lifting device and remove the lifting slingers.
22. Install the tension rod and transverse link bolts.
23. Connect the lower steering column joint to the steering rack.
24. Install the air conditioning tube clamps.
25. Install the rear engine gussets.
26. Install the oil filter bracket with a new oil filter.
27. Install the engine undercover.
28. Lower the vehicle.
29. Fill the crankcase to the proper level.
30. Connect the negative battery cable. Start the engine and check for leaks.

### Maxima

1. Disconnect the negative battery cable.
2. Raise the front of the vehicle and support safely.
3. Drain the oil pan.
4. Remove the engine lower covers.
5. Using a suitable jack and block of wood, support the engine in the area of the crank pulley.
6. Remove the engine mounting insulator fasteners.

7. Remove the center crossmember.
8. Remove the oil pan bolts in the proper sequence.
9. Insert a seal cutter between the oil pan and the cylinder block.
10. Tapping the cutter with a hammer, slide it around the entire edge of the oil pan. Do not drive the seal cutter into the oil pump or rear seal retainer portion or the aluminum mating surface will be deformed.
11. Lower the oil pan from the cylinder block and remove it.

### To install:

12. Carefully scrape the old gasket material away from the pan and cylinder block mounting surfaces and then apply a thin continuous bead of liquid gasket around the oil pan and to the 4 corners of the cylinder block mounting surface. Do the same to the oil pan gasket; both upper and lower surfaces. Wait 5 minutes and then install the pan. Wait 30 minutes before refilling the crankcase to allow the sealant to cure properly.
13. Install the oil pan and tighten the mounting bolts from the inside, out, to 5–6 ft. lbs. (7–8 Nm) in the proper sequence.
14. Install the center crossmember assembly.
15. Install the engine mount insulator fasteners.
16. Lower the engine.
17. Connnect the front exhaust pipe.
18. Install the engine lower covers.
19. Fill the crankcase to the proper level.
20. Connect the negative battery cable. Start the engine and check for leaks.

### 1988–89 Stanza

1. Disconect the negative battery cable.
2. Drain the oil pan.
3. Raise and support the front of the vehicle safely.
4. Remove the front exhaust tube section and the center crossmember.
5. Remove the oil pan bolts.
6. Insert a seal cutter between the oil pan and the cylinder block.
7. Tapping the cutter with a hammer, slide it around the entire edge of the oil pan. Do not drive the seal cutter into the oil pump or rear seal retainer portion or the aluminum mating surface will be deformed.
8. Lower the oil pan from the cylinder block and remove it.

### To install:

9. Carefully scrape the old gasket material away from the pan and cylinder block mounting surfaces and then apply a thin continuous bead of liquid gasket around the oil pan and to the 4 corners of the cylinder block mounting surface. Do the same to the oil pan gas-

ket; both upper and lower surfaces. Wait 5 minutes and then install the pan. Wait 30 minutes before refilling the crankcase to allow the sealant to cure properly.

10. Install the oil pan and tighten the mounting bolts from the inside, out, to 4–5 ft. lbs. (5–7 Nm).

11. Install the center crossmember and front exhaust tube section.

12. Lower the vehicle.

13. Fill the crankcase to the proper level.

14. Connect the negative battery cable. Start the engine and check for leaks.

### Pulsar, Sentra and 1990–92 Stanza

#### (EXCEPT SR20DE ENGINE)

1. Disconnect the negative battery cable.

2. Raise the vehicle and support safely.

3. Drain the oil pan.

4. Remove the right side splash cover.

5. Remove the right side undercover.

6. Remove the center member (2WD vehicles only).

7. Remove the forward section of the exhaust pipe.

8. Remove the front buffer rod and its bracket (1988 vehicles only).

9. Remove the engine gussets (1988 vehicles only).

10. Remove the oil pan bolts.

11. Insert a seal cutter between the oil pan and the cylinder block.

12. Tapping the cutter with a hammer, slide it around the entire edge of the oil pan. Do not drive the seal cutter into the oil pump or rear seal retainer portion or the aluminum mating surface will be deformed.

13. Lower the oil pan from the cylinder block and remove it.

**To install:**

14. Carefully scrape the old gasket material away from the pan and cylinder block mounting surfaces and then apply a thin continuous bead of liquid gasket around the oil pan and to the 4 corners of the cylinder block mounting surface. Do the same to the oil pan gasket; both upper and lower surfaces. Wait 5 minutes and then install the pan. Wait 30 minutes before refilling the crankcase to allow the sealant to cure properly.

15. Install the oil pan and tighten the mounting bolts from the inside, out, to 5–6 ft. lbs. (7–8 Nm).

16. Install the engine gussets (1988 vehicles only).

17. Install the front buffer rod and its bracket (1988 vehicles only).

18. Install the forward section of the exhaust pipe using new gaskets.

19. Install the center member (2WD vehicles only).

20. Install the right side undercover.

21. Install the right side splash cover.

22. Lower the vehicle.

23. Fill the crankcase to the proper level.

24. Connect the negative battery cable. Start the engine and check for leaks.

### SR20DE ENGINE)

1. Raise and support the vehicle safely. Remove the engine under cover and drain the oil.

2. Remove the steel oil pan bolts in the proper sequence. Remove the steel oil pan. Insert tool KV10111100 or equivalent between steel oil pan and aluminum oil pan to pry apart.

3. Remove the oil baffle bolts and oil baffle. Remove the front tube.

4. Set a suitable jack under the transaxle and raise the engine with and engine hoist.

5. If equipped with an automatic transaxle, remove the transaxle shift control cable.

6. Remove the compressor gussets, the rear cover plate and all aluminum oil pan bolts. Loosen aluminum oil pan bolts in the proper sequence.

7. Remove the 2 engine-to-transaxle bolts and refit the them into vacant holes at the bottom of the oil pan. Remove the aluminum oil pan. Use tool KV10111100 or equivalent to pry oil pan from block. Remove the engine to transaxle bolts.

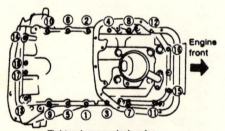

Tighten in numerical order.

**Aluminum oil pan installation torque sequence—SR20DE engine**

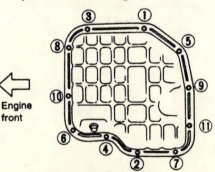

Tighten in numerical order.

**Steel oil pan installation torque sequence—SR20DE engine**

**To install:**

8. Clean the oil pan rail of all liquid gasket and apply a new bead of ⅛″ thickness to the oil pan rail.

9. Install the aluminum oil pan and torque bolts 1–16 to 12–14 ft. lbs. (16–19 Nm) and bolts 17–18 to 5–6 ft. lbs. (6–8 Nm) in the opposite order of removal.

10. Install the 2 engine to transaxle bolts, rear cover plate, compressor gussets, automatic transmission shift control cable (if equipped), center member, front tube and baffle plate.

11. Clean the oil pan rail of all liquid gasket and apply a new bead of ⅛″ thickness to the oil pan rail.

12. Install the steel oil pan and install bolts untill snug. Tighten bolts in the reverse order of removal and wait 30 minuites before refilling crankcase with oil.

## Oil Pump

### REMOVAL & INSTALLATION

#### CA18DE and CA20E Engines

1. Disconnect the negative battery cable.

2. Drain the oil pan.

3. Remove all accessory drive belts.

4. Remove the alternator.

5. Remove the timing belt covers.

6. Remove the timing belt.

7. On 200SX and the Stanza Wagon, unbolt the engine from its mounts and lift or jack the engine up from the unibody. On the Stanza (except Wagon) and Pulsar, remove the center member from the body.

8. Remove the oil pan.

9. Remove the oil pump assembly along with the oil strainer. Remove the O-ring from the oil pump body and replace it.

10. Replace the front seal.

**To install:**

11. If installing a new or rebuilt oil pump, first pack the pump full of petroleum jelly to prevent the pump from cavitating when the engine is started. Apply RTV sealer to the front oil seal end of the pan prior to installation.

12. Install the pump and torque the oil pump mounting bolts to 8–12 ft. lbs. (12–16 Nm). Make sure the oil pump body O-ring is properly seated.

13. Install the oil pan.

14. On the Stanza (except Wagon) and Pulsar, install the center member. On 200SX and the Stanza Wagon, lower and re-mount the engine.

15. Install the timing belt.

16. Install the timing belt covers.

17. Install the alternator.

18. Install and tension the drive belts.

19. Fill the crankcase to the proper level.

20. Connect the negative battery cable. Start the engine and check for leaks.

### E16i Engine

1. Disconnect the negative battery cable.

2. Drain the oil pan.

3. Remove all accessory drive belts.

4. Remove the alternator.

5. Disconnect the oil pressure gauge harness.

6. Remove the oil filter.

7. Remove the oil pump and gasket.

**To install:**

8. If installing a new or rebuilt oil pump, first pack the pump full of petroleum jelly to prevent the pump from cavitating when the engine is started.

9. Mount the pump on the engine using a new gasket. Torque the pump mounting bolts to 7–9 ft. lbs. (10–12 Nm).

10. Install a new oil filter.

11. Connect the oil pressure gauge harness.

12. Install the alternator.

13. Install and tension the drive belts.

14. Fill the crankcase to the proper level.

15. Connect the negative battery cable. Start the engine and check for leaks.

### GA16i Engine and 1990–92 Stanza Engine (KA24E)

The oil pump used on the GA16i engine consists of an inner and outer gear located in the front cover. Removal of the front cover is necessary to gain access to the oil pump.

1. Disconnect the negative battery cable.

2. Remove the front cover with the strainer tube.

3. Loosen the oil pump cover retaining screw and mounting bolts and separate the oil pump cover from the front cover.

4. Remove the oil pump inner and outer gears.

**To install:**

5. Thoroughly clean the oil pump cover mating surfaces and the gear cavity.

6. Install the outer gear into the cavity.

7. Install the inner gear so the grooved side is facing up (towards the oil pump cover). Make sure the gears mesh properly and pack the pump cavity with petroleum jelly.

8. Install the oil pump cover. On GA16i engines, torque the retaining screws to 2.2–3.6 ft. lbs. (3–5 Nm) and the bolts to 3.6–5.1 ft. lbs. (5–7 Nm).

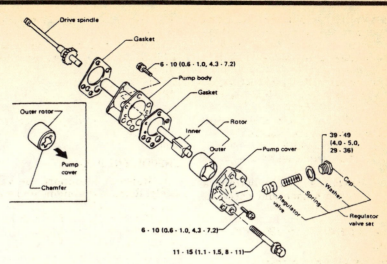

**Align the punch mark on the drive spindle with the oil hole—240SX**

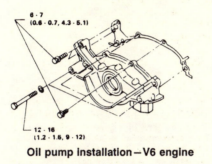

**Oil pump installation—V6 engine**

On KA24E engines, torque the cover screws to 2.2–3.6 ft. lbs. (3–5 Nm) and the bolts to 12–15 ft. lbs. (16–21 Nm).

9. Install the front cover with a new seal.

10. Connect the negative battery cable. Start the engine and check for leaks.

### GA16DE, KA24DE and SR20DE Engines

1. Remove the drive belts.

2. Remove the cylinder head and oil pans.

3. Remove the oil strainer and baffle plate.

4. Remove the front cover assembly. Remove the oil pump.

**To install:**

5. Clean the mating surfaces of liquid gasket and apply a fresh bead of 1/8 in. thickness.

6. Coat the oil pump gears with oil. Using a new oil seal and O-ring, install the front cover assembly.

7. Install the oil strainer, baffle plate, oil pans, cylinder head and drive belts.

### KA24E Engine (240SX)

1. Disconnect the negative battery cable.

2. Drain the oil pan.

3. Turn the crankshaft so No. 1 piston is at TDC on its compression stroke.

4. Remove the distributor cap and mark the position of the distributor rotor in relation to the distributor base with a piece of chalk.

5. Remove the splash shield.

6. Remove the oil pump body with the drive spindle assembly.

**To install:**

7. To install, fill the pump housing with engine oil, align the punch mark on the spindle with the hole in the pump. No. 1 piston should be at TDC on its compression stroke.

8. With a new gasket and seal placed over the drive spindle, install the oil pump and drive spindle assembly. Make sure the tip of the drive spindle fits into the distributor shaft notch securely. The distributor rotor should be pointing to the matchmark made earlier.

9. Install the splash shield.

10. Install the distributor cap.

11. Fill the crankcase to the proper level.

12. Connect the negative battery cable. Start the engine and check for leaks. Check the ignition timing.

### VG30E, VG30ET, VG30DE and VG30DETT Engines

1. Disconnect the negative battery cable.

2. Remove the oil pan.

3. Remove the timing belt.

4. Remove the crankshaft timing sprocket using a suitable puller.

5. Remove the timing belt plate.

6. Remove the oil pump strainer and pick-up tube from the oil pump.

7. Remove the mounting bolts and remove the oil pump and gasket.

8. Replace the oil pump seal.

**To install:**

9. Before installing the oil pump, remove the front cover and pack the pump's cavity with petroleum jelly, then make sure the O-ring is fitted properly. Torque the front cover screws to 3–4 ft. lbs. (4–5 Nm).

10. Mount the oil pump with a new gasket. Torque the 8mm retaining bolts to 16–22 ft. lbs. (22–29 Nm) and the 6mm bolts to 5–6 ft. lbs. (6–8 Nm).

11. Install the oil pump strainer and pick-up tube with a new O-ring. Torque the pick-up tube mounting bolts to 12–15 ft. lbs. (16–21 Nm).

12. Install the timing belt plate.

13. Install the crankshaft timing sprocket.

14. Install the timing belt.

15. Install the oil pan.

16. Connect the negative battery cable. Start the engine and check for leaks.

## CHECKING

### CA18DE, CA20E, VG30E, VG30ET, VG30DE and VG30DETT Engines

1. Remove the oil pump cover and gasket.

2. Disassemble the regulator valve components. Visually inspect all parts for wear and damage.

3. Make sure the regulator valve moves smoothly in the valve bore. Make sure the valve spring is sturdy.

4. Coat the regulator valve with clean engine oil and check that it falls into the valve bore by its own weight. Assemble the regulator valve components. Torque the valve cap to 29–36 ft. lbs. (39–49 Nm).

5. Inspect the oil pressure relief valve for movement, cracks and damage by pushing the ball in. If necessary, install a new valve by prying the old valve out and tapping the new valve in place.

6. Check the body-to-outer gear clearance. It should be 0.0043–0.0079 in. (0.11–0.20mm).

7. Check the inner gear-to-crescent clearance. It should be 0.0047–0.0091 in. (0.12–0.23mm).

8. Check the outer gear-to-crescent clearance. It should be 0.0083–0.0126 in. (0.21–0.32mm).

9. Check the body (housing)-to-inner gear clearance. It should be 0.0020–0.0035 in. (0.05–0.09mm).

10. Check the body (housing)-to-outer gear clearance. It should be 0.0020–0.0043 in. (0.05–0.11mm).

11. If any of the clearances exceed the specified limits, replace the gear set or the entire oil pump assembly.

12. Coat the inner and outer gears with clean engine oil prior to installation.

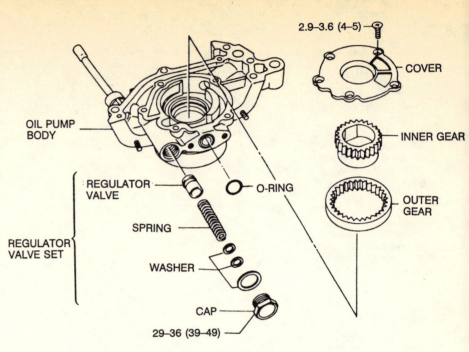

**Oil pump assembly – C-Series engines**

13. Install the oil pump cover with a new gasket. Tighten the cover screws to 3–4 ft. lbs. (4–5 Nm).

### E16i and KA24E (240SX) Engines

**NOTE: Do not disassemble the inner rotor and drive gear.**

1. Disassemble the regulator valve components. Visually inspect all parts for wear and damage.

2. Make sure the regulator valve moves smoothly in the valve bore. Make sure the valve spring is sturdy.

3. Coat the regulator valve with clean engine oil and check that it falls into the valve bore by its own weight. Assemble the regulator valve components. Torque the valve cap to 29–36 ft. lbs. (39–49 Nm).

4. Inspect the oil pressure relief valve for movement, cracks and damage by pushing the ball in. If necessary, install a new valve by prying the old valve out and tapping the new valve in place.

5. Check the rotor tip clearance. It should be less than 0.0047 in. (0.12mm).

6. Check the outer rotor-to-body clearance. It should be 0.0059–0.0083 in. (0.15–0.21mm).

7. With the pump body gasket installed, check the side clearance. It should be 0.0020–0.0047 in. (0.05–0.12mm) for E16i engine; and 0.0016–0.0031 in. (0.04–0.08mm) on KA24E engines.

8. If any of the clearances exceed the specified limits, replace the gear set or the entire oil pump assembly.

9. Coat the inner and outer gears with clean engine oil prior to installation.

### GA16i and KA24E (1990–92 Stanza) Engines

1. Remove the oil pump cover and gasket.

2. Disassemble the regulator valve components. Visually inspect all parts for wear and damage.

3. Make sure the regulator valve moves smoothly in the valve bore. Make sure the valve spring is sturdy.

4. Coat the regulator valve with clean engine oil and check that it falls into the valve bore by its own weight. Assemble the regulator valve components. Torque the valve cap to 29–36 ft. lbs. (39–49 Nm).

5. Inspect the oil pressure relief valve for movement, cracks and damage by pushing the ball in. If necessary, install a new valve by prying the old valve out and tapping the new valve in place.

6. Check the body-to-outer gear clearance. It should be 0.0043–0.0079 in. (0.11–0.20mm).

7. Check the inner gear-to-crescent clearance. It should be 0.0085–0.0129 in. (0.217–0.327mm).

8. Check the outer gear-to-crescent clearnce. It should be 0.0083–0.0126 in. (0.21–0.32mm).

9. Check the body-to-inner gear

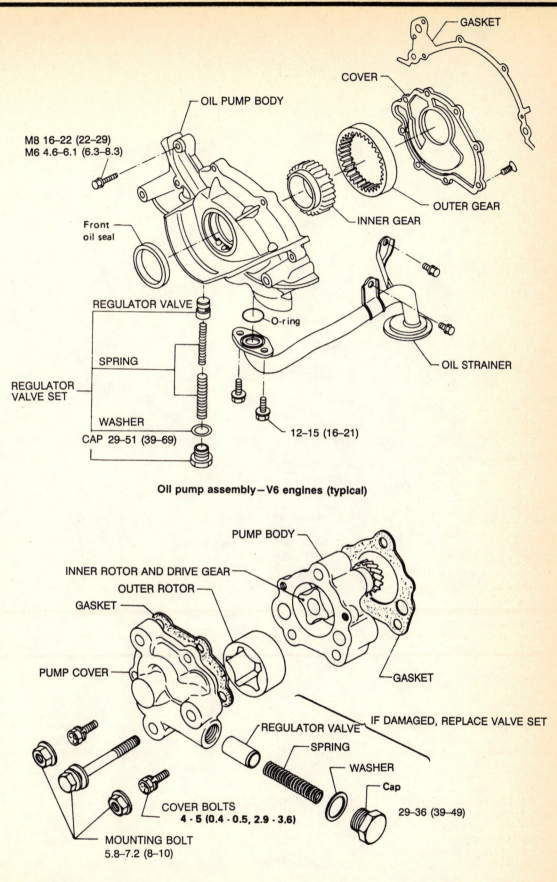

**Oil pump assembly—V6 engines (typical)**

**Oil pump assembly—E16i engine**

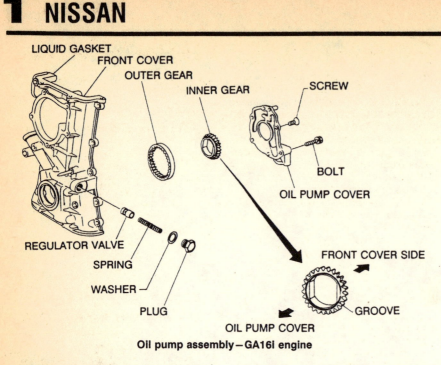

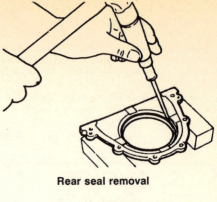

Rear seal removal

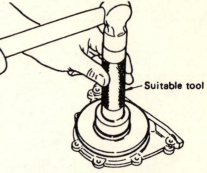

Suitable tool

Rear seal installation

Oil pump assembly—GA16i engine

clearance. It should be 0.0020–0.0035 in. (0.05–0.09mm).

10. Check the body-to-outer gear clearance. It should be 0.0020–0.0043 in. (0.05–0.11mm).

11. On GA16i engines, check the clearance between the inner gear and the braised portion of the housing. It should be 0.0018–0.0036 in. (0.045–0.091mm). To do this, measure the diameter of the front cover seal opening with an inside micrometer, then measure the diameter of the inner gear race. Subtract the 2 readings to obtain the clearance.

12. If any of the clearances exceed the specified limits, replace the gear set or the oil pump assembly.

13. Coat the inner and outer gears with clean engine oil prior to installation.

14. Install the oil pump cover. On GA16i engines, torque the retaining screws to 2.2–3.6 ft. lbs. (3–5 Nm) and the bolts to 3.6–5.1 ft. lbs. (5–7 Nm). On KA24E engines, torque the cover screws to 2.2–3.6 ft. lbs. (3–5 Nm) and the bolts to 12–15 ft. lbs. (16–21 Nm).

### GA16DE Engine

1. Check the following clearances with a suitable feeler gauge:
   a. The body-to-outer gear clearance 0.0043–0.0079 in.
   b. The inner gear-to-crescent clearance 0.0085–0.0129 in.
   c. The outer gear-to-crescent clearance 0.0083–0.0126 in.
   d. The housing-to-inner gear clearance 0.0020–0.0035 in.
   e. The housing-to-outer gear clearance 0.0020–0.0043 in.

2. If any clearance exceeds the limit, replace the gear set or the entire gear assembly.

### KA24DE and SR20DE Engines

1. Remove the oil pump cover.

2. Body to outer gear clearance should be 0.0045–0.0079 in. (0.114–0.200mm).

3. Inner gear to outer gear clearance should be less than 0.071 in. (0.18mm). If not within specification, replace the gear set.

4. Lay a straightedge across the surface of the gears and check the gear to body clearance. If not within specification, replace the front cover.

5. Body to inner gear clearance should be 0.0020–0.0035 in. (0.05–0.09mm). If not within specification, replace the front cover.

6. Body to outer gear clearance should be 0.0020–0.0043 in. (0.05–0.11mm). If not within specification, replace the front cover.

7. Subtract the outside diameter of the inner gear collar from the inside diameter of the front cover raised portion. Clearance should be 0.0018–0.0036 in. (0.045–0.091mm). If not within specification, replace the front cover.

8. Assemble the oil pump using a new oil seal and O-ring. Lightly coat the gears with oil and install the oil pump cover. Tighten the oil pump cover bolts to 5–6 ft. lbs. (6–8 Nm). Tighten the oil pump gear bolt to 3–4 ft. lbs. (4–5 Nm).

## Rear Main Bearing Oil Seal

### REMOVAL & INSTALLATION

1. Remove the transmission or transaxle.

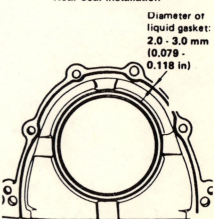

Diameter of liquid gasket:
2.0 - 3.0 mm (0.079 - 0.118 in)

On most engines, apply a 0.08–0.12 in. (2–3mm) of liquid gasket to the rear oil seal retainer

2. Remove the flywheel or drive plate.

3. Remove the rear oil seal retainer from the block.

4. Using a suitable prying tool, remove the oil seal from the retainer.
**To install:**

5. Thoroughly scrape the surface of the retainer to remove any traces of the existing sealant or gasket material.

6. Wipe the seal bore with a clean rag.

7. Apply clean engine oil to the new oil seal and carefully install it into the retainer using the proper seal installation tool.

8. Install the rear oil seal retainer into the engine, along with a new gasket. Apply a 0.08–0.12 in. (2–3mm) of liquid gasket to the rear oil seal retainer prior to installation as necessary. Torque the bolts to 3–6 ft. lbs. (4–8 Nm).

9. Install the flywheel or driveplate.

10. Install the transmission or transaxle.

# ENGINE COOLING

## Radiator

### REMOVAL & INSTALLATION

1. Disconnect the negative battery cable.

2. Drain the cooling system.

3. Remove the undercover, if equipped.

4. Disconnect the reservoir tank hose.

5. Disconnect all temperature switch connectors.

6. Remove the front bumper on the 1988 Maxima and 1988–89 300ZX.

7. Disconnect and plug the transmission or transaxle cooling lines from the bottom of the radiator, if equipped.

8. On rear wheel drive vehicles, remove the fan shroud and position the shroud over the fan and clear of the radiator. On front wheel drive vehicles, discharge the air conditioning system, then unbolt and remove the condenser and radiator fan assembly from the radiator if necessary.

9. Disconnect the upper and lower hoses from the radiator.

10. Remove the radiator retaining bolts or the upper supports.

11. Lift the radiator off the mounts and out of the vehicle.

**To install:**

12. Lower the radiator onto the mounts and bolt in place.

13. Install the lower shroud, if removed.

14. Connect the upper and lower radiator hoses.

15. On rear wheel drive vehicles, install the fan shroud. On front wheel drive vehicles, install the condenser and radiator fan assembly as necessary.

16. Connect the transaxle or transmission cooling lines, if removed.

17. On 1988 Maxima and 1988–89 300ZX, install the front bumper.

18. Plug in the temperature switch connectors.

19. Connect the reservoir tank hose.

20. Fill the cooling system to the proper level.

21. Connect the negative battery cable.

22. Start the engine and check for leaks.

## Electric Cooling Fan

### TESTING

#### Maxima

1. Warm up the engine to normal

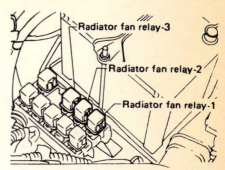

Radiator fan relay locations — Maxima

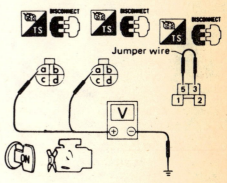

Checking radiator fan voltage — Maxima

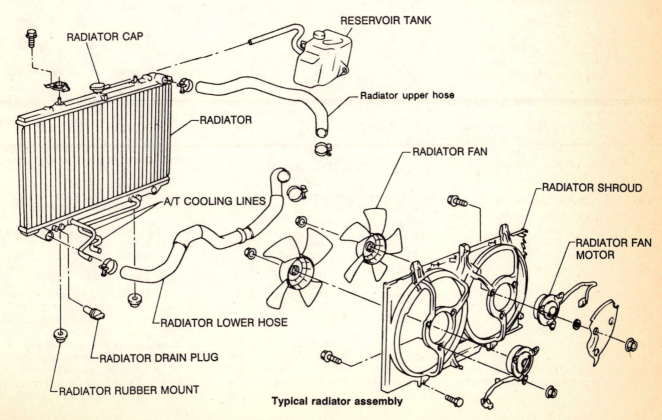

Typical radiator assembly

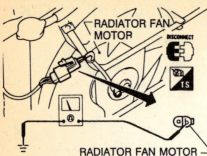

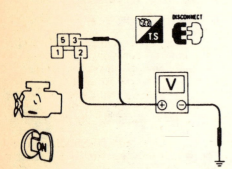

**Checking radiator fan voltage — Pulsar and Sentra**

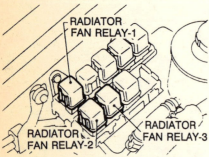

**Checking radiator fan voltage — Stanza**

**Radiator fan relay locations — Stanza**

operating temperature, then shut it off.

2. Remove radiator fan relay No. 1.

3. Connect a jumper wire between terminals **3** and **5** of the relay.

4. Disconnect the cooling fan and condenser motor wiring harness connectors.

5. Turn the ignition switch to the **ON** position.

6. Check for voltage between terminal **A** of the fan motor harness connector and ground. Battery voltage should exist.

7. If battery voltage does not exist, check the ground circuit harness for continuity, inspect the harness connectors or replace the fan motor.

### Pulsar and Sentra

1. Warm up the engine to normal operating temperature, then shut it off.

---

2. Disconnect the cooling fan motor wiring harness connector.

3. Turn the ignition switch to the **ON** position.

4. Check for voltage beteen terminal **A** of the fan motor harness connector and ground. Battery voltage should exist.

5. If battery voltage does not exist, check the ground circuit harness for continuity, check the radiator fan relays, or replace the fan motor.

### Stanza

1. Warm up the engine to normal operating temperature, then shut it off.

2. Remove radiator fan relays No. 1 and 2.

3. Turn the ignition switch to the **ON** position.

4. Check for voltage beteen terminals **2** and **3** of the relays and ground. Battery voltage should exist.

5. If battery voltage does not exist, check the ground circuit harness for continuity, check the radiator fan relay(s), inspect the harness connectors or replace the fan motor.

## REMOVAL & INSTALLATION

1. Disconnect the negative battery cable.

2. Unplug the condenser and radiator fan motor wiring harness connectors.

3. Remove the radiator shroud bolts.

4. Separate the shroud and cooling fan assembly from the radiator and remove.

**To install:**

5. Mount the radiator shroud and cooling fan assembly onto the radiator.

6. Install the radiator shroud bolts.

7. Plug in the radiator and condenser fan motor harness connectors.

8. Connect the negative battery cable.

## Heater Core

### REMOVAL & INSTALLATION

#### 200SX, 240SX, 300ZX

1. Disconnect the negative battery cable.

2. Set the TEMP lever to the **HOT** position and drain the cooling system.

3. Disconnect the heater hoses from the driver's side of the heater unit.

4. Remove the console box and the floor mats.

5. Remove the instrument panel lower covers from both the driver's and passenger's sides of the vehicle. Remove the lower cluster lids.

6. Remove the left side ventilator

---

duct. On 240SX, detach the defroster duct from the upper center heater unit opening.

7. Remove the radio, equalizer and stereo cassette deck as required.

8. Remove the instrument panel-to-transmission tunnel stay.

9. Remove the rear heater duct from the floor of the vehicle.

10. Remove the center ventilator duct.

11. Remove the left and right side ventilator ducts from the lower heater outlets.

12. Disconnect and label the wiring harness connections.

13. Separate the heating unit Remove the 2 screws at the bottom sides of the heater unit and the 1 screw at the top of the unit and remove the unit together with the heater control assembly.

14. Separate the heater case halves and slide the core from the case.

**To install:**

15. Install the heater core and assemble the heater case halves. Use new gaskets and seals as required.

16. Mount the heater unit/control assembly and install the upper and lower attaching screws.

17. Plug in the wiring harness connectors.

18. Connect the left and right side ducts to the lower heater outlets.

19. Connect the center ventilator duct.

20. Connect the rear heater duct.

21. Attach the instrument panel-to-transmission stay.

22. Install the cassette deck, equalizer and radio.

23. On 240SX, connect the upper defroster duct to the upper center heater opening. Connect the left side ventilator duct.

24. Install the lower cluster lids and lower instrument panel covers.

25. Install the floor mats and console box.

26. Install the front seats. Torque the seat bolts to 32–41 ft. lbs. (43–55 Nm).

27. Connect the heater hoses. Use new grommets as required.

28. Fill the cooling system to the proper level.

29. Connect the negative battery cable.

#### Maxima

1. Disconnect the negative battery cable.

2. Set the TEMP lever to the **HOT** position.

3. Drain the cooling system.

4. Disconnect the heater hoses from the driver's side of the heater unit.

5. Remove the front floor mats.

6. Remove the instrument panel

lower covers from both the driver's and passenger's sides of the vehicle.

7. Remove the left side ventilator duct.

8. Remove the instrument panel.

9. Remove the rear heater duct from the floor of the vehicle.

10. Disconnect the wiring harness connectors.

11. Separate the heating unit from the cooling unit. Remove the 2 screws at the bottom sides of the heater unit and the 1 screw from the top of the unit. Lift out the heater together with the heater control assembly.

12. Remove the center vent cover and heater control assembly, loosening the clips and screws.

13. Remove the screws securing the door shafts.

14. Remove the clips from the case and split the case. Remove the core.

15. Separate the heater case halves and slide the core from the case.

**To install:**

16. Install the heater core and assemble the heater case halves. Use new gaskets and seals as required.

17. Install the door shaft retaining screws.

18. Install the heater control assembly and center vent cover.

19. Mount the heater unit/control assembly and install the upper and lower attaching screws.

20. Plug in the wiring harness connectors.

21. Install the rear heater duct.

22. Install the instrument panel.

23. Install the left side ventilator duct.

24. Install the instrument panel lower covers.

25. Install the floor mats.

26. Connect the heater hoses. Use new grommets as required.

27. Fill the cooling system to the proper level.

28. Connect the negative battery cable.

### Pulsar and Sentra

1. Disconnect the negative battery cable.

2. Set the TEMP lever to the maximum **HOT** position and drain the engine coolant.

3. Disconnect the heater hoses at the engine compartment.

4. Remove the instrument panel assembly.

5. Remove the heater control assembly.

6. If equipped with air conditioning, separate the heating unit from the cooling unit.

7. Remove the heater unit assembly.

8. Remove the case clips and split the case. Remove the core.

**To install:**

9. Install the heater core and assemble the heater case halves. Use new gaskets and seals as required. Always check the operation of the air mix door when re-attaching the heater case halves.

10. Mount the heater unit and connect it the cooling unit, if equipped.

11. Install the heater control assembly.

12. Install the instrument panel.

13. Connect the heater hoses. Use new grommets as required.

14. Fill and bleed the cooling system.

15. Connect the negative battery cable.

### Stanza

1. Disconnect the negative battery cable.

2. Set the TEMP lever to the maximum HOT position and drain the engine coolant.

3. Disconnect the heater hoses at the engine compartment.

4. Remove the instrument panel assembly.

5. Remove the heater control assembly.

6. Remove pedal bracket mounting bolts, steering column mounting bolts, brake and clutch pedal cotter pins.

7. Move the pedal bracket and steering column to the left.

8. Disconnect the air mix door control cable and heater valve control lever, then remove the control lever.

9. Remove the core cover and remove the core.

**To install:**

10. Install the core and cover. Use new seals and gaskets as required.

11. Install the control and heater valve levers. Connect the air mix door control cable.

12. Move the steering column and brake pedal bracket to the right. Install the clutch and brake pedal cotter pins and steering column and brake pedal bolts.

13. Install the heater control assembly.

14. Install the instrument panel.

15. Connect the heater hoses to the core. Use new grommets as required.

16. Fill and bleed the cooling system.

17. Connect the negative battery cable.

## Water Pump

### REMOVAL & INSTALLATION

#### 4 Cylinder Engine

1. Disconnect the negative battery cable.

2. Drain the coolant from the radiator and cylinder block.

3. Remove all the drive belts.

4. Unbolt the water pump pulley and the water pump attaching bolts.

5. Separate the water pump with the gasket, if installed, from the cylinder block.

6. Remove all gasket material or sealant from the water pump mating surfaces. All sealant must be removed from the groove in the water pump surface also.

**To install:**

7. Apply a continuous bead of high temperature liquid gasket to the water pump housing mating surface. The housing must be attached to the cylinder block within 5 minutes after the sealant is applied. After the pump housing is bolted to the block, wait at least 30 minutes for the sealant to cure before starting the engine.

8. Position the water pump (and gasket) onto the block and install the attaching bolts. Torque the small retaining bolts to about 5 ft. lbs. and large retaining bolts 12–14 ft. lbs.

9. Install the water pump pulley.

10. Install the drive belts and adjust the tension.

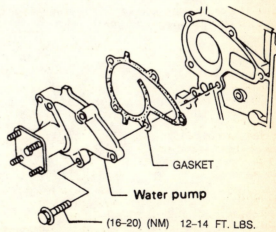

GASKET

**Water pump**

(16–20) (NM) 12–14 FT. LBS.

**Water pump assembly—CA20E engine**

DIAMETER OF LIQUID GASKET BEAD:
0.079–0.118 IN. (2.0–3.0MM)

**Apply a continuous bead oh high
temperature sealant to the water
pump housing mating surface**

11. Fill the cooling system to the proper level.
12. Connect the negative battery cable.

### 6 Cylinder Engine

1. Disconnect the negative battery cable and drain the coolant from the radiator and the left side drain cocks on the cylinder block. On 1989–92 Maxima and 1990–92 300ZX, there are 2 cylinder block drain plugs; one on the right side of the cylinder block behind the right halfshaft boot and one on the left side of the block next to the oil level gauge.
2. On 1990–92 300ZX, remove the undercover and the radiator.
3. Remove the radiator shroud.
4. Remove the power steering, compressor and alternator drive belts.
5. Remove the cooling fan and coupling.
6. Disconnect the water pump hoses.
7. On 1990–92 300ZX, unbolt and remove the inlet and outlet pipes from the block.
8. Remove the water pump pulley, then the upper and lower timing covers.

**NOTE: Be careful not to get coolant on the timing belt and to avoid deforming the timing cover, make sure there is enough clearance between the timing cover and the hose clamp.**

9. Remove the water pump retaining bolts, note different lengths, and remove the pump.
10. Make sure the gasket sealing surfaces are clean and free of all the old gasket material.
**To install:**
11. Mount the water pump and gasket onto the cylinder block. Torque the retaining bolts to 12–15 ft. lbs. (16–21 Nm).
12. Install the upper and lower timing belt covers and crankshaft pulley.
13. On 1990–92 300ZX, install the inlet and outlet pipes and torque the

nuts and bolts to 12–14 ft. lbs. (16–19 Nm).
14. Connect the water pump hoses.
15. Install the cooling fan and coupling.
16. Install and tension the drive belts.
17. Install the radiator shroud.
18. On 1990–92 300ZX, install the undercover and radiator.
19. Fill the cooling system and connect the negative battery cable.

## Thermostat

### REMOVAL & INSTALLATION

1. Disconnect the negative battery cable and drain the coolant from the radiator and the left side drain cocks on the cylinder block. On 1989–92 Maxima and 1990–92 300ZX, there are 2 cylinder block drain plugs; one on the right side of the cylinder block behind the right halfshaft boot and one on the left side of the block next to the oil level gauge.
2. On 1990–92 300ZX, remove the undercover.
3. On GA16i engines, disconnect the water temperature switch connector from the thermostat housing.
4. Remove the radiator hose from the water outlet side and remove the bolts securing the water outlet to the cylinder head.

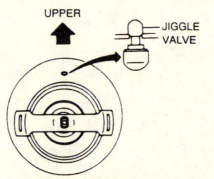

**Always be sure the jiggle valve is facing upward when installing the thermostat**

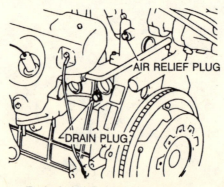

**Typical air relief plug location fc. bleeding the cooling system**

5. On 200SX (V6) and 300ZX, remove the radiator shroud, drive belts for 1990–92 300ZX, cooling fan and coupling and water inlet pipe.
6. Remove the thermostat and clean off the old gasket or sealant from the mating surfaces.
**To install:**
7. Install the thertmostat with a new gasket. When installing the thermostat, be sure to install a new gasket or sealant and be sure the air bleed hole in the thermostat is facing the left side or upward on the engine. The jiggle valve must always face up. Also make sure the new thermostat to be installed is equipped with a air bleed hole. Some thermostats have the word TOP stamped next to the jiggle valve. Again, the word TOP and the jiggle valve must be facing up.
8. On 200SX (V6) and 300ZX, install the water inlet pipe, cooling fan and coupling, drive belts for 1990–92 300ZX and radiator shroud.
9. Install the water outlet and upper radiator hose.
10. On GA16i engines, connect the water temperature switch connector to the thermostat housing.
11. On 1990–92 300ZX, install the undercover.
12. Fill the cooling system and connect the negative battery cable.

## Cooling System Bleeding

1. Remove the radiator cap.
2. Fill the radiator and reservoir tank with the proper type of coolant. If equipped with an air relief plug, remove the plug and add coolant until it spills out the air relief opening. Install the plug.
3. Install and tighten the radiator cap.
4. Start the engine and allow the coolant to come up to operating temperature. On 4 cylinder engine, allow the electric cooling fan to come on at least once. Run the heater at full force and with the temperature lever in the HOT position. Be sure the heater control valve is functioning.
5. Shut the engine off and recheck the coolant level, refill as necessary.

## ENGINE ELECTRICAL

**NOTE: Disconnecting the negative battery cable on some vehicles may interfere with the functions of the on board computer**

systems and may require the computer to undergo a relearning process, once the negative battery cable is reconnected.

## Distributor

NOTE: The CA18DE (used in the 1988–89 Pulsar) and VG30DE and VG30DETT engines (used in the 1990–92 300ZX) do not use a conventional distributor and high tension wires. Instead these engines use small ignition coils fitted directly to each spark plug. The ECU controls the coils by means of a crank angle sensor and other engine parameter gathering equipment.

### REMOVAL

1. Disconnect the negative battery cable.
2. Release the retaining clips and lift the distributor cap straight up. It will be easier to install the distributor if the wiring is not disconnected from the cap. If the wires must be removed from the cap, label the wires according to cylinder number to aid in installation and avoid confusion.
3. Disconnect the distributor wiring harness.
4. Disconnect and label the vacuum lines, if equipped.

Distributor shaft and housing alignment marks — V-Series engines, except 1990–92 300ZX

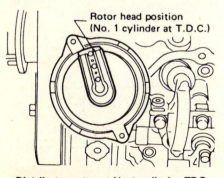

Distributor rotor at No.1 cylinder TDC postion — V series engines (except 1990–92 300ZX)

5. Note the position of the rotor in relation to the base. Scribe a mark on the base of the distributor and on the engine block to facilitate reinstallation. Align the marks with the direction the rotor is pointing.
6. Remove the bolt(s) which hold the distributor to the engine.
7. Lift the distributor assembly from the engine.

NOTE: Once the distributor is removed, try not to disturb the position of the rotor.

## INSTALLATION

### Timing Not Disturbed

1. Insert the distributor shaft and assembly into the engine.
2. Align the distributor and engine matchmarks with the rotor. Make sure the vacuum advance diaphragm is pointed in the same direction as it was pointed originally. This will be done automatically if the marks on the engine and the distributor are lined up with the rotor. On 240SX, make sure the distributor driving spindle is properly aligned before inserting the distributor into the front cover.
3. Install the distributor hold-down bolt and clamp. Leave the screw loose enough so the distributor can be moved with moderate hand pressure.

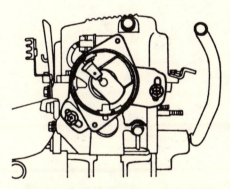

Distributor rotor at No.1 cylinder TDC postion — 1990–92 Stanza

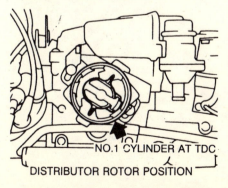

Distributor rotor at No.1 cylinder TDC postion — GA16i engines

4. Connect the vacuum lines, if equipped.
5. Connect the primary wire to the coil.
6. Install the distributor cap on the distributor housing. Secure the distributor cap with the spring clips.
7. Install the spark plug wires if removed. Make sure the wires are pressed all the way into the top of the distributor cap and firmly onto the spark plug.
8. Set the ignition timing.

### Timing Disturbed

NOTE: If the crankshaft has been turned or the engine disturbed in any manner (i.e., disassembled and rebuilt) while the distributor was removed or if the marks were not drawn, it will be necessary to initially time the engine. Follow the procedure given below.

1. It is necessary to place the No. 1 cylinder in the firing position to correctly install the distributor. To locate this position, the ignition timing marks on the crankshaft front pulley are used.
2. Remove the No. 1 cylinder spark plug. Turn the crankshaft until the piston in the No. 1 cylinder is moving up on the compression stroke. This can be determined by placing a thumb over the spark plug hole and feeling the air being forced out of the cylinder. Stop turning the crankshaft when the timing marks are aligned. On 240SX, the driving spindle must be properly aligned to accept the distributor.
3. Oil the distributor housing lightly where the distributor mounts to the block.
4. Install the distributor so the rotor, which is mounted on the shaft, points toward the No. 1 spark plug terminal tower position when the cap is installed. Lay the cap on top of the distributor and make a mark on the side of the distributor housing just below the No. 1 spark plug terminal. Make sure the rotor points toward that mark when installing the distributor.
5. When the distributor shaft has reached the bottom of the hole, move the rotor back and forth slightly until the driving lug on the end of the shaft enters the slots cut in the end of the oil pump shaft and the distributor assembly slides down into place.
6. When the distributor is correctly installed, the reluctor teeth should be aligned with the pick-up coil. This can be accomplished by rotating the distributor body after it has been installed in the engine. Once again, line up the marks made before the distributor was removed.
7. Install the distributor hold-down bolt.

8. Install the spark plug into the No. 1 spark plug hole and continue with the remainder of the distributor installation procedure.

## Ignition Timing

NOTE: The 200SX (CA20E) and 1988–89 Stanza models use a dual electronic ignition. The firing order is 1–3–4–2 and the rotor is designed with a 135 degree offset to fire both spark plugs at the same time.

## ADJUSTMENT

### 200SX, 240SX, 1988–89 300ZX, Maxima, 1988 Pulsar, 1988 Sentra and Stanza

1. Locate the timing marks on the crankshaft pulley and the front of the engine.
2. Clean off the timing marks.
3. Use chalk or white paint to color the mark on the crankshaft pulley and the mark on the scale which will indicate the correct timing when aligned with the notch on the crankshaft pulley.
4. Connect a tachometer to the engine.
5. Attach a timing light to the engine, according to the manufacturer's instructions.
6. Start the engine and allow to reach normal operating temperature.
7. Check that the idle speed is set to specifications. Adjust as necessary.
8. Aim the timing light and illuminate the timing marks. If the marks on the pulley and the engine are aligned when the light flashes, the timing is correct. Turn off the engine and remove the tachometer and the timing light. If the marks are not in alignment, proceed with the following steps.
9. On 240SX and 1990–92 Stanza, disconnect the throttle sensor harness connector.
10. Loosen the distributor lockbolt(s) just enough so the distributor can be turned with little effort.

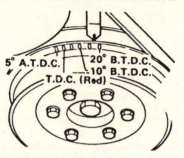

Ignition timing marks—240SX and 1990–92 Stanza

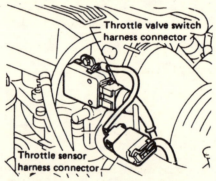

Throttle harness connector location on 240SX

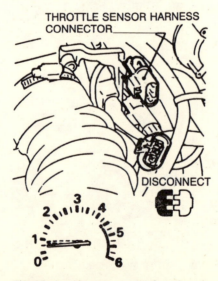

THROTTLE SENSOR HARNESS CONNECTOR

DISCONNECT

Throttle harness connector location on 1990–92 Stanza

11. Start the engine.
12. With the timing light aimed at pulley and the marks on the engine, turn the distributor in the direction of rotor rotation to retard the spark, and in the opposite direction of rotor rotation to advance the spark. Align the marks on the pulley and the engine with the flashes of the timing light. Tighten the hold-down bolt.
13. Disconnect the test equipment. On 240SX and 1990–92 Stanza, connect the throttle harness connector.

### 1990–92 300ZX and 1988–89 Pulsar (CA18DE Engine)

NOTE: The CA18DE, VG30DE and VG30DETT engines do not utilize a conventional distributor and high tension wires. Instead they use small ignition coils fitted directly to each spark plug. The ECU controls the coils by means of a crank angle sensor from which it receives piston position and engine speed information. The ECU takes the information from the crank angle sensor and sends it to the power transistor which controls the engine timing.

1. Run the engine until it reaches normal operating temperature.
2. Check the idle speed and adjust as necessary.
3. On CA18DE engine, disconnect the air duct and both air hoses at the throttle chamber.
4. On CA18DE engine, remove the

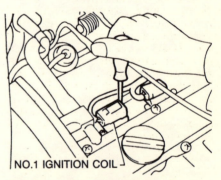

NO.1 IGNITION COIL

Removal and Installation of the No. 1 ignition coil—CA18DE engine

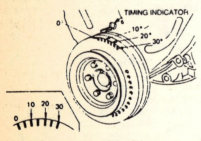

300ZX V6 timing marks

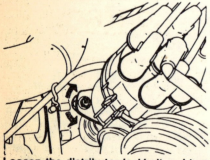

Loosen the distributor lockbolt and turn the distributor slightly to advance (upper arrow) or retard (lower arrow) the timing

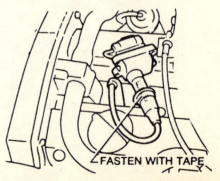

FASTEN WITH TAPE

Timing light connection—CA18DE engine

ornament cover between the camshaft covers. The acceleration wire need not be removed to remove the ornament cover.

5. Remove the ignition coil at the No. 1 cylinder.

6. Connect the No. 1 ignition coil to the No. 1 spark plug with a suitable high tension wire.

7. Use an inductive pick-up type timing light and clamp it to the wire connected in Step 6.

8. Reconnect the air duct and hoses and then start the engine.

9. Check the ignition timing. If not to specifications, turn off the engine and loosen the 3 crank angle sensor mounting bolts slightly.

**NOTE: The crank angle sensor can be found attached to the upper front cover.**

10. Restart the engine and adjust the timing by turning the sensor body slightly until the timing is within specifications. Clockwise rotation retards the timing and counterclockwise rotation advances it.

### 1989–90 Pulsar (GA16i Engine) and 1989–92 Sentra (GA16i, CA16DE and SR20DE Engines)

1. Run the engine until the water temperature indicator points to the middle of the gauge.

2. Run the engine for 1–2 minutes with no load; all electrical accessories in the **OFF** position.

3. Connect a timing light to the engine and illuminate the timing marks. If the timing is not within specification, proceed to adjust.

4. To adjust the timing, stop the engine and disconnect the throttle sensor connector. Loosen the distributor hold-down bolt just enough to allow the distributor to be turned by hand.

5. Start the engine and race it 2–3 times with no load and then allow the engine to run at idle speed.

6. Adjust the ignition timing by rotating the distributor either clockwise or counterclockwise.

7. Tighten the distributor hold-down bolt and stop the engine.

8. Connect the throttle sensor connector and remove the timing light.

## Alternator

### PRECAUTIONS

The following precautions must be observed to prevent alternator and regulator damage:

● Be absolutely sure of correct polarity when installing a new battery or connecting a battery charger.

● Do not short across or ground any alternator or regulator terminals.

● Disconnect the battery ground cable before replacing any electrical unit.

● Never operate the alternator with any of the leads disconnected.

● When steam cleaning the engine, be careful not to subject the alternator to excessive heat or moisture.

● When charging the battery, remove it from the vehicle or disconnect the alternator output terminal.

### BELT TENSION ADJUSTMENT

The correct belt tension for all alternators is about ¼–½ in. play on the longest span of the belt.

1. Loosen the alternator pivot and mounting bolts.

2. Pry the alternator toward or away from the engine until the tension is correct. Use a hammer handle or wooden prybar.

3. When the tension is correct, tighten the bolts and check the adjustment. Be careful not to over-tighten the belt, which will lead to alternator bearing failure.

### REMOVAL & INSTALLATION

1. Disconnect the negative battery cable.

2. Disconnect the 2 lead wires and harness connector from the alternator.

3. Loosen the drive belt adjusting bolt and remove the belt.

4. Unscrew the alternator attaching bolts and remove the alternator from the vehicle. On the 1988–89 300ZX, first remove the front stabilizer bar bolts and pull the stabilizer bar down. On 1990–92 300ZX, remove the lower radiator hose bracket and pull the hose upward to gain the clearance to remove the alternator.

5. Installation is in the reverse order of removal. Adjust the drive belt tension.

## Starter

### REMOVAL & INSTALLATION

1. Disconnect the negative battery cable.

2. Remove the starter heat shield (300ZX) and harness clamps, if equipped. On 1990–92 Stanza with automatic transaxle, remove the harness connectors from the harness connector bracket.

3. Disconnect and label the wires from the terminals on the solenoid.

4. Remove the 2 bolts which secure the starter to the flywheel housing and pull the starter forward and out.

5. On 1991–92 Sentra vehicles remove the starter motor from under vehicle on SR20DE engine. On GA16DE engine (manual transaxle) remove the starter motor from the transaxle side and from the engine side on automatic transaxle applications.

6. To install, reverse the removal procedure. Check the starter for proper operation.

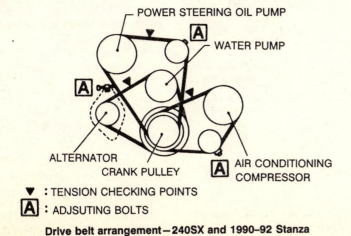

: TENSION CHECKING POINTS

A : ADJSUTING BOLTS

**Drive belt arrangement—240SX and 1990–92 Stanza**

## EMISSION CONTROLS

Please refer to "Emission Controls" in the Unit Repair section for system maintenance procedures. Due to the complex nature of modern electronic engine control systems, comprehensive diagnosis and testing procedures fall outside the confines of this repair manual. For complete information on diagnosis, testing and repair procedures concerning all modern engine and emission control systems, please refer to "Chilton's Guide to Fuel Injection and Electronic Engine Controls".

# FUEL SYSTEM

## Fuel System Service Precaution

Failure to conduct fuel system maintenance and repairs in a safe manner may result in serious personal injury. Maintenance and testing of the vehicle's fuel system components can be accomplished safely and effectively by adhering to the following rules and guidelines.

• To avoid the possibility of fire and personal injury, always disconnect the negative battery cable unless the repair or test procedure specifically requires that battery voltage be applied.

• Always relieve the fuel system pressure prior to disconnecting any fuel system component (injector, fuel rail, pressure regulator, etc.), fitting or fuel line connection. Exercise extreme caution whenever relieving fuel system pressure to avoid exposing skin, face and eyes to fuel spray. Be advised that fuel under pressure may penetrate the skin or any part of the body that it comes in contact with.

• Always place a shop towel or cloth around the fitting or connection prior to loosening to absorb any excess fuel due to spillage. Ensure that all fuel spillage (should it occur) is quickly removed from engine surfaces. Ensure that all fuel soaked cloths or towels are deposited into a suitable waste container.

• Always have a properly charged Class B dry chemical or $CO_2$ fire extinguisher in the vicinity of the work area and always ensure work areas are adequately ventilated.

• Do not allow fuel spray or fuel vapors to come in contact with spark or open flame. Remember that smoking and fuel maintenance do not mix!

• Always use a backup wrench when loosening and tightening fuel line connection fittings. This will prevent unnecessary stress and torsion to fuel line piping. Always follow the proper torque specifications.

• Always replace worn fuel fitting O-rings with new ones. Do not substitute fuel hose or equivalent, where rigid fuel pipe is called for.

• Always use common sense.

## RELIEVING FUEL SYSTEM PRESSURE

1. Remove the fuel pump fuse from the fuse block, fuel pump relay or disconnect the harness connector at the tank while engine is running.

2. It should run and then stall when the fuel in the lines is exhausted. When the engine stops, crank the starter for about 10 seconds to make sure all pressure in the fuel lines is released.

3. Install the fuel pump fuse, relay or harness connector after repair is made.

## Fuel Tank

### REMOVAL & INSTALLATION

1. Disconnect the negative battery cable.

2. Drain the fuel from the tank unit.

3. Remove the access plate from the trunk or rear seat area.

4. Disconnect all fuel lines and connections.

5. Raise and safely support the vehicle.

6. Remove the fuel tank protector if so equipped. Disconnect the fuel filler tube or filler hose at the fuel tank.

7. Remove the gas tank assembly strap retaining bolts and slowly lower the tank assembly down from the vehicle.

8. Installation is the reverse of the removal procedure. Replace all gas tank line hose clamps as necessary. Always torque gas tank assembly strap retaining bolts evenly.

## Fuel Filter

### REMOVAL & INSTALLATION

――――― CAUTION ―――――
*Make sure to relieve the fuel system pressure before replacing the fuel filter.*

1. Relieve the fuel system pressure.
2. Disconnect the negative battery cable.
3. Loosen the fuel hose clamps and disconnect the hoses from the filter.

**NOTE: On the Stanza 4WD Wagon, the fuel filter is found in-line, under the floor, near the fuel pump.**

4. Remove the bolt securing the filter to the bracket.
5. Remove the filter.
6. Install the new filter. Connect the fuel hoses and tighten the clamps.

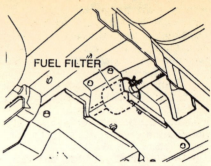

**The fuel filter is found under the floor on the Stanza wagons (4WD)**

8. Replace the fuel pump fuse, relay or connector.
9. Connect the negative battery cable. Start the engine and check for leaks.

## Electric Fuel Pump

### PRESSURE TESTING

#### *Except Pulsar and Sentra With GA16i Engine*

1. Relieve the fuel system pressure.
2. Remove the air duct, if required.
3. Connect a fuel pressure gauge between the fuel feed pipe and the fuel filter outlet.
4. Start the engine and read the fuel pressure. If the pressure is not as specified, replace the pump. If the pump output pressure is okay, go to Step 5 to check the pressure regulator.
5. Stop the engine and disconnect the fuel pressure regulator vacuum hose from the intake manifold.
6. Plug the intake manifold with a rubber cap.
7. On VG30E engines for 1988 200ZX, 1988–89 300ZX and 1988–89 Maxima, connect a jumper wire from terminal No. 108 of the ECU to a suitable body ground.
8. Connect a vacuum pump to the fuel pressure regulator.
9. On all except VG30E engines, start the engine and alternately increase and decrease the vacuum while

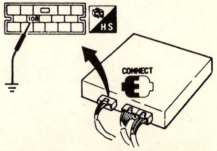

**On VG30E engine—1988 200ZX, 1988–89 300ZX and 1988–89 Maxima—jump terminal 108 of the ECU to a body ground**

watching the gauge. On VG30E engine, turn the ignition switch to the **ON** position without starting the engine. Fuel pressure should decrease as the vacuum is increased. If the pressure is incorrect, replace the pressure regulator. After replacement of the regulator, repeat the pressure test. If still incorrect, check the fuel lines for kinks or blockage, and replace the pump as necessary.

### *Pulsar and Sentra With GA16I Engine*

1. Relieve the fuel system pressure.
2. Disconnect the fuel inlet hose from the electro-injection unit.
3. Connect a pressure gauge to the electro-injection unit inlet opening and connect the fuel inlet hose to the gauge.
4. Start the engine and check the fuel line and gauge connections for fuel leaks.
5. Read the fuel pressure. If the pressure is not as specified, replace the pump.
6. Release the fuel system pressure and disconnect the gauge.
7. Connect the fuel inlet hose to the electro-injection unit.

## REMOVAL & INSTALLATION

The fuel pump is located in the fuel tank on all models except the 2WD Stanza Wagon. On 2WD Stanza Wagon the fuel pump is located in line to the fuel tank. In tank fuel pumps are accessible either by lifting up the rear seat or through an opening in the trunk compartment.

1. Relieve the pressure from the fuel system, then disconnect the negative battery cable.
2. Open the trunk, remove the mat and flip up the fuel pump access plate in the trunk floor. If there is no access plate in the luggage compartment, check under the rear seats.
3. On 2WD Stanza Wagon, clamp the hose between the fuel tank and the fuel pump to prevent gas from spilling out of the tank. Disconnect and plug the fuel outlet hose and remove the pump from the mounting bracket.
4. Disconnect the inlet and outlet tubes from the fuel pump.
5. Unbolt and remove the pump from the top of the fuel tank. Discard the O-ring seal or gasket.
**To install:**
6. Install the pump with a new gasket or O-ring seal. Tighten the pump retaining bolts and connect the fuel hoses. Be sure to use new clamps and that all hoses are properly seated on the fuel pump and the fuel pump hoses.

7. Install the fuel pump access plate.
8. Connect the pump wiring harness.
9. Connect the negative battery cable.

## Fuel Injection

### IDLE SPEED ADJUSTMENT

Before adjusting the idle speed, visually check the following items first: air cleaner for clogging, hoses and ducts for leaks, EGR valve for proper operation, all electrical connectors, gaskets and the throttle valve and throttle valve switch operation.

### *1988–89 Stanza and 200SX (CA20E ENGINE)*

1. Connect a tachometer and timing light to the engine.
2. Turn all electrical accessories and air conditioner to the **OFF** position.
3. Warm up engine to normal operating temperature.
4. Run the engine at 2000 rpm for about 2 minutes without load.
5. Race the engine 2–3 times and allow to idle.
6. Check the idle speed.
7. If the idle speed is not within specifications, disconnect the Auxiliary Air Control (AAC) valve and throttle valve switch harness connectors.
8. Adjust the idle speed by turning the idle speed adjusting screw.
9. Connect the AAC and throttle valve switch connectors.
10. Check the timing and adjust as necessary.
11. Stop the engine and remove test equipment.

### *240SX and 1990–92 Stanza*

1. Connect a tachometer and timing light to the engine.
2. Turn all electrical accessories and air conditioner to the **OFF** position.
3. Warm up engine to normal operating temperature.
4. Run the engine at 2000 rpm for about 2 minutes without load.
5. Race the engine 2–3 times and allow to idle.
6. Check the idle speed in the **N** position for both manual and automatic transmission models.
7. To adjust the idle speed, first disconnect the throttle sensor harness connector.
8. Adjust the idle speed by turning the idle speed adjusting screw.
9. Stop the engine. Connect the throttle sensor harness connector.
10. Remove the test equipmemt.

### *300ZX and 1988 Maxima*

1. Connect a tachometer and timing light to the engine.
2. Turn all electrical accessories and air conditioner to the **OFF** position.
3. Warm up engine to normal operating temperature.
4. Run the engine at 2000 rpm for about 2 minutes without load.
5. On 1988–89 300ZX non-turbo and Maxima, disconnect harness connector at idle-up solenoid valve.
6. Race the engine 2–3 times and allow to idle.
7. Check the timing and adjust as necessary.
8. Check the idle speed. To adjust the idle speed on 1988–89 300ZX non-turbo and Maxima, turn idle speed adjusting screw. Connect idle-up solenoid on 300ZX and Maxima models.
9. To adjust idle speed on 1988–89 300ZX turbo and all 1990–92 300ZX models, stop engine and disconnect harness connector at Auxiliary Air Control (AAC) valve. Start engine and adjust idle speed to specifications. Stop engine and reconnect control valve. Start engine and ensure idle speed is correct.
10. Remove the test equipment.

**Idle-up solenoid location on VG30E engines**

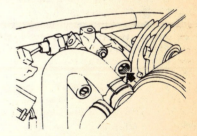

**Idle speed adjustment screw location on VGE30 engines**

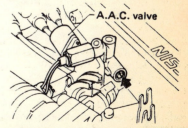

**AAC valve location on 1988–89 300ZX turbo engines**

## 1989–92 Maxima

1. Connect a tachometer and timing light to the engine.

2. Turn all electrical accessories and air conditioner to the **OFF** position.

3. Warm up engine to normal operating temperature.

4. Run the engine at 2000 rpm for about 2 minutes without load.

5. Race the engine 2–3 times and allow to idle for 1 minute.

6. Check the timing and adjust as necessary.

7. Check the idle speed in the **N** position for both manual and automatic transaxle models.

8. To adjust the idle speed, close the Auxiliary Air Control (AAC) valve by turning the diagnostic mode selector on the ECU fully clockwise.

9. Adjust the idle speed by turning the idle speed adjusting screw with transaxle in the **N** position.

10. Operate the AAC valve by turning the diagnostic mode selector on the ECU. fully conterclockwise.

11. Stop the engine and remove the test equipment.

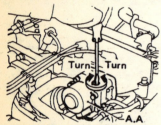

**Idle speed adjusting screw—1989–92 Maxima**

## Pulsar and Sentra

1. Connect a tachometer and timing light to the engine.

2. Turn all electrical accessories and air conditioner to the **OFF** position.

3. Warm up engine to normal operating temperature.

4. Run the engine at 2000 rpm for about 2 minutes without load.

5. Race the engine 2–3 times and allow to idle for 1 minute.

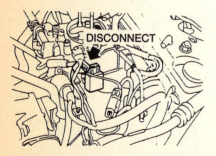

**Throttle valve switch harness connector location—1988 Pulsar and Sentra with E16i engine**

**Idle speed adjustment—SR20De engine**

6. Check the timing and adjust as necessary.

7. Check the idle speed and adjust as necessary.

8. Stop the engine and disconnect the throttle sensor connector.

9. Start the engine and adjust the idle speed by turning the throttle adjusting screw.

10. Stop the engine and reconnect the throttle valve switch connector.

11. Remove the test equipment.

# IDLE MIXTURE ADJUSTMENT

## 1988–89 Stanza and 200SX (CA20E ENGINE)

1. Connect a tachometer and timing light to the engine.

2. Turn all electrical accessories and air conditioner to the **OFF** position.

3. Warm up engine to normal operating temperature.

4. Check the idle speed and ignition timing. Adjust as necessary.

5. Run the engine at 2000 rpm for about 2 minutes without any load. The green ECU inspection light should flash on and off at least 9 times in 10 seconds at 2000 rpm.

6. Race the engine 2–3 times and allow to idle.

7. Set the ECU to the No. 2 diagnosis mode and disconnect the throttle valve switch connector. The red and green lights on the ECU should flash together. If they do, then the idle mixture is correct and no further adjustment is required. If they don't, then continue with the remainder of the procedure.

8. Stop the engine and remove the air flow meter from the vehicle.

9. Drill a small hole in the seal plug which covers the variable resistor and remove the plug from the air flow meter.

10. Install the air flow meter.

11. Warm up engine to normal operating temperature.

12. Set the ECU to the No. 2 diagnosis mode, then adjust the idle mixture by turning the variable resistor until the red and green lights on the ECU flash together. If the mixture still can't be adjusted, replace the air flow meter.

13. Install a new seal plug and tap it into place with a suitable tool.

14. Connect the throttle valve switch connector and remove the test equipment.

## 200SX (VG30E ENGINE), 240SX, 300ZX, Maxima, and 1990–92 Stanza

1. Connect a tachometer and timing light to the engine.

2. Turn all electrical accessories and air conditioner to the **OFF** position.

3. Warm up engine to normal operating temperature.

4. Check the idle speed and ignition timing. Adjust as necessary.

5. Run the engine at 2000 rpm for about 2 minutes without any load. The green ECU inspection lamp should flash on and off at least 5 times in 10 seconds at 2000 rpm.

6. Race the engine 2–3 times and allow to idle.

7. Set the ECU to the No. 2 diagnosis mode by turning the diagnostic mode selector screw on ECU fully counterclockwise. Disconnect the throttle valve switch connector. The red and green lights on the ECU should flash together. If they do, then the idle mixture is correct and no further adjustment is required. If they don't, then continue with the remainder of the procedure.

8. Stop the engine and disconnect the engine temperature sensor harness connector from the sensor. Connect a 2.5 kilo-ohm resistor across the terminals of the engine temperature harness connector. The sensor is located on the cylinder head.

9. On 240SX and 1990–92 Stanza, disconnect the AIV hose and plug the AIV pipe. On 1990–92 300ZX, disconnect the AIV control solenoid valve harness connector.

10. Start the engine and run for 5 minutes, then race the engine 2–3 times and allow to idle.

11. Check the CO content and make sure the engine runs smoothly. The idle mixture on these vehicles is controlled by the ECU, and is not adjustable. However, the following components should be checked before identifying the ECU as the source of the problem.

Exhaust gas sensor(s)
Exhaust gas sensor harness
Fuel pressure regulator
Air flow meter
Fuel injectors
Engine temperature sensor

12. Stop the engine. Remove the resistor from the engine temperature switch harness connector and plug in the connector. Connect the AIV hose.

13. Remove the test equipment.

## Pulsar and Sentra

1. Connect a tachometer and timing light to the engine.

2. Turn all electrical accessories and air conditioner to the **OFF** position.

3. Warm up engine to normal operating temperature.

4. Check the idle speed and ignition timing. Adjust as necessary.

5. Run the engine at 2000 rpm for about 2 minutes without any load. The green ECU inspection lamp should flash on and off at least 5 times in 10 seconds at 2000 rpm.

6. Race the engine 2–3 times and allow to idle.

7. Set the ECU to the No. 2 diagnosis mode. The red and green lights on the ECU should flash together. If they do, then the idle mixture is correct and no further adjustment is required. If they don't then continue with the remainder of the procedure.

8. Stop the engine.

9. On E16i and GA16i engines, remove the throttle body from the vehicle. On CA18DE engine, remove the air flow meter from the vehicle.

10. Drill a small hole in the seal plug which covers the variable resistor and remove the plug from the air flow meter or throttle body.

11. Install the throttle body or air flow meter.

12. Warm up engine to normal operating temperature.

13. Set the ECU to the No. 2 diagnosis mode, then adjust the idle mixture by turning the variable resistor until the red and green lights on the ECU flash together. Turning counterclockwise lowers the CO content and clockwise raises it. If the mixture still can't be adjusted, replace the air flow meter or the throttle body.

14. Install a new seal plug and tap it into place with a suitable tool.

15. Remove the test equipment.

# Fuel Injector

## REMOVAL & INSTALLATION

### 200SX (VG30E Engine), 300ZX and 1988 Maxima

1. Relieve the fuel system pressure.
2. Disconnect the negative battery cable.

3. Disconnect the hoses and electrical wiring from the intake collector. Label each hose and wire to ensure proper placement during installation.

4. On 200SX, remove the intake collector cover.

5. Remove the intake collector and gasket.

6. Remove the fuel tube retaining bolts.

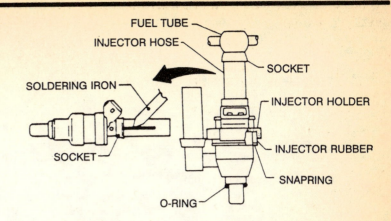

**Removing the injector braided reinforcement hose**

7. Remove the injector retaining bolts and remove the injector, fuel tubes and pressure regulator as an assembly.

8. Using a soldering iron or hot, sharp knife, slice the braided reinforcement hose from the socket end to the fuel tube end. Be careful not to allow the tool to contact the injector tail piece or the socket plastic connector. Pull the hose from the injector and repeat the procedure for the remaining injectors.

**To install:**

9. Clean the exterior of the injector tail piece and fuel tube end. Install new O-rings.

10. Wet the inside of the new fuel tube with clean fuel.

11. Push the end of the rubber hose and hose socket onto the injector tail piece and fuel tube end as far as it will go. Clamps are not required. Repeat the procedure for the remaining injectors.

12. Position and install the injector, fuel tube and pressure regulator assembly. Install the injector and fuel tube retaining bolts. Pressurize the fuel system and check for leaks at all fuel connections.

13. Install the intake collector.

14. On 200SX, install the intake collector cover and gasket. Position the gasket so the silicone rubber portion is facing down.

15. Connect all the hoses and electrical wiring to the intake collector.

16. Connect the negative battery cable.

### 1989–92 Maxima

1. Relieve the fuel system pressure.
2. Disconnect the negative battery cable.

3. Disconnect the automatic speed control device cable and accelerator cable from the intake manifold collector.

4. Disconnect the Auxiliary Air Control (AAC) valve, throttle sensor and idle switch connectors.

5. Disconnect the air cut valve water hose. Plug the end to prevent leakage.

6. Disconnect the PCV hoses.

7. Disconnect the vacuum gallery, power valve actuator, master brake cylinder and EGR control valve vacuum hoses.

8. Loosen and disconnect the EGR flare tube.

9. Remove the upper manifold collector from the engine.

10. Disconnect the engine ground harness from the lower intake collector manifold and remove the manifold from the engine.

11. Disconnect pressure regulator vacuum hose, fuel supply and return tubes and injector electrical connectors.

12. Remove the fuel injector tube assembly.

13. Withdraw the injectors from the fuel tube.

**To install:**

14. Insert the fuel injector(s) into the fuel tubes with new O-rings.

15. Install the injector and fuel tube assembly.

16. Connect the injector electrical connectors, fuel supply and return tubes and pressure regulator vacuum hose. Pressurize the fuel system and check for leaks at all fuel connections.

17. Install the lower intake collector manifold and connect the engine ground harness.

18. Install the upper collector manifold.

19. Connect and tighten the EGR flare tube.

20. Connect the vacuum and PCV hoses, air cut valve water hose and electrical connectors.

21. Connect the accelerator cable and automatic speed control device cable to the intake manifold collector. Adjust the cables.

22. Connect the negative battery cable.

### 200SX (CA20E Engine), 1988–89 Stanza and Pulsar (CA18DE Engine)

1. Relieve the fuel system pressure.
2. Disconnect the negative battery cable.
3. Disconnect the ECU and ignition wires.
4. Disconnect the fuel supply and return hoses. Plug the hoses to prevent fuel leakage.
5. Disconnect the pressure regulator vacuum hose.
6. Remove the fuel tube retaining bolts.
7. Remove the injector retaining bolts and remove the injector, fuel tubes and pressure regulator as an assembly. Be careful not to smack the injectors or bend the fuel tube.
8. Using a soldering iron or hot, sharp knife, slice the braided reinforcement hose from the socket end to the fuel tube end. Be careful not to allow the tool to contact the injector tail piece or the socket plastic connector. Pull the hose from the injector and repeat the procedure for the remaining injectors.

**To install:**
9. Clean the exterior of the injector tail piece and fuel tube end. Install new O-rings.
10. Wet the inside of the new fuel tube with clean fuel.
11. Push the end of the rubber hose and hose socket onto the injector tail piece and fuel tube end as far as it will go. Clamps are not required. Repeat the procedure for the remaining injectors.
12. Position and install the injector, fuel tube and pressure regulator assembly. Install the injector and fuel tube retaining bolts. Pressurize the fuel system and check for leaks at all fuel connections.
13. Connect the pressure regulator vacuum hose.
14. Connect the fuel supply and return hoses.
15. Connect the ECU and ignition wires.
16. Connect the negative battery cable.

### 240SX

1. Relieve the fuel system pressure.
2. Disconnect the negative battery cable.
3. Remove the BPT valve.
4. Remove the fuel tube retaining bolts.
5. Remove the fuel tube and injector assembly from the intake manifold.
6. Withdraw the injectors from the fuel tube.

**To install:**
7. Clean the injector tail piece and insert the injectors into the fuel tube with new O-rings.
8. Position the injector and fuel tube assembly onto the intake manifold and install the injector tube retaining bolts.
9. Pressurize the fuel system and check for leaks at all fuel connections.
10. Install the BPT valve.
11. Connect the negative battery cable.

### Pulsar and Sentra (E16i and GA16i Engines)

1. Relieve the fuel system pressure.
2. Disconnect the negative battery cable.
3. Remove the injector cover plates.
4. Using the proper tool, carefully withdraw the fuel injector straight up from the throttle body. Be careful not to damage the injector terminals during removal.
5. Remove the injector upper and lower O-rings. Install a new lower O-ring.

**To install:**
6. Using a 13mm socket or suitable tool, carefully push the injector into the throttle body. Make sure the injector terminals are aligned properly. Be careful not to bend the injector terminals during installation.
7. Position the new upper injector O-ring and install it with a 19mm socket or other suitable tool.

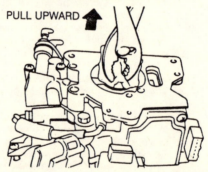

PULL UPWARD

**Injector removal on E16i and GA16i engines**

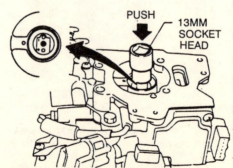

PUSH — 13MM SOCKET HEAD

**Injector installation on E16i and GA16i engines. Note Injector terminal alignment**

8. Install the lower (white) injector cover plate. Do not over tighten the cover screws.
9. Install the injector cover without the rubber boot. Make sure the 2 O-rings (large and small) properly seated in the cover. Make sure there is a good connection between the injector terminal and the injector cover terminal. When this connection is verified, install the cover boot.
10. Connect the negative battery cable.
11. Start the engine and check for leaks at all fuel connections.

### 1991–92 Sentra (GA16DE and SR20DE Engines)

1. Relieve the fuel system pressure. Disconnect the negative battery cable.
2. Disconnect the fuel injector wiring harness connectors and vacuum line from the fuel pressure regulator.
3. Disconnect the fuel hoses from the fuel tube assembly.
4. Remove the injectors with fuel tube assembly.
5. Installation is the reverse of the removal procedure. Install injectors with fuel tube assembly to intake manifold torque all reataining bolts in two steps to 15–20 ft. lbs. Check for fuel leaks after installation is complete.

### 1990–92 Stanza

1. Relieve the fuel system pressure.
2. Disconnect the negative battery cable.
3. Disconect the air duct.
4. Disconnect the supply and return hoses from the fuel tube. Plug the ends to prevent leakage.
5. Disconnect the vacuum line from the fuel pressure regulator.
6. Detach the accelerator cable bracket.
7. Disconnect the fuel injector wiring harness connectors.
8. Remove the fuel tube retaining bolts.
9. Pull the fuel tube and injector assembly from the intake manifold. Remove the injector assembly out from the No. 4 injector side.

**To install:**
10. Remove the O-rings and insulators and install new ones.
11. Install the injector and fuel tube assembly into the intake manifold.
12. Install the injector tube retaining bolts.
13. Connect the injector wiring harness conectors.
14. Attach the accelerator cable bracket.
15. Connect the pressure regulator vacuum line.
16. Connect the fuel supply and return hoses.
17. Connect the air duct.

18. Connect the negative battery cable.
19. Start the engine and check for leaks at all fuel connections.

# DRIVE AXLE

## Halfshaft

### REMOVAL & INSTALLATION

#### Front Wheel Drive

This procedure applies to all 2WD drive vehicles and to the front halfshafts on 4WD vehicles. Removal and installation of the rear halfshafts on 4WD vehicles is described below.

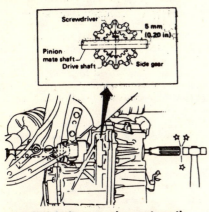

Left halfshaft removal on automatic transaxle vehicles—Maxima, Stanza and Stanza Wagon

Removing halfshaft

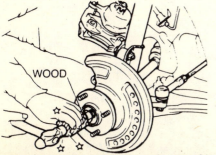

Separating the halfshaft from the steering knuckle

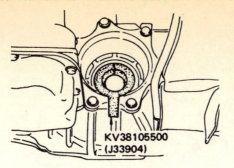

KV38105500
(J33904)

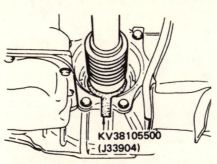

KV38105500
(J33904)

Halfshaft alignment tools used on front wheel drive vehicles

NOTE: Installation of the halfshafts will require a special tool for the spline alignment of the halfshaft end and the transaxle case. Do not perform this procedure without access to this tool or suitable equivalent. The tool is J-34296, J-34297 or J-33904 depending on the vehicle.

1. Raise the vehicle and support safely.
2. Remove the wheel and tire assembly.
3. Withdraw the cotter pin from the castellated nut on the wheel hub.
4. Depress the brake pedal and remove the wheel bearing locknut.
5. Remove the brake caliper assembly without disconnecting the brake line. Support the caliper with wire.
6. Separate the halfshaft from the steering knuckle by tapping it with a block of wood and a mallet.
7. Remove the tie rod ball joint. Remove the 3 mounting nuts for the lower ball joint and then pull it down.

NOTE: Always use a new nut when replacing the tie rod ball joint.

8. Using a suitable tool, reach through the engine crossmember and carefully tap the right side inner CV-joint out of the transaxle case.
9. Using a block of wood and a suitable jack, support the engine under the oil pan.
10. Remove the support bearing bracket and bearing retainer bolts from the engine and then withdraw the right halfshaft (except Pulsar with E16i and GA16i and Sentra).

11. On vehicles with manual transaxles, carefully insert a small prybar between the left CV-joint inner flange and the transaxle case mounting surface and pry the halfshaft out of the case. Withdraw the shaft from the steering knuckle and remove it.
12. On vehicles with automatic transaxles, insert a dowel through the right side halfshaft hole and use a small mallet to tap the left halfshaft out of the transaxle case. Withdraw the shaft from the steering knuckle and remove it.

NOTE: Be careful not to damage the pinion mating shaft and the side gear while tapping the left halfshaft out of the transaxle case.

To install:
13. When installing the shafts into the transaxle, use a new oil seal and then install an alignment tool along the inner circumference of the oil seal.
14. Insert the halfshaft into the transaxle, align the serrations and then remove the alignment tool.
15. Push the halfshaft, then press-fit the circular clip on the shaft into the clip groove on the side gear.

NOTE: After insertion, attempt to pull the flange out of the side joint to make sure the circular clip is properly seated in the side gear and will not come out.

16. Connect the tie rod end ball joint.
17. Insert the driveshaft into the steering knuckle.
18. Mount the brake caliper assembly.
19. Install the wheel bearing locknut. Torque the nut to 174–231 ft. lbs. (235–314 Nm) on Maxima and Stanza; 145–203 ft. lbs. (196–275 Nm) on 1988–89 Pulsar; 145–203 ft. lbs. (196–275 Nm) on Sentra and 1990 Pulsar. When tightening the nut, apply the brake pedal.
20. Install a new cotter pin into the wheel bearing locknut.
21. Mount the wheel and tire assembly.
22. Lower the vehicle.

#### Rear Wheel Drive

**EXCEPT SENTRA (4WD) AND STANZA WAGON (4WD)**

NOTE: When removing the rear halfshafts, cover the CV-boots with cloth to prevent damage.

1. Raise and support the rear of the vehicle safely.
2. Remove the rear wheel and tire assembly.
3. Remove the adjusting cap and

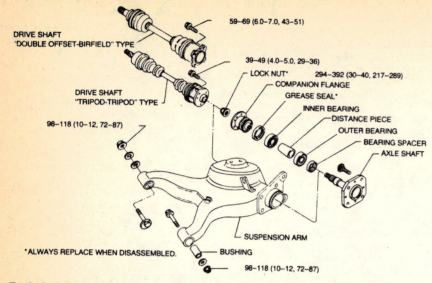

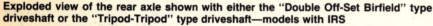

**Exploded view of the rear axle shown with either the "Double Off-Set Birfield" type driveshaft or the "Tripod-Tripod" type driveshaft—models with IRS**

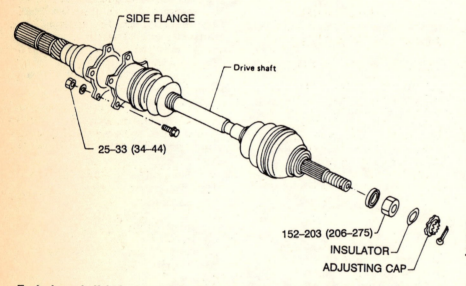

**Typical rear halfshaft assembly on rear wheel drive vehicles (1990–92 300ZX shown)**

cotter pin from the wheel bearing locknut.

4. Apply the parking brake and remove the rear wheel locknut.

5. On 200SX and 1988–89 300ZX, remove the spring seat stay.

6. Disconnect the halfshaft from the differential side by removing the flange bolts.

7. Grasp the halfshaft at the center and extract if from the wheel hub by prying it with a suitable prybar or with the use of a wood block and mallet.

**NOTE: To protect the threads of the shaft, temporarily install the locknut when loosening the shaft from the wheel hub.**

**To install:**

8. Insert the shaft into the wheel hub and temporarily install the locknut.

**NOTE: Take care not to damage the oil seal or either end of the halfshaft during installation.**

9. Connect the halfshaft to the differential and install the flange bolts. On 240SX and 300ZX, torque the flange bolts to 25–33 ft. lbs. (34–44 Nm). On 200SX with CA20E and VG30E engines, torque the flange bolts to 29–36 ft. lbs. (39–49 Nm).

10. On 200SX and 1988–89 300ZX, install the spring seat stay.

11. Apply the parking brake and

tighten the locknut. Torque the locknut to 152–210 ft. lbs. (206–284 Nm) on 200SX and 1988–89 300ZX; 174–231 ft. lbs. on 240SX and 154–203 ft. lbs. (206–275 Nm) on 1990–92 300ZX.

12. Install a new locknut cotter pin and install the adjusting cap.

13. Mount the rear wheel and tire assembly.

14. Lower the vehicle.

### Sentra (4WD) and Stanza Wagon (4WD)

This procedure applies to removal and installation of the rear halfshafts only.

**NOTE: When removing the rear halfshafts, cover the CV-boots with cloth to prevent damage.**

1. Raise and support the rear of the vehicle safely.

2. Remove the rear wheel and tire assembly.

3. Remove the adjusting cap, insulator and cotter pin from the wheel bearing locknut.

4. Apply the parking brake and remove the rear wheel locknut.

5. Disconnect the brake line. Use a brake line wrench or suitable equivalent. Plug the line to prevent leakage of brake fluid.

6. Disconnect the parking brake cable.

7. Grasp the halfshaft at the center and extract if from the wheel hub by prying it with a suitable prybar or with the use of a wood block and mallet.

8. Remove the transverse link and radius rod attaching bolts.

**NOTE: Before removing the transverse rod bolts, matchmark the toe-in adjusting bolt to the adjustment degree plate.**

9. Pry the halfshaft from the differential using a small prybar.

10. Remove the knuckle attaching bolts and remove the wheel hub, baffle plate, knuckle and halfshaft as a unit. Be careful not to damage the differential drive gear oil seal during removal.

**To install:**

11. Mount the wheel hub, baffle plate, knuckle and driveshaft and temporarily install the wheel bearing locknut.

12. Insert the halfshaft into the transaxle and properly align the splines.

13. Push the halfshaft, then press-fit the circular clip on the shaft into the clip groove on the side gear.

**NOTE: After insertion, attempt to pull the flange out of the side joint to make sure the circular clip is properly seated in the side gear and will not come out.**

14. Tighten the knuckle attaching bolts.

15. Install the transverse link and radius rod attaching (fixing) bolts. Make sure the toe-in bolt matchmarks are aligned properly.

16. Connect the parking brake cable and brake line.

17. Install the rear wheel bearing nut and adjust the rear wheel bearing pre-load.

18. Install adjusting cap, insulator and a new locknut cotter pin.

19. Mount the rear wheel and tire assembly.

20. Lower the vehicle.

21. Adjust the parking brake cable and bleed the brakes.

## CV-Boot

### REMOVAL & INSTALLATION

#### Transaxle Side

1. Remove the halfshaft and mount in a protected jaw vise.

2. Remove the boot bands.

3. Matchmark the slide joint housing and spider assembly to the halfshaft.

4. Remove the slide joint housing from the halfshaft.

5. Remove the spider snapring.

6. Remove the spider assembly from the halfshaft.

7. Cover the driveshaft splined end with tape to protect the CV-boot.

8. Remove the CV-boot.

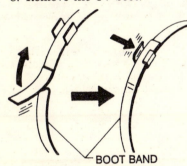

**Installing the CV-boot bands**

**To install:**

9. Install the CV-boot with a new boot band.

10. Install the spider assembly. Make sure the matchmarks are aligned properly.

11. Install a new spider snapring. Make sure the snapring seats evenly in the groove of the shaft.

12. Pack the CV-boot with grease.

13. Install the remaining boot bands. Tighten and crimp the bands using the proper tool.

#### Wheel Side

1. Remove the halfshaft and mount in a protected jaw vise.

2. Matchmark the joint assembly to the shaft.

3. Remove the joint assembly from the shaft using a suitable puller. Install the axle nut to prevent damage to the threads when removing the joint.

4. Remove the boot bands.

5. Cover the halfshaft splined end with tape to protect the CV-boot.

6. Remove the CV-boot.

**To install:**

7. Install the CV-boot with a new boot band.

8. Install the joint assembly by tapping lightly. Make sure the axle nut is installed to prevent damage to the threads. Make sure the matchmarks are aligned properly.

9. Pack the CV-boot with the proper grade and amount of grease.

10. Install the remaining boot bands. Tighten and crimp the bands using the proper tool.

## Driveshaft and U-Joints

### REMOVAL & INSTALLATION

#### 200SX, 240SX and 300ZX

1. Release the hand brake.

2. Raise and safely support the vehicle. On 300ZX, remove the the front pipe and the heat shield plate.

3. Matchmark the flanges on the driveshaft and differential so the driveshaft can be reinstalled in its original orientation; this will help maintain drive line balance.

4. Unbolt the rear flange and the center bearing.

5. Withdraw the driveshaft from the transmission and pull the driveshaft down and back to remove.

6. Plug the transmission extension housing to prevent oil leakage.

**To install:**

7. Lubricate the sleeve yoke splines with clean engine oil prior to installation. Insert the driveshaft into the transmission and align the flange matchmarks.

8. Install the flange and the center bearing bolts.

9. On 200SX and 240SX, torque the center bearing support bracket bolts to 19–29 ft. lbs. (25–39 Nm). On 1990–92 300ZX, torque the center bearing bolts to 43–58 ft. lbs. (59–78 Nm).

10. On 200SX with CA20E and VG30E engines, torque the flange bolts to 29–33 ft. lbs. (39–44 Nm); 240SX and 1988–89 300ZX torque to 29–33 ft. lbs. (39–44 Nm). On 1990–92 300ZX turbo, torque the flange bolts to 47–54 ft. lbs. On 1990–92 300ZX non-turbo, torque the flange bolts to 29–33 ft. lbs. (39–44 Nm).

11. On 300ZX, install the the front pipe and the heat shield plate.

#### Sentra (4WD) and Stanza Wagon (4WD)

1. Raise and safely support the vehicle. Mark the relationship of the driveshaft flange to the differential flange.

2. Unbolt the center bearing bracket.

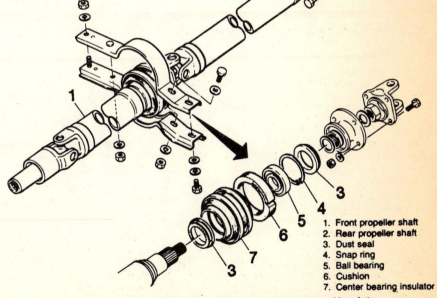

1. Front propeller shaft
2. Rear propeller shaft
3. Dust seal
4. Snap ring
5. Ball bearing
6. Cushion
7. Center bearing insulator

**Two piece driveshaft with center bearing and three U-points**

3. Unbolt the driveshaft flange from the differential flange.

4. Pull the driveshaft back under the rear axle. Plug the rear of the transmission to prevent oil or fluid loss.

5. To install, align the flange matchmarks made in Step 1. Torque the front and rear flange bolts to 25–33 ft. lbs. (34–44 Nm). On Sentra torque the center bracket bolts to 19–29 ft. lbs. (25–39 Nm). On Stanza Wagon, torque the center bearing bolts to 23–31 ft. lbs. (31–42 Nm).

## Front Axle Shaft, Bearing and Seal

### REMOVAL & INSTALLATION

#### 200SX and 1988–89 300ZX

1. Raise and support the vehicle safely.

2. Remove the front wheels. Work off center hub cap by using thin tool. If necessary tap around it with a soft hammer while removing. Pry off cotter pin and take out adjusting cap. Apply the parking brake firmly and remove the wheel bearing nut. The nut will require a good deal of force to remove it.

3. Unbolt the caliper and move it aside. Do not disconnect the hose from the caliper. Do not allow the caliper to hang by the hose; support the caliper with a length of wire or rest it on a suspension member.

4. Remove the wheel hub, disc brake rotor and bearing from the spindle. During removal, capture the outer bearing to prevent it from hitting the ground.

5. To replace the bearing outer race, drive it out with a suitable brass drift and mallet.

**To install:**

6. Install the new bearing outer race using a suitable race installation tool.

7. Install a new oil seal so the words "BEARING SIDE" face the inner side of the hub. Coat the lip of the seal with multi-purpose grease.

8. Pack the bearings, hub, hub cap and hub cap O-ring with multi-purpose grease. If the hub cap O-ring is crimped, replace it.

9. Install the inner and outer bearings.

10. Install the wheel hub and rotor disc onto the spindle.

11. Coat the threaded portion of the spindle shaft and the contact surface between the lock washer and outer wheel bearing with multi-purpose grease.

12. Install the wheel bearing locknut and adjust the bearing pre-load. Use a new cotter pin.

13. Mount the brake caliper assembly.

14. Install the front wheels and lower the vehicle.

#### 240SX

1. Raise and support the vehicle safely.

2. Remove the front wheels.

3. Work off center hub cap by using thin tool. If necessary tap around it with a soft hammer while removing. Pry off cotter pin and take out adjusting cap.

4. Apply the parking brake firmly and remove the wheel bearing nut. The nut will require a good deal of force to remove it.

5. Unbolt the caliper and move it aside. Do not disconnect the hose from the caliper. Do not allow the caliper to hang by the hose; support the caliper with a length of wire or rest it on a suspension member.

6. Pull the brake disc and wheel hub from the spindle.

7. Separate the tie rod and lower ball joints using the proper tool.

8. Place matchmarks on the strut lower bracket and camber adjusting pin for assembly reference. Remove the lower bracket bolts and nuts. Remove the wheel hub and knuckle assembly.

9. Remove the bearing retaining ring from the wheel hub.

10. Press the bearing assembly from the wheel hub. Apply pressure from the outside of the hub to remove the bearing.

**To install:**

11. Press the new bearing assembly into the hub from the inside.

**NOTE: Do not press the on the inner race of the wheel bearing assembly. Do not lubricate the surfaces of mating surfaces of the**

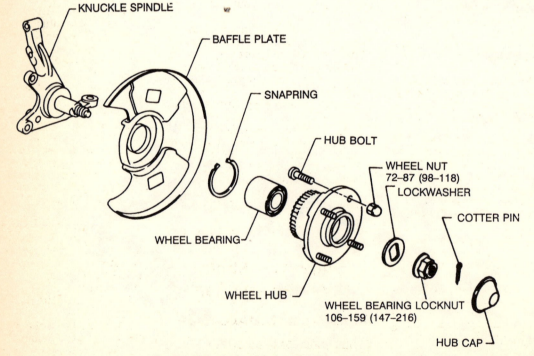

**Front axle and wheel hub assembly—240SX**

KNUCKLE SPINDLE

BAFFLE PLATE

SNAPRING

HUB BOLT

WHEEL NUT 72–87 (98–118)

LOCKWASHER

COTTER PIN

WHEEL BEARING

WHEEL HUB

WHEEL BEARING LOCKNUT 106–159 (147–216)

HUB CAP

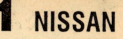

wheel bearing outer race and wheel with grease or oil. Be careful not to damage the grease seal.

12. Install the bearing retaining ring.

13. Coat the lip of the grease seal with multi-purpose grease.

14. Manuever the wheel hub and axle assembly onto the lower mounting bracket and install the bracket bolts and nuts. Make sure the matchmarks on the bracket and the camber adjusting pin are aligned properly.

15. Connect the lower and tie rod ball joints.

16. Push the brake disc and wheel hub onto the spindle.

17. Install the brake caliper assembly.

18. Apply the parking brake and torque the wheel bearing locknut to 108–159 ft. lbs. (147–216 Nm). Mount a dial indicator so the stylus of the dial rests on the face of the hub and check the wheel bearing axial endplay by attempting to rock the wheel hub in and out. The endplay should be 0.0012 in. or less.

19. Install a new locknut cotter pin. Install the bearing hub cap after packing it with multi-purpose grease.

20. Mount the the front wheels and lower the vehicle.

### 1990–92 300ZX

1. Raise and support the vehicle safely.

2. Remove the front wheels.

3. Unbolt the caliper and move it aside. Do not disconnect the hose from the caliper. Do not allow the caliper to hang by the hose; support the caliper with a length of wire or rest it on a suspension member.

4. Separate the tie rod and lower ball joints using the proper tool.

**NOTE: The steering knuckle is made of an aluminum alloy. Be careful no to strike it when removing the ball joints.**

5. Remove the kin pin lower nut and remove the steering knuckle assembly.

6. Remove the hub cap, wheel bearing locknut, sensor rotor (with ABS) or washer (without ABS).

7. Remove the wheel hub with a suitable drift.

8. Remove the wheel bearing retaining ring.

9. Press the wheel bearing from the knuckle.

10. Drive out the wheel bearing inner race to the outside of the wheel hub.

11. Remove the grease seal and splash guard (baffle plate).

**To install:**

12. From the outside of the knuckle,

press the new wheel bearing assembly into the knuckle.

**NOTE: Do not press the on the inner race of the wheel bearing assembly. Do not lubricate the surfaces of mating surfaces of the wheel bearing outer race and wheel with grease or oil. Be careful not to damage the grease seal.**

13. Install the bearing retaining ring. Make sure it seats evenly in the groove of the knuckle.

14. Coat the lip of the grease seal with multi-purpose grease and install.

15. Install the splash guard.

16. Press the wheel hub into the steering knuckle.

17. Install the washer (without ABS), sensor rotor (with ABS) and wheel bearing locknut. Torque the locknut to 152–210 ft. lbs. (206–284 Nm). Stake the locknut tabs using a small cold chisel.

18. Place the hub cap onto the knuckle and tap it into place using a rubber or plastic mallet. Once the cap is seated lightly into the knuckle, install the cap retaining bolts and torque to 8–12 ft. lbs. (11–16 Nm).

19. Mount the steering knuckle assembly and tighten the lower king pin nut.

20. Connect the tie rod and lower ball joints using the proper tool.

21. Install the brake caliper assembly.

22. Prior to checking the bearing pre-load, spin the wheel hub at least 10 revolutions in both directions to seat the bearing. Check the wheel bearing preload and axial end play as follows:

a. Pre-load—connect a spring scale of known calibration to a wheel hub bolt and measure the turning torque. If an NSK wheel bearing is used, the turning torque should be 1.3–8.4 lbs. (5.9–37.3 N). For NTN bearings, the turning torque should be 1.8–13.0 lbs. (7.8–57.9 N).

b. Axial endplay—mount a dial indicator so the stylus of the dial rests on the face of the hub and check the wheel bearing axial endplay by attempting to rock the wheel hub in and out. The endplay should be 0.0020 in. (0.05mm) or less.

23. Mount the front wheels and lower the vehicle.

## Rear Axle Shaft, Bearings and Seal

### REMOVAL & INSTALLATION

### 200SX and 1988–89 300ZX

1. Block the front wheels.

2. Raise and support the vehicle safely. Remove the front wheels.

3. Apply the parking brake firmly. This helps hold the stub axle while removing the axle nut. Also, hold the stub axle at the outside while removing the nut from the axle shaft side. The nut will require a good deal of force to remove, so be sure to hold the stub axle firmly. Discard the axle nut and replace with new nut.

4. On vehicles with rear disc brakes, unbolt the caliper and move it aside. Do not disconnect the hose from the caliper. Do not allow the caliper to hang by the hose; support the caliper with a length of wire or rest it on a suspension member.

5. Remove the brake disc on vehicles with rear disc brakes. Remove the brake drum on vehicles with drum brakes.

6. Remove the stub axle with a slide hammer and an adapter. The outer wheel bearing will come off with the stub axle.

7. Unbolt and remove the companion flange from the lower arm.

8. Remove and discard the grease seal and inner bearing from the lower arm using a drift made for the purpose or a length of pipe of the proper diameter. The outer bearing can be removed from the stub axle with a puller. If the grease seal or the bearings are removed, new parts must be used on assembly.

**To install:**

9. Clean all the parts to be reused in solvent.

10. Sealed-type bearings are used. When the new bearings are installed, the sealed side must face out. Install the sealed side of the outer bearing facing the wheel, and the sealed side of the inner bearing facing the differential.

11. Press the outer bearing onto the stub axle.

12. The bearing housing is stamped with an A, C or no mark. Select a spacer (distance piece) on the stub axle that matches the letter stamped on the bearing housing except is there is no mark. Bearing housings with no mark always accept a B spacer.

13. Install the stub axle into the lower arm.

14. Install the new inner bearing into the lower arm with the stub axle in place. Install a new grease seal.

15. Install the companion flange onto the stub axle.

16. Install a new stub axle nut. Tighten to 152–210 ft. lbs. (206–284 Nm).

17. Install the brake disc or drum, and the caliper if removed.

18. Install the rear wheels and lower the vehicle.

### 240SX and 1990–92 300ZX

1. Block the front wheels.

2. Raise and support the rear of the vehicle and remove the rear wheels. Remove the cotter pin, adjusting cap and insulator.

3. Apply the parking brake firmly to hold the rear halfshaft while removing the axle nut. Hold the stub axle at the outside while removing the nut from the axle shaft side. The nut will require a good deal of force to remove.

4. Unbolt the caliper and move it aside. Do not disconnect the hose from the caliper. Do not allow the caliper to hang by the hose; support the caliper with a length of wire or rest it on a suspension member. Remove the brake disc.

5. Separate the halfhaft from the axle housing by lightly tapping it. Cover the driveshaft boots with a shop towel to prevent damage.

6. Unbolt and remove the axle housing from the vehicle. Remove the 4 bolts that hold the wheel bearing, flange and hub to the axle housing.

7. Press the wheel bearing from the axle hub. Mount the hub in a vise and remove the inner race using a bearing replacer/puller tool. Discard the inner race. If the grease seals are being replaced, replace them as a set.

8. Clean all parts in a suitable solvent. Check the wheel hub and axle housing for cracks, preferably using the dye penetrant method. Check the wheel bearing seating surface for roughness, seizure or other damage that may interfere with proper bearing function. Check the rubber bushing for wear.

**To install:**

9. Place the hub on a block of wood and seat the inner race using a suitable drift. Be careful not to damage the grease seals during installation of the inner race.

10. Press the bearing into the hub using a suitable drift.

11. Mount the axle housing. Torque the axle housing bolts to 58–72 ft. lbs. (78–98 Nm) on both the 240SX and 1990–92 300ZX.

12. Insert the halfshaft into the wheel hub. Lubricate the halfshaft splines prior to installation. Make sure the splines are aligned properly.

13. Install the caliper assembly.

14. Install the wheel bearing locknut. On 240SX, torque the nut to 174–231 ft. lbs. (235–314 Nm). On 1990–92 300ZX, torque the nut to 152–203 ft. lbs. (206–275 Nm). Install the insulator and fit adjusting cap. Install a new cotter pin.

15. On 1990–92 300ZX, check the axial endplay as follows before mounting the rear wheels: mount a dial indicator so the stylus of the dial rests on the face of the hub and check the wheel bearing axial endplay by attempting to rock the wheel hub in and out. The endplay should be 0.0020 in. (0.05mm) or less.

16. Mount the rear wheels and lower the vehicle.

## Front Wheel Hub, Knuckle and Bearings

### REMOVAL & INSTALLATION

#### Maxima, Pulsar, Sentra and Stanza

1. Raise and support the vehicle safely.

2. Remove the front wheels.

3. Remove the brake rotor.

4. Remove the cotter pin, adjusting cap and insulator.

5. Apply the parking brake firmly and remove the wheel bearing nut. The nut will require a good deal of force to remove it.

6. Unbolt the caliper and move it aside. Do not disconnect the hose from the caliper. Do not allow the caliper to hang by the hose; support the caliper with a length of wire or rest it on a suspension member.

7. Separate the tie rod end from the steering knuckle using the proper tool.

8. Disconnect the halfshaft from the transaxle using the proper tool or by tapping on it with a block of wood and a mallet.

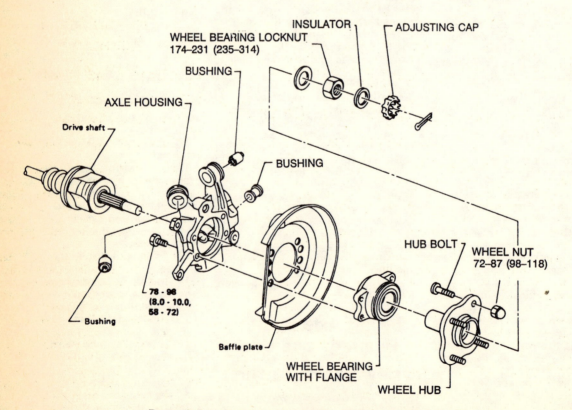

Rear axle housing assembly–240SX shown–1990–92 300ZX similar

**NOTE: Cover the CV-boots with cloth to prevet damage when removing the halfshafts.**

9. Remove the nuts and bolt that attach the knuckle to the strut. Make sure to place a visible matchmark on the adjusting pin and knuckle mounting bracket before removing these fasteners.

10. Remove the lower arm bolts.

11. On Pulsar and Sentra, loosen the lower ball joint nut and separate the knuckle from the lower ball joint stud using the proper tool.

12. Remove the knuckle and hub assembly.

13. Drive out the hub and outside inner race with a suitable tool.

14. Withdraw the outside inner race from the wheel hub.

15. On Maxima and Stanza, remove the outer and grease seals from the hub at this time, then press the outer race from the hub.

16. On Pulsar and Sentra, press the inside inner race from the hub. Set the race aside for use in removal of the wheel bearing.

17. Remove the wheel bearing retainer with the proper tool. On Maxima and Stanza, there are retainers on both sides of the hub. After both retainers are removed, the bearing can be pressed from the hub at this time.

18. On Pulsar and Sentra, place the inside inner race set aside in Step 16 on top of the wheel bearing and press the bearing out of the hub. Apply pressure to the inside of the knuckle to remove the bearing.

19. Clean all parts in a suitable solvent. Check the wheel hub and axle housing for cracks, preferrably using the dye penetrant method. Check the wheel bearing seating surface for roughness, seizure or other damage that may interfere with proper bearing function.

**To install:**

20. On Maxima and Stanza, install the inner bearing retainer.

21. Press the new bearing into the knuckle by applying pressure to the outside of the knuckle. Do not exceed 3.3 tons of pressure.

**NOTE: Do not press the on the inner race of the wheel bearing assembly. Do not lubricate the surfaces of mating surfaces of wheel bearing outer race and wheel with grease or oil. Be careful not to damage the grease seal.**

22. Install the remaining bearing retainer. Make sure it seats evenly in the groove of the knuckle.

23. Coat the lip of the seal with multi-purpose grease. On Maxima and Stanza, install the inner and outer grease seals. Make sure the lip of the seal(s) faces the inside of the hub.

24. Press the hub into the knuckle. Do not exceed 3.3 tons of pressure.

25. Clamp the knuckle portion in a vise and apply a pre-load of 3.5–5.0 tons to the outside (wheel bolt side) of the bearing with a suitable press. Spin the knuckle several turns in both directions and make sure the bearing spins freely and does not bind.

26. Mount the knuckle and hub assembly.

27. On Pulsar and Sentra, connect the lower ball joint to the knuckle.

28. Install the lower arm bolts.

29. Install the knuckle-to-strut fasteners. Make sure the adjusting pin matchmarks are aligned properly.

30. Install the halfshafts.

31. Connect the tire rod end to the steering knuckle using the proper tool.

32. Install the brake caliper assembly.

33. Install the wheel bearing locknut. Torque the nut to 174–231 ft. lbs. (235–314 Nm) on Maxima and Stanza; 145–203 ft. lbs. (196–275 Nm) on 1988–89 Pulsar; 145–203 ft. lbs. (196–275 Nm) on Sentra and 1990 Pulsar. When tightening the nut, apply the brake pedal.

34. Install the insulator and adjusting cap. Install a new cotter pin into the wheel bearing locknut.

35. Check the axial endplay as follows: mount a dial indicator so the stylus of the dial rests on the face of the hub and check the wheel bearing axial endplay by attempting to rock the wheel hub in and out. The endplay should be 0.0020 in. (0.05mm) or less.

36. Mount the front wheels.

37. Lower the vehicle.

## Differential Carrier

### REMOVAL & INSTALLATION

1. Raise the rear of the vehicle and support safely. Drain the oil from the differential. Position a floor jack underneath the differential unit.

2. Disconnect the brake hydraulic lines and the parking brake cable. On 240SX, remove the brake caliper leaving the brake line connected. Plug the brake lines to prevent lakage.

3. Disconnect the sway bar from the control arms on either sides (not required on 1990–92 300ZX).

4. Remove the rear exhaust pipe.

5. Disconnect the driveshaft and the rear axle shafts.

6. Remove the rear shock absorbers from the control arms. On 1990–92 300ZX, remove the nuts that attach the differential rear cove to the suspension member.

7. Unbolt the differential unit from the chassis at the differential mounting insulator. On 1990–92 300ZX, remove the mounting member from the front of the final drive.

8. Lower the rear assembly out of the vehicle using the floor jack. It is best to have at least one other person helping to balance the assembly. After the final drive is removed, support the center suspension member to prevent damage to the insulators.

9. During installation, torque the rear cover-to-insulator nuts to 72–87 ft. lbs. (98–118 Nm); mounting insulator-to-chassis bolts to 22–29 ft. lbs. (30–39 Nm); strut nuts to 51–65 ft. lbs. (69–81 Nm); sway bar-to-control arm nuts to 12–15 ft. lbs. (16–21 Nm). On 240SX and 300ZX, torque the drive shaft flange bolts to 25–33 ft. lbs. (34–44 Nm); on 200SX with CA20E and VG30E engines, torque the flange bolts to 29–36 ft. lbs. (39–49 Nm).

# MANUAL TRANSMISSION

For further information on transmissions/transaxles, please refer to "Chilton's Guide to Transmission Repair".

## Transmission Assembly

### REMOVAL & INSTALLATION

#### 200SX, 240SX and 300ZX

1. Disconnect the negative battery cable.

2. Raise and support the vehicle safely.

3. On 1988–89 300ZX, remove the exhaust front pipe, catalytic converter and exhaust manifold conecting tube. On 1990–92 300ZX, remove the exhaust pipe section from the manifold and remove the support bracket from the transmission.

4. Unbolt the driveshaft at the rear and remove. If there is a center bearing, unbolt it from the crossmember. Seal the end of the transmission extension housing to prevent leakage.

5. Disconnect the speedometer drive cable from the transmission.

6. On 200SX, 1988–89 300ZX non-turbocharged and all 1990–92 300ZX, remove the shifter lever. On 1988–89 300ZX turbocharged, remove the shift knob and console boot finisher. On 240SX, disconnect the control rod front the shift lever.

**NOTE: On the 1988–89 300ZX turbo, the shifter boot must not be removed from the shift lever.**

7. Remove the clutch operating cylinder from the clutch housing.

8. Support the engine with a large wood block and a jack under the oil pan. Do not place the jack under the oil pan drain plug.

9. Unbolt the transmission from the crossmember. Support the transmission with a jack and remove the crossmember.

10. Lower the rear of the engine to allow clearance.

11. Unplug the back-up light, neutral and overdrive switch connectors.

12. Unbolt the transmission. Lower and remove it to the rear.

**NOTE: The transmission bolts are different lengths. Tagging the transmission-to-engine bolts upon removal will facilitate proper tightening during installation.**

**To install:**

13. Raise the transmission onto the engine and install the mounting bolts. Torque the bolts as follows:

   a. 200SX with 4 cylinder engine—tighten bolts (1) and (2) to 29–36 ft. lbs. (39–49 Nm) and bolt (3) to 22–29 ft. lbs. (29–39 Nm).

   b. 200SX (V6) and 1988–89 300ZX—tighten the long mounting bolts (65mm and 60mm) to 29–36 ft. lbs. (39–49 Nm). Tighten the short bolts (55mm and 25mm) to 22–29 ft. lbs. (29–39 Nm).

   c. 240SX—tighten bolts (1), (2) and (4) to 29–36 ft. lbs. (39–49 Nm) and bolt (3) to 22–29 ft. lbs. (29–39 Nm)

   d. 1990–92 300ZX—tighten bolts (1), (2) and (3) to 29–36 ft. lbs. (39–49 Nm). Tighten bolts (4) and (5) to 22–29 ft. lbs. (29–39 Nm).

14. Plug in the back-up light, neutral and overdrive switch connectors.

15. Install the crossmember.

16. Install the clutch operating cylinder.

17. Install the shifter lever, shift knob and console boot finisher or control rod.

18. Connect the speedometer drive cable.

19. Install the driveshaft. Torque the flange bolts to 29–33 ft. lbs. (34–44 Nm). On 1990–92 300ZX, torque the center bearing bracket nuts to 19–29 ft. lbs. (25–39 Nm).

20. On 1990–92 300ZX, connect the exhaust tube section to the manifolds and attach the support bracket to the transmission. On 1988–89 300ZX, install the exhaust front tube, catalytic converter and exhaust manifold conecting tube.

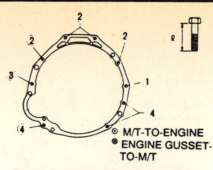

Transmission mounting bolt locations on 1988–89 300ZX and 200SX (V6); bolt (1) is 65mm, bolt (2) is 60mm, bolt (3) is 55mm and bolt 4 is 25mm

⊙ M/T-TO-ENGINE
⊗ ENGINE GUSSET-TO-M/T

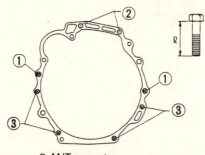

⊙ M/T to engine
⊗ Engine gusset to M/T

Transmission mounting bolt locations on 200SX (4 cylinder); bolt (1) is 75mm, bolt (2) is 65mm and bolt (3) is 25mm

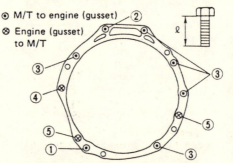

⊙ M/T to engine (gusset)
⊗ Engine (gusset) to M/T

Transmission mounting bolt locations on 1990–92 300ZX; bolt (1) is 100mm, bolt (2) is 65mm, bolt (3) is 60mm, bolt (4) is 55mm and bolt (5) is 25mm

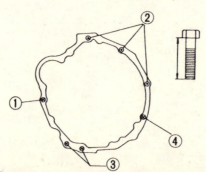

Transmission mounting bolt locations on 240SX; bolt (1) is 70mm, bolt (2) is 60mm, bolt (3) is 30mm and bolt (4) is 25mm

21. Lower the vehicle and connect the negative battery cable.

# MANUAL TRANSAXLE

For further information on transmissions/transaxles, please refer to "Chilton's Guide to Transmission Repair".

## Transaxle Assembly

### REMOVAL & INSTALLATION

#### Except 1990–92 Stanza

1. Disconnect the negative battery cable.

2. Remove the battery and battery bracket.

3. Remove the air duct, air cleaner box and air flow meter.

4. Raise the front of the vehicle and support safely.

5. Drain the transaxle oil.

6. On Stanza Wagon (4WD) and Sentra (4WD) vehicles, remove the transfer case.

7. Withdraw the halfshafts from the transaxle. On Stanza Wagon (4WD), remove only the left halfshaft.

**NOTE: When removing halfshafts, use care not to damage the lip of the oil seal. After shafts are removed, insert a steel bar or wooden dowel of suitable diameter to prevent the side gears from rotating and falling into the differential case.**

8. On 1989–92 Maxima, remove the clutch operating cylinder from the transaxle.

9. Remove the wheel well protector(s).

10. Separate the control rod and support rod from the transaxle.

11. Remove the engine gusset securing bolt and the engine mounting.

12. Remove the clutch control cable from the operating lever.

13. Disconnect speedometer cable from the transaxle.

14. Disconnect the wires from the reverse (back-up), neutral and overdrive switches. On 1989–92 Maxima, disconnect the speed and position switch sensors from the transaxle also.

15. Support the engine by placing a jack under the oil pan, with a wooden block placed between the jack and pan for protection.

16. Support the transaxle with a hydraulic floor jack.

17. Remove the engine mounting securing bolts.

**NOTE: Most of the transaxle mounting bolts are different lenghts. Tagging the bolts upon removal will facilitate proper tightening during installation.**

18. Remove the bolts attaching the transaxle to the engine.

19. Using the hydraulic floor jack as a carrier, carefully lower the transaxle down and away from the engine.

**To install:**

20. Before installing, clean the mating surfaces on the engine rear plate and clutch housing. On Sentra (4WD) and Stanza Wagon (4WD), apply sealant KP510–00150 or equivalent.

21. Apply a light coat of a lithium-based grease to the spline parts of the clutch disc and the transaxle input shaft.

22. Raise the transaxle into place and bolt it to the engine. Install the engine mounts. Torque the tranasxle mounting bolts as follows:

a. 1988 Maxima—tighten bolts (1), (2) and (3) to 32–43 ft. lbs. (43–58 Nm). Tighten bolt (4) to 22–30 ft. lbs. (30–40 Nm) and bolt (5) to 12–15 ft. lbs. (16–21 Nm).

b. 1989–92 Maxima—tighten bolt (1) to 12–15 ft. lbs. (16–21 Nm), bolt (2) to 22–30 ft. lbs. (30–40 Nm), bolts (3) and (4) to 32–43 ft. lbs. (43–58 Nm). Torque the front and rear gusset bolts to 22–30 ft. lbs. (30–40 Nm).

c. 1988 Pulsar/Sentra (E16S and E16i)—tighten bolts (1) and (3) to 12–15 ft. lbs. (16–22 Nm). Tighten bolts (2) and (4) to 14–22 ft. lbs. (20–29 Nm). Bolts (3) and (4) are found all Sentra models.

d. 1988 Pulsar (CA18DE)—On CA18DE engines, tighten bolts (1) and (2) to to 32–43 ft. lbs. (43–58 Nm) and bolts (3) to 22–30 ft. lbs. (30–40 Nm).

e. 1989 Pulsar (CA18DE)—tighten bolts (1) and (2) to 32–43 ft. lbs. (43–58 Nm) and bolt (3) to 22–30 ft. lbs. (30–40 Nm).

f. Pulsar and 2WD Sentra—tighten all bolts to 12–15 ft. lbs. (16–21 Nm).

g. Sentra 4WD—torque all the bolts to 22–30 ft. lbs.

h. 1988–89 Stanza—tighten bolts (1), (2) and (3) to 32–43 ft. lbs. (39–49 Nm). Tighten bolt (4) to 22–30 ft. lbs. (30–40 Nm).

23. On 1989–92 Maxima, connect the speed and position switch sensor wires. Connect the reverse (back-up), neutral and overdrive switch wires.

24. Connect the speedometer cable to the transaxle.

25. Connect the clutch cable to the operating lever.

26. Connect the control and support rods to the transaxle.

27. Install the wheel well protectors.

28. On 1989–92 Maxima, install the clutch operating cylinder.

29. Install the halfshafts.

30. On Stanza Wagon (4WD) and Sentra (4WD) vehicles, install the transfer case.

31. Lower the vehicle.

32. Install the air duct, air cleaner box and air flow meter.

33. Install the battery and battery bracket.

34. Connect the negative battery cable.

35. Remove the filler plug and fill the transaxle to the proper level with fluid that meets API GL-4 specifications.

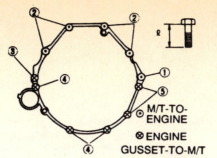

**Transaxle mounting bolt locations on 1988 Maxima; bolt (1) is 65mm, bolt (2) is 55mm, bolt (3) is 60mm and bolts (4) and (5) are 25mm**

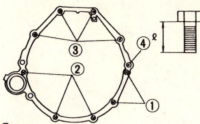

**Transaxle mounting bolt locations on 1989–92 Maxima; bolts (1) and (2) are 25mm, bolt (3) is 55mm and bolt (4) is 65mm**

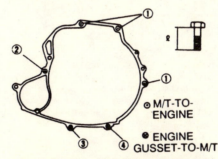

**Transaxle mounting bolt locations on 1988 Pulsar/Sentra (E16S and E16i); bolt (1) is 70mm, bolt (2) is 40mm, bolt (3) is 25mm, bolt (4) is 20mm**

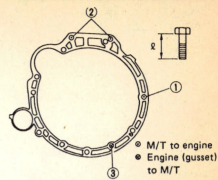

**Transaxle mounting bolt locations on 1989 Pulsar (CA18DE engine); bolt (1) is 125mm, bolt (2) is 65mm, bolt (3) is 45mm. Bolt (1) has a nut**

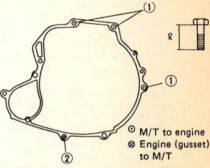

**Transaxle mounting bolt locations on 1989–91 Pulsar and 2WD Sentra (GA16i engine); bolt (1) is 70mm and bolt (2) is 25mm**

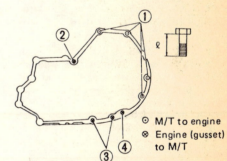

**Transaxle mounting bolt locations on 1988–91 Sentra 4WD; bolt (1) is 70mm, bolt (2) is 40mm, bolt (3) is 20mm), bolt (4) is 55mm**

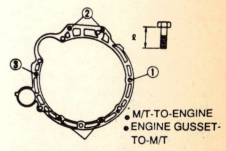

**On 1988–89 Stanza; bolt (1) is 120mm, bolt (2) is 65mm, bolt (3) is 70mm, bolt (4) is 25mm. Bolt (1) has a nut**

Fill to the level of the plug hole. Apply a thread sealant to the threads of the filler plug and install the plug in the transaxle case.

### 1990–92 Stanza

1. Disconnect the negative battery cable.
2. Remove the battery and battery bracket.
3. Remove the air cleaner box with the air flow meter.
4. Remove the AIV unit.
5. Remove the clutch operating cylinder from the transaxle.
6. Remove the clutch hose clamp.
7. Raise and support the vehicle safely.
8. Disconnect the speedometer cable from the transaxle.
9. Disconnect the position switch and all electrical connectors from the transaxle. Tag each wire.
10. Remove the breather hose clamp from the transaxle.
11. Remove the starter.
12. Disconnect the shift control rod from the transaxle.
13. Drain the transaxle fluid.
14. Remove the front exhaust tube.
15. Withdraw the halfshafts from the transaxle.

**NOTE: When removing halfshafts, use care not to damage the lip of the oil seal. After shafts are removed, insert a steel bar or wooden dowel of suitable diameter to prevent the side gears from rotating and falling into the differential case.**

16. Support the engine by placing a jack under the oil pan, with a wooden block placed between the jack and pan for protection.
17. Support the transaxle with a suitable floor jack.
18. Remove the rear and left engine mounts.
19. Remove the bolts attaching the transaxle to the engine.

**NOTE: The transaxle mounting bolts are different lengths. Tagging the bolts upon removal will facilitate proper tightening during installation.**

20. Using the jack as a carrier, carefully lower the transaxle down and away from the vehicle.

**NOTE: Be careful not to strike any adjacent parts or input shaft (the shaft protruding from the transaxle which fits into the clutch assembly) when removing the transaxle from the vehicle.**

**To install:**
21. Before installing, clean the mat-

ing surfaces on the engine rear plate and clutch housing.
22. Apply a light coat of a lithium-based grease to the spline parts of the clutch disc and the transaxle input shaft.
23. Raise the transaxle into place and install the mounting bolts. Tighten bolts (1) and (2) to 29–36 ft. lbs. (39–49 Nm). Tighten bolts (3) and (4) to 22–30 ft. lbs. (30–40 Nm).
24. Install the rear and left engine mounts.
25. Remove the transaxle and engine supports.
26. Install the halfshafts.
27. Install the front exhaust tube with new gaskets.
28. Connect the shift control rod.
29. Install the starter.
30. Connect the electrical and position switch wiring.
31. Connect the speedometer cable.
32. Lower the vehicle.
33. Install the clutch hose clamp.

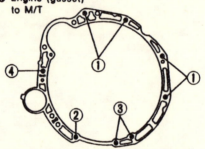

① M/T to engine (gusset)
② Engine (gusset) to M/T

**Transaxle mounting bolt locations on 1990–92 Stanza; bolt (1) is 45mm, bolt (2) is 25mm), bolt (3) is 30mm, bolt (4) is 40mm**

34. Install the clutch operating cylinder.
35. Install the AIV unit.
36. Install the air cleaner box and air flow meter.
37. Install the battery bracket and battery.
38. Connect the negative battery cable.
39. Remove the filler plug and fill the transaxle to the proper level with fluid that meets API GL–4 specifications. Fill to the level of the plug hole. Apply a thread sealant to the threads of the filler plug and install the plug in the transaxle

---

# CLUTCH

## Clutch Assembly

### REMOVAL & INSTALLATION

1. Remove the transmission or transaxle.
2. Insert a clutch aligning bar or similar tool all the way into the clutch disc hub. This must be done so as to support the weight of the clutch disc during removal.
3. Mark the clutch assembly-to-flywheel relationship with paint or a center punch so the clutch assembly can be assembled in the same position from which it is removed.
4. Loosen the pressure plate bolts in criss-cross fashion, a turn at a time to gradually relieve the spring pressure. Remove the bolts once the spring pressure is relieved.
5. Remove the pressure plate and

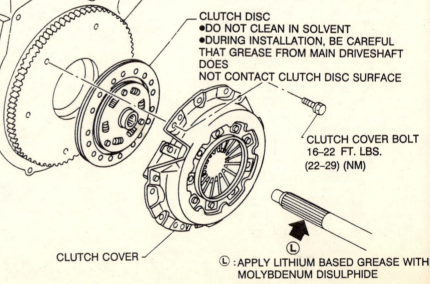

— FLYWHEEL

— CLUTCH DISC
●DO NOT CLEAN IN SOLVENT
●DURING INSTALLATION, BE CAREFUL THAT GREASE FROM MAIN DRIVESHAFT DOES NOT CONTACT CLUTCH DISC SURFACE

CLUTCH COVER BOLT 16–22 FT. LBS. (22–29) (NM)

CLUTCH COVER —

Ⓛ :APPLY LITHIUM BASED GREASE WITH MOLYBDENUM DISULPHIDE

**Typical clutch assembly**

clutch disc. Inspect the pressure plate or scoring for roughness, and reface or replace as necessary. Slight roughness can be smoothed with a fine emery cloth. Inspect the clutch disc for worn or oily facings, loose rivets and broken or loose springs, and replace.

6. Remove the release mechanism. On Pulsar and Sentra, the clutch lever is removed by aligning the lever retaining pins with the clutch cavity, then driving out the pins with a suitable pin punch. Inspect the release sleeve and lever contact surfaces for wear, rust or any other damage. Replace if necessary.

7. Inspect the pressure plate for wear, scoring, etc., and reface or replace as necessary. Minor imperfections or discoloration may be removed with emery cloth.

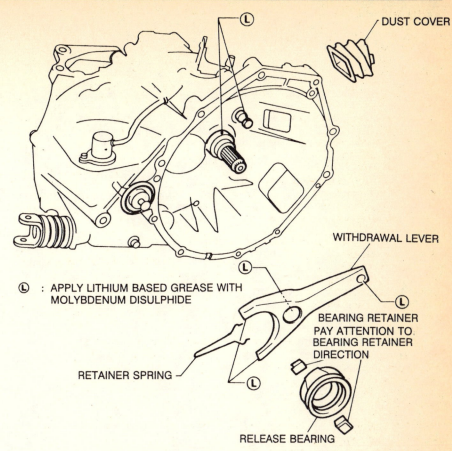

Ⓛ : APPLY LITHIUM BASED GREASE WITH MOLYBDENUM DISULPHIDE

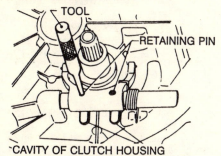

**Clutch lever retaining pin removal— Pulsar and Sentra**

**Clutch release mechanism—except Pulsar and Sentra**

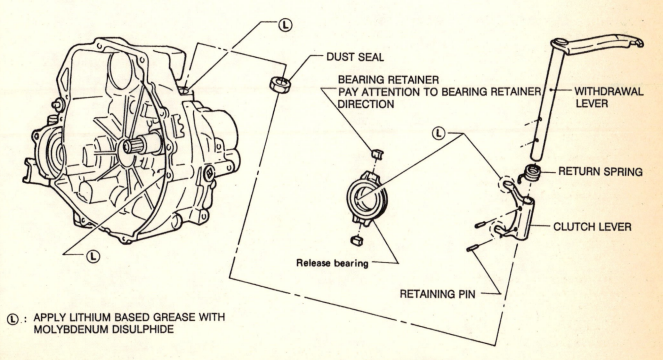

Ⓛ : APPLY LITHIUM BASED GREASE WITH MOLYBDENUM DISULPHIDE

**Clutch release mechanism—Pulsar and Sentra**

8. Inspect the release bearing. The bearing should roll freely and quietly. It should not have any cracks, pitting or wear. Replace as necessary.

**To install:**

9. Apply multi-purpose grease to the bearing sleeve inside groove, the contact point of the withdrawal lever and bearing sleeve, the contact surface of the lever ball pin and lever.

10. Apply a small amount of lithium based grease to the transmission splines.

11. Install the disc on the splines and slide it back and forth a few times. Remove the disc and remove any excess grease on the hub. Be sure no grease contacts the disc or pressure plate.

**NOTE: Take special care to prevent any grease or oil from getting on the clutch facing. During assembly, keep all disc facings, flywheel and pressure plate clean and dry. Grease, oil or dirt on these parts will result in a slipping clutch when assembled.**

12. Install the disc, aligning it with a splined dummy shaft.

13. Install the pressure plate and torque the bolts to 16–22 ft. lbs. (22–29 Nm) on all vehicles except 240SX, and 1990–92 300ZX. On 240SX and 1990–92 300ZX, torque the bolts to 25–33 ft. lbs. (34–44 Nm).

14. Remove the dummy shaft.

15. Install the transmission or transaxle.

## PEDAL HEIGHT/FREE-PLAY ADJUSTMENT

### Hydraulic Clutch

1. Pedal height is adjusted by moving the pedal stopper or clutch switch.

2. Pedal free-play is adjusted at the master cylinder pushrod by turning the locknut.

3. If the pushrod is non-adjustable, free-play is adjusted by placing shims between the master cylinder and the firewall. On a few vehicles, pedal free-play can also be adjusted at the operating (slave) cylinder pushrod.

### Mechanical Clutch

1. Loosen the locknut and adjust

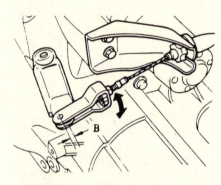

**Clutch withdrawal lever adjustment on Pulsar and Sentra. Arrow shows locknut adjustment**

the pedal height by means of the pedal stopper. Tighten the locknut.

2. Push the withdrawal lever in by hand until resistance is felt. Adjust withdrawal lever play at the lever tip end with the locknuts. Withdrawal lever play should be 0.0198–0.138 in. (2.5–3.5mm).

3. Depress and release the clutch pedal several times and then recheck the withdrawal lever play again. Readjust if necessary.

4. Measure the pedal free travel at the center of the pedal pad.

## Clutch Cable

### REMOVAL & INSTALLATION

1. Disconnect the negative battery cable.

2. Remove the floor mats.

3. Working from inside the engine compartment, loosen the adjusting nuts and locknut and disconnect the clutch cable from the withdrawal lever.

4. Working from inside the vehicle, disconnect the clutch cable from the clutch pedal.

5. Working from inside the engine compartment, remove the 2 nuts that attach the end of the cable to the fire wall.

6. From inside the engine compartment, pull the clutch cable through the firewall and remove it.

## CLUTCH PEDAL SPECIFICATIONS

| Model | Pedal Height above Floor in. (mm) | Pedal Free-play in. (mm) |
|---|---|---|
| 200 SX | 7.44–7.83 (189–199) | 0.04–0.12 (1–3) |
| CA20E, VG30E | 7.72–8.11 (196–206) | 0.04–0.12 (1–3) |
| 240SX | 7.32–7.72 (186–196) | 0.04–0.12 (1–3) |
| 300ZX | | |
| 1988–89 | 7.68–8.07 (195–205) | 0.04–0.12 (1–3) |
| 1990–92 (VG30DE) | 7.60–7.99 (193–203) | 0.04–0.12 (1–3) |
| 1990–92 (VG30DETT) | 7.05–7.44 (179–189) | 0.04–0.12 (1–3) |
| Maxima | | |
| 1988 | 6.73–7.13 (171–181) | 0.04–0.12 (1–3) |
| 1989–92 | 6.50–6.89 (165–175) | 0.04–0.12 (1–3) |
| Pulsar, Sentra | 6.38–6.77 (162–172) | 0.492–0.689 (12.5–17.5)① |
| Stanza Sedan | | |
| 1988–89 | 6.73–7.13 (171–181) | 0.04–0.12 (1–3) |
| 1990–92 | 6.50–6.89 (165–175) | 0.04–0.12 (1–3) |
| Stanza Wagon | 9.29–9.69 (236–246) | 0.04–0.12 (1–3) |

① Withdrawal lever play—0.098–0.138 (2.5–3.5)

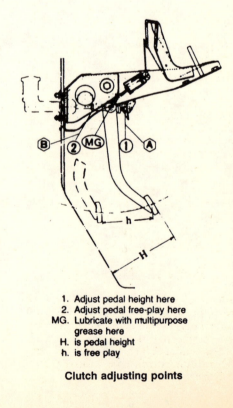

1. Adjust pedal height here
2. Adjust pedal free-play here
MG. Lubricate with multipurpose grease here
H. is pedal height
h. is free play

**Clutch adjusting points**

**To install:**

7. Route the clutch cable through the passenger compartment.

8. Position the cable end over the studs on the firewall and install the 2 mounting nuts. Torque the nuts to 6–8 ft. lbs. (9–11 Nm).

9. Connect the clutch cable to the clutch pedal.

10. Connect the clutch cable to the withdrawal lever.

11. Lubricate the pedal fulcrum pin and pivot points with lithium based grease.

12. Adjust the cable and the clutch switch.

13. Check the clutch for proper engagement.

14. Install the floor mats.

15. Connect the negative battery cable.

## Clutch Master Cylinder

### REMOVAL & INSTALLATION

1. Disconnect the negative battery cable.

2. Disconnect the clutch pedal arm from the pushrod.

3. Disconnect the clutch hydraulic line from the master cylinder. Plug the end of line to prevent leakage.

4. Remove the nuts attaching the master cylinder and remove the master cylinder and pushrod toward the engine compartment side.

5. Install the master cylinder in the reverse order of removal.

6. Bleed the clutch hydraulic system and make all necessary clutch adjustments.

## Clutch Slave Cylinder

### REMOVAL & INSTALLATION

1. Remove the slave cylinder attaching bolts and the pushrod from the shift fork.

2. Disconnect the flexible fluid hose from the slave cylinder and remove the unit form the vehicle. Plug the end of the hose.

3. Install the slave cylinder in the reverse order of removal and bleed the clutch hydraulic system.

## Hydraulic Clutch
## System Bleeding

Bleeding is required to remove air trapped in the hydraulic system. This operation is necessary whenever the system has been leaking or opened for maintenance. The bleed screw is located on the clutch slave (operating) cylinder.

Some vehicles are also equipped with a clutch damper mechanism. The clutch damper mechanism is bled in exactly the same manner as the operating cylinder. It should be bled along with the operating cylinder.

1. Remove the bleed screw dust cap.

2. Attach a transparent vinyl tube to the bleed screw, immersing the free end in a clean container of clean brake fluid.

3. Fill the master cylinder with the proper fluid.

4. Open the bleed screw about ¾ turn.

5. Depress the clutch pedal quickly. Hold it down. Have an assistant tighten the bleed screw. Allow the pedal to return slowly.

6. Repeat Steps 2 and 5 until no more air bubbles are seen in the fluid container.

7. Remove the bleed tube. Replace the dust cap. Refill the master cylinder.

8. Bleed the clutch damper, if equipped.

# AUTOMATIC TRANSMISSION

For further information on transmissions/transaxles, please refer to "Chilton's Guide to Transmission Repair".

## Transmission Assembly

### REMOVAL & INSTALLATION

#### 200SX, 240SX and 300ZX

1. Disconnect the battery cable.

2. Remove the accelerator linkage.

3. Detach the shift linkage.

4. Disconnect the neutral safety switch and downshift solenoid wiring.

5. Raise and safely support the vehicle. Remove the drain plug and drain the torque converter. If there is no converter drain plug, drain the transmission. If there is no transmission drain plug, remove the pan to drain. Replace the pan to keep out dirt.

6. Remove the front exhaust pipe.

7. Remove the vacuum tube and speedometer cable.

8. Disconnect the fluid cooler and charging tubes. Plug the tube ends to prevent leakage.

9. Lower the driveshaft and remove the starter.

10. Support the transmission with a jack under the oil pan. Support the engine also.

11. Remove the rear crossmember.

12. Mark the relationship between the torque converter and the driveplate. Remove the bolts holding the converter to the driveplate through the access hole at the front, under the engine by rotating the crankshaft. Unbolt the transmission from the engine and remove it.

**NOTE: The transmission bolts are different lengths. Tag each bolt according to location to ensure proper installation. This is particularly important on the 240SX and 1990–92 300ZX.**

13. Check the driveplate runout with a dial indictator. Runout must be no more than 0.020 in.

**To install:**

14. If the torque converter was removed from the engine for any reason, after it is installed, the distance from the face of the converter to the edge of the converter housing must be checked prior to installing the transmission. This is done to ensure proper installation of the torque converter. On 200SX and 1988–89 300ZX, the dimension should be 1.38 in. (35mm) or more. On 240SX and 1990–92 300ZX (non-turbocharged), the dimension should be 1.02 in. (26mm) or more. On 1990–92 300ZX (turbocharged), the dimension should be 0.98 in. (25mm) or more.

15. Raise the transmission and bolt the driveplate to the converter and transmission to the engine. Torque the driveplate-to-torque converter and converter housing-to-engine bolts to 29–36 ft. lbs. (39–49 Nm) on all except 240SX and 1990–92 300ZX. On these vehicles, torque the transmission mounting bolts as follows: On 240SX, tighten bolts (1) and (2) to 29–36 ft. lbs. (39–49 Nm); tighten bolt (3) to 22–29 ft. lbs. (29–39 Nm); tighten the gusset-to-engine bolts to 22–29 ft. lbs. (29–39 Nm). On 1990–92 300ZX tighten bolts (1), (2), (3), (6) and (7) to 29–36 ft. lbs. (39–49 Nm). Tighten bolts (2) and (5) to 22–29 ft. lbs. (29–39 Nm). Tighten the engine gusset bolts to 22–29 ft. lbs. (29–39 Nm).

**NOTE: After the converter is installed, rotate the crankshaft several times to make sure the transmission rotates freely and does not bind.**

16. Install the rear crossmember.

17. Remove the engine and transmission supports.

18. Install the starter and connect the driveshaft. Torque the flange bolts to 29–33 ft. lbs. (34–44 Nm) on all except 1990–92 300ZX (turbo). On 1990–

# 1 NISSAN

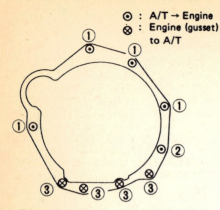

Transmission mounting bolt locations on 240SX; bolt (1) is 40mm, bolt (2) is 50mm, bolt (3) is 25mm and the gusset bolts are 20mm

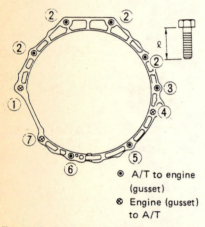

⊙ A/T to engine (gusset)
⊗ Engine (gusset) to A/T

Transmission mounting bolt locations on 1990–92 300ZX (turbo and non-turbo)

92 300ZX (turbo), torque the flange bolts to 40–47 ft. lbs. (54–64 Nm).

19. Unplug, connect and tighten the fluid cooler tubes.
20. Connect the speedometer cable and the vacuum tube.
21. Connect the front exhaust pipe using new gaskets.
22. Connect the switch wiring to the transmission.
23. Connect the shift linkage.
24. Connect the negative battery cable, fill the transmission to the proper level and make any necessary adjustment.
25. Perform a road test and check the fluid level.

## SHIFT LINKAGE ADJUSTMENT

### 200SX, 240SX and 300SX

If the detents cannot be felt or the pointer indicator is improperly aligned while shifting from the P range to

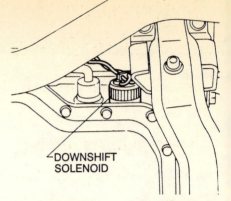

Manual control linkage adjustment—200SX, 240SX and 300ZX

range 1, the linkage should be adjusted.
1. Place the shifter in the P position.
2. Loosen the locknuts.
3. Tighten the outer locknut X until it touches the trunnion, pulling the selector lever toward the R range side without pushing the button.
4. Back off the outer locknut X ¼–½ turns and then tighten the inner locknut Y to 5–11 ft. lbs. (8–15 Nm).
5. Move the selector lever from P to 1. Make sure it moves smoothly.

NOTE: The 1988–92 300ZX has an automatic transmission interlock system. This interlock system prevents the transmission selector from being shifted from the P position unless the brake pedal is depressed.

## KICKDOWN SWITCH ADJUSTMENT

When the accelerator pedal is depressed, a click can be heard just before the pedal bottoms out. If the click is not heard, loosen the locknut and extend the switch until the pedal lever makes contact with the switch and the switch clicks.

On 1990–92 300ZX, before adjusting the kickdown switch, make sure the accelerator cable is properly adjusted. Then, check the clearance between the stopper rubber and the threaded end of the switch with the accelerator cable fully depressed. The clearance should be 0.012–0.039 in. (0.3–1.0mm). If the clearance is not as

Downshift solenoid location—200SX and 1987–89 300ZX

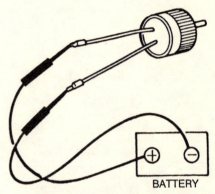

Check the downshift solenoid by applying battery voltage

specified, adjust by loosening the switch locknut and turning the switch in or out. Tighten the locknut and check the clearance again.

## DOWNSHIFT SOLENOID CHECK

### 200SX and 1988–89 300ZX

The solenoid is controlled by a downshift switch on the accelerator linkage inside the vehicle. To test the switch and solenoid operation, preform the following:
1. Turn the ignition to the ON position.
2. Push the accelerator all the way down to actuate the switch.
3. The solenoid should "click" when actuated. The solenoid is screwed into the outside of the case. If there is no click, check the switch, wiring, and solenoid.
4. To remove the solenoid, first drain 2–3 pints of fluid, then unscrew the unit.
5. Apply battery voltage to the switch and listen for the click. If no click is audible, replace the switch or repair the wiring.

# AUTOMATIC TRANSAXLE

For further information on transmissions/transaxles, please refer to "Chilton's Guide to Transmission Repair".

## Transaxle Assembly

### REMOVAL & INSTALLATION

#### 1988 Maxima

NOTE: The engine/transaxle unit must be removed and installed as a unit. After removal, the transaxle may be separated from the engine.

1. Remove the transaxle/engine as an assembly.
2. Remove the transaxle-to-engine mounting bolts and then carefully draw out the rear plate.
3. Remove the bolts securing the torque converter to the driveplate.
4. Before removing the torque converter, use chalk or paint to matchmark at least 2 parts so they may be replaced in their original positions during installation. Remove the torque converter.
5. Check the driveplate runout with a dial indicator. Runout must be no more than 0.020 in.
6. If the torque converter was removed from the engine for any reason, after it is installed, the distance from the face of the converter to the edge of the converter housing must be checked prior to installing the transaxle. This is done to ensure proper installation of the torque converter. The dimension should be 0.709 in. (18mm) or more.
7. During installation of the transaxle/engine assembly, observe the following:

 a. When installing the torque converter to the driveplate, be certain the matchmarks made during removal are in alignment. Apply Loctite® or a similar sealing compound to the converter-to-driveplate bolts before installation.

 b. After the torque converter has been reinstalled, rotate the crankshaft a few times to ensure that the transaxle rotates freely, with no binding.

 c. Adjust the control cable and check the inhibitor switch.

 d. After installation of the engine/transaxle assembly into the vehicle, fill the transaxle and engine with the proper amounts of fluids, then road test the vehicle.

#### Pulsar, Sentra, Stanza and 1989–92 Maxima

1. Disconnect the negative battery cable.
2. Raise and support the vehicle safely.
3. Remove the left front tire.
4. Drain the transaxle fluid.
5. Remove the left side fender protector.
6. Remove the halfshafts.

NOTE: Be careful not to damage the oil seals when removing the halfshafts. After removing the halfshafts, install a suitable bar so the side gears will not rotate and fall into the differential case.

7. On Stanza Wagon, disconnect and remove the forward exhaust pipe.
8. Disconnect the speedometer cable.
9. Disconnect the throttle wire (cable) connection.
10. Remove the control cable rear end from the unit and remove the oil level gauge tube.
11. Place a suitable jack under the transaxle and engine. Do not place the jack under the oil pan drain plug. Support the engine with wooden blocks placed between the engine and the center member.
12. Disconnect the oil cooler and charging tubes. Plug the tube ends to prevent leakage.
13. Remove the engine motor mount securing bolts, as required.
14. Remove the starter motor and disconnect all electrical wires from the transaxle.
15. Loosen and remove all but 3 of the bolts holding the transaxle to the engine. Leave the 3 bolts in to support the weight of the transaxle while removing the converter bolts.
16. Remove the driveplate or dust covers.
17. Remove the bolts holding the torque torque converter to the driveplate. Rotate the crankshaft to gain access to each bolt. Before separating the torque converter, place chalk marks on 2 parts for alignment purposes during installation.

NOTE: The transaxle bolts are different lengths. Tag each bolt according to location to ensure proper installation.

18. Remove the 3 temporary bolts. Move the jack gradually until the transaxle can be lowered and removed from the vehicle through the left side wheel housing.
19. Check the driveplate runout with a dial indictator. Runout must be no more than 0.020 in.

**To install:**

20. If the torque converter was re-

moved from the engine for any reason, after it is installed, the distance from the face of the converter to the edge of the converter housing must be checked prior to installing the transaxle. This is done to ensure proper installation of the torque converter. On Maxima, the distance should be 0.71 in. (18mm) or more. On Pulsar with RL3F01A transaxles, it should be 0.831 in. (21mm) or more. On Pulsar with RL4F02A transaxles, it should be 0.748 in. (19mm) or more. On Stanza, it should be 0.75 in. (19mm) or more.

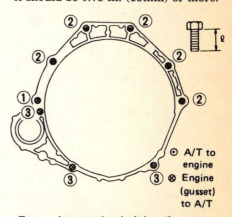

Transaxle mounting bolt locations on 1989–92 Maxima; bolt (1) is 60mm, bolt (2) is 45mm, bolt (3) is 25mm

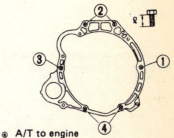

Transaxle mounting bolt locations on 1988–89 Stanza; bolt (1) is 85mm, bolt (2) is 50mm, bolt (3) is 70mm, bolt (4) is 25mm

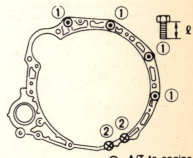

Transaxle mounting bolt locations on 1990–92 Stanza; bolt (1) is 45mm and bolt (2) is 20mm

21. Raise the transaxle onto the engine and install the torque coverter-to-driveplate bolts. Torque the bolts to specification. Install 3 bolts to support the transaxle while tighten the converter bolts.

**NOTE: After the converter is installed, rotate the crankshaft several times to make sure the transaxle rotates freely and does not bind.**

22. Install the driveplate or dust covers.
23. Install the transaxle mounting bolts. On 1989–92 Maxima and 1988–92 Stanza, torque the bolts as follows: On 1989–92 Maxima, tighten bolts (1) and (3) to 22–30 ft. lbs. (30–40 Nm) and bolts (2) to 29–36 ft. lbs. (39–49 Nm). On 1988–89 Stanza, tighten bolts (1), (2) and (3) to 29–36 ft. lbs. Tighten bolts (4) to 22–30 ft. lbs. (30–40 Nm). On 1990–92 Stanza, tighten bolts (1) to 29–36 ft. lbs. (39–49 Nm) and bolts (2) to 22–30 ft. lbs. (30–40 Nm)
24. Connect the transaxle wiring and install the starter.
25. Install the engine mounts, if removed.
26. Connect the oil cooler and charging tubes.
27. Remove the engine and transaxle supports.
28. Install the oil level gauge tube and control cable rear end.
29. Connect the throttle wire (cable) connection.
30. Connect the speedometer cable.
31. On Stanza Wagon, install the front exhaust pipe using new gaskets.
32. Install the halfshafts.
33. Install the left side fender protector.
34. Mount the left front tire and lower the vehicle.
35. Fill the transaxle and engine with the proper amounts of fluids.
36. Adjust the control cable and throttle wire.
37. Check the inhibitor switch for proper operation.
38. Road test the vehicle.

## THROTTLE WIRE ADJUSTMENT

The throttle wire is adjusted by means of double nuts on the throttle body.

**NOTE: On 1989–92 Maxima and 1990–92 Stanza, there is no throttle wire adjustment.**

### Except 1990 Pulsar

1. Loosen the adjusting nuts.
2. With the throttle fully opened, turn the threaded shaft inward as far

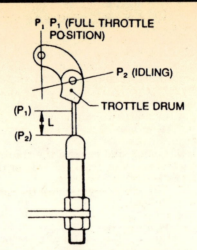

Throttle wire stroke—Sentra, 1988–89 Pulsar and 1988 Maxima

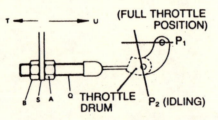

Throttle wire adjustment—Sentra, 1988–89 Pulsar and 1987–88 Maxima

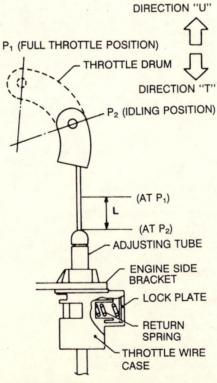

Throttle wire stroke adjustment—1990 Pulsar

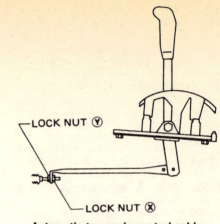

Automatic transaxle control cable adjustment—all vehicles

as it will go and then tighten the first nut against the bracket.
3. Back off the first nut ¾–1¼ turns on the 1988 Maxima; and 2¾–3¼ turns on the 1988–89 Stanza (including Wagon) and then tighten the second nut against the bracket. On 1988–89 Pulsar back off the nut 2¾–3¼ turns (RL4F02A transaxles) and 1–1½ turns (RL3F01A transaxles) and tighten the nut.
4. Tighten both double nuts to 5.8–7.2 ft. lbs. (8–10 Nm). The throttle drum should be held securely in the full open position.
5. On 1988–89 Stanza and and 1988 Maxima vehicles, check that the throttle wire stroke between full throttle and idling is 1.54–1.69 in. (39–43mm). On the 1988–90 Pulsar/Sentra it should be 1.079–1.236 in. (27.4–31.4mm).

### 1990 Pulsar

1. Remove the air cleaner cover.
2. While pressing on the lock plate, move the adjusting tube in the proper direction.
3. Return the lock plate to its original position.
4. Move the throttle drum from position $P_1$ to $P_2$ quickly.
5. Check that the throttle wire stroke (**L**) between full throttle and idling is 1.079–1.236 in. (27.4–31.4mm). Marking the throttle wire with paint dabs or a colored marker will help in measuring the throttle wire stroke.
6. Adjust the throttle wire stroke only if the throttle and accelerator wires are installed. After adjustment, make sure the parting line is straight.

## CONTROL CABLE ADJUSTMENT

On all vehicles, move the selector from the **P** range through each gear to the **1** range. At each gear selection, the detent should be felt. If the detents cannot be felt or if the gear shift indicator pointer is not aligned properly, then the control, cable must be adjusted as follows:

1. Position the control lever (gear selector) in **P**.

2. Connect the control cable end to the lever in the transaxle unit and tighten the cable securing bolt.

3. Move the control lever from **P** to the **1** position. Be certain the lever works smoothly and quietly.

4. Position the lever in **P** once again. Make sure the lever locks into this position.

5. Loosen the cable adjusting locknuts.

6. While holding the select rod horizontal, tighten locknut **X** until it contacts the end of the rod. Then tighten locknut **Y**.

7. Move the control lever through all of its detents again and check for smooth and quiet operation.

8. Lubricate the spring washer at the end of the cable with multi-purpose grease.

# TRANSFER CASE

## Transfer Case Assembly

### REMOVAL & INSTALLATION

#### Sentra and Stanza Wagon

1. Disconnect the negative battery cable.

2. Drain the gear oil from the transaxle and the transfer case.

3. Disconnect and remove the forward exhaust pipe.

4. Using chalk or paint, matchmark the flanges on the driveshaft and then unbolt the driveshaft from the transfer case.

5. On Sentra, unbolt and remove the transaxle support rod from the transfer case.

6. Unbolt and remove the transfer control actuator from the side of the transfer case as necessary.

7. Disconnect and remove the right side halfshaft.

8. Disconnect the speedometer gear from the transfer case.

9. Unbolt and remove the front, rear and side transfer case gussets (support members).

10. Use a hydraulic floor jack and a block of wood to support the transfer case, remove the transfer case-to-transaxle mounting bolts and then remove the case.

**To install:**

11. Lubricate the lips of the transfer side oil seal (in transaxle), adapter oil seal (in transfer) and driveshaft oil seal. Use a suitable multi-purpose grease.

12. Apply KP510–00150 or equivalent sealant to the ring gear oil seal seating surface prior to installation of the transfer case.

13. Raise and and mount the transfer. Tighten the transfer case-to-transaxle mounting bolts and the transfer case gusset mounting bolts to 22–30 ft. lbs. (30–40 Nm) on 1988 vehicles. On all other years, torque the transfer rear gusset bolts to 29–36 ft. lbs. (39–49 Nm).

**NOTE: Be careful not to damage the transaxle oil seal when inserting thew splined portion of the transfer ring gear into the transaxle.**

14. Install the front, rear and side transfer case gussets.

15. Connect the speedometer cable.

16. Install the right side halfshaft.

17. Connect the transfer control actuator to the side of the transfer case as necessary.

18. On Sentra, connect the transfer support rod to the transfer case.

19. Connect the driveshaft to the transfer case by aligning the matchmarks. Torque the driveshaft bolts to 25–33 ft. lbs. (34–44 Nm) on both Sentra and Stanza.

**NOTE: When connecting the drive shaft, be careful not to damage the driveshaft and adapter oil seals.**

20. Connect the forward exhaust pipe using new gaskets.

21. Fill the transfer case to the proper level with gear oil. The transfer case and the transaxle use different types and weights of lubricant.

22. Connect the negative battery cable.

23. Check the transfer case for proper operation.

# FRONT SUSPENSION

## MacPherson Strut

### REMOVAL & INSTALLATION

1. Raise and support the vehicle safely.

2. Remove the front wheels.

3. Disconnect and plug the brake line if it interferes with removal of the strut.

4. Disconnect the tension rod and stabilizer bar from the transverse link.

5. Unbolt the steering arm from the lower end of the strut.

6. Support the bottom of the strut with a jack or equivalent. On 240SX, place matchmarks on the strut lower bracket and camber adjusting pin for assembly reference.

7. Open the hood and remove the nuts holding the top of the strut. On 300ZX and Maxima equipped with adjustable or sonar suspension shocks, disconnect the electrical lead from the actuating unit.

8. Lower the jack slowly and cautiously until the strut assembly can be removed.

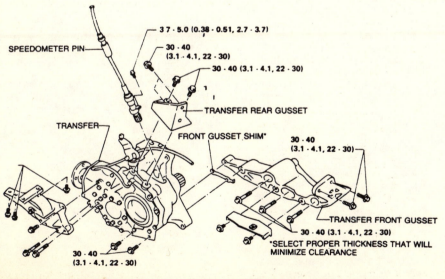

SPEEDOMETER PIN
3 7 - 5.0 (0.38 - 0.51, 2.7 - 3.7)
30 - 40 (3.1 - 4.1, 22 - 30)
30 - 40 (3.1 - 4.1, 22 - 30)
TRANSFER
TRANSFER REAR GUSSET
FRONT GUSSET SHIM*
30 - 40 (3.1 - 4.1, 22 - 30)
TRANSFER FRONT GUSSET
30 - 40 (3.1 - 4.1, 22 - 30)
30 - 40 (3.1 - 4.1, 22 - 30)
*SELECT PROPER THICKNESS THAT WILL MINIMIZE CLEARANCE

**Transfer case removal – Stanza 4WD (Sentra 4WD similar)**

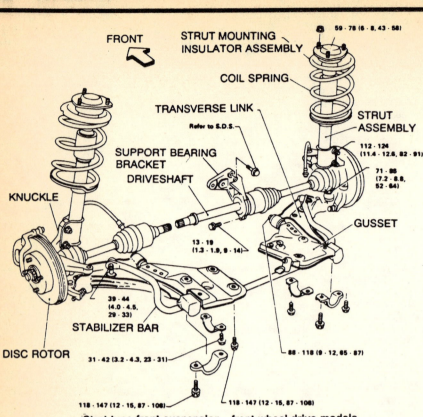

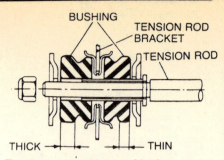

Tension rod bushing positioning — rear wheel drive models

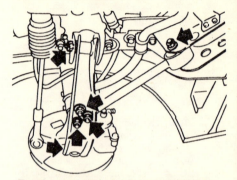

Tension rod and stabilizer bar ataching points — 240SX

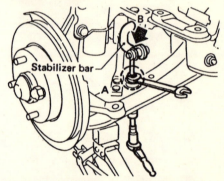

Hold the stabilizer connecting rod with a wrench when removing and installing the mounting nuts

Strut-type front suspension — front wheel drive models

9. During installation, observing the following:

a. The self locking nuts holding the top of the strut must be replaced.

c. On 240SX, make sure the matchmarks on the bracket and the camber adjusting pin are aligned properly.

d. On 1989–92 Maxima with sonar suspension, before installing the actuator ensure the output shaft on the inside of the actuating unit is aligned with the shock absorber control rod. If this is not done, the actuator will be damaged.

## Tension Rod and Stabilizer Bar

### REMOVAL & INSTALLATION

#### 200SX, 240SX and 300SX

1. Raise and support the vehicle safely.

2. Remove the tension rod-to-frame lock nuts.

3. Remove the 2 mounting bolts at the transverse link, lower control arm, and then slide out the tension rod.

4. On 240SX, to remove the tension rod, remove the bolt and nut that holds the rod to the tension rod bracket (through the bushing), then swing the rod upward and remove the tranverse link bolts, nuts, bushings and washers. If the bushings are worn replace them.

5. Unbolt the stabilizer bar at each transverse link or connecting rod. On 240SX, engage the flats of stabilizer bar connecting rod with a wrench to keep the rod from moving when removing the nuts.

6. Remove the 4 stabilizer bar bracket bolts, and remove the stabilizer bar.

7. During installation observe the following:

a. Tighten the stabilizer bar-to-transverse link bolts to 12–16 ft. lbs. (16–22 Nm) and 34–38 ft. lbs. (46–52 Nm) on 240SX.

b. Tighten the stabilizer bar bracket bolts to 22–29 ft. lbs. (29–39 Nm) and 29–36 ft. lbs. (39–49 Nm) on 240SX.

c. Tighten the tension rod-to-transverse link nuts to 31–43 ft. lbs. (42–59 Nm). On 240SX, torque the plain nuts to 65–80 ft. lbs. (88–108 Nm) and the nuts with bushings and washers to 14–22 ft. lbs. (20–29 Nm). Make sure to hold the connecting rod stationary.

d. Tighten the tension rod-to-frame nut (bushing end) to 33–40 ft. lbs. (44–54 Nm). Always use a new locknut when reconnecting the tension rod to the frame.

e. Be certain the tension rod bushings are installed properly. Make sure the stabilzer bar ball joint socket is properly positioned.

**NOTE: Never tighten any bolts or nuts to their final torque unless the vehicle is resting, unsupported, on the wheels (unladen).**

#### Pulsar, Sentra, Stanza Wagon and 1989–92 Maxima

1. Raise and support the vehicle safely. Disconnect the parking brake cable at the equalizer on the Stanza Wagon.

2. On the Stanza Wagon (4WD), remove the mounting nuts for the transaxle support rod and the transaxle control rod.

3. Disconnect the front exhaust

pipe at the manifold and position it aside (not required on Maxima).

4. On the Stanza Wagon (4WD), matchmark the flanges and then separate the driveshaft from the transfer case.

5. Remove the stabilizer bar-to-transverse link (lower, control arm) mounting bolts. Engage the flats of stabilizer bar connecting rod with a wrench to keep the rod from moving when removing (and installing) the bolts.

6. Matchmark the stabilizer bar to the mounting clamps.

7. Remove the stabilizer bar mounting clamp bolts and then pull the bar out, around the link and exhaust pipe.

8. Installation is the reverse of the removal procedure. Never tighten the mounting bolts unless the vehicle is resting on the ground with normal weight upon the wheels. On Pulsar and Sentra, be sure the stabilizer bar ball joint socket is properly positioned.

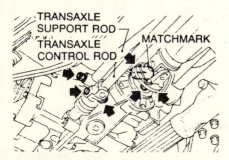

**Removing the stabilizer bar on the Stanza wagon (4wd)**

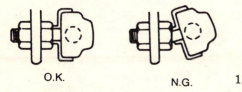

**Ball joint socket positioning**

## Lower Ball Joints

### INSPECTION

#### Dial Indicator Method

1. Raise and support the vehicle safely.

2. Clamp a dial indicator to the transverse link and place the tip of the dial on the lower edge of the brake caliper.

3. Zero the indicator.

4. Make sure the front wheels are straight ahead and the brake pedal is fully depressed.

5. Insert a long prybar between the

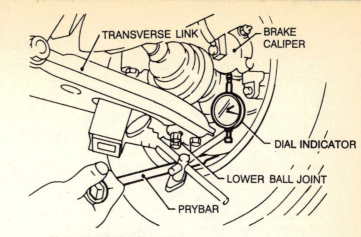

**Measuring ball joint endplay with a dial indicator**

transverse link and the inner rim of the wheel.

6. Push down and release the prybar and observe the reading (deflection) on the dial indicator. Take several readings and use the maximum dial indicator deflection as the ball joint vertical endplay. Make sure to **0** the indicator after each reading. If the reading is not within specifications, replace the transverse link or the ball joint. Ball joint vertical endplay specifications are as follows:

    200SX and 240SX – 0 in. (0mm)
    300ZX
      1988–89 – 0.098 in. (2.5mm) or less

      1990–92 – 0 in. (0mm)
    Maxima
      1988 – 0.098 in. (2.5mm) or less
      1989–92 – 0 in. (0mm)
    Pulsar
      1988 – 0.098 in. (2.5mm) or less
      1989–90 – 0 in. (0mm)
    Sentra
      1988–92 – 0 in. (0mm)
    Stanza
      1988–89 – 0.004–0.039 in. (0.1–1.0mm)
      1990–92 – 0 in. (0mm)
      Stanza Wagon – 0.098 in. (2.5mm) or less

#### Visual Approximation Method

The lower ball joint should be replaced when play becomes excessive. An effective way to visually approximate ball joint verticle endplay without the use of a dial indicator is to preform the following:

1. Raise and safely support the vehicle until the wheel is clear of the ground. Do not place the jack under the ball joint; it must be unloaded.

2. Place a long prybar under the tire and move the wheel up and down. Keep one hand on top of the tire while doing this.

3. If ¼ in. or more of play exists at the top of the tire, the ball joint should

be replaced. Be sure the wheel bearings are properly adjusted before making this measurement. A double check can be made; while the tire is being moved up and down, observe the ball joint. If play is seen, replace the ball joint.

### REMOVAL & INSTALLATION

#### Rear Wheel Drive

On 200SX and 1988–89 300SX, there is a plugged hole in the bottom of the joint for installation of a grease fitting. The ball joint should be greased every 30,000 miles.

**NOTE: The transverse link (lower control arm) must be removed and then the ball joint must be pressed out.**

1. Raise and support the vehicle safely.

2. Remove the front wheels.

3. Separate the knuckle arm from the tie rod using the proper tool.

4. Separate the knuckle arm from the strut.

5. Remove the stabilizer bar and tension rod.

6. Remove the transverse link and knuckle arm.

7. Separate the knuckle arm from the ball joint with a suitable press.

8. Replace the transverse link/ball joint assembly.

9. Installation is the reverse of the removal procedure.

#### Front Wheel Drive

1. Raise and support the vehicle safely.

2. Remove the front wheels.

3. Remove the wheel bearing locknut.

4. Separate the tie rod end ball joint from the steering knuckle with a ball joint remover, being careful not to

damage the ball joint dust cover if the ball joint is to be used again.

5. On 1989–92 Maxima and 1990–92 Stanza, loosen, but do not remove the strut upper nuts.

6. Remove the nut that attaches the ball joint to the transverse link.

7. Separate the halfshaft from the knuckle by lightly taping the end of the shaft.

8. Separate the ball joint from the knuckle using the proper tool.

9. Tighten the ball stud attaching nut (from ball joint-to-steering knuckle) to 22–29 ft. lbs. (30–39 Nm), and the ball joint-to-transverse link bolts to 40–47 ft. lbs. (54–64 Nm) except on Stanza. On Stanza, torque the bolts to 56–80 ft. lbs. (76–108 Nm).

## Lower Control Arm (Transverse Link)

### REMOVAL & INSTALLATION

#### 200SX, 240SX and 300ZX

1. Raise and support the vehicle safely.

2. Remove the front wheels.

3. Remove the cotter pin and castle nut from the side rod (steering arm) ball joint and separate the ball joint from the side rod using the proper tool.

4. Separate the steering knuckle arm from the MacPherson strut.

5. Remove the tension rod and stabilizer bar from the lower arm.

6. Remove the nuts or bolts connecting the lower control arm (transverse link) to the suspension crossmember.

7. Remove the lower control arm (transverse link) with the suspension ball joint and knuckle arm still attached.

8. When installing the control arm, temporarily tighten the nuts and/or bolts securing the control arm to the suspension crossmember. Tighten them fully only after the vehicle is sitting on its wheels. Lubricate the ball joints after assembly.

#### 1988–89 Maxima

1. Raise and support the vehicle safely.

2. Remove the front wheels.

3. Remove the nut fastening the link between the stabilizer bar and the control arm to the control arm.

4. Remove the 3 nuts fastening the ball joint to the lower control arm.

5. Remove the 2 bolts attaching the front and rear hinge joints of the control arm to the body.

6. Remove the control arm.

7. Installation is the reverse of the removal procedure. Tighten all bolts and nuts until they are snug enough to support the weight of the vehicle, but not quite fully tightened. Lower the vehicle so it rests on the ground. Tighten the forward bolts attaching the hinge joint to the body to 65–87 ft. lbs. (88–118 Nm). Tighten the rear hinge joint bolts to 87–108 ft. lbs. (118–147 Nm) and the ball joint mounting nuts to 56–80 ft. lbs. (76–108 Nm). Check the front end alignment.

### 1989–92 Maxima and 1990–92 Stanza

1. Raise the vehicle and support it safely.

2. Unbolt and remove the stabilizer bar. The bar is removed by unfastening the clamp bolts and the bolts that hold the bar to the transverse link gusset plate. When removing the clamps, note the relationship between the clamp and paint mark on the bar.

3. Unbolt and remove the transverse link and gusset.

4. Inspect the transverse link, gusset and bushings for cracks, damage and deformation.

5. To install, bolt the transverse link and gusset into place. Lower the vehicle and torque the the bolts and nuts in the proper sequence as illustrated. Torque the nuts to 30–35 ft. lbs. (41–51 Nm) and the bolts to 87–108 ft. lbs. (118–147 Nm). The vehicle

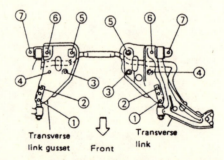

**Transverse link and gusset bolt torque sequence—1989–92 Maxima and 1990–92 Stanza**

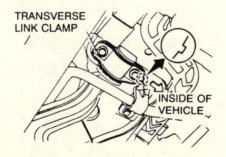

**Transverse link clamp positioning—Pulsar and Sentra**

must at curb weight and the tires must be on the ground. After installation is complete, check the front end alignment.

### Pulsar and Sentra

1. Raise the vehicle and support it safely.

2. Remove the front wheels.

3. Remove the wheel bearing locknut.

4. Remove the tie rod ball joint with a suitable puller.

5. Remove the lower strut-to-knuckle mounting bolts and separate the strut from the knuckle.

6. Separate the outer end of the halfshaft from the steering knuckle by carefully tapping it with a rubber mallet. Be sure to cover the CV-joints with a shop rag.

7. Using a suitable ball joint removal tool, separate the lower ball joint stud from the steering knuckle.

8. Unbolt and remove the transverse link and ball joint as an assembly.

9. Installation is the reverse of the removal procedure. Make sure the tab on the transverse link clamp is pointing in the proper direction. Final tightening of all bolts should take place with the weight of the vehicle on the wheels. Check wheel alignment.

### 1988–89 Stanza

**NOTE: Always use new nuts when installing the ball joint to the control arm.**

1. Raise the vehicle and support it safely.

2. Remove the front wheels.

3. Remove the lower ball joint bolts from the control arm.

**NOTE: If equipped with a stabilizer bar, disconnect it at the control arm.**

4. Remove the control arm-to-body bolts.

5. Remove the gusset.

6. Remove the control arm.

7. Installation is the reverse of the removal procedure using the following torque specifications: gusset-to-body bolts to 87–108 ft. lbs. (118–147 Nm); control arm securing nut to 87–108 ft. lbs. (118–147 Nm) and lower ball joint-to-control arm nuts to 56–80 ft. lbs. (76–108 Nm). When installing the link, tighten the nut securing the link spindle to the gusset. Final tightening should be made with the weight of the vehicle on the wheels.

**NOTE: On the Stanza Wagon, make sure to torque the gusset bolts in the proper sequence.**

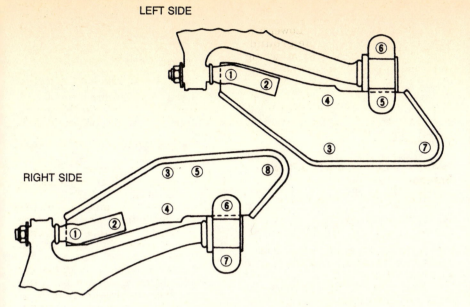

LEFT SIDE

RIGHT SIDE

Transverse link gusset bolt torque sequence—Stanza wagon

# Front Wheel Bearings

## ADJUSTMENT

NOTE: For wheel bearing procedures on front wheel drive vehicles, please refer to the "Drive Axle" section.

### 200SX and 1988–89 300ZX

1. Raise and support the vehicle safely.
2. Remove the front wheels.
3. While rotating the brake disc, torque wheel bearing lock nut to 18–22 ft. lbs.
4. Loosen locknut approximately 60 degrees on all vehicles. Install adjusting cap and align groove of nut with hole in spindle. If alignment cannot be obtained, change position of adjusting cap. Also, if alignment cannot be obtained, loosen locknut slightly but not more than 15 degrees.
5. Install the front wheels and lower the vehicle.

### 240SX

There is no procedure for torquing the front wheel bearings due to the design of the bearing. Once the final torque is applied to the wheel bearing axle nut and the axial play is checked, no further adjustment is either necessary or possible.

Check the torque of the wheel bearing locknut. This value is 108–159 ft. lbs. (147–216 Nm). Then, mount a dial indicator to the face of the hub and check the axial play. It should not exceed 0.0012 in. (0.03mm). If the axial play is not as specified, replace the wheel bearing.

### 1990–92 300ZX

1. Raise the vehicle and suppport safely.
2. Remove the front wheels.
3. Prior to checking the bearing pre-load, spin the wheel hub at least 10 revolutions in both directions to seat the bearing.
4. To check the pre-load: connect a spring scale of known calibration to a wheel hub bolt and measure the turning torque. If an NSK wheel bearing is used, the turning torque should be 1.3–8.4 lbs. (5.9–37.3 N). For NTN bearings, the turning torque should be 1.8–13.0 lbs. (7.8–57.9 N).
5. To check the axial endplay: mount a dial indicator so the stylus of the dial rests on the face of the hub and check the wheel bearing axial endplay by attempting to rock the wheel hub in and out. The endplay should be 0.0020 in. (0.05mm) or less.
6. Mount the front wheels and lower the vehicle.

## REMOVAL & INSTALLATION

### 200SX and 1988–89 300ZX

1. Raise and support the vehicle safely.
2. Remove the front wheels. Work off center hub cap by using thin tool. If necessary tap around it with a soft hammer while removing. Pry off cotter pin and take out adjusting cap. Apply the parking brake firmly and remove the wheel bearing nut. The nut will require a good deal of force to remove it.
3. Unbolt the caliper and move it aside. Do not disconnect the hose from the caliper. Do not allow the caliper to hang by the hose; support the caliper with a length of wire or rest it on a suspension member.
4. Remove the wheel hub, disc brake rotor and bearing from the spindle. During removal, capture the outer bearing to prevent it from hitting the ground.
5. To replace the bearing outer race, drive it out with a suitable brass drift and mallet.
**To install:**
6. Install the new bearing outer race using a suitable race installation tool.
7. Install a new oil seal so the words "BEARING SIDE" face the inner side of the hub. Coat the lip of the seal with multi-purpose grease.
8. Pack the bearings, hub, hub cap and hub cap O-ring with multi-purpose grease. If the hub cap O-ring is crimped, replace it.
9. Install the inner and outer bearings.
10. Install the wheel hub and rotor disc onto the spindle.
11. Coat the threaded portion of the spindle shaft and the contact surface between the lockwasher and outer wheel bearing with multi-purpose grease.
12. Install the wheel bearing locknut and adjust the bearing pre-load as described above. Use a new cotter pin.
13. Mount the brake caliper assembly.
14. Install the front wheels and lower the vehicle.

### 240SX

1. Raise and support the vehicle safely.
2. Remove the front wheels.
3. Work off center hub cap by using a suitable thin tool. If necessary tap around it with a soft hammer while removing. Pry off cotter pin and take out adjusting cap.
4. Apply the parking brake firmly and remove the wheel bearing nut. The nut will require a good deal of force to remove it.
5. Unbolt the caliper and move it aside. Do not disconnect the hose from the caliper. Do not allow the caliper to hang by the hose; support the caliper with a length of wire or rest it on a suspension member.
6. Pull the brake disc and wheel hub from the spindle.
7. Separate the tie rod and lower ball joints using the proper tool.
8. Place matchmarks on the strut lower bracket and camber adjusting

pin for assembly reference. Remove the lower bracket bolts and nuts. Remove the wheel hub and knuckle assembly.

9. Remove the bearing retaining ring from the wheel hub.

10. Press the bearing assembly from the wheel hub. Apply pressure from the outside of the hub to remove the bearing.

**To install:**

11. Press the new bearing assembly into the hub from the inside.

NOTE: **Do not press the on the inner race of the wheel bearing assembly. Do not lubricate the surfaces of mating surfaces of the wheel bearing outer race and wheel with grease or oil. Be careful not to damage the grease seal.**

12. Install the bearing retaining ring.

13. Coat the lip of the grease seal with multi-purpose grease.

14. Manuever the wheel hub and axle assembly onto the lower mounting bracket and install the bracket bolts and nuts. Make sure the matchmarks on the bracket and the camber adjusting pin are aligned properly.

15. Connect the lower and tie rod ball joints.

16. Push the brake disc and wheel hub onto the spindle.

17. Install the brake caliper assembly.

18. Check the wheel bearing pre-load.

19. Install a new locknut cotter pin. Install the bearing hub cap after packing it with multi-purpose grease.

20. Mount the the front wheels and lower the vehicle.

### 1990–92 300ZX

1. Raise and support the vehicle safely.

2. Remove the front wheels.

3. Unbolt the caliper and move it aside. Do not disconnect the hose from the caliper. Do not allow the caliper to hang by the hose; support the caliper with a length of wire or rest it on a suspension member.

4. Separate the tie rod and lower ball joints using the proper tool.

NOTE: **The steering knuckle is made of an aluminum alloy. Be careful no to strike it when removing the ball joints.**

5. Remove the kinpin lower nut and remove the steering knuckle assembly.

6. Remove the hub cap, wheel bearing locknut, sensor rotor (with ABS) or washer (without ABS).

7. Remove the wheel hub with a suitable drift.

8. Remove the wheel bearing retaining ring.

9. Press the wheel bearing from the knuckle.

10. Drive out the wheel bearing inner race to the ouside of the wheel hub.

11. Remove the grease seal and splash guard (baffle plate).

**To install:**

12. From the outside of the knuckle, press the new wheel bearing assembly into the knuckle.

NOTE: **Do not press the on the inner race of the wheel bearing assembly. Do not lubricate the surfaces of mating surfaces of the wheel bearing outer race and wheel with grease or oil. Be careful not to damage the grease seal.**

13. Install the bearing retaining ring. Make sure it seats evenly in the groove of the knuckle.

14. Coat the lip of the grease seal with multi-purpose grease and install.

15. Install the spash guard.

16. Press the wheel hub into the steering knuckle.

17. Install the washer (without ABS), sensor rotor (with ABS) and wheel bearing locknut. Torque the locknut to 152–210 ft. lbs. (206–284 Nm). Stake the locknut tabs using a small cold chisel.

18. Place the hub cap onto the knuckle and tap it into place using a rubber or plastic mallet. Once the cap is seated lightly into the knuckle, install the cap retaining bolts and torque to 8–12 ft. lbs. (11–16 Nm).

19. Mount the steering knuckle assembly and tighten the lower king pin nut.

20. Connect the tie rod and lower ball joints using the proper tool.

21. Install the brake caliper assembly.

22. Ajust the wheel bearing pre-load and axial endplay.

23. Mount the front wheels and lower the vehicle.

# REAR SUSPENSION

## Shock Absorbers

### REMOVAL & INSTALLATION

#### 200SX and Stanza Wagon (2WD)

1. Open the trunk and remove the cover panel, if necessary, to expose the shock mounts. Pry off the mount covers, if equipped.

2. Remove the 2 nuts holding the top of the shock absorber.

3. Unbolt the bottom of the shock absorber.

4. Remove the shock absorber.

5. Installation is the reverse of removal. Final tightening of the lower end of the shock absorber should be performed with the wheels on the ground in the unladen position.

### 1988–89 300ZX

#### WITH ADJUSTABLE SHOCKS

1. Open the hatch and remove the luggage side trim.

2. Disconnect the sub-harness connector from the top of the shock.

3. Remove the 2 upper retaining nuts.

4. Remove the lower thru-bolt.

5. Remove the shock absorber.

6. Installation is the reverse of the removal procedure. Final tightening of the shock absorber upper and lower end should be performed with the wheels on the ground in the unladen position. Torque the bottom bolt to 43–58 ft. lbs. (59–78 Nm) and top nuts to 23–31 ft. lbs. (31–42 Nm)

#### WITHOUT ADJUSTABLE SHOCKS

1. Open the hatch and remove the luggage side trim.

2. Remove the 2 upper retaining nuts.

3. Remove the lower thru-bolt.

4. Remove the shock absorber.

5. Installation is the reverse of the removal procedure. Final tightening of the shock absorber upper and lower end should be performed with the wheels on the ground in the unladen position. Torque the bottom bolt to 43–58 ft. lbs. (59–78 Nm) and the 2 top nuts to 23–31 ft. lbs. (31–42 Nm).

## MacPherson Strut

### REMOVAL & INSTALLATION

#### 240SX and 1990–92 300ZX

1. Block the front wheels.

2. Raise and support the vehicle safely.

NOTE: **The vehicle should be far enough off the ground so the rear spring does not support any weight.**

3. Working inside the luggage compartment, turn and remove the caps above the strut mounts. Remove the strut mounting nuts.

4. Remove the mounting bolt for the strut at the lower arm (transverse link) and then lift out the strut.

5. Installation is in the reverse order of removal. Install the upper end first and secure with the nuts snugged

down but not fully tightened. Attach the lower end of the strut to the transverse link and the tighten the upper nuts to 12–14 ft. lbs. (16–19 Nm). Tighten the lower mounting bolt to 65–80 ft. lbs. (88–108 Nm).

### Pulsar and Sentra (2WD)

1. Raise and support the rear of the vehicle safely.
2. Remove the rear wheels.
3. Disconnect the brake tube and parking brake cable.
4. If necessary, remove the brake assembly and wheel bearing.
5. Disconnect the parallel links and radius rod from the strut or knuckle.
6. Support the strut assembly.
7. Remove the strut upper end nuts and then remove the strut from the vehicle.
8. Installation is the reverse of the removal procedure. Tighten the radius rod-to-knuckle nuts to 43–61 ft. lbs. (59–83 Nm), the strut-to-knuckle and parallel link-to-knuckle bolts to 72–87 ft. lbs. (98–118 Nm) and the strut-to-body nuts to 18–22 ft. lbs. (25–29 Nm).

### Sentra (4WD) and Stanza Wagon (4WD)

1. Block the front wheels.
2. Raise and support the vehicle safely.
3. Position a suitable floor jack under the transverse link on the side of the strut to be removed. Raise it just enough to support the strut.
4. Open the rear of the vehicle and remove the 3 nuts that attach the top of the strut to the body.
5. Remove the rear wheels.
6. Remove the brake line from its bracket and position it aside. Do not disconnect the brake line.
7. Remove the 2 lower strut-to-knuckle mounting bolts.
8. Carefully lower the floor jack and remove the strut.
9. Installation is the reverse order of removal. Final tightening of the strut mounting bolts should take place with the wheels on the ground and the vehicle unladen. Tighten the upper strut-to-body nuts to 33–40 ft. lbs. (45–60 Nm). Tighten the lower strut-to-knuckle bolts to 111–120 ft. lbs. (151–163 Nm).

### 1988 Maxima and 1988–89 Stanza

#### RIGHT STRUT

1. Unclip the rear brake line at the strut. Do not disconnect it.
2. Remove the radius rod mounting bolt, radius rod mounting bracket.
3. Remove the 2 parallel link mounting bolts.

4. Remove the rear seat and parcel shelf.
5. On Maxima with adjustable suspension, disconnect the sub-harness connector and the connector from the cap. Grasp the cap connector from both sides during removal to avoid damage. This connector is very sensitive.
6. Position a suitable floor jack under the strut and raise it just enough to support the strut.

NOTE: **Do not support the strut at the parallel links or the radius rods.**

7. Remove the 3 upper strut mounting nuts and then lift out the strut and rear axle assembly.
8. Installation is the reverse of the removal procedure. Tighten all bolts sufficiently to safely support the vehicle and then lower the vehicle to the ground so it rests on its own weight. Tighten the upper strut mounting nuts to 23–31 ft. lbs. (31–42 Nm); the radius rod bracket bolts to 43–58 ft. lbs. (59–78 Nm) and the parallel link mounting bolts to 65–87 ft. lbs. (88–118 Nm).

#### LEFT STRUT

1. Unclip the rear brake line at the strut. Do not disconnect it.
2. Remove the radius rod mounting bolt.
3. Remove the stabilizer bar connecting bracket.
4. Remove the suspension crossmember mounting nuts.
5. Remove the strut upper mounting nuts.
6. Remove the left suspension assembly and the crossmember.
7. Installation is the reverse of the removal procedure. Tighten all bolts sufficiently to safely support the vehicle and then lower the vehicle to the ground so it rests on its own weight. Tighten the upper strut mounting nuts to 23–31 ft. lbs. (31–42 Nm); the radius rod bracket bolts to 43–58 ft. lbs. (59–78 Nm) and the parallel link mounting bolts to 65–87 ft. lbs. (88–118 Nm).

### 1989–92 Maxima and 1990–92 Stanza

1. Unclip the rear brake line at the strut. Do not disconnect it.
2. Disconnect the parking brake at the equalizer.
3. Remove the parallel link mounting bolts, radius rod mounting bolts, stabilizer mounting bolts, stabilizer connecting brackets and parking brake cable mounting bracket bolts.
4. Remove the rear seat and parcel shelf.

5. Remove the 3 upper strut mounting nuts and then lift out the strut.
6. Installation is the reverse of the removal procedure. Tighten all bolts sufficiently to safely support the vehicle and then lower the vehicle to the ground so it rests on its own weight. Tighten the upper strut mounting nuts to 31–40 ft. lbs. (42–54 Nm); parallel link mounting bolts to 65–87 ft. lbs. (88–118 Nm); connecting rod bracket nuts to 30–35 ft. lbs. (41–47 Nm); stabilizer bar mounting bolts to 43–58 ft. lbs. (59–78 Nm) and radius rod mounting bolts to 65–87 ft. lbs. (88–118 Nm).

## Coil Springs
### ——— CAUTION ———
*Coil springs are under considerable tension and can exert enough force to cause bodily injury. Exercise extreme caution when working with them.*

### REMOVAL & INSTALLATION

#### 200SX and 1988–89 300ZX

This suspension is similar to the IRS MacPherson strut type, except this type utilizes separate coil springs and shock absorbers, instead of strut units.

1. Compress the coil spring with a suitable spring compressor.
2. Raise the vehicle and support safely.
3. Compress the coil spring until it is of sufficient length to be removed. Remove the spring.
4. When installing the spring, be sure the upper and lower spring seat rubbers are not twisted and have not slipped off when installing the coil spring.

#### Stanza Wagon (2WD)

1. Raise the vehicle and support safely.
2. Remove the rear wheels.
3. Release the parking brake.
4. Remove the inner hub cap, the cotter pin and the wheel bearing locknut. Remove the brake drum.
5. Disconnect and plug the hydraulic brake line.
6. Disconnect the parking brake cable.
7. Remove the 4 brake backing plate mounting bolts and then slide the backing plate along with the inner wheel bearing off of the rear axle.
8. Disconnect the rear stabilizer bar.
9. Unbolt the anchor arm bracket and then remove the inner bushing bracket mounting bolts. Remove the torsion bar.
10. Installation is in the reverse or-

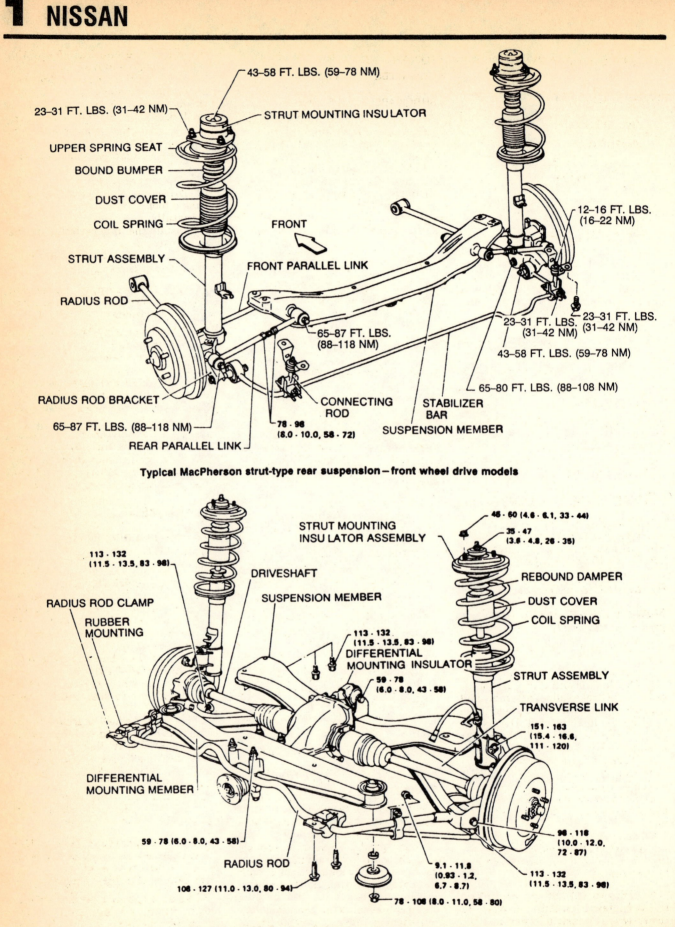

43–58 FT. LBS. (59–78 NM)

STRUT MOUNTING INSULATOR

23–31 FT. LBS. (31–42 NM)

UPPER SPRING SEAT

BOUND BUMPER

DUST COVER

COIL SPRING

FRONT

STRUT ASSEMBLY

FRONT PARALLEL LINK

RADIUS ROD

12–16 FT. LBS. (16–22 NM)

65–87 FT. LBS. (88–118 NM)

23–31 FT. LBS. (31–42 NM)

23–31 FT. LBS. (31–42 NM)

43–58 FT. LBS. (59–78 NM)

65–80 FT. LBS. (88–108 NM)

RADIUS ROD BRACKET

65–87 FT. LBS. (88–118 NM)

REAR PARALLEL LINK

78 · 98 (8.0 · 10.0, 58 · 72)

CONNECTING ROD

STABILIZER BAR

SUSPENSION MEMBER

**Typical MacPherson strut-type rear suspension — front wheel drive models**

STRUT MOUNTING INSULATOR ASSEMBLY

45 · 60 (4.6 · 6.1, 33 · 44)

35 · 47 (3.6 · 4.8, 26 · 35)

113 · 132 (11.5 · 13.5, 83 · 98)

DRIVESHAFT

SUSPENSION MEMBER

REBOUND DAMPER

DUST COVER

COIL SPRING

RADIUS ROD CLAMP

RUBBER MOUNTING

113 · 132 (11.5 · 13.5, 83 · 98)

DIFFERENTIAL MOUNTING INSULATOR

59 · 78 (6.0 · 8.0, 43 · 58)

STRUT ASSEMBLY

TRANSVERSE LINK

151 · 163 (15.4 · 16.6, 111 · 120)

DIFFERENTIAL MOUNTING MEMBER

59 · 78 (6.0 · 8.0, 43 · 58)

RADIUS ROD

106 · 127 (11.0 · 13.0, 80 · 94)

9.1 · 11.8 (0.93 · 1.2, 6.7 · 8.7)

78 · 108 (8.0 · 11.0, 58 · 80)

98 · 118 (10.0 · 12.0, 72 · 87)

113 · 132 (11.5 · 13.5, 83 · 98)

**MacPherson strut rear suspension — Stanza wagon (4WD)**

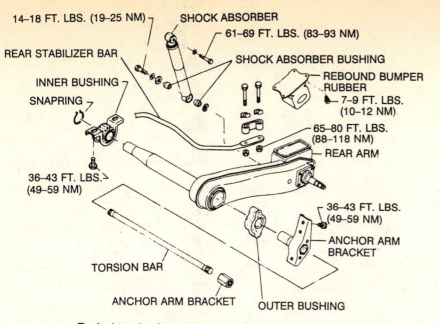

14–18 FT. LBS. (19–25 NM)
SHOCK ABSORBER
61–69 FT. LBS. (83–93 NM)
REAR STABILIZER BAR
SHOCK ABSORBER BUSHING
INNER BUSHING
REBOUND BUMPER RUBBER
SNAPRING
7–9 FT. LBS. (10–12 NM)
65–80 FT. LBS. (88–118 NM)
REAR ARM
36–43 FT. LBS. (49–59 NM)
36–43 FT. LBS. (49–59 NM)
ANCHOR ARM BRACKET
TORSION BAR
ANCHOR ARM BRACKET
OUTER BUSHING

**Typical torsion bar rear suspension — Stanza wagon (2wd)**

der of removal. Tighten the inner bushing and anchor arm mounting bolts to 36–43 ft. lbs. (49–59 Nm). Tighten the stabilizer bar bolts to 65–80 ft. lbs. (88–108 Nm).

## Rear Wheel Bearings

**NOTE: For wheel bearing procedures on rear wheel drive models, please refer to "Rear Axle Shaft" in the Drive Axle section.**

### REMOVAL & INSTALLATION

#### Maxima, Pulsar, Sentra (2WD) and Stanza (2WD)

1. Raise and support the vehicle safely.
2. Remove the rear wheels.
3. On Maxima and 1990–92 Stanza, remove the brake caliper assembly and support it with wire. The brake hose need not be disconnected. Do not depress the brake pedal while the caliper is supported or the piston will pop out.
4. Work off center hub cap by using thin tool. If necessary tap around it with a soft hammer while removing.
5. Remove the cotter pin, take out adjusting cap and wheel bearing lock nut.
6. Remove drum or disc with bearing inside. On Maxima and 1990–92 Stanza, a disc rotor is used instead of a brake drum.

**NOTE: On all Pulsar and Sentra vehicles, a circular clip holds inner wheel bearing in brake hub. On 1989–92 Maxima, Pulsar, Sen-**

tra and 1990–92 Stanza, the rear wheel bearing is a sealed unit which combines the bearing, inner and outer races and grease seal. This bearing is retained by a circlip.

7. Remove bearing from drum using long brass drift pin or an arbor press (1989–92 Maxima, Pulsar, Sentra and 1990–92 Stanza).
8. Pack the bearings.
9. Installation is the reverse of the removal procedire: During installation, observe the following:
   a. On 1989–92 Maxima, Pulsar, Sentra and 1990–92 Stanza, the bearing must be pressed into the brake drum or brake disc.
   b. Do not press the inner race of the bearing; do not coat the wheel bearing and outer hub mating surfaces with oil or grease and do not damage the grease seal.
   c. Adjust wheel bearings as outlined below.

#### Sentra (4WD) and Stanza (4WD)

1. Raise and support the vehicle safely.
2. Remove wheel bearing locknut while depressing brake pedal.
3. Disconnect brake hydraulic line and parking brake cable.
4. Separate halfshaft from knuckle by slightly tapping it with suitable tool. Cover axle boots with waste cloth so as not to damage them when removing halfshaft.
5. Remove all knuckle retaining bolts and nuts. Make a matchmark before removing adjusting pin.

6. Separate the hub from the knuckle using a suitable tool.
7. Drive out the inner (outside) race using a suitable press.
8. Remove the outer grease seal.
9. Drive the inner race (inside) from the hub. The inner grease seal will be removed with it.
10. Remove inner and outer circular clips.
11. Remove the bearings.
12. Drive out the outer race using a suitable tool.

**To install:**

13. Install the inner circlip in the knuckle groove.
14. Press in the new outer race from the outside of the knuckle.

**NOTE: Do not apply grease the wheel bearing outer race and knuckle surfaces.**

15. Pack the bearings and the grease seal lip with grease.
16. Install the outer circlip in the knuckle groove.
17. Install the inner races uisng the proper tool, then install the inner grease seal. Be careful not to damage the grease seal.
18. Press the hub into the knuckle.
19. Complete the installation of the remaining components in reverse of the removal procedure. Adjust the wheel bearings as described below.

### ADJUSTMENT

#### 1988 Maxima and 1988–89 Stanza 2WD

Before adjusting the rear wheel bearings on these vehicles apply multi-purpose grease to the following parts: threaded portion of the wheel spindle, mating surfaces of the lock washer and outer wheel bearing, inner hub cap and grease seal lip.

1. Tighten the wheel bearing nut to 18–25 ft. lbs. (25–34 Nm).
2. Turn the wheel several times in both directions to seat the bearing correctly.
3. Loosen the wheel bearing nut until there is no pre-load and then tighten it to 6.5–8.7 ft. lbs. (9–12 Nm). Turn the wheel several times again and then retighten it to the same torque again.
4. Install the adjusting cap and align any of its slots with the hole in the spindle.

**NOTE: If necessary, loosen the locknut as much as 15 degrees in order to align the spindle hole with one in the adjusting cap.**

5. Rotate the hub in both directions several times while measuring its starting torque and axial play. The axial play should be 0 in. (0mm). The

starting torque with grease seal should be 6.9 inch lbs. or less. When measured at wheel hub bolt, starting torque should be 3.1 lbs. (13.7 N).

6. Correctly measure the rotation from the starting force toward the tangential direction against the hub bolt. The above figures do not allow for any "dragging" resistance. When measuring starting torque, confirm that no "dragging" exists. No wheel bearing axial play can exist at all.

7. Spread the cotter pin and install the inner hub cap.

### 1989–92 Maxima, Pulsar, Sentra, 1990–92 Stanza 2WD and Stanza 4WD

Due to a bearing change on these models, there is no procedure for torquing the rear wheel bearings. Once the final torque is applied to the rear wheel bearing axle nut and the axial play is checked, no further adjustment is either necessary or possible.

Check the torque of the wheel bearing locknut. This value is 137–188 ft. lbs. on Maxima, Pulsar, Sentra 2WD and 1990–92 Stanza. On Sentra/Stanza 4WD, the torque value is 174–231 ft. lbs. Rotate the hub and make sure the bearing turn smoothly and quietly. Then, mount a dial indicator to the face of the hub and check the axial play. It should not exceed 0.0020 in. (0.05mm). If the axial play is not as specified, replace the necessary component.

## Rear Axle Assembly

### REMOVAL & INSTALLATION

1. Raise and support the vehicle safely.
2. Remove the rear wheels.
3. Disconnect the brake line and parking brake cable.
4. Work off center hub cap by using thin tool. If necessary tap around it with a soft hammer while removing.
5. Remove the cotter pin, take out adjusting cap and wheel bearing lock nut.
6. Remove drum and wheel hub assembly.
7. Unbolt and remove the knuckle/spindle assembly.
8. Installation is the reverse of the removal procedure. Adjust the rear wheel bearings and bleed the brakes.

# STEERING

## Steering Wheel

### —— CAUTION ——
*On vehicles equipped with an air bag, turn the ignition switch to OFF position. The negative battery cable must be disconnected and wait 10 minutes after the cable is disconnected before working on the system. Failure to do so may result in deployment of the air bag and possible personal injury.*

### REMOVAL & INSTALLATION

1. Position the wheels in the straight-ahead direction. The steering wheel should be right-side up and level.
2. Disconnect the negative battery cable.
3. Look at the back of the steering wheel. If there are countersunk screws in the back of the steering wheel spokes, remove the screws and pull off the horn pad. Some vehicles have a horn wire running from the pad to the steering wheel. Disconnect it.

**NOTE: There are 3 other types of horn buttons or rings. The first simply pulls off. The second, which is usually a large, semi-triangular pad, must be pushed up, then pulled off. The third must be pushed in and turned clockwise.**

4. Remove the rest of the horn switching mechanism, noting the relative location of the parts. Remove the mechanism only if it interferes with removal of the steering wheel.
5. Matchmark the top of the steering column shaft and the steering wheel flange.
6. Remove the attaching nut and remove the steering wheel with a puller.

**NOTE: Do not strike the shaft with a hammer; which may cause the column to collapse.**

**To install:**
7. Install the steering wheel by aligning the punch marks. Do not drive or hammer the wheel into place, or the collapsible steering column may collapse. Before installing the horn pad, apply multi-purpose grease to the surface of the cancel pin and horn contact slip ring.
8. Tighten the steering wheel nuts to 22–29 ft. lbs. (29–39 Nm).
9. Reinstall the horn button, pad, or ring.
10. Connect the negative battery cable.

## Steering Column

### REMOVAL & INSTALLATION

1. Disconnect the negative battery cable.
2. Remove the steering wheel.
3. Remove the steering column covers.

4. Disconnect the combination switch and steering lock switch wiring.
5. Remove most of the steering column support bracket and clamp nuts and bolts. Leave a few of the fasteners loosely installed to support the column while disconnecting it from the steering gear.
6. Remove the bolt from the column lower joint.
7. Remove the temporarily installed column support bracket bolts and withdraw the column from the lower joint.
8. Withdraw the column spline shaft from the lower joint and remove the steering column. Be careful not to tear the column tube jacket insulator during removal.
**To install:**
9. Insert the column spline shaft into the lower joint and install all column fasteners finger-tight.
10. Install the lower joint bolt. The cutout portion of the spline shaft must perfectly aligned with the bolt. Torque the bolt to 17–22 ft. lbs. (23–30 Nm). Tighten the steering bracket and clamp fasteners gradually. While tightening, make sure no stress is placed on the column.
11. Connect the combination switch and steering lock switch wiring.
12. Install the steering column covers.
13. Install the steering wheel.
14. Connect the negative battery cable.
15. After the installation is complete, turn the steering wheel from stop to stop and make sure it turns smoothly. The number of turns to the left and right stops must be equal.

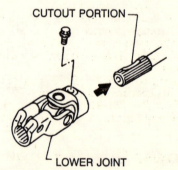

**The cutout portion of the steering column spline shaft must perfectly aligned with the bolt**

## Manual Steering Rack and Pinion

### REMOVAL & INSTALLATION
### Sentra

1. Raise and support the vehicle safely and remove the wheels.

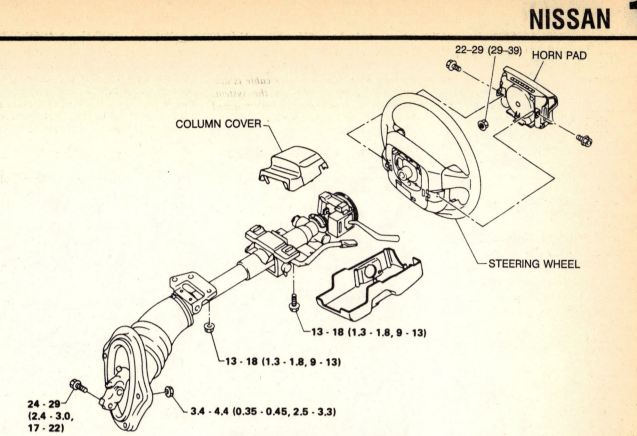

COLUMN COVER

22–29 (29–39)  HORN PAD

STEERING WHEEL

13 - 18 (1.3 - 1.8, 9 - 13)

13 - 18 (1.3 - 1.8, 9 - 13)

24 - 29
(2.4 - 3.0,
17 - 22)

3.4 - 4.4 (0.35 - 0.45, 2.5 - 3.3)

Steering column assembly – 1990 Pulsar

2. Disconnect the tie rod from the steering knuckle and loosen the steering gear attaching bolts.

3. Remove the bolt securing the lower joint to the steering gear pinion and remove the lower joint from the pinion.

4. Remove the bolts holding the steering gear housing to the body, and remove the steering gear and linkage assembly from the vehicle.

5. Installation is the reverse order of the removal procedure. When fitting the lower U-joint, make sure the attaching bolt is aligned perfectly with the cut out in the splined end of the steering column shaft. Torque the steering gear mounting clamp bolts to 54–72 ft. lbs. (73–97 Nm). Torque the tie rod end nuts to 22–29 ft. lbs. (29–39 Nm).

## Power Steering Rack and Pinion

### REMOVAL & INSTALLATION

#### 200SX

1. Raise and support the vehicle safely.

2. Remove the air cleaner and remove the bolt securing the U-joint to the worm shaft.

3. Disconnect the hoses from the power steering gear and plug the hoses to prevent leakage.

4. Remove the pitman arm from the sector shaft using a suitable tool and remove the steering gear mounting bolts.

5. Remove the exhaust pipe mounting nut.

6. Disconnect the control cable or linkage for the transmission and position it aside.

7. Remove the steering gear from the vehicle.

8. Installation is the reverse of the removal procedure. Torque the mounting clamp bolts to 29–36 ft. lbs. (39–49 Nm) and the tie rod end nuts to 40–72 ft. lbs. (54–98 Nm). Torque the worm shaft U-joint bolt to 17–22 ft. lbs. (24–29 Nm). Refill the power steering pump, start the engine and bleed the system.

#### 300ZX

1. Block the rear wheels. Raise and support the vehicle safely.

2. Position an oil catch pan under the power steering gear, remove the hydraulic lines from the gear and drain the oil. Plug the lines to prevent leakage.

3. Loosen the steering column lower joint shaft bolt.

4. Before disconnecting the lower ball joint set the steering gear assembly in neutral by making the wheels straight. Loosen the bolt and disconnect the lower joint. Matchmark the

pinion shaft to the pinion housing to record the neutral gear position.

5. Remove the tie rod end-to-knuckle arm cotter pins and castle nuts.

6. Separate the tie rods from the knuckle arms using a suitable puller.

7. Remove the steering gear housing-to-suspension crossmember bolts.

8. Position a floor jack under the engine and raise it just enough to support the engine. Loosen the engine mounting bolts and raise the engine about ½ in.

9. Remove the steering gear and linkage from the vehicle.

**To install:**

10. Installation is the reverse of the removal procedure observing the following:

   a. Tighten the gear housing mounting bracket bolts to 29–36 ft. lbs. (39–49 Nm) on 1988–89 vehicles, and 65–80 ft. lbs. (88–108 Nm) on 1990–92 vehicles.

   b. Torque the tie rod end nuts to 22–29 ft. lbs. (29–39 Nm).

   c. On 1990–92 vehicles, torque the high pressure hydraulic line fitting to 22–26 ft. lbs. (36–40 Nm) and lower pressure fitting to 27–30 ft. lbs. (36–40 Nm).

   d. When attaching the lower joint, set the left and right dust boots to equal deflection. Refill power steering pump, start the engine and bleed the system.

**NOTE: On 1990–92 vehicles, the**

O-ring in the lower pressure hydraulic line fitting is larger than the O-ring in the high pressure line. Make sure the O-rings are installed in the proper fittings. Observe the torque specification given for the hydraulic line fittings. Over-tightening will cause damage to the fitting threads and O-rings.

### Pulsar, Sentra, Stanza, Maxima and 240SX

1. Raise and support the vehicle safely and remove the wheels.
2. Disconnect the power steering hose from the power steering gear and plug all hoses to prevent leakage.
3. Disconnect the side rod studs from the steering knuckles.
4. On Pulsar and Sentra, support the transaxle with a suitable transmission jack and remove the exhaust pipe and rear engine mounts.
5. On other vehicles, remove the lower joint assembly from the steering gear pinion. Before disconnecting the lower ball joint set the steering gear assembly in neutral by making the wheels straight. Loosen the bolt and disconnect the lower joint. Matchmark the pinion shaft to the pinion housing to record the neutral gear position.
6. Remove the steering gear and linkage assembly from the vehicle.
**To install:**
7. Installation is the reverse of the removal procedure observing the following:
   a. Make sure the pinion shaft and pinion housing are aligned properly.
   b. Torque the high pressure hydraulic line fitting to 11–18 ft. lbs. (15–25 Nm) and lower pressure fitting to 20–29 ft. lbs. (27–39 Nm).
   c. When attaching the lower joint, set the left and right dust boots to equal deflection.
   d. On Maxima and Stanza, torque the gear housing mounting bracket bolts to 54–72 ft. lbs. (73–97 Nm) using the proper sequence.
8. Refill the power steering pump, start the engine and bleed the system. Refill the power steering pump, start the engine and bleed the system.

NOTE: On most vehicles, the O-ring in the lower pressure hydraulic line fitting is larger than the O-ring in the high pressure line. Make sure the O-rings are installed in the proper fittings. Observe the torque specification given for the hydraulic line fittings. Over-tightening will cause damage to the fitting threads and O-rings.

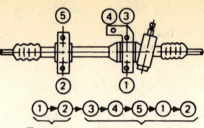

Gear housing mounting bracket bolt torque sequence—Stanza and Maxima

## Power Steering Pump

### REMOVAL & INSTALLATION

1. On the 200SX, remove the air cleaner duct and air cleaner.
2. Loosen the idler pulley locknut and turn the adjusting nut counterclockwise, in order to remove the power steering belt.
3. Remove the drive belt on the air conditioning compressor, if so equipped.
4. Loosen the power steering hoses at the pump and remove the bolts holding the power steering pump to the bracket.
5. Disconnect and plug the power steering hoses and remove the pump from the vehicle.
6. Installation is the reverse of the removal procedure. Fill and bleed the power steering system.

### BELT ADJUSTMENT

1. Loosen the tension adjustment and mounting bolts.
2. Move the pump toward or away from the engine so the belt deflects ¼–½ in. midway between the idler pulley and the pump pulley under moderate thumb pressure.
3. Tighten the bolts and recheck the tension adjustment.

### SYSTEM BLEEDING

1. Check the level in the power steering pump reservoir. Add fluid as necessary to the proper level.
2. Safely raise and support the vehicle until the wheels are just off the ground.
3. With the engine running, quickly turn the steering wheel all the way to the left and all the way to the right 10 times.
4. Stop the engine and check to see if any more fluid is required in the pump reservoir. Add fluid as necessary.
5. If all the air cannot be bled from

the system, repeat Steps 3–4 until all the air is removed from the system.

## Tie Rod Ends

### REMOVAL & INSTALLATION

A ball joint remover tool or equivalent, is required for this operation.
1. Raise and support the vehicle safely.
2. Locate the faulty tie rod end. It will have a lot of play in it and the dust cover will probably be torn.
3. Remove the cotter key and nut from the tie rod stud. Note the position of the tie rod end in relation to the rest of the steering linkage.
4. Loosen the lock nut holding the tie rod to the rest of the steering linkage.
5. Free the tie rod ball joint from either the relay rod or steering knuckle by using a ball joint remover or equivalent tool.
6. Unscrew and remove the tie rod end, counting the number of turns it takes to completely free it.
**To install:**
7. Install the new tie rod end, turning it in exactly the same number of turns for removal. Make sure it is correctly positioned in relation to the rest of the steering linkage.
8. Fit the ball joint and nut. Torque the tie rod end to 22–36 ft. lbs. (29–39 Nm) on all vehicles except 200SX. On 200SX, torque the tie rod end nut to 40–72 ft. lbs. (54–98 Nm). Once the specified torque is reached, tighten further until the nut groove is aligned with the first pin hole. Install a new cotter pin.
9. Check and adjust the toe of the vehicle as needed.

# BRAKES

For all brake system repair and service procedures not detailed below, please refer to "Brakes" in the Unit Repair section.

## Master Cylinder

### REMOVAL & INSTALLATION

1. Clean the outside of the cylinder thoroughly, particularly around the cap and fluid lines.
2. Disconnect the fluid lines and cap them to keep dirt out.
3. On vehicles with a fluid level gauge, disconnect the electrical connector.
4. Remove the clevis pin connecting

the pushrod to the brake pedal arm inside the vehicle.

5. Unbolt the master cylinder from the firewall and remove along with gasket. If the pushrod is not adjustable, there will be shims between the cylinder and the firewall. These shims, or the adjustable pushrod, are used to adjust brake pedal free-play.

6. Installation of the master cylinder is the reverse of the removal procedure. Bleed the brakes.

## Proportioning Valve

The proportioning valve is incorporated into the master cylinder. Consequently, removal and installation procedures are limited to replacement of the master cylinder unit as a whole.

## Power Brake Booster

### REMOVAL & INSTALLATION

1. Remove the master cylinder.
2. Remove the vacuum hose at the power brake booster.
3. Remove the pushrod from the brake pedal.
4. From under the instrument panel, remove the cowl-to-booster nuts. Remove the brake booster.

5. Installation is in the reverse order of removal. Bleed the brake system.

## Brake Calipers

### REMOVAL & INSTALLATION

1. Raise the vehicle and support safely.
2. Remove the front or rear wheels.
3. Disconnect the brake line from the caliper. Remove the metal gaskets from the brake hose fitting and discard them.
4. Disconnect the parking brake cable.
5. Remove the brake pads if they interfere with caliper removal.
6. Remove the brake caliper mounting bolts.
7. Remove the brake caliper assembly.
8. Installation is the reverse of the removal procedure. Torque the caliper bolts to 40–72 ft. lbs. (54–98 Nm). Use new brake hose fitting gaskets. Bleed the brake system and adjust the parking brake cable.

## Front Disc Brake Pads

### REMOVAL & INSTALLATION

#### 200SX and Maxima

##### TYPE AD22V

AD22V type front disc brakes are used on 200SX with CA20E engines.
1. Raise the vehicle and support safely.
2. Remove the front wheels.
3. Remove the lower caliper guide pin.
4. Rotate the brake caliper body upward.
5. Remove the brake pad retainer and the inner and outer pad shims.
6. Remove the brake pads.

**NOTE: Do not depress the brake pedal when the caliper body is raised. The brake piston will be forced out of the caliper.**

**To install:**

7. Clean the piston end of the caliper body and the pin bolt holes. Be careful not to get oil on the brake rotor.
8. Pull the caliper body to the outer side and install the inner brake pad.
9. Install the outer pad, shim and pad retainer.
10. Reposition the caliper body and then tighten the guide pin bolt to 23–30 ft. lbs. (31–41 Nm).
11. Apply the brakes a few times to seat the pads before driving out on the road.

##### TYPES CL25VB AND CL28VB

CL28VB type front disc brakes are used on 200SX with VG30E engines and 1988 Maxima. CL25VB type brakes are used on 1989–92 Maxima.
1. Raise the vehicle and support safely.
2. Remove the front wheels.
3. Remove the pin (lower) bolt from the caliper.
4. Swing the caliper body upward on the upper bolt.
5. Remove the pad retainers and inner and outer shims.

**NOTE: Do not depress the brake pedal when the cylinder body is in the raised position or the piston will pop out of the cylinder.**

**To install:**

6. Check the level of fluid in the master cylinder. If the fluid is near the maximum level, use a clean syringe to remove fluid until the level is down well below the lip of the reservoir.
7. Use a large C-clamp or piston expansion tool to press the caliper piston back into the caliper, to allow room for the installation of the thicker new pads.

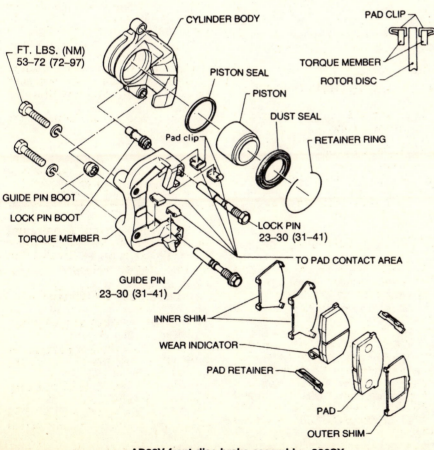

AD22V front disc brake assembly—200SX

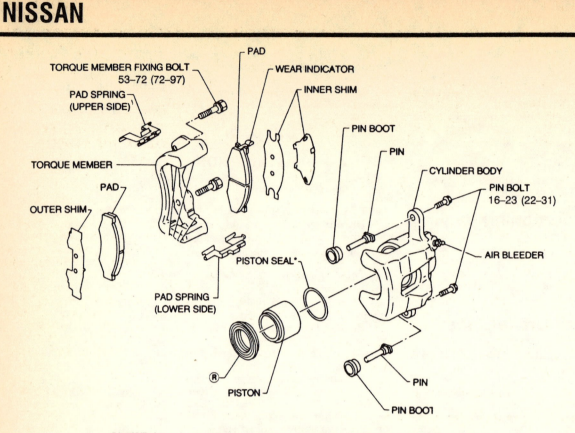

**TORQUE MEMBER FIXING BOLT**
53–72 (72–97)

**PAD SPRING (UPPER SIDE)**

**PAD**

**WEAR INDICATOR**

**INNER SHIM**

**PIN BOOT**

**PIN**

**TORQUE MEMBER**

**CYLINDER BODY**

**PIN BOLT** 16–23 (22–31)

**PAD**

**OUTER SHIM**

**AIR BLEEDER**

**PISTON SEAL***

**PAD SPRING (LOWER SIDE)**

**PISTON**

**PIN**

**PIN BOOT**

CL28VB front brake disc assembly—200SX and 1988–89 300ZX (non-turbo)

8. Install the new pads, utilizing new shims, in reverse order. Torque the lower pin bolt to 16–23 ft. lbs. (22–31 Nm) on both types of brakes.

## 240SX

### TYPES CL22VB AND CL25VA

CL22VB type front disc brakes are used on vehicles without ABS and CL25VA type brake are used on vehicles with ABS.
1. Raise and support the vehicle safely.
2. Remove the front wheels.
3. Remove the pin (lower) bolt from the caliper.
4. Swing the caliper body upward on the upper bolt.
5. Remove the pad retainers and inner and outer shims.

**NOTE: Do not depress the brake pedal when the cylinder body is in the raised position or the piston will pop out of the cylinder.**

6. Check the level of fluid in the master cylinder. If the fluid is near the maximum level, use a clean syringe to remove fluid until the level is down well below the lip of the reservoir.
7. Use a large C-clamp or piston expansion tool to press the caliper piston back into the caliper, to allow room for the installation of the thicker new pads.

8. Install the new pads, utilizing new shims, in reverse order. Torque the lower and main pin bolts to 16–23 ft. lbs. (22–31 Nm) on both CL22VB and CL25VA type front disc brakes.

## 1988–89 300ZX

### TYPES CL28VE AND CL28VB

CL28VE type front disc brakes are used on turbocharged engines and CL28VB type brakes are used on non-turbocharged engines.
1. Raise and support the vehicle safely.
2. Remove the front wheels.
3. Remove the lower pin bolt which retains the caliper to the torque member.
4. Rotate the caliper up and aside, exposing the pads. Do not try to move the caliper sideways.
5. Remove the pad retainers, the inner and outer shims, then the pads.
**To install:**
6. Clean the piston end and pin bolts.
7. Install a new inner pad. Rotate the caliper back down into place, slightly open the bleeder screw, then using a long bar, lever the caliper to the outside to press the piston into place. Rotate the caliper back up and aside.
8. Lightly coat the sliding surfaces of the torque member with grease. Install a new outer pad with the inner

and outer shims. Install the pad retainers; be careful not to install them upside down.
9. Rotate the caliper down and install the pin bolt. Tighten to 16–23 ft. lbs. (22–31 Nm).
10. Apply the brakes a few times to seat the pads. Check the master cylinder level and add fluid if necessary. Bleed the brakes if necessary.

## 1990–92 300ZX

### TYPES OPZ25V AND PZ25VA

OPZ25VA type front disc brakes are used on turbocharged engines. OPZ25V brakes are used on non-turbocharged engines.
1. Raise the vehicle and support safely.
2. Remove the front wheels.
3. Remove the clip from the pad pin and remove the pad pin.
4. Remove the cross spring.
5. Withdraw the outer pad and insert and temporarily insert it between the lower piston and the rotor.
6. Using a suitable tool, push the upper piston back and insert the new pad so it contacts the upper piston.
7. Withdraw the old pad.
8. Push the piston back with a suitable tool to prevent it from popping out.
9. Pull out the new pad and re-install it in the correct position.

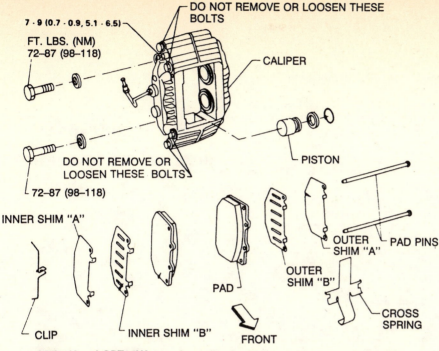

7 · 9 (0.7 · 0.9, 5.1 · 6.5)

FT. LBS. (NM)
72–87 (98–118)

DO NOT REMOVE OR LOOSEN THESE BOLTS

CALIPER

PISTON

DO NOT REMOVE OR LOOSEN THESE BOLTS

72–87 (98–118)

INNER SHIM "A"

OUTER SHIM "A"

PAD PINS

OUTER SHIM "B"

PAD

CROSS SPRING

CLIP

INNER SHIM "B"

FRONT

**OPZ25V and OPZ25VA type front disc brake assembly – 1990–92 300ZX**

10. Repeat steps 5–9 for the inner pad.
11. Install the cross spring, pad pin and pad clip.

### *Pulsar, Sentra and Stanza*
### TYPES AD18B, AD18V, CL18B, CL25VA AND CL28VA

CL18B, AD18B and AD18V type front disc brakes are used on Pulsar and Sentra depending on engine application. CL28VA type brakes are used on 1988–89 Stanza and Stanza Wagon. The 1990–92 Stanza uses CL25VA front disc brakes on both ABS equipped and non-ABS vehicles.

1. Raise the vehicle and support safely.
2. Remove the front wheels.
3. Remove the bottom guide pin (Stanza and Sentra) or the lock pin (Pulsar) from the caliper and swing the caliper cylinder body upward.
4. Remove the brake pad retainers and the pads.
**To install:**
5. Install the brake pads and caliper assembly.
6. Install the wheels and lower the vehicle.
7. Apply the brakes a few times to seat the pads. Check the master cylinder and add fluid if necessary. Bleed the brakes, if necessary.

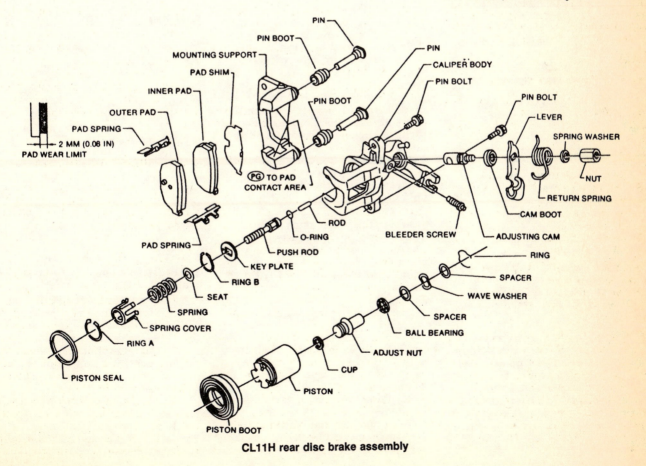

PIN

PIN BOOT

MOUNTING SUPPORT

PAD SHIM

PIN

CALIPER BODY

PIN BOLT

INNER PAD

PIN BOOT

PIN BOLT

LEVER

OUTER PAD

SPRING WASHER

PAD SPRING

NUT

2 MM (0.08 IN)
PAD WEAR LIMIT

PG TO PAD CONTACT AREA

RETURN SPRING

CAM BOOT

ADJUSTING CAM

PAD SPRING

ROD

BLEEDER SCREW

RING

O-RING

SPACER

PUSH ROD

WAVE WASHER

KEY PLATE

RING B

SPACER

SEAT

BALL BEARING

SPRING

ADJUST NUT

SPRING COVER

RING A

CUP

PISTON

PISTON SEAL

PISTON BOOT

**CL11H rear disc brake assembly**

## Rear Disc Brake Pads

### REMOVAL & INSTALLATION

#### 200SX, 240SX, Maxima and 1990–92 Stanza With ABS

#### TYPES CL11H AND CL9H

CL11H type rear disc brakes are used on 200SX with CA20E engines and on the 1988 Maxima. CL9H rear disc brake are used on 240SX and 1989–92 Maxima on both ABS equipped and non-ABS vehicles. CL9H rear disc brakes are also used on 1990–92 Stanza with ABS.

1. Raise and support the vehicle safely.
2. Remove the rear wheels.
3. Release the parking brake and remove the cable bracket bolt.
4. Remove the pin bolts and lift off the caliper body.
5. Pull out the pad springs and then remove the pads and shims.

**To install:**

6. Clean the piston end of the caliper body and the area around the pin holes. Be careful not to get oil on the rotor.
7. Using the proper tool, carefully turn the piston clockwise back into the caliper body. Take care not to damage the piston boot.
8. Coat the pad contact area on the mounting support with a silicone based grease.
9. Install the pads, shims and the pad springs. Always use new shims.
10. Position the caliper body in the mounting support and tighten the pin bolts.
11. Mount the wheels, lower the vehicle and bleed the system if necessary.

#### TYPE CL14HB

CL14HB type rear disc brakes are used on 200SX with VG30E engines.

1. Raise and support the vehicle safely.
2. Remove the rear wheels.
3. Release the parking brake and remove the cable bracket bolt.
4. Remove the 2 pin bolts and the lock spring. Remove the caliper and suspending it above the disc so as to avoid putting any strain on the hose.
5. Remove the pad retainers, pads, and shims.

**NOTE: Do not depress the brake pedal when the cylinder body is in the raised position or the piston will pop out. Avoid damaging the piston seal when removing/installing the pads and retainers.**

6. Check the level of fluid in the master cylinder. If the fluid is near the maximum level, use a clean syringe to remove fluid until the level is down well below the lip of the reservoir. Then, press the caliper piston back into the caliper by turning it clockwise. The piston has a helical groove on the outer diameter. This will allow room for the installation of the thicker new pads.
7. Install the new pads using new shims in reverse order of the removal procedure.

#### 300ZX

#### TYPES CL14HB AND OPZ11VB

CL14HB rear disc brakes are used on 1988–89 vehicles. OPZ11VB rear disc brakes are used on 1990–92 vehicles.

1. Raise and support the vehicle safely.
2. Remove the rear wheels.
3. Disconnect the parking brake cable.
4. Remove the clip at the outside of the pad pins.
5. Remove the pad pins. Hold the anti-squeal springs in place by hand.
6. On 1990–92 vehicles, remove the cross spring.
7. Remove the pads.

**NOTE: When the pads are removed, do not depress the brake or else the piston will pop out.**

8. Clean the end of the piston with clean brake fluid. Lightly coat the caliper-to-pad, the yoke-to-pad, the retaining pin-to-pad and the retaining pin-to-bracket surfaces with brake grease.
9. Push in on the piston while at the same time turning it clockwise into the bore. Then, with a lever between the rotor and yoke, push the yoke over until there is clearance to install the pads, equally.
10. Install the cross spring (1990–92 vehicles) shims, the pads, the anti-squeal springs and the pins. Install the clip. Note that the inner pad has a tab which must fit into the piston notch. Make sure the piston notch is centered to allow for proper pad installation.
11. Apply the brakes a few times to center the pads. Check the master cylinder fluid level and add fluid, if necessary.

## Brake Rotor

### REMOVAL & INSTALLATION

1. Safely raise and support the vehicle.
2. Remove the front or rear wheels.
3. Remove the front or rear caliper assembly and suspend it with a piece of wire. Leave the brake hose connected.

**NOTE: Do not allow the caliper to hang by the brake hose unsupported.**

4. As required, pry off the grease cap, then remove the cotter pin, adjusting cap, insulator and wheel bearing locknut.
5. Remove the hub/rotor assembly.
6. Installation is the reverse of the removal procedure.

## Brake Drums

### REMOVAL & INSTALLATION

1. Raise and support the vehicle safely.
2. Remove the rear wheels.
3. Release the parking brake lever fully.
4. If required, remove the wheel bearing grease cap, cotter pin and locknut.
5. Remove the brake drum. On some vehicles, there are 2 threaded service holes in each drum which accept 8mm bolts. If the drums are hard to remove, insert the bolts into the service holes and screw them in to force the drum away from the axle.
6. Installation is the reverse of the removal procedure.

## Brake Shoes

### REMOVAL & INSTALLATION

#### Pulsar, Sentra and Stanza

1. Raise and support the vehicle safely.
2. Remove the rear wheels and the drums.
3. Release the parking brake lever.
4. Remove the anti-rattle spring and the pin from the brake shoes. To remove the anti-rattle spring and pin, push the spring/pin assembly into the brake shoe, turn it 90 degrees and release it; the retainer cap, spring, washer and pin will separate.
5. Support the brake shoe assembly and remove the return springs and brake shoes.

**NOTE: If the brake shoes are difficult to remove, loosen the brake adjusters. Use a C-clamp or heavy rubber band around the cylinder to prevent the piston from popping out.**

6. Clean the backing plate and check the wheel cylinder for leaks.
7. Lubricate the backing plate pads and the screw adjusters with lithium base grease.
8. Install the brake shoes and springs.
9. Install the drum assembly.
10. Adjust brakes and bleed the system if necessary.

## Wheel Cylinder

### REMOVAL & INSTALLATION

1. Raise and support the vehicle safely.
2. Remove the tire and wheel assembly.
3. Remove the brake drum and brake shoes.
4. Disconnect the hydraulic line from the wheel cylinder. Plug the line to prevent leakage.
5. Remove the wheel cylinder from the brake backing plate.
6. Remove the dust boot and take out the piston. Discard the piston cup. The dust boot can be reused although it is best to replace it.
7. Wash all of the components in clean brake fluid.
8. Inspect the piston and piston bore. Replace any components that are severely corroded, scored or worn. The piston and piston bore may be polished lightly with crocus cloth; move the cloth around the piston bore, not in and out.
9. Wash the wheel cylinder and piston in clean brake fluid.
10. Coat all new components to be installed with clean brake fluid.
11. Assemble the cylinder and install it on the backing plate. Connect the hydraulic line.
12. Install the brake shoes and brake drum.
13. Install the wheel and tire assembly.
14. Lower the vehicle.
15. Bleed the brake system.

## Parking Brake Cable

### ADJUSTMENT

1. Pull up the hand brake lever, counting the number of notches for full engagement. Full engagement should be:

 200SX: 7–8 notches
 240SX: 6–8 notches
 300ZX
  1988–89: 8–10 notches
  1990–92: 8–10 notches
 Maxima
  1988: 11–13 notches
  1989–92: 8–11 notches
 Pulsar: 7–11 notches
 Sentra
  1988: 11–13 notches
  1989–92: 7–11 notches
 Stanza sedan
  1988: 11–13 notches
  1989–92: 11–13 notches
 Stanza Wagon
  2WD: 11–17 notches
  4WD: 8–9 notches

2. Release the parking brake.

3. Except on 200SX, adjust the lever stroke by loosening the locknut and tightening the adjusting nut to reduce the number of notches necessary for engagement. Tighten the locknut. The locknut and adjuster can be found inside the handbrake assembly, in the passenger compartment. Some vehicles just have an adjusting nut. Access to the locknut is gained by removing the parking brake console or through an access hole in the console itself. On 200SX, the lever stroke is adjusted by turning the equalizer under the vehicle.
4. Check the adjustment and repeat as necessary.
5. After adjustment, check to see that the rear brake levers, at the calipers, return to their full off positions when the lever is released, and that the rear cables are not slack when the lever is released.
6. To adjust the parking brake light, bend the light switch plate down so the light comes on when the lever is engaged 1–2 notches.

### REMOVAL & INSTALLATION

#### Front Cable

1. Remove the parking brake console box.

2. Remove the heat insulator, if equipped.
3. Remove the front passenger seat, if required.
4. Disconnect the warning lamp switch plate connector.
5. Unbolt the lever from the floor.
6. Working from under the vehicle, remove the locknut, adjusting nut and equalizer.
7. Pull the front cable out through the compartment and remove it from the vehicle.

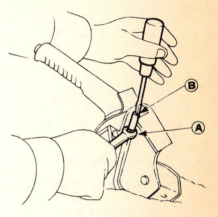

**Typical parking brake adjustment**

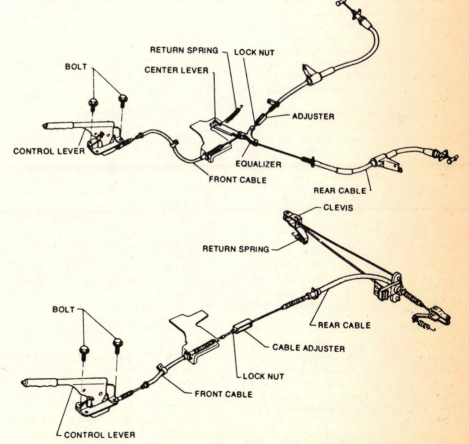

**Two common types of parking brake cables – most vehicles are similar**

NOTE: On some vehicles it may be necessary to separate the front cable from the lever by breaking the pin.

8. Installation is the reverse of the removal procedure. Adjust the lever stroke.

### Rear Cable

1. Back off on the adjusting nut or equalizer to loosen the cable tension.
2. Working from underneath the vehicle, disconnect the cable at the equalizer.
3. Remove the cable lock plate from the rear suspension member.
4. Disconnect the cable from the rear brakes.
5. Disconnect the cable from the suspension arm.
6. Remove the cable.
7. Installation is the reverse of the removal procedure. Adjust the lever stroke.

## Brake System

## Bleeding

### PRECAUTIONS

- Carefully monitor the brake fluid level in the master cylinder at all times during the bleeding procedure. Keep the reservoir full at all times.
- Only use brake fluid that meets or exceeds DOT 3 specifications.
- Place a suitable container under the master cylinder to avoid spillage of brake fluid.
- Do not allow brake fluid to come in contact with any painted surface. Brake fluid makes excellent paint remover.
- Make sure to use the proper bleeding sequence.

### BLEEDING PROCEDURE

The brake bleeding sequence varys from vehicle to vehicle and whether the vehicle is equipped with ABS or not. Bleeding sequences are as follows:

**200SX, 240SX (without ABS) and 1988–89 300ZX**—left rear caliper, right rear caliper, right front caliper, left front caliper.

**240SX (with ABS) and 1990–92 300ZX**—left rear caliper, right rear caliper, right front caliper, left front caliper, front side air bleeder on ABS actuator, rear side air bleeder on ABS actuator

**Maxima**—left rear caliper, right front caliper, right rear caliper, left front caliper

**Pulsar, Sentra, Stanza**—left wheel cylinder or caliper, right front caliper, right rear wheel cylinder or caliper, left front caliper

To bleed the brakes, use the following procedure:

1. If equipped with ABS, turn the ignition switch to the **OFF** position and disconnect the connectors from the ABS actuator. Wait a few minutes to allow for the system to bleed down, then disconnect the negative battery cable.
2. Connect a transparent vinyl tube to the bleeder valve. Submerge the tube in a container half filled with clean brake fluid.
3. Fully depress the brake pedal several times.
4. With the brake pedal depressed, open the air bleeder valve to release the air.
5. Close the air bleeder valve.
6. Release the brake pedal slowly.
7. Repeat Steps 3–6 until clear fluid flows from the air bleeder valve.
8. Check the fluid level in the master cylinder reservoir and add as necessary.

## Anti-Lock Brake System Service

### RELIEVING ANTI-LOCK BRAKE SYSTEM PRESSURE

To relieve the pressure from the ABS system, turn the ignition switch to the **OFF** position. Disconnect the connectors from the ABS actuator. Wait a few minutes to allow for the system to bleed down, then disconnect the negative battery cable.

## ABS Actuator

### REMOVAL & INSTALLATION

1. Relieve the pressure from the ABS system.
2. Disconnect the negative battery cable.
3. Disconnect the electrical harness connectors from the actuator.
4. Disconnect the fluid lines from the actuator. Plug the ends of the lines to prevent leakage.
5. On 240SX, remove the relay bracket.
6. Remove the actuator mounting bolts and nuts.
7. Remove the actuator from the mounting bracket.
**To install:**
8. Position the actuator onto the mounting bracket.
9. Install the actuator mounting fasteners.
10. On 240SX, install the relay bracket.

11. Connect the fluid lines and the harness connectors.
12. Connect the negative battery cable.
13. Bleed the brake system.

## ABS Front Wheel Sensor

### REMOVAL & INSTALLATION

1. Raise and support the vehicle safely.
2. Remove the front wheels.
3. Disconnect the sensor harness connector.
4. Detach the sensor mounting brackets.
5. Unbolt the sensor from the rear of the steering knuckle.
6. Withdraw the sensor from the sensor rotor. Remove the sensor mounting brackets from the sensor wiring.

NOTE: During removal and installation, take care not to damage the sensor or the teeth of the rotor.

**To install:**
7. Transfer the mounting brackets to the new sensor. Insert the sensor through the opening in the the rear of the knuckle and engage the sensor with the rotor teeth.
8. Install the sensor mounting bolts. Check and adjust the sensor-to-rotor clearance as described below. Once the clearance is set, tighten the sensor mounting bolt(s) to 8–12 ft. lbs. (11–16 Nm) on 240SX (8–11 ft. lbs. on 1992 Sentra) and 300ZX and 13–17 ft. lbs. (18–24 Nm) on Maxima and Stanza.
9. Position and install the sensor mounting brackets. Make the sure the sensor wiring is routed properly.
10. Connect the sensor harness connector.
11. Mount the front wheels and lower the vehicle.

### WHEEL SENSOR CLEARANCE ADJUSTMENT

1. Install the sensor.
2. Check the clearance between the edge of the sensor and rotor teeth using a feeler gauge. Clearances should be as follows:
   a. On 240SX, front wheel sensor clearance should be 0.0108–0.0295 in. (0.275–0.75mm).
   b. On 300ZX, front wheel sensor clearance should be 0.0087–0.0280 in. (0.22–0.71mm).
   c. On Maxima and Stanza, the clearance should be 0.008–0.039 in. (0.2–1.0mm).

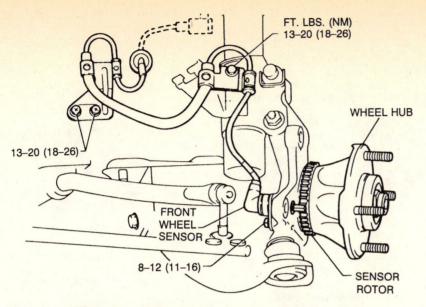

FT. LBS. (NM)
13–20 (18–26)

WHEEL HUB

13–20 (18–26)

FRONT
WHEEL
SENSOR

8–12 (11–16)

SENSOR
ROTOR

**ABS front wheel sensor removal and installation—240SX**

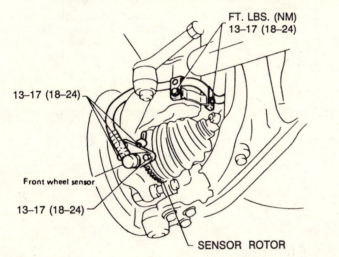

FT. LBS. (NM)
13–17 (18–24)

13–17 (18–24)

Front wheel sensor

13–17 (18–24)

SENSOR ROTOR

**ABS front wheel sensor removal and installation—Maxima and Stanza**

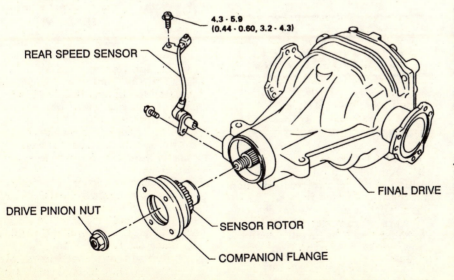

4.3 - 5.9
(0.44 - 0.60, 3.2 - 4.3)

REAR SPEED SENSOR

DRIVE PINION NUT

SENSOR ROTOR

COMPANION FLANGE

FINAL DRIVE

**ABS rear wheel sensor removal and installation—240SX**

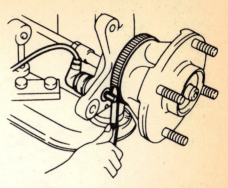

**Checking front wheel sensor-to-rotor clearance**

3. To adjust the clearance, loosen the sensor mounting bolt(s) and move the sensor back and forth until the clearance is as specified.

4. Once the clearance is set, tighten the sensor mounting bolt(s) to 8–12 ft. lbs. (11–16 Nm) on 240SX and 300ZX and 13–17 ft. lbs. (18–24 Nm) on Maxima and Stanza.

## ABS Rear Wheel Sensor

### REMOVAL & INSTALLATION

#### 240SX, 1990–92 300ZX, Maxima and Stanza

1. Raise and support the vehicle safely.

2. Remove the rear wheels.

3. Disconnect the sensor harness connector.

4. Detach the sensor mounting brackets.

5. Remove the sensor mounting bolts.

6. On Maxima and Stanza, withdraw the sensor from the rear gusset. On 240SX, the sensor is located on the side of the differential carrier near the driveshaft companion flange. On 300ZX, there are 2 sensors on the side of the differential near each halfshaft.

7. Remove the sensor mounting brackets from the sensor wiring.

**To install:**

8. Transfer the mounting brackets to the new sensor.

9. Install the sensor. Check and adjust the sensor-to-rotor clearance as described below. Once the clearance is set, tighten the sensor mounting bolt(s) to to 13–20 ft. lbs. (18–26 Nm).

10. Install the sensor mounting brackets. Make the sure the sensor wiring is routed properly.

11. Connect the sensor harness connector.

12. Mount the rear wheels and lower the vehicle.

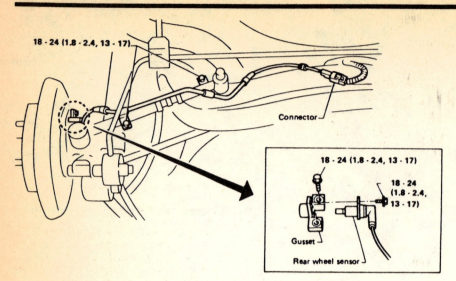

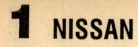

**ABS rear wheel sensor removal and installation—Maxima and Stanza**

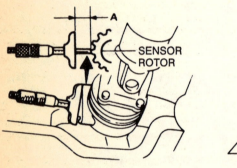

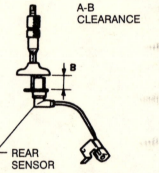

**Checking rear wheel sensor-to-rotor clearance on 240SX**

## WHEEL SENSOR

## CLEARANCE ADJUSTMENT

1. Install the rear wheel sensor.
2. Check the clearance between the edge of the sensor and rotor teeth using a feeler gauge. Clearances should be as follows:

a. On 240SX, rear wheel sensor clearance should 0.0138–0.0246 in. (0.035–0.625mm).

b. On 300ZX, rear wheel sensor clearance should be 0.0024–0.0366 in. (0.06–0.93mm).

c. On Maxima and Stanza, the clearance should be 0.008–0.039 in. (0.2–1.0mm).

3. To adjust the clearance, loosen the sensor mounting bolt(s) and move the sensor back and forth until the clearance is as specified.

4. Once the clearance is set, tighten the sensor mounting bolt(s) to to 13–20 ft. lbs. (18–26 Nm).

# CHASSIS ELECTRICAL

## Air Bag

### DISARMING

On vehicles equipped with an air bag, turn the ignition switch to OFF position. The negative battery cable must be disconnected and wait 10 minutes after the cable is disconnected before working on the system. SRS sensors must always be installed with the arrow marks facing the front of the vehicle.

## Heater Blower Motor

### REMOVAL & INSTALLATION

1. Disconnect the negative battery cable.
2. Remove all panels and ducting necessary to gain access to the blower motor.
3. Disconnnect the blower motor harness wiring connectors.
4. Remove the blower motor retaining screws and lower the motor/wheel from the intake housing. On some models, release the clips that attach the blower casing to the intake housing to remove the blower motor.
**To install:**
5. Transfer the old blower wheel to the shaft of the new motor.
6. Raise the blower/wheel assembly up and onto the intake housing. Use a new gasket, if required.
7. Install the blower motor retaining screws or lock the clips.
8. Connect the blower motor wiring.
9. Install all ducting and panels.
10. Connect the negative battery cable.
11. Check the blower for proper operation at all speeds.

## Windshield Wiper Motor

### REMOVAL & INSTALLATION

*200SX, 240SX, Stanza and Stanza Wagon*

#### FRONT

1. Disconnect the negative battery cable and make sure the wiper switch is in the **OFF** position.
2. Remove the wiper arm.
3. Remove the cowl cover and disconnect the wiper harness connector(s).
3. Remove the wiper motor bolts.
4. Maneuver the wiper motor so the wiper motor link exits the oblong opening in the front cowl top panel. Then, pull the motor straight out and disconnect the ball joint from the motor and wiper links.
5. Remove the wiper motor.
6. Remove the wiper link pivot blocks on the driver's and passenger's sides.
7. Withdraw the wiper link and pivot blocks as one unit from the oblong opening on the left side (driver's) of the cowl top.
**To install:**
8. Lubricate the ball joints and pivot points with multi-purpose grease.

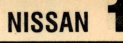

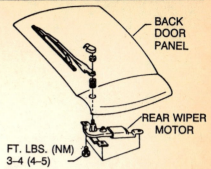

Rear wiper assembly—240SX

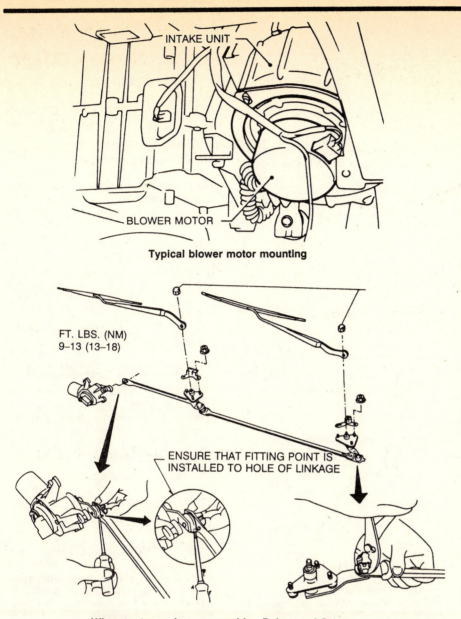

Typical blower motor mounting

FT. LBS. (NM)
9–13 (13–18)

ENSURE THAT FITTING POINT IS
INSTALLED TO HOLE OF LINKAGE

Wiper motor and arm assembly—Pulsar and Sentra

9. Position the wiper link and pivot block as one unit in the cowl top through the oblong hole.

10. Before installing the pivot blocks on the cowl top, hold the end of the motor side link at the hole in the front cowl top panel and insert the motor link ball pin into the wiper link hole.

11. Mount the wiper motor and install the bolts.

12. Connect the wiper motor wiring and install the cowl cover.

13. Attach the wiper arm. To reduce wiper arm looseness, prior to connecting the wiper arm, make sure the motor spline shaft and pivot area is completely free of debris and corrosion. Wire brush as necessary.

**NOTE: On 200SX, one wiper arm is longer than the other. The driver's side arm is marked with a "D" and the passenger's side with an "A". Make sure they are installed on their respective sides.**

14. Connnect the negative battery cable and check the wipers for proper operation.

### REAR

1. Disconnect the negative battery cable.

2. Lift up the rear hatch.

3. Separate the rear wiper arm from the motor shaft.

4. Disconnect the wiper motor wiring harness connector.

5. Unbolt and remove the rear wiper motor from the hatch.

6. Installation is the reverse of the removal procedure. Check the wipers for proper operation.

### Pulsar and Sentra

The wiper motor is on the firewall under the hood. The operating linkage is on the firewall inside the vehicle.

1. Disconnect negative battery cable. Detach the motor wiring plug.

2. Working from inside the vehicle, remove the nut connecting the linkage to the wiper shaft.

3. Unbolt and remove the wiper motor from the firewall.

4. Installation is the reverse of the removal procedure. To reduce wiper arm looseness, prior to connecting the wiper arm, make sure the motor spline shaft and pivot area is completely free of debris and corrosion. Wire brush as necessary.

### 300ZX and Maxima

The wiper motor and operating linkage is on the firewall under the hood.

1. Disconnect the negative battery cable.

2. Lift the wiper arms. Remove the securing nuts and detach the arms.

3. Remove the air intake grille.

4. Remove the nuts holding the wiper pivots to the body.

5. Open the hood and unscrew the motor from the firewall.

6. Disconnect the wiring connector and remove the wiper motor with the linkage.

7. Installation is the reverse of the removal procedure. To reduce wiper arm looseness, prior to connecting the wiper arm, make sure the motor spline shaft and pivot area is completely free of debris and corrosion. Wire brush as necessary.

**NOTE: If the wipers do not park correctly, adjust the position of the automatic stop cover on the wiper motor.**

# Windshield Wiper Switch

## REMOVAL & INSTALLATION

### Front

The windshield wiper switch is part of

the combination switch, which is mounted on the steering column.

### Rear

#### 200SX, 240SX, 300ZX, STANZA AND SENTRA

On Stanza Wagon the rear window wiper/washer is located left-side of the instrument panel. On Sentra Wagon the rear window wiper/washer is located right-side of the instrument panel. On all other vehicles, the rear window wiper switch is located on the right side of the instrument panel.

1. Remove the instrument cluster.
2. Remove the nut that attaches the combination switch to the dash.
3. Disconnect the electrical connectors from the rear of the switch, then remove it.
4. Installation is the reverse of the removal procedure.

## Instrument Cluster

### REMOVAL & INSTALLATION

#### 200SX and 240SX

NOTE: On 240SX, when removing the Head-Up Display (HUD) finisher, be careful not to scratch the HUD's reflective surface. To prevent this, cover the finisher and reflective surface with a protective covering.

1. Disconnect the negative battery cable.
2. Remove the steering wheel and steering wheel covers, as required.
3. Remove the screws holding the cluster lid in place and remove the lid.
4. On 200SX, remove the 2 screws and 7 pawls to release the cluster. On 240SX, the cluster is held with 3 screws.
5. Carefully withdraw the cluster from the instrument panel and disconnect the speedometer cable (analog) and electrical wiring from the rear of the cluster. Make sure the wiring is labeled clearly to avoid confusion during installation.
6. Remove the cluster. Be careful not to damage the printed circuit.
7. Installation is the reverse of the removal procedure.

#### 300ZX

1. Disconnect the negative battery cable.
2. Remove the steering wheel and steering wheel covers.

3. To remove the combination switch, first remove the combination switch lower mounting nut, then remove the switch.
4. Remove the left and right instrument switches by removing the hooks and fasteners.
5. Remove the cluster lids and cluster retaining screws.
6. Carefully withdraw the cluster from the instrument panel and disconnect the speedometer cable and electrical wiring from the rear of the cluster. Make sure the wiring is labeled clearly to avoid confusion during installation.
7. Remove the cluster. Be careful not to damage the printed circuit.
8. Installation is the reverse of the removal procedure.

#### Maxima

NOTE: On 1989–92 Maxima, when removing the Head-Up Display (HUD) finisher, be careful not to scratch the HUD's reflective surface. To prevent this, cover the finisher and reflective surface with a protective covering.

1. Disconnect the negative battery cable.
2. Remove the instrument panel lower cover.
3. Remove the steering wheel and steering wheel covers.
4. Remove the cluster lids.
5. Genlty withdraw the combination meter assembly from the instrument pad and disconnect the speedometer cable (analog).
6. Disconnect the wiring and remove the cluster. Make sure the wiring is marked clearly to avoid confusion during installation.
7. Remove the cluster. Be careful not to damage the printed circuit.
8. Installation is the reverse of the removal procedure.

#### Pulsar, Sentra and Stanza

1. Disconnect the negative battery cable.
2. Remove the steering wheel and the steering column covers.
3. Remove the instrument cluster lid by removing its screws.
4. Remove the instrument cluster screws.
5. Gently withdraw the cluster from the instrument pad and disconnect all wiring and speedometer cable. Make sure the wires are marked clearly to avoid confusion during installation. Be careful not to damage the printed circuit.

6. Remove the cluster.
7. Installation is the reverse of removal.

## Speedometer

NOTE: If equipped with a digital speedometer, the entire cluster assembly must be replaced if the speedometer is faulty.

### REMOVAL & INSTALLATION

#### Analog (Needle Type) Speedometers

1. Disconnect the negative battery cable.
2. Remove the cluster.
3. Disconnect the speedometer cable and remove the speedometer fasteners.
4. Carefully remove the speedometer from the cluster. Be careful not to damage the printed circuit board.
5. Installation is the reverse of the removal procedure.

## Concealed Headlights
### —— CAUTION ——
*Before attempting to manually operate the concealed (retractable) headlights, first disconnect the negative battery cable. Otherwise the headlights and motor shaft may suddenly move and injure hand and fingers.*

### MANUAL OPERATION

NOTE: If the headlights are frozen and inoperative, carefully melt the ice before attempting the manual operation procedure. Operation of a frozen headlight will drain the battery and may cause damage to the motor and operating linkages.

1. Switch the headlight and retractable headlight switches to the OFF position.
2. Disconnect the negative battery cable.
3. Remove the rubber cap from the motor shaft.
4. Manually turn the motor shaft in the counterclockwise position until the headlights are in the desired position (open or closed).
5. Install the motor shaft cap.
6. Connect the negative battery cable.
7. Check the head lights for proper operation.

# SERIAL NUMBER IDENTIFICATION

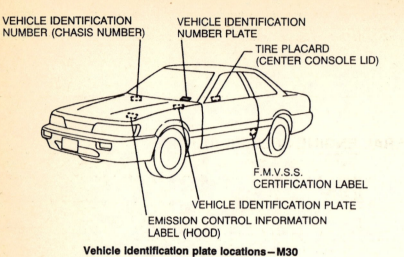

Vehicle identification plate locations – M30

## Vehicle Identification Number

The vehicle identification number plate is located at the upper left corner of the dash panel, as viewed through the windshield.

## Engine Number

The engine number is located at the rear of the engine block. It is centrally positioned on Q45, slightly right of center on M30 and at the left side on the G20.

## Chassis Number

The chassis number plate is located in the engine compartment, at the upper right portion of the firewall.

## Transaxle Number

The G20 manual transaxle identification number is located at the top of the

case near the bellhousing. The G20 automatic transaxle identification number is located at the top of the case on the govenor cap.

## Transmission Number

The automatic transmission identification number for both the M30 and Q45 is located at the right rear of the case on the tailshaft.

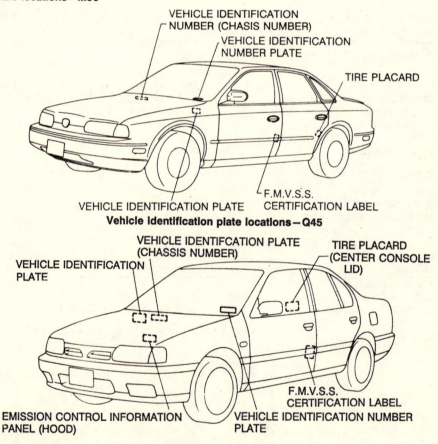

Vehicle identification plate locations – Q45

Vehicle identification plate locations – G20

# SPECIFICATIONS
## ENGINE IDENTIFICATION

| Year | Model | Engine Displacement cu. in. (cc/liter) | Engine Series Identification | No. of Cylinders | Engine Type |
|------|-------|----------------------------------------|------------------------------|------------------|-------------|
| 1990 | Q45 | 274 (4494/4.5) | VH45DE | 8 | DOHC |
| | M30 | 181 (2960/3.0) | VG30 | 6 | SOHC |

## ENGINE IDENTIFICATION

| Year | Model | Engine Displacement cu. in. (cc/liter) | Engine Series Identification | No. of Cylinders | Engine Type |
|------|-------|----------------------------------------|------------------------------|------------------|-------------|
| 1991–92 | Q45 | 274 (4494/4.5) | VH45DE | 8 | DOHC |
| | M30 | 181 (2960/3.0) | VG30 | 6 | SOHC |
| | G20 | 122 (1998/2.0) | SR20DE | 4 | DOHC |

SOHC—Single Overhead Camshaft
DOHC—Double Overhead Camshaft

## GENERAL ENGINE SPECIFICATIONS

| Year | Model | Engine Displacement cu. in. (cc) | Fuel System Type | Net Horsepower @ rpm | Net Torque @ rpm (ft. lbs.) | Bore × Stroke (in.) | Compression Ratio | Oil Pressure @ rpm |
|------|-------|----------------------------------|------------------|----------------------|------------------------------|---------------------|-------------------|--------------------|
| 1990 | Q45 | 274 (4494) | MPFI | 278 @ 6000 | 280 @ 4000 | 3.66 × 3.26 | 10.2:1 | 67–81 @ 3000 |
| | M30 | 181 (2960) | MPFI | 162 @ 5200 | 180 @ 3600 | 3.43 × 3.27 | 9.0:1 | 53–67 @ 3200 |
| 1991–92 | Q45 | 274 (4494) | MPFI | 278 @ 6000 | 280 @ 4000 | 3.66 × 3.26 | 10.2:1 | 67–81 @ 3000 |
| | M30 | 181 (2960) | MPFI | 162 @ 5200 | 180 @ 3600 | 3.43 × 3.27 | 9.0:1 | 53–67 @ 3200 |
| | G20 | 122 (1998) | MPFI | 140 @ 6400 | 132 @ 4800 | 3.38 × 3.38 | 10.0:1 | 46–57 @ 3200 |

MPFI—Multi-Point Fuel Injection

## ENGINE TUNE-UP SPECIFICATIONS

| Year | Model | Engine Displacement cu. in. (cc) | Spark Plugs Type | Gap (in.) | Ignition Timing (deg.) MT | AT | Compression Pressure (psi) | Fuel Pump (psi) | Idle Speed (rpm) MT | AT | Valve Clearance In. | Ex. |
|------|-------|----------------------------------|------------------|-----------|---------------------------|----|----------------------------|-----------------|---------------------|----|---------------------|-----|
| 1990 | Q45 | 274 (4494) | PFR6B-11 | 0.040 | — | 15B | 185 @ 300 rpm | 34 | — | 750 | Hyd. | Hyd. |
| | M30 | 181 (2960) | PFR6B-11 | 0.040 | — | 15B | 173 @ 300 rpm | 43 | — | 800 | Hyd. | Hyd. |
| 1991 | Q45 | 274 (4494) | PFR6B-11 | 0.040 | — | 15B | 185 @ 300 rpm | 34 | — | 750 | Hyd. | Hyd. |
| | M30 | 181 (2960) | PFR6B-11 | 0.040 | — | 15B | 173 @ 300 rpm | 43 | — | 800 | Hyd. | Hyd. |
| | G20 | 122 (1998) | PFR6B-11 | 0.040 | 15B | 15B | 178 @ 300 rpm | 43 | 800 | 800 | Hyd. | Hyd. |
| 1992 | SEE UNDERHOOD STICKER | | | | | | | | | | | |

Hyd.—Hydraulic

## FIRING ORDERS

**NOTE: To avoid confusion, always replace spark plug wires one at a time.**

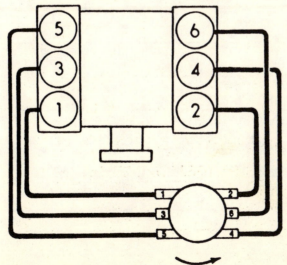

**3.0L Engine**
**Engine Firing Order: 1–2–3–4–5–6**
**Distributor Rotation: Counterclockwise**

## FIRING ORDERS

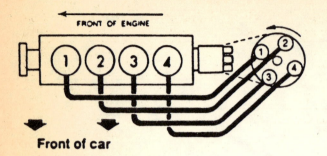

**2.0L Engine**
**Engine Firing Order: 1–3–4–2**
**Distributor Rotation: Counterclockwise**

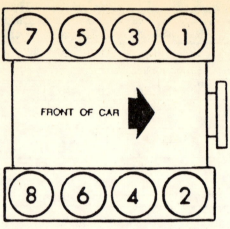

**4.5L Engine**
**Engine Firing Order: 1–8–7–3–6–5–4–2**
**Distributorless Ignition System**

## CAPACITIES

| Year | Model | Engine Displacement cu. in. (cc) | Engine Crankcase (qts.) with Filter | without Filter | Transmission (pts.) 4-Spd | 5-Spd | Auto. | Drive Axle (pts.) | Fuel Tank (gal.) | Cooling System (qts.) |
|---|---|---|---|---|---|---|---|---|---|---|
| 1990 | Q45 | 274 (4494) | 6½ | 6 | — | — | 18¼ | 3⅛ | 22½ | 11 |
| | M30 | 181 (2960) | 4½ | 4¼ | — | — | 17½ | 2¾ | 16 | 9½ |
| 1991–92 | Q45 | 274 (4494) | 6½ | 6 | — | — | 18¼ | 3⅛ | 22½ | 11 |
| | M30 | 181 (2960) | 4½ | 4¼ | — | — | 17½ | 2¾ | 16 | 9½ |
| | G20 | 122 (1998) | 3⅝ | 3⅝ | — | 7½ | 17¾ | — | 16 | ① |

① 6½ qts.—Manual transaxle
6⅞ qts.—Automatic transaxle

## CAMSHAFT SPECIFICATIONS

| Year | Engine Displacement cu. in. (cc) | Journal Diameter 1 | 2 | 3 | 4 | 5 | Lobe Lift ① In. | Ex. | Bearing Clearance | Camshaft End Play |
|---|---|---|---|---|---|---|---|---|---|---|
| 1990 | 274 (4494) | 1.0211–1.0218 | 1.0211–1.0218 | 1.0211–1.0218 | 1.0211–1.0218 | 1.0211–1.0218 | 1.4929–1.5004 | 1.3889–1.3964 | 0.0018–0.0059 | 0.0028–0.0079 |
| | 181 (2960) | 1.8866–1.8874 | 1.8472–1.8480 | 1.8472–1.8480 | 1.8472–1.8480 | 1.6701–1.6709 | 1.5566–1.5641 | 1.5566–1.5641 | 0.0024–0.0041 | 0.0012–0.0024 |
| 1991–92 | 274 (4494) | 1.0211–1.0218 | 1.0211–1.0218 | 1.0211–1.0218 | 1.0211–1.0218 | 1.0211–1.0218 | 1.4929–1.5004 | 1.3889–1.3964 | 0.0018–0.0059 | 0.0028–0.0079 |
| | 181 (2960) | 1.8866–1.8874 | 1.8472–1.8480 | 1.8472–1.8480 | 1.8472–1.8480 | 1.6701–1.6709 | 1.5566–1.5641 | 1.5566–1.5641 | 0.0024–0.0041 | 0.0012–0.0024 |
| | 122 (1998) | 1.0998–1.1006 | 1.0998–1.1006 | 1.0998–1.1006 | 1.0998–1.1006 | 1.0998–1.1006 | 1.5121–1.5196 | 1.4929–1.5004 | 0.0018–0.0034 | 0.0022–0.0055 |

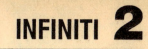
## CRANKSHAFT AND CONNECTING ROD SPECIFICATIONS

All measurements are given in inches.

| Year | Engine Displacement cu. in. (cc) | Crankshaft | | | | Connecting Rod | | |
| | | Main Brg. Journal Dia. | Main Brg. Oil Clearance | Shaft End-play | Thrust on No. | Journal Diameter | Oil Clearance | Side Clearance |
|---|---|---|---|---|---|---|---|---|
| **1990** | 274 (4494) | ① | 0.0005–0.0020 | 0.0039–0.0118 | 3 | ② | 0.0008–0.0026 | 0.0079–0.0157 |
| | 181 (2960) | ③ | 0.0011–0.0035 | 0.0020–0.0118 | 4 | 1.9667–1.9675 | 0.0006–0.0035 | 0.0079–0.0157 |
| **1991–92** | 274 (4494) | ① | 0.0005–0.0020 | 0.0039–0.0118 | 3 | ② | 0.0008–0.0026 | 0.0079–0.0157 |
| | 181 (2960) | ③ | 0.0011–0.0035 | 0.0020–0.0118 | 4 | 1.9667–1.9675 | 0.0006–0.0035 | 0.0079–0.0157 |
| | 122 (1998) | ④ | 0.0002–0.0009 | 0.0039–0.0102 | 3 | ⑤ | 0.0008–0.0018 | 0.0079–0.0138 |

① Grade No. 0—2.5180–2.5183
  Grade No. 1—2.5178–2.5180
  Grade No. 2—2.5176–2.5178
  Grade No. 3—2.5173–2.5176
② Grade No. 0—2.0460–2.0462
  Grade No. 1—2.0457–2.0460

Grade No. 2—2.0455–2.0457
③ Grade No. 0—2.4790–2.4793
  Grade No. 1—2.4787–2.4790
  Grade No. 2—2.4784–2.4787
④ Grade No. 0—2.1643–2.1646
  Grade No. 1—2.1641–2.1643

Grade No. 2—2.1639–2.1641
Grade No. 3—2.1636–2.1639
⑤ Grade No. 0—1.8885–1.8887
  Grade No. 1—1.8883–1.8885
  Grade No. 2—1.8880–1.8883

## VALVE SPECIFICATIONS

| Year | Engine Displacement cu. in. (cc) | Seat Angle (deg.) | Face Angle (deg.) | Spring Test Pressure (lbs.) | Spring Installed Height (in.) | Stem-to-Guide Clearance (in.) | | Stem Diameter (in.) | |
| | | | | | | Intake | Exhaust | Intake | Exhaust |
|---|---|---|---|---|---|---|---|---|---|
| **1990** | 274 (4494) | 45.25 | 44.75 | 120.4 | 1.86① | 0.0017②–0.0039 | 0.0018②–0.0039 | 0.275 | 0.314 |
| | 181 (2960) | 45.25 | 45 | ③ | ④ | | | 0.274 | 0.314 |
| **1991–92** | 274 (4494) | 45.25 | 44.75 | 120.4 | 1.86① | 0.0017②–0.0039 | 0.0018②–0.0039 | 0.275 | 0.314 |
| | 181 (2960) | 45.25 | 45 | ③ | ④ | | | 0.274 | 0.314 |
| | 122 (1998) | 45.15–45.45 | 44.53–45.07 | 128–144 | 1.18 | 0.0008–0.0021 | 0.0016–0.0029 | 0.235 | 0.234 |

① Free height
② Maximum
③ Inner—57.3
  Outer—117.7
④ Inner—1.74
  Outer—2.02

## PISTON AND RING SPECIFICATIONS

All measurements are given in inches.

| Year | Engine Displacement cu. in. (cc) | Piston Clearance | Ring Gap | | | Ring Side Clearance | | |
| | | | Top Compression | Bottom Compression | Oil Control | Top Compression | Bottom Compression | Oil Control |
|---|---|---|---|---|---|---|---|---|
| **1990** | 274 (4494) | 0.0004–0.0012 | 0.0106–0.0390 | 0.0154–0.0390 | 0.0079–0.0390 | 0.0016–0.0040 | 0.0012–0.0040 | — |
| | 181 (2960) | 0.0010–0.0018 | 0.0083–0.0390 | 0.0071–0.0390 | 0.0079–0.0390 | 0.0016–0.0040 | 0.0012–0.0040 | — |
| **1991–92** | 274 (4494) | 0.0004–0.0012 | 0.0106–0.0390 | 0.0154–0.0390 | 0.0079–0.0390 | 0.0016–0.0040 | 0.0012–0.0040 | — |
| | 181 (2960) | 0.0010–0.0018 | 0.0083–0.0390 | 0.0071–0.0390 | 0.0079–0.0390 | 0.0016–0.0040 | 0.0012–0.0040 | — |
| | 122 (1998) | 0.0004–0.0012 | 0.0079–0.0118 | 0.0138–0.0197 | 0.0079–0.0236 | 0.0018–0.0031 | 0.0012–0.0026 | — |

## TORQUE SPECIFICATIONS
All readings in ft. lbs.

| Year | Engine Displacement cu. in. (cc) | Cylinder Head Bolts | Main Bearing Bolts | Rod Bearing Bolts | Crankshaft Pulley Bolts | Flywheel Bolts | Manifold Intake | Manifold Exhaust | Spark Plugs |
|---|---|---|---|---|---|---|---|---|---|
| 1990 | 274 (4494) | ① | ② | ③ | 260–275 | 61–69 | 12–15 | 20–23 | 15–20 |
|  | 181 (2960) | ④ | 67–74 | ③ | 90–98 | 61–69 | 12–14 | 13–16 | 15–20 |
| 1991–92 | 274 (4494) | ① | ② | ③ | 260–275 | 61–69 | 12–15 | 20–23 | 15–20 |
|  | 181 (2960) | ④ | 67–74 | ③ | 90–98 | 61–69 | 12–14 | 13–16 | 15–20 |
|  | 122 (1998) | ⑤ | ⑥ | ③ | 105–112 | 61–69 | 13–15 | 13–15 | 15–20 |

NOTE: Always tighten bolts in specified sequence.
① ⓐ Tighten bolts to 22 ft. lbs. (29 Nm)
  ⓑ Tighten bolts to 69 ft. lbs. (93 Nm)
  ⓒ Loosen bolts completely.
  ⓓ Tighten bolts to 18–25 ft. lbs. (25–34 Nm)
  ⓔ Turn bolts 90 to 95 degrees clockwise or if angle wrench is not available, tighten bolts to 69–72 ft. lbs. (93–98 Nm)
② See text

③ Step 1: 10–12 ft. lbs.
  Step 2: An additional 60–65 degrees or tighten to a final torque of 28–33 ft. lbs.
④ Step 1: 22 ft. lbs.
  Step 2: 43 ft. lbs.
  Step 3: Loosen all bolts completely
  Step 4: 22 ft. lbs.
  Step 5: An additional 60–65 degrees or tighten to a final torque of 40–47 ft. lbs.
⑤ ⓐ Tighten all bolts to 29 ft. lbs. (39 Nm)
  ⓑ Tighten all bolts to 58 ft. lbs. (78 Nm)
  ⓒ Loosen all bolts completely

ⓓ Tighten all bolts to 25–33 ft. lbs. (34–44 Nm)
ⓔ Turn all bolts 90 degrees–100 degrees clockwise
ⓕ Turn all bolts an additional 90 degrees–100 degrees clockwise
• Do not turn any bolt 180 degrees–200 degrees clockwise all at once
⑥ ⓐ Tighten bolts to 24–28 ft. lbs. (32–38 Nm)
  ⓑ Turn all bolts 45 degrees–50 degrees clockwise

## BRAKE SPECIFICATIONS
All measurements in inches unless noted.

| Year | Model | Lug Nut Torque (ft. lbs.) | Master Cylinder Bore | Brake Disc Minimum Thickness | Brake Disc Maximum Runout | Standard Brake Drum Diameter | Minimum Lining Thickness Front | Minimum Lining Thickness Rear |
|---|---|---|---|---|---|---|---|---|
| 1990 | Q45 | 72–87 | 1.06 | ① | 0.003 | — | 0.080 | 0.080 |
|  | M30 | 76–90 | 1.00 | ② | 0.003 | — | 0.080 | 0.080 |
| 1991–92 | Q45 | 72–87 | 1.06 | ① | 0.003 | — | 0.080 | 0.080 |
|  | M30 | 76–90 | 1.00 | ② | 0.003 | — | 0.080 | 0.080 |
|  | G20 | 76–90 | 0.937 | ③ | 0.003 | — | 0.080 | 0.080 |

① Front: 1.024 Rear: 0.315
② Front: 0.787 Rear: 0.354
③ Front: 0.790 Rear: 0.310

## WHEEL ALIGNMENT

| Year | Model | | Caster Range (deg.) | Caster Preferred Setting (deg.) | Camber Range (deg.) | Camber Preferred Setting (deg.) | Toe-in (in.) | Steering Axis Inclination (deg.) |
|---|---|---|---|---|---|---|---|---|
| 1990 | Q45 | front | 5¾P–7¼P | 6½P | 1½N–0 | ¾N | 1/32 | 12–13½ |
|  |  | rear | — | — | 1½N–½N | 1N | 1/8 | — |
|  | M30 | front | 4P–5½P | 4¾P | ½N–1P | ¾P | 0 | 12–13½ |
|  |  | rear | — | — | 1N–¼P | ⅜N | 1/16 | — |
| 1991–92 | Q45 | front | 5¾P–7¼P | 6½P | 1½N–0 | ¾N | 1/32 | 12–13½ |
|  |  | rear | — | — | 1½N–½N | 1N | 1/8 | — |
|  | M30 | front | 4P–5½P | 4¾P | ½N–1P | ¾P | 0 | 12–13½ |
|  |  | rear | — | — | 1N–¼P | ⅜N | 1/16 | — |
|  | G20 | front | 1–2½P | 2P | ¾N–¾P | 0 | 0–¼P | 13¾–15¼ |
|  |  | rear | — | — | 1¾N–¼P | 1¼N | ¼N–¼P | — |

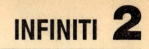

# ENGINE MECHANICAL

**NOTE: Disconnecting the negative battery cable on some vehicles may interfere with the functions of the on board computer systems and may require the computer to undergo a relearning process, once the negative battery cable is reconnected.**

## Engine Assembly

### REMOVAL & INSTALLATION

#### G20

1. Disconnect the negative battery cable. Raise and support the vehicle safely. Remove the engine under cover. Matchmark the hood with the hood hinges and remove.
2. Drain the coolant from both the cylinder block and radiator.
3. Drain the engine oil.
4. Release fuel system pressure and remove fuel line.
5. Label and remove all vacuum lines and wiring harness connectors.
6. Remove exhaust tubes, ball joints and drive shafts.
7. Remove the radiator and fans.
8. Remove the drive belts.
9. Remove the alternator, compressor and power steering pump from the engine and lay them aside. do not disconnect the compressor or power steering pump lines.
10. Support the engine with a hoist and the transmission with a suitable jack. Raise the engine and transaxle slightly and remove the center member.
11. Remove the bolts from the rear engine mount and slowly lower the hoist and transaxle jack.
12. Remove the engine and transaxle from beneath the vehicle.
**To install:**
13. Install the center member on the engine (if removed). Ensure that all insulators are correctly positioned on the brackets. Tighten bolts to 57–72 ft. lbs. (77–98 Nm).
14. If equipped with manual transaxle, ensure that the distance between the center of the insulator through-bolt and the center member is 2.28–2.36 in. (58–60mm). Tighten through-bolt to 46–58 ft. lbs. (62–78 Nm).
15. Carefully install the engine and tighten the center member-to-frame bolts. Install the rear engine mount.
16. Install the alternator, compressor and power steering pump.
17. Connect all vacuum hoses and wiring harness connectors. Connect the fuel line.
18. Install the exhaust tubes, ball joints, drive shafts, the radiator and fans, the drive belts.
19. Fill the coolant system with anti-freeze and the crankcase with oil.
20. Install the engine under cover and hood.

#### M30

1. Mark the hood hinge relationship and remove the hood and engine undercover.
2. Release the fuel system pressure and disconnect the negative battery cable. Raise and support the vehicle safely.
3. Drain the cooling system and the oil pan.
4. Remove the air cleaner and disconnect the throttle cable.
5. Disconnect or remove the following:
   Drive belts
   Ignition wire from the coil to the distributor
   Ignition coil ground wire and the engine ground cable
   Block connector from the distributor
   Fusible links
   Engine harness connectors
   Fuel and fuel return hoses
   Upper and lower radiator hoses
   Heater inlet and outlet hoses
   Engine vacuum hoses
   Carbon canister hoses and the air pump air cleaner hose
   Any interfering engine accessory: power steering pump, air conditioning compressor or alternator
6. Remove the air pump air cleaner.
7. Remove the carbon canister.
8. Remove the auxiliary fan, washer tank, grille and radiator (with fan assembly).
9. Disconnect the speedometer cable.
10. Remove the spring pins from the transaxle gear selector rods.
11. Install engine slingers to the block and connect a suitable lifting device to the slingers.
12. Disconnect the exhaust pipe at both the manifold connection and the clamp holding the pipe to the engine.
13. Drain the transaxle gear oil.
14. Lower the shifter and selector rods and remove the bolts from the motor mount brackets. Remove the nuts holding the front and rear motor mounts to the frame.
15. Lift the engine/transaxle assembly up and away from the vehicle.
**To install:**
16. Lower the engine and transaxle assembly into the vehicle. When lowering the engine onto the frame, make sure to keep it as level as possible.
17. Check the clearance between the frame and transaxle and make sure the engine mount bolts are seated in the groove of the mounting bracket.
18. After installing the motor mounts, adjust and install the buffer rods. The front should be 3.50–3.58 in. (89–91mm), and the rear, 3.90–3.98 in. (99–101mm).
19. Raise the shifter and selector rods to their normal operating positions.
20. Connect the exhaust pipe to the manifold connection and the clamp holding the pipe to the engine.
21. Disconnect the lifting device and remove the engine slingers.
22. Insert the spring pins into the transaxle gear selector rods.
23. Connect the speedometer cable.
24. Install the auxiliary fan, washer tank, grille and radiator (with fan assembly).
25. Install the carbon canister.
26. Install the air pump air cleaner.
27. Install or connect all hoses, belts, harnesses, connectors and components that were necessary to remove the engine.
28. Connect the throttle cable and install the air cleaner.
29. Fill the transaxle and cooling system to the proper levels.
30. Install the hood and connect the negative battery cable.
31. Make all the necessary engine adjustments. Charge the air conditioning system.
32. Tighten the following to the proper torque:
   Front engine mount bracket-to-engine bolts to 33–43 ft. lbs.
   Front engine mount-to-bracket bolts to 29–36 ft. lbs.
   Rear engine mount-to-crossmember bolts to 16–21 ft. lbs.
   Rear crossmember-to-transaxle bolts to 32–41 ft. lbs.

#### Q45

1. Disconnect the negative battery cable.
2. Relieve the pressure from the fuel system.
3. Mark the relation of the hood to the hinge brackets and remove the hood.
4. Raise and safely support the vehicle.
5. Remove the engine splash shield.
6. Drain the coolant and the engine oil.
7. Disconnect the transmission cooler lines from the radiator.
8. Remove the radiator hoses and remove the radiator and shroud.
9. Tag and disconnect all vacuum hoses, fuel lines and electrical connectors.

10. Disconnect the exhaust pipes from the exhaust manifolds.

11. Mark the position of the drive-shaft on the flanges and remove the driveshaft.

12. Remove the accessory drive belts.

13. Remove the alternator, air conditioning compressor and power steering pump.

14. Remove the lower steering joint.

15. Remove the sway bar, transverse link and tension rod with bracket.

16. Place a suitable jack under the transmission and disconnect the transmission rear mount.

17. Remove the suspension member attaching bolts.

18. Remove the engine mounting bolts.

19. Attach a suitable hoist to the engine. Lower the transmission jack and the hoist and lower the engine and transmission from under the vehicle.

**To install:**

20. Raise the engine and transmission into position.

21. Install the engine mounting nuts and bolts and tighten to 41 ft. lbs. (55 Nm).

22. Install the suspension member bolts.

23. Install and tighten the rear mount-to-body bolts to 41 ft. lbs. (55 Nm).

24. Remove the hoist and the transmission jack.

25. Install the sway bar, transverse link and the tension rod with bracket.

26. Install the lower steering joint.

27. Install the alternator, air conditioning compressor and power steering pump.

28. Install and adjust the accessory drive belts.

29. Install the radiator and shroud. Install the radiator hoses.

30. Install the driveshaft, aligning the marks that were made during the removal procedure.

31. Connect the exhaust pipes to the exhaust manifolds.

32. Connect all electrical connectors, fuel lines and vacuum hoses.

33. Fill the crankcase with the proper type of engine oil to the required level. Fill the cooling system with the proper type and quantity of coolant.

34. Install the hood, aligning the marks that were made during the removal procedure.

35. Connect the negative battery cable, start the engine and check for leaks.

## Engine Mount

### REMOVAL & INSTALLATION

#### G20

1. Disconnect the negative battery cable.

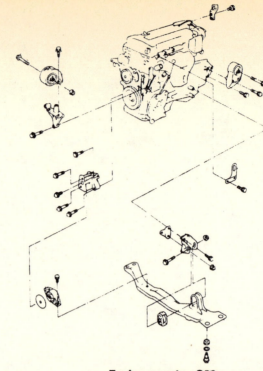

**Engine mounts – G20**

2. Matchmark the engine mount to its frame mounting location.

3. Raise the vehicle and support safely, if necessary. Using the proper equipment, support the weight of the engine.

4. Inspect all mounts to determine which is defective. A defective mount will have the rubber portion of the mount separated from the metal backing or stud.

5. Remove all bolts and nuts that attach the mount to the engine, transaxle or frame and remove the mount assembly from the vehicle.

6. Remove the through bolt and separate the insulator from the bracket, as required.

**To install:**

7. Installation is the reverse of removal.

8. If equipped with manual transaxle, ensure that the distance between the center of the front mounting bracket through-bolt and the center member is 2.28–2.36 in. (58–60mm). Tighten through-bolt to 46–58 ft. lbs. (62–78 Nm).

9. Tighten center member bolts to 57–72 ft. lbs. (77–98 Nm); rear fluid engine mount to 32–41 ft. lbs. (43–55 Nm); front fluid engine mount to 36–43 ft. lbs. (49–59 Nm).

#### M30

1. Disconnect the negative battery cable.

2. Matchmark the engine mount to its frame mounting location.

3. Raise the vehicle and support safely, if necessary. Using the proper equipment, support the weight of the engine.

4. Inspect all mounts to determine which is defective. A defective mount will have the rubber portion of the mount separated from the metal backing or stud.

5. Remove all bolts and nuts that attach the mount to the engine, transmission or frame and remove the mount assembly from the vehicle.

6. Remove the through bolt and separate the insulator from the bracket, as required.

7. Installation is the reverse of removal.

8. Tighten bolts as follows: engine mount-to-frame 29–36 ft. lbs. (39–49 Nm); engine mount-to-engine 33–43 ft. lbs. (44–59 Nm); transmission mount-to-crossmember 16–21 ft. lbs. (22–28 Nm); transmission mount-to-transmission 21–41 ft. lbs. (43–55 Nm).

#### Q45

1. Disconnect the negative battery cable.

2. Matchmark the engine mount to its frame mounting location.

3. Raise the vehicle and support safely, if necessary. Using the proper equipment, support the weight of the engine.

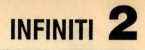

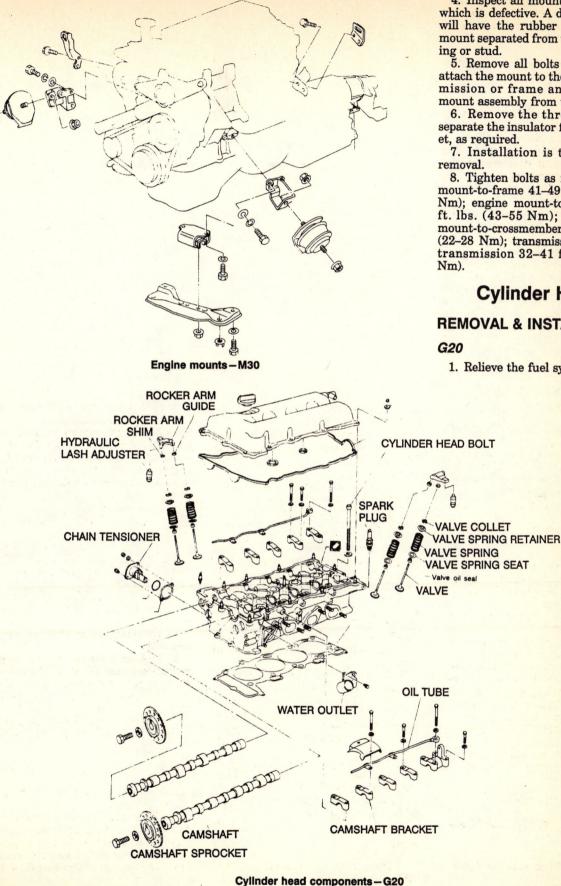

**Engine mounts—M30**

4. Inspect all mounts to determine which is defective. A defective mount will have the rubber portion of the mount separated from the metal backing or stud.

5. Remove all bolts and nuts that attach the mount to the engine, transmission or frame and remove the mount assembly from the vehicle.

6. Remove the through bolt and separate the insulator from the bracket, as required.

7. Installation is the reverse of removal.

8. Tighten bolts as follows: engine mount-to-frame 41–49 ft. lbs. (55–67 Nm); engine mount-to-engine 32–41 ft. lbs. (43–55 Nm); transmission mount-to-crossmember 16–21 ft. lbs. (22–28 Nm); transmission mount-to-transmission 32–41 ft. lbs. (43–55 Nm).

## Cylinder Head

### REMOVAL & INSTALLATION

*G20*

1. Relieve the fuel system pressure

**Cylinder head components—G20**

and Disconnect the negative battery cable.

2. Drain the coolant from the radiator and engine block. Remove the radiator.

3. Remove the right front wheel and engine side cover.

4. Remove the air duct to the intake manifold.

5. Remove the drive belts, water pump pulley, alternator and power steering pump.

6. Label and remove the vacuum hoses, fuel hoses and wire harness connectors.

7. Remove all the spark plugs, the AIV valve and resonator.

8. Remove the rocker cover and oil separator. Loosen rocker cover bolts, using 2–3 steps, in the opposite sequence of tightening

9. Remove the intake manifold supports.

10. Remove the oil filter bracket and power steering oil pump bracket.

11. Set No. 1 piston at TDC on the compression stroke by rotating the crankshaft.

12. Remove the chain tensioner.

13. Remove the distributor. Do not turn the rotor with the distributor removed.

14. Remove the timing chain guide, camshaft sprockets, camshafts, brackets, oil tubes and baffle plate. The camshaft bracket bolts must be loosened in sequence to prevent damage to the camshafts or the head.

15. Remove the cylinder block water hose and heater hoses.

16. Remove the starter motor and water pipe bolt.

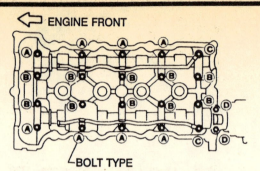

**Camshaft bracket bolt type—G20**

17. Remove the cylinder head outside bolts. Remove the inside cylinder head bolts by loosening them, using 2–3 steps, in the reverse order of the tightening sequence.

18. Remove the cylinder head with the intake and exhaust manifolds attached.

**To install:**

19. Apply a continuous bead of liquid gasket to the mating surface of the cylinder block before installing the head gasket.

20. Install the the gasket and cylinder head on the block.

NOTE: Cylinder head bolts may be reused providing the dimension from the bottom of the head to the end of the bolt does not exceed 6.228 in. (158.2mm). If the dimension exceeds the specification, install replacement cylinder head bolts.

21. Tighten cylinder head bolts as follows:

   a. Tighten all bolts to 29 ft. lbs. (39 Nm) using the proper sequence.

   b. Tighten all bolts to 58 ft. lbs. (78 Nm) using the proper sequence.

   c. Loosen all bolts completely.

   d. Tighten all bolts to 25–33 ft. lbs. (34–44 Nm) using the proper sequence.

   e. Tighten all bolts an additional 90–100 degrees.

22. Install the cylinder head outside bolts.

23. Install the water pipe bolt, starter motor and water hoses.

24. Clean the left hand camshaft end bracket and coat with liquid gasket. Install the camshafts, camshaft brackets, oil tubes and baffle plate. Ensure the left camshaft ket is at 12 o'clock and the right camshaft key is at 10 o'clock.

25. The procedure for tightening camshaft bolts must be followed exactly to prevent camshaft damage. Tighten bolts as follows:

   a. Tighten right camshaft bolts 9 and 10 (in that order) to 1.5 ft. lbs. (2 Nm) then tighten bolts 1 through

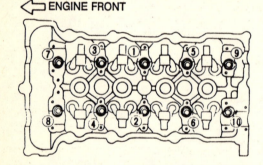

**Cylinder head inside bolt torque sequence—G20**

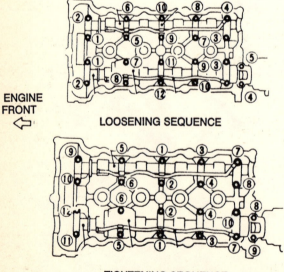

**Camshaft bracket loosening and tightening sequence—G20**

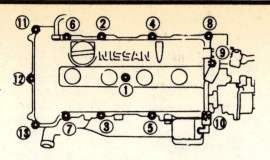

**Rocker cover tightening sequence—G20**

8 (in that order) to the same specification.

b. Tighten left camshaft bolts 11 and 12 (in that order) to 1.5 ft. lbs. (2 Nm) then tighten bolts 1 through 10 (in that order) to the same specification.

c. Tighten all bolts in sequence to 4.5 ft. lbs. (6 Nm).

d. Tighten all bolts in sequence to 6.5–8.5 ft. lbs. (9–12 Nm) for type A, B and C bolts, and 13–19 ft. lbs. (18–25 Nm) for type D bolts.

26. Line up the mating marks on the timing chain and camshaft sprockets and install the sprockets. Tighten sprocket bolts to 101–116 ft. lbs. (137–157 Nm).

27. Install the timing chain guide, distributor (ensure that rotor head is at 5 o'clock position), chain tensioner, oil filter bracket and power steering oil pump bracket.

28. Install intake manifold supports. Clean the rocker cover and mating surfaces and apply a continious bead of liquid gasket to the mating surface.

29. Install the rocker cover and oil separator. Tighten the rocker cover bolts as follows:

a. Tighten nuts 1, 10, 11, and 8 in that order to 3 ft. lbs. (4 Nm).

b. Tighten nuts 1 through 13 as indicated in the figure to 6–7 ft. lbs. (8–10 Nm).

30. Install the AIV and resonator, spark plugs, power steering pump, alternator water pump pulley and drive belts, air duct to the intake manifold and the radiator.

31. Install all vacuum and fuel hoses, and reconnect all electrical connections.

32. Install the engine side cover, right front wheel and engine under cover.

33. Refill the cooling system.

### M30

1. Relieve the fuel system pressure and disconnect the negative battery cable.

2. Drain the cooling system.

3. Remove the timing belt.

**NOTE: do not rotate either the crankshaft or camshaft from this point onward or the valves could be bent by hitting the tops of the pistons.**

4. Disconnect and tag all vacuum and water hoses connected to the intake collector.

5. Remove the distributor, ignition wires and disconnect the accelerator and cruise control (ASCD) cables from the intake manifold collector.

6. Remove the collector cover and the collector from the intake manifold. Disconnect and tag all harness connectors and vacuum lines to gain access to the cover retaining bolts on these models.

7. Remove the intake manifold and fuel tube assembly. Loosen the intake manifold bolts starting from the front of the engine and proceed in criss-cross pattern towards the center.

8. Remove the exhaust collector bracket.

9. Remove the exhaust manifold covers.

10. Disconnect the exhaust manifold from the exhaust pipe.

11. Remove the camshaft pulleys and the rear timing cover securing bolts. Remove the rocker arm covers.

12. Separate the air conditioning compressor and alternator from the their mounting brackets. Remove the mounting brackets. Do not disconnect the refrigerant lines from the compressor or serious injury will result.

13. Remove the cylinder head bolts in the correct sequence. Lift the cylinder head off the engine block with the exhaust manifolds attached. It may be necessary to tap the head lightly with a rubber mallet to loosen it.

**To install:**

14. Make sure the No. 1 cylinder is set at TDC on its compression stroke as follows:

a. Align the crankshaft timing mark with the mark on the oil pump housing.

b. The knock pin in the front end of the camshaft should be facing upward.

**NOTE: do not rotate crankshaft and camshaft separately because valves will hit piston head.**

15. Install the cylinder head with a new gasket. Apply clean engine oil to the threads and seats of the bolts and install the bolts with washers in the correct position. Note that bolts 4, 5, 12, and 13 are 4.95 in. (127mm) long. The other bolts are 4.13 in. (106mm) long.

16. Torque the bolts in the proper sequence as follows:

a. Torque all bolts, in sequence, to 22 ft. lbs. (29 Nm).

b. Torque all bolts, in sequence, to 43 ft. lbs. (58 Nm).

c. Loosen all bolts completely.

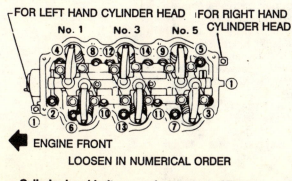

**Cylinder head bolt removal sequence—M30**

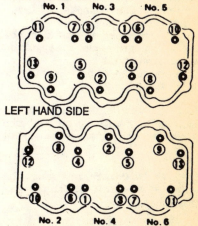

**Cylinder head bolt tightening sequence—M30**

d. Torque all bolts, in sequecne, to 22 ft. lbs. (29 Nm).

e. Torque all bolts, in sequence, to 40–47 ft. lbs (54–64 Nm). Using an angle torque wrench, torque them 60–65 degrees tighter rather than going to 40–47 ft. lbs. (54–64 Nm)

17. Install the alternator and air conditioner compressor mounting brackets. Mount the compressor and alternator.

18. Install the rear timing cover bolts. Install the camshaft pulleys. Make sure the pulley marked R3 goes on the right and that marked L3 goes on the left. Align the timing marks if necessary and then install the timing belt and adjust the belt tension.

19. Connect the exhaust manifold to the exhaust pipe.

20. Install the exhaust manifold covers.

21. Install the exhaust collector bracket.

22. Install the intake manifold and fuel tube assembly.

23. Install the intake manifold collector cover.

24. Connect the accelerator and cruise control cables to the intake manifold and install the distributor and ignition wires.

25. Connect the vacuum and water hoses to the intake collector.

26. Install and tension the timing belt.

27. Fill the cooling system and connect the negative battery cable.

28. Make all the necessary engine adjustments.

### Q45

1. Disconnect the negative battery cable.

2. Remove the engine and transmission assembly from the vehicle.

3. Remove the suspension member and engine mounts from the engine.

4. Remove the air compressor bracket and the exhaust manifolds.

5. Remove the cooling fan with coupling and the engine gusset.

6. Separate the engine from the transmission and mount the engine on a suitable workstand.

7. Remove the oil pan. Remove the intake collector.

8. Disconnect the injector harness connector and remove the injector tube assembly with injector. Loosen bolts in opposite sequence of torquing..

**NOTE: Be careful not to let the rubber washer fall into the intake manifold.**

9. Remove the intake manifold.
10. Remove the ornamental rocker cover and remove the ignition coils and spark plugs.

11. Bring the No. 1 piston to TDC on the compression stroke.

12. Use a suitable puller to remove the crankshaft pulley.

13. Remove the rocker cover.

14. Remove the crank angle sensor and the Valve Timing Control (VTC) solenoid.

15. Remove the chain tensioners and the upper front covers.

16. Remove the front timing chain cover.

**NOTE: The timing chain will not be disengaged or dislocated from the crankshaft sprocket unless the front cover is removed. The cast portion of the front cover is located on the lower side of the crankshaft sprocket so the timing chain is not disengaged from the sprocket.**

17. Remove the VTC assembly and the camshaft sprocket.

18. Remove the oil pump chain and the timing chains.

**NOTE: do not attempt to disassemble the VTC assembly since they are difficult to reassemble accurately in the field. If it should be disassembled, the VTC assembly must be replaced with a new one.**

19. Remove the camshaft brackets in the reverse order of torquing sequence. Use 2–3 steps. Remove the camshafts. Mark the parts so they can be reinstalled in their original positions.

20. Remove the rocker arm and hydraulic lash adjuster. Be sure to identify each adjuster so it can be reinstalled in it's original position.

21. Remove the cylinder head and gasket. Loosen the head bolts in 2–3 steps working from the outside bolts in towards the center bolts.

**To install:**

22. Make sure all mating surfaces are clean before installation.

23. Check the cylinder head surface for warpage using a feeler gauge and a suitable straightedge. If the cylinder head is warped more than 0.004 in. (0.1mm) it must be resurfaced or replaced. The total amount machined from the head or head and block combined, cannot total more than 0.008 in. (0.2mm).

24. Make sure the No. 1 piston is still at TDC of the compression stroke, then turn the crankshaft until the No. 1 piston is at approximately 45 degrees before TDC on the compression stroke. At this point, the No. 3 piston will be at the same height as the No. 1 piston to prevent interference of the valves and pistons.

25. Install the cylinder heads with new gaskets. Temporarily tighten the cylinder head bolts to avoid damaging the cylinder head gaskets. Be sure to install washers between the bolts and the cylinder heads. Do not rotate the crankshaft or camshaft separately or the valves will hit the pistons.

26. Install the hydraulic lash adjusters and check them as follows:

a. When the rocker arm can be moved at least 0.04 in. (1.0mm) by pushing at the hydraulic lash adjuster location, it indicates that there is air in the high pressure chamber. Noise will be emitted from the hydraulic lash adjuster if the engine is started without bleeding the air.

b. Remove the hydraulic lash adjuster and dip in a container filled with engine oil. While pushing the top of the plunger down, insert a suitable thin rod through the hole in the top of the plunger and lightly push the check ball. Air is completely bled when the plunger no longer moves.

**NOTE: Air cannot be bled from the lash adjusters by running the engine.**

27. Install the rocker arms, camshafts and camshaft brackets on the right bank and tighten in the proper sequence to 9–10 ft. lbs (12–14 Nm).

28. Install the VTC assembly and the exhaust cam sprocket on the right bank.

29. After making sure the camshafts are still correctly positioned, turn the crankshaft clockwise to bring the No. 1 piston to TDC on the compression stroke.

30. Install the timing chain on the right bank, aligning the mating marks on the chain with those on the crankshaft and camshaft sprockets.

31. Install the chain tensioner on the right bank.

32. Turn the crankshaft approximately 120 degrees clockwise from the point where the No. 1 piston is at TDC

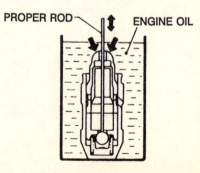

**Hydraulic lash adjuster bleeding—Q45**

on the compression stroke. At this point, the valves on the left bank still remain unlifted.

33. Correctly position the camshafts for the left cylinder head and tighten brackets in the proper sequence to 9–10 ft. lbs (12–14 Nm). Install the VTC assembly and the exhaust cam sprocket.

34. Install the timing chain on the left bank, aligning the mating marks on the chain with those on the crankshaft and camshaft sprockets.

35. Install the oil pump chain and sprockets.

36. Install the oil pump chain guides. Place a 0.04 in. (1.0mm) feeler gauge between the upper chain guide and chain before assembling the chain guides. The force applied to the chain is equivalent to the upper chain guide weight.

37. Apply suitable sealer and install the front covers.

38. Install the chain tensioner for the left bank.

39. Apply suitable sealer to the rubber plugs and install them on the cylinder head.

40. Install the crank angle sensor, VTC solenoid, rocker cover and crank pulley.

41. Bring the piston in No. 1 cylinder to TDC on the compression stroke.

42. Tighten the cylinder head bolts

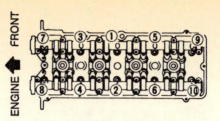

**Cylinder head torque sequence—Q45**

in the proper torque sequence as follows:

a. Tighten the bolts in sequence to 22 ft. lbs. (29 Nm).
b. Tighten the bolts in sequence to 69 ft. lbs. (93 Nm).
c. Loosen the bolts completely.
d. Tighten the bolts in sequence to 18–25 ft. lbs. (25–34 Nm).
e. Turn the bolts in sequence 90–95 degrees or 69–72 ft. lbs. (93–98 Nm).

43. Install the intake manifold bolts in their proper positions on the cylinder head and lightly tighten the mounting bolts.

44. Connect the injector tube assemblies, including the fuel injectors, to the intake manifolds and lightly tighten the mounting bolts.

**NOTE: Be careful not to let the rubber washer fall into the intake manifold.**

45. Install the intake collector and lightly tighten the mounting bolts.

46. Tighten the intake manifold mounting bolts at the cylinder head, remove the intake collectors and tighten the intake manifolds to 12–15 ft. lbs. (16–21 Nm).

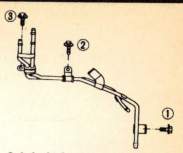

**Sub-fuel tubes torque sequence**

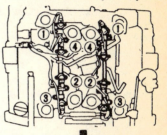

**Engine front**

**Injector tube torque sequence**

47. Tighten the sub-fuel tubes, in sequence, first to 3.1–4.3 ft. lbs. (4.2–5.9 Nm) and then to 6.2–8.0 ft. lbs. (8.4–10.8 Nm).

48. Tighten the injector tube assemblies, in sequence, first to 6.9–8.0 ft. lbs. (9.3–10.8 Nm) and then to 15–20 ft. lbs. (21–26 Nm).

49. Install the intake collectors and tighten to 9–11 ft. lbs. (12–15 Nm).

50. Install the exhaust manifolds.

51. Install the rocker covers and tighten in the proper sequence to 5–7 ft. lbs. (7–10 Nm).

52. Installation of the remaining components is the reverse of the removal procedure.

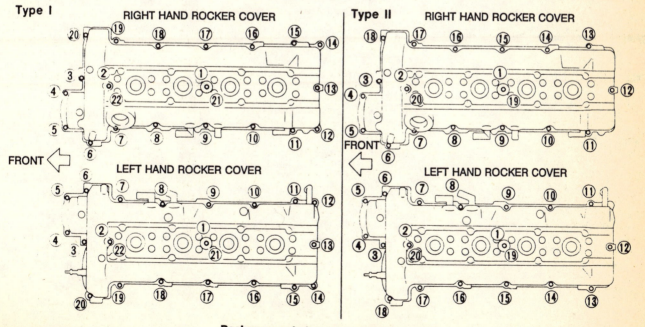

**Rocker cover bolt torque sequence—Q45**

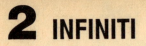

## Valve Lifters

### REMOVAL & INSTALLATION

#### M30

1. Relieve the fuel system pressure and disconnect the negative battery cable.
2. Drain the cooling system.
3. Remove the timing belt.

**NOTE: do not rotate either the crankshaft or camshaft from this point onward or the valves could be bent by hitting the tops of the pistons.**

4. Disconnect and tag all vacuum and water hoses connected to the intake collector.
5. Remove the distributor, ignition wires and disconnect the accelerator and cruise control (ASCD) cables from the intake manifold collector.
6. Remove the collector cover and the collector from the intake manifold. Disconnect and tag all harness connectors and vacuum lines to gain access to the cover retaining bolts on these models.
7. Remove the intake manifold and fuel tube assembly. Loosen the intake manifold bolts starting from the front of the engine and proceed in criss-cross pattern towards the center.
8. Remove the exhaust collector bracket.
9. Remove the exhaust manifold covers.
10. Disconnect the exhaust manifold from the exhaust pipe.
11. Remove the camshaft pulleys and the rear timing cover securing bolts. Remove the rocker arm covers.
12. Separate the air conditioning compressor and alternator from the their mounting brackets. Remove the mounting brackets.
13. Remove the rocker shafts with the rocker arms. The bolts should be loosened in 2–3 steps.
14. Remove the hydraulic valve lifters and the lifter guide. Hold the valve lifter with wire so they do not fall from the lifter guide.
**To install:**
15. Install the valve lifters into the valve lifter guide.
16. Assemble the lifters to their original position and hold all the lifters with wire to prevent the lifters from falling out. After installing them, remove the wire.
17. Install the rocker shafts with the rocker arms. Tighten the bolts gradually in 2–3 stages. Before tightening, be sure to set camshaft lobe at the position where lobe is not lifted or the valve closed. Set each cylinder 1 at a time or follow the procedure below.

The cylinder head, intake manifold, collector and timing belt must be installed:
   a. Set No. 1 piston at TDC of the compression stroke and tighten rocker shaft bolts for Nos. 2, 4 and 6 cylinders.
   b. Set No. 4 piston at TDC of the compression stroke and tighten rocker shaft bolts for Nos. 1, 3 and 5 cylinders.
   c. Torque specification for the rocker shaft retaining bolts is 13–16 ft. lbs. (18–22 Nm).
18. Install the alternator and air conditioner compressor mounting brackets. Mount the compressor and alternator.
19. Install the rear timing cover bolts. Install the camshaft pulleys. Make sure the pulley marked R3 goes on the right and that marked L3 goes on the left. Align the timing marks if necessary and then install the timing belt and adjust the belt tension.
20. Connect the exhaust manifold to the exhaust pipe.
21. Install the exhaust manifold covers.
22. Install the exhaust collector bracket.
23. Install the intake manifold and fuel tube assembly.
24. Install the intake manifold collector cover.
25. Connect the accelerator and cruise control cables to the intake manifold and install the distributor and ignition wires.
26. Connect the vacuum and water hoses to the intake collector.
27. Install and tension the timing belt.
28. Fill the cooling system and connect the negative battery cable.
29. Make all the necessary engine adjustments.

## Hydraulic Lash Adjusters

### REMOVAL & INSTALLATION

#### G20

1. Relieve the fuel system pressure and Disconnect the negative battery cable.
2. Drain the coolant from the radiator and engine block. Remove the radiator.
3. Raise and support the vehicle safely. Remove the right front wheel and engine side cover.
4. Remove the air duct to the intake manifold.
5. Remove the drive belts, water pump pulley, alternator and power steering pump.
6. Label and remove the vacuum

hoses, fuel hoses and wire harness connectors.
7. Remove all the spark plugs, the AIV valve and resonator.
8. Remove the rocker cover and oil separator. Loosen rocker cover bolts, using 2–3 steps, in the opposite sequence of tightening
9. Remove the intake manifold supports.
10. Remove the oil filter bracket and power steering oil pump bracket.
11. Set No. 1 piston at TDC on the compression stroke by rotating the crankshaft.
12. Remove the chain tensioner.
13. Remove the distributor. Do not turn the rotor with the distributor removed.
14. Remove the timing chain guide, camshaft sprockets, camshafts, brackets, oil tubes and baffle plate. The camshaft bracket bolts must be loosened in sequence to prevent damage to the camshafts or the head.
15. Remove the hydraulic lash adjuster and rocker arm assembly.
**To install:**
16. Install the hydraulic lash adjusters and check them as follows:
   a. When the rocker arm can be moved at least 0.04 in. (1.0mm) by pushing at the hydraulic lash adjuster location, it indicates that there is air in the high pressure chamber. Noise will be emitted from the hydraulic lash adjuster if the engine is started without bleeding the air.
   b. Remove the hydraulic lash adjuster and dip in a container filled with engine oil. While pushing the top of the plunger down, insert a suitable thin rod through the hole in the top of the plunger and lightly push the check ball. Air is completely bled when the plunger no longer moves.

**NOTE: Air cannot be bled from the lash adjusters by running the engine.**

17. Clean the camshaft end bracket and coat with liquid gasket. Install the camshafts, camshaft brackets, oil tubes and baffle plate. Ensure the left camshaft ket is at 12 o'clock and the right camshaft key is at 10 o'clock.
18. The procedure for tightening camshaft bracket bolts must be followed exactly to prevent camshaft damage. Tighten bolts as follows:
   a. Tighten right camshaft bolts 9 and 10 (in that order) to 1.5 ft. lbs. (2 Nm) then tighten bolts 1 through 8 (in that order) to the same specification.
   b. Tighten left camshaft bolts 11 and 12 (in that order) to 1.5 ft. lbs. (2 Nm) then tighten bolts 1 through

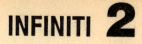

10 (in that order) to the same specification.

c. Tighten all bolts in sequence to 4.5 ft. lbs. (6 Nm).

d. Tighten all bolts in sequence to 6.5–8.5 ft. lbs. (9–12 Nm) for type A, B and C bolts, and 13–19 ft. lbs. (18–25 Nm) for type D bolts.

19. Line up the mating marks on the timing chain and camshaft sprockets and install the sprockets. Tighten sprocket bolts to 101–116 ft. lbs. (137–157 Nm).

20. Install the timing chain guide, distributor (ensure that rotor head is at 5 o'clock position) and chain tensioner.

21. Install intake manifold supports. Clean the rocker cover and mating surfaces and apply a continious bead of liquid gasket to the mating surface.

22. Install the rocker cover and oil separator. Tighten the rocker cover bolts as follows:

a. Tighten nuts 1, 10, 11, and 8 in that order to 3 ft. lbs. (4 Nm).

b. Tighten nuts 1 through 13 in the proper sequence to 6–7 ft. lbs. (8–10 Nm).

23. Installation of the remaining components is the reverse of removal procedures.

### Q45

1. Disconnect the negative battery cable.

2. Remove the engine and transmission assembly from the vehicle.

3. Remove the suspension member and engine mounts from the engine.

4. Remove the air compressor bracket.

5. Remove the cooling fan with coupling and the engine gusset.

6. Separate the engine from the transmission and mount the engine on a suitable workstand.

7. Remove the oil pan.

8. Remove the ornamental rocker cover and remove the ignition coils and spark plugs.

9. Bring the No. 1 piston to TDC on the compression stroke.

10. Use a suitable puller to remove the crankshaft pulley.

11. Remove the rocker cover.

12. Remove the crank angle sensor and the Valve Timing Control (VTC) solenoid.

13. Remove the chain tensioners and the upper front covers.

14. Remove the front timing chain cover.

**NOTE: The timing chain will not be disengaged or dislocated from the crankshaft sprocket unless the front cover is removed. The cast portion of the front cover is located on the lower side of the crankshaft sprocket so the timing chain is not disengaged from the sprocket.**

15. Remove the VTC assembly and the camshaft sprocket.

16. Remove the oil pump chain and the timing chains.

**NOTE: do not attempt to disassemble the VTC assembly since they are difficult to reassemble accurately in the field. If it should be disassembled, the VTC assembly must be replaced with a new one.**

17. Remove the camshaft brackets and the camshafts. Mark the parts so they can be reinstalled in their original positions.

18. Remove the rocker arm and hydraulic lash adjuster. Be sure to identify each adjuster so it can be reinstalled in it's original position.

**To install:**

19. Make sure all mating surfaces are clean before installation.

20. Install the hydraulic lash adjusters and check them as follows:

a. When the rocker arm can be moved at least 0.04 in. (1.0mm) by pushing at the hydraulic lash adjuster location, it indicates that there is air in the high pressure chamber. Noise will be emitted from the hydraulic lash adjuster if the engine is started without bleeding the air.

b. Remove the hydraulic lash adjuster and dip in a container filled with engine oil. While pushing the top of the plunger down, insert a suitable thin rod through the hole in the top of the plunger and lightly push the check ball. Air is completely bled when the plunger no longer moves.

**NOTE: Air cannot be bled from the lash adjusters by running the engine.**

21. Install the rocker arms, camshafts and camshaft brackets on the right bank.

22. Install the VTC assembly and the exhaust cam sprocket on the right bank.

23. Make sure the camshafts are still correctly positioned and the piston in the No. 1 cylinder is still at TDC.

24. Install the timing chain on the right bank, aligning the mating marks on the chain with those on the crankshaft and camshaft sprockets.

25. Install the chain tensioner on the right bank.

26. Turn the crankshaft approximately 120 degrees clockwise from the point where the No. 1 piston is at TDC on the compression stroke. At this point, the valves on the left bank still remain unlifted.

27. Correctly position the camshafts for the left cylinder head. Install the VTC assembly and the exhaust cam sprocket.

28. Install the timing chain on the left bank, aligning the mating marks on the chain with those on the crankshaft and camshaft sprockets.

29. Install the oil pump chain and sprockets.

30. Install the oil pump chain guides. Place a 0.04 in. (1.0mm) feeler gauge between the upper chain guide and chain guides before assembling the chain guides. The force applied to the chain is equivalent to the upper chain guide weight.

31. Apply suitable sealer and install the front covers.

32. Install the chain tensioner for the left bank.

33. Apply suitable sealer to the rubber plugs and install them on the cylinder head.

34. Install the crank angle sensor, VTC solenoid, rocker cover and crank pulley.

35. Installation of the remaining components is the reverse of the removal procedure.

## Rocker Arms

### REMOVAL & INSTALLATION

### G20

1. Relieve the fuel system pressure and Disconnect the negative battery cable.

2. Drain the coolant from the radiator and engine block. Remove the radiator.

3. Raise and support the vehicle safely. Remove the right front wheel and engine side cover.

4. Remove the air duct to the intake manifold.

5. Remove the drive belts, water pump pulley, alternator and power steering pump.

6. Label and remove the vacuum hoses, fuel hoses and wire harness connectors.

7. Remove all the spark plugs, the AIV valve and resonator.

8. Remove the rocker cover and oil separator. Loosen rocker cover bolts, using 2 through 3 steps, in the opposite sequence of tightening

9. Remove the intake manifold supports.

10. Remove the oil filter bracket and power steering oil pump bracket.

11. Set No. 1 piston at TDC on the compression stroke by rotating the crankshaft.

12. Remove the chain tensioner.

13. Remove the distributor. Do not

turn the rotor with the distributor removed.

14. Remove the timing chain guide, camshaft sprockets, camshafts, brackets, oil tubes and baffle plate. The camshaft bracket bolts must be loosened in sequence to prevent damage to the camshafts or the head.

15. Remove rocker arm assembly.

**To install:**

16. Check the hydraulic lash adjusters to ensure they did not bleed down during disassembly. If bleed down has occured, remove the lash adjuster and reprime.

**NOTE: Air cannot be bled from the lash adjusters by running the engine.**

17. Clean the camshaft end bracket and coat with liquid gasket. Install the camshafts, camshaft brackets, oil tubes and baffle plate. Ensure the left camshaft ket is at 12 o'clock and the right camshaft key is at 10 o'clock.

18. The procedure for tightening camshaft bracket bolts must be followed exactly to prevent camshaft damage. Tighten bolts as follows:

  a. Tighten right camshaft bolts 9 and 10 (in that order) to 1.5 ft. lbs. (2 Nm) then tighten bolts 1 through 8 (in that order) to the same specification.

  b. Tighten left camshaft bolts 11 and 12 (in that order) to 1.5 ft. lbs. (2 Nm) then tighten bolts 1 through 10 (in that order) to the same specification.

  c. Tighten all bolts in sequence to 4.5 ft. lbs. (6 Nm).

  d. Tighten all bolts in sequence to 6.5–8.5 ft. lbs. (9–12 Nm) for type A, B and C bolts, and 13–19 ft. lbs. (18–25 Nm) for type D bolts.

19. Line up the mating marks on the timing chain and camshaft sprockets and install the sprockets. Tighten sprocket bolts to 101–116 ft. lbs. (137–157 Nm).

20. Install the timing chain guide, distributor (ensure that rotor head is at 5 o'clock position) and chain tensioner.

21. Install intake manifold supports. Clean the rocker cover and mating surfaces and apply a continious bead of liquid gasket to the mating surface.

22. Install the rocker cover and oil separator. Tighten the rocker cover bolts as follows:

  a. Tighten nuts 1, 10, 11, and 8 in that order to 3 ft. lbs. (4 Nm).

  b. Tighten nuts 1 through 13 in the proper sequence to 6–7 ft. lbs. (8–10 Nm).

32. Installation of the remaining components is the reverse of removal procedures.

## M30

1. Relieve the fuel system pressure and disconnect the negative battery cable.

2. Drain the cooling system.

3. Remove the timing belt.

**NOTE: do not rotate either the crankshaft or camshaft from this point onward or the valves could be bent by hitting the tops of the pistons.**

4. Disconnect and tag all vacuum and water hoses connected to the intake collector.

5. Remove the distributor, ignition wires and disconnect the accelerator and cruise control (ASCD) cables from the intake manifold collector.

6. Remove the collector cover and the collector from the intake manifold. Disconnect and tag all harness connectors and vacuum lines to gain access to the cover retaining bolts on these models.

7. Remove the intake manifold and fuel tube assembly. Loosen the intake manifold bolts starting from the front of the engine and proceed in crisscross pattern towards the center.

8. Remove the exhaust collector bracket.

9. Remove the exhaust manifold covers.

10. Disconnect the exhaust manifold from the exhaust pipe.

11. Remove the camshaft pulleys and the rear timing cover securing bolts. Remove the rocker arm covers.

12. Separate the air conditioning compressor and alternator from their mounting brackets. Remove the mounting brackets.

13. Remove the rocker shafts with the rocker arms. The bolts should be loosened in 2–3 steps.

**To install:**

14. Install the rocker shafts with the rocker arms. Tighten the bolts gradually in 2–3 stages. Before tightening, be sure to set camshaft lobe at the position where lobe is not lifted or the valve closed. Set each cylinder 1 at a time or follow the procedure below. The cylinder head, intake manifold, collector and timing belt must be installed:

  a. Set No. 1 piston at TDC of the compression stroke and tighten rocker shaft bolts for Nos. 2, 4 and 6 cylinders.

  b. Set No. 4 piston at TDC of the compression stroke and tighten rocker shaft bolts for Nos. 1, 3 and 5 cylinders.

  c. Torque specification for the rocker shaft retaining bolts is 13–16 ft. lbs. (18–22 Nm).

15. Install the alternator and air conditioner compressor mounting brack-ets. Mount the compressor and alternator.

16. Install the rear timing cover bolts. Install the camshaft pulleys. Make sure the pulley marked R3 goes on the right and that marked L3 goes on the left. Align the timing marks, if necessary, and then install the timing belt and adjust the belt tension.

17. Connect the exhaust manifold to the exhaust pipe.

18. Install the exhaust manifold covers.

19. Install the exhaust collector bracket.

20. Install the intake manifold and fuel tube assembly.

21. Install the intake manifold collector cover.

22. Connect the accelerator and cruise control cables to the intake manifold and install the distributor and ignition wires.

23. Connect the vacuum and water hoses to the intake collector.

24. Install and tension the timing belt.

25. Fill the cooling system and connect the negative battery cable.

26. Make all the necessary engine adjustments.

## Q45

1. Disconnect the negative battery cable.

2. Remove the engine and transmission assembly from the vehicle.

3. Remove the suspension member and engine mounts from the engine.

4. Remove the air compressor bracket.

5. Remove the cooling fan with coupling and the engine gusset.

6. Separate the engine from the transmission and mount the engine on a suitable workstand.

7. Remove the oil pan.

8. Remove the ornamental rocker cover and remove the ignition coils and spark plugs.

9. Bring the No. 1 piston to TDC on the compression stroke.

10. Use a suitable puller to remove the crankshaft pulley.

11. Remove the rocker cover.

12. Remove the crank angle sensor and the Valve Timing Control (VTC) solenoid.

13. Remove the chain tensioners and the upper front covers.

14. Remove the front timing chain cover.

**NOTE: The timing chain will not be disengaged or dislocated from the crankshaft sprocket unless the front cover is removed. The cast portion of the front cover is located on the lower side of the crankshaft sprocket so the**

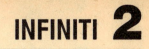

**timing chain is not disengaged from the sprocket.**

15. Remove the VTC assembly and the camshaft sprocket.

16. Remove the oil pump chain and the timing chains.

**NOTE: do not attempt to disassemble the VTC assembly since they are difficult to reassemble accurately in the field. If it should be disassembled, the VTC assembly must be replaced with a new one.**

17. Remove the camshaft brackets and the camshafts. Mark the parts so they can be reinstalled in their original positions.

18. Remove the rocker arms. Be sure to identify each rocker arm so it can be reinstalled in it's original position.

**To install:**

19. Make sure all mating surfaces are clean before installation.

20. Install the rocker arms, camshafts and camshaft brackets on the right bank. Properly lubricate the rocker arms and camshafts prior to installation.

21. Install the VTC assembly and the exhaust cam sprocket on the right bank.

22. Make sure the camshafts are still correctly positioned and the piston in the No. 1 cylinder is still at TDC.

23. Install the timing chain on the right bank, aligning the mating marks on the chain with those on the crankshaft and camshaft sprockets.

24. Install the chain tensioner on the right bank.

25. Turn the crankshaft approximately 120 degrees clockwise from the point where the No. 1 piston is at TDC on the compression stroke. At this point, the valves on the left bank still remain closed.

26. Correctly position the camshafts and rocker arms for the left cylinder head. Properly lubricate the rocker arms and camshafts prior to installation. Install the VTC assembly and the exhaust cam sprocket.

27. Install the timing chain on the left bank, aligning the mating marks on the chain with those on the crankshaft and camshaft sprockets.

28. Install the oil pump chain and sprockets.

29. Install the oil pump chain guides. Place a 0.04 in. (1.0mm) feeler gauge between the upper chain guide and chain guides before assembling the chain guides. The force applied to the chain is equivalent to the upper chain guide weight.

30. Apply suitable sealer and install the front covers.

31. Install the chain tensioner for the left bank.

32. Apply suitable sealer to the rubber plugs and install them on the cylinder head.

33. Install the crank angle sensor, VTC solenoid, rocker cover and crank pulley.

34. Installation of the remaining components is the reverse of the removal procedure.

## Intake Manifold

### REMOVAL & INSTALLATION

#### G20

1. Disconnect the negative battery cable.

2. Properly relieve the fuel system pressure.

3. Drain the cooling system.

4. Tag and disconnect the fuel lines, vacuum hoses and electrical connectors. Disconnect the throttle linkage.

5. Remove the intake manifold collector. Loosen bolts in the reverse order of the torquing sequence.

6. Remove the injector tube assembly and remove the intake manifolds. Loosen bolts in the reverse order of the torquing sequence.

**To install:**

7. Make sure all mating surfaces are clean prior to installation.

8. Install the intake manifold bolts, in their proper positions, on the cylinder head and lightly tighten the mounting bolts.

9. Connect the injector tube assemblies, including the fuel injectors, to the intake manifolds and lightly tighten the mounting bolts.

10. Install the intake collector and lightly tighten the mounting bolts.

11. To tighten the intake manifold mounting bolts at the cylinder head, remove the intake collector bolts and tighten the intake manifolds in sequence to 13–15 ft. lbs. (18–21 Nm).

12. Tighten the injector tube assemblies, in sequence, first to 6.9–8.0 ft. lbs. (9.3–10.8 Nm) and then to 15–20 ft. lbs. (21–26 Nm).

13. Install the intake collector and tighten the bolts in sequence to 12–15 ft. lbs. (16–21 Nm).

14. Reconnect the fuel lines, vacuum hoses and electrical connectors. Disconnect the throttle linkage.

15. Refill the cooling system, connect the negative battery cable and start engine and test for leaks.

#### M30

1. Relieve the fuel system pressure, disconnect the negative battery cable and drain the cooling system.

2. Remove the distributor and the ignition wires.

3. Disconnect the ASCD and accelerator wires from the intake manifold collector.

4. Disconnect the harness connectors for the AAC valve, throttle sensor and idle switch.

5. Disconnect the air cut out valve water hose.

6. Disconnect the PCV valve hoses.

7. Disconnect the vacuum hoses from the vacuum gallery, swirl control valve, master brake cylinder, EGR control valve and EGR flare tube.

8. Loosen the upper collector cover bolts in proper sequence and remove the upper intake manifold collector from the engine. Remove the collector gasket.

9. Disconnect the engine ground harness.

10. Loosen the lower collector bolts, in sequence, and remove the lower intake manifold collector from the engine.

11. Disconnect the harness connectors for all injectors, engine temperature switch and sensor, power valve control solenoid valve, EGR control solenoid valve, EGR. temperature sensor (California only).

12. Disconnect the vacuum gallery hoses.

13. Disconnect the pressure regulator valve vacuum hose, heater hose, fuel feed and return hose.

14. Remove the intake manifold and fuel tube assembly. Loosen intake manifold bolts in numerical order.

**To install:**

15. Install the intake manifold and fuel tube assembly with a new gasket. Tighten the manifold bolts and nuts, in 2–3 stages, in sequence.

16. Connect the hoses and electrical wires to the intake manifold and fuel tube.

17. Install the upper and lower collector and collector cover with new gaskets. Tighten collector to intake manifold bolts, in 2–3 stages, by reversing the removal sequence.

18. Connect the vacuum lines, hoses, cables and brackets to the collector cover and collector assembly.

19. Install the distributor and ignition wires.

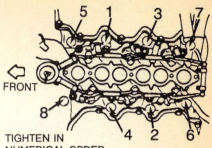

TIGHTEN IN NUMERICAL ORDER

**Intake manifold installation torque sequence—M30**

20. Fill the cooling system to the proper level and connect the negative battery cable.

21. Make all the necessary engine adjustments.

### Q45

1. Disconnect the negative battery cable.

2. Properly relieve the fuel system pressure.

3. Drain the cooling system.

4. Tag and disconnect the fuel lines, vacuum hoses and electrical connectors. Disconnect the throttle linkage.

5. Remove the intake manifold collector.

6. Remove the injector tube assembly and remove the intake manifolds.

**To install:**

7. Make sure all mating surfaces are clean prior to installation.

8. Install the intake manifold bolts, in their proper positions, on the cylinder head and lightly tighten the mounting bolts.

9. Connect the injector tube assemblies, including the fuel injectors, to the intake manifolds and lightly tighten the mounting bolts.

**NOTE: Be careful not to let the rubber washer fall into the intake manifold.**

10. Install the intake collector and lightly tighten the mounting bolts.

11. Tighten the intake manifold mounting bolts at the cylinder head, remove the intake collectors and tighten the intake manifolds to 12–15 ft. lbs. (16–21 Nm).

12. Tighten the sub-fuel tubes, in sequence, first to 3.1–4.3 ft. lbs. (4.2–5.9 Nm) and then to 6.2–8.0 ft. lbs. (8.4–10.8 Nm).

13. Tighten the injector tube assemblies, in sequence, first to 6.9–8.0 ft. lbs. (9.3–10.8 Nm) and then to 15–20 ft. lbs. (21–26 Nm).

14. Install the intake collector and tighten to 9–11 ft. lbs. (12–15 Nm).

15. Install the remaining components in the reverse order of their removal.

## Exhaust Manifold

### REMOVAL & INSTALLATION

#### G20

1. Disconnect the negative battery cable. Raise and support the vehicle safely.

2. Remove the undercover and dust covers, if equipped. Disconnect the exhaust pipe at the manifold flange.

3. Remove the AIV, AIV tube and attaching bracket.

4. Disconnect the exhaust gas sen-

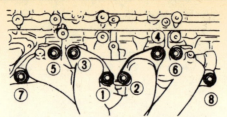

Exhaust manifold tightening sequence—G20

sor electrical connection and remove the sensor.

5. Remove the exhaust manifold cover.

6. Remove the exhaust manifold nuts in reverse order of torquing sequence.

7. Remove the exhaust manifold and gasket.

**To install:**

8. Clean the gasket mating surface and intall a new exhaust manifold gasket.

9. Install the exhaust manifold and tighten the manifold nuts, in sequence, to 27–35 ft. lbs. (37–48 Nm).

10. Install the exhaust manifold cover and exhaust gas sensor. Reconnect the sensor electrical connection.

11. Install the AIV, AIV tube and attaching bracket.

12. Install the exhaust pipe to the manifold flange and tighten the nuts to 30–35 ft. lbs. (41–48 Nm).

13. Lower the vehicle, start the engine and check for leaks.

#### M30

1. Disconnect the negative battery cable. Raise and support the vehicle safely.

3. Remove the air cleaner or collector assembly, if necessary for access.

4. Remove the heat shield(s), if equipped.

5. Disconnect the exhaust pipe from the exhaust manifold.

6. Remove or disconnect the temperature sensors, oxygen sensors, air induction pipes, bracketry and other attachments from the manifold.

7. Loosen and remove the exhaust manifold attaching nuts and remove the manifold(s) from the block. Discard the exhaust manifold gaskets and replace with new.

8. Clean the gasket surfaces and check the manifold for cracks and warpage.

**To install:**

9. Install the exhaust manifold with a new gasket. Torque the manifold fasteners from the center outward in several stages.

10. Install or connect the temperature sensors, oxygen sensors, air induction pipes, brackets and other attachments to the manifold.

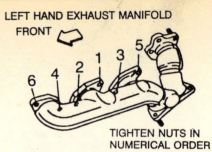

LEFT HAND EXHAUST MANIFOLD
FRONT

TIGHTEN NUTS IN NUMERICAL ORDER

**Left hand exhaust manifold installation torque sequence—M30**

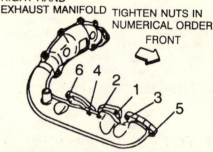

RIGHT HAND EXHAUST MANIFOLD   TIGHTEN NUTS IN NUMERICAL ORDER
FRONT

**Right hand exhaust manifold installation torque sequence—M30**

11. Connect the exhaust pipe to the manifold or turbo outlet using a new gasket.

12. Install the heat shields.

13. Install the air cleaner or collector assembly.

14. Install the under covers and dust covers.

15. Connect the negative battery cable.

#### Q45

1. Disconnect the negative battery cable. Raise and support the vehicle safely.

2. Remove the undercover and dust covers, if equipped. Disconnect the exhaust pipe at the manifold flange.

3. Disconnect the exhuast gas sensor electrical connection and if necessary, remove the sensor.

4. Remove the exhaust manifold nuts in reverse order of torquing sequence.

5. Remove the exhaust manifold and gasket.

**To install:**

6. Clean the gasket mating surface and intall a new exhaust manifold gasket.

7. Install the exhaust manifold and tighten the manifold nuts, in sequence, to 20–23 ft. lbs. (27–31 Nm).

8. Install exhaust gas sensor (if removed) and tighten to 30–37 ft. lbs. (40–50 Nm. Reconnect the sensor electrical connection.

9. Install the exhaust pipe to the manifold flange and tighten the nuts

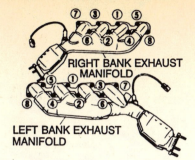

Exhaust manifold torque sequence—Q45

**Front timing cover gasket sealing surface—G20**

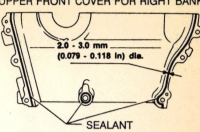

**Upper front right cover sealant application areas—Q45**

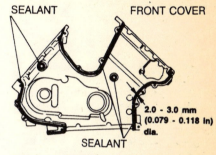

**Front cover sealant application areas—Q45**

to 33– 44 ft. lbs. (45–60 Nm).

13. Lower the vehicle, start the engine and check for leaks.

# Timing Chain Front Cover

## REMOVAL & INSTALLATION

### G20

1. Disconnect the negative battery cable.
2. Drain the engine oil and coolant.
3. Remove the cylinder head.
4. Raise and support the vehicle safely. Remove the oil pan, oil strainer and baffle plate.
5. Remove the crankshaft pulley using a suitable puller. Removal of the radiator may be necessary to gain clearance.
6. Place a suitable jack under the main bearing beam. Remove the front engine mount.
7. Loosen the front cover bolts in 2–3 steps and remove the front cover.

**To install:**

8. Clean all mating surfaces of liquid gasket material.
9. Apply a continious bead of liquid gasket to the mating surface of the timing cover. Install the oil pump drive spacer and front cover. Tighten front cover bolts to 5–6 ft. lbs. (6–8 Nm). Wipe excess liquid gasket material.
10. Install front engine mount.
11. Install crankshaft pulley and tighten bolt to 105–112 ft. lbs.(142–152 Nm). Set No. 1 piston at TDC on the compression stroke.
12. Install the oil strainer and baffle. Install the oil pan.
13. Before installing the cylinder head, place a bead of liquid gasket at the parting line between the front cover and the engine block.
14. Install the cylinder head.
15. Lower the vehicle, connect the negative battery cable, start the engine and check for leaks.

### Q45

1. Disconnect the negative battery cable.
2. Remove the engine and transmission assembly from the vehicle.
3. Remove the suspension member and engine mounts from the engine.
4. Remove the air compressor bracket.
5. Remove the cooling fan with coupling and the engine gusset.
6. Separate the engine from the transmission and mount the engine on a suitable workstand.
7. Remove the oil pan.
8. Remove the ornamental rocker cover and remove the ignition coils and spark plugs.
9. Bring the No. 1 piston to TDC on the compression stroke.
10. Use a suitable puller to remove the crankshaft pulley.
11. Remove the rocker cover.
12. Remove the crank angle sensor and the Valve Timing Control (VTC) solenoid.
13. Remove the chain tensioners and the upper front covers.
14. Remove the front timing chain cover.
15. Installation is the reverse of the removal procedure. Make sure all mating surfaces are clean prior to installation. Apply a suitable sealant to the proper locations on the timing chain covers.

UPPER FRONT COVER FOR LEFT BANK

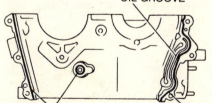

**Upper front left cover sealant application areas—Q45**

16. Tighten the cover bolts to 4.6–6.1 ft. lbs. (6.3–8.3 Nm) and the crankshaft pulley bolt to 260–275 ft. lbs. (353–373 Nm).

# Front Cover Oil Seal

## REPLACEMENT

### G20

1. Raise and support the vehicle safely. Remove the engine under cover, right wheel and engine side cover.
2. Remove the drive belts.
3. Remove the crankshaft pulley using a suitable puller.
4. Pry the front seal out using a pry bar taking care not to damage the front cover.
5. Install a new seal lubricated with engine oil using a seal driver.
6. Install the crankshaft pulley, drive belts, engine covers and right wheel.
7. Start engine and check for leaks.

### Q45

1. Disconnect the negative battery cable.
2. Raise and safely support the vehicle.
3. Remove the engine splash shield.
4. Remove the cooling fan and the engine gusset.
5. Remove the necessary accessory drive belts.
6. Remove the lower rear plate in order to remove the crankshaft pulley bolt.

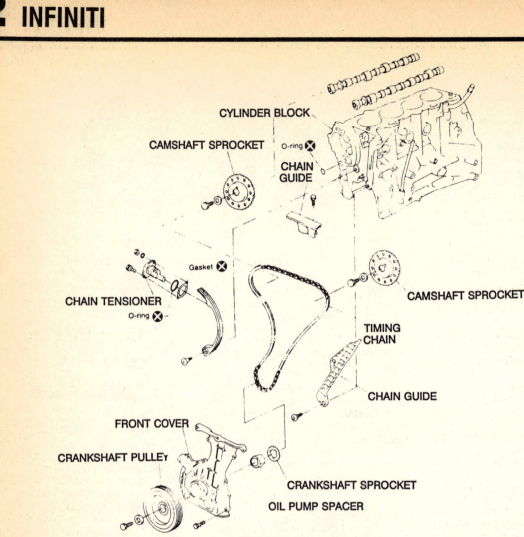

CYLINDER BLOCK

CAMSHAFT SPROCKET

O-ring ✕

CHAIN GUIDE

CAMSHAFT SPROCKET

CHAIN TENSIONER

O-ring ✕

Gasket ✕

TIMING CHAIN

CHAIN GUIDE

FRONT COVER

CRANKSHAFT PULLEY

CRANKSHAFT SPROCKET

OIL PUMP SPACER

**Timing chain assembly—G20**

7. Remove the crankshaft pulley bolt and the crankshaft pulley.

8. Use a suitable tool to remove the front cover oil seal.

9. Installation is the reverse of the removal procedure. Lubricate the seal lip prior to installation. Tighten the crank pulley bolt to 260–275 ft. lbs. (353–373 Nm).

## Timing Chain and Sprockets

### REMOVAL & INSTALLATION

#### G20

1. Relieve the fuel system pressure and Disconnect the negative battery cable.

2. Drain the coolant from the radiator and engine block. Remove the radiator.

3. Raise and support the vehicle safely. Remove the right front wheel and engine side cover and lower the vehicle.

4. Remove the drive belts, water pump pulley, alternator and power steering pump.

5. Label and remove the vacuum hoses, fuel hoses and wire harness connectors.

6. Remove the cylinder head.

7. Raise and support the vehicle safely.

8. Remove the oil pan.

9. Remove the crankshaft pulley using a suitable puller.

10. Remove the engine front mount.

11. Remove the front cover.

12. Remove the timing chain guides and timing chain. Check the timing chain for excessive wear at the roller links. Replace the chain if necessary.

**To install:**

13. Install the crankshaft sprocket. Position the crankshaft so that No.1 piston is set at TDC (keyway at 12 o'clock, mating mark at 4 o'clock) fit timing chain to crankshaft sprocket so that mating mark is in line with mating mark on crankshaft sprocket. The mating marks on the camshaft sprockets should be silver. The mating mark on the crankshaft sprocket should be gold.

14. Install the timing chain and timing chain guides.

15. Install front engine mount.

16. Install the crankshaft pulley and set No.1 piston at TDC on the compression stroke.

17. Install the oil strainer, baffle plate and oil pan.

18. Install the cylinder head, camshafts, oil tubes and baffles. Position the left camshaft key at 12 o'clock and the right camshaft key at 10 o'clock.

19. Install the camshaft sprockets by lining up the mating marks on the timing chain with the mating marks on the camshaft sprockets. Tighten the camshaft bolts to 101–116 ft. lbs. (137–157 Nm).

20. Install the timing chain guide and distributor. Ensure rotor is at 5 o'clock position.

21. Install the chain tensioner. Press the cam stopper down and the press-in sleeve untill the hook can be engaged on the pin. When tensioner is bolted in position the hook will release automatically. Ensure the arrow on the outside faces the front of the engine.

22. Install all other components in reverse order of removal.

### Q45

1. Disconnect the negative battery cable.
2. Remove the engine and transmission assembly from the vehicle.
3. Remove the suspension member and engine mounts from the engine.
4. Remove the air compressor bracket.
5. Remove the cooling fan with coupling and the engine gusset.
6. Separate the engine from the transmission and mount the engine on a suitable workstand.
7. Remove the oil pan.
8. Remove the ornamental rocker cover and remove the ignition coils and spark plugs.
9. Bring the No. 1 piston to TDC on the compression stroke.
10. Use a suitable puller to remove the crankshaft pulley.
11. Remove the rocker cover.
12. Remove the crank angle sensor and the VTC (Valve Timing Control) solenoid.
13. Remove the chain tensioners and the upper front covers.
14. Remove the front timing chain cover.

**NOTE: The timing chain will not be disengaged or dislocated from the crankshaft sprocket unless the front cover is removed. The cast portion of the front cover is located on the lower side of the crankshaft sprocket so the timing chain is not disengaged from the sprocket.**

15. Remove the VTC assembly and the camshaft sprocket.
16. Remove the oil pump chain and the timing chains.

**NOTE: do not attempt to disassemble the VTC assembly since they are difficult to reassemble accurately in the field. If it should be disassembled, the VTC assembly must be replaced with a new one.**

17. Use a suitable tool to remove the crankshaft sprocket.
**To install:**
18. Make sure all mating surfaces are clean before installation.
19. Install the VTC assembly and the exhaust cam sprocket on the right bank.
20. Make sure the camshafts are still correctly positioned and the piston in the No. 1 cylinder is still at TDC.
21. Install the timing chain on the right bank, aligning the mating marks on the chain with those on the crankshaft and camshaft sprockets.

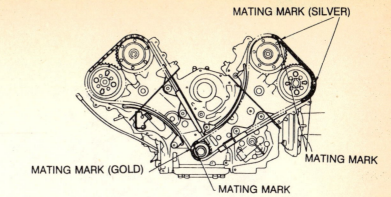

Left bank timing chain alignment—Q45

Right bank timing chain alignment—Q45

22. Install the chain tensioner on the right bank.
23. Turn the crankshaft approximately 120 degrees clockwise from the point where the No. 1 piston is at TDC on the compression stroke. At this point, the valves on the left bank still remain unlifted.
24. Correctly position the camshafts and rocker arms for the left cylinder head. Properly lubricate the rocker arms and camshafts prior to installation. Install the VTC assembly and the exhaust cam sprocket.
25. Install the timing chain on the left bank, aligning the mating marks on the chain with those on the crankshaft and camshaft sprockets.
26. Install the oil pump chain and sprockets.
27. Install the oil pump chain guides. Place a 0.04 in. (1.0mm) feeler gauge between the upper chain guide and chain before assembling the chain guides. The force applied to the chain is equivalent to the upper chain guide weight.
28. Apply suitable sealer and install the front covers.
29. Install the chain tensioner for the left bank.
30. Apply suitable sealer to the rubber plugs and install them on the cylinder head.
31. Install the crank angle sensor, VTC solenoid, rocker cover and crank pulley.

32. Installation of the remaining components is the reverse of the removal procedure.

## Timing Belt Front Cover

### REMOVAL & INSTALLATION

#### M30

1. Disconnect the negative battery cable.
2. Raise and support the front of the vehicle safely.
3. Remove the engine undercovers.
4. Drain the cooling system.
5. Remove the right front wheel.
6. Remove the engine side cover.
7. Remove the alternator, power steering and air conditioning compressor drive belts from the engine. When removing the power steering drive belt, loosen the idler pulley from the right side wheel housing.
8. Remove the upper radiator and water inlet hoses; remove the water pump pulley.
9. Remove the idler bracket of the compressor drive belt.
10. Remove the crankshaft pulley with a suitable puller.
11. Remove the upper and lower timing belt covers and gaskets.
**To install:**
12. Install the upper and lower timing belt covers with new gaskets.
13. Install the crankshaft pulley. Torque the pulley bolt to 90–98 ft. lbs. (123–132 Nm).
14. Install the compressor drive belt idler bracket.
15. Install the water pump pulley and torque the nuts to 12–15 ft. lbs. (16–21 Nm); install the upper radiator and water inlet hoses.
16. Install the drive belts.
17. Install the engine side cover.
18. Mount the front right wheel.
19. Install the engine undercovers.
20. Lower the vehicle.
21. Fill the cooling system and connect the negative battery cable.

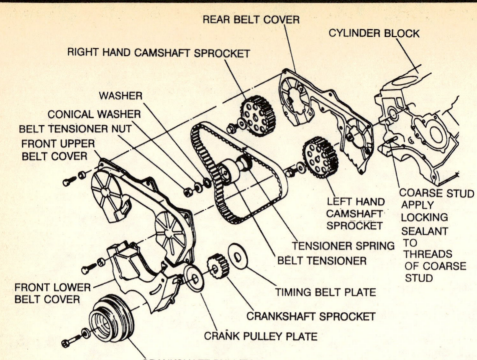

RIGHT HAND CAMSHAFT SPROCKET

REAR BELT COVER

CYLINDER BLOCK

WASHER
CONICAL WASHER
BELT TENSIONER NUT
FRONT UPPER
BELT COVER

LEFT HAND
CAMSHAFT
SPROCKET

COARSE STUD
APPLY
LOCKING
SEALANT
TO
THREADS
OF COARSE
STUD

TENSIONER SPRING
BELT TENSIONER

FRONT LOWER
BELT COVER

TIMING BELT PLATE

CRANKSHAFT SPROCKET

CRANK PULLEY PLATE

CRANKSHAFT PULLEY

**Timing belt installation—M30**

## OIL SEAL REPLACEMENT

### M30

1. Disconnect the negative battery cable.
2. Remove the timing belt.
3. Remove the crankshaft sprocket.
4. Remove the oil pan and oil pump.
5. Using a suitable tool, pry the oil seal from the front cover.

**NOTE: When removing the oil seal, be careful not the gouge or scratch the seal bore or crankshaft surface.**

6. Wipe the seal bore with a clean rag.
7. Lubricate the lip of the new seal with clean engine oil.
8. Install the seal into the front cover with a suitable seal installer.
9. Install the oil pump and oil pan.
10. Install the crankshaft sprocket.
11. Install the timing belt.
12. Connect the negative battery cable.

## Timing Belt and Tensioner

### ADJUSTMENT

### M30

1. Disconnect the negative battery cable.
2. Remove timing belt front covers.

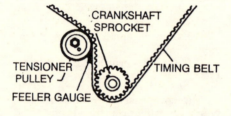

CRANKSHAFT
SPROCKET

TENSIONER
PULLEY

TIMING BELT

FEELER GAUGE

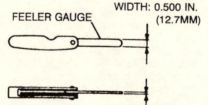

FEELER GAUGE

WIDTH: 0.500 IN.
(12.7MM)

THICKNESS:
0.0138 IM. (0.35MM)

**Setting timing belt tension—M30**

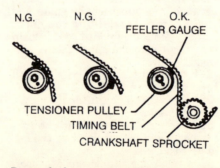

N.G.       N.G.       O.K.
FEELER GAUGE

TENSIONER PULLEY
TIMING BELT
CRANKSHAFT SPROCKET

**Proper feeler gauge position for setting timing belt tension—M30**

3. Set engine to TDC No. 1 cylinder on its compression stroke.
4. Loosen the tensioner locknut, keeping the tension steady with the hexagonal wrench.
5. Turn tensioner 70–80 degrees clockwise with the hexagonal wrench. Temporarily tighten locknut.
6. Turn crankshaft clockwise at least 2 times, then slowly set the engine to TDC No. 1 cylinder on its compression stroke.
7. Push the middle of the timing belt between the right hand camshaft sprocket and tensioner pulley with a force of 22 lbs. (98 N).
8. Loosen the tensioner locknut, keeping the tensioner steady with the hexagonal wrench.
9. Set a feeler gauge 0.0138 in. (0.35mm) thick and 0.500 in. (12.7mm) wide between the timing belt and the tensioner pulley.
10. Turn the crankshaft clockwise and until the feeler gauge is on the tensioner pulley behind the timing belt.
11. Tighten the tensioner locknut, keeping tensioner steady with the hexagonal wrench.
12. Turn the crankshaft clockwise to remove the feeler gauge.
13. Turn the crankshaft clockwise at least 2 times, then slowly set the engine to TDC No. 1 on its compression stroke.
14. Install the timing belt covers.
15. Connect negative battery cable.

## REMOVAL & INSTALLATION

### M30

1. Disconnect the negative battery cable.
2. Raise and support the front of the vehicle safely.
3. Remove the engine undercovers.
4. Drain the cooling system.
5. Remove the front right side wheel.
6. Remove the engine side cover.
7. Remove the alternator, power steering and air conditioning compressor drive belts from the engine. When removing the power steering drive belt, loosen the idler pulley from the right side wheel housing.
8. Remove the upper radiator and water inlet hoses; remove the water pump pulley.
9. Remove the idler bracket of the compressor drive belt.
10. Remove the crankshaft pulley with a suitable puller.
11. Remove the upper and lower timing belt covers and gaskets.
12. Rotate the engine with a socket wrench on the crankshaft pulley bolt to align the punch mark on the left hand camshaft pulley with the mark on the upper rear timing belt cover; align the punchmark on the crankshaft with the notch on the oil pump housing; temporarily install the crankshaft pulley bolt to allow for crankshaft rotation.
13. Use a hex wrench to turn the belt tensioner clockwise and tighten the tensioner locknut just enough to hold the tensioner in position. Then, remove the timing belt.

**To install:**

14. Before installing the timing belt confirm that No. 1 cylinder is at TDC of the compression stroke. Install tensioner and tensioner spring. If stud is removed apply locking sealant to threads before installing.
15. Swing tensioner fully clockwise with hexagon wrench and temporarily tighten locknut.
16. Point the arrow on the timing belt toward the front belt cover. Align the white lines on the timing belt with the punch marks on all 3 pulleys.

**NOTE: There are 133 total timing belt teeth. If timing belt is installed correctly there will be 40 teeth between left hand and right hand camshaft sprocket timing marks. There will be 43 teeth between left hand camshaft sprocket and crankshaft sprocket timing marks.**

17. Loosen tensioner locknut, keeping tensioner steady with a hexagon wrench.
18. Swing tensioner 70–80 degrees

clockwise with hexagon wrench and temporarily tighten locknut.
19. Turn crankshaft clockwise 2–3 times, then slowly set No. 1 cylinder at TDC of the compression stroke.
20. Push middle of timing belt between right hand camshaft sprocket and tensioner pulley with a force of 22 lbs.
21. Loosen tensioner locknut, keeping tensioner steady with a hexagon wrench.
22. Insert a 0.138 in. (0.35mm) thick and 0.5 in. (12.7mm) wide feeler gauge between the bottom of tensioner pulley and timing belt. Turn crankshaft clockwise and position gauge completely between tensioner pulley and timing belt. The timing belt will move about 2.5 teeth.
23. Tighten tensioner locknut, keeping tensioner steady with a hexagon wrench.
24. Turn crankshaft clockwise or counterclockwise and remove the gauge.
25. Rotate the engine 3 times, then set No. 1, to TDC, on its compression stroke.
26. Install the upper and lower timing belt covers with new gaskets.
27. Install the crankshaft pulley. Torque the pulley bolt to 90–98 ft. lbs. (123–132 Nm).
28. Install the compressor drive belt idler bracket.
29. Install the water pump pulley and torque the nuts to 12–15 ft. lbs. (16–21 Nm). Install the upper radiator and water inlet hoses.
30. Install the drive belts.
31. Install the engine side cover.
32. Mount the front right wheel.
33. Install the engine undercovers.
34. Lower the vehicle.
35. Fill the cooling system and connect the negative battery cable.

## Timing Sprockets

### REMOVAL & INSTALLATION

### M30

1. Disconnect the negative battery cable.
2. Set the No. 1 piston to TDC of the compression stroke.
3. Remove the timing belt covers.
4. Remove the timing belt.
5. Using a suitable spanner wrench and a socket wrench, remove the camshaft pulley bolt and washer. Remove the front plate, O-ring and spring from the right (intake) camshaft to gain access to the sprocket bolt. The left camshaft sprocket is held in place by plate and 4 bolts.
6. Using a suitable puller, remove the crankshaft gear and timing belt plates from the crankshaft. Be careful

not to gouge or scratch the surface of the crankshaft when removing the gear.
7. Inspect the timing gear teeth for wear and replace, as necessary.

**To install:**

8. Install the crankshaft gear with new Woodruff® keys.
9. Install the camshaft sprockets. Torque the sprocket bolts to 58–65 ft. lbs. (78–88 Nm); 90–98 ft. lbs. (123–132 Nm) for right (intake) and 10–14 ft. lbs. (14–19 Nm) for the left (exhaust).

**NOTE: The right hand and left hand camshaft pulleys are different. Install them in their correct positions. The right hand pulley has an R3 identification mark and the left hand pulley has an L3.**

10. Install the timing belt.
11. Install the timing belt covers.
12. Connect the negative battery cable.

## Camshaft

### REMOVAL & INSTALLATION

### G20

1. Disconnect the negative battery cable. Remove the rocker cover and oil separator.
2. Rotate the crankshaft until the No.1 piston is at TDC on the compression stroke. Then rotate the crankshaft until the mating marks on the camshaft sprockets line up with the mating marks on the timing chain.
3. Remove the timing chain tensioner.
4. Remove the distributor.
5. Remove the timing chain guide.
6. Remove the camshaft sprockets. Use a wrench to hold the camshaft while loosening the sprocket bolt.
7. Loosen the camshaft bracket bolts in the opposite order of the torquing sequence.
8. Remove the camshaft.

**To install:**

9. Clean the left hand camshaft end bracket and coat the mating surface with liquid gasket. Install the camshafts, camshaft brackets, oil tubes and baffle plate. Ensure the left camshaft key is at 12 o'clock and the right camshaft key is at 10 o'clock.
10. The procedure for tightening camshaft bolts must be followed exactly to prevent camshaft damage. Tighten bolts as follows:
    a. Tighten right camshaft bolts 9 and 10 (in that order) to 1.5 ft. lbs. (2 Nm) then tighten bolts 1–8 (in that order) to the same specification.
    b. Tighten left camshaft bolts 11 and 12 (in that order) to 1.5 ft. lbs.

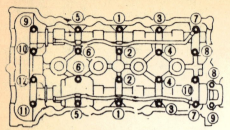

**Camshaft bracket bolt torque sequence G20**

(2 Nm) then tighten bolts 1–10 (in that order) to the same specification.

c. Tighten all bolts in sequence to 4.5 ft. lbs. (6 Nm).

d. Tighten all bolts in sequence to 6.5–8.5 ft. lbs. (9–12 Nm) for type A, B and C bolts, and 13–19 ft. lbs. (18–25 Nm) for type D bolts.

11. Line up the mating marks on the timing chain and camshaft sprockets and install the sprockets. Tighten sprocket bolts to 101–116 ft. lbs. (137–157 Nm).

12. Install the timing chain guide, distributor (ensure that rotor head is at 5 o'clock position) and chain tensioner.

13. Clean the rocker cover and mating surfaces and apply a continious bead of liquid gasket to the mating surface.

14. Install the rocker cover and oil separator. Tighten the rocker cover bolts as follows:

a. Tighten nuts 1, 10, 11, and 8 in that order to 3 ft. lbs. (4 Nm).

b. Tighten nuts 1–13 as indicated in the figure to 6–7 ft. lbs. (8–10 Nm).

### M30

1. Disconnect the negative battery cable.

2. Drain the cooling system.

3. Remove the timing belt.

4. Remove the collector assembly.

5. Remove the intake manifold.

6. Remove the cylinder head.

7. Remove the rocker shafts with rocker arms. Bolts should be loosened in several steps in the proper sequence.

8. Remove hydraulic valve lifters and lifter guide. Hold hydraulic valve lifters with wire so they will not drop from lifter guide.

9. Using a dial gauge measure the camshaft endplay. If the camshaft endplay exceeds the limit (0.0012–0.0024 in.), select the thickness of a cam locate plate so the endplay is within specification. For example: if camshaft endplay measures 0.0031 in. (0.08mm) with shim 2 used, then change shim 2 to shim 3 so the camshaft endplay is 0.0020 in. (0.05mm).

10. Remove the camshaft front oil seal and slide camshaft out the front of the cylinder head assembly.

**To install:**

11. Install camshaft, locater plates, cylinder head rear cover and front oil seal. Set camshaft knock pin at 12 o'clock position. Install cylinder head with new gasket to engine.

12. Install valve lifter guide assembly. Assemble valve lifters in their original position. After installing them in the correct location remove the wire holding them in lifter guide.

13. Install rocker shafts in correct position with rocker arms. Tighten bolts, in 2–3 stages, to 13–16 ft. lbs. (18–22 Nm). Before tightening, be sure to set camshaft lobe at the position where lobe is not lifted or the valve closed. Set each cylinder 1 at a time or follow the procedure below. The cylinder head, intake manifold, collector and timing belt must be installed:

a. Set No. 1 piston at TDC of the compression stroke and tighten rocker shaft bolts for Nos. 2, 4 and 6 cylinders.

b. Set No. 4 piston at TDC of the compression stroke and tighten rocker shaft bolts for Nos. 1, 3 and 5 cylinders.

c. Torque specification for the rocker shaft retaining bolts is 13–16 ft. lbs. (18–22 Nm).

14. Fill the cooling system to the proper level.

15. Connect the negative battery cable.

### Q45

1. Disconnect the negative battery cable.

2. Remove the engine and transmission assembly from the vehicle.

3. Remove the suspension member and engine mounts from the engine.

4. Remove the air compressor bracket.

5. Remove the cooling fan with coupling and the engine gusset.

6. Separate the engine from the transmission and mount the engine on a suitable workstand.

7. Remove the oil pan.

8. Remove the ornamental rocker cover and remove the ignition coils and spark plugs.

9. Bring the No. 1 piston to TDC on the compression stroke.

10. Use a suitable puller to remove the crankshaft pulley.

11. Remove the rocker cover.

12. Remove the crank angle sensor and the Valve Timing Control (VTC) solenoid.

13. Remove the chain tensioners and the upper front covers.

14. Remove the front timing chain cover.

**NOTE: The timing chain will not be disengaged or dislocated from the crankshaft sprocket unless the front cover is removed. The cast portion of the front cover is located on the lower side of the crankshaft sprocket so the timing chain is not disengaged from the sprocket.**

15. Remove the VTC assembly and the camshaft sprocket.

16. Remove the oil pump chain and the timing chains.

**NOTE: do not attempt to disassemble the VTC assembly since they are difficult to reassemble accurately in the field. If it should be disassembled, the VTC assembly must be replaced with a new one.**

17. Remove the camshaft brackets and the camshafts. Mark the parts so they can be reinstalled in their original positions.

18. Remove the rocker arms. Be sure to identify each rocker arm so it can be reinstalled in it's original position.

**To install:**

19. Make sure all mating surfaces are clean before installation.

20. Install the rocker arms, camshafts and camshaft brackets on the right bank. Properly lubricate the rocker arms and camshafts prior to installation. Tighten the camshaft bracket bolts to 9–10 ft. lbs. (12–14 Nm) in the proper sequence.

21. Install the VTC assembly and the exhaust cam sprocket on the right bank.

22. Make sure the camshafts are still correctly positioned and the piston in the No. 1 cylinder is still at TDC.

23. Install the timing chain on the right bank, aligning the mating marks on the chain with those on the crankshaft and camshaft sprockets.

24. Install the chain tensioner on the right bank.

25. Turn the crankshaft approximately 120 degrees clockwise from the point where the No. 1 piston is at TDC on the compression stroke. At this point, the valves on the left bank still remain unlifted.

26. Correctly position the camshafts and rocker arms for the left cylinder head. Properly lubricate the rocker arms and camshafts prior to installation. Tighten the camshaft bracket bolts to 9–10 ft. lbs. (12–14 Nm) in the proper sequence. Install the VTC assembly and the exhaust cam sprocket.

27. Install the timing chain on the left bank, aligning the mating marks on the chain with those on the crankshaft and camshaft sprockets.

28. Install the oil pump chain and sprockets.

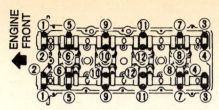

**Camshaft bracket torque sequence—Q45**

29. Install the oil pump chain guides. Place a 0.04 in. (1.0mm) feeler gauge between the upper chain guide and chain before assembling the chain guides. The force applied to the chain is equivalent to the upper chain guide weight.

30. Apply suitable sealer and install the front covers.

31. Install the chain tensioner for the left bank.

32. Apply suitable sealer to the rubber plugs and install them on the cylinder head.

33. Install the crank angle sensor, VTC solenoid, rocker cover and crank pulley.

34. Installation of the remaining components is the reverse of the removal procedure.

## Piston and Connecting Rod

### POSITIONING

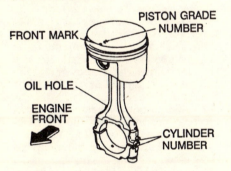

## ENGINE LUBRICATION

### Oil Pan

#### REMOVAL & INSTALLATION

*G20*

1. Raise and support the vehicle safely. Remove the engine under cover and drain the oil.

2. Remove the steel oil pan bolts in the proper sequence. Remove the steel

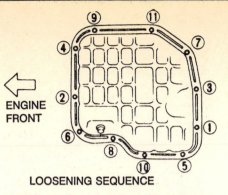

**LOOSENING SEQUENCE**

**Steel oil pan bolt removal sequence—G20**

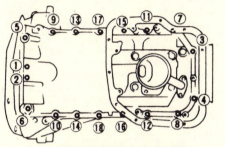

**LOOSENING SEQUENCE**

**ENGINE FRONT** ➡

**Aluminum oil pan bolt removal sequence—G20**

oil pan. Insert tool KV10111100 between steel oil pan and aluminum oil pan to pry apart.

3. Remove the oil baffle bolts and oil baffle. Remove the front tube.

4. Set a suitable jack under the transaxle and raise the engine with and engine hoist.

5. If equipped with an automatic transaxle, remove the transaxle shift control cable.

6. Remove the compressor gussets, the rear cover plate and all aluminum oil pan bolts. Loosen aluminum oil pan bolts in the proper sequence.

7. Remove the two engine to transaxle bolts and refit the them into vacant vacant holes at the bottom of the oil pan. Remove the aluminum oil pan. Use tool KV10111100 to pry oil pan from block. Remove the engine to transaxle bolts.

**To install:**

8. Clean the oil pan rail of all liquid gasket and apply a new bead of ⅛" thickness to the oil pan rail.

9. Install the aluminum oil pan and torque bolts 1–16 to 12–14 ft. lbs. (16–19 Nm) and bolts 17–18 to 5–6 ft. lbs. (6–8 Nm) in the opposite order of removal.

10. Install the two engine to transaxle bolts, rear cover plate, compressor gussets, automatic transmission shift

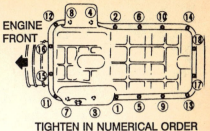

**TIGHTEN IN NUMERICAL ORDER**

**Oil pan bolt loosening sequence—M30**

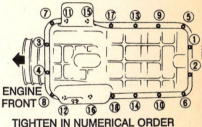

**TIGHTEN IN NUMERICAL ORDER**

**Oil pan bolt tightening sequence—M30**

control cable (if equipped), center member, front tube and baffle plate.

11. Clean the oil pan rail of all liquid gasket and apply a new bead of ⅛" thickness to the oil pan rail.

12. Install the steel oil pan and install bolts untill snug. Tighten bolts in the reverse order of REMOVAL & wait 30 minuites before refilling crankcase with oil.

*M30*

1. Raise and safely support the vehicle.

2. Drain the engine oil in a suitable container. Remove the oil level gauge.

3. Remove the air duct.

4. Disconnect the air conditioning and brake booster vacuum hoses from their mounting brackets.

5. Remove the upper radiator mounting bolts and the automatic transmission oil cooler line mounting bolts.

6. Remove the oil pan mounting bolts, loosen them in numerical order. remove the oil pan using the proper tool to remove.

7. Loosen the front exhaust tube mounting bolts and remove the front stabilizer bar mounting brackets. Remove the right side stabilizer mounting bolt.

8. Loosen the left side stabilizer mounting bolt. Position a suitable transmission jacking device under the transmission case.

9. Remove the engine mounting bolts. Slowly, raise the transmission jack and remove the oil pan.

10. Thoroughly clean the mounting surfaces. Apply the proper sealant to the oil pump gasket, the rear oil seal retainer and the oil pan mounting surface.

11. The installation is the reverse of the removal procedure. Install the bolts in the reverse order of the removal. Tighten to 5.1–5.8 ft. lbs.

### Q45

1. Disconnect the negative battery cable.
2. Raise the vehicle and support safely.
3. Remove the engine undercover.
4. Drain the engine oil
5. Remove the fan coupling with the fan.
6. Remove the drive belts, alternator, air compressor and engine gusset.
7. Remove the steering lower joint.
8. Support the transmission.
9. Attach a suitable lifting device and raise the engine.
10. Remove the suspension member assembly.
11. Remove the oil pan bolts and nuts.
12. Remove the oil pan from the engine block. Be careful not to damage the mating surface on the engine block.

**To install:**
13. Remove all gasket material from mating surfaces on the block and oil pan.
14. Apply a continuous bead of liquid gasket to the mating surface on the oil pan. Ensure that the bead is 0.138–0.177 in. (3.5–4.5mm) wide.
15. Install the oil pan. Install attaching bolts and nuts in sequence.
16. Complete the installation of the oil pan by reversing the removal procedure.

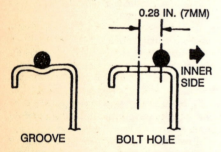

**Oil pan liquid sealant bead—all engines**

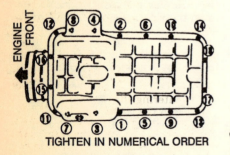

**TIGHTEN IN NUMERICAL ORDER**

**Oil pan installation torque sequence— Q45**

17. Allow gasket material to set for 30 minutes before filling the engine with oil.

## Oil Pump

### REMOVAL & INSTALLATION

### G20

1. Remove the drive belts.
2. Remove the cylinder head and oil pans.
3. Remove the oil strainer and baffle plate.
4. Remove the front cover assembly.

**To install:**
5. Clean the mating surfaces of liquid gasket and apply a fresh bead of ⅛″ thickness.
6. Coat the oil pump gears with oil. Using a new oil seal and O-ring, install the front cover assembly.
7. Install the oil strainer, baffle plate, oil pans, cylinder head and drive belts.

### M30

1. Raise and safely support the vehicle.
2. Drain the engine oil in a suitable container. Remove the oil level gauge.
3. Remove the oil pan.
4. Remove the oil pump mounting bolts and lift out the oil pump.
5. Always replace with a new oil seal and gasket. Apply oil to the inner and outer gears when installing.
6. The installation is the reverse of the removal procedure. Tighten the long mounting bolt to 9–12 ft. lbs. and the short bolts to 4.3–5.1 ft. lbs.

### Q45

1. Disconnect the negative battery cable.
2. Remove the engine and transmission assembly from the vehicle.
3. Remove the suspension member and engine mounts from the engine.
4. Remove the air compressor bracket.
5. Remove the cooling fan with coupling and the engine gusset.
6. Separate the engine from the

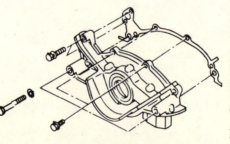

**Oil pump assembly—M30**

transmission and mount the engine on a suitable workstand.
7. Remove the oil pan.
8. Remove the ornamental rocker cover and remove the ignition coils and spark plugs.
9. Bring the No. 1 piston to TDC on the compression stroke.
10. Use a suitable puller to remove the crankshaft pulley.
11. Remove the rocker cover.
12. Remove the crank angle sensor and the Valve Timing Control (VTC) solenoid.
13. Remove the chain tensioners and the upper front covers.
14. Remove the front timing chain cover.

**NOTE: The timing chain will not be disengaged or dislocated from the crankshaft sprocket unless the front cover is removed. The cast portion of the front cover is located on the lower side of the crankshaft sprocket so the timing chain is not disengaged from the sprocket.**

15. Remove the VTC assembly and the camshaft sprocket.
16. Remove the oil pump chain and the timing chains.
17. Remove the mounting bolts and lift out the oil pump.

**To install:**
18. Thoroughly clean the mounting surfaces. Apply engine oil to the gears.
19. Install the oil pump with a new seal and gasket. Tighten the long bolts to 12–15 ft. lbs. and the short bolts to 3.3–4.3 ft. lbs.
20. Make sure all mating surfaces are clean before installation.
21. Install the VTC assembly and the exhaust cam sprocket on the right bank.
22. Make sure the camshafts are still correctly positioned and the piston in the No. 1 cylinder is still at TDC.
23. Install the timing chain on the right bank, aligning the mating marks on the chain with those on the crankshaft and camshaft sprockets.
24. Install the chain tensioner on the right bank.
25. Turn the crankshaft approximately 120 degrees clockwise from the point where the No. 1 piston is at TDC on the compression stroke. At this point, the valves on the left bank still remain unlifted.
26. Correctly position the camshafts and rocker arms for the left cylinder head. Properly lubricate the rocker arms and camshafts prior to installation. Install the VTC assembly and the exhaust cam sprocket.
27. Install the timing chain on the left bank, aligning the mating marks on the chain with those on the crankshaft and camshaft sprockets.

28. Install the oil pump chain and sprockets.

29. Install the oil pump chain guides. Place a 0.04 in. (1.0mm) feeler gauge between the upper chain guide and chain before assembling the chain guides. The force applied to the chain is equivalent to the upper chain guide weight.

30. Apply suitable sealer and install the front covers.

31. Install the chain tensioner for the left bank.

32. Apply suitable sealer to the rubber plugs and install them on the cylinder head.

33. Install the crank angle sensor, VTC solenoid, rocker cover and crank pulley.

34. Installation of the remaining components is the reverse of the removal procedure.

## Rear Main Bearing Oil Seal

The rear main oil seal is a solid type seal located in the rear oil seal retainer at the rear of the engine.

### REMOVAL & INSTALLATION

1. Raise and safely support the vehicle. Remove the transmission.

2. Remove the flywheel or drive plate.

3. Remove the rear oil seal retainer from the block.

4. Using a suitable prying tool, remove the oil seal from the retainer.

5. Thoroughly scrape the surface of the retainer to remove any traces of the existing sealant or gasket material.

6. Wipe the seal bore with a clean rag.

7. Apply clean engine oil to the new oil seal and carefully install it into the retainer using the proper seal installation tool.

8. Install the rear oil seal retainer into the engine, along with a new gasket.

9. Install the driveplate and transmission. Lower the vehicle.

# ENGINE COOLING

## Radiator

### REMOVAL & INSTALLATION

#### G20

1. Disconnect the negative battery cable. Drain the coolant system, remove the upper radiator hose and reservoir tank.

2. Remove the lower radiator hose and transmission cooler lines.

3. Unplug the radiator fan motor connector and remove the radiator fan.

4. Remove all radiator attaching bolts and remove the radiator.

**To install:**

5. Lower the radiator into position. Take care not to damage the radiator fins as this will effect cooling efficiency.

6. Install all attaching bolts and tighten securely.

7. Install the radiator fan and reconnect the radiator fan motor connector.

8. Install the radiator upper and lower hoses, and the reservoir tank.

9. Fill the cooling system, start the engine and allow it to reach normal operating temperature. Bleed the cooling system and check for leaks.

#### M30 and Q45

1. Disconnect the negative battery cable.

2. Drain the coolant.

3. On the Q45, remove the plastic cover over the radiator. Remove the upper hose and coolant reserve tank hose from the radiator.

4. Unbolt the shroud and move it backward in order to remove the fan and coupling. Remove the fan to water pump bolts and remove the fan, coupling, water pump pulley and shroud.

5. Raise the vehicle and support safely. Remove the lower hose from the radiator.

6. Disconnect and plug the automatic transmission cooler hoses. Disconnect the coolant thermo switch. Lower the vehicle.

7. Remove the mounting brackets or unbolt the radiator from the support and carefully lift out of the engine compartment.

8. Remove the cooling fans from the radiator.

**To install:**

9. Lower the radiator into position.

10. Install the mounting brackets or bolts.

11. Raise the vehicle and support safely. Connect the automatic transmission cooler lines and the thermo switch connector.

12. Connect the lower hose. Lower the vehicle.

13. Install the shroud, pulley, coupling and fan. Torque the water pump pulley nuts to 7 ft. lbs. (10 Nm). Adjust the belt.

14. Connect the upper hose and coolant reserve tank hose.

15. On the M30, open the air release plug. Fill the cooling system and check for leaks.

16. Connect the negative battery cable, run the vehicle until the thermostat opens, fill the radiator completely and check the automatic transmission fluid level. Recheck for coolant leaks.

17. Once the vehicle has cooled, recheck the coolant level.

## Heater Core

### REMOVAL & INSTALLATION

#### G20

It should be possible to remove the heater core without removing the dashboard.

1. Disconnect the negative battery cable.

2. With the temperature control lever set to the **HOT** position, drain the cooling system.

3. Disconnect the heater hoses a the drivers side of the heater unit.

4. Remove the glove compartment and the front panel from the center console.

5. Remove the radio and heater/air conditioner controls to remove the lower portion of the center console.

6. Disconnect the output vent ducts and remove the heater unit.

7. Disassemble the housing to remove the heater core.

**To install:**

8. Install the heater core and assemble the heater unit housing. Use new gaskets and seals as required, and check for smooth movement of the doors and linkage.

9. Install the heater unit and attach the ducts. Take care not to damage the gasket between the heater and cooling units.

10. Install the lower center console, the radio, and the heater controls. Before completing the assembl, connect the battery and adjust the door motor linkage.

11. Install the glove compartment and console panel.

12. Connect the heater hoses and refill the cooling system with the temperature control set at **HOT**. Bleed the cooling system.

#### M30

1. Disconnect the negative battery cable and allow 10 minutes to elapse before entering the vehicle.

2. Drain the coolant.

3. Disconnect the heater hoses from the heater core tubes and plug them.

4. Remove the steering column covers.

5. Remove the front pillar garnish and lower instrument covers.

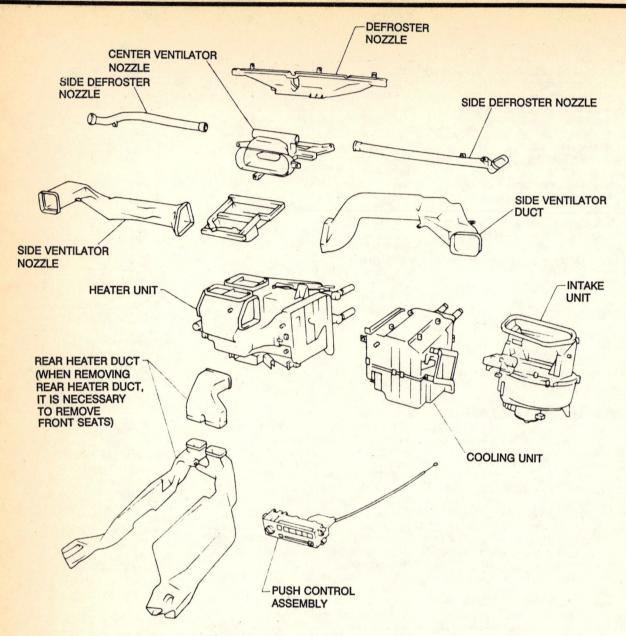

**Heater and air conditioner assembly—G20**

6. Remove the cluster lid and instrument cluster.

7. Remove the radio bezel, radio and climate control switch assembly.

8. Remove the glove box.

9. Remove the instrument reinforcement and the shift lever cover.

10. Remove the console assembly.

11. Remove the defroster grille and sensors.

12. Remove the hood lock cable bracket and rear heater ducts.

13. Remove the fuse block and disconnect the Super Multiple Junction (SMJ).

14. Remove the steering column mounting bolts and lower the column.

15. Remove the caps that cover the instrument panel securing screws, remove the screws and remove the instrument panel assembly.

16. Remove the air distribution ducts from the heater unit.

17. Disconnect all wires and cables that connect to the unit.

18. Remove the mounting bolts and nuts and remove the heater unit from the vehicle.

19. Disassemble and remove the heater core from the unit.

**To install:**

20. Clean the inside of the unit out, install the heater core and assemble the unit.

21. Install the unit to the vehicle and connect all wires and cables. Install the air distribution ducts.

22. Install the instrument panel assembly and snap the screw caps in place.

23. Raise and secure the steering column.

24. Connect the SMJ and install the fuse block.

25. Install the rear heater ducts and hood lock cable bracket.

26. Install the defroster grille and sensors.

27. Install the console assembly and shift lever cover.

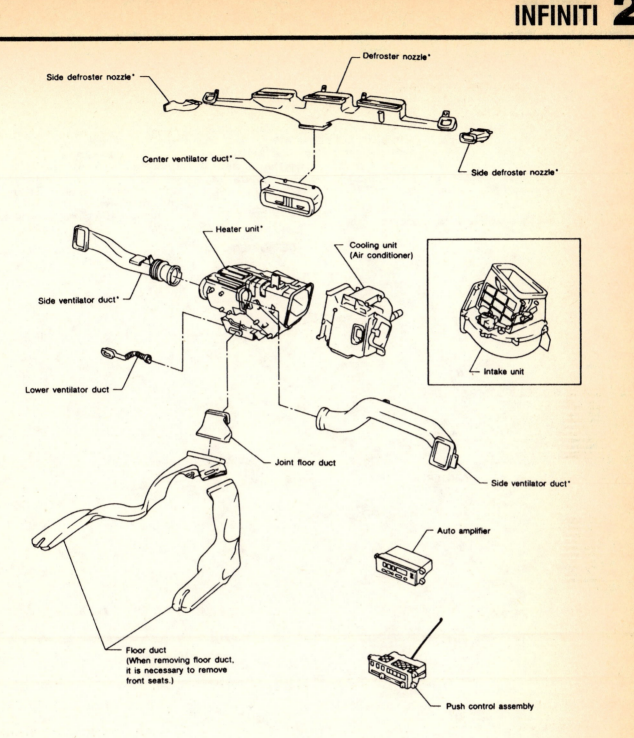

Side defroster nozzle*

Defroster nozzle*

Side defroster nozzle*

Center ventilator duct*

Heater unit*

Cooling unit
(Air conditioner)

Side ventilator duct*

Intake unit

Lower ventilator duct

Joint floor duct

Side ventilator duct*

Auto amplifier

Floor duct
(When removing floor duct,
it is necessary to remove
front seats.)

Push control assembly

: For removal, it is necessary to remove instrument assembly.

**Instrument panel assembly—Q45**

28. Install the instrument reinforcement and glove box.

29. Install the climate control switch assembly, radio and bezel.

30. Install the instrument cluster and lid.

31. Install the lower instrument panel covers and pillar garnish.

32. Install the steering column covers.

33. Connect the heater core tubes to the heater core tubes.

34. Open the air release plug. Fill the cooling system and check for leaks.

35. Connect the negative battery cable, run the vehicle until the thermostat opens, fill the radiator completely and check the automatic transmission fluid level. Recheck for coolant leaks.

36. Once the vehicle has cooled, recheck the coolant level.

### Q45
1. In order to open the hot water valve, perform the following:

a. Turn the ignition switch to the **ON** position.

b. Within 10 seconds, press the **OFF** switch on the climate control switch assembly for at least 5 seconds.

c. Press the temp-hotter switch 3 times.

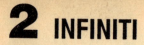

d. Press the defroster switch 2 times.

e. The air conditioning switch panel should display Code 43.

f. Wait for 10 seconds before turning the ignition switch off.

2. Disconnect the negative battery cable and allow 10 minutes to elapse before entering the vehicle.

3. Drain the coolant.

4. Disconnect the heater hoses from the heater core tubes and plug them.

**NOTE: Since this vehicle is** equipped with an air bag, it is imperative that the exact steering wheel Removal & Installation procedure under Steering is followed. The air bag module is a fragile component. Always place it with the pad side facing upward. Do not allow oil, grease or water to come in contact with the module. Do not drop the module; if it is damaged in any way, do not reinstall it to the steering wheel.

5. Remove the steering wheel and column covers.

6. Remove the shifter lever bezel.

7. Remove the ash tray assembly.

8. Remove the radio and climate control switch bezel.

9. Remove the lower instrument panel covers.

10. Remove the front and rear floor console assemblies.

11. Remove the cruise control main switch/outside mirror control switch assembly.

12. Remove the cluster lid and instrument cluster.

13. Remove the glove box and glove box cover.

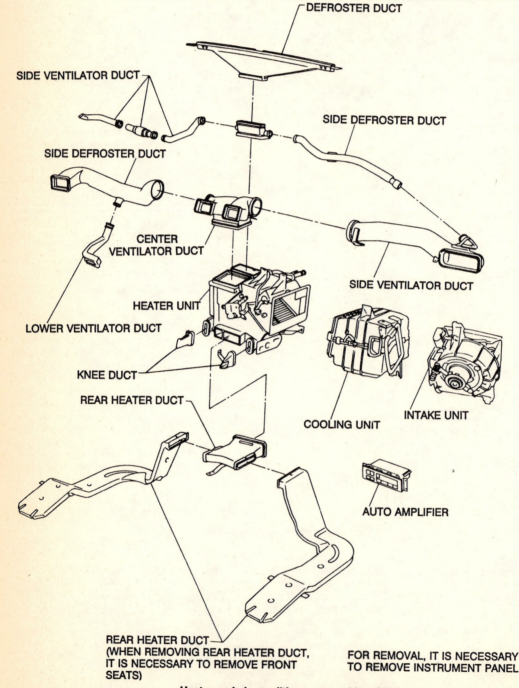

**Heater and air conditioner assembly—Q45**

14. Remove the cover on the lower right side of the instrument panel.

15. Remove the defroster grille.

16. Remove the radio and climate control switch assemblies.

17. Remove the remaining mounting screws remove the instrument panel assembly.

18. Remove the air distribution ducts from the heater unit.

19. Disconnect all wires and cables that connect to the unit.

20. Remove the mounting bolts and nuts and remove the heater unit from the vehicle.

21. Disassemble and remove the heater core from the unit.

**To install:**

22. Clean the inside of the unit out, install the heater core and assemble the unit. Connect the heater hoses.

23. Install the unit to the vehicle and connect all wires and cables. Install the air distribution ducts.

24. Install the instrument panel assembly. Install the cover on the lower right side.

25. Install the radio and climate control switch assemblies.

26. Install the defroster grille.

27. Install the glove box cover and glove box assembly.

28. Install the instrument cluster and cluster lid.

29. Install the cruise control main switch/outside mirror control switch assembly.

30. Install the console assemblies.

31. Install the lower instrument panel covers.

32. Install the radio and climate control switch bezel.

33. Install the ash tray assembly.

34. Install the shifter lever bezel.

35. Install the steering wheel and column covers.

36. Fill the cooling system and check for leaks.

37. Connect the negative battery cable, run the vehicle until the thermostat opens, fill the radiator completely and check the automatic transmission fluid level. Recheck for coolant leaks.

38. Once the vehicle has cooled, recheck the coolant level.

## Water Pump

### REMOVAL & INSTALLATION

#### G20

1. Drain the coolant from the radiator and engine block. The drain plug in the engine block is located at the left front of the cylinder block.

2. Remove the drive belts.

3. Loosen the water pump attaching bolts and remove the water pump. Take care not to drip coolant on the drive belts.

4. Clean all mating surfaces and place a 2–3mm bead of liquid gasket on the water pump mating surface.

5. Install water pump and tighten bolts to 12–15 ft. lbs. (16–21 Nm).

6. Using a radiator cap tester, or equivalent, check the system for leaks.

7. Refill with coolant and bleed the system of air.

#### M30

1. Disconnect the negative battery cable.

2. Drain the coolant from the radiator and from the drain plugs on both sides of the cylinder block.

3. Remove the timing belt covers.

**NOTE: Use the proper precautions to avoid getting coolant on the timing belt.**

4. Note the positioning of the clamp and disconnect the hose from the water pump.

5. Remove the water pump mounting bolts and remove the pump from the engine.

**To install:**

6. Thoroughly clean and dry the mating surfaces, bolts and bolt holes.

7. Apply liquid gasket to the water pump and install to the engine. Torque the bolts to 14 ft. lbs. (19 Nm).

8. Connect the hose and install the clamp in the same position as when it was removed to provide adequate clearance between it and the timing belt cover.

9. Open the air release plug. Fill the cooling system and check for leaks using a pressure tester before continuing.

10. Install the timing belt covers and all related parts.

11. Connect the negative battery cable, run the vehicle until the thermostat opens and fill the radiator completely. Recheck for coolant leaks.

12. Once the vehicle has cooled, recheck the coolant level.

#### Q45

1. Disconnect the negative battery cable.

2. Drain the coolant from the radiator and from the drain cocks on both sides of the cylinder block.

3. Unbolt the shroud and move it backward in order to remove the fan and coupling. Remove the fan to water pump bolts and remove the fan, coupling, water pump pulley and shroud.

4. Remove all necessary accessories to gain access to the water pump.

5. Note the positioning of the clamp and disconnect the hose from the water pump.

6. Remove the water pump mounting bolts and remove the pump from the engine.

**To install:**

7. Thoroughly clean and dry the mating surfaces, bolts and bolt holes.

8. Apply liquid gasket to the water pump and install to the engine. Torque the bolts to 14 ft. lbs. (19 Nm).

9. Connect the hose and install the clamp in the same position as when it was removed. Fill the cooling system and check for leaks using a pressure tester before continuing.

10. Install all removed accessories.

11. Install the shroud, pulley, cou-

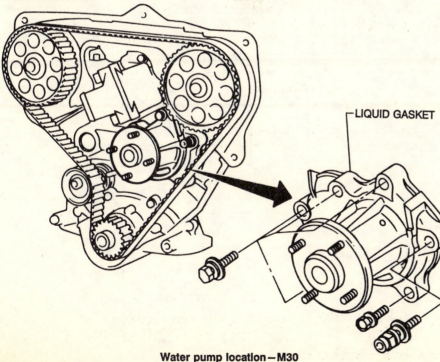

LIQUID GASKET

**Water pump location—M30**

pling and fan. Torque the water pump pulley nuts to 7 ft. lbs. (10 Nm). Adjust all belts.

12. Connect the negative battery cable, run the vehicle until the thermostat opens and fill the radiator completely. Recheck for coolant leaks.

13. Once the vehicle has cooled, recheck the coolant level.

## Thermostat

### REMOVAL & INSTALLATION

#### G20

1. Drain the engine coolant.
2. Remove the lower radiator hose.
3. Remove the water inlet, then remove the thermostat.
4. Install the new thermostat with the air bleeder or jiggle valve facing upward.
5. Clean all mating surfaces and ap-

ply a 2–3mm bead of liquid gasket to the water inlet.

6. Install the water pump inlet and tighten bolts to 5–6 ft. lbs. (6–8 Nm).
7. Install the lower radiator hose, refill and bleed the coolant system and check for leaks.

#### M30

1. Disconnect the negative battery cable. Drain the cooling system to below thermostat level.
2. Disconnect the upper radiator hose from the thermostat housing.
3. Remove the thermostat housing and thermostat.

**To install:**

4. Thoroughly clean and dry the mating surfaces, bolts and bolt holes.
5. Install the thermostat with the **UPR** mark and arrow at the top.
6. Apply liquid gasket to the thermostat housing. Install the housing and torque the bolts to 14 ft. lbs. (19 Nm).

7. Open the air release plug and fill the cooling system.
8. Connect the negative battery cable, run the vehicle until the thermostat opens and fill the radiator completely. Recheck for coolant leaks.
9. Once the vehicle has cooled, recheck the coolant level.

#### Q45

1. Disconnect the negative battery cable. Drain the cooling system to below thermostat level.
2. Remove the front ornament cover.
3. Disconnect the upper hose from the coolant inlet.
4. Remove the inlet and thermostat.

**To install:**

5. Thoroughly clean and dry the mating surfaces, bolts and bolt holes.
6. Install the thermostat with the jiggle valve at the top.

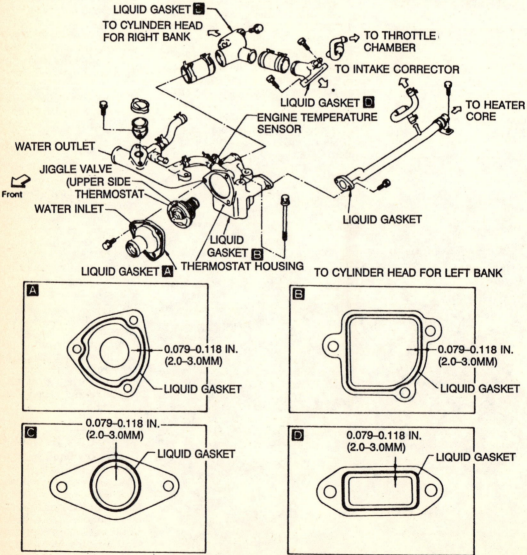

Thermostat location—Q45

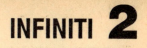

7. Apply liquid gasket to the inlet. Install and torque the bolts to 14 ft. lbs. (19 Nm).

8. Fill the cooling system.

9. Connect the negative battery cable, run the vehicle until the thermostat opens and fill the radiator completely. Recheck for coolant leaks.

10. Once the vehicle has cooled, recheck the coolant level.

## Cooling System Bleeding

### G20

1. Set the heater temperature control lever to **MAX** hot position. Remove the radiator cap, air relief plug (located at the thermostat housing) and the air bleeder cap (located near the heater core).

2. Refill the reservoir bottle to the **MAX** line. Reinstall the the air relief plug when coolant spills from the hole. Reinstall the air bleeder cap.

3. Install a steel wire between the negative pressure valve and the seat of the radiator cap. Install the cap and warm the engine to normal operating temperature.

4. Run the engine at 2500 rpm for 10 seconds and return to idle. Repeat this 2–3 times. Turn the engine off and allow car to cool.

5. Remove the radiator cap and check the coolant level. If necessary refill the radiator with coolant up to the filler neck. Repeat Steps 9 and 10 several times.

6. Remove the radiator cap and remove the steel wire. Install the cap and warm the engine and check for the sound of coolant flow with engine running from idle to 4000 rpm. If a sound is heard, bleed air from the cooling system as follows:

   a. Cool engine and remove the air bleeder cap on the heater inlet hose.

   b. Attach a suitable transparent hose at the air bleeder pipe and put the opposite end of the hose into the coolant reservoir.

   c. Install the radiator cap with the steel wire inserted and check for proper connection of all coolant related hoses.

   d. Start the engine and check for bubbles in the reservoir tank.

   e. Set the heater control lever to **MAX** cool and run the engine up to 2300 rpm until the bubbles disappear in the hose.

   f. After bubbles disappear, set the heater control lever to **MAX** hot and listen for coolant system sound. If sound is heard, perform Steps A–E again.

   g. After all air has been bled from the system, remove the steel wire

from the radiator cap, remove the transparent hose, install the air bleeder cap and check the coolant reservoir to ensure it is full.

### M30

The M30 is equipped with a air release plug in line with a coolant hose on the right side of the ornamental collector cover. When filling the coolant system open the plug to bleed air from the system.

### Q45

The Q45 uses a thermostat which is equipped with a jiggle valve. This valve bleeds air as the system is being filled, thus the cooling system requires no further bleeding.

# ENGINE ELECTRICAL

**NOTE: Disconnecting the negative battery cable on some vehicles may interfere with the functions of the on board computer systems and may require the computer to undergo a relearning process, once the negative battery cable is reconnected.**

## Distributor

### REMOVAL

#### G20 and M30

1. Disconnect the negative battery cable.

2. Remove the splash shield (if equipped). Disconnect the distributor connectors.

3. Unscrew the distributor cap hold-down screws and lift off the distributor cap with all ignition wires still connected.

4. Matchmark the rotor to the distributor housing and the distributor housing to the engine.

**NOTE: do not crank the engine during this procedure. If the engine is cranked, the matchmark must be disregarded.**

5. Remove the hold-down bolt.

6. Remove the distributor from the engine.

### INSTALLATION

#### Timing Not Disturbed

1. Install a new distributor housing O-ring.

2. Install the distributor in the engine so the rotor is aligned with the matchmark on the housing and the housing is aligned with the matchmark on the engine. Make sure the distributor is fully seated and the distributor gear is fully engaged.

3. Install and snug the hold-down bolt.

4. Connect the distributor pickup lead wires.

5. Install the distributor cap and tighten the screws. Install the splash shield.

6. Connect the negative battery cable.

7. Adjust the ignition timing and tighten the hold-down bolt.

#### Timing Disturbed

1. Install a new distributor housing O-ring.

2. Position the engine so the No. 1 piston is at TDC of its compression stroke and the mark on the vibration damper is aligned with **0** on the timing indicator.

3. Install the distributor in the engine so the rotor is aligned with the position of the No. 1 ignition wire on the distributor cap (4–5 o'clock position on the G20). Make sure the distributor is fully seated and that the distributor shaft is fully engaged.

**NOTE: There are distributor cap runners inside the cap on 3.0L engine. Make sure the rotor is pointing to where the No. 1 runner originates inside the cap.**

4. Install and snug the hold-down bolt.

5. Connect the distributor pickup lead wires.

6. Install the distributor cap and tighten the screws. Install the splash shield, if equipped.

7. Connect the negative battery cable.

8. Adjust the ignition timing and tighten the hold-down bolt.

## Distributorless Ignition

### REMOVAL & INSTALLATION

#### Q45

##### POWER TRANSISTOR UNIT

1. Disconnect the negative battery cable.

2. Remove the air intake duct, if necessary.

3. Disconnect the connector.

4. Remove the bolts that attach the unit to the ornamental rocker cover.

5. Remove the unit from the engine.

6. The installation is the reverse of the removal procedure.

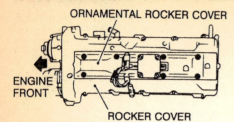

ORNAMENTAL ROCKER COVER

ENGINE FRONT

ROCKER COVER

**Ornamental rocker cover—4.5L engine**

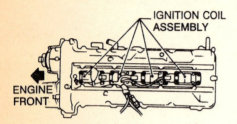

IGNITION COIL ASSEMBLY

ENGINE FRONT

**Ignition coil assembly—4.5L engine**

## IGNITION COIL

1. Disconnect the negative battery cable.
2. Remove the air intake duct, if necessary.
3. Disconnect the power transistor unit connector.
4. Remove the ornamental rocker cover.
5. Remove the ignition coil bracket mounting bolts and pull out the bracket with the ignition coils.
6. Separate the coil from the bracket and remove from the engine.
7. The installation is the reverse of the removal procedure.

## CRANK ANGLE SENSOR

1. Disconnect the negative battery cable.
2. Remove the air intake duct.
3. Matchmark the position of the crankshaft sensor assembly to the head.
4. Disconnect the connector, remove the mounting bolts and remove the crank angle sensor from the engine.
5. The installation is the reverse of the removal procedure.
6. Check the ignition timing and adjust, if necessary.

# Ignition Timing

## ADJUSTMENT

1. Start the engine, set the parking brake and run the engine until at normal operating temperature. Keep all lights and accessories off.
2. Connect a timing light to the No. 1 cylinder spark plug wire.
3. Use the Nissan Consult System Checking tool in the Data Monitor

mode to check engine rpm. Adjust, if necessary.
4. Aim the timing light at the timing scale.
5. On the G20, run the engine at 2000 rpm for 2 minuites and race engine 2–3 times under no load. Return engine to idle. Turn engine OFF and disconnect the throttle sensor harness connector. Start engine and race at 2000–3000 rpm 2–3 times. Check igntion timing with a timing light. Specification is 13–17° BTDC (manual transmission) and 13–17° BTDC in **N** (automatic transmission). Adjust timing as necessary by loosening distributor holddown clamp and rotating distributor.
6. On the M30 and Q45, run the engine at 2000 rpm for 2 minuites and race engine 2–3 times under no load. Return engine to idle. Check ignition timing with a timing light. Specification is 13–17° BTDC. Adjust timing as necessary by loosening distributor holddown clamp and rotating distributor.

# Alternator

## PRECAUTIONS

Several precautions must be observed with alternator equipped vehicles to avoid damage to the unit.
• If the battery is removed for any reason, make sure it is reconnected with the correct polarity. Reversing the battery connections may result in damage to the one-way rectifiers.
• When utilizing a booster battery as a starting aid, always connect the positive to positive terminals and the negative terminal from the booster battery to a good engine ground on the vehicle being started.
• Never use a fast charger as a booster to start vehicles.
• Disconnect the battery cables when charging the battery with a fast charger.
• Never attempt to polarize the alternator.
• do not use test lamps of more than 12 volts when checking diode continuity.
• do not short across or ground any of the alternator terminals.
• The polarity of the battery, alternator and regulator must be matched and considered before making any electrical connections within the system.
• Never separate the alternator on an open circuit. Make sure all connections within the circuit are clean and tight.
• Disconnect the battery ground terminal when performing any service on electrical components.

• Disconnect the battery if arc welding is to be done on the vehicle.

## BELT TENSION ADJUSTMENT

### G20

1. Disconnect the negative battery cable.
2. Loosen the nut that secures the T-bolt to the slotted adjustment bracket.
3. Turn the adjustment bolt until the belt deflects approximately 0.28–0.31 in. (alternator) and 0.16–0.20 in. (power steering) at its longest expanse.
4. Tighten the T-bolt nut to 12–16 ft. lbs. (16–22 Nm).
5. Connect the negative battery cable.

### M30

1. Disconnect the negative battery cable.
2. Loosen the nut that secures the T-bolt to the slotted adjustment bracket.
3. Turn the adjustment bolt until the belt deflects approximately 0.3 in. at its longest expanse.
4. Tighten the T-bolt nut to 11 ft. lbs. (15 Nm).
5. Connect the negative battery cable.

### Q45

1. Disconnect the negative battery cable.
2. Loosen the nut that secures the T-bolt to the alternator belt idler pulley.
3. Turn the adjustment bolt until the belt deflects approximately 0.3 in. at its longest expanse.
4. Tighten the T-bolt nut to 24 ft. lbs. (32 Nm).
5. Connect the negative battery cable.

## REMOVAL & INSTALLATION

### G20 and M30

1. Disconnect the negative battery cable.
2. Loosen the alternator belt and remove from the pulley.
3. Remove the adjusting bracket.
4. Disconnect the harness connector and cable from the rear of the alternator.

**NOTE: The front mounting bolt cannot be removed separately because of insufficient clearance between the alternator and engine coolant inlet tube.**

5. Remove the rear mounting bolt loosen the front mounting bolt.

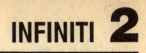

6. Remove the alternator with the front mounting bolt.

**To install:**

7. The installation is the reverse of the removal procedure. Torque the mounting bolts to 15 ft. lbs. (20 Nm).

8. Adjust the belt so it deflects approximately 0.3 in. at its longest expanse.

9. Connect the negative battery cable and check the alternator for proper operation.

### Q45

1. Disconnect the negative battery cable.

2. Remove the radiator shroud and cooling fan.

3. Drain a sufficient amount of coolant and remove the upper radiator hose.

4. Remove the upper alternator bracket and the air conditioner pipe mounting bracket.

5. Remove the idler pulley and belt.

6. Remove the 2 power steering cooler pipe mounting screws.

7. Remove the mounting through bolt.

8. Pull the alternator toward the radiator and remove the harness heat shield.

9. Disconnect the wires from the rear of the alternator and remove from the vehicle.

**To install:**

10. Position the alternator and connect the wires. Install the heat shield.

11. Install the mounting through bolt loosely.

12. Install the 2 power steering cooler pipe mounting screws.

13. Install the idler pulley and belt.

14. Install the air conditioner pipe mounting bracket and upper alternator bracket. Tighten the through bolt.

15. Adjust the belt so it deflects approximately 0.3 in. at its widest expanse.

16. Install the upper radiator hose and refill the cooling system.

17. Install the cooling fan and radiator shroud.

18. Connect the negative battery cable and check the alternator for proper operation.

## Starter

### REMOVAL & INSTALLATION

1. Disconnect the negative battery cable.

2. Raise the vehicle and support safely.

3. Remove the engine undercover.

4. Remove exhaust components, as required, in order to gain access to the starter.

5. Remove the starter mounting bolts and remove the starter.

6. The installation is the reverse of the removal procedure. Torque the mounting bolts to 25 ft. lbs. (34 Nm).

7. Connect the negative battery cable and check the starter for proper operation.

# EMISSION CONTROLS

**Please refer to "Emission Controls" in the Unit Repair section for system maintenance procedures. Due to the complex nature of modern electronic engine control systems, comprehensive diagnosis and testing procedures fall outside the confines of this repair manual. For complete information on diagnosis, testing and repair procedures concerning all modern engine and emission control systems, please refer to "Chilton's Guide to Fuel Injection and Electronic Engine Controls".**

# FUEL SYSTEM

## Fuel System Service Precautions

Safety is the most important factor when performing not only fuel system maintenance but any type of maintenance. Failure to conduct maintenance and repairs in a safe manner may result in serious personal injury or death. Maintenance and testing of the vehicle's fuel system components can be accomplished safely and effectively by adhering to the following rules and guidelines.

● To avoid the possibility of fire and personal injury, always disconnect the negative battery cable unless the repair or test procedure requires that battery voltage be applied.

● Always relieve the fuel system pressure prior to disconnecting any fuel system component (injector, fuel rail, pressure regulator, etc.), fitting or fuel line connection. Exercise extreme caution whenever relieving fuel system pressure to avoid exposing skin, face and eyes to fuel spray. Please be advised that fuel under pressure may penetrate the skin or any part of the body that it contacts.

● Always place a shop towel or cloth around the fitting or connection prior to loosening to absorb any excess fuel due to spillage. Ensure that all fuel spillage (should it occur) is quickly removed from engine surfaces. Ensure that all fuel soaked cloths or towels are deposited into a suitable waste container.

● Always keep a dry chemical (Class B) fire extinguisher near the work area.

● do not allow fuel spray or fuel vapors to come into contact with a spark or open flame.

● Always use a backup wrench when loosening and tightening fuel line connection fittings. This will prevent unnecessary stress and torsion to fuel line piping. Always follow the proper torque specifications.

● Always replace worn fuel fitting O-rings with new. Do not substitute fuel hose or equivalent where fuel pipe is installed.

### RELIEVING FUEL SYSTEM PRESSURE

1. Disable the fuel system either by pulling the fuel pump fuse, located in the interior fuse box, or by disconnecting the fuel pump relay or module located in the trunk.

2. Start the engine and run until it stalls.

3. Crank the engine 2–3 more times to ensure that all pressure is relieved.

4. Disconnect the negative battery cable. Install or reconnect the fuse, relay or module.

5. Erase the created code using a Nissan Consult Tester, or equivalent, when servicing is finished.

## Fuel Tank

### REMOVAL & INSTALLATION

1. Relieve the fuel system pressure.

2. Disconnect the negative battery cable. Raise and support the rear of the vehicle safely.

3. Using the proper equipment, drain the fuel tank.

4. Remove the fuel tank and filler neck protective plates. Remove the filler neck to quarter panel attaching bolts. Disconect the ventilation pipes and remove the fuel filler assembly.

5. Disconnect the wiring harness connector for the fuel pump/sending unit assembly.

6. Place a suitable jack under the center of the tank and apply slight pressure. Remove the tank retaining bolts.

7. Lower the tank and disconnect the fuel hoses from the pump/sending

unit assembly and plug them. Some vehicles are equipped with an inspection cover under the rear seat. Remove this cover to gain access to the fuel hoses prior to lowering the fuel tank.

8. Remove the fuel tank from the vehicle.

**To install:**

9. If the pump/sending unit was removed from the fuel tank, use a new O-ring and install the assembly on the fuel tank.

10. Install the fuel tank. Torque the retaining bolts to 24 ft. lbs. (33 Nm).

11. Connect all fuel lines and harness connections. Connect the filler neck and overflow tube.

12. Install the protective plates.

13. Lower the vehicle. Install the bolts that attach the filer neck to the quarter panel.

14. Connect the negative battery cable, start the engine and check for leaks.

## Fuel Filter

### REMOVAL & INSTALLATION

— **CAUTION** —

*do not use conventional fuel filters, hoses or clamps when servicing this fuel system. They are not compatible with the high pressures of the injection system and could fail, causing personal injury. Use only components specifically designed for fuel injection.*

1. Relieve the fuel system pressure.
2. Disconnect the negative battery cable.
3. Disconnect the fuel hoses from the fuel filter, located in the right side of the engine compartment.
4. Remove the filter mounting screws and remove from the vehicle.
5. Inspect all hoses and clamps for damage of any type. Replace parts, as required.
6. The installation is the reverse of the removal.

## Fuel Pump

The fuel pump for all Infiniti models is located inside the fuel tank at the fuel gauge sender unit.

### PRESSURE TESTING

1. Relieve the fuel system pressure.
2. Disconnect the fuel hose between the fuel filter and the fuel tube leading to the engine.
3. Install an appropriate fuel pressure gauge between the filter and tube.
4. Start the engine and check for fuel leaks.

5. Observe the fuel pressure. The specification is 34 psi at idle and 43 psi when the fuel pressure regulator vacuum hose is pinched off.

6. Stop the engine, disconnect the vacuum hose to the pressure regulator and plug it.

7. Connect a hand-held vacuum pump to the regulator.

8. Start the engine and observe the fuel pressure as the vacuum is varied. The fuel pressure should decrease as the vacuum is increased.

### REMOVAL & INSTALLATION

#### G20

1. Release the fuel system pressure.
2. Remove the inspection hole cover located beneth the rear seat.
3. Disconnect the connectors and fuel tubes.
4. Remove the fuel gauge locking ring using tool SST-X38879, or equivalent.
5. Remove the fuel gauge assembly and disconnect the tubes and connector.
6. Remove the fuel pump by sliding it out on an angle.

**To install:**

7. Use a new O-ring on the fuel gauge assembly locking ring.
8. Install the new fuel pump and attach all fuel lines and connectors.
9. Using tool SST-X38879, or equivalent, tighten the locking ring to 22–26 ft. lbs. (30–35 Nm).
10. Install the inspection cover and test fuel system pressure at the injectors.

#### M30 and Q45

1. Relieve the fuel system pressure.
2. Disconnect the negative battery cable.
3. Remove the fuel tank.
4. Disconnect the wiring harness. Remove the fuel tank sender unit attaching bolts. Remove the fuel tank sender and discard the O-ring.
5. Remove the fuel pump from the sender unit.

**To install:**

6. Install the new fuel pump on the sender unit assembly.
7. Using a new O-ring, install the sender unit in the fuel tank. Tighten the bolts to 2 ft. lbs. (2–3 Nm).
8. Connect the wiring harness and install the fuel tank. Tighten the fuel tank attaching strap bolts to 20–27 ft. lbs. (26–36 Nm).
9. Connect the negative battery cable, start the engine and check for leaks.

## Fuel Injection

### IDLE SPEED ADJUSTMENT

The idle speed is controlled by the ECCS control unit. Adjustment is not required.

### IDLE MIXTURE ADJUSTMENT

The idle mixture is controlled by the ECCS control unit. Adjustment is not required.

## Fuel Injector

### REMOVAL & INSTALLATION

#### G20

1. Disconnect the negative battery cable. Relieve fuel system pressure.
2. Disconnect injector harness connectors.
3. Disconnect vacuum hose from pressure regulator.
4. Disconnect fuel hoses from fuel tube assembly.
5. Remove injectors with fuel tube assembly. Loosen bolts in reverse order of torquing sequence.
6. To remove injector, push out of the fuel tube assembly.

**NOTE: do not remove injector by pinching connector.**

**To install:**

7. Replace or clean injector as necessary.
8. Install injector on fuel tube as-

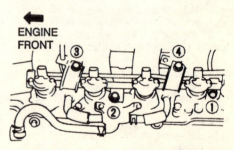

**Fuel tube torquing sequence—G20**

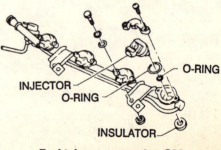

**Fuel tube components—G20**

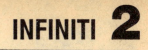
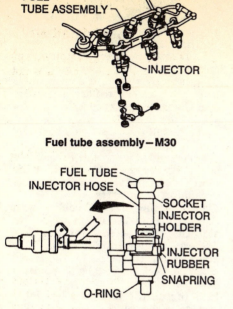

**Fuel tube assembly—M30**

**Injector assembly—M30**

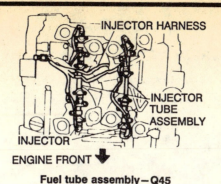

**Fuel tube assembly—Q45**

## Halfshaft

### REMOVAL & INSTALLATION

*G20*

1. Raise and support the vehicle safely. Remove the wheel bearing lock nut.
2. Remove the brake caliper assembly and rotor. Using a piece of wire, position the caliper so that it is not supported by the brake line.
3. Separate the tie-rod from the ball joint.
4. Separate the kingpin from the knuckle.
5. Remove the halfshaft from the wheel hub/knuckle by lightly tapping it with a wood drift. Take care not to damage the CV boots.
6. Remove the halfshaft from the transaxle by prying outward with a suitable tool at the transaxle case.
7. On automatic transaxle models, remove the left halfshaft by tapping it out with a drift from the right side of the transaxle case. Take care not to damage the pinion mate shaft and side gear.

**To install:**

8. Drive a new oil seal into the transaxle. Set tool KV38106800, or equivalent, along the inner circumference of the oil seal.
9. Insert the halfshaft into the transaxle. Ensure that the serrations are aligned. Remove the tool.
10. Push the halfshaft inward and install the circular clip in the groove of the side gear. After inserting the clip, pull outward on the flange of the slide joint to ensure the clip is properly meshed with the side gear. If if pulls out, the clip was not installed properly.
11. Install the halfshaft into the wheel hub/knuckle. Tighten the upper knuckle nut to 72–87 ft. lbs. (98–118 Nm) and wheel bearing lock nut to 174–231 ft. lbs. (235–314 Nm).
12. Using a dial indicator, check wheel bearing axial end play. Specification calls for 0.0020 in. (0.05mm) or less.

*M30*

1. Raise the vehicle and support safely.
2. Remove the 6 bolts and nuts attaching the outer CV-joint to the companion flange.
3. Remove the inner CV-joint from the differential carrier by prying with a suitable tool.

**To install:**

4. Install the inner CV-joint into the differential carrier.
5. Connect the outer CV-joint to the companion flange with the 6 bolts and

---

sembly using a new O-ring and insulator. Lubricate O-rings with silicone oil.

9. Install injectors with fuel tube assembly onto intake manifold. Tighten fuel tube assembly bolts in sequence to 7–8 ft. lbs. (9–10 Nm), and then retighten to 15–20 ft. lbs. (21–26 Nm).
10. Install fuel hoses, lubricating them with silicone oil.
11. Connect the injector harness connector, start the engine and check for leaks.

### M30

1. Relieve the fuel system pressure. Disconnect the negative battery cable.
2. Disconnect the cruise control and throttle cables from the throttle body.
3. Remove the intake manifold collector.
4. Disconnect the vacuum hose from the fuel pressure regulator.
5. Disconnect and plug the fuel hoses.
6. Disconnect all injector harness connectors.
7. Disconnect the fuel temperature sensor connector.
8. Remove the injector fuel fuel tube assembly retaining bolts and remove the assembly from the engine.
9. Remove the injector(s) and short fuel hose(s) from the fuel tube. Do not reuse the rubber hose(s).

**To install:**

10. Wet the inside of the new rubber hose(s) with fuel.
11. Push the end of the rubber hose with hose sockets into the injector tail piece and fuel tube end as far as they

---

will go. Clamps are not used at these connections.

12. Install the injector fuel tube assembly.
13. Connect the fuel temperature sensor connector.
14. Connect all injector harness connectors.
15. Connect the fuel hoses and the regulator vacuum hose.
16. Install the intake manifold collector.
17. Connect the cruise control and throttle cables to the throttle body.
18. Connect the negative battery cable and check for leaks.

### Q45

1. Relieve the fuel system pressure. Disconnect the negative battery cable.
2. Drain the coolant.
3. Remove the EGR control valve.
4. Remove the intake manifold collector.
5. Disconnect the harness connector(s) from the fuel injector(s).
6. Remove the injector(s) from the injector tube assembly. Do not reuse the O-ring(s).

**To install:**

7. Using new O-ring(s), install the injector(s) to the injector tube.
8. Connect the harness connector(s).
9. Install the intake manifold collector.
10. Install the EGR control valve.
11. Fill the cooling system.
12. Connect the negative battery cable and check for leaks.

---

# DRIVE AXLE

**NOTE: Final tightening of any suspension component must be performed with the suspension unladen with the tires on the ground.**

---

nuts. Tighten to 20–27 ft. lbs. (27–37 Nm).

6. Lower the vehicle.

### Q45

1. Raise the vehicle and support safely.

2. Remove the rear wheel.

3. Remove the differential side flange bolts and nuts and separate shaft.

4. Remove the cotter pin, adjusting cap, insulator, wheel bearing locknut and washer from halfshaft.

5. Remove the halfshaft by lightly tapping it with a copper hammer.

6. Remove the halfshaft assembly from the vehicle.

**To install:**

7. Insert halfshaft into wheel hub and install washer and wheel bearing locknut. Temporarily tighten the locknut.

8. Connect the halfshaft with the differential side flange. Install the nuts and bolts and tighten to 25–33 ft. lbs. (34–44 Nm).

9. Tighten the wheel bearing locknut to 152–203 ft. lbs. (206–275 Nm). Install the insulator, adjusting cap and a new cotter pin.

10. Install the rear wheel.

11. Lower the vehicle.

## CV-Boot

### REMOVAL & INSTALLATION

#### G20

1. Raise and support the vehicle safely.

2. Remove halfshaft assembly from vehicle and place in a suitable working fixture.

3. Remove the boot bands. Matchmark the transaxle side slide joint housing and the inner race before separating the joint assembly.

4. Remove the snapring and disassemble the slide joint housing.

5. Matchmark the inner race and halfshaft. Remove the snapring, then remove the ball cage, inner race and balls as a unit.

6. Cover the axle serrations with tape so as not to damage the boot. Remove the snapring and slide the boot off the shaft.

7. Install the wheel bearing locknut on the wheel side joint assembly. Matchmark the halfshaft and joint assembly. Using a suitable puller, separate the joint assembly.

**NOTE: The wheel side joint assembly cannot be disassembled.**

8. Cover the axle serrations with tape so as not to damage the boot. Remove the snapring and slide the boot off the shaft.

**To install:**

9. Install the transaxle side boot and joint assembly. Ensure that all snaprings are secure. If a snapring is loose or damaged, replace it. Ensure that the matchmarks made during assembly are mated.

10. Install the wheel side boot and joint by setting the joint assembly on the halfshaft. Lightly tap the joint to seat it on the shaft. Ensure that the matchmarks made during disassembly are mated.

11. Pack the joint assemblies with 3.6–4.2 Oz (105–125 ml) of grease. Install the boots so that the length is 3.86 in. (98.5mm) for the wheel side and 3.96 in. (100.5mm) for the transaxle side. Lock the boot bands securely in place.

12. Install the halfshaft assembly and lower the vehicle.

#### M30

1. Raise the vehicle and support safely.

2. Remove the halfshaft from the vehicle and place in a vise.

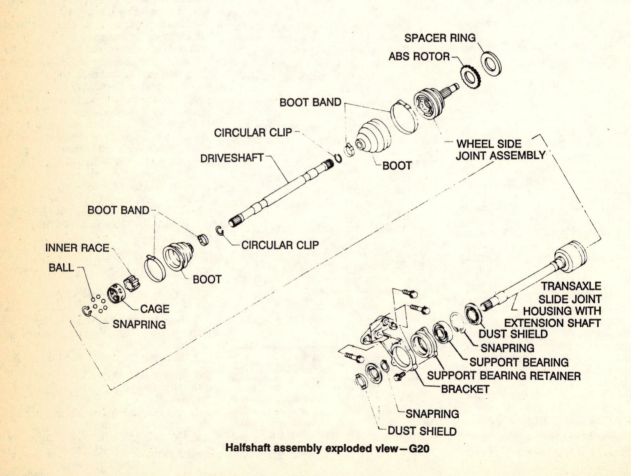

**Halfshaft assembly exploded view—G20**

3. Remove the plug seal from the slide joint housing by lightly tapping around the slide joint housing.

4. Remove the boot bands.

5. Put matchmarks on the slide joint housing, halfshaft and spider assembly before separating the joint assembly.

6. Remove the snapring on the halfshaft and remove spider assembly.

7. Remove the CV-joint housing.

8. Remove the boot from the shaft.

**NOTE: Cover the shaft splines with tape to protect the boot.**

**To install:**

9. Install boot onto shaft.

10. Install CV-joint housing onto shaft.

11. Install spider assembly onto shaft observing matchmarks made on disassembly. Ensure that the spider assembly chamfer faces the shaft.

12. Install snapring onto shaft.

13. With the CV-joint housing held vertically in the vise, install the coil spring, spring cap and new plug seal.

**NOTE: The CV-joint housing is held vertically to prevent the coil spring from tilting or falling over.**

14. Pack the halfshaft with the 6.52–6.88 oz. (185–195 g) of grease.

15. Set the boot so it does not swell or deform when installed.

16. Install a new large boot band and lock in place.

17. Install a new small boot band and lock in place.

18. Install halfshaft assembly in vehicle.

19. Lower vehicle.

### Q45

1. Raise the vehicle and support safely.

2. Remove the halfshaft assembly from the vehicle and place in a vise.

3. Remove the boot bands on both inner and outer joints.

4. Put matchmarks on the slide joint housing and inner race before separating the joint assembly.

5. Remove large snapring retaining slide joint and remove slide joint from halfshaft.

6. Put matchmarks on the inner race and the halfshaft.

7. Remove small snapring and remove the ball cage, inner race and balls as a unit.

8. Remove the boot.

9. Before separating the joint assembly on the wheel side, put matchmarks on the halfshaft and joint assembly.

**NOTE: The joint on the wheel side cannot be disassembled.**

10. Separate the joint assembly from the halfshaft using a slide hammer or equivalent.

11. Remove the boot.

**To install:**

12. Apply tape to the halfshaft splines to prevent damage to the boots.

13. Install a new small boot band and a new boot on the wheel side of the halfshaft.

14. Set the joint assembly onto the halfshaft and seat the joint by lightly tapping it. Ensure that the matchmarks are aligned when assembling.

15. Pack the halfshaft with 6.00–6.70 oz. (170–190 g).

16. Set boot so it does not swell or deform when installed in the vehicle.

17. Lock new larger and smaller boot band securely with a suitable tool.

18. Install a new small boot band and a new boot on the differential side of the halfshaft.

19. Install the ball cage, inner race and balls as a unit. Ensure that the matchmarks are aligned when assembling.

20. Install a new large snapring.

21. Pack the halfshaft with 6.35–7.05 oz. (180–200 g) of grease.

22. Install slide joint housing and install a new small snapring.

23. Set the boot so it does not swell or deform when installed in the vehicle.

24. Lock the new larger and smaller boot bands securely with a suitable tool.

25. Install the halfshaft assembly in the vehicle.

26. Install the rear wheel.

27. Lower the vehicle.

## Driveshaft and U-Joints

### REMOVAL & INSTALLATION

#### M30 and Q45

1. Raise the vehicle and support safely.

2. Put matchmarks on the flanges and separate driveshaft from the differential carrier.

3. Remove driveshaft from the transmission and plug the rear opening of the extension housing.

4. Remove the bolts attaching the center bearing bracket.

5. Remove driveshafts from vehicle.

6. Inspect driveshaft runout. Runout should not exceed 0.024 in. (0.6mm).

**To install:**

7. Temporarily install the differential companion flange to the flange yoke. Observe the alignment marks made during removal.

8. Turn the driveshaft until alignment marks face straight upward. Securely fasten the driveshaft so the lower side wall of the concave flange yoke touches the lower side wall of the convex companion flange.

9. Remove the plug in the rear extension housing and install the driveshaft into the transmission.

10. Install the bolts attaching the center bearing bracket.

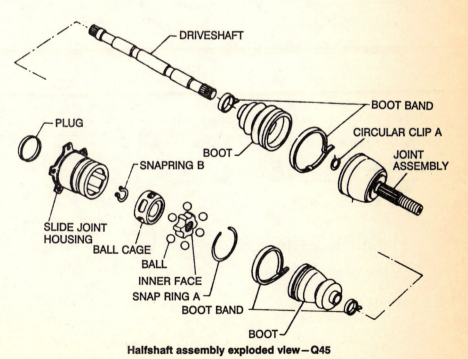

**Halfshaft assembly exploded view—Q45**

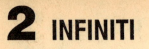
## Front Wheel Hub and Knuckle

### REMOVAL & INSTALLATION

#### G20

1. Raise and support the vehicle safely. Remove the wheel bearing lock nut.
2. Remove the brake caliper assembly and rotor. Using a piece of wire, position the caliper so that it is not supported by the brake line.
3. Separate the tie-rod from the ball joint.
4. Separate the kingpin from the knuckle.
5. Remove the halfshaft from the wheel hub/knuckle.
6. Remove lower ball joint nut and using tool HT2520000, or equivalent. Separate the knuckle from the transverse link and remove the wheel hub/knuckle from the vehicle.

**To install:**

7. Install the wheel hub/knuckle on the vehicle and tighten the lower ball joint nut to 52–64 ft. lbs. (71–86 Nm).
8. Install the halfshaft into the wheel hub/knuckle and tighten the kingpin nut to 72–87 ft. lbs. (98–118 Nm).
9. Install the tie-rod, wheel bearing lock nut and brake assembly.

## Pinion Seal

### REMOVAL & INSTALLATION

#### M30 and Q45

1. Raise the vehicle and support safely.
2. Remove the driveshaft.
3. Loosen the drive pinion nut.
4. Remove the companion flange using a suitable puller.
5. Remove the pinion seal using a suitable seal puller.

**To install:**

6. Apply a multi-purpose grease to the sealing lips of the new pinion seal. Install the new seal into the carrier using a suitable seal installer.
7. Install the companion flange and drive pinion nut. Tighten to 137–217 ft. lbs. (186–294 Nm).
8. Install the driveshaft.
9. Lower the vehicle.

## Differential Carrier

### REMOVAL & INSTALLATION

#### M30

1. Raise the vehicle and support safely.
2. Remove the driveshaft.

**NOTE: Plug rear opening in transmission extension housing.**

3. Remove the halfshafts.
4. Support the weight of the differential carrier.
5. Remove the nuts and bolts securing the differential carrier to the suspension member.
6. Remove the bolts and nuts securing the differential mounting insulator to the body.
7. Move the differential carrier toward the rear of the vehicle with the jack.
8. Lower the differential carrier using the jack.

**To install:**

9. Position the differential carrier in the vehicle.
10. Install bolts and nuts securing the differential mounting insulator to the body. Tighten bolts to 22–29 ft. lbs. (29–39 Nm). Tighten the nuts to 43–58 ft. lbs. (59–78 Nm).
11. Install the differential carrier to the suspension member. Tighten the nuts to 43–65 ft. lbs. (59–88 Nm).
12. Remove the jack.
13. Install the halfshafts.
14. Install the driveshaft.
15. Install the exhaust tube.
16. Lower the vehicle.

#### Q45

1. Raise the vehicle and support safely.
2. Remove the exhaust tube.
3. Remove the driveshaft.

**NOTE: Plug rear opening in transmission extension housing.**

4. Remove the halfshafts.
5. Remove the nuts securing the differential carrier rear cover to suspension member.
6. Support the weight of the differential carrier.
7. Remove the differential carrier mounting member from the front of the differential carrier.
8. Move the differential carrier forward together with the jack. Remove the rear cover stud bolts from the suspension member.
9. Lower the differential carrier using the jack.

**To install:**

10. Position the differential carrier in the vehicle.
11. Install the nuts securing the differential carrier rear cover to the suspension member. Tighten to 72–87 ft. lbs. (98–118 Nm).
12. Install the differential carrier mounting member to the front of the differential carrier. Tighten to 72–87 ft. lbs. (98–118 Nm).
13. Remove the jack.
14. Install the halfshafts.
15. Install the driveshaft.
16. Install the exhaust tube.
17. Lower the vehicle.

# MANUAL TRANSAXLE

## Transaxle Assembly

### REMOVAL & INSTALLATION

#### G20

1. Disconnect the negative battery cable and disconnect the air duct.
2. Disconnect the clutch control cable and speedometer cable from the transaxle.
3. Disconnect the back-up light switch, neutral switch and ground harness connectors.
4. Remove the starter, shift control rod and support rod from the transaxle.
5. Drain the gear oil from the transaxle and remove the exhaust front tube.
6. Remove the halfshafts.
7. Support the engine with a suitable jack under the oil pan.
8. Remove the rear and left engine mounts
9. Raise the jack and remove the lower transaxle housing bolts. Lower the jack and remove the upper housing bolts. Keep the bolts in order as they are different lengths and must be returned to the same position.
10. Lower the transaxle.

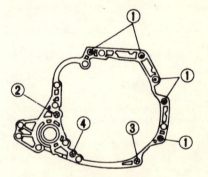

1. 51–59 ft. lbs. (70–79 Nm) – 2.17 in. (55mm) length
2. 51–59 ft. lbs. (70–79 Nm) – 2.56 in. (65mm) length
3. 22–30 ft. lbs. (30–40 Nm) – 1.38 in. (35mm) length
4. 22–30 ft. lbs. (30–40 Nm) – 1.77 in. (45mm) length

**Transaxle mounting bolt torque specifications**

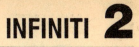

**To install:**

11. Raise the transaxle into place and install the attaching bolts. Tighten bolts to the torque specified.

12. Install the rear and left engine mounts.

13. Install the driveshafts.

14. Install the shift control rods, support rod and starter on the transaxle.

15. Connect the back-up light switch, neutral switch and ground harness connectors.

16. Connect the clutch control cable and speedometer cable from the transaxle.

17. Connect the air duct and install the negative battery cable. Road test the vehicle.

## CLUTCH

## Clutch Assembly

### REMOVAL & INSTALLATION

1. Disconnect the negative battery cable.

2. Raise and support the vehicle safely.

3. Remove the transaxle.

4. Insert tool KV30101000, or equivalent, into the clutch disc hub and loosen pressure plate bolts in 2–3 steps in sequence.

5. Remove the pressure plate and clutch disc as an assembly.

6. Remove the release bearing by pulling the bearing retainers outward from the transaxle case.

7. Inspect the clutch disc for surface wear. Measure from the friction surface to the top of the rivets. Wear limit is 0.012 in. (0.3mm). Replace clutch disc as necessary.

8. Inspect the contact surface of the flywheel for burns or discoloration. Check flywheel runout. Maximum runout is 0.0059 in. (0.15mm)

9. Using tools ST20050100 and ST20050010, or equivalent, check pressure plate diaphragm springs. Measure from the pressure plate/flywheel mating surface to the top of the diaphragm spring. Height should be 1.201–1.280 in. (30.5–32.5mm). Replace pressure plate as necessary.

10. Inspect the release bearing for damage. Spin the bearing to see that it rolls freely.

**To install:**

11. Lightly lubricate the transaxle input shaft, input shaft collar, clutch lever assembly and the clutch release bearing with a lithium based grease.

NOTE: Keep clutch disc and all clutch components clean during installation. Do not allow grease to contact the clutch disc.

12. Insert tool KV30101000, or equivalent, into the clutch disc hub. Install the clutch disc and pressure plate on the tool and tighten the pressure plate bolts to 16–22 ft. lbs. (22–29 Nm) in 2–3 steps using the sequence provided. Remove the tool.

13. Install release bearing in the transaxle. Ensure that the bearing retainer clips are fully engaged.

14. Install the transaxle.

15. Adjust clutch pedal height and free-play.

16. Lower vehicle, connect negative battery cable and road test vehicle.

### PEDAL HEIGHT/FREE-PLAY ADJUSTMENT

1. Adjust pedal height with pedal stopper or automatic speed control device (ASCD) cancel switch. Pedal height specification is 6.28–6.67 in. (159.5–169.5mm) from the top of the pedal to the floot well (when measured at a 90 degree angle to the top of the pedal).

2. Adjust the withdrawl lever play on the top of the transaxle, by pushing the withdrawl lever until resistance is felt and then adjusting the nut. Turn the adjusting nut 2.5–3.5 turns back and then tighten the lock nut. Withdrawl lever play should be 0.0098–0.138 in. (2.5–3.5mm). Tighten the locknut to 2–3 ft. lbs. (3–4 Nm).

3. As a final check, measure pedal free travel at the center of the pedal pad. Pedal free travel should be 0.425–0.594 in. (10.8–15.1mm).

4. On U.S. models only, adjust the clearance between the stopper rubber and the threaded end of the clutch interlock switch while depressing the clutch pedal fully. Adjust the clearance to 0.039–0.004 in. (0.1–1.0mm).

## Clutch Cable

### REMOVAL & INSTALLATION

1. Raise and support the vehicle safely.

2. Loosen the lock nut and adjusting nut on the clutch cable at the withdrawl lever and disconnect the cable.

3. Disconnect the cable from the clutch pedal under the dash.

4. Remove any clips or ties holding the cable to the chassis and remove the cable.

**To install:**

5. Install the cable using the original routing.

6. Connect the cable at the clutch pedal and withdrawl lever.

7. Adjust the pedal height and free-play.

8. Lower the vehicle and road test.

## AUTOMATIC TRANSMISSION

For further information on transmissions/transaxles, please refer to "Chilton's Guide to Transmission Repair".

## Transmission Assembly

### REMOVAL & INSTALLATION

#### M30 and Q45

1. Disconnect the negative battery cable.

2. Raise the vehicle and support safely.

3. Remove the exhaust tube.

4. Remove the fluid charging line.

5. Remove the oil cooler line.

6. Plug fluid charging and oil cooler fittings after removing lines.

7. Remove the control linkage from the selector lever.

8. Disconnect the neutral safety switch and solenoid harness connectors.

9. Disconnect the speedometer cable.

10. Remove the driveshaft. Insert plug into rear seal opening to prevent loss of fluid.

11. Remove the starter motor.

12. Support the transmission safely.

13. Remove the gusset securing the transmission to the engine. Remove the bolts attaching the transmission to the engine.

NOTE: The bolts securing the transmission to the engine are of differing lengths. Note the length of the bolts as they are removed.

14. Remove the bolts securing the torque converter to the flexplate.

15. Support the engine safely. Avoid jacking directly under the oil pan drain plug.

16. Remove the transmission from the vehicle.

**To install:**

17. Position the transmission in the vehicle and install the torque converter-to-flexplate bolts. Tighten to 33–43 ft. lbs. (44–59 Nm).

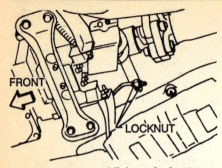

**Manual control linkage locknut**

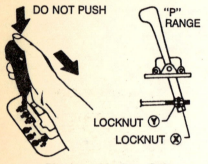

**Piston positioning—Q45**

18. Secure the transmission to the engine. Torque the:
  60mm bolts to 29–36 ft. lbs. (39–49 Nm)
  50mm bolts to 29–36 ft. lbs. (39–49 Nm)
  45mm bolts to 29–36 ft. lbs. (39–49 Nm)
  25mm bolts to 22–29 ft. lbs. (29–39 Nm)
  20mm gusset bolts to 22–29 ft. lbs. (29–39 Nm)
19. Install the starter motor.
20. Install the driveshaft.
21. Connect the speedometer cable.
22. Connect the neutral safety switch and solenoid harness connectors.
23. Install the control linkage to the selector lever.
24. Install the fluid charging and oil cooler lines.
25. Connect the exhaust tube.
26. Lower the vehicle.
27. Connect negative battery cable.

## SHIFT LINKAGE ADJUSTMENT

1. Place the selector lever in **P** range.
2. Loosen the locknuts.
3. Without pushing the button, pull selector lever toward **R** and tighten locknut X until it touches trunnion.
4. Back off locknut X one turn and tighten locknut Y to 8–11 ft. lbs. (11–15 Nm).

## THROTTLE LINKAGE ADJUSTMENT

Adjust throttle wire endplay to 0.04–0.12 in. (1–3mm). Tighten locknut to 6–7 ft. lbs. (8–10 Nm).

# AUTOMATIC TRANSAXLE

For further information on transmissions/transaxles, please refer to "Chilton's Guide to Transmission Repair".

## Transaxle Assembly

### REMOVAL & INSTALLATION

#### G20

1. Disconnect the negative battery cable and the air duct.
2. Raise and support the vehicle safely. Disconnect the transaxle solenoid harness and inhibitor switch harness connector. Disconnect the throttle wire at the engine side.
3. Drain the transaxle fluid.
4. Disconnect the control cable and transaxle coolant lines.
5. Remove the halfshafts, exhaust front tube and starter.
6. Remove the rear plate cover and the bolts securing the torque converter to the drive plate. Rotate the crankshaft to gain access to the bolts.
7. Support the engine with a suitable stand and use a suitable jack to support the transaxle.
8. Remove the transaxle mounting bolts and the transaxle-to-engine bolts. Lower the transaxle.
**To install:**
9. Place a straightedge across the bellhousing of the transaxle and measure the distance to the mounting bosses on the torque converter. The distance should be 0.626 in. (15.9mm). If not, the torque converter is not installed correctly.
10. Check the drive plate runout with a dial indicator. Maximum allowable runout is 0.008 in. (0.2mm).
11. Raise the transaxle into position and install the torque converter bolts. Tighten bolts to 33–43 ft. lbs. (44–59 Nm). Rotate the crankshaft to gain access to the bolts.
12. Install the halfshafts, exhaust front tube and starter.
13. Connect the control cable and transaxle coolant lines.
14. Connect the transaxle solenoid

harness and inhibitor switch harness connector. Disconnect the throttle wire at the engine side.
15. Fill the transaxle with lubricant, install the negative battery cable and road test the vehicle.

## CONTROL CABLE ADJUSTMENT

The control cable is adjusted by loosening the locknut on the manual shaft (located at the top of the transaxle) and sliding the cable. After adjustment, move the selector lever from Park to Low range and make sure that the selector lever moves smoothly without making a sliding noise.

## THROTTLE WIRE ADJUSTMENT

1. Turn ignition switch **OFF**.
2. Move adjusting tube toward the transaxle side while pressing the lock plate. Then return the lock plate to lock the adjusting tube.
3. Put a mark on the throttle wire to use as a reference while measuring.
4. Move the throttle drum from the idling position to the full throttle position quickly. The adjusting tube should move tn the direction of the engine side depressing the lock plate.
5. Ensure that the throttle wire stroke is 1.54–1.69 in. (39–43mm). If the throttle drum is too far toward the transaxle, kickdown range will greatly increase. If the throttle drum is too far toward the engine, kickdown will not occur.

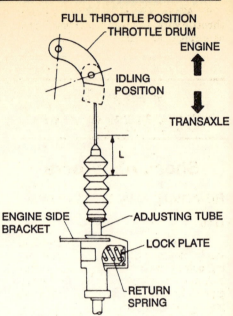

**Throttle wire adjustment—G20**

6. After properly adjusting the throttle wire, ensure the parting line is as straight as possible.

# FRONT SUSPENSION

## Shock Absorbers

### REMOVAL & INSTALLATION

#### G20

1. Raise and support the vehicle safely. Remove the shock absorber fixing bolt at the lower suspension member, and the three nuts inside the engine compartment. Do not remove the piston rod lock nut.

2. Remove the shock absorber assembly and place in a suitable holding device.

3. Using a prybar to hold the spring, loosen the piston rod lock nut.

4. Compress the spring with a spring compressor so that the shock mounting insulator can be turned by hand.

5. Remove the piston rod lock nut. Remove the shock absorber.

**To install:**

6. Inspect all components carefully for damage or wear. Replace as necessary.

7. Install shock absorber and tighten rod lock nut to 13–17 ft. lbs. (18–24 Nm).

8. Install the shock absorber assembly in the vehicle. Ensure the bend in the lower shock bracket faces rearward on the left side and forward on the right side of the vehicle.

9. Install the upper spring seat with the cutout facing the inside of the vehicle.

10. Tighten the upper shock mounting bolts to 31–40 ft. lbs. (42–54 Nm) and the lower through-bolt to 82–93 ft. lbs. (112–126 Nm). Final tightening must take place with the suspension loaded (vehicle at normal ride height).

#### Q45

1. Remove the upper shock absorber mounting insulator bolts.

2. Raise and safely support the vehicle.

3. Remove the lower shock mounting bolt and lift out the shock assembly.

4. Lower the vehicle.

5. The installation is the reverse of the removal procedure. Keep the following torques in mind:

a. Tighten the upper mounting bolts to 30–35 ft. lbs.

b. Tighten the piston rod locknut to 13–17 ft. lbs.

c. Tighten the lower mounting bolt to 80–94 ft. lbs.

## MacPherson Strut

### REMOVAL & INSTALLATION

#### M30

1. Disconnect the negative battery cable.

1. GASKET
2. UPPER MOUNTING
3. UPPER RUBBER SEAT
4. BOUND BUMPER RUBBER
5. DUST COVER
6. BOUND BUMPER RUBBER
7. COIL SPRING
8. SHOCK ABSORBER
9. THIRD LINK
10. CAP
11. WHEEL HUB AND STEERING KNUCKLE ASSEMBLY
12. ADJUSTING CAP
11. WHEEL HUB AND STEERING KNUCKLE ASSEMBLY

12. INSULATOR
13. ADJUSTING CAP
14. COTTER PIN
15. TRANSVERSE LIK
16. CONNECTING ROD
17. STABILIZER
18. GUSSET PIN
19. COTTER PIN
20. DRIVE SHAFT
21. UPPER LINK BRACKET
22. UPPER LINK
23. BUSHING
24. WASHER

2. Disconnect the sub-harness connector strut actuator mounting bolt.

3. Remove the strut assembly mounting nut. Do not remove the piston rod locknut on the vehicle.

4. Raise and safely support the vehicle. Remove the tension rod nuts and the strut-to-steering knuckle mounting bolts. Make sure the brake hose is not twisted.

5. Remove the strut assembly.

6. The installation is the reverse of the removal procedure. Keep the following torques in mind:

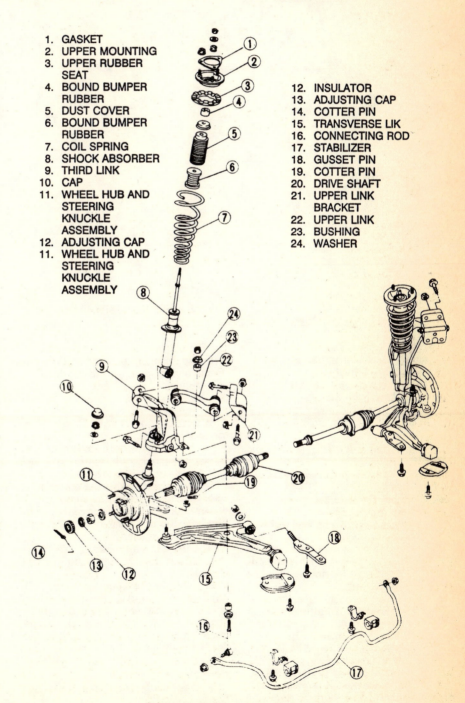

Front suspension components – G20

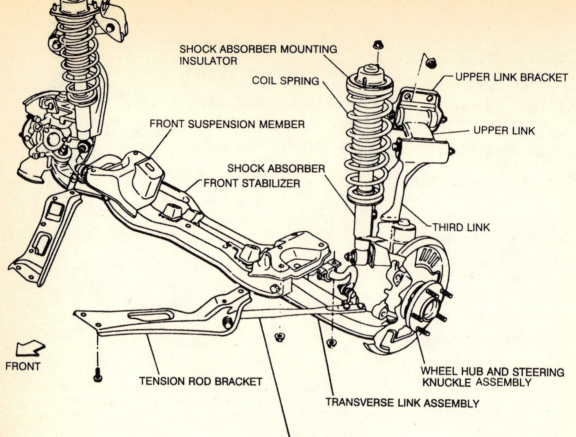

**Front suspension components—Q45**

a. Tighten the upper mounting bolts to 30–35 ft. lbs.

b. Tighten the piston rod locknut to 13–17 ft. lbs.

c. Tighten the lower mounting bolt to 80–94 ft. lbs.

## Coil Springs

### REMOVAL & INSTALLATION

#### G20

1. Raise and support the vehicle safely. Remove the shock absorber fixing bolt at the lower suspension member, and the three nuts inside the engine compartment. Do not remove the piston rod lock nut.

2. Remove the shock absorber assembly and place in a suitable holding device.

3. Using a pry bar to hold the spring, loosen the piston rod lock nut.

4. Compress the spring with a spring compressor so that the shock mounting insulator can be turned by hand.

5. Remove the piston rod lock nut. Remove the coil spring from shock absorber.

**To install:**

6. Inspect all components carefully for damage or wear. Replace as necessary.

7. Install the coil spring on the shock absorber and tighten rod lock nut to 13–17 ft. lbs. (18–24 Nm).

8. Install the coil spring assembly in the vehicle. Ensure the bend in the lower shock bracket faces rearward on the left side and forward on the right side of the vehicle.

9. Install the upper spring seat with the cutout facing the inside of the vehicle.

10. Tighten the upper shock mounting bolts to 31–40 ft. lbs. (42–54 Nm) and the lower through-bolt to 82–93 ft. lbs. (112–126 Nm). Final tightening must take place with the suspension loaded (vehicle at normal ride height).

#### M30

1. Disconnect the negative battery cable.

2. Disconnect the sub-harness connector strut actuator mounting bolt.

3. Remove the strut assembly mounting nut. Do not remove the piston rod locknut on the vehicle.

4. Raise and safely support the vehicle. Remove the tension rod nuts and the steering knuckle mounting bolts. Make sure the brake hose is not twisted.

5. Secure the strut assembly in suitable holding fixture and loosen the piston rod locknut. Do not remove it.

6. Compress the spring with the proper tool so the shock absorber mounting insulator can be turned by hand.

7. Remove the piston rod locknut and the coil spring assembly.

8. Remove the gland packing with the proper tool. Retract the piston, by pushing it down until it bottoms.

9. Slowly, remove the piston rod from the cylinder together with the piston guide.

**To install:**

10. Inspect the rubber parts for deterioration.

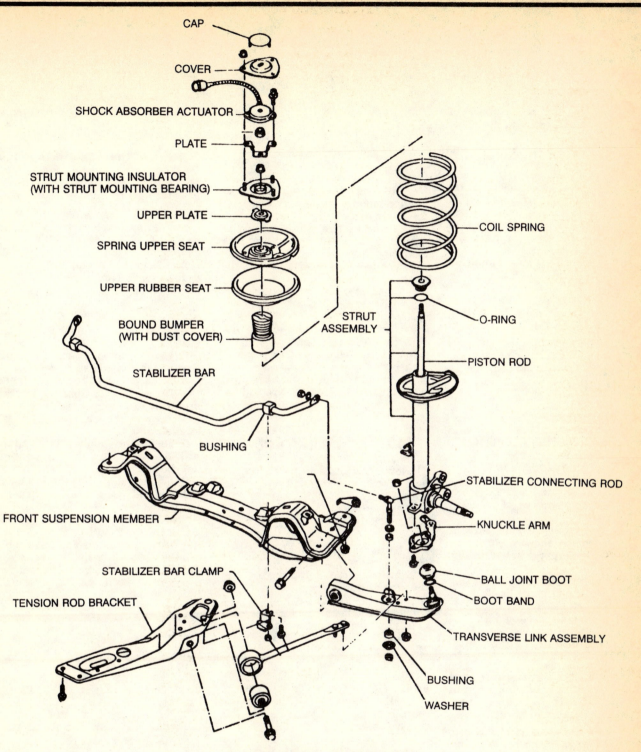

CAP

COVER

SHOCK ABSORBER ACTUATOR

PLATE

STRUT MOUNTING INSULATOR
(WITH STRUT MOUNTING BEARING)

UPPER PLATE

SPRING UPPER SEAT

UPPER RUBBER SEAT

BOUND BUMPER
(WITH DUST COVER)

STABILIZER BAR

BUSHING

FRONT SUSPENSION MEMBER

STABILIZER BAR CLAMP

TENSION ROD BRACKET

STRUT
ASSEMBLY

COIL SPRING

O-RING

PISTON ROD

STABILIZER CONNECTING ROD

KNUCKLE ARM

BALL JOINT BOOT

BOOT BAND

TRANSVERSE LINK ASSEMBLY

BUSHING

WASHER

**Front suspension components—M30**

11. Lubricate the sealing lip of the gland packing.

12. Install the gland packing while covering the piston rod with tape so not to damage the oil sealing lip.

13. Tighten the gland packing to 51–94 ft. lbs. without the special tool.

14. The installation is the reverse of the removal procedure. The flat por-tion of the spring goes in the top position.

15. Install the spring seat with it's cutout facing the outer side of the ve-hicle. Tighten the following:

   a. The upper cover mounting bolts to 22–29 ft. lbs.

   b. The upper piston rod locknut to 43–58 ft. lbs.

   c. The lower strut-to-knuckle arm mounting bolts to 53–72 ft. lbs.

**Q45**

1. Remove the upper shock absorb-er mounting insulator bolts.

2. Raise and safely support the vehicle.

3. Remove the lower shock mount-

ing bolt and lift out the shock assembly.

4. Secure the shock absorber in a suitable holding fixture.

5. Loosen the piston rod locknut. Do not remove the locknut.

6. Compress the spring with the proper tool so the shock absorber mounting insulator can be turned by hand.

7. Remove the piston rod locknut. Remove the spring assembly, dust cover and rubber seat.

8. Remove the shock absorber. Inspect the rubber parts for deterioration.

9. The installation is the reverse of the removal procedure. Keep the following torques in mind:

a. Tighten the upper mounting bolts to 30–35 ft. lbs.

b. Tighten the piston rod locknut to 13–17 ft. lbs.

c. Tighten the lower mounting bolt to 80–94 ft. lbs.

**NOTE: When installing the coil spring, be careful not to reverse the top and bottom direction. The top end is flat.**

## Kingpins

### REMOVAL & INSTALLATION

#### Third Link and Upper Link
##### G20

1. Raise and support the vehicle safely.

2. Remove the cap and kingpin nut.

3. Remove the shock absorber attaching nuts and upper link attaching bolts.

4. Remove the stabilizer connecting rod, third link and upper link.

**To install:**

5. Pack kingpin housing with 0.14 oz (4 g) of multi-purpose grease. Pack the cap with 0.35 oz (10 g) of multi-purpose grease.

**NOTE: Final tightening must be done with vehicle at normal ride height with tires on ground and suspension loaded.**

6. Install the third link and cap. Tighten kingpin bolt to 72–87 ft. lbs. (98–118 Nm) and stabilizer connecting rod bolt to 12–16 ft. lbs. (16–22 Nm).

7. Install the upper link. Tighten upper link-to-third link through bolt to 82–93 ft. lbs. (112–126 Nm) and upper link-to-bracket bolt to 65–90 ft. lbs. (88–123 Nm).

##### Q45

1. Raise and safely support the vehicle. Support the wheel assembly with a suitable jacking device.

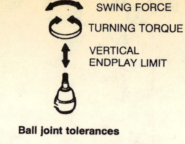

SWING FORCE

TURNING TORQUE

VERTICAL ENDPLAY LIMIT

**Ball joint tolerances**

2. Remove the cap and the upper kingpin mounting nut. Do not remove the lower nut.

3. Remove the shock absorber mounting nut and the upper link mounting bolts.

4. Remove the third link and the upper link.

5. Installation is the reverse of removal. Upper link bushings cannot be disassembled.

6. Always install the upper link with the 'A' facing the axle and the side without a character facing the vehicle body.

7. Tighten the upper kingpin mounting nut to 72–87 ft. lbs. and the lower kingpin mounting nut to 65–80 ft. lbs.

## Lower Ball Joints

The lower ball joints are part of the the lower transverse arm and replaced as an assembly.

### INSPECTION

1. Turn the ball joint at least 10 revolutions before checking.

2. Measure the swing force using the proper tool. The G20 and Q45 should be 1.8–11.9 ft. lbs. and the M30 should read 5.5–18.1 ft. lbs.

3. The turning torque should read 4.3–30.4 inch lbs. on the G20 and Q45; 13–43 inch lbs. on the M30.

4. The vertical endplay should be 0 in. (0mm) on the G20 and Q45; 0.004–0.051 in. (0.1–1.3mm) on the M30.

5. After inspecting, if the play exceeds these specifications replace the transverse arm.

## Lower Control Arm

### REMOVAL & INSTALLATION

#### G20

1. Raise and support the vehicle safely.

2. Remove the stabilizer.

3. Support the steering knuckle with a suitable jack and remove the lower ball joint nut.

4. Remove the bolts attaching the

lower control arm to the chassis. Remove the lower control arm.

**To install:**

5. Check the lower ball joint for damage or wear. If present, replace the lower control arm assembly. The ball joint is not servicable seprately.

6. Installation is the reverse of removal.

**NOTE: Final tightening must be done with the vehicle at normal ride height, tires on the ground and the chassis loaded.**

7. Tighten lower control arm bolts to 87–108 ft. lbs. (118–147 Nm) and gusset nut to 69–87 ft. lbs. (93–118 Nm). Tighten ball joint nut to 52–64 ft. lbs. (71–86 Nm).

#### M30

1. Raise and safely support the vehicle.

2. Remove the bolts and disconnect the the tension and stabilizer bar.

3. Remove the bolt and disconnect the transverse arm from the knuckle arm, using the proper tool.

4. Remove the transverse arm and joint assembly.

5. Install the stabilizer bar with the ball joint socket in a straight position, not cocked.

6. The installation is the reverse of the removal procedure. Tighten the following to:

a. The stabilizer bar mounting bolt to 14–22 ft. lbs.

b. The tension rod mounting bolts to 35–43 ft. lbs.

c. The steering knuckle mounting bolt to 71–88 ft. lbs.

#### Q45

1. Raise and safely support the vehicle. Support the wheel assembly with a suitable jacking device.

2. Remove the mounting bolts and disconnect the tension rod and stabilizer bar.

3. Remove the bolt and disconnect the transverse arm from the knuckle arm, using the proper tool.

4. Remove the transverse arm and joint assembly.

5. The installation is the reverse of the removal procedure. The final tightening must be at curb weight with the tires on the ground.

6. Tighten the following to:

a. The stabilizer bar mounting bolt to 14–22 ft. lbs.

b. The tension rod mounting bolts to 72–87 ft. lbs.

c. The steering knuckle mounting bolt to 65–80 ft. lbs.

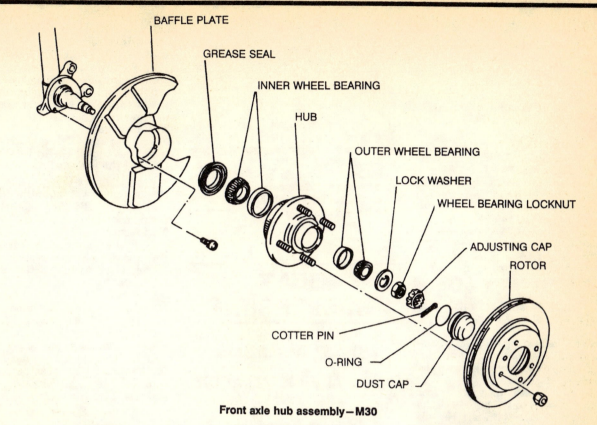

BAFFLE PLATE
GREASE SEAL
INNER WHEEL BEARING
HUB
OUTER WHEEL BEARING
LOCK WASHER
WHEEL BEARING LOCKNUT
ADJUSTING CAP
ROTOR
COTTER PIN
O-RING
DUST CAP

**Front axle hub assembly—M30**

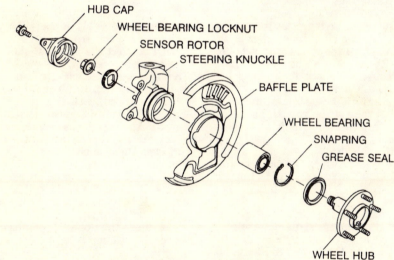

HUB CAP
WHEEL BEARING LOCKNUT
SENSOR ROTOR
STEERING KNUCKLE
BAFFLE PLATE
WHEEL BEARING
SNAPRING
GREASE SEAL
WHEEL HUB

**Front axle hub assembly—Q45**

# Stabilizer Bar

## REMOVAL & INSTALLATION

1. Raise and support the vehicle safely.

2. Using a backup wrench to support the connecting rod, remove the stabilizer to connecting rod bolt.

3. Remove the stabilizer bracket bolts. Remove the stabilizer.

**To install:**

4. Install the stabilizer with the paint mark to the right of the bracket when viewed from the front of the vehcile. Install the bracket with the elongated hole toward the rear of the vehicle. Tighten the bracket bolts to 29–36 ft. lbs. (39–49 Nm). On the M30 tighten bolts to 40–47 ft. lbs. (54–64 Nm).

**NOTE: Final tightening must be done with the vehicle at normal ride height, tires on the ground and the chassis loaded.**

5. Ensure that the ball socket on the connecting rod is straight, then attach the connecting rod and tighten the bolt to 30–38 ft. lbs. (41–51 Nm). Use a backup wrench to keep the connecting rod straight.

# Front Wheel Bearings

## PRELOAD ADJUSTMENT

### M30

1. Thoroughly clean all parts to prevent dirt entry.

2. Apply the recommended multi-purpose grease to the following components:

a. The rubbing surface of the spindle.

b. The contact surface between the lock washer and the outer wheel bearing.

c. The inside of the dust cap.

d. The grease seal lip.

3. Tighten the wheel bearing lock to 25–29 ft. lbs. Turn the wheel hub several times in both directions to seat the wheel bearing correctly.

4. Again, tighten the wheel bearing to the specified torque. Turn back the wheel bearing locknut 90 degrees.

5. Install the adjusting cap and the locknut. Do not turn the nut back for cotter pin insertion. Align the cotter pin by re-tightening the nut within 15 degrees.

6. Measure the wheel bearing preload and the axle endplay limit with the proper tool. The wheel bearing

preload, measure at the wheel hub bolt should be 3.1 lbs. or less. The axle endplay limit is 0.0020 in. (0.05mm).

7. Repeat procedure until the correct bearing preload is obtained.

## REMOVAL & INSTALLATION

### M30

1. Raise and safely support the vehicle. Remove the brake caliper assembly and the brake rotor. The brake line need not be disconnected.

2. Remove the wheel hub and the wheel bearing from the spindle.

3. Secure the hub in a suitable holding fixture. Drive out the outer race with the proper tool.

4. Inspect all the components for damage or excessive wear.

**To install:**

5. Install the bearing outer race with the proper tool until it seat in the hub.

6. Coat the bearing with the recommended multi-purpose grease and install. Pack the grease seal lip with the recommended grease.

7. Install the seal with the proper tool until it seats in the hub. Pack the hub and dust cap with the recommended grease.

8. Adjust the wheel bearing preload.

9. The remainder of the installation is the reverse of the removal procedure.

### Q45

1. Raise and safely support the vehicle. Remove the brake caliper assembly and the brake rotor. The brake line need not be disconnected.

2. Disconnect the tie rod and transverse arm from the steering knuckle assembly with the proper tool.

**NOTE: The steering knuckle is made from aluminum alloy, Be careful not to hit the knuckle.**

3. Remove the kingpin lower nut and the steering knuckle assembly. Secure the steering knuckle in a suitable holding fixture.

4. Remove the dust cap and the wheel bearing locknut. Remove the wheel hub with the proper tool.

5. Remove the circular clip and press out the bearing assembly from the steering knuckle with the proper tools.

6. Drive out the wheel bearing inner race from the wheel hub and remove the grease seal with the suitable tools.

**To install:**

7. Press a new wheel bearing assembly into the steering knuckle from outside the of the steering knuckle. The maximum press load is 3.9 tons.

Do not press the inner race of the wheel bearing assembly.

8. Install the circular clip into the groove of the steering knuckle. Apply a multi-purpose grease to the sealing and install the grease seal and splash guard.

9. Press the wheel hub onto the steering knuckle with the proper tool. The maximum press load is 3.3 tons.

10. Tighten the wheel bearing locknut to 152–210 ft. lbs.

11. Stake the wheel bearing locknut and install the dust cap.

12. The remainder of the installation is the reverse of the removal procedure.

# REAR SUSPENSION

## Shock Absorbers

### REMOVAL & INSTALLATION

### G20

1. Raise and support the vehicle safely.

2. Remove the rear seat to gain access to the top shock abosorber bolts. Remove the 3 top shock mount bolts.

3. Remove the rear stabilizer conecting rod where it attaches the knuckle assembly.

4. Remove the shock absorber through bolts at the knuckle assembly and remove the shock absorber assembly.

5. Set the shock absorber assembly in a vise using attachment ST25652000,or equivalent. Loosen the piston rod lock nut but do not remove.

6. Compress the spring with a suitable tool so that the strut mounting insulator can be turned by hand.

7. Remove the piston rod lock nut and spring with compressor attached.

**To install:**

8. Replace the bound rubber bumpers. Install the coil spring on the shock absorber and tighten the piston rod locknut to 43–58 ft. lbs. (59–78 Nm). Gradually release the spring compressor. When the coil spring is located correctly, there should be 2 identification color codes on the lower side.

9. Installation is the reverse of removal.

10. Tighten the shock assembly upper attaching bolts to 31–40 ft. lbs. (42–54 Nm); lower attaching bolts to 72–87 ft. lbs. (98–118 Nm) and the stabilizer bar connecting rod bolts to 30–35 ft. lbs. (41–47 Nm)

### M30

1. Disconnect the negative battery cable.

2. Remove the rear parcel shelf. Disconnect the sub-harness connector.

3. Remove the strut mounting cap.

4. Remove the shock absorber actuator mounting bolts and the upper end mounting nuts.

5. Raise and safely support the vehicle. Disconnect the hydraulic brake line and the parking brake cable.

6. Disconnect the propeller shaft. Remove the lower mounting bolt.

7. Remove the shock absorber and spring assembly.

**To install:**

8. Place the shock absorber and spring assembly into postion. It may be necessary to install the propeller shaft first.

9. Tighten the lower mounting bolt to 43–58 ft. lbs. and the upper mounting insulator bolts to 23–31 ft. lbs.

10. Install the brake line and parking brake cable. Lower the vehicle.

11. Connect the sub-harness connector and install the rear parcel shelf. Connect the negative battery cable and test drive the vehicle.

### Q45

1. Raise and safely support the vehicle. Remove the exhaust tube.

2. Disconnect the propeller shaft at the rear of the vehicle.

3. Disconnect the parking brake cable from the front of the vehicle.

4. If equipped, with High Capacity Actively Controlled Steering (HICAS). Remove the ball joints by removing the snaping and pressing out the ball joint from the axle housing with proper tools.

5. Remove the tire and wheel assembly. Remove the brake caliper assembly. It is not neccessary to disconnect the brake line.

6. Remove the upper shock absorber end nuts. Do not remove the piston rod nut.

7. Remove the rear suspension mounting nuts. Draw out the rear axle and rear suspension assembly.

8. Remove the shock absorber upper and lower mounting nuts. Do not remove the piston rod nut.

9. Remove the shock absorber and spring assembly.

**To install:**

10. Install the shock absorber and spring assembly. It may be necessary to install the rear axle and suspension assembly prior to installing the shock assembly.

11. Tighten the lower shock mounting bolt to 57–72 ft. lbs. and the upper spring seat mounting bolts to 12–14 ft. lbs.

1. GASKET
2. STRUT MOUNTING INSULATOR
3. UPPER SPRING SEAT
4. DUST COVER
5. COIL SPRING
6. BOUND BUMPER
7. STRUT ASSEMBLY
8. CONNECTING ROD
9. KNUCKLE ASSEMBLY
10. BAFFLE PLATE
11. WHEEL HUB BEARING
12. COTTER PIN
13. CAP
14. PARALLEL LINK
15. MOUNTING BRACKET
16. BUSHING
17. CLAMP
18. STABILIZER BAR
19. RADIUS ROD

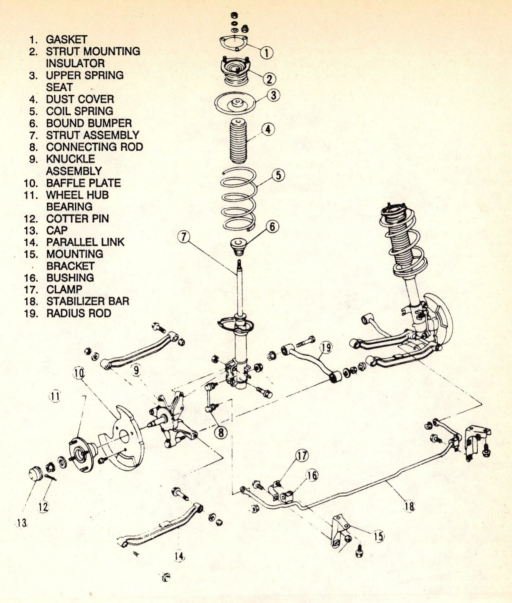

**Rear suspension assembly—G20**

Install the brake caliper, wheel and tire, parking brake cable, propeller shaft and exhaust tube.

13.
Lower the vehicle and test drive.

## Coil Springs

### REMOVAL & INSTALLATION

#### G20

1. Raise and support the vehicle safely.

2. Remove the shock absorber assembly.

3. Set the shock absorber assembly in a vise using attachment ST25652000, or equivalent. Loosen the piston rod lock nut but do not remove.

4. Compress the spring with a suitable tool so that the strut mounting insulator can be turned by hand.

5. Remove the piston rod lock nut and spring with compressor attached.
**To install:**

6. Replace the bound rubber bumpers. Install the coil spring on the shock absorber and tighten the piston rod locknut to 43–58 ft. lbs. (59–78 Nm). Gradually release the spring compressor. When the coil spring is located correctly, there should be 2 identification color codes on the lower side.

7. Install the shock absorber assembly. Lower the vehcile.

8. Final tightening of all rubber parts should take place with the tires on the ground and the chassis at normal ride height.

#### M30

1. Raise and support the vehicle safely.

2. Remove the rear parcel shelf and disconnect the shock absorber actuator wiring connector.

3. Remove the strut mounting cap, spacer and insulator bolts.

4. Remove the lower mounting bolt. Remove the shock absorber assembly.

5. Place the shock absorber assembly in an appropriate holding fixture and loosen the piston lock nut.

6. Compress the coil spring with a

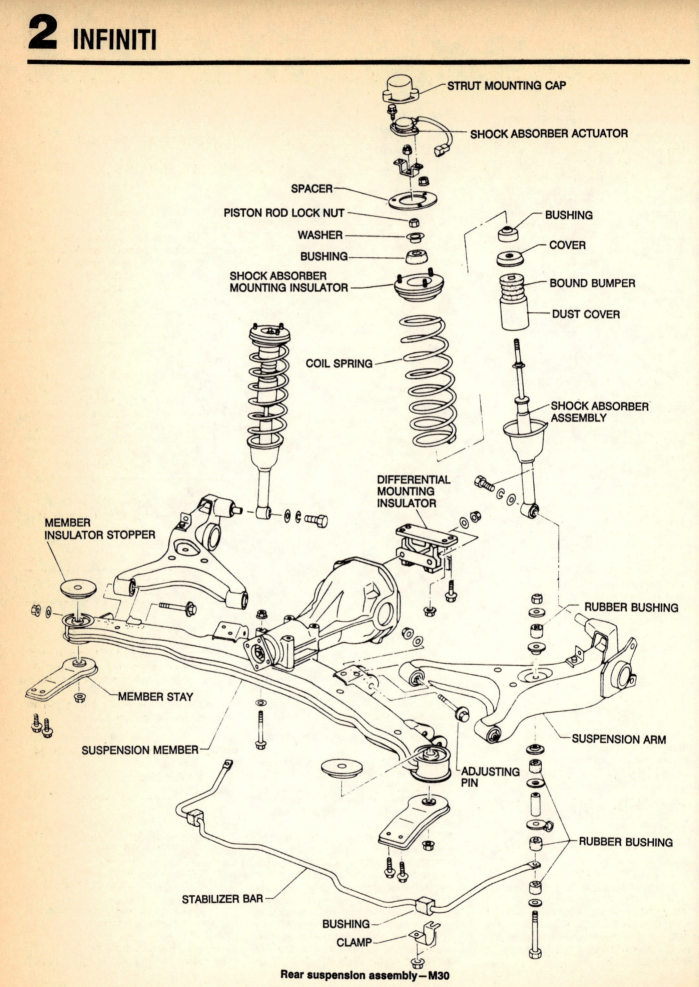

STRUT MOUNTING CAP

SHOCK ABSORBER ACTUATOR

SPACER

PISTON ROD LOCK NUT

WASHER

BUSHING

SHOCK ABSORBER
MOUNTING INSULATOR

BUSHING

COVER

BOUND BUMPER

DUST COVER

COIL SPRING

SHOCK ABSORBER
ASSEMBLY

DIFFERENTIAL
MOUNTING
INSULATOR

MEMBER
INSULATOR STOPPER

RUBBER BUSHING

MEMBER STAY

SUSPENSION ARM

SUSPENSION MEMBER

ADJUSTING
PIN

STABILIZER BAR

RUBBER BUSHING

BUSHING

CLAMP

**Rear suspension assembly — M30**

spring compressor, then remove the lock nut. Remove the coil spring with the compressor still attached.

**To install:**

7. Install the new coil spring with the spring compressor attached.

8. Assemble the shock absorber components and tighten the piston rod lock nut.

9. Installation is the reverse of removal.

10. Tighten the lower shock mount bolt to 43–58 ft. lbs. (59–78 Nm); shock insulator bolts to 23–31 ft. lbs. (31–42 Nm).

11. Final tightening of all rubber parts should take place with the tires on the ground and the chassis at normal ride height.

### Q45

1. Raise and support the vehicle safely.

2. Remove the upper shock assembly attaching nuts. It may be necessary to remove the rear parcel shelf to gain access to the nuts.

3. Remove the lower shock assembly mounting bolt at the axle assembly.

4. Place the shock absorber assembly in a suitable holding fixture and loosen the piston rod lock nut.

5. Using a spring compressor, compress the coil spring, then remove the piston rod lock nut. Remove the coil spring with the compressor attached.

**To install:**

6. Install the spring compressor, if removed, and assemble the shock absorber assembly. Remove the spring compressor.

7. Installation is the reverse of removal.

8. Tighten the piston rod lock nut to 13–17 ft. lbs. (18–24 Nm); upper shock mount nuts to 12–14 ft. lbs. (16–19 Nm); lower shock mount bolts to 57–72 ft. lbs. (77–98 Nm).

9. Final tightening of all rubber parts should take place with the tires on the ground and the chassis at normal ride height.

## Rear Control Arm

### REMOVAL & INSTALLATION

#### G20

1. Raise and support the vehicle safely.

2. Remove the brake caliper assembly and rotor.

3. Support the suspension under the knuckle assembly with a floor jack.

4. Remove the parallel link attaching bolts. Remove the parallel link.

5. Installation is the reverse of removal.

6. Tighten all parallel link bolts to 80–94 ft. lbs. (108–127 Nm).

### M30

1. Raise and support the vehicle. Remove the axle shaft assembly.

2. Remove the stabilizer bar bolt and disconnect the parking brake cable.

3. Disconnect the lower shock absorber bolt.

4. Matchmark the suspension arm to the pin and remove the pin.

5. Remove the lower suspension arm.

6. The installation is the reverse of the removal procedure. Adjust the rear alignment after installing the lower arm.

7. When installing, tighten the suspension arm pin to 72–87 ft. lbs. after installing the wheels and placing the vehicle on the ground under the unladen condition.

### Q45

1. Raise and safely support the vehicle. Remove the exhaust tube.

2. Disconnect the propeller shaft at the rear of the vehicle.

3. Disconnect the parking brake cable from the front of the vehicle.

4. If equipped, with High Capacity Actively Controlled Steering (HICAS). Remove the ball joints by removing the snapring and pressing out the ball joint from the axle housing with proper tools.

5. Remove the tire and wheel assembly. Remove the brake caliper assembly. It is not neccessary to disconnect the brake line.

6. Remove the upper shock absorber end nuts. Do not remove the piston rod nut.

7. Remove the rear suspension mounting nuts. Draw out the rear axle and rear suspension assembly.

8. The installation is the reverse of the removal procedure. Tighten the lower arm adjusting pin bolts to 57–72 ft. lbs.

## Rear Wheel Bearings

### REMOVAL & INSTALLATION

#### G20

1. Raise and support the vehicle safely.

2. Remove the rear wheel and tire assembly.

3. Remove the rear wheel hub cap, cotter pin, lock nut, washer and wheel hub bearing.

**NOTE: The wheel bearing is integral with the hub and cannot be serviced separately.**

4. Installation is the reverse of removal. Tighten the wheel bearing lock nut to 137–188 ft. lbs. (186–255 Nm).

## Rear Axle Assembly

### REMOVAL & INSTALLATION

#### G20

1. Raise and support the vehicle safely.

2. Remove the rear wheel, disc brake caliper and rotor assembly.

3. Remove the rear parcel shelf to gain access to the upper shock mount and remove the shock absorber assembly.

4. Remove the stabilizer bar from the connecting rods. Remove the radius rods and parallel links from the rear hub assembly only.

**To install:**

5. Attach the parallel links and radius rods to the rear hub assembly. Tighten the parallel link bolts to 80–94 ft. lbs. (108–127 Nm) and the radius rod bolts to 65–80 ft. lbs. (88–108 Nm).

6. Install the stabilizer bar. Tighten the stabilizer bar-to-connecting rod nuts to 30–35 ft. lbs. (41–47 Nm).

7. Install the shock absorber assembly.

8. Install the rear disc brake rotor and caliper. Install the rear wheel and tire.

# STEERING

## Steering Wheel
### —— CAUTION ——

*On vehicles equipped with an air bag, the negative battery cable must be disconnected, before working on the system. Failure to do so may result in deployment of the air bag and possible personal injury.*

### REMOVAL & INSTALLATION

#### Except Air Bag

1. Disconnect the negative battery cable.

2. Ensure that the steering wheel and front tires are positioned in the straight ahead position.

3. Using an appropriate tool, pry the horn pad off the steering wheel.

4. Remove the steering wheel lock nut.

5. Using an appropriate puller, remove the steering wheel.

**To install:**

6. Apply multi-purpose grease to the entire surface of the trun signal

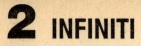

cancel pin and the horn contact clip ring.

7. Install the steering wheel and tighten the lock nut to 22–29 ft. lbs. (29–39 Nm).

8. Install the horn pad. Reconnect the negative battery cable.

### With Air Bag

1. Make sure the wheels are pointing straight ahead. Disconnect the negative battery cable and allow 10 minutes to elapse.

2. Remove the lower lid from the steering column and disconnect the air bag module connector.

**NOTE: The air bag module is a fragile component. Always place it with the pad side facing upward. Do not allow oil, grease or water to come in cantact with the module. Do not drop the module; if it is damaged in any way, do not reinstall it to the steering wheel.**

3. Remove the side access lids, remove the left and right T50H Torx® bolts and discard them. These bolts are specially coated and should not be reused.

4. Carefully remove the air bag module and place in a safe location with the pad side facing upward.

5. Disengage the spiral cable and disconnect the horn connector. Remove the steering wheel hold-down nut.

6. Using an appropriate puller, remove the steering wheel.

7. Attach the spiral cable to the stopper.

8. Remove the steering column covers.

9. Disconnect the connector, remove the 4 mounting screws and remove the spiral cable.

10. Disconnect all combination switch connectors from underneath the steering column.

11. Remove the screws that fasten the combination switch to the steering column and remove from the vehicle.

**To install:**

12. Feed the wires down the column and install the combination switch to the steering column.

13. Connect the spiral cable connectors and install to the column. Disengage the stopper by pulling the 2 pin guides on the spiral cable unit.

14. Pull the spiral cable through the steering wheel opening and install the steering wheel, setting the pin guides.

15. Connect the horn connector and engage the spiral cable with the pawls in the steering wheel.

16. Install the hold-down nut and torque to 25 ft. lbs. (34 Nm).

17. Carefully position the air bag module. Install new Torx® bolts and torque to 15 ft. lbs. (20 Nm). Connect the air bag module connector.

18. Install the 3 access lids and the column covers.

19. Connect the negative battery cable.

20. Using the Nissan Consult System Checking tool, conduct self-diagnosis to ensure the system is operating properly.

21. If the Consult tool is not available, perform the following:

a. From the passanger seat, turn the ignition switch to the **ON** position.

b. Observe the **AIR BAG** warning light on the instrument cluster.

c. The warning light should illuminate for about 7 seconds, then go out.

d. If the warning light illuminates in any sequence except the above, perform the proper diagnostics before continuing.

## Steering Column

### REMOVAL & INSTALLATION

1. Disconnect the negative battery cable.

2. Remove the steering wheel.

3. Remove the upper and lower steering column covers.

4. Disconnect the steering column multi-function switch connectors.

5. Remove the bolts attaching the lower steering column bracket to the firewall.

6. Remove the set bolt from the steering column lower joint.

7. Remove the bolts attaching the steering column to the instrument panel.

8. Remove the steering column from the vehicle.

**To install:**

9. Position the steering column in the vehicle.

**NOTE: Ensure that the lower steering column engages in the lower joint before the steering column is permanently attached.**

10. Install and finger-tighten the bolts attaching the steering column to the instrument panel.

11. Tighten steering column-to-lower joint set bolt.

**NOTE: When attaching the coupling, ensure that set bolt faces the cutout portion in the splines of the lower steering column shaft.**

12. Install the bolts attaching the lower steering column bracket to the firewall. Tighten to 5.8–7.2 ft. lbs. (24–29 Nm).

13. Tighten the steering column-to-

instrument panel bolts to 9–13 ft. lbs. (13–18 Nm).

14. Install the steering wheel.

15. Install the negative battery cable.

## Power Steering Rack

### ADJUSTMENT

1. With rack assembly removed from the vehicle and installed in a vise, set the rack to the neutral position without fluid in the gear.

2. Coat the adjusting screw with locking sealant and install the screw.

3. Lightly tighten the locknut.

4. Tighten the adjusting screw to 43–52 ft. lbs. (4.9–5.9 Nm).

5. Loosen the adjusting screw and retighten to 1.7 inch lbs. (0.2 Nm).

6. Move rack over its entire stroke several times.

7. Measure pinion rotating torque with the range of 180 degrees from the neutral position. Stop the gear at the point of maximum torque.

8. Loosen the adjusting screw, the retighten to 43 inch lbs. (4.9 Nm).

9. Loosen the adjusting screw 70–110 degrees.

10. Prevent the adjusting screw from turning and tighten the locknut to specified torque.

11. Measure the pinion rotating torque. Within ±100 from the neutral position: Average rotating torque should be 6.9–11.3 inch lbs. (0.8–1.3 Nm). Maximum torque deviation is 3.5 inch lbs. (0.4 Nm).

12. Check rack sliding force as follows:

a. Install the steering gear in the vehicle., but do not connect the tie rod-to-knuckle arm.

b. Connect all piping and fill with steering fluid.

c. Start the engine and bleed the air completely.

d. Disconnect the steering column lower joint from the gear.

e. Keep the engine at idle and make sure steering fluid has reached normal operating temperature.

f. While pulling tie rod slowly in the ±0.453 in. (±11.5mm) range from the neutral position, make sure the rack sliding force is within specification. On G20 and M30, the average rack sliding force should be 53–64 lbs. (235–284 N). On Q45, the average rack sliding force should be 37–51 lbs. (167–226 N).

g. Check sliding force outside the above range. Maximum allowable sliding force is not more than 9 lbs. (39 N) above the normal value.

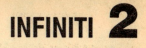

## REMOVAL & INSTALLATION

1. Disconnect the negative battery cable.
2. Raise the vehicle and support safely.
3. Remove the front wheels.
4. Disconnect the outer tie rods from the steering knuckle.
5. Remove the set screw from the lower steering column universal joint. Disconnect the shaft from the joint.
6. Remove the power steering fluid lines from the rack assembly.
7. Remove the bolts attaching the power steering rack assembly to the body.
8. Remove the rack assembly from the vehicle.
9. Complete the installation of the power steering rack assembly by reversing the removal procedure. Pay close attention to the following:
   a. Tighten the rack mounting bolts to 62–80 ft. lbs. (84–108 Nm).
   b. Initially, tighten the tie rod-to-steering knuckle nuts bolts to 22–29 ft. lbs. (29–39 Nm). Tighten the nut further to expose first pin hole and install a new cotter pin.
   c. Tighten the pinion shaft-to-universal joint set screw to 17–22 ft. lbs. (24–29 Nm).
   d. On G20 and M30 models, tighten low pressure power steering lines to 20–29 ft. lbs. (27–39 Nm). Tighten high pressure lines to 11–18 ft. lbs. (15–25 Nm).
   e. On Q45 models, tighten low pressure power steering lines to 27–30 ft. lbs. (36–40 Nm). Tighten high pressure lines to 22–26 ft. lbs. (30–35 Nm).

## Power Steering Pump

### REMOVAL & INSTALLATION

1. Disconnect the negative battery cable.
2. Remove the power steering belt pump drive belt.
3. Disconnect the power steering fluid lines.
4. Remove the power steering pump mounting bolts and remove the pump.
5. Complete the installation of the power steering pump by reversing the removal procedure.

### BELT ADJUSTMENT

1. Loosen the power steering pump tension locknut.
2. On the G20 and M30, using a suitable belt tension gauge, adjust the belt tension to 0.55–0.63 in. (14–16mm) with a force of 22 lbs. (98 N) applied at the midpoint of the belt run between the crankshaft and power steering pump pulleys.
3. On the Q45, using a suitable belt tension gauge, adjust the belt tension to 0.35–0.39 in. (9–10mm) with a force of 22 lbs. (98 N) applied at the midpoint of the belt run between the crankshaft and power steering pump pulleys for vehicles without Super HICAS. Vehicles with Super HICAS, adjust the tension to 0.28–0.31 in. (7–8mm) with a force of 22 lbs. (98 N) applied at the midpoint of the belt run between the crankshaft and power steering pump pulleys.
4. Tighten the power steering pump tension locknut.

### SYSTEM BLEEDING

1. Raise and support the vehicle safely.
2. Ensure that the reservoir is full.
3. Quickly turn the wheels from side to side lightly touching the steering stops.
4. Repeat steps 2 and 3 until the fluid level no longer decreases in the reservoir.
5. Start the engine.
6. Air in the system may cause one or all of the following:
   a. Air bubbles to appear in the reservoir.
   b. Generation of a clicking noise in the oil pump.
   c. Excessive buzzing in the oil pump.

## Tie Rod Ends

### REMOVAL & INSTALLATION

1. Raise the vehicle and support safely.
2. Remove the front wheel.
3. Matchmark the position of tie rod end locknut on the threaded section of the tie rod.
4. Loosen the tie rod end locknut.
5. Remove the cotter pin and tie rod end nut.
6. Separate the tie rod end from the steering knuckle using a suitable tool.
7. Remove the tie rod end from the tie rod.
**To install:**
8. Install the new tie rod end on the tie rod.
9. Install the tie rod end on the steering knuckle. Initially, tighten the tie rod-to-steering knuckle nuts bolts to 22–29 ft. lbs. (29–39 Nm). Tighten the nut further to expose first pin hole and install a new cotter pin.
10. Adjust the toe-in to the matchmark made on the threaded section of the tie rod. Tighten the locknut.
11. Install the front wheel.

12. Lower the vehicle.
13. Check alignment to verify proper toe-in setting.

# BRAKES

For all brake system repair and service procedures not detailed below, please refer to "Brakes" in the Unit Repair section.

## Master Cylinder

### REMOVAL & INSTALLATION

**NOTE: Prevent brake fluid from coming in contact with painted surfaces. Clean up any spills immediately.**

1. Loosen the brake line flare nuts and remove brake lines from master cylinder fittings.
2. Remove the master cylinder mounting nuts.
3. Remove the master cylinder.
**To install:**
4. Bench bleed the master cylinder.
5. Install the master cylinder in the vehicle. Tighten bolts to 6–8 ft. lbs. (8–11 Nm).
6. Connect the brake lines to the master cylinder and finger-tighten the flare nuts.
7. Bleed the air from the brake lines. Tighten the flare nuts.

## Proportioning Valve

The proportioning valve is integral to the master cylinder and cannot be serviced or removed separately.

## Power Brake Booster

### REMOVAL & INSTALLATION

1. Remove the master cylinder.
2. Remove the clevis pin connecting the brake pedal to the booster input rod.
3. Remove the brake pedal bracket to booster mounting nuts.
4. Remove the brake booster.
5. Complete the installation of the brake booster by reversing the removal procedure. Tighten the brake booster nuts to 9–12 ft. lbs. (13–16 Nm).

## Brake Caliper

### REMOVAL & INSTALLATION

**NOTE: Prevent brake fluid from coming in contact with**

painted surfaces. Clean up any spills immediately.

1. Raise the vehicle and support safely.
2. Remove the wheel.
3. Loosen the brake hose connecting bolt.
4. Remove the bolts connecting the caliper to the torque member.
5. Slide the caliper out from the rotor and remove the pad, shim and shim cover.
6. Remove the brake hose connecting bolt from the caliper.
7. Remove the caliper from the vehicle.
8. Complete the installation of the brake caliper by reversing the removal procedure. Tighten the caliper bolts to 16–23 ft. lbs. (22–31 Nm). Bleed the air from the system.

## Disc Brake Pads

### REMOVAL & INSTALLATION

1. Remove the cap from the master cylinder reservoir and extract a small amount of brake fluid from the reservoir.
2. Raise the vehicle and support safely.
3. Remove the wheel.
4. On Q45 models, if servicing the right front brake, disconnect the sensor harness by pushing the connector pin and pulling the connector. Remove the bracket from the cylinder body. If servicing the right rear brake, remove the sensor harness by pushing it toward the pad, turning it counterclockwise and removing it.
5. Remove the lower pin bolt.
6. Pivot the caliper body upward and remove pad retainers, inner and outer shims and pads.
**To install:**
7. Place the old pad in place over the caliper cylinders. Use a C-clamp to compress the cylinder pistons to allow for the added thickness of the new pads.
8. Install the new pads and install caliper on rotor. Install pin bolts.
9. Install connector harness, if removed. Pump brakes to seat pads and then refill master cylinder.

## Brake Rotor

### REMOVAL & INSTALLATION

1. Raise the vehicle and support safely.
2. Remove the wheel.
3. Remove the caliper from the torque member and support using a length of mechanics wire.

4. Remove the bolts attaching the torque member and remove.
5. Remove the rotor from the hub assembly.
6. Complete the installation of the brake rotor by reversing the removal procedure.

## Parking Brake Cable

### ADJUSTMENT

#### Shoe Clearance (except G20)

1. Remove adjuster hole plug and turn the adjuster wheel down until the brake is locked.

**NOTE: Ensure that the parking brake control lever is completely released.**

2. Return the adjuster wheel 7–8 notches on the M30 and 5–6 latches on the Q45.
3. Install the adjuster hole plug and ensure that there is not drag between the shoes and the brake drum when rotating the wheel.

#### Parking Brake Cable

1. On the M30 and Q45, adjust shoe clearance before adjusting the parking brake cable.
2. Loosen the adjuster locknut.
3. Rotate the adjuster to adjust cable.
4. Tighten locknut.
5. On G20 models, pull the lever control handle with 44 lbs. (196 N) of force. The parking brake should be set in 7–8 notches.
6. On M30 models, pull the lever control handle with 44 lbs. (196 N) of force. The parking brake should be set in 8–9 notches.
7. On Q45 models, depress the parking brake pedal with 44 lbs. (194 N) of force. The parking brake should be set within the pedal stroke of 3.54–4.13 in. (90–105mm).

### REMOVAL & INSTALLATION

#### G20

1. Remove the center console and disconnect the warning lamp connector.
2. Remove the retaining bolts and slacken off the adjusting nut.
3. Remove the cable mounting bracket and lock spring at the rear caliper.
4. Remove the brake cable.
5. Installation is the reverse of removal.
6. Tighten cable holddown bracket bolts to 2–3 ft. lbs. (3–4 Nm). Adjust the brake cable.

#### M30

##### FRONT CABLE

1. It is necessary to cut the carpet directly behind the parking brake handle in order to access the front cable.
2. Remove the bolts attaching the parking brake handle and disconnect the parking brake front cable.
3. Remove the bolts attaching the bracket at the point where the cable passes through the floor.
4. Raise the vehicle and support safely.
5. Pull the cable through the hole in the floor and disconnect from the rear cable.
6. Connect the new cable and feed into the hole.
7. Connect the cable to the parking brake lever and install the floor bracket and parking brake handle bolts.
8. Adjust cable.

##### REAR CABLE

1. Raise the vehicle and support safely.
2. Remove rear wheels.
3. Remove the bolts attaching the rear disc brake caliper mounting bracket. Remove bracket with caliper attached. Support using a length of mechanics wire.
4. Remove 2 bolts attaching rear brake rotor and remove rotor.
5. Disconnect parking brake cable end from toggle lever. Remove cable from backing plate mounting.
6. Remove cable brackets.
7. Disconnect rear cable from equalizer.
8. Complete the installation of the rear parking brake cable by reversing the removal procedure. Pay close attention to the following:
   a. Install the rear parking brake cable into the backing plate by tapping the flanged section of the cable cover with a hammer and punch.
   b. Check the shoe clearance adjustment before adjusting the cable.
   c. Adjust parking brake cable.

#### Q45

##### FRONT CABLE

**NOTE: It is possible to remove the front parking brake cable without removing the pedal assembly.**

1. Raise the vehicle and support safely.
2. Disconnect the front cable from the equalizer.
3. Lower the vehicle.
4. Remove the clip retaining the cable end to the pedal assembly.
5. Remove the center console.
6. Remove the cable brackets and

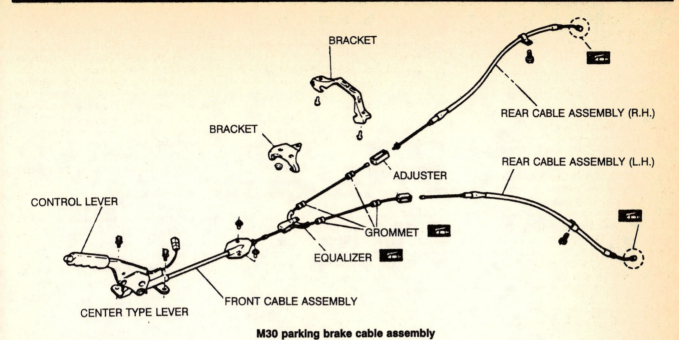

**M30 parking brake cable assembly**

remove the cable from the floor grommet.

7. Complete the installation of the front parking brake cable by reversing the removal procedure.

**REAR CABLE**

1. Raise the vehicle and support safely.
2. Remove rear wheels.
3. Remove the bolts attaching the rear disc brake caliper mounting bracket. Remove bracket with caliper attached. Support using a length of mechanics wire.
4. Remove 2 bolts attaching rear brake rotor and remove rotor.
5. Disconnect parking brake cable end from toggle lever. Remove cable from backing plate mounting.
6. Remove cable brackets.
7. Disconnect rear cable from equalizer.
8. Complete the installation of the rear parking brake cable by reversing the removal procedure. Pay close attention to the following:

   a. Install the rear parking brake cable into the backing plate by tapping the flanged section of the cable cover with a hammer and punch.

   b. Check the shoe clearance adjustment before adjusting the cable.

   c. Adjust parking brake cable.

# Brake System Bleeding

1. Fill the brake master cylinder reservoir with brake fluid.
2. Raise and safely support the vehicle.

3. Connect a length of vinyl hose to the bleeder plug.
4. Submerge one end of the vinyl hose in a container filled with brake fluid. Connect the other end of the vinyl hose to the wheel cylinder bleeder plug.
5. Have an assistant slowly depress the brake pedal and hold it.
6. Open the bleeder plug of the

nyl hose to the wheel cylinder bleeder plug.

5. Have an assistant slowly depress the brake pedal and hold it.
6. Open the bleeder plug of the

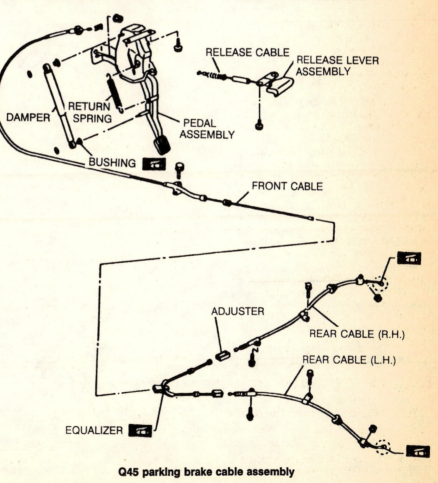

**Q45 parking brake cable assembly**

right rear wheel cylinder ⅓–½ turn until the bubbles stop coming out of the tube. Close the bleeder plug.

7. Have the assistant release the brake pedal.

**NOTE: The assistant must keep the brake pedal depressed until the bleeder plug is closed.**

8. Continue the above procedure until air bubbles are no longer observed in the brake fluid.

9. Remove the vinyl tube and replace the bleeder plug cap.

10. Bleed the system without anti-lock brakes in the following order:
   a. Left rear
   b. Right rear
   c. Left front
   d. Right front

11. Bleed the system with anti-lock brakes as follows:
   a. For G20 vehicles, bleed the system in this order: left rear, right front, right rear and left front.
   b. M30 and Q45 vehicles should be bled in this order: left rear, right rear, left front, right front, front side bleeder on ABS actuator and rear side bleeder on the ABS actuator.

12. Check the brake fluid level in the master cylinder reservoir frequently during the bleeding operation.

## Anti-Lock Brake System Service

### PRECAUTIONS

• Carefully monitor the brake fluid level in the master cylinder at all times during the bleeding procedure. Keep the reservoir full at all times.

• Only use brake fluid that meets or exceeds DOT 3 specifications.

• Place a suitable container under the master cylinder to avoid spillage of brake fluid.

• do not allow brake fluid to come in contact with any painted surface.

• Make sure to use the proper bleeding sequence.

### RELIEVING ANTI-LOCK BRAKE SYSTEM PRESSURE

To relieve the pressure from the ABS system, turn the ignition switch to the **OFF** position. Disconnect the connectors from the ABS actuator. Wait a few minutes to allow for the system to bleed down, then disconnect the negative battery cable.

## Wheel Speed Sensor

### REMOVAL & INSTALLATION

#### Front

1. Raise and safely support the front of the vehicle.

2. Remove the tire and wheel.

3. On some models, it may be necessary to remove the inner fender liner.

4. With the ignition switch **OFF**, disconnect the wheel speed sensor lead from the ABS harness. Remove any retaining bolts or clips holding the harness in place.

**NOTE: Clips and retainers must be reinstalled in their exact original location. Take careful note of the position of each retainer and of the correct harness routing during removal.**

5. Remove the single bolt holding the speed sensor.

6. Carefully remove the sensor straight out of its mount. Do not subject the sensor to shock or vibration; protect the tip of the sensor at all times.

**To install:**

7. Fit the sensor into position. Make certain the sensor sits flush against the mounting surface; it must not be crooked.

8. Install the retaining bolt. Correct bolt tightness for all vehicles is 9 ft. lbs. (12 Nm).

9. Route the sensor cable correctly and install the harness clips and retainers. The cable must be in its origi-

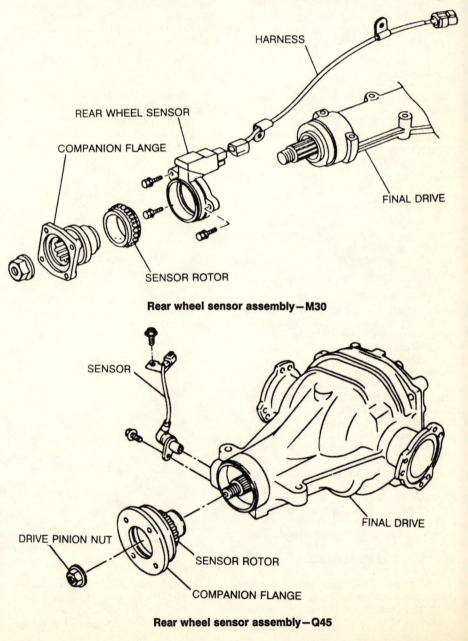

Rear wheel sensor assembly—M30

Rear wheel sensor assembly—Q45

nal position and completely clear of moving components.

10. Connect the sensor cable to the ABS harness.

11. Install the inner fender liner if it was removed.

12. Install the wheel and tire.

13. Lower the vehicle to the ground.

### Rear

1. Raise and safely support the rear of the vehicle.

2. For G20, remove the tire and wheel.

3. Disconnect the wheel speed sensor lead from the ABS harness. Remove any retaining bolts or clips holding the harness in place.

**NOTE: Clips and retainers must be reinstalled in their exact original location. Take careful note of the position of each retainer and of the correct harness routing during removal.**

4. Remove the single bolt holding the speed sensor.

5. Carefully remove the sensor straight out of its mount. Do not subject the sensor to shock or vibration; protect the tip of the sensor at all times.

**To install:**

6. Fit the sensor into position. Make certain the sensor sits flush against the mounting surface; it must not be crooked.

7. Install the retaining bolt. Tighten the bolt to 9 ft. lbs. (12 Nm).

8. Route the sensor cable correctly and install the harness clips and retainers. The cable must be in its original position and completely clear of moving components.

9. Connect the sensor cable to the ABS harness.

10. On the G20, install the wheel and tire.

11. Lower the vehicle to the ground.

## Hydraulic Actuator

### REMOVAL & INSTALLATION

1. Disconnect the negative battery cable.

2. Drain the brake fluid from the system. Use a syringe or similar tool to empty the master cylinder reservoir. Connect a plastic tube to each brake bleeder. Proceed as if bleeding the brakes; pump each line clear of fluid by operating the brake pedal.

3. Disconnect the wiring connectors at the actuator.

4. Apply dots of colored paint to identify each actuator brake line and its correct port. Using tool GG 94310000 or its equivalent, carefully disconnect each brake line from the actuator.

5. Remove the retaining nuts holding the actuator. Make certain the brake lines are out of the way, then remove the actuator from the engine compartment.

**To install:**

6. Install the actuator into the engine compartment.

7. Connect the brake lines to the actuator temporarily, finger tight only. Make certain each is in the correct location.

8. Tighten the actuator mounting bolts to 12 ft. lbs. (16 Nm.)

9. Tighten the actuator brake line fittings to 11 ft. lbs. (15 Nm).

10. Connect the wiring connectors to the actuator.

11. Refill the system with DOT 3 brake fluid from unopened containers. Since the system was drained, a substantial amount may be required.

12. Bleed the system at all 4 wheels and at the ABS actuator if required. Each line may require repeated bleeding to eliminate all air within.

13. Connect the negative battery cable.

# CHASSIS ELECTRICAL

### CAUTION
*It is possible for the air bag to inflate for 10 minutes after the battery has been disconnected. Therefore, disconnect the negative battery cable and wait 10 minutes before working on the system. Failure to do so may result in deployment of the air bag and possible personal injury.*

## Air Bag

### DISARMING

Before servicing any component, turn the ignition switch **OFF**, disconnect the negative battery cable and wait for at least 10 minutes. This will disarm the air bag.

## Heater Blower Motor

### REMOVAL & INSTALLATION

1. Disconnect the negative battery cable. Remove the lower right side instrument panel cover.

2. Remove the screws that attach the blower housing to the intake unit.

3. Remove the housing and remove the blower motor from the housing.

4. The installation is the reverse of the removal procedure.

5. Connect the negative battery cable and check the climate control system for proper operation.

## Windshield Wiper Motor

### REMOVAL & INSTALLATION

1. Disconnect the negative battery cable.

2. Disconnect the leads at the motor.

3. Remove the motor mounting bolts.

4. Pull the motor out and remove the wiper motor linkage attaching nut.

5. Remove the motor from the firewall.

6. The installation is the reverse of the removal procedure.

7. Connect the negative battery cable and check all windshield wiper and washer functions for proper operation.

## Instrument Cluster

### REMOVAL & INSTALLATION

#### Except Q45

1. Disconnect the negative battery cable.

2. Remove the steering column covers.

3. Remove the screws that fasten the cluster lid to the instrument panel and remove the lid.

4. Remove the screws that fasten the instrument cluster to the instrument panel, pull the cluster out, disconnect all connectors and remove the cluster.

5. Disassemble the cluster, as required.

6. The installation is the reverse of the removal procedure.

7. Connect the negative battery cable and check all gauges for proper operation.

#### Q45

1. Disconnect the negative battery cable.

2. Remove the steering column covers.

3. Remove the gear shifter bezel from the console.

4. Remove the ash tray assembly.

5. Remove the screws that fasten the radio and climate control switch bezel to the instrument panel. Pull the bezel down and out, disconnect the rear window defogger switch and remove the bezel.

6. Remove the cruise control main

switch/outside mirror control switch assembly.

7. Remove the screws that fasten the cluster lid to the instrument panel and remove the lid.

8. Remove the screws that attach the instrument cluster to the instrument panel, pull the cluster out, disconnect all connectors and remove the cluster.

9. Disassemble the cluster, as required.

**To install:**

10. Assemble the cluster, connect all connectors and install to the instrument panel.

11. Connect the negative battery cable and check all gauges for proper operation. If everything is operating properly, disconnect the negative battery cable and proceed.

12. Install the cluster lid and cruise control main switch/outside mirror control switch assembly.

13. Install the radio and climate control switch bezel to the instrument panel.

14. Install the ash tray and gear shifter bezel.

15. Install the steering column covers.

16. Connect the negative battery cable and check all gauges for proper operation.

## Radio

### REMOVAL & INSTALLATION

1. Disconnect the negative battery cable.

2. Remove the trim panel surrounding the radio and heater control panel.

3. Remove the radio attaching screws.

4. Disconnect the radio wiring harness and remove the radio.

5. Installation is the reverse of removal.

6. Before installing the radio, ensure that the fuse located at the rear of the radio is good.

## Combination Switch

### REMOVAL & INSTALLATION

**NOTE: On vehicles equipped with an airbag, it is imperative that the exact steering wheel Removal & Installation procedure is followed. The air bag module is a fragile component. Always place it with the pad side facing upward. Do not allow oil, grease or water to come in contact with the module. Do not drop the module; if it is damaged in any way, do not reinstall it to the steering wheel.**

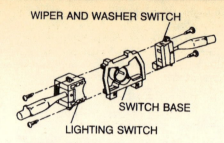

**Combination switch assembly—G20 and M30**

### Except Q45

On the G20 and M30, the combination switch assembly is made up of 3 units— the windsheild wiper/washer switch is located to the right side of the steering column, the combination switch base is attached to the steering column, and the headlight, dimmer and turn signal switch is located to the right side of the steering column. The 2 switches can be removed without removing the switch base.

1. Disconnect the negative battery cable.

2. Remove the steering column covers. Disconnect the connector.

3. Remove the combination switch mounting screws and remove the switch from the switch base.

4. The installation is the reverse of the removal procedure.

5. Connect the negative battery cable and check all functions of the combination switch for proper operation.

### Q45

On the Q45, the combination switch assembly cannot be disassembled and refers to all column-mounted stalk switches as a single unit.

Before replacing the switch, unplug the existing switch and plug in the replacement one to make sure all functions operate properly.

1. Make sure the wheels are pointing straight ahead. Disconnect the negative battery cable and allow 10 minutes to elapse.

2. Remove the steering wheel.

3. Disconnect all combination switch connectors from underneath the steering column.

4. Remove the screws that fasten the combination switch to the steering column and remove from the vehicle.

5. The installation is the reverse of the removal procedure.

6. Connect the negative battery cable and check all functions of the combination switch for proper operation.

## Combination Switch Base

### REMOVAL & INSTALLATION

**NOTE: On vehicles equipped with airbags, it is imperative that the exact steering wheel Removal & Installation procedure under Steering is followed. The air bag module is a fragile component. Always place it with the pad side facing upward. Do not allow oil, grease or water to come in contact with the module. Do not drop the module; if it is damaged in any way, do not reinstall it to the steering wheel.**

### G20

1. Make sure the wheels are point-

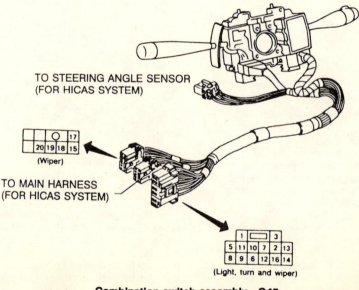

**Combination switch assembly—Q45**

ing straight ahead. Disconnect the negative battery cable and allow 10 minutes to elapse.

2. Remove the steering wheel.

3. Disconnect all combination and windshield wiper switch connectors and remove the switches from the switch base.

4. Insert a suitable tool between the combination switch base and the steering column. Lift the base and pull outward to remove.

5. The installation is the reverse of the removal procedure.

6. Connect the negative battery cable and check all functions of the combination and windshield wiper switches for proper operation.

### M30

1. Make sure the wheels are pointing straight ahead. Disconnect the negative battery cable and allow 10 minutes to elapse.

2. Remove the steering wheel.

3. Disconnect all combination and windshield wiper switch connectors and remove the switches from the switch base.

4. To remove the combination switch base, remove the base attaching screw and turn after pushing it.

5. The installation is the reverse of the removal procedure.

6. Connect the negative battery cable and check all functions of the combination and windshield wiper switches for proper operation.

## Ignition Lock/Switch

### REMOVAL & INSTALLATION

**NOTE: On vehicles equipped with airbags, it is imperative that the exact steering wheel Removal & Installation procedure under Steering is followed. The air bag module is a fragile component. Always place it with the pad side**

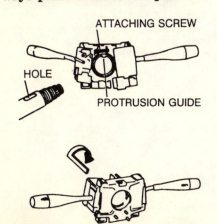

ATTACHING SCREW

HOLE

PROTRUSION GUIDE

**Combination switch base removal—M30**

facing upward. Do not allow oil, grease or water to come in contact with the module. Do not drop the module; if it is damaged in any way, do not reinstall it to the steering wheel.**

1. Make sure the wheels are pointing straight ahead. Disconnect the negative battery cable and allow 10 minutes to elapse.

2. Remove the steering wheel and combination switch or switch base.

3. Disconnect the ignition switch wiring.

4. Lower the steering column.

5. Using a hacksaw blade, cut a groove into the heads of the special self-shearing screws and remove the screws.

6. Remove the assembly from the column.

**To install:**

7. With the key inserted in the switch, install the assembly onto the column with new self-shearing screws. Tighten the screws gradually, testing the key for binding often. Tighten the screws until the heads shear off.

8. Raise and secure the steering column.

9. Install the combination switch or switch base, and steering wheel.

10. Connect the negative battery cable and check the ignition switch for proper operation in all positions.

## Stoplight Switch

### ADJUSTMENT

1. Measure the free height of the brake pedal at its bottom edge. The specification is 6.0 in. (152mm) for the manual transmission and 6.0–7.0 in. (152–177mm) for the automatic transaxle on the G20; 8.0 in. (205mm) for M30 and 7.4 in. (190mm) for Q45. Adjust by loosening the booster input rod locknut and turning the input rod.

2. The stoplight switch is to the right of the cruise control cancel switch on the bracket above the brake pedal. Adjust both switches during this procedure.

3. Measure the clearance between the threaded end of the switches and the pedal stopper. The specification is 0.025 in. (0.06mm) for both.

4. Adjust be loosening the locknut and turning each switch.

5. Check the pedal free-play. The specification is 0.08 in. (2.0mm); 0.04–0.12 in. (1–3mm) for the G20.

6. Make sure the brake lights illuminate when the pedal is depressed and they go out when the pedal is released.

7. Also, make sure the cruise control cancels when the brake pedal is depressed.

### REMOVAL & INSTALLATION

1. Disconnect the negative battery cable.

2. Remove the locknut.

3. Remove the switch from the bracket above the brake pedal.

4. The installation is the reverse of the removal procedure.

5. Adjust the switch.

6. Connect the negative battery cable and check the switch for proper operation.

## Neutral Safety Switch

### ADJUSTMENT

1. Disconnect the negative battery cable.

2. Raise the vehicle and support safely.

3. Disconnect the manual control linkage from the manual shift shaft.

4. Set the manual shift shaft in the **N** detent.

5. Loosen the neutral safety switch mounting bolts.

6. Align the switch with the shift shaft by inserting a suitable pin in the alignment holes.

7. Tighten the switch mounting bolts and connect the control linkage.

8. Make sure the vehicle does not start in any gear except **P** or **N** and does start in both **P** and **N**.

### REMOVAL & INSTALLATION

1. Disconnect the negative battery cable.

2. Raise the vehicle and support safely.

3. Disconnect the wires to the switch.

4. Remove the switch mounting screws.

5. Remove the switch from the transmission.

6. The installation is the reverse of the removal procedure.

7. Adjust the switch.

8. Make sure the vehicle does not start in any gear except **P** or **N** and does start in both **P** and **N**.

## Clutch Switch

### ADJUSTMENT

1. Ensure that the clutch pedal height and free travel adjustments are within specification.

2. With the clutch pedal fully depressed, measure the clearance between the rubber stopper and the threaded end of the clutch switch. Clearance should be 0.004–0.039 in. (0.1–1.0mm).

3. If the clearance is not within specificaiton, adjust the switch by loosening the locknut and adjusting the switch.

## REMOVAL & INSTALLATION

1. Disconnect the negative battery cable.
2. Disconnect the wiring harness from the clutch switch.
3. Loosen the locknut and remove the clutch switch.
4. Installation is the reverse of removal.
5. Adjust the switch.

# Fuses, Circuit Breakers and Relays

## LOCATION

A fuse, fusible link and relay box is located in the engine compartment, near the battery. Release the latch and remove the protective covering to access the desired component. The radio has its own fuse behind it. Other various relays are located throughout the vehicle.

There is a second fuse box located behind an access door to the left of the steering column on the instrument panel. The circuit breaker for the power door locks and seats is located near this fuse box. The circuit breaker for the power windows and the sunroof is located behind the left side kick panel.

# Computers

## LOCATION

### G20

**ABS Acutator** — is located at the right front of the engine compartment.
**ABS Control Unit** — is located at the right side kick panel.
**ASCD Actuator** — is located at the rear center of the engine compartment.
**ASCD Control Unit** — is located under the dash to the left of the steering column.

**Automatic Seat Belt Control Unit** — is located under the console.
**Combination Flasher Unit** — is located under the dash to the right of the steering column.
**Diagnostic Connector** — is located at the fuse block.
**ECCS Control Unit** — is located under the front of the console.
**Electronic Control Unit (ECU)** — see Electronic Concentrated Control System (ECCS) Unit.
**Shift Lock Control Unit (automatic transmission)** — is located under the left side of the dash.
**Theft Warning Control Unit** — is located under the dash to the right of the steering column.

### M30

**Sonar Suspension Control Unit** — located to the left of the rear seat, behind the trim panel
**Automatic Transmission Control Unit** — located on the left side kick panel.
**Time Control Unit** — located on the left side kick panel.
**Shift Lock Control Unit** — located under the left side of the instrument panel.
**Automatic Speed Control Device (ASCD) Control Unit** — located to the left of the rear seat, behind the trim panel.
**Theft Warning Control Unit** — located on the left side kick panel.
**Anti-Lock Brake System (ABS) Control Unit** — located in the top front of the trunk.
**Electronic Concentrated Control System (ECCS) Unit (for engine control)** — located on the right side kick panel.
**Air Bag Control Unit** — located in the rear of the console.

### Q45

**Fuel Pump Control Module** — located at the top front of the trunk.
**High Captivity Actively Controlled Steering (HICAS) Control Unit (for 4WS)** — located at the top front of the trunk.
**Automatic Transmission Control Unit** — located on the left side kick panel.

**Time Control Unit** — located on the left side kick panel.
**Shift Lock Control Unit** — located on the left side kick panel.
**Automatic Drive Positioner Control Unit** — located to the left of the steering column.
**Automatic Speed Control Device (ASCD) Control Unit** — located to the left of the console.
**Power Steering Control Unit** — located to the left of the console.
**Theft Warning Control Unit** — located behind the glove box.
**Anti-Lock Brake System (ABS) Control Unit** — located behind the glove box.
**Electronic Concentrated Control System (ECCS) Unit (for engine control)** — located on the right side kick panel.
**Right Side Power Seat Control Unit** — located under the right front seat.
**Left Side Power Seat Control Unit** — located under the left front seat.
**Air Bag Control Unit** — located in the rear of the console.

# Flasher

## LOCATION

The combination flasher unit is located under the instrument panel to the right of the steering column on the G20 and M30, and near the interior fuse box on the Q45.

# Cruise Control

## ADJUSTMENT

1. Adjust the throttle cable so it has 0.08 in. (2mm) free-play.
2. With no play in the cruise control cable, loosen the locknut and turn the adjusting nut ½–1 turn to prevent response delay.
3. Tighten the locknut.

# SPECIFICATIONS

## ENGINE IDENTIFICATION

| Year | Model | Engine Displacement cu. in. (cc/liter) | Engine Series Identification (VIN) | No. of Cylinders | Engine Type |
|---|---|---|---|---|---|
| 1988 | Van | 146 (2389/2.4) | Z24i | 4 | OHC |
| | Pick-Up 2WD | 146 (2389/2.4) | Z24i | 4 | OHC |
| | Pick-Up 2WD | 181 (2960/3.0) | VG30i | 6 | DOHC |
| | Pick-Up 4WD | 146 (2389/2.4) | Z24i | 4 | OHC |
| | Pick-Up 4WD | 181 (2960/3.0) | VG30i | 6 | DOHC |
| | Pathfinder | 146 (2389/2.4) | Z24i | 4 | OHC |
| | Pathfinder | 181 (2960/3.0) | VG30i | 6 | DOHC |
| 1989 | Pick-Up 2WD | 146 (2389/2.4) | Z24i | 4 | OHC |
| | Pick-Up 2WD | 181 (2960/3.0) | VG30i | 6 | DOHC |
| | Pick-Up 4WD | 146 (2389/2.4) | Z24i | 4 | OHC |
| | Pick-Up 4WD | 181 (2960/3.0) | VG 30i | 6 | DOHC |
| | Pathfinder 2WD | 181 (2960/3.0) | VG30i | 6 | DOHC |
| | Pathfinder 4WD | 146 (2389/2.4) | Z24i | 4 | OHC |
| | Pathfinder 4WD | 181 (2960/3.0) | VG30i | 6 | DOHC |
| 1990 | Axxess 2WD | 146 (2389/2.4) | KA24E | 4 | OHC |
| | Axxess 4WD | 146 (2389/2.4) | KA24E | 4 | OHC |
| | Pick-Up 2WD | 146 (2389/2.4) | KA24E | 4 | OHC |
| | Pick-Up 2WD | 181 (2960/3.0) | VG30E | 6 | DOHC |
| | Pick-Up 4WD | 146 (2389/2.4) | KA24E | 4 | OHC |
| | Pick-Up 4WD | 181 (2960/3.0) | VG30E | 6 | DOHC |
| | Pathfinder | 181 (2960/3.0) | VG30E | 6 | DOHC |
| 1991–92 | Pick-Up 2WD | 146 (2389/2.4) | KA24E | 4 | OHC |
| | Pick-Up 2WD | 181 (2960/3.0) | VG30E | 6 | DOHC |
| | Pick-Up 4WD | 146 (2389/2.4) | KA24E | 4 | OHC |
| | Pick-Up 4WD | 181 (2960/3.0) | VG30E | 6 | DOHC |
| | Pathfinder | 181 (2960/3.0) | VG30E | 6 | DOHC |

OHC—Overhead cam
DOHC—Dual overhead cam

## GENERAL ENGINE SPECIFICATIONS

| Year | Model | Engine Displacement cu. in. (cc) | Fuel System Type | Net Horsepower @ rpm | Net Torque @ rpm (ft. lbs.) | Bore × Stroke (in.) | Compression Ratio | Oil Pressure @ rpm |
|---|---|---|---|---|---|---|---|---|
| 1988 | Van | 146 (2389) | EFI | 103 @ 4800 | 134 @ 2800 | 3.50 × 3.78 | 8.3:1 | 55 @ 3000 |
| | Pick-Up | 146 (2389) | EFI | 103 @ 4800 | 134 @ 2800 | 3.50 × 3.78 | 8.3:1 | 55 @ 3000 |
| | Pick-Up | 181 (2960) | EFI | 152 @ 5200 | 162 @ 3600 | 3.43 × 3.27 | 9.0:1 | 60 @ 3200 |
| | Pathfinder | 146 (2389) | EFI | 103 @ 4800 | 134 @ 2800 | 3.50 × 3.78 | 8.3:1 | 55 @ 3000 |
| | Pathfinder | 181 (2960) | EFI | 152 @ 5200 | 162 @ 3600 | 3.43 × 3.27 | 9.0:1 | 60 @ 3200 |
| 1989 | Pick-Up | 146 (2389) | EFI | 103 @ 4800 | 134 @ 2800 | 3.50 × 3.78 | 8.3:1 | 55 @ 3000 |
| | Pick-Up | 181 (2960) | EFI | 152 @ 5200 | 162 @ 3600 | 3.43 × 3.27 | 9.0:1 | 60 @ 3200 |
| | Pathfinder | 146 (2389) | EFI | 103 @ 4800 | 134 @ 2800 | 3.50 × 3.78 | 8.3:1 | 55 @ 3000 |
| | Pathfinder | 181 (2960) | EFI | 152 @ 5200 | 162 @ 3600 | 3.43 × 3.27 | 9.0:1 | 60 @ 3200 |

## GENERAL ENGINE SPECIFICATIONS

| Year | Model | Engine Displacement cu. in. (cc) | Fuel System Type | Net Horsepower @ rpm | Net Torque @ rpm (ft. lbs.) | Bore × Stroke (in.) | Compression Ratio | Oil Pressure @ rpm |
|---|---|---|---|---|---|---|---|---|
| 1990 | Axxess | 146 (2389) | MFI | 138 @ 5600 | 148 @ 4400 | 3.50 × 3.78 | 8.6:1 | 65 @ 3000 |
| | Pick-Up | 146 (2389) | MFI | 138 @ 5600 | 148 @ 4400 | 3.50 × 3.78 | 8.6:1 | 65 @ 3000 |
| | Pick-Up | 181 (2960) | MFI | 153 @ 4800 | 180 @ 4000 | 3.43 × 3.27 | 9.0:1 | 60 @ 3200 |
| | Pathfinder | 146 (2389) | MFI | 138 @ 5600 | 148 @ 4400 | 3.50 × 3.78 | 8.6:1 | 65 @ 3000 |
| | Pathfinder | 181 (2960) | MFI | 153 @ 4800 | 180 @ 4000 | 3.43 × 3.27 | 9.0:1 | 60 @ 3200 |
| 1991-92 | Pick-Up | 146 (2389) | MFI | 138 @ 5600 | 148 @ 4400 | 3.50 × 3.78 | 8.6:1 | 65 @ 3000 |
| | Pick-Up | 181 (2960) | MFI | 153 @ 4800 | 180 @ 4000 | 3.43 × 3.27 | 9.0:1 | 60 @ 3200 |
| | Pathfinder | 146 (2389) | MFI | 138 @ 5600 | 148 @ 4400 | 3.50 × 3.78 | 8.6:1 | 65 @ 3000 |
| | Pathfinder | 181 (2960) | MFI | 153 @ 4800 | 180 @ 4000 | 3.43 × 3.27 | 9.0:1 | 60 @ 3200 |

EFI—Electronic fuel injection
MFI—Multi fuel injection

## ENGINE TUNE-UP SPECIFICATIONS

| Year | Model | Engine Displacement cu. in. (cc) | Spark Plugs Type | Gap (in.) | Ignition Timing (deg.) MT | Ignition Timing (deg.) AT | Compression Pressure (psi) | Fuel Pump (psi) | Idle Speed (rpm) MT | Idle Speed (rpm) AT | Valve Clearance In. | Valve Clearance Ex. |
|---|---|---|---|---|---|---|---|---|---|---|---|---|
| 1988 | Van | 146 (2389) | BPR5ES① | 0.033 | 10 | 10 | 173 | 36 | 800 | 750② | 0.008 | 0.009 |
| | Pick-Up | 146 (2389) | BPR5ES① | 0.033 | 10 | 10 | 173 | 36 | 800 | 750② | 0.008 | 0.009 |
| | Pick-Up | 181 (2960) | BCPR5ES-11 | 0.041 | 12 | 12 | 173 | 36 | 800 | 750② | Hyd. | Hyd. |
| | Pathfinder | 146 (2389) | BPR5ES① | 0.033 | 10 | 10 | 173 | 36 | 800 | 750② | 0.008 | 0.009 |
| | Pathfinder | 181 (2960) | BCPR5ES-11 | 0.041 | 12 | 12 | 173 | 36 | 800 | 750② | Hyd. | Hyd. |
| 1989 | Pick-Up | 146 (2389) | BPR5ES① | 0.033 | 10 | 10 | 173 | 36 | 800 | 750② | 0.008 | 0.009 |
| | Pick-Up | 181 (2960) | BCPR5ES-11 | 0.041 | 12 | 12 | 173 | 36 | 800 | 750② | Hyd. | Hyd. |
| | Pathfinder | 146 (2389) | BPR5ES① | 0.033 | 10 | 10 | 173 | 36 | 800 | 750② | 0.008 | 0.009 |
| | Pathfinder | 181 (2960) | BCPR5ES-11 | 0.041 | 12 | 12 | 173 | 36 | 800 | 750② | Hyd. | Hyd. |
| 1990 | Axxess | 146 (2389) | ZFR5E-11 | 0.033 | 15 | 15 | 175 | 33 | 650 | 750③ | Hyd. | Hyd. |
| | Pick-Up | 146 (2389) | ZFR5E-11 | 0.041 | 15 | 15 | 192 | 33 | 800 | 750③ | Hyd. | Hyd. |
| | Pick-Up | 181 (2960) | BKR6EY | 0.033 | 15 | 15 | 173 | 33 | 750 | 750② | Hyd. | Hyd. |
| | Pathfinder | 146 (2389) | ZFR5E-11 | 0.041 | 15 | 15 | 192 | 33 | 800 | 750③ | Hyd. | Hyd. |
| | Pathfinder | 181 (2960) | BKR6EY | 0.033 | 15 | 15 | 173 | 33 | 750 | 750② | Hyd. | Hyd. |
| 1991-92 | Pick-Up | 146 (2389) | ZFR5E-11 | 0.041 | 15 | 15 | 192 | 33 | 800 | 750③ | Hyd. | Hyd. |
| | Pick-Up | 181 (2960) | BKR6EY | 0.033 | 15 | 15 | 173 | 33 | 750 | 750③ | Hyd. | Hyd. |
| | Pathfinder | 146 (2389) | ZFR5E-11 | 0.041 | 15 | 15 | 192 | 33 | 800 | 750③ | Hyd. | Hyd. |
| | Pathfinder | 181 (2960) | BKR6EY | 0.033 | 15 | 15 | 173 | 33 | 750 | 750② | Hyd. | Hyd. |

Hyd.—Hydraulic
① Intake and exhaust sides
② Transmission in drive
③ Transmission in neutral

## FIRING ORDER

NOTE: To avoid confusion, always replace spark plug wires one at a time.

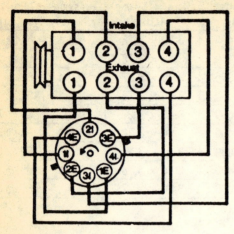

**2.4L (Z24I) Engine**
Engine Firing Order: 1–3–4–2
Distributor Rotation: Counterclockwise

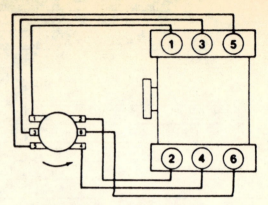

**3.0L (VG30I and VG30E) Engines**
Engine Firing Order: 1–2–3–4–5–6
Distributor Rotation: Counterclockwise

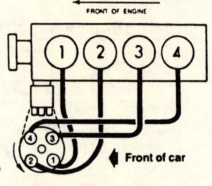

**2.4L (KA24E) Engine**
Engine Firing Order: 1–3–4–2
Distributor Rotation: Counterclockwise

## CAPACITIES

| Year | Model | Engine Displacement cu. in. (cc) | Engine Crankcase with Filter | without Filter | Transmission (pts.) 4-Spd | 5-Spd | Auto. | Drive Axle (pts.) | Fuel Tank (gal.) | Cooling System (qts.) |
|------|-------|------|------|------|------|------|------|------|------|------|
| 1988 | Van | 146 (2389) | 4.4 | 3.9 | — | 4.25 | 14.8 | 2.8 | 17.1 | 9.6 |
| | Pick-Up | 146 (2389) | ⑥ | ⑦ | 3.6 | ③ | 14.8 | ⑤ | 15.9 | 9.0 |
| | Pick-Up | 181 (2960) | ① | ② | — | ④ | 14.8 | ⑤ | 21.1 | 10.5 |
| | Pathfinder | 146 (2389) | ⑥ | ⑦ | 3.6 | ③ | 14.8 | ⑤ | 15.9 | 9.0 |
| | Pathfinder | 181 (2960) | ① | ② | — | ④ | 14.8 | ⑤ | 21.1 | 10.5 |
| 1989 | Pick-Up | 146 (2389) | ⑥ | ⑦ | 3.6 | ③ | 14.8 | ⑤ | 15.9 | 9.0 |
| | Pick-Up | 181 (2960) | ① | ② | — | ④ | 14.8 | ⑤ | 21.1 | 10.5 |
| | Pathfinder | 146 (2389) | ⑥ | ⑦ | 3.6 | ③ | 14.8 | ⑤ | 15.9 | 9.0 |
| | Pathfinder | 181 (2960) | ① | ② | — | ④ | 14.8 | ⑤ | 21.1 | 10.5 |
| 1990 | Axxess | 146 (2389) | 3.8 | 3.4 | — | 10.0 | 15.8 | 2.1 | — | 8.0 |
| | Pick-Up | 146 (2389) | ⑩ | ⑪ | — | ③ | 16.8 | ⑤ | 15.9 | ⑨ |
| | Pick-Up | 181 (2960) | ① | ② | — | ④ | 16.8⑫ | ⑤ | 21.1 | ⑧ |
| | Pathfinder | 146 (2389) | ⑩ | ⑪ | — | ③ | 16.8 | ⑤ | 15.9 | ⑨ |
| | Pathfinder | 181 (2960) | ① | ② | — | ④ | 16.8⑫ | ⑤ | 21.1 | ⑧ |

## CAPACITIES

| Year | Model | Engine Displacement cu. in. (cc) | Engine Crankcase with Filter | Engine Crankcase without Filter | Transmission (pts.) 4-Spd | Transmission (pts.) 5-Spd | Transmission (pts.) Auto. | Drive Axle (pts.) | Fuel Tank (gal.) | Cooling System (qts.) |
|---|---|---|---|---|---|---|---|---|---|---|
| 1991-92 | Pick-Up | 146 (2389) | ⑩ | ⑪ | — | ③ | 16.8 | ⑤ | 15.9 | ⑨ |
| | Pick-Up | 181 (2960) | ① | ② | — | ④ | 16.8⑫ | ⑤ | 21.1 | ⑧ |
| | Pathfinder | 146 (2389) | ⑩ | ⑪ | — | ③ | 16.8 | ⑤ | 15.9 | ⑨ |
| | Pathfinder | 181 (2960) | ① | ② | — | ④ | 16.8⑫ | ⑤ | 21.1 | ⑧ |

① 2WD—4.25
  4WD—3.6
② 2WD—3.9
  4WD—3.1
③ 2WD—4.3
  4WD—8.5
④ 2WD—5.1
  4WD—7.6

⑤ 4WD front—4 cylinder engine—R180A—2.8
  4WD front—V6 engine—R200A—3.1
  4WD rear—4 cylinder engine—C200—2.8
  2WD—4 cylinder engine—H190A—3.1
  2WD or 4WD rear—V6 engine—H233B—5.9
⑥ 2WD—4.0
  4WD—4.5
⑦ 2WD—3.5
  4WD—4.0

⑧ 2WD—11.4
  4WD—12.4
⑨ 2WD—8.6
  4WD—9.5
⑩ 2WD—4.1
  4WD—3.5
⑪ 2WD—3.8
  4WD—3.1

## CAMSHAFT SPECIFICATIONS

All measurements given in inches.

| Year | Engine Displacement cu. in. (cc) | Journal Diameter 1 | Journal Diameter 2 | Journal Diameter 3 | Journal Diameter 4 | Journal Diameter 5 | Lobe Lift In. | Lobe Lift Ex. | Bearing Clearance | Camshaft End Play |
|---|---|---|---|---|---|---|---|---|---|---|
| 1988 | 146 (2389) | 1.2961–1.2968 | 1.2961–1.2968 | 1.2961–1.2968 | 1.2961–1.2968 | 1.2961–1.2968 | NA | NA | 0.0024–0.0041 | 0.008 |
| | 181 (2960) | 1.8866–1.8874 | 1.8472–1.8480 | 1.8472–1.8480 | 1.8472–1.8480 | 1.6701–1.6709 | NA | NA | 0.0018–0.0035 | 0.0012–0.0024 |
| 1989 | 146 (2389) | 1.2961–1.2968 | 1.2961–1.2968 | 1.2961–1.2968 | 1.2961–1.2968 | 1.2961–1.2968 | NA | NA | 0.0024–0.0041 | 0.008 |
| | 181 (2960) | 1.8866–1.8874– | 1.8472–1.8480 | 1.8472–1.8480 | 1.8472–1.8480 | 1.6701–1.6709 | NA | NA | 0.0018–0.0035 | 0.0012–0.0024 |
| 1990 | 146 (2389) | 1.2967–1.2974 | 1.2967–1.2974 | 1.2967–1.2974 | 1.2967–1.2974 | 1.2967–1.2974 | NA | NA | 0.0018–0.0035 | 0.0028–0.0059 |
| | 181 (2960) | 1.8866–1.8874 | 1.8472–1.8480 | 1.8472–1.8480 | 1.8472–1.8480 | 1.6701–1.6709 | NA | NA | 0.0024–0.0041 | 0.0012–0.0024 |
| 1991-92 | 146 (2389) | 1.2967–1.2974 | 1.2967–1.2974 | 1.2967–1.2974 | 1.2967–1.2974 | 1.2967–1.2974 | NA | NA | 0.0018–0.0035 | 0.0028–0.0059 |
| | 181 (2960) | 1.8866–1.8874– | 1.8472–1.8480 | 1.8472–1.8480 | 1.8472–1.8480 | 1.6701–1.6709 | NA | NA | 0.0024–0.0041 | 0.0012–0.0024 |

NA—Not available

## CRANKSHAFT AND CONNECTING ROD SPECIFICATIONS

All measurements are given in inches.

| Year | Engine Displacement cu. in. (cc) | Crankshaft Main Brg. Journal Dia. | Crankshaft Main Brg. Oil Clearance | Crankshaft Shaft End-play | Crankshaft Thrust on No. | Connecting Rod Journal Diameter | Connecting Rod Oil Clearance | Connecting Rod Side Clearance |
|---|---|---|---|---|---|---|---|---|
| 1988 | 146 (2389) | 2.3599–2.3604 | ① | 0.0020–0.0071 | 3 | 1.9670–1.9675 | 0.0005–0.0021 | 0.008–0.012 |
| | 181 (2960) | 2.4790–2.4793 | 0.0011–0.0022 | 0.0020–0.0067 | 4 | 1.9670–1.9675 | 0.0006–0.0021 | 0.008–0.014 |
| 1989 | 146 (2389) | 2.3599–2.3604 | ① | 0.0020–0.0071 | 3 | 1.9670–1.9675 | 0.0006–0.0019 | 0.008–0.012 |
| | 181 (2960) | 2.4790–2.4793 | 0.0011–0.0022 | 0.0020–0.0067 | 4 | 1.9670–1.9675 | 0.0006–0.0021 | 0.008–0.014 |

## CRANKSHAFT AND CONNECTING ROD SPECIFICATIONS

All measurements are given in inches.

| Year | Engine Displacement cu. in. (cc) | Crankshaft Main Brg. Journal Dia. | Main Brg. Oil Clearance | Shaft End-play | Thrust on No. | Connecting Rod Journal Diameter | Oil Clearance | Side Clearance |
|---|---|---|---|---|---|---|---|---|
| 1990 | 146 (2389) | 2.5057–2.5060 | 0.0008–0.0019 | 0.0020–0.0071 | 3 | 2.3603–2.3612 | 0.0004–0.0014 | 0.008–0.016 |
| | 181 (2960) | 2.4790–2.4793 | 0.0011–0.0022 | 0.0020–0.0067 | 4 | 1.9667–1.9675 | 0.0006–0.0021 | 0.008–0.014 |
| 1991–92 | 146 (2389) | 2.5057–2.5060 | 0.0008–0.0019 | 0.0020–0.0071 | 3 | 2.3603–2.3612 | 0.0004–0.0014 | 0.008–0.016 |
| | 181 (2960) | 2.4790–2.4793 | 0.0011–0.0022 | 0.0020–0.0067 | 4 | 1.9667–1.9675 | 0.0006–0.0021 | 0.008–0.014 |

① No. 1 and 5—0.0008–0.0024
   No. 2, 3 and 4—0.0008–0.0030

## VALVE SPECIFICATIONS

| Year | Engine Displacement cu. in. (cc) | Seat Angle (deg.) | Face Angle (deg.) | Spring Test Pressure (lbs.) | Spring Installed Height (in.) | Stem-to-Guide Clearance (in.) Intake | Exhaust | Stem Diameter (in.) Intake | Exhaust |
|---|---|---|---|---|---|---|---|---|---|
| 1988 | 146 (2389) | 45 | 45.5 | ② | ① | 0.0008–0.0021 | 0.0016–0.0029 | 0.3136–0.3142 | 0.3128–0.3134 |
| | 181 (2960) | 45 | 45.5 | ③ | ④ | 0.0008–0.0021 | 0.0016–0.0029 | 0.3136–0.3142 | 0.3128–0.3134 |
| 1989 | 146 (2389) | 45 | 45.5 | ② | ① | 0.0008–0.0021 | 0.0016–0.0029 | 0.3136–0.3142 | 0.3128–0.3134 |
| | 181 (2960) | 45 | 45.5 | ③ | ④ | 0.0008–0.0021 | 0.0016–0.0029 | 0.2742–0.2748 | 0.3128–0.3134 |
| 1990 | 146 (2389) | 45 | 45.5 | ⑤ | ⑥ | 0.0008–0.0021 | 0.0016–0.0029 | 0.2742–0.2748 | 0.3128–0.3134 |
| | 181 (2960) | 45 | 45.5 | ③ | ④ | 0.0008–0.0021 | 0.0012–0.0021 | 0.2742–0.2748 | 0.3136–0.3138 |
| 1991–92 | 146 (2389) | 45 | 45.5 | ⑤ | ⑥ | 0.0008–0.0021 | 0.0016–0.0029 | 0.2742–0.2748 | 0.3128–0.3134 |
| | 181 (2960) | 45 | 45.5 | ③ | ④ | 0.0008–0.0021 | 0.0012–0.0021 | 0.2742–0.2748 | 0.3136–0.3138 |

① Outer—1.58 in.
   Inner—1.34 in.
② Outer—51 lbs.
   Inner—24 lbs.
③ Outer—118 lbs.
   Inner—57 lbs.
④ Outer—1.18 in.
   Inner—0.98 in.
⑤ Outer intake—136 lbs.
   Outer exhaust—144 lbs.
   Inner intake—64 lbs.
   Inner exhaust—74 lbs.
⑥ Outer intake—1.48 in.
   Outer exhaust—1.34 in.
   Inner intake—1.28 in.
   Inner exhaust—1.15 in.

## PISTON AND RING SPECIFICATIONS

All measurements are given in inches.

| Year | No. Cylinder Displacement cu. in. (liter) | Piston Clearance | Ring Gap Top Compression | Bottom Compression | Oil Control | Ring Side Clearance Top Compression | Bottom Compression | Oil Control |
|---|---|---|---|---|---|---|---|---|
| 1988 | 146 (2389) | 0.0010–0.0018 | 0.011–0.015 | 0.010–0.014 | 0.008–0.023 | 0.0016–0.0029 | 0.0012–0.0025 | NA |
| | 181 (2960) | 0.0010–0.0018 | 0.008–0.017 | 0.007–0.017 | 0.008–0.029 | 0.0016–0.0029 | 0.0012–0.0025 | 0.0006–0.0075 |

## PISTON AND RING SPECIFICATIONS
All measurements are given in inches.

| Year | No. Cylinder Displacement cu. in. (liter) | Piston Clearance | Ring Gap | | | Ring Side Clearance | | |
|------|------|------|------|------|------|------|------|------|
| | | | Top Compression | Bottom Compression | Oil Control | Top Compression | Bottom Compression | Oil Control |
| **1989** | 146 (2389) | 0.0010–0.0018 | 0.011–0.015 | 0.010–0.014 | 0.008–0.023 | 0.0016–0.0029 | 0.0012–0.0025 | NA |
| | 181 (2960) | 0.0010–0.0018 | 0.008–0.017 | 0.007–0.017 | 0.008–0.029 | 0.0016–0.0029 | 0.0012–0.0025 | 0.0006–0.0075 |
| **1990** | 146 (2389) | 0.0008–0.0016 | 0.012–0.020 | 0.017–0.027 | 0.008–0.027 | 0.0016–0.0031 | 0.0012–0.0028 | 0.0026–0.0053 |
| | 181 (2960) | 0.0010–0.0018 | 0.008–0.017 | 0.007–0.017 | 0.008–0.029 | 0.0016–0.0029 | 0.0012–0.0025 | NA |
| **1991–92** | 146 (2389) | 0.0008–0.0016 | 0.012–0.020 | 0.017–0.027 | 0.008–0.027 | 0.0016–0.0031 | 0.0012–0.0028 | 0.0026–0.0053 |
| | 181 (2960) | 0.0010–0.0018 | 0.008–0.017 | 0.007–0.017 | 0.008–0.029 | 0.0016–0.0029 | 0.0012–0.0025 | NA |

NA—Not available

## TORQUE SPECIFICATIONS
All readings in ft. lbs.

| Year | Engine Displacement cu. in. (cc) | Cynlinder Head Bolts | Main Bearing Bolts | Rod Bearing Bolts | Crankshaft Pulley Bolts | Flywheel Bolts | Manifold | | Spark Plugs |
|------|------|------|------|------|------|------|------|------|------|
| | | | | | | | Intake | Exhaust | |
| **1988** | 146 (2389) | 61 | 38 | 33 | 102 | ③ | 14 | 15 | 18 |
| | 181 (2960) | 47 | 74 | 33 | 62 | 80 | ① | 15 | 18 |
| **1989** | 146 (2389) | 61 | 38 | 33 | 102 | ③ | 14 | 15 | 18 |
| | 181 (2960) | 47 | 74 | 33 | 62 | 80 | ① | 15 | 18 |
| **1990** | 146 (2389) | 61 | 38 | ② | 116 | ③ | 14 | 15 | 18 |
| | 181 (2960) | 47 | 74 | ② | 98 | 80 | ① | 15 | 18 |
| **1991–92** | 146 (2389) | 61 | 38 | ② | 116 | ③ | 14 | 15 | 18 |
| | 181 (2960) | 47 | 74 | ② | 98 | 80 | ① | 15 | 18 |

① Bolt—12–14
  Nut—17–20
② 10–12 ft. lbs., plus, 60–65 degrees
③ Manual—112
  Automatic—76

## BRAKE SPECIFICATIONS
All measurements in inches unless noted

| Year | Model | Lug Nut Torque (ft. lbs.) | Master Cylinder Bore | Brake Disc | | Standard Brake Drum Diameter | Minimum Lining Thickness | |
|------|------|------|------|------|------|------|------|------|
| | | | | Minimum Thickness | Maximum Runout | | Front | Rear |
| **1988** | Van | 78 | 1.000 | 0.945 | 0.0028 | 10.24 | 0.079 | 0.059 |
| | Pick-Up | 98 | ① | ③ ④ | 0.0028 | ② | 0.079 | 0.059 |
| | Pathfinder | 98 | ① | ③ ④ | 0.0028 | ② | 0.079 | 0.059 |
| **1989** | Pick-Up | 98 | ① | ③ ④ | 0.0028 | ⑤ | 0.079 | 0.059 |
| | Pathfinder | 98 | ① | ③ ④ | 0.0028 | ⑤ | 0.079 | 0.059 |

## BRAKE SPECIFICATIONS

All measurements in inches unless noted

| Year | Model | Lug Nut Torque (ft. lbs.) | Master Cylinder Bore | Brake Disc Minimum Thickness | Brake Disc Maximum Runout | Standard Brake Drum Diameter | Minimum Lining Thickness Front | Rear |
|---|---|---|---|---|---|---|---|---|
| 1990 | Axxess | 78 | 0.938 | 0.787 | 0.0028 | ⑥ | 0.079 | 0.059 |
|  | Pick-Up | 98 | 0.938 | ③ ④ | 0.0028 | ⑦ | 0.079 | 0.059 |
|  | Pathfinder | 98 | 0.938 | ③ ④ | 0.0028 | 10.24 | 0.079 | 0.059 |
| 1991–92 | Pick-Up | 98 | 0.938 | ③ ④ | 0.0028 | ⑦ | 0.079 | 0.059 |
|  | Pathfinder | 98 | 0.938 | ③ ④ | 0.0028 | 10.24 | 0.079 | 0.059 |

① 2WD light duty—LT26B: 0.938 and 1.000 in.
Except 2WD light duty—LT26B: 0.938 in.
② 2WD light duty—LT26B: 10.24 in.
2WD light duty—LT26B: 8.66 in.
③ 2WD with 4 cylinder—CL28VA: 0.787 in.
Except 2WD with 4 cylinder—CL28VD: 0.945 in.

④ Sports package—AD14VB—0.630 in.
⑤ 2WD with 4 cylinder—LT26B—10.24 in.
2WD/4WD heavy duty—DS25B and DS25C—10.00 in.
Sports package—AD14VB—11.26 in.
Sports package—DS19HB—7.48 in.

⑥ 2WD—5 passenger: 9.00 in.
4WD and 2WD—7 passenger: 10.24 in.
⑦ Except 4WD Pick-Up—LT26B: 10.24 in.
4WD Pick-Up—LT30A: 11.61 in.

## WHEEL ALIGNMENT

| Year | Model | Caster Range (deg.) | Caster Preferred Setting (deg.) | Chamber Range (deg.) | Chamber Preferred Setting (deg.) | Toe-in (in.) | Steering Axis Inclination (deg.) |
|---|---|---|---|---|---|---|---|
| 1988 | Van | 3/4P–2 1/4P | 1 1/2P | 1/2N–1P | 1/4P | 0.04 | 9–10 |
|  | Pick-Up 2WD | 1/6N–5/6P | 1/3P | 1/12N–1 1/12P | 11/24P | 0.12 | 9 |
|  | Pick-Up 4WD | 5/16P–1 5/6P | 11/12P | 1/6P–1 1/6P | 2/3P | 0.16 | 8 |
|  | Pathfinder 2WD | 1/6N–5/6P | 1/3P | 1/12N–1 1/12P | 11/24P | 0.12 | 9 |
|  | Pathfinder 4WD | 5/6P–1 5/6P | 11/12P | 1/6P–1 1/6P | 2/3P | 0.16 | 8 |
| 1989 | Pick-Up 2WD | 1/6N–5/6P | 1/3P | 1/12N–1 1/12P | 11/24P | 0.12 | 9 |
|  | Pick-Up 4WD | 5/6P–1 5/6P | 11/12P | 1/6P–1 1/6P | 2/3P | 0.16 | 8 |
|  | Pathfinder | 5/6P–1 5/6P | 11/12P | 1/6P–1 1/6P | 2/3P | 0.16 | 8 |
| 1990 | Axxess 2WD | 1/4N–1 1/4P | 1/2P | 1/3N–1P | 1/3P | 0.08 | 14 |
|  | Axxess 4WD | 1/12N–1 5/12P | 2/3P | 7/12N–1 1/12P | 1/6P | 0.08 | 14 |
|  | Pick-Up 2WD | 1/6N–5/6P | 1/3P | 1/12N–1 1/12P | 11/24P | 0.16 | 9 |
|  | Pick-Up 4WD | 5/6P–1 5/6P | 11/12P | 1/6P–1 1/6P | 2/3P | 0.16 | 8 |
|  | Pathfinder | 5/6P–1 5/6P | 11/12P | 1/6P–1 1/6P | 2/3P | 0.16 | 8 |
| 1991–92 | Pick-Up 2WD | 1/6N–5/6P | 1/3P | 1/12N–1 1/12P | 11/24P | 0.16 | 9 |
|  | Pick-Up 4WD | 5/6P–1 5/6P | 11/12P | 1/6P–1 1/6P | 2/3P | 0.16 | 8 |
|  | Pathfinder | 5/6P–1 5/6P | 11/12P | 1/6P–1 1/6P | 2/3P | 0.16 | 8 |

N—Negative
P—Positive

# ENGINE MECHANICAL

**NOTE: Disconnecting the negative battery cable on some vehicles may interfere with the functions of the on board computer systems and may require the computer to undergo a relearning process when the battery cable is reconnected. This usually requires only a few minutes of driving.**

## Engine

### REMOVAL & INSTALLATION

*Pick-Up and Pathfinder*

On 1990–92 vehicles equipped with the 3.0L engine, the transmission must be removed before removing the engine. If equipped with the 2.4L engine, the engine and transmission are removed together. On vehicles with 4WD, the front torsion bar must be removed to remove the transfer case.

1. Relieve the fuel system pressure.
2. Disconnect the battery cables and remove the battery.
3. Using a scribing tool, mark the location of the hood hinges on the body and remove the hood.
4. Drain the engine oil and the cooling system, including the block drains. Dispose of old fluids properly.
5. Remove the air cleaner. Wrap a shop rag around the fuel filter outlet and disconnect the hose.
6. Raise and safely support the vehicle. If equipped, remove the splash pan from under the engine.
7. To remove the radiator:
    a. Remove the upper and lower radiator hoses.
    b. If equipped with an automatic transmission, disconnect and plug the transmission oil cooler lines from the radiator.
    c. Remove the lower radiator shroud.
    d. Remove the bracket bolts and lift the radiator and shroud out together.
8. If equipped with air conditioning, loosen the belt tension and remove the belt. Disconnect the wiring, remove the compressor and secure it out of the way. Do not disconnect the pressure hoses.
9. If equipped with power steering, remove the drive belt and the power steering pump and secure it out of the way. Do not disconnect the pressure hoses.
10. Label and disconnect all wiring and vacuum hoses.

11. Disconnect the heater hoses from the engine and disconnect the throttle cable.
12. Remove the starter.
13. Matchmark the driveshaft flange at the rear pinion flange and remove the driveshaft. Plug the extension housing opening to prevent the oil from draining out.
14. If equipped with 4WD, matchmark both front driveshaft flanges so the shaft can be installed in the same position. Remove the driveshaft.
15. Disconnect the exhaust pipe from the manifold(s) and from the catalytic converter and remove the pipe.
16. Disconnect the speedometer cable and the wiring from the transmission.
17. If equipped an automatic transmission:
    a. Disconnect the selector lever and throttle cables from the transmission.
    b. Remove the dipstick tube and disconnect the cooler lines.
    c. Remove the torque converter housing dust cover. Matchmark the converter with the driveplate for reassembly; these are balanced together at the factory. Remove the torque converter-to-driveplate (flywheel) bolts. Use a wrench on the crankshaft pulley bolt to rotate the crankshaft to expose the hidden torque converter bolts.
18. On vehicles with a manual transmission:
    a. Remove the shifter knob and boot and remove the snapring to lift the shift lever out of the transmission. Stuff a rag in the opening to keep dirt out of the transmission.
    b. Without disconnecting the hydraulic hose, remove the clutch slave cylinder from the transmission and secure it aside.
19. If equipped with 4WD:
    a. Working under the vehicle, measure and note the length of the threads on the torsion bar adjustment. At the front of the bar, pull the boot back and matchmark the bar to the mounting plate. The spline on the bar must be re-installed in the same position on the plate.
    b. Remove the locknut and adjustment nut from both torsion bars. Remove the 3 nuts at the mounting plate and remove the bars. Mark the bars left and right side for proper installation.
    c. Remove the transfer case shift lever assembly from the transfer case.
    d. If necessary, the transfer case can be removed at this point so the jack will be available to remove the transmission.

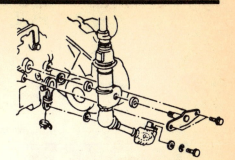
Removing the transfer case shift lever on 4WD Pick-Up and Pathfinder

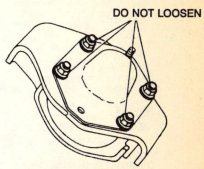
DO NOT LOOSEN
Do not remove these engine mount nuts—Pick-Up and Pathfinder

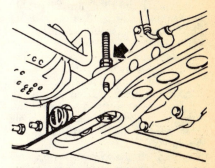
Measure thread length before removing torsion bar on 4WD Pick-Up and Pathfinder

    e. If equipped with a 3.0L engine, remove the gusset securing the engine to the transmission.
20. Using a chain hoist, attach it to the engine and lift the engine slightly to take the weight off the mounts. Using an appropriate transmission jack, properly support the transmission and remove the transmission mount and crossmember.
21. Remove the transmission-to-engine bolts and move the transmission back away from the engine. On automatic transmissions, secure the torque converter so it does not fall out. Lower the transmission from the vehicle.

**NOTE: When removing the engine mounts, do not loosen the 4 mount cover nuts. The mount is fluid filled and will not function properly if the fluid leaks out.**

22. Check to make sure all wires and hoses have been disconnected. Remove the front engine mount bolts and carefully lift the engine out.

**To install:**

23. Carefully guide the engine into place and start the mount bolts. Tighten the bolts temporarily.

24. On manual transmission:

   a. Lightly grease the input shaft splines. On 4WD, apply a silicone sealant to the engine block or rear plate to seal the engine to the transmission.

   b. Fit the transmission into place and start all the engine-to-transmission bolts. Make sure the input shaft fits properly into the clutch disc and pilot bearing.

   c. Torque the 2.36 in. (60mm) and 2.56 in. (65mm) engine-to-transmission bolts to 36 ft. lbs. (49 Nm).

   d. Torque the remaining bolts to 18 ft. lbs. (25 Nm) on the 2.4L cylinder engine, 29 ft. lbs. (39 Nm) on the 3.0L engine.

25. On automatic transmission:

   a. Use a dial indicator to check the driveplate runout while turning the crankshaft. Maximum allowable runout is 0.020 in. (0.5mm); if beyond specifications, replace the driveplate.

   b. Measure and adjust how far the torque converter is recessed into the transmission housing. The distance between the front mounting surface of the transmission and the torque converter-to-driveplate bolt boss should be at least 1.024 in. (26mm).

   c. Install the transmission and torque transmission-to-engine bolts to 36 ft. lbs. (49 Nm). Torque to transmission-to-engine gusset bolts to 29 ft. lbs. (39 Nm).

26. Install the crossmember and torque the crossmember-to-chassis bolts to 38 ft. lbs. (52 Nm) on 2WD or 31 ft. lbs. (42 Nm) on 4WD.

27. Install the rear transmission mount bolts, loosen the engine mount bolts, then torque all the mount bolts to 31 ft. lbs. (42 Nm), starting at the rear.

28. On automatic transmission, align the matchmarks on the driveplate and torque converter, install the bolts and torque to 36 ft. lbs. (49 Nm). Turn the crankshaft after tightening the bolts to make sure there is no binding at the driveplate.

29. If the torsion bars were removed, install them in their original location. Make sure the splines are in their original position and set the adjustment to its original position.

30. If the transfer case was removed, apply silicone sealant to seal the case to the transmission. Install the trans-

fer case and torque the bolts to 30 ft. lbs. (41 Nm). Install the shift lever.

31. When installing the driveshafts, be sure to align the matchmarks. Torque the bolts on the front driveshaft (4WD) to 33 ft. lbs. (44 Nm). On single piece rear driveshafts, torque the bolts to 65 ft. lbs. (88 Nm). On 2 piece driveshafts, torque the bolts to 33 ft. lbs. (44 Nm). Torque the center bearing bracket bolts to 16 ft. lbs. (22 Nm).

32. When installing the exhaust system, use new gaskets and torque the flange bolts to 27 ft. lbs. (36 Nm).

33. Install the remaining components in order of removal and connect the wiring and hoses.

## Van

The engine and transmission are removed together from under the vehicle. The crossmember under the engine and the suspension leading link attached to it must also be removed.

1. Locate and remove the fuel pump fuse. Run the engine until it stalls, then disconnect the battery cables.

2. Wrap a rag around the fuel filter outlet and remove the hose.

3. Drain the engine oil and the cooling system, including the block drains. Dispose of old fluids properly.

4. Remove the air cleaner duct and place a clean rag in the throttle body to prevent dirt from entering the engine. Remove the distributor cap and spark plug wires as an assembly. Remove the rotor.

5. Disconnect the cooling system hoses from the engine. If equipped with an automatic transmission, disconnect and plug the transmission oil cooler lines from the radiator.

6. If equipped with air conditioning, loosen the belt tension and remove the belt. Disconnect the wiring, remove the compressor and secure it out of the way. Do not disconnect the pressure hoses.

7. If equipped with power steering, remove the drive belt and the power steering pump and secure it out of the way. Do not disconnect the pressure hoses.

8. Label and disconnect all wiring and vacuum hoses that can be reached from above. Disconnect the accelerator cable.

9. Raise and safely support the vehicle.

10. Disconnect the speedometer cable and all wiring from the transmission. To disconnect the transmission shift linkage without disturbing the adjustments, remove the pin clips and slide the levers off the shafts. Remove the cables and the mounting bracket from the transmission.

11. Matchmark the driveshaft to the

differential flange and remove the driveshaft. Plug the transmission opening to prevent oil leakage.

12. Without disconnecting the hydraulic line, remove the clutch release cylinder from the transmission and secure it out of the way.

13. Disconnect the exhaust pipe from the manifold and remove the pipe from the catalytic converter.

14. Remove the leading links that connect the front suspension to the crossmember. The rubber bushings are mounted on the link and are not interchangable, identify them for reassembly.

15. Check to make sure all wiring, cables and hoses are disconnected. Support the engine and transmission with a jack and remove the rear transmission mount.

16. Remove the crossmember bolts and lower the engine and transmission from the vehicle.

17. If equipped with an automatic transmission, matchmark the torque converter to the driveplate and remove the torque converter-to-driveplate bolts. Push the torque converter back so it does not fall out.

18. Separate the engine and transmission and install the engine on a work stand to remove the crossmember and mounts.

**To install:**

19. If equipped with a manual transmission, lightly grease the input shaft spline before joining the engine and transmission. Torque the long bolts to 36 ft. lbs. (49 Nm) and the short bolts to 29 ft. lbs. (39 Nm).

20. If equipped with an automatic transmission:

   a. Use a dial indicator to check the driveplate runout while turning the crankshaft. Maximum allowable runout is 0.020 in. (0.5mm); if beyond specifications, replace the driveplate.

   b. Measure and adjust how far the torque converter is recessed into the transmission housing. The distance between the front mounting surface of the transmission and the torque converter-to-driveplate bolt boss should be at least 1.380 in. (35mm).

   c. Join the engine and transmission and torque the long bolts to 36 ft. lbs. (49 Nm), the short bolts to 24 ft. lbs. (32 Nm).

   d. Align the matchmarks on the torque converter and driveplate and install the bolts. Torque the bolts to 36 ft. lbs. (49 Nm). Turn the crankshaft to make sure there is no binding at the driveplate.

21. Raise the engine and transmission into place and start all the mounting bolts. If the front mount fasteners are already tight, loosen them and

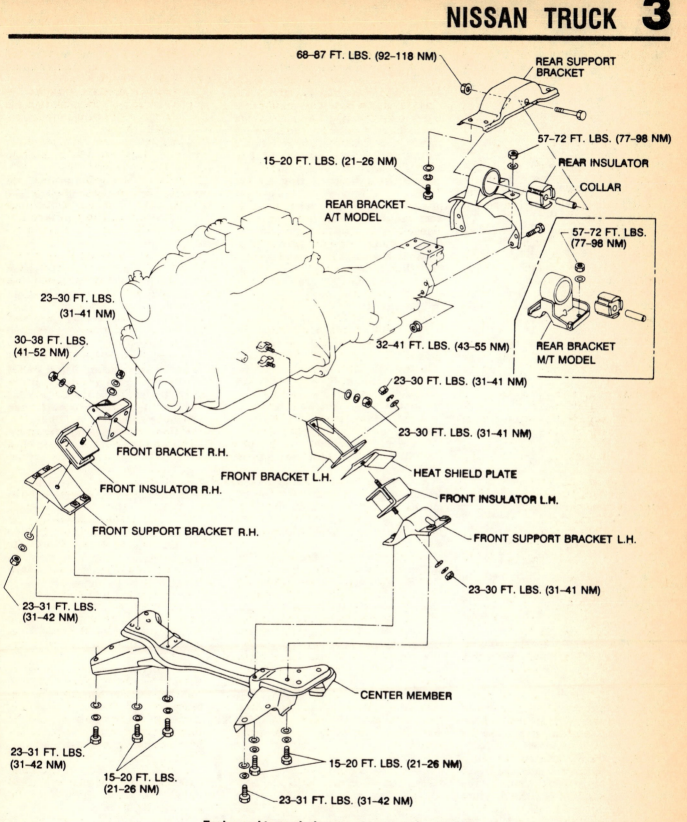

68–87 FT. LBS. (92–118 NM)

REAR SUPPORT BRACKET

57–72 FT. LBS. (77–98 NM)

15–20 FT. LBS. (21–26 NM)

REAR INSULATOR

COLLAR

REAR BRACKET A/T MODEL

57–72 FT. LBS. (77–98 NM)

23–30 FT. LBS. (31–41 NM)

30–38 FT. LBS. (41–52 NM)

32–41 FT. LBS. (43–55 NM)

REAR BRACKET M/T MODEL

23–30 FT. LBS. (31–41 NM)

23–30 FT. LBS. (31–41 NM)

FRONT BRACKET R.H.

FRONT BRACKET L.H.

HEAT SHIELD PLATE

FRONT INSULATOR R.H.

FRONT INSULATOR L.H.

FRONT SUPPORT BRACKET R.H.

FRONT SUPPORT BRACKET L.H.

23–30 FT. LBS. (31–41 NM)

23–31 FT. LBS. (31–42 NM)

CENTER MEMBER

23–31 FT. LBS. (31–42 NM)

15–20 FT. LBS. (21–26 NM)

15–20 FT. LBS. (21–26 NM)

23–31 FT. LBS. (31–42 NM)

**Engine and transmission mount torque values on Van**

torque the rear mount bolts, then the crossmember bolts, then the front mount bolts.

22. Install the front suspension links and torque the bolts and the nut to 30 ft. lbs. (40 Nm).

23. Install the driveshaft with the matchmarks aligned and torque the bolts to 33 ft. lbs. (44 Nm).

24. Use new gaskets to install the exhaust pipe and torque the bolts to 25 ft. lbs. (34 Nm).

25. Connect the shifter cables and wiring to the transmission. On auto-matic transmissions, install the dipstick tube and connect the cooling system lines. On manual transmissions, install the clutch release cylinder.

26. Install the remaining components and connect the wiring, hoses and control cables.

## Axxess

The engine and transaxle are lowered as a unit from the vehicle but the unit must be supported from above to remove the mount member. On 4WD models, the front crossmember bar must be removed. On all models, the halfshafts must be removed. The torque on the front axle nut is very high and an assistant is required to hold the brake pedal when tightening or loosening it.

1. Locate and remove the fuel pump fuse. Run the engine until it stalls, then disconnect the battery cables.

2. Wrap a rag around the fuel filter outlet and remove the hose.

3. Drain the engine oil and the cooling system, including the block drains. Dispose of old fluids properly.

4. Remove the air duct, the battery and the air cleaner and air flow meter assembly.

5. Disconnect the cooling system hoses from the engine. If equipped with an automatic transaxle, disconnect and plug the transaxle oil cooler lines from the radiator.

6. If equipped with air conditioning, loosen the belt tension and remove the belt. Disconnect the wiring, remove the compressor and secure it out of the way. Do not disconnect the pressure hoses.

7. If equipped with automatic transaxle, disconnect the transaxle-throttle control cable from the throttle. The nut towards the cable end is the locknut; mark the position of the adjusting nut and loosen the locknut to disconnect the cable. Disconnect the shifter cable from the transaxle.

8. Label and disconnect all wiring and vacuum hoses. Disconnect the accelerator cable.

9. Disconnect the speedometer cable and all wiring from the transaxle. If equipped with a manual transaxle, remove the clutch release cylinder without disconnecting the hydraulic line and secure it out of the way.

10. Raise and safely support the vehicle. Disconnect the manual transaxle shift linkage and the support rod.

11. If equipped with power steering, remove the drive belt and the power steering pump and secure it out of the way. Do not disconnect the pressure hoses.

12. Disconnect the exhaust pipe from the manifold and remove the pipe from the catalytic converter.

13. On 4WD models, matchmark the drive flanges and disconnect the driveshaft from the transfer case. If it is decided that the driveshaft is in the way of engine removal, matchmark the rear flange and remove the entire driveshaft. Do not disassemble the driveshaft and protect the CV-joint boot when moving the driveshaft.

14. Make sure the vehicle is securely supported and have an assistant hold the brake pedal. Remove the front axle cotter pin, adjusting cap and washer and loosen the axle nut. The torque is very high; if possible, loosen and tighten this nut with the wheels installed and the vehicle on the ground.

15. Without disconnecting the hydraulic hose, remove the brake calipers and hang them from the body. Do not let the caliper hang by the hose. Be sure to remove the caliper, pads and carrier as an assembly. Do not remove the sliding pin bolts.

16. Disconnect the tie rod end from the steering knuckle. Turn the knuckle all the way out at the front and use a soft hammer to tap the axle out of the hub.

17. Carefully pry the right inner CV-joint from the transaxle or transfer case.

18. On 2WD with automatic transaxle, insert a thin drift pin through the right side of differential and tap the left inner CV-joint out. Be careful not to damage the mate pinion shaft or side gear inside the differential.

19. On all other models, pry the left CV-joint out the same way as the right.

20. Carefully support the engine and transaxle from above and remove the mount member from 2WD or crossmember from 4WD.

21. Support the engine and transaxle with floor jacks, remove the remaining mounts and lower the unit out of the vehicle. Remove the starter.

22. Before removing the automatic transaxle from the engine, matchmark the torque converter to the driveplate for re-assembly and remove the torque converter–to–driveplate bolts. When separating the engine and transaxle, be careful that the torque converter does not fall out.

**To install:**

23. If equipped with a manual transaxle, lightly grease the input shaft spline before joining the engine and transaxle. Torque the long bolts (1¾ in. or longer) to 36 ft. lbs. (49 Nm) and the short bolts (1½ or shorter) to 30 ft. lbs. (40 Nm).

24. If equipped with an automatic transaxle:

a. Use a dial indicator to check the driveplate runout while turning the crankshaft. Maximum allowable runout is 0.020 in. (0.5mm); if beyond specifications, replace the driveplate.

b. Measure and adjust how far the torque converter is recessed into the transaxle housing. The distance between the front mounting surface of the transaxle and the torque converter–to–driveplate bolt boss should be at least ¾ in. (19mm).

c. Join the engine and transaxle and torque the bolts to 33 ft. lbs. (44 Nm).

d. Align the matchmarks on the torque converter and driveplate and install the bolts. Torque the bolts to 43 ft. lbs. (59 Nm). Turn the crankshaft to make sure there is no binding at the driveplate.

25. Install the engine and transaxle and start all the mount bolts. When all the mounts and support members are in place, torque the bolts as shown.

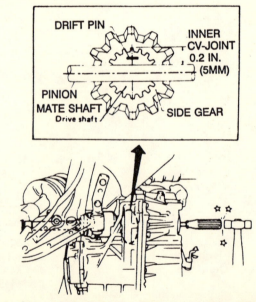

**When inserting a tool to push the left inner CV-joint out of the differential, be careful not to damage the pinion mate shaft or side gear—Axxess with 2WD and automatic transaxle**

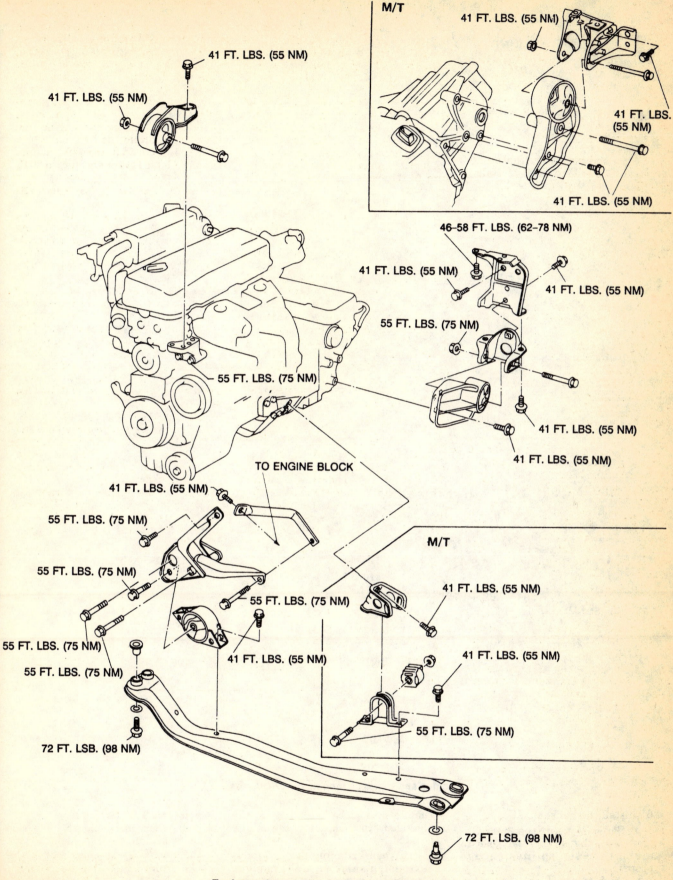

**M/T**

41 FT. LBS. (55 NM)

41 FT. LBS. (55 NM)

41 FT. LBS. (55 NM)

41 FT. LBS. (55 NM)

41 FT. LBS. (55 NM)

41 FT. LBS. (55 NM)

46–58 FT. LBS. (62–78 NM)

41 FT. LBS. (55 NM)

41 FT. LBS. (55 NM)

55 FT. LBS. (75 NM)

41 FT. LBS. (55 NM)

41 FT. LBS. (55 NM)

55 FT. LBS. (75 NM)

TO ENGINE BLOCK

41 FT. LBS. (55 NM)

55 FT. LBS. (75 NM)

55 FT. LBS. (75 NM)

55 FT. LBS. (75 NM)

55 FT. LBS. (75 NM)

55 FT. LBS. (75 NM)

41 FT. LBS. (55 NM)

72 FT. LSB. (98 NM)

**M/T**

41 FT. LBS. (55 NM)

41 FT. LBS. (55 NM)

55 FT. LBS. (75 NM)

72 FT. LSB. (98 NM)

**Engine and transaxle mounts on 2WD Axxess**

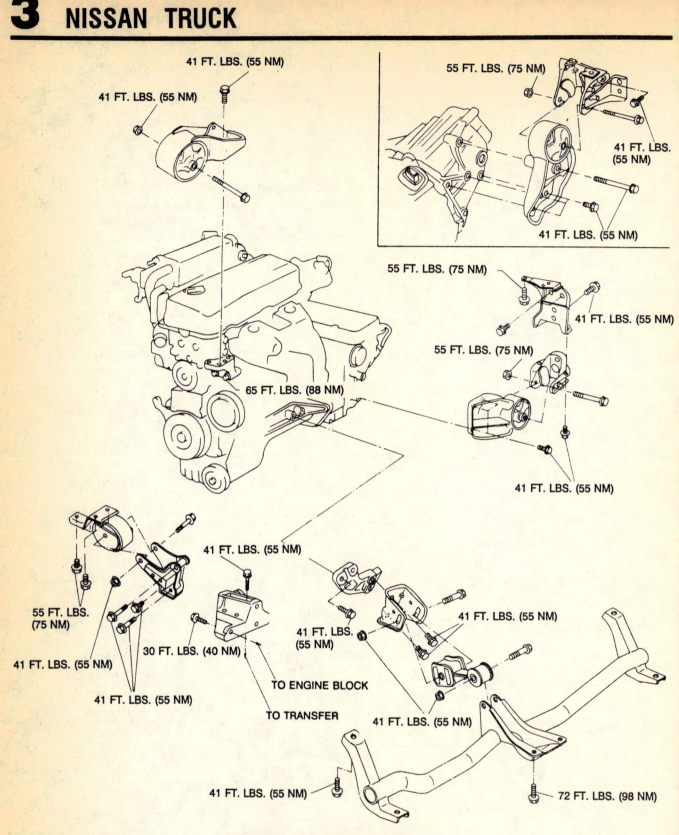

41 FT. LBS. (55 NM)

41 FT. LBS. (55 NM)

55 FT. LBS. (75 NM)

41 FT. LBS. (55 NM)

41 FT. LBS. (55 NM)

55 FT. LBS. (75 NM)

41 FT. LBS. (55 NM)

65 FT. LBS. (88 NM)

55 FT. LBS. (75 NM)

41 FT. LBS. (55 NM)

41 FT. LBS. (55 NM)

55 FT. LBS. (75 NM)

41 FT. LBS. (55 NM)

30 FT. LBS. (40 NM)

41 FT. LBS. (55 NM)

41 FT. LBS. (55 NM)

41 FT. LBS. (55 NM)

TO ENGINE BLOCK

TO TRANSFER

41 FT. LBS. (55 NM)

41 FT. LBS. (55 NM)

41 FT. LBS. (55 NM)

72 FT. LBS. (98 NM)

**Engine and transaxle mounts on 4WD Axxess**

26. Install the halfshafts:

a. Carefully insert the inner CV-joint into the differential gear to make sure the splines engage properly.

b. Push the shaft in to click the circlip into place. Pull out on the halfshaft to make sure the clip is seated.

c. When installing the right side extension shaft on 2WD models, torque the support bearing bracket bolts to 26 ft. lbs. (35 Nm).

d. When installing the left side halfshaft on 4WD models, torque the inner CV-joint bolts to 36 ft. lbs. (45 Nm).

e. Make sure the outer axle

splines are clean and insert the axle into the hub. Connect the tie rod end to the steering knuckle and torque the nut to 29 ft. lbs. (39 Nm) and tighten as required to install a new cotter pin.

    f. Install the washer and nut onto the axle but do not torque the nut yet.

27. Install the brake calipers and torque the carrier bolts to 72 ft. lbs. (97 Nm).

28. On 4WD models, connect the driveshaft and torque the bolts to 33 ft. lbs. (44 Nm). If the driveshaft was removed, torque the center bearing support bolts to 30 ft. lbs. (41 Nm).

29. When installing the exhaust pipe, use new gaskets and torque the manifold flange nuts to 37 ft. lbs. (50 Nm), the catalytic converter flange bolts to 31 ft. lbs. (42 Nm).

30. Complete the installation of the remaining components. When the vehicle is resting on at least 3 wheels, have an assistant hold the brake pedal and torque the front axle nuts to 231 ft. lbs. (314 Nm). Install the adjusting cap and an new cotter pin.

## Cylinder Head

### REMOVAL & INSTALLATION

#### 2.4L Engine

1. Relieve the fuel system pressure. Disconnect the negative battery cable.
2. Remove the air cleaner. Disconnect the accelerator cable from the throttle body.
3. Drain the engine coolant, including the block drain.
4. Label and disconnect all wiring and hoses as required.
5. Remove the intake and exhaust manifolds.
6. Remove the steering pump, alternator and/or air conditioner compressor as required and remove the brackets as required. When removing the steering pump or air conditioner compressor, disconnect the drive belt, remove the unit pump and move it aside; do not disconnect the pressure hoses.
7. Remove the distributor cap and rotor and disconnect the wires from the spark plugs.
8. Remove the valve cover.
9. Rotate the crankshaft until the No. 1 cylinder is on the TDC of its compression stroke. Make sure the TDC mark on the crankshaft pulley is aligned with the pointer. The silver link on the timing chain should be aligned with the mark on the camshaft sprocket and the knock pin on the camshaft will be at the top.
10. To remove the camshaft sprocket:

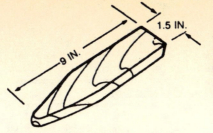

**Make a wooded wedge to support the timing chain when removing 2.4L engine cylinder head**

**Remove the camshaft sprocket with chain attached—2.4L engine**

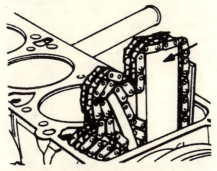

**Support the chain with the wedge to keep it engaged with the crankshaft sprocket**

    a. Fabricate a wooden wedge tool to hold the timing chain in place.

    b. Remove the camshaft sprocket bolt and the camshaft sprocket. Hold the sprocket up to keep tension on the chain.

    c. Install the wedge tool and rest the chain on the tool with the driver's side of the chain pulled snug against the crankshaft sprocket. If the chain falls off the crankshaft sprocket or if the crankshaft is turned, the front cover must be removed to properly set the valve timing.

11. Remove the cylinder head-to-timing chain cover bolts.
12. Carefully loosen the cylinder head bolts one turn at a time in the reverse order of the tightening sequence. When all bolts are loose, remove the bolts and remove the cylinder head.

**To install:**

13. Throughly clean all gasket sur-

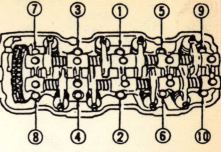

**Cylinder head bolt torque sequence— 1988–89 2.4L engine**

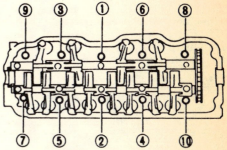

**Cylinder head bolt torque sequence— 1990–92 2.4L engine**

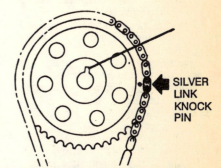

**To install the camshaft sprocket, the knock pin will be at the top and the silver link will align with the mark**

faces and inspect the head and block for damage to the surfaces. Before installing, check the cylinder head for warping. The limit is 0.006 in. (0.15mm). Make sure the threads on the bolts and in the block are clean and that the bolts turn easily in the threads. Do not oil the threads.

14. Make sure the camshaft knock pin is at the top; both valves for No. 1 cylinder will be closed.

15. Install the new gasket and carefully install the cylinder head. Torque the cylinder head bolts in the sequence shown in 5 steps:

    Step 1—22 ft. lbs. (29 Nm)
    Step 2—58 ft. lbs. (78 Nm)
    Step 3—loosen all bolts
    Step 4—22 ft. lbs. (29 Nm)
    Step 5—54–61 ft. lbs. (74–83 Nm)

16. Correctly position the camshaft sprocket into the timing chain with

the silver link aligned with the mark on the sprocket. Install the sprocket onto the camshaft, install the sprocket bolt but do not fully torque it yet.

17. Carefully turn the crankshaft 2 full turns and make sure the timing marks still line up. If not, remove the camshaft sprocket and try again. Torque the sprocket bolt to 87–116 ft. lbs. (118–157 Nm).

18. Adjust the valves.

19. Use a silicone sealer when installing the rubber covers at each end of the camshaft. Install the valve cover with a new gasket and torque the bolts in a circular pattern to 7 ft. lbs. (10 Nm). Loosen all the bolts and torque them again in the same pattern.

20. Complete the installation of the remaining components. Change the oil before running the engine.

### 3.0L Engine

1. Relieve the fuel system pressure. Disconnect the negative battery cable.

2. Remove the air cleaner. Disconnect the accelerator cable from the throttle body.

3. Drain the engine coolant, including the block drain.

4. Label and disconnect all wiring and hoses as required.

5. Disconnect the exhaust pipes and on 1988–89 models, remove the exhaust manifolds.

6. Remove the distributor and spark plug wires as an assembly.

7. Remove the timing belt covers and the timing belt.

8. On 1988–89 models with throttle body fuel injection:

   a. Disconnect the wiring and the hoses from the throttle body.

   b. Carefully loosen the intake manifold bolts 1 turn at a time in the reverse order of the torque sequence. This is important to prevent warping the manifold.

   c. Remove the bolts and lift the manifold off.

9. On 1990–92 models with multipoint fuel injection:

   a. Remove the upper intake manifold section (5 bolts).

   b. Label and disconnect the wiring to the fuel injectors and disconnect the fuel supply and return hoses.

   c. Remove the injectors and rail as an assembly. Place the assembly where it will stay clean.

   d. Loosen the intake manifold bolts 1 turn at a time in the reverse order of the torque sequence. This is important to prevent warping the manifold.

   e. Remove the bolts and lift the manifold off.

10. Mark the camshaft sprockets left and right for proper installation and remove them.

11. Remove the rear timing belt cover.

12. Without disconnecting the hydraulic or coolant hoses, remove the power steering pump and the air conditioner compressor and secure them out of the way. Remove the brackets from the cylinder heads.

13. Remove the rocker arm covers.

**NOTE: It may be necessary to remove the rocker shafts and valve lifter guide to provide access to the cylinder head bolts. Before removing the valve lifter guide, secure the valve lifters with a safety wire to keep them in their original positions.**

14. To prevent warping the heads, loosen the cylinder head bolts 1 turn at a time in the reverse order of the torque sequence. When they are all loose, remove the bolts and lift the heads off the engine.

**To install:**

15. Throughly clean all gasket surfaces and inspect the head and block for damage to the surfaces. Before installing, check the cylinder head for warping. The limit is 0.004 in. (0.10mm). Make sure the threads on the bolts and in the block are clean and that the bolts turn easily in the threads. Do not oil the threads.

16. Set the crankshaft to TDC on No. 1 cylinder and make sure the mark on the sprocket aligns with the mark on the oil pump body. Make sure the knock pin on the camshaft is at the top.

17. On 1990–92 models, use new gaskets and install the exhaust manifolds. Torque the nuts or bolts in the proper sequence to 16 ft. lbs. (22 Nm).

18. Apply sealant to the block cooling system drain plugs and install the plugs.

19. Make sure the new head gaskets are properly fitted and install the cylinder heads. When installing the bolts, the long bolts go into positions 4, 5, 12 and 13; the flat side of the washer goes towards the head.

20. Torque the cylinder head bolts in the proper sequence in five steps:

   Step 1—22 ft. lbs. (30 Nm)
   Step 2—43 ft. lbs. (58 Nm)
   Step 3—loosen all bolts
   Step 4—22 ft. lbs. (30 Nm)
   Step 5—40–47 ft. lbs. (54–64 Nm)

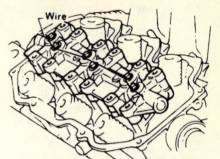

Secure the lifters with wire before removing the guide assembly—3.0L engine

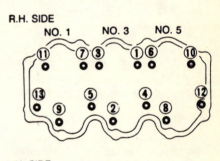

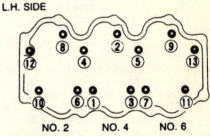

Cylinder head bolt torque sequence—3.0L engine

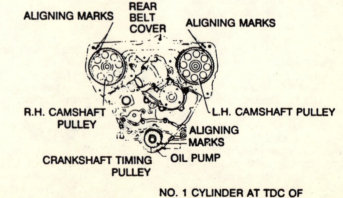

NO. 1 CYLINDER AT TDC OF COMPRESSION STROKE

**View of the camshaft sprocket timing marks—3.0L engine**

or;
Step 5 alternate—22 ft. lbs. (30 Nm) plus 65 degrees

21. If the lifter guide and rocker arms were removed, install them now and tighten the bolts 1 turn at a time to draw the shafts down evenly against the valve springs without bending the shafts. Torque the bolts to 16 ft. lbs. (22 Nm).

22. Install the rocker arm covers and torque the bolts to 25 inch lbs. (3 Nm).

23. Install the rear timing belt cover and the camshaft sprockets. Make sure the sprockets are on the correct side and torque the sprocket bolts to 65 ft. lbs. (88 Nm).

24. Make sure the crankshaft and camshafts are properly positioned to install the timing belt. Be careful if it is necessary to turn either shaft; this is not a free wheeling engine and the valves will contact the pistons if the crankshaft is turned without the timing belt in place.

25. Install the timing belt, set the tension and turn the crankshaft 2 full turns to make sure the timing marks still align properly.

26. Use a new gasket to install the intake manifold and torque the nuts bolts in the proper sequence in 3 steps. Torque the nuts to 20 ft. lbs. (27 Nm) and the bolts to 14 ft. lbs. (20 Nm).

27. On 1988–89 models, use new gaskets and install the exhaust manifolds; torque the manifold nuts to 16 ft. lbs. (22 Nm).

28. Connect the exhaust pipes to the manifolds and torque the bolts to 20 ft. lbs. (27 Nm).

29. Install the remaining components using new gaskets, O-rings or seals as required. Adjust belt tensions and change the oil before starting the engine.

30. When the engine is first started, the hydraulic valve lifters may be noisy. Run the engine for 10–20 minutes at about 1000 rpm. If the noise has not subsided, the lifter will probably never pump up and must be replaced.

## Valve Lash

### ARRANGEMENT

#### 2.4L Engine
I–E–E–I–I–E–E–I (front-to-rear)

#### 3.0L Engine
**RIGHT SIDE**
E–I–E–I–E–I (front-to-rear)

**LEFT SIDE**
I–E–I–E–I–E (front-to-rear)

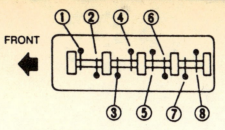

**FRONT**

Valve numbers for adjustment—1988 2.4L engine

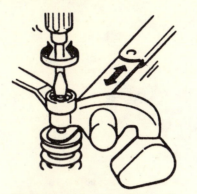

Check the clearance between the valve stem and the adjuster screw—1988 2.4L engine

## ADJUSTMENT

### 1988 2.4L Engine

**NOTE: Adjustment can be made with the engine hot or cold.**

1. Disconnect the negative battery cable. Remove the valve cover.

2. Using a socket wrench on the crankshaft pulley bolt, rotate the crankshaft until the No. 1 cylinder is on the TDC of the compression stroke. Both camshaft lobes on No. 1 will be down.

3. Check and/or adjust valves 1, 2, 4 and 6. Loosen the locknut, adjust the valve and tighten the locknut to 16 ft. lbs. (22 Nm). Check the clearance again after tightening the locknut.

4. Rotate the crankshaft 180 degrees to position the No. 4 cylinder on the TDC of its compression stroke. Both camshaft lobes will be pointed down.

5. Adjust valves 3, 5, 7 and 8 and check again with the locknut tightened.

6. Clean the gasket mounting surfaces and install the rocker arm cover with a new gasket.
Intake valve clearance: 0.008 in. (0.21mm) cold or 0.012 in. (0.30mm) hot.
Exhaust valve clearance: 0.009 in. (0.23mm) cold or 0.012 in. (0.30mm) hot.

## Rocker Arms and Valve Lifters

### REMOVAL & INSTALLATION

#### 2.4L Engine
On 1989–92 models, the hydraulic lifters are built into the rocker arms. Do not allow the arms to lay on their side or they will become air bound. Keep the rocker arms upright or lay them in a pan of new engine oil. On all models, the same bolts that hold the rocker arm assembly also hold the camshaft bearing caps. To avoid damage to the bearing surfaces, the camshaft sprocket must be removed.

1. Relieve the fuel system pressure and disconnect the negative battery cable.

2. Remove the rocker arm cover and turn the crankshaft to align the timing marks at TDC on No. 1 cylinder.

3. Use a wire tie or wire to secure the timing chain to the camshaft sprocket.

4. Hold the camshaft sprocket to loosen the bolt and remove the sprocket. Secure the sprocket so the chain

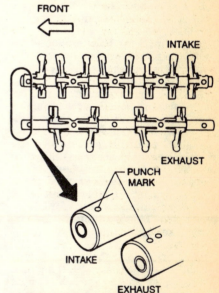

**FRONT**

**INTAKE**

**EXHAUST**

**PUNCH MARK**

**INTAKE**

**EXHAUST**

Make sure the rocker arm shafts are returned to their correct position—2.4L engine with hydraulic adjusters shown

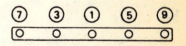

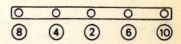

Rocker arm shaft tightening sequence—2.4L engine

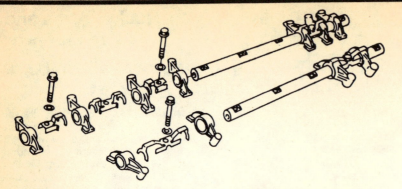

**Rocker arm assembly on 2.4L engine with hydraulic lash adjusters**

**Rocker arm assembly on 2.4L engine with manual lash adjusters**

does not fall off the crankshaft sprocket.

5. Loosen each rocker shaft bolt 1 turn at a time to prevent bending the shafts.

6. When all the bolts are loose, remove the rocker arm shafts with the bolts still in the shafts. This will hold the assembly together.

7. If the rocker arms are to be removed from the shafts, mark them so they can be returned into their original position. Remove the bolts from the shaft assembly and remove the parts. Keep the rocker arms upright or lay them in a pan of new engine oil. Note the punch marks on the front of each shaft that tell which shaft is for the intake side and which is for the exhaust side. This is important for correct rocker arm oiling.

**To install:**

8. Lubricate the shafts with engine oil and assemble them with the punch marks facing up. Use the bolts to hold the assembly together. Make sure the camshaft and the bearing surfaces are in good condition and lubricate with engine oil. Make sure the pin on the camshaft sprocket end is up.

9. Install the rocker arm shafts and tighten the bolts in the proper sequence 1 turn at a time to draw the shafts down evenly against the valve springs without bending the shafts. Torque the bolts to 16 ft. lbs. (22 Nm).

10. Install the camshaft sprocket and remove the tie securing the chain. Install the sprocket bolt but don't torque it yet. Rotate the crankshaft 2 full turns to make sure the timing marks line up. When the valve timing is cor-

rect, torque the sprocket bolt to 116 ft. lbs. (157 Nm).

11. If required, adjust the valves.

12. Use a silicone sealer on the rubber end plugs and install the rocker arm cover with a new gasket. Torque the bolts to 7 ft. lbs. (10 Nm) in a crisscross pattern starting at the middle. Install the remaining components.

13. When the engine is first started, the hydraulic valve lifters may be noisy. Run the engine for 10–20 minutes at about 1000 rpm. If the noise has not subsided, the lifter will probably never pump up and must be replaced.

### 3.0L Engine

1. Relieve the fuel system pressure and disconnect the negative battery cable.

2. Remove the rocker arm covers.

3. Turn the crankshaft to align the timing marks at TDC on No. 1 cylinder. Remove the distributor cap and matchmark the position of the rotor to the distributor body and to the engine. Remove the distributor.

4. Loosen each rocker shaft bolt 1 turn at a time to prevent bending the shafts.

5. When all the bolts are loose, remove the rocker arm shafts with the bolts still in the shafts. This will hold the assembly together.

6. If the lifters are to be removed:

a. Secure the valve lifters in the guide assembly with safety wire to keep them in their original positions, then remove the entire assembly.

b. Before removing a lifter from the guide assembly, tag the lifters to make sure they are returned to their original position. Do not disassemble a lifter.

c. Keep the lifters upright to prevent air from getting in or lay them down in a pan of new engine oil.

d. Check the lifter for signs of wear or damage. Measure the outside diameter of the lifter and the inside diameter of the bore it came from. The clearance should be 0.0017–0.0026 in. (0.043–0.066mm).

7. If the rocker arms are to be removed from the shafts, mark them so they can be returned into their original position. Remove the bolts from the shaft assembly and remove the rockers. Tag each shaft to tell which shaft is for the intake side and which is for the exhaust side. This is important for correct rocker arm oiling.

**To install:**

8. Lubricate the shafts with new engine oil and install the rockers in their original positions. Lubricate the lifters and install them into their original positions. Wire the lifters into the guide assembly.

9. Make sure the engine is at TDC on No. 1 cylinder. Install the left bank lifter guide assembly, remove the safety wire and install the rocker arm shafts. Tighten the bolts 1 turn at a time to draw the shafts down evenly. Torque the bolts to 16 ft. lbs. (22 Nm).

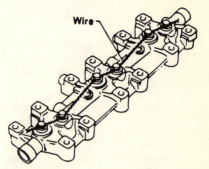

**Hold the lifters in place with wire before removing the guide assembly— 3.0L engine**

ROCKER SHAFT DIRECTION

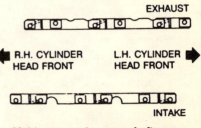

**Make sure rocker arm shafts are installed in their original position— 3.0L engine**

10. Rotate the crankshaft to bring cylinder No. 4 to TDC. Set the right bank lifter guide assembly into place, remove the safety wire and install the rocker arm shafts. Tighten the bolts 1 turn at a time to 16 ft. lbs. (22 Nm).

11. Use new gaskets to install the rocker arm covers and torque the bolts to 24 inch lbs. (3 Nm). Install the remaining components.

12. When the engine is first started, the hydraulic valve lifters may be noisy. Run the engine for 10–20 minutes at about 1000 rpm. If the noise has not subsided, the lifter will probably never pump up and must be replaced.

## Intake Manifold

### REMOVAL & INSTALLATION

#### 2.4L Engine

##### EXCEPT 1990 AXXESS

1. Release the fuel pressure. Disconnect the negative battery cable.

2. Remove the air cleaner assembly together with all of the attending hoses. Remove the EGR tube.

3. Label and disconnect all wiring and hoses as required.

4. Drain the engine coolant to a level below the thermostat housing, then, disconnect the upper coolant hose from the thermostat housing.

5. Disconnect the throttle linkage from the throttle body. The throttle body and/or fuel injectors can be removed from the manifold at this point or the entire assembly can be removed.

6. Remove the manifold bracket, if equipped, and remove the bolts and the intake manifold.

**To install:**

7. Clean the gasket mounting surfaces and use new gaskets. Install the manifold and tighten the bolts in 2 steps working from the center out. Torque the bolts to 15 ft. lbs. (21 Nm).

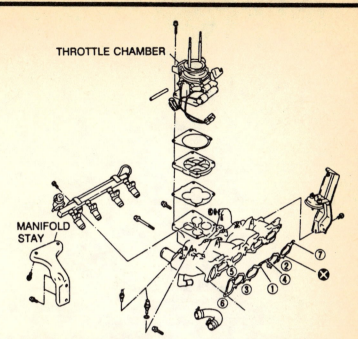

THROTTLE CHAMBER

MANIFOLD STAY

**Intake manifold assembly on 1990–92 2.4L engine except Axxess**

8. If it was removed, install the throttle body with a new gasket and torque the nuts to 13 ft. lbs. (18 Nm). Use new O-rings to install the injectors.

9. Install the remaining components and connect the wiring and hoses. Fill the cooling system and run the engine to check ignition timing and idle speed.

##### 1990 AXXESS

1. Release the fuel pressure. Disconnect the negative battery cable.

2. Remove the air duct from the throttle body. Remove the EGR tube.

3. Label and disconnect the electrical wiring and hoses as required.

4. Drain the engine coolant to a level below the thermostat housing, then, disconnect the upper coolant hose from the thermostat housing.

5. Disconnect the throttle linkage

and vacuum lines from the throttle body.

6. Remove the throttle body-to-intake manifold collector bolts and the throttle body.

7. Remove the intake manifold stays.

8. Remove the intake manifold collector-to-intake manifold, the collector and the gasket.

9. Remove the intake manifold-to-engine bolts and the intake manifold.

10. Clean the gasket mounting surfaces and install new gaskets.

11. Install the manifold and torque the bolts in 2 steps, working from the center out, to 15 ft. lbs. (21 Nm).

12. Install the collector with a new gasket and torque the bolts in 2 steps to 15 ft. lbs. (21 Nm).

13. If the fuel injectors were removed, use new O-rings and gaskets to install them.

14. Install the remaining components and connect the wiring and hoses. Fill the cooling system and run the engine to check ignition timing and idle speed.

#### 3.0L Engine

##### 1988–89

1. Relieve the fuel system pressure and disconnect the negative battery cable.

2. Drain the cooling system to a level below the intake manifold.

3. Remove the air cleaner. Disconnect the accelerator linkage from the throttle body.

4. Remove the upper radiator hose from the water outlet housing and the exhaust tube from the EGR valve. If

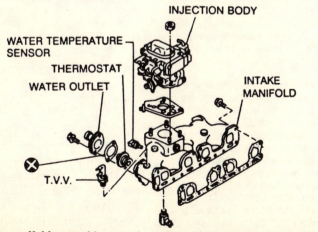

INJECTION BODY

WATER TEMPERATURE SENSOR

THERMOSTAT

WATER OUTLET

INTAKE MANIFOLD

T.V.V.

**Intake manifold assembly on 2.4L engine with throttle body injection**

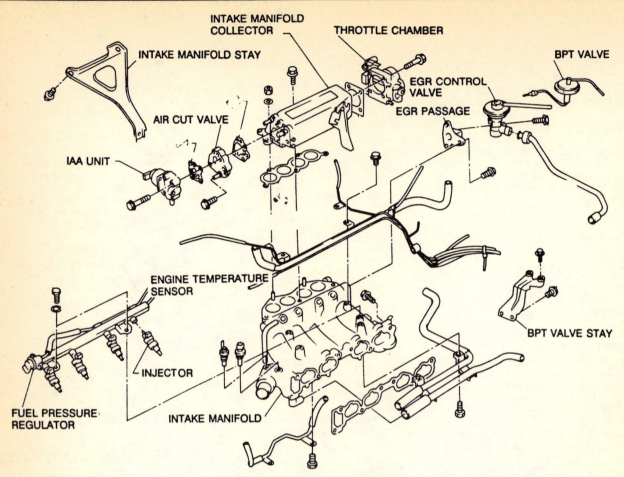

INTAKE MANIFOLD COLLECTOR

THROTTLE CHAMBER

INTAKE MANIFOLD STAY

BPT VALVE

EGR CONTROL VALVE

AIR CUT VALVE

EGR PASSAGE

IAA UNIT

ENGINE TEMPERATURE SENSOR

BPT VALVE STAY

FUEL PRESSURE REGULATOR

INJECTOR

INTAKE MANIFOLD

**Intake manifold assembly on Axxess**

necessary, remove the EGR valve-to-intake manifold nuts and the EGR valve.

5. Using a shop rag, wrap it around the fuel line and disconnect it from the throttle body. Remove the throttle body-to-intake manifold nuts, the throttle body and the heater mixture assembly.

6. To prevent warping, loosen the intake manifold nuts and bolts 1 or 2 turns at a time in the reverse of the torque sequence. Remove the manifold.

**To install:**

7. Clean the gasket surfaces and install new gaskets.

8. Install the intake manifold and torque the nuts and bolts in 2 steps in the proper sequence. Torque the nuts to 20 ft. lbs. (27 Nm) and the bolts to 14 ft. lbs. (19 Nm).

9. Use new gaskets to install the remaining components. Torque the EGR valve nuts to 17 ft. lbs. (23 Nm) and the throttle body nuts to 13 ft. lbs. (18 Nm).

10. Refill the cooling system and run the engine to check ignition timing and idle speed.

ELECTRO INJECTION UNIT
17–20 FT. LBS. (24–27 NM)

9–13 FT. LBS. (12–18 NM)

12–14 FT. LBS. (16–20 NM)

MEXTURE HEATER

EGR VALVE

WATER OUTLET

13–17 FT. LBS. (18–23 NM)

GASKET

INTAKE MANIFOLD

**Intake manifold assembly on 1988–89 3.0L engine**

### 1990–92

1. Release the fuel system pressure and disconnect the negative battery cable.2. Drain the cooling system to a level below the intake manifold.

3. Remove the air duct from the throttle body. Disconnect the accelerator linkage from the throttle body.

4. Remove the upper radiator hose from the water outlet housing and the exhaust tube from the EGR valve. If necessary, remove the EGR valve-to-intake manifold nuts and the EGR valve.

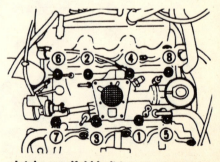

**Intake manifold bolt torque sequence— 1988–89 3.0L engine**

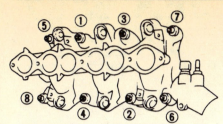

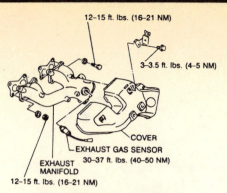

**Intake manifold bolt torque sequence—1990–92 3.0L engine**

5. Label and disconnect the wiring and hoses as required.

6. Remove the 5 intake manifold collector-to-intake manifold bolts and the lift the collector off the engine.

7. Remove the fuel rail and the injectors as an assembly from the intake manifold.

8. To prevent warping, loosen the intake manifold nuts and bolts 1 or 2 turns at a time in the reverse of the torque sequence. Remove the manifold.

**To install:**

9. Clean the gasket surfaces and install new gaskets.

10. Install the intake manifold and torque the nuts and bolts in the proper sequence in the following steps:

Step 1: all to 43 inch lbs. (5 Nm).

Step 2: bolts to 14 ft. lbs. (20 Nm), nuts to 20 ft. lbs. (27 Nm).

Step 3: repeat Step 2.

11. Use new O-rings and install the fuel injectors and rail assembly. Connect the wiring.

12. Use a new gasket and install the intake manifold collector. Torque the bolts to 12 ft. lbs. (16 Nm).

13. Install the remaining components and connect the wiring and hoses. Refill the cooling system and run the engine to check ignition timing and idle speed.

## Exhaust Manifold

### REMOVAL & INSTALLATION

#### 2.4L Engine

1. Disconnect the negative battery cable.

2. If equipped, remove the hot air duct from the exhaust manifold cover.

3. Disconnect the spark plug wires from the exhaust side of the engine; if necessary, remove the spark plugs from the exhaust side of the engine.

4. If necessary, raise and safely support the vehicle.

5. If equipped, remove the air induction tubes from the exhaust manifold. Remove the EGR tube from the exhaust manifold.

6. Remove the hot air cover and the exhaust pipe from the exhaust manifold.

12–15 ft. lbs. (16–21 NM)

3–3.5 ft. lbs. (4–5 NM)

COVER

EXHAUST GAS SENSOR 30–37 ft. lbs. (40–50 NM)

EXHAUST MANIFOLD

12–15 ft. lbs. (16–21 NM)

**Exhaust manifold—2.4L engine**

7. Remove the exhaust manifold-to-engine nuts and the manifold from the engine.

**To install:**

8. Clean the gasket mounting surfaces and install new gaskets.

9. Install the manifold and torque the nuts/bolts to 15 ft. lbs. (20 Nm), working from the center to the ends, in 2 steps.

10. Use new gaskets and connect the exhaust pipe to the manifold. Torque the nuts to 27 ft. lbs. (36 Nm).

11. Install the remaining components and run the engine to check for leaks.

#### 3.0L Engine

**LEFT SIDE**

1. Disconnect the negative battery cable.

2. Remove the hot air tube from the exhaust manifold cover. Remove the exhaust manifold cover-to-exhaust manifold bolts and cover.

3. Remove the EGR and the AIR tubes from the exhaust manifold, if equipped.

**NOTE: If the alternator is in the way, remove the drive belt and the alternator.**

4. Raise and safely support the vehicle.

5. Remove the exhaust pipe-to-exhaust manifold nuts and separate the exhaust pipe from the manifold.

6. Remove the exhaust manifold-to-cylinder head bolts and the manifold from the engine.

R.H. EXHAUST MANIFOLD

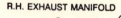

FRONT

L.H. EXHAUST MANIFOLD

FRONT

**Exhaust manifolds—3.0L engine**

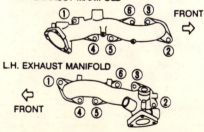

7. Clean the gasket mounting surfaces.

8. To install, use new gaskets and reverse the removal procedures. Torque the exhaust manifold-to-cylinder head nuts to 16 ft. lbs. (22 Nm) and the exhaust pipe-to-exhaust manifold bolts to 20 ft. lbs. (27 Nm).

**RIGHT SIDE**

1. Disconnect the negative battery cable.

2. Remove the upper/lower exhaust manifold cover-to-exhaust manifold bolts and covers.

3. Remove the AIR tube from the exhaust manifold, if equipped.

4. Raise and safely support the vehicle.

5. Remove the exhaust pipe-to-exhaust manifold bolts and separate the exhaust pipe from the manifold.

6. Remove the exhaust manifold-to-cylinder head bolts and the manifold from the engine.

7. Clean the gasket mounting surfaces.

8. To install, use new gaskets and reverse the removal procedures. Torque the exhaust manifold-to-cylinder head nuts to 16 ft. lbs. (22 Nm) and the exhaust pipe-to-exhaust manifold bolts to 20 ft. lbs. (27 Nm).

## Timing Chain Front Cover

### REMOVAL & INSTALLATION

#### 2.4L Engine

**EXCEPT AXXESS**

1. Disconnect the negative battery cable. Drain the cooling system. Remove the upper and lower coolant hoses from the engine and the radiator.

2. Loosen the alternator adjusting bolt and remove the drive belt. Remove the alternator bracket-to-engine bolts and move the alternator aside.

3. If equipped with air conditioning, remove the drive belt. If necessary, remove the air conditioner compressor and move it aside without disconnecting the coolant hoses.

4. If equipped with power steering, remove the drive belt.

5. Rotate the crankshaft to position the No. 1 cylinder on TDC of it's compression stroke.

6. Drain the oil and remove the oil pan.

7. Remove the distributor cap. Matchmark the rotor to the distributor housing and the distributor housing to the timing chain cover. Remove the distributor hold-down bolt and the distributor.

8. Remove the oil pump-to-timing

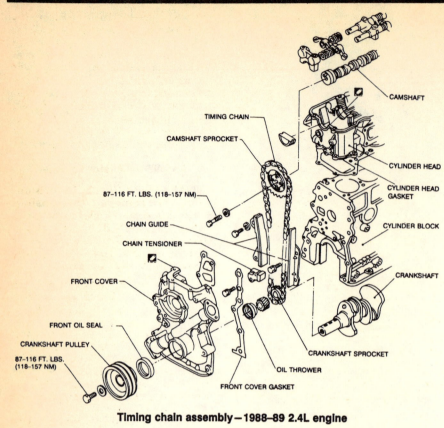

**Timing chain assembly—1988–89 2.4L engine**

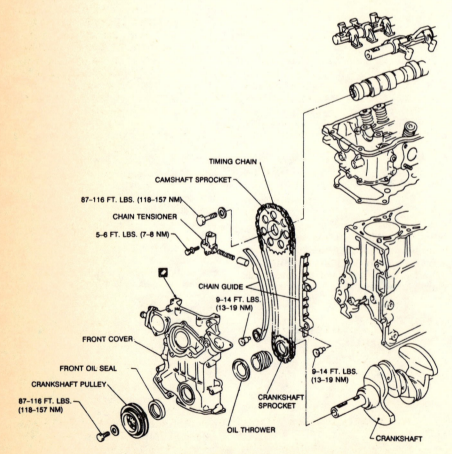

**Timing chain assembly—1990–92 2.4L engine except Axxess**

cover bolts, the oil pump and its drive spindle.

9. On RWD vehicles, remove the cooling fan-to-water pump bolts, the fan, the fan coupling if equipped and the water pump pulley.

10. Remove the crankshaft pulley-to-crankshaft bolt and the crankshaft pulley.

11. Remove the timing chain cover-to-cylinder head bolts, the timing chain cover-to-engine bolts, and remove the cover. Clean the gasket mounting surfaces.

**To install:**

NOTE: Whenever the timing cover is removed, replace the oil seal.

12. Install a new oil seal and use new gaskets and silicone sealant as necessary to install the front cover.

13. Install the oil pan.

14. When installing the oil pump, place the new gasket over the shaft and make sure the drive spindle mark aligns with the hole in the pump body. This will align the shaft properly for the distributor.

15. Install the distributor and make sure the rotor aligns with the matchmark.

16. Install the crankshaft pulley and torque the bolt to 116 ft. lbs. (157 Nm).

17. Install the remaining components and refill the cooling system. Run the engine to check ignition timing and idle speed.

**AXXESS**

The right side engine mount must be removed, an engine hoist is required.

1. Disconnect the negative battery cable. Drain the cooling system. Remove the upper and lower coolant hoses from the engine and the radiator.

2. Loosen the alternator adjusting bolt and remove the drive belt. Remove the alternator and the adjusting bracket.

3. If equipped with air conditioning, remove the drive belt. If necessary, remove the air conditioner compressor and move it aside without disconnecting the coolant hoses.

4. If equipped with power steering, remove the drive belt.

5. Rotate the crankshaft to position the No. 1 cylinder on TDC of it's compression stroke.

6. Raise and safely support the vehicle and remove the underpan.

7. Remove the crankshaft pulley and the oil pump drive boss.

8. Drain the oil and remove the oil pan and the oil pick-up tube and strainer.

9. Remove the rocker arm cover.

10. Attach a chain hoist to the en-

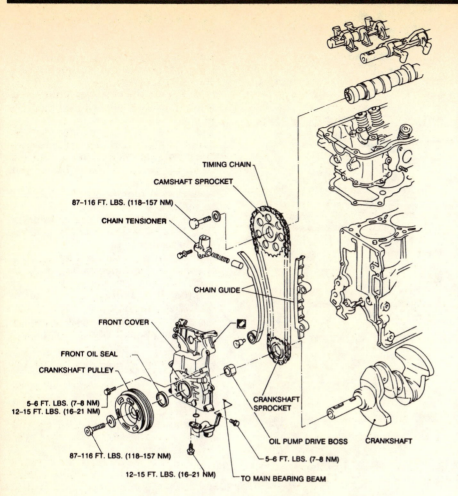

**Timing chain assembly on Axxess**

TIMING CHAIN

CAMSHAFT SPROCKET

87–116 FT. LBS. (118–157 NM)

CHAIN TENSIONER

CHAIN GUIDE

FRONT COVER

FRONT OIL SEAL

CRANKSHAFT PULLEY

5–6 FT. LBS. (7–8 NM)
12–15 FT. LBS. (16–21 NM)

87–116 FT. LBS. (118–157 NM)

12–15 FT. LBS. (16–21 NM)

TO MAIN BEARING BEAM

CRANKSHAFT SPROCKET

OIL PUMP DRIVE BOSS

CRANKSHAFT

5–6 FT. LBS. (7–8 NM)

gine, remove the right side mount and lower the engine slightly.

11. Remove the bolts and remove the front cover.

**To install:**

12. Install a new front cover oil seal and lubricate the seal with lithium grease. Use new gaskets, O-rings or silicone sealant as necessary to install the front cover, the oil pick-up tube and the oil pan.

13. Raise the engine, install the engine mount and torque the nuts and bolts to 41 ft. lbs. (55 Nm).

14. Install the oil pump drive boss and the crankshaft pulley. Torque the pulley bolt to 116 ft. lbs. (157 Nm).

15. Install the remaining components, adjust the drive belt tensions and refill the cooling system. Run the engine to check ignition timing and idle speed.

## Front Cover Oil Seal

### REPLACEMENT

#### 2.4L Engine

1. Disconnect the negative battery cable.

2. Remove the radiator shroud as required and remove crankshaft pulley.

3. Carefully pry the front oil seal out of the timing cover without damaging the crankshaft.

4. Lubricate the new seal with light grease. Using an oil seal installation tool, drive the new oil seal into the timing cover until it seats. Clean all oil and grease away from the seal and crankshaft area.

5. To complete the installation, reverse the removal procedures. Torque the crankshaft pulley-to-crankshaft bolt to 116 ft. lbs. (157 Nm). Start the engine, allow it reach normal operating temperatures and check for leaks.

## Timing Chain and Sprockets

### REMOVAL & INSTALLATION

#### 2.4L Engine

1. Disconnect the negative battery cable.

2. Rotate the crankshaft to align the timing marks on the crankshaft

pulley at TDC of No. 1 cylinder. Remove the timing chain cover and the rocker arm cover.

3. Make sure the No. 1 piston is at TDC of its compression stroke; the No. 1 camshaft lobes will both be down. The timing marks on the camshaft sprocket and crankshaft sprocket should align with the silver links on the timing chain. If the chain has no silver links, paint alignment marks on the chain.

4. Remove the chain tensioner.

**NOTE: When the chain tensioner bolts are removed, the tensioner will come apart. Hold on to the piston and don't drop any of the parts into the oil pan. There is no need to remove the chain guide unless it is being replaced.**

5. Hold the camshaft sprocket from turning, remove the bolt and remove the sprocket along with the chain.

**To install:**

6. Inspect the timing chain for cracked links, wear and/or damage; if necessary, replace the chain. Inspect the guides and sprockets for wear or damage and replace as necessary. If replacing a sprocket, always replace the chain.

7. Install the timing chain and camshaft sprocket, making sure to align all the timing marks. Install the camshaft sprocket bolt but do not torque it yet.

8. Install the chain tensioner and torque the bolts to 72 inch lbs. (8 Nm).

9. Rotate the crankshaft 2 full turns and make sure the timing marks still align. When the chain is correctly installed, torque the camshaft sprocket bolt to 116 ft. lbs. (157 Nm).

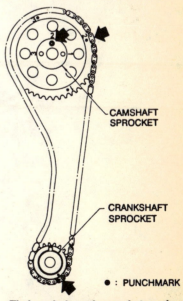

CAMSHAFT SPROCKET

CRANKSHAFT SPROCKET

● : PUNCHMARK

**Timing chain and sprocket marks on 2.4L engine; later models may have only 1 timing mark on the camshaft sprocket**

10. Install the front cover, crankshaft pulley and all remaining components. Run the engine to check ignition timing and idle speed.

## Timing Belt Front Cover

### REMOVAL & INSTALLATION

#### 3.0L Engine

1. Disconnect the negative battery cable and remove the engine under cover.

2. Drain the coolant and remove the hoses and the lower fan shroud. Remove the radiator and main shroud as an assembly.

3. Remove the accessory drive belts and remove the fan and water pump pulley.

4. Remove the spark plugs and the fresh air intake tube to the rocker arm cover.

5. Remove the idler pulley bracket and the water inlet hose.

6. Remove the crankshaft pulley bolt and use a puller to remove the crankshaft pulley. Put a spacer (a stack of washers or a large nut) on the pulley bolt and install the bolt so the crankshaft can be turned with the socket or wrench.

7. Remove the front timing belt covers. To remove the rear covers, the timing belt and camshaft sprockets must be removed.

8. Installation is the reverse of removal. Torque the crankshaft pulley bolt to 98 ft. lbs. (132 Nm).

### OIL SEAL REPLACEMENT

#### 3.0L Engine

The front oil seal is a part of the oil pump.

1. Remove the oil pump.
2. Carefully pry the oil seal from the oil pump.
3. Lubricate the new seal with light grease. Using an oil seal installation tool, drive the new oil seal into the oil pump housing until it seats. Clean all oil and grease away from the seal.
4. To complete the installation, use new gaskets and reverse the removal procedures.

## Timing Belt and Tensioner

### ADJUSTMENT

#### 3.0L Engine

1. This procedure is for adjusting the belt tension only if the belt has not been removed. If the belt was removed, see the Removal and Installation procedure. Disconnect the negative battery cable and remove the front timing belt covers.

2. Loosen the tensioner pulley locknut and allow the spring to hold the pulley against the belt.

3. Set a 0.014 in. (0.35mm) feeler gauge between the belt and pulley on the crankshaft side of the pulley. The feeler gauge should be at least ½ in. (12.7mm) wide.

4. Rotate the crankshaft clockwise to make the feeler gauge roll up between the tensioner pulley and the belt. Make sure the gauge is centered on the tensioner pulley.

5. Push in on the belt halfway between the tensioner pulley and the camshaft sprocket with a force of 22 lbs. (98 N) and torque the locknut to 43 ft. lbs. (58 Nm).

6. Rotate the crankshaft to remove the feeler gauge. Install the covers.

### REMOVAL & INSTALLATION

#### 3.0L Engine

1. Disconnect the negative battery cable and remove the timing belt cover.

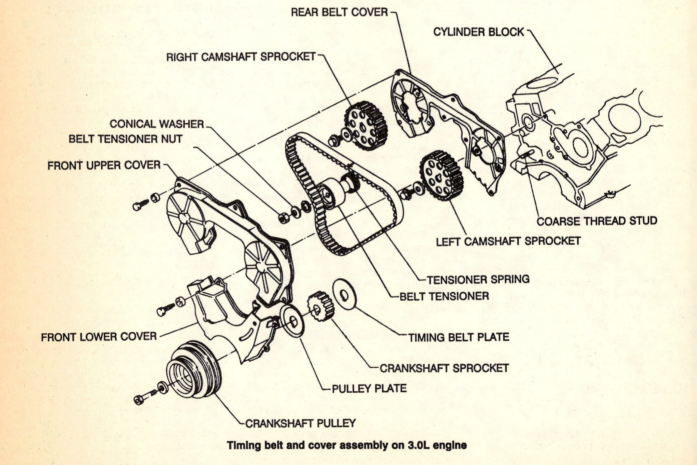

Timing belt and cover assembly on 3.0L engine

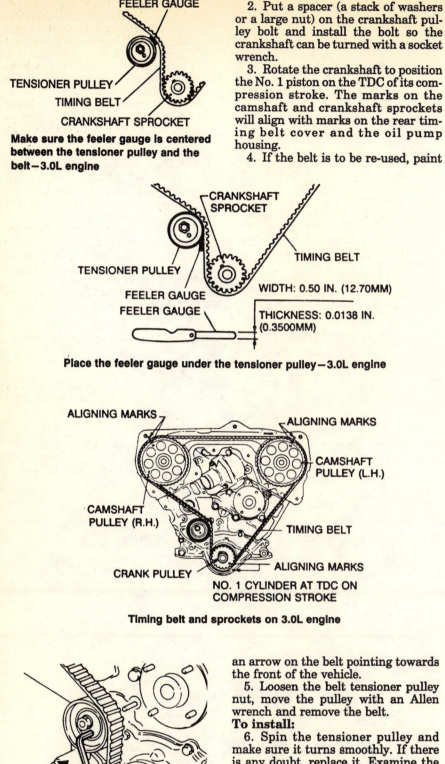

Make sure the feeler gauge is centered between the tensioner pulley and the belt—3.0L engine

CRANKSHAFT SPROCKET
TENSIONER PULLEY
FEELER GAUGE
FEELER GAUGE
TIMING BELT
WIDTH: 0.50 IN. (12.70MM)
THICKNESS: 0.0138 IN. (0.3500MM)

Place the feeler gauge under the tensioner pulley—3.0L engine

ALIGNING MARKS
ALIGNING MARKS
CAMSHAFT PULLEY (L.H.)
CAMSHAFT PULLEY (R.H.)
TIMING BELT
CRANK PULLEY
ALIGNING MARKS
NO. 1 CYLINDER AT TDC ON COMPRESSION STROKE

Timing belt and sprockets on 3.0L engine

Move the tensioner pulley with an Allen wrench

2. Put a spacer (a stack of washers or a large nut) on the crankshaft pulley bolt and install the bolt so the crankshaft can be turned with a socket wrench.

3. Rotate the crankshaft to position the No. 1 piston on the TDC of its compression stroke. The marks on the camshaft and crankshaft sprockets will align with marks on the rear timing belt cover and the oil pump housing.

4. If the belt is to be re-used, paint an arrow on the belt pointing towards the front of the vehicle.

5. Loosen the belt tensioner pulley nut, move the pulley with an Allen wrench and remove the belt.

**To install:**

6. Spin the tensioner pulley and make sure it turns smoothly. If there is any doubt, replace it. Examine the belt for wear or damage, replace as necessary.

7. Make sure all the sprockets are correctly aligned with the timing marks. Be careful when turning the crankshaft or camshafts, this is not a free wheeling engine.

8. Turn the tensioner pulley clockwise to move it out of the way, install the timing belt and allow the tensioner

to slowly return on its spring. Make sure all the timing marks are still aligned. When the belt is correctly installed, there will be 40 teeth between the camshaft sprocket timing marks and 43 teeth between the crankshaft and left camshaft sprocket timing marks.

9. Turn the tensioner approximately 70–80 degrees clockwise with the wrench and tighten the locknut.

10. To adjust the belt tension, turn the crankshaft clockwise several times and slowly set the No. 1 piston to TDC of the compression stroke.

11. Set a 0.014 in. (0.35mm) feeler gauge between the belt and pulley on the crankshaft side of the pulley. The feeler gauge should be at least ½ in. (12.7mm) wide.

12. Rotate the crankshaft clockwise to make the feeler gauge roll up between the tensioner pulley and the belt. Make sure the gauge is centered on the tensioner pulley.

13. Loosen the tensioner pulley locknut, push in on the belt halfway between the tensioner pulley and the camshaft sprocket with a force of 22 lbs. (98 N) and torque the locknut to 43 ft. lbs. (58 Nm).

14. Rotate the crankshaft to remove the feeler gauge. Install the covers.

## Timing Sprockets

### REMOVAL & INSTALLATION

#### 3.0L Engine

1. Disconnect the negative battery cable.

2. Remove the timing belt cover and the timing belt.

3. Use an appropriate tool to prevent the camshafts from turning and remove the sprocket bolts. Pull the sprockets straight off.

4. Installation is the reverse of removal. Torque the camshaft sprocket bolts to 65 ft. lbs. (88 Nm). Install the timing belt.

## Camshaft

### REMOVAL & INSTALLATION

#### 2.4L Engine

The same bolts that hold the rocker arm assembly also hold the camshaft bearing caps and on 1988 models, the rocker arm shaft holder is the bearing cap. On 1989–92 models, the hydraulic lifters are built into the rocker arms. If the rocker arm shafts are disassembled, do not allow the arms to lay on their side or they will become air bound. Keep the rocker arms upright or lay them in a pan of new engine oil.

1. Relieve the fuel system pressure

and disconnect the negative battery cable.

2. Remove the rocker arm cover and turn the crankshaft to align the timing marks at TDC on No. 1 cylinder.

3. If the timing chain is not being removed, use a wire tie or wire to secure the timing chain to the camshaft sprocket.

4. Hold the camshaft sprocket to loosen the bolt and remove the sprocket. Secure the sprocket so the chain does not fall off the crankshaft sprocket.

5. Loosen each rocker shaft bolt 1 turn at a time to prevent bending the shafts.

6. When all the bolts are loose, remove the rocker arm shafts with the bolts still in the shafts. This will hold the assembly together.

7. If they are not already identified, mark the bearing caps so they can be installed in their original position facing the same direction. Lift the caps off and lift the camshaft out.

**To install:**

8. Inspect the camshaft and the bearings:

   a. Make sure the camshaft and the bearing surfaces are in good condition.

   b. Install the bearing caps without the camshaft, torque the rocker arm shaft bolts to specification and measure the inside diameter of the bearing circle.

   c. Measure the diameter of the camshaft bearings.

   d. The difference between the measurements is the camshaft journal clearance; it should be no more than 0.0047 in. (0.12mm)

   e. Install the camshaft without the rocker arms and torque the bolts to specification. The camshaft endplay should be no more than 0.008 in. (0.2mm).

9. Lubricate the camshaft with engine oil and set it in place. Make sure the pin on the sprocket end is up.

10. Install the rocker arm shafts and tighten the bolts in the proper sequence 1 turn at a time to draw the shafts down evenly against the valve springs without bending the shafts. Torque the bolts to 16 ft. lbs. (22 Nm).

11. Install the camshaft sprocket and remove the tie securing the chain. In-

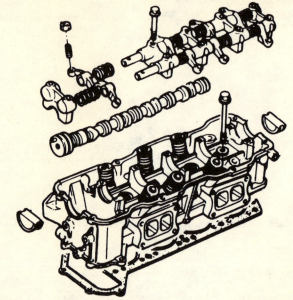

**Camshaft removal on 1988 2.4L engine; the rocker arm shaft holders are also the bearing caps**

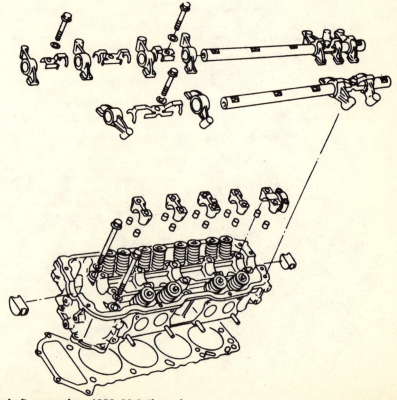

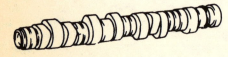

**Camshaft removal on 1989–92 2.4L engine**

stall the sprocket bolt but don't torque it yet. Rotate the crankshaft 2 full turns to make sure the timing marks line up. When the valve timing is correct, torque the sprocket bolt to 116 ft. lbs. (157 Nm).

12. On 1988 models, adjust the valves.

13. Use a silicone sealer on the rubber end plugs and install the rocker arm cover with a new gasket. Torque the bolts to 7 ft. lbs. (10 Nm) in a criss-cross pattern starting at the middle. Install the remaining components.

14. When the engine is first started, the hydraulic valve lifters may be noisy. Run the engine for 10–20 minutes at about 1000 rpm. If the noise has not subsided, the lifter will probably never pump up and must be replaced.

### 3.0L Engine

The camshafts can be removed without removing the cylinder heads. When removing the timing belt covers, the radiator must be removed. This should provide the clearance for removing the camshafts.

1. Relieve the fuel system pressure and disconnect the negative battery cable.

2. Remove the rocker arm covers.

3. Turn the crankshaft to align the timing marks at TDC on No. 1 cylinder. Remove the timing belt cover and the timing belt.

4. Hold the camshafts from turning and remove the camshaft sprockets. Remove the rear timing belt cover.

5. Loosen each rocker shaft bolt 1 turn at a time to prevent bending the shafts. When all the bolts are loose, remove the rocker arm shafts with the bolts still in the shafts. This will hold the assembly together.

6. Secure the valve lifters in the guide assembly with safety wire to keep them in their original positions, then remove the entire assembly.

**NOTE: Before removing a lifter from the guide assembly, tag the lifters to make sure they are returned to their original position. Keep the lifters upright to keep them from becoming air bound or lay them down in a pan of new engine oil. Do not disassemble a lifter.**

7. Remove the plates from the front and rear of the cylinder heads and pry the oil seals out. Remove the bolt at the rear of the camshafts and remove the locating plates. Carefully withdraw the camshafts out towards the front.

**To install:**

8. Inspect the camshaft and the bearing surfaces:

a. Make sure the camshaft and the bearing surfaces are in good condition.

b. Measure the inside diameter of the bearing circle.

c. Measure the diameter of the camshaft bearings.

d. The difference between the measurements is the camshaft journal clearance; it should be no more than 0.0059 in. (0.15mm)

e. To check endplay, install the camshaft and the locating plates and torque the bolts to 65 ft. lbs. (88 Nm). The camshaft endplay should be no more than 0.0024 in. (0.06mm).

9. Lubricate the camshaft with engine oil and carefully set it in place. Install the locating plate at the rear and torque the bolt to 65 ft. lbs. (88 Nm). Turn the camshaft so the pin on the sprocket end is up.

10. Install the rear camshaft cover plate with a new gasket.

11. Lubricate a new camshaft front oil seal with grease and use an appropriate seal installation tool to carefully drive the new seal into place. Make sure the seal seats in the cylinder head.

12. With the rocker arm assemblies removed, all the valves will be closed. The rear timing belt cover, sprockets and timing belt can be installed without risk of damage to valves or pistons. Adjust timing belt tension according to correct procedure.

13. Make sure the engine is at TDC on No. 1 cylinder. Install the left bank lifter guide assembly, remove the safety wire and install the rocker arm shafts. Tighten the bolts 1 turn at a time to draw the shafts down evenly. Torque the bolts to 16 ft. lbs. (22 Nm).

14. Rotate the crankshaft to bring cylinder No. 4 to TDC. Set the right bank lifter guide assembly into place, remove the safety wire and install the rocker arm shafts. Tighten the bolts 1 turn at a time to 16 ft. lbs. (22 Nm).

15. Use new gaskets to install the rocker arm covers and torque the bolts to 24 inch lbs. (3 Nm). Install the remaining components.

16. When the engine is first started, the hydraulic valve lifters may be noisy. Run the engine for 10–20 minutes at about 1000 rpm. If the noise has not subsided, the lifter will probably never pump up and must be replaced.

## Piston and Connecting Rod

### POSITIONING

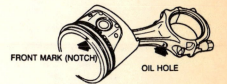

**Piston and rod orientation on 2.4L engine**

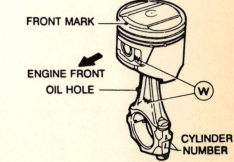

**Piston and rod orientation on 3.0L engine**

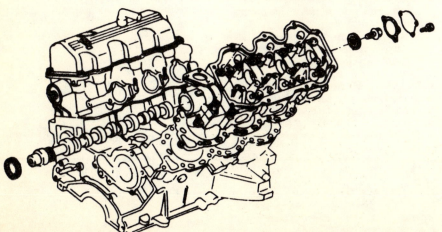

**Camshaft removal on 3.0L engine can be done without removing the cylinder head**

# ENGINE LUBRICATION

## Oil Pan

### REMOVAL & INSTALLATION

#### 2.4L Engine

##### EXCEPT AXXESS

1. Raise and safely support the vehicle.
2. Remove the engine undercover and drain the engine oil.
3. On 4WD models, perform the following procedures:
   a. Remove the bolt from the front differential carrier member.
   b. Position a floor jack under the front differential carrier and remove the mounting bolts.
   c. Remove the transmission-to-rear engine mount bracket nuts.
   d. Remove the engine mount nuts and bolts.
   e. Attach an engine hoist and raise the engine slightly.
4. On 2WD models, remove the front crossmember.
5. Remove the oil pan-to-engine bolts. Insert a seal cutter tool between the cylinder block and the oil pan and tap it around the circumference of the pan with a hammer. Remove the oil pan.

**NOTE: Be careful not to drive the seal cutter into the oil pump or rear oil seal retainer as damage may occur.**

**To install:**

6. Clean the gasket mounting surfaces.
7. Apply a continuous ⅛ in. bead of silicone sealant to the oil pan mounting surface; be sure to trace sealant bead to the inside of the bolt holes where there is no groove.
8. Install the oil pan and torque the bolts in sequence to 60 inch lbs. (7 Nm).
9. To complete the installation, reverse the removal procedures.
10. Wait at least 30 minutes and re-

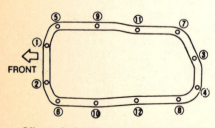

Oil pan bolt tightening sequence on 2.4L engine

fill the crankcase. Start the engine and allow it to reach normal operating temperatures and check for leaks.

##### AXXESS

1. Raise and safely support the vehicle.
2. Drain the engine oil.
3. Remove the front exhaust tube and the front side gusset.
4. On 2WD models, remove the crossmember.
5. Remove the oil pan-to-engine bolts. Insert a seal cutter tool between the cylinder block and the oil pan and tap it around the circumference of the pan with a hammer. Remove the oil pan.

**NOTE: Be careful not to drive the seal cutter into the oil pump or rear oil seal retainer as damage may occur.**

**To install:**

6. Clean the gasket mounting surfaces.
7. Apply a continuous ⅛ in. bead of silicone sealant to the oil pan mounting surface; be sure to trace sealant bead to the inside of the bolt holes where there is no groove.
8. Install the oil pan and torque the bolts in sequence to 7 ft. lbs. (10 Nm).
9. To complete the installation, reverse the removal procedures.
10. Wait at least 30 minutes and refill the crankcase. Start the engine and allow it to reach normal operating temperatures and check for leaks.

#### 3.0L Engine

1. Raise and safely support the vehicle.
2. Remove the undercover and drain the engine oil.
3. On 2WD models, remove the stabilizer bar bracket bolts.
4. On 4WD models, remove the front driveshaft and disconnect the halfshafts at the transfer case. Position a floor jack under the front differential carrier and remove the mounting bolts.
5. On 2WD models, remove the front crossmember.
6. Remove the idler arm and the starter motor.
7. On 4WD models, remove the transmission-to-rear engine mount bracket nuts and the engine mount nuts/bolts.
8. Remove the engine gussets.
9. On 4WD models, attach a hoist to the engine and raise the engine slightly.
10. Remove the oil pan-to-engine bolts in the correct sequence to avoid warping the pan. Insert a seal cutter tool between the cylinder block and the oil pan and tap the tool around the

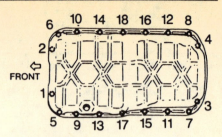

Oil pan bolt loosening sequence on 3.0L engine—tighten the bolts in the reverse of this sequence

circumference with a hammer to remove the oil pan.

**NOTE: Be careful not to drive the seal cutter into the oil pump or rear oil seal retainer for damage may occur.**

11. Clean the gasket mounting surfaces.

**To install:**

12. Apply silicone sealant to the oil pump and oil seal retainer gasket.
13. Apply a continuous ⅛ in. bead of sealant to the oil pan mounting surface; be sure to trace sealant bead to the inside of the bolt holes where there is no groove.
14. Install the oil pan and torque the bolts in sequence to 60 inch lbs. (7 Nm).
15. To complete the installation, reverse the removal procedures.
16. Wait at least 30 minutes and refill the crankcase. Start the engine and allow it to reach normal operating temperatures and check for leaks.

## Oil Pump

### REMOVAL & INSTALLATION

#### 2.4L Engine

##### EXCEPT AXXESS

The oil pump is an external type, mounted to the right side of the crankshaft pulley.

1. Disconnect the negative battery cable.
2. Rotate the crankshaft to position

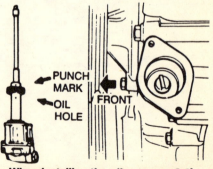

When installing the oil pump on 2.4L engine, align the mark on the shaft with the oil hole

Oil pump on Axxess engine is part of the front cover

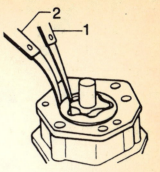

Inspecting oil pump rotor clearance—
2.4L engine except Axxess

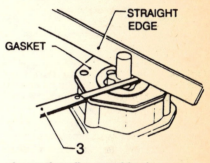

Inspecting oil pump side clearance—
2.4L engine except Axxess

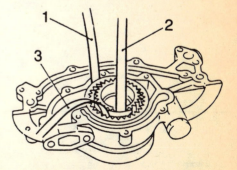

Inspecting oil pump rotor clearance on
3.0L and 2.4L Axxess engines

Oil pump on 3.0L engine is on the front of the engne block

the No. 1 cylinder on the TDC of the compression stroke.

3. If equipped with a splash pan, remove it. If necessary, remove the stabilizer bar.

4. Remove the oil pump-to-housing bolts and the oil pump from the engine.

5. Clean the gasket mounting surfaces.

**To install:**

6. Install a new gasket onto the pump and fill the pump with oil.

7. Align the distributor drive spindle punch mark with the oil hole on the oil pump. This will properly align the drive spindle with the distributor.

8. Insert the oil pump into the housing until the drive spindle tang fits into the distributor shaft notch. Torque the oil pump-to-engine housing bolts to 11 ft. lbs. (15 Nm).

9. Start the engine to check the ignition timing and to check for leaks.

### AXXESS

The oil pump rides on the crankshaft and is attached to the front cover.

1. Disconnect the negative battery cable.

2. Raise and safely support the vehicle. Drain the cooling system.

3. Drain the engine oil.

4. Remove the oil pan and the front cover.

5. Remove the oil pump cover-to-front cover bolts, the cover and the oil pump gears.

**NOTE: Whenever the oil pump is removed, replace the oil seal.**

6. Inspect and/or replace the oil pump gears.

7. Using petroleum jelly, pack the oil pump cavity and reverse the removal procedures.

### *3.0L Engine*

The oil pump is mounted at the front of the engine behind the crankshaft pulley.

1. Disconnect the negative battery cable.

2. Raise and safely support the vehicle. Drain the cooling system and the crankcase.

3. Remove the oil pan and the timing belt.

4. Remove the crankshaft timing sprocket using a wheel puller and the timing belt plate.

5. Remove the oil pump strainer and the pickup tube from the oil pump.

6. Remove the oil pump-to-engine bolts and the oil pump from the engine.

7. Clean the gasket mounting surfaces.

**NOTE: Whenever the oil pump is removed, replace the oil seal.**

8. To install, use new gaskets or silicone sealant. Pack the oil pump cavity with petroleum jelly and reverse the removal procedures. Torque as follows:

Oil pump-to-engine:
6mm bolts—60 inch lbs. (7 Nm)
8mm bolts—12 ft. lbs. (16 Nm)
Pickup tube-to-oil pump bolts—15 ft. lbs. (21 Nm)

## CHECKING

To check the oil pump clearances, the oil pump must be removed from the engine and disassembled. If the parts do not meet specifications, replace the oil pump as an assembly.

### *2.4L Engine*

#### EXCEPT AXXESS

Using a feeler gauge, check the following clearances:

Inner rotor tip-to-outer rotor—0.0047 in. (0.12mm) max.

Outer rotor-to-housing—0.0059–0.0083 in. (0.15–0.21mm)

Side clearance (with gasket)—0.0016–0.0031 in. (0.04–0.07mm)

#### AXXESS

Using a feeler gauge, check the following clearances:

Pump body-to-outer gear—0.0043–0.0079 in. (0.11–0.20mm)

Inner gear-to-cressent—0.0087–0.0130 in. (0.22–0.33mm)

Outer gear-to-cressent—0.0083–0.0126 in. (0.21–0.32mm)

Housing-to-inner gear—0.0020–0.0035 in. (0.05–0.09mm)

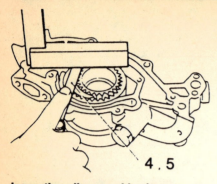

**Inspecting oil pump side clearance on 3.0L and 2.4L Axxess engines**

Housing-to-outer gear – 0.0020–0.0043 in. (0.05–0.11mm)

### 3.0L Engine

Using a feeler gauge, check the following clearances:
Pump body-to-outer gear – 0.0043–0.0079 in. (0.11–0.20mm)
Inner gear-to-cressent – 0.0047–0.0091 in. (0.12–0.23mm)
Outer gear-to-cressent – 0.0083–0.0126 in. (0.22–0.33mm)
Housing-to-inner gear – 0.0020–0.0035 in. (0.05–0.09mm)
Housing-to-outer gear – 0.0020–0.0043 in. (0.05–0.11mm)

## Rear Main Bearing Oil Seal

### REMOVAL & INSTALLATION

#### Except Axxess

1. Disconnect the negative battery cable.
2. Raise and safely support the vehicle. Remove the starter.
3. Remove the transmission from the vehicle.
4. If equipped with a manual transmission, remove the clutch-to-flywheel bolts and the clutch assembly from the vehicle.
5. Remove the flywheel-to-crankshaft bolts and the flywheel from the engine.

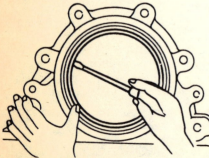

**Removing the rear oil seal from the retainer; the transmission and flywheel must be removed**

6. Remove the rear oil seal retainer-to-engine bolts, the rear oil seal retainer-to-oil pan bolts and the retainer.
7. Carefully pry the rear oil seal from the retainer; be careful not to damage the mounting surfaces. Clean the oil seal mounting surfaces.
8. Using an appropriate oil seal installation tool, lubricate the new oil seal lips with engine oil and drive the the seal into the retainer until it seats.
9. To complete the installation, reverse the removal procedures. Start the engine and check for leaks.

### Axxess

1. Disconnect the negative battery cable.
2. Raise and safely support the vehicle. Remove the starter.
3. On 2WD models, remove the halfshafts from the transaxle.
4. On 4WD models, remove the driveshafts and halfshaft from the transaxle/transfer case assembly.
5. Remove the transaxle-to-engine bolts, the transaxle-to-transfer case bolts for 4WD, and lower the transaxle from the vehicle.
6. If equipped with a manual transaxle, remove the clutch-to-flywheel bolts and the clutch assembly from the vehicle.
7. Remove the flywheel-to-crankshaft bolts and the flywheel from the engine.
8. Remove the rear oil seal retainer-to-engine bolts, the rear oil seal retainer-to-oil pan bolts and the retainer.
9. Carefully pry the rear oil seal from the retainer; be careful not to damage the mounting surfaces. Clean the oil seal mounting surfaces.
10. Using an appropriate oil seal installation tool, lubricate the new oil seal lips with engine oil and drive the the seal into the retainer until it seats.
11. To complete the installation, reverse the removal procedures. Start the engine and check for leaks.

# ENGINE COOLING

## Radiator

### REMOVAL & INSTALLATION

#### Axxess

1. Disconnect the negative battery cable and the wiring for the electric fans.
2. Remove the fan shroud bolts and remove the shroud and fans as an assembly.
3. Raise and safely support the vehicle and drain the cooling system.
4. Disconnect the hoses from the radiator. If equipped with an automatic transaxle, disconnect the plug the oil cooler lines.
5. Remove the upper radiator-to-chassis bolts and lift the radiator from the vehicle.
6. Installation is the reverse of removal. Make sure the lower radiator mounting rubbers are in place before installing radiator.
7. If equipped with an automatic transmission, check and/or refill the transmission.

#### Except Axxess

1. Disconnect the negative battery cable.
2. Drain the engine cooling system and disconnect the radiator hoses. If equipped with an automatic transmission, disconnect and plug the transmission oil cooler lines at the radiator.
3. On Pick-Up and Pathfinder, there is a lower section that can be removed from the fan shroud. Remove this section, unbolt the 2 upper radiator brackets and lift the radiator and shroud out together.
4. On Van, if the shroud will not clear the fan, unbolt the shroud and move it back away from the radiator. Remove the bolts and lift the radiator out.
5. Installation is the reverse of removal. Make sure the lower radiator mounting rubbers are in place before installing radiator.
6. If equipped with an automatic transmission, check and/or refill the transmission.

## Electric Cooling Fan

### REMOVAL & INSTALLATION

#### Axxess

1. Disconnect the negative battery cable and the wiring for the electric fans.
2. Remove the fan shroud bolts and remove the shroud and fans as an assembly.
3. Remove the nut in the center of the fan blade and pull the blade off the motor.
4. Remove the bolts to remove the motors from the shroud.
5. Installation is the reverse of removal.

### TESTING

The cooling fans are controlled by the

ECU; testing must be performed on the vehicle.

1. Start the engine and turn the air conditioner and blower fan **ON**. Both fans should operate at low speed.

2. If the air conditioner compressor operates but both fans do not operate, check for power to the fan relays under the hood. These relays are operated by the main ECU.

3. To check high speed operation, stop the engine, disconnect the engine coolant temperature sensor, in the cylinder head near the oil filler cap, and start the engine. Both fans should run at high speed.

4. If either fan does not operate under any condition, stop the engine and unplug the connectors at the fans. Use jumper wires to provide 12 volts directly to the motors: the black wire and the yellow/black wire are both ground wires.

# Heater Core

## REMOVAL & INSTALLATION

### Pick-Up, Pathfinder and Van

1. The dashboard must be removed. Disconnect the negative battery cable. On vehicles with theft protected radios, obtain the security code.

2. Set the temperature control to full hot and drain the cooling system.

3. Disconnect the heater hoses at the engine compartment.

4. Remove the ash tray and remove the screws holding the center console face cover. Remove the cover, heater controls, radio and center vent.

5. Disconnect the control cables and wiring as needed to remove the dashboard.

6. Disconnect the ducts and remove the heater unit. Remove the clips or screws and split the case to remove the heater core. Note how the air flow control doors fit into the case.

**To install:**

7. Install the heater core and assemble the case halves. Use a new gasket and make sure the air flow doors work properly.

8. Install the heater unit and use a new gasket to seal it to the cooling unit or blower fan housing. Connect the ducts.

9. Install the instrument panel.

10. Install the heater control assembly, center vent and radio.

11. Adjust the heater controls and air flow doors as required.

12. Connect the heater hoses, fill the cooling system and start the engine to test the system.

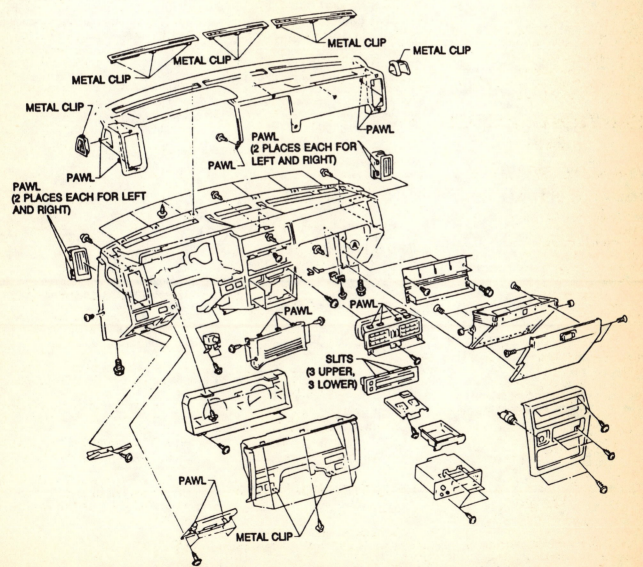

**Pick-Up and Pathfinder dashboard assembly must be removed to remove the heater core**

## Axxess

1. The heater unit can be removed without removing the dashboard. Disconnect the negative battery cable. On vehicles with theft protected radios, obtain the security code.

2. Set the temperature control to full hot and drain the cooling system.

3. Disconnect the heater hoses at the engine compartment.

4. Remove the glove compartment, ash tray assembly and the radio.

5. Disconnect the heater control cables and wiring as required and remove the control assembly.

6. Disconnect the ducting and remove the heater unit. Split the case to remove the heater core. Note the placement of the air flow control doors.

**To install:**

7. Install the heater core and assemble the case halves. Use a new gasket and make sure the air flow doors work properly.

8. Install the heater unit and use a new gasket to seal it to the cooling unit or blower fan housing. Connect the ducts.

9. Install the heater control assembly and radio.

10. Adjust the heater control cables and rods.

11. Connect the heater hoses, re-fill the cooling system and start the engine to test the system.

# Water Pump

## REMOVAL & INSTALLATION
### Axxess

1. Disconnect the negative battery

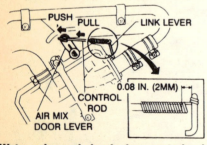

**Water valve and air mix door control rod adjustment-Pick-Up, Pathfinder and Van.**

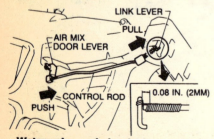

**Water valve and air mix door control rod adjustment-Axxess**

cable and drain the cooling system. Don't forget the block drain.

2. Remove the upper radiator hose to provide working room and loosen the alternator to remove the drive belt from the pulleys.

3. Disconnect the hoses and remove the bolts to remove the water pump and thermostat housing assembly from the block.

4. Remove the pulley bolts to remove the pulley from the pump. Remove the bolts to remove the pump from the housing.

**To install:**

5. Make sure all gasket surfaces are clean and use a new gasket or silicone sealer when installing the pump to the housing.

6. Install the housing to the block with a new gasket or silicone sealer.

7. Connect the hoses, install the belts and fill the cooling system to check for leaks.

## Van, Pick-Up and Pathfinder With 2.4L Engine

1. Disconnect the negative battery cable and drain the cooling system. Don't forget the block drain.

2. Remove the upper radiator hose to provide working room and loosen the alternator to remove the drive belt from the pulleys.

3. On Pick-Up and Pathfinder, remove the lower section of the fan

**Water pump replacement on 2.4L engine in Pick-Up, Pathfinder and Van**

shroud and remove the screws to lift the shroud from the engine. Hold the pulley and remove the nuts to remove the fan and pulley from the water pump.

4. On Van, remove the shroud screws and push the shroud back away from the radiator. Remove the fan pulley nuts and lift the fan and shroud out together.

5. Remove the bolts and remove the water pump from the engine.

**To install:**

6. Make sure all gasket surfaces are clean and use a new gasket or silicone sealer when installing the pump to the engine. Torque the 6mm bolts to 7 ft. lbs. (10 Nm) and the 8mm bolts to 12 ft. lbs. (16 Nm).

7. On Van, lower the shroud and fan into place and push the shroud back against the engine.

8. Install the fan clutch, fan and pulley and torque the nuts or bolts to 7 ft. lbs. (10 Nm).

9. Install the fan shroud and drive belts and fill the cooling system to check for leaks.

## Pick-Up and Pathfinder With 3.0L Engine

1. The timing belt cover must be removed. Disconnect the negative battery cable and drain the cooling system. Don't forget the block drain.

2. Remove the radiator hoses and, on automatic transmission, disconnect and plug the fluid cooling lines.

3. Remove the lower section of the fan shroud and remove the screws to lift the shroud from the engine. Remove the bracket bolts and lift the radiator out of the vehicle.

4. Remove all the accessory drive belts.

5. Hold the pulley and remove the nuts to remove the fan and pulley from the water pump.

6. Remove the timing belt covers.

7. Remove the bolts to remove the water pump from the engine.

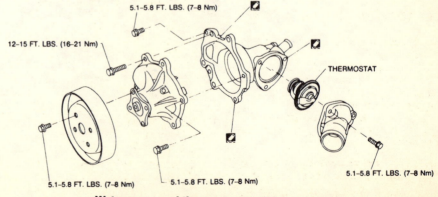

**Water pump and thermostat assembly on Axxess**

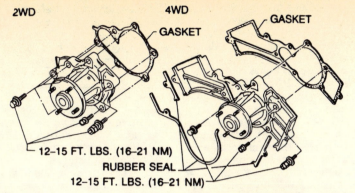

2WD      4WD       GASKET

GASKET

12–15 FT. LBS. (16–21 NM)

RUBBER SEAL

12–15 FT. LBS. (16–21 NM)

**The timing belt cover must be removed to remove the water pump on 3.0L engine—on 4WD, the pump is part of the rear belt cover**

**To install:**

8. Make sure all gasket surfaces are clean and use a new gasket or silicone sealer when installing the pump to the engine. Torque the bolts to 15 ft. lbs. (21 Nm).

9. Install the timing belt covers. On 4WD models, make sure the sealing surfaces are clean and carefully install the rubber seal when installing the cover. The timing belt must be properly protected from dirt and oil.

10. Install the pulley, fan clutch and the fan.

11. Install the accessory drive belts and adjust the tension.

12. Install the radiator and fan shroud and connect the cooling system hoses.

13. Fill the system and check for leaks.

## Thermostat

The factory-installed thermostat opening temperature is 180°F (USA) or 190°F (Canada). On the Z24i engine, the thermostat is located on the right front-side of the intake manifold; on the KA24E engine used with the Axxess, the thermostat is mounted in the water pump housing, attached to the left side of the engine; on the all other engines, the thermostat is located above the water pump.

### REMOVAL & INSTALLATION

1. Disconnect the negative battery cable.

2. Drain the engine coolant to a level below the thermostat housing.

3. Disconnect the coolant hose from the thermostat water outlet.

4. Remove the water outlet-to-thermostat housing bolts, gasket and thermostat.

**NOTE: The thermostat spring must face the inside of the engine.**

5. Clean the gasket mounting surfaces.

**NOTE: If the thermostat is equipped with an air bleed or jiggle valve, be sure to position it in the upward direction.**

6. To install, use a new gasket or sealant and reverse the removal proce-

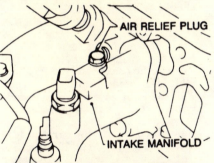

AIR RELIEF PLUG

INTAKE MANIFOLD

**Air relief plug location on Pick-Up, Pathfinder and Van with 2.4L engine.**

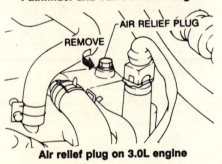

AIR RELIEF PLUG

REMOVE

**Air relief plug on 3.0L engine**

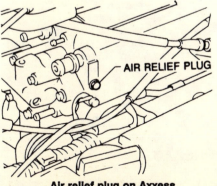

AIR RELIEF PLUG

**Air relief plug on Axxess**

dures. Torque the thermostat housing bolts to 6 ft. lbs. (8 Nm) on the 1990–92 2.4L engine or 15 ft. lbs. (21 Nm) on all except 1990–92 2.4L engine.

## Cooling System Bleeding

1. Set the heater temperature control to **HOT** and open the air relief plug. Pour coolant into the radiator until it comes out the relief plug, then close the plug.

2. Fill the reservoir and run the engine to warm it to operating temperature.

3. When the engine is cool again, check the coolant level in the reservoir.

---

# ENGINE ELECTRICAL

**NOTE: Disconnecting the negative battery cable on some vehicles may interfere with the functions of the on board computer systems and may require the computer to undergo a relearning process when the battery cable is reconnected. This usually requires only a few minutes of driving.**

## Distributor

### REMOVAL

1. Disconnect the negative battery cable.

2. Remove the distributor cap without disconnecting the spark plug wires. Unplug the distributor connector.

3. Rotate the crankshaft to TDC of No. 1 cylinder, if possible. Mark the position of the rotor to the distributor body and to the engine.

4. Remove the hold-down bolt and lift the distributor out of the engine.

DISTRIBUTOR DRIVE GEAR

MARK ON SHAFT

PROTRUDING MARK ON HOUSING

INDENTED MARK ON HOUSING

**Some distributors have alignment marks on the shaft and body—3.0L engine shown**

## INSTALLATION

### Timing Not Disturbed

1. If necessary, install a new O-ring on the distributor body. Lightly oil the O-ring and make sure the distributor mounting boss is clean.

2. If the crankshaft was not rotated with the distributor removed, align the rotor with the mark on the distributor body and insert the distributor into place. Some distributors have alignment marks on the shaft and housing. Align the shaft mark with the protruding mark on the housing.

3. The rotor may turn as the distributor is pushed in; remove it and turn the rotor back or forward 1 tooth and try again. When installing the distributor, it is important to make sure the rotor points to the mark made on the engine.

4. Check and adjust ignition timing as required.

### Timing Disturbed

1. If the crankshaft was turned or if no alignment marks were made when the distributor was removed, make sure the engine is at TDC of No. 1 cylinder.

   a. Remove the spark plug from No. 1 cylinder.

   b. Rotate the crankshaft while holding a thumb over the spark plug hole to determine that the is coming up on the compression stroke.

   c. Align the red TDC mark on the crankshaft pulley with the pointer on the cover.

2. Check the O-ring on the distributor body and replace as necessary. Lightly lubricate the O-ring and make sure the mounting boss is clean.

3. Align the marks on the distributor shaft and body and install the distributor. The rotor may turn as the distributor is pushed in; remove it and turn the rotor back or forward 1 tooth and try again. When installing the distributor, it is important to make sure the rotor points to the mark made on the engine.

4. Check and adjust ignition timing as required.

## Ignition Timing

### ADJUSTMENT

The ignition timing is controlled by the ECU, but a basic setting is required if the distributor has been removed. Always check and adjust ignition timing and idle speed together.

1. Locate the timing marks on the crankshaft pulley and the front of the engine. The timing marks are in 5 degree increments and the TDC mark is always painted red.

2. Connect a tachometer and a timing light to the engine, according to the manufacturer's instructions. Make sure the wires do not interfere with the fan.

3. Make sure all lights and accessories are switched **OFF** and run the engine to warm it to normal operating temperature.

4. With the transmission out of gear, run the engine at 2000 rpm for about 2 minutes, then check idle speed and ignition timing. If timing and idle speed are different from specification, look for another engine problem such as a vacuum leak or bad electrical connection. If no other obvious problem is found, a full diagnostic test should be run.

5. Check idle speed; on engines with throttle body fuel injection, ignition timing is not adjustable.

   a. On all 1988–89 models, idle speed should be 800 rpm with manual transmission, 750 rpm in **D** with automatic transmission.

   b. On 1990–92 models with automatic transmission, idle speed should be 750 rpm in **N**.

6. To adjust timing on 3.0L engines with multi-point fuel injection:

   a. If timing is not correct, disconnect the wiring for the air control valve at the back of the intake manifold. Idle speed should be 700 rpm. The adjusting screw is on the same body assembly as the air control valve.

   b. Reconnect the wiring, idle speed should be about 750 rpm. Do not change it with the wiring connected.

   c. Check and adjust timing as required to 12 degrees BTDC on 1988–89 models or 15 degrees BTDC on 1990–92 models. Adjust by rotating the distributor. Idle speed should remain at about 750 rpm.

7. To adjust timing on the 2.4L engine with multi-point fuel injection:

   a. Check idle speed at about 800 rpm. If not correct, disconnect the throttle sensor wiring and adjust the speed to less than 800 rpm.

   b. Check and adjust ignition timing to 15 degrees BTDC on Axxess or 10 degrees BTDC on Pick-Up, Pathfinder and Van.

8. Run the engine at 2000 rpm for about 2 minutes and check idle speed and timing again. If idle speed or timing are not correct, other problems exist with the engine control system and a full diagnostic test must be run.

## Alternator

### PRECAUTIONS

Several precautions must be observed with alternator equipped vehicles to avoid damage to the unit.

● If the battery is removed for any reason, make sure it is reconnected with the correct polarity. Reversing the battery connections may result in damage to the one-way rectifiers.

● When utilizing a booster battery as a starting aid, always connect the positive to positive terminals and the negative terminal from the booster battery to a good engine ground on the vehicle being started.

● Never use a fast charger as a booster to start vehicles.

● Disconnect the battery cables when charging the battery with a fast charger.

● Never attempt to polarize the alternator.

● Do not use test lights of more than 12 volts when checking diode continuity.

● Do not short across or ground any of the alternator terminals.

● The polarity of the battery, alternator and regulator must be matched and considered before making any electrical connections within the system.

● Never separate the alternator on an open circuit. Make sure all connections within the circuit are clean and tight.

● Disconnect the battery ground terminal when performing any service on electrical components.

● Disconnect the battery if arc welding is to be done on the vehicle.

## BELT TENSION ADJUSTMENT

Belt tension can be checked with a gauge made for the purpose. If a tension gauge is not available, belt deflection can be measured in inches. Press on the belt with 22 lbs. (10 kg) of force at a point halfway between the alternator and water pump pulleys. Deflection should be 0.200–0.310 in. (5–8mm) on the 3.0L engine or 0.310–0.470 in. (8–12mm) on the 2.4L engine.

1. Loosen the alternator's pivot bolt and the tension adjuster lock bolt.

2. Turn the adjuster bolt as required until the tension is correct.

3. Tighten the bolts and recheck the tension. If new belts have been installed, run the engine for a few minutes, then check tension again. The ideal adjustment is toward the looser end of the specification, belts adjusted too tight will cause bearing failure.

### REMOVAL & INSTALLATION

1. Disconnect the negative battery cable.

2. Label and disconnect the wiring from the alternator.

3. Loosen the drive belt tension and remove the belt from the pulley.

4. Remove the alternator-to-bracket bolts and the alternator from the vehicle.

5. To install, reverse the removal procedures. Adjust the drive belt tension and torque the lower bracket bolt to 35 ft. lbs. (47 Nm), the adjuster lock bolt to 10 ft. lbs. (13 Nm).

6. Connect all wiring before connecting the battery cable. Terminal **E** is always alternator ground.

## Voltage Regulator

The voltage regulator on all models is an internal part of the alternator and cannot be removed separately. The regulator can be replaced when rebuilding the alternator.

## Starter

### REMOVAL & INSTALLATION

1. If necessary, raise and safely support the vehicle.

2. Disconnect the negative battery cable.

3. Disconnect the electrical connectors from the starter, taking note of the positions for reinstallation purposes.

4. Remove the starter-to-engine bolts and the starter from the vehicle.

5. To install, reverse the removal procedures. Torque the starter mounting bolts to 29–36 ft. lbs. (39–49 Nm).

# EMISSION CONTROLS

## Emission Warning Lamp

The check engine light is located on the instrument panel of California vehicles only and indicates an emission performance malfunction.

### RESETTING

1. Turn the ignition switch **ON**.

2. If the check engine light turns **ON**, perform the self-diagnosis procedures to determine the malfunction.

3. Turn the ignition switch **OFF**.

4. Locate and repair the malfunction.

**NOTE: When the malfunction is** repaired and the fault code memory cleared, the check engine light will stay OFF.

# FUEL SYSTEM

## Fuel System Service Precautions

• Keep a Class B dry chemical fire extinguisher available.

• Always relieve the fuel system pressure before disconnecting any fitting.

• Make sure the work area is well ventilated to minimize the possibility of explosion.

• Turn off any source of ignition, such as a heater or welding equipment before beginning work on a fuel system.

• Always use new O-rings or gaskets and do not replace the metal fuel pipes with hose.

• Always us a back-up wrench when opening or closing a fuel line. Wrap a rag around the fitting to catch any fuel spilled.

• Deposit of fuel soaked rags or clothing in a proper safety container.

### RELIEVING FUEL SYSTEM PRESSURE

1. Locate the fuel pump fuse or relay and remove it.

2. Start the engine and allow it to run.

3. After the engine stalls, crank it 2–3 times to make sure the pressure is released.

4. Turn the ignition switch **OFF** and replace the fuse. There may still be some pressure in the system, make sure to take proper precautions when loosening any fittings.

## Fuel Filter

### REMOVAL & INSTALLATION

#### Axxess

The fuel filter is located under the driver's side and attached to the chassis; it is concealed by a cover plate.

1. Relieve the fuel pressure.

2. Raise and safely support the vehicle.

3. Remove the fuel filter cover plate.

4. Loosen the hose clamps and remove the filter.

5. Installation is the reverse of removal. Be sure to use a high pressure type filter and that the flow direction arrow on the filter points to the front of the vehicle.

#### Except Axxess

On Pick-Up and Pathfinder, the fuel filter is located in the right side of the engine compartment, near the power steering fluid reservoir. On Van, the filter is next to the cruise control vacuum actuator.

1. Release the fuel pressure.

2. Loosen the hose clamps at the fuel inlet and outlet lines and slide each line off the filter nipples.

3. Remove the fuel filter.

4. Installation is the reverse of removal. Be sure to use a high pressure type filter and that the flow direction arrow on the filter points to the engine.

## Electric Fuel Pump

The fuel pump is located in the fuel tank which must be removed to remove the fuel pump.

### SYSTEM PRESSURE TEST

1. Relieve the fuel system pressure.

2. Disconnect the fuel filter outlet hose and install a 0–60 psi gauge on a Tee fitting. Connect the fuel hose to the other leg of the Tee.

3. Start the engine, check for leaks and note the system pressure on the gauge. At idle, the pressure should be more than 33 psi.

4. Disconnect the vacuum hose from the pressure regulator. The pressure should increase to about 43 psi.

5. If the pressure is not correct, check for a system leak or a faulty injector or pressure regulator before removing the pump.

### PUMP DELIVERY TEST

1. Relieve the fuel system pressure and disconnect the outlet hose from the filter.

2. Connect a length of hose that has an inside diameter of ¼ in. (6mm). The diameter of the hose is important for accurate measurements.

3. Raise the end of the hose above the level of the pump. Turn the ignition switch **ON** and catch the gasoline in a graduated container. Pump output should be 1400cc in a minute or less.

### REMOVAL & INSTALLATION

1. Relieve the fuel system pressure. Disconnect the negative battery cable.

2. Siphon the fuel from the fuel

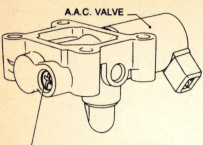

Idle speed adjustment on engines with multi-point fuel injection is on the Idle Air Adjusting unit—3.0L engine shown

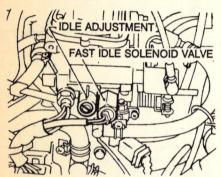

Idle speed adjustment on engines with throttle body fuel injection is on the throttle body

tank or, if fuel tank is equipped with a drain plug, remove the plug and drain the fuel into a proper fuel container.

3. Raise and safely support the vehicle.

4. Disconnect the fuel lines and the electrical connector from the fuel pump assembly. For 4WD models, remove the fuel tank protector from the bottom of the fuel tank.

5. Remove the fuel tank filler tube-to-vehicle bolts or nuts and the outer plate.

6. Remove the fuel tank-to-chassis bolts and lower the tank from the vehicle.

7. Remove the fuel pump assembly-to-tank screws and lift the assembly from the tank.

8. To install, use a new fuel pump assembly-to-tank O-ring and reverse the removal procedures. Torque the fuel pump assembly-to-tank screws to 24 inch lbs. (3 Nm) and the fuel tank protectors-to-chassis bolts to 26 ft. lbs. (35 Nm).

## Fuel Injection

### IDLE SPEED ADJUSTMENT

**NOTE: Idle speed and ignition timing must be checked together.**

1. Visually inspect the air cleaner for clogging, the hoses/ducts for leaks, the EGR valve operation, the electrical connectors, the gaskets, the throttle valve and throttle sensor operation and the AIV hose.

2. Start the engine and allow it to reach normal operating temperature.

3. Operate the engine under no-load for 2 minutes at about 2000 rpm. Make sure all accessories and lights are **OFF**. Race the engine 2–3 times, then let it at idle speed for 1 minute.

4. To adjust idle speed on engines with throttle body fuel injection, turn the large adjusting screw that is next to the fast idle solenoid valve on the throttle body. Do not turn the throttle stop screw.

5. To adjust idle speed on the 3.0L engine with multi-point fuel injection:

   a. Disconnect the wiring for the Auxiliary Air Control (AAC) valve at the back of the intake manifold. Idle speed should drop to about 700 rpm. The adjusting screw is on the same body assembly as the AAC.

   b. Reconnect the wiring, idle speed should be about 750 rpm. Do not change it with the wiring connected. If idle speed is not correct, look for another problem in the engine control system.

   c. Check and adjust timing as required to 15 degrees BTDC by rotating the distributor. Idle speed should remain at about 750 rpm.

6. To adjust timing on the 2.4L engine with multi-point fuel injection:

   a. Check idle speed at about 800 rpm. If it is not correct, disconnect the throttle sensor wiring and adjust the speed to less than 800 rpm. The adjustment is on the throttle body Idle Air Adjusting (IAA) unit that has small engine coolant hoses connected to it.

   b. Check and adjust ignition timing to 15 degrees BTDC.

7. Run the engine at 2000 rpm for about 2 minutes and check idle speed and timing again. If idle speed or timing are not correct, other problems exist with the engine control system and a full diagnostic test must be run.

## Fuel Injector

### REMOVAL & INSTALLATION

#### 1988–89

The injectors are in the throttle body, 1 for the 2.4L engine or 2 for the 3.0L engine. The throttle body assembly must be removed and the injectors pushed out from the bottom.

1. Relieve the fuel system pressure.

2. Drain about 1⅛ qt. (1L) of coolant from the engine.

3. From the throttle body, remove or disconnect the following items:

a. Air cleaner
b. Label and disconnect all wiring
c. Accelerator cable
d. Fuel and coolant hoses

4. Remove the throttle body-to-intake manifold nuts and the throttle body.

5. Remove the rubber seal and the injector harness grommet from the throttle body.

6. Remove the injector cover-to-injector body screws and the cover from the throttle body.

7. Turn the throttle valve to the fully open position. Place a soft hollow tube, with and inside diameter of not less than ¼ in., on the bottom of the fuel injectors and tap the injectors from the throttle body. Do not use a solid rod or the injector will be damaged.

**NOTE: If the injector tip becomes deformed by the tube, it must be replaced.**

8. If replacing an injector with a new one, perform the following operation:

   a. Disconnect the faulty injector wires from the electrical connector, then cut the injector wires from the metal terminals and pull the injector wiring from the harness tube.

   b. Install the new wiring into the harness tube and connect new terminals to the injector wires.

   c. Install the terminals into the electrical harness connector.

**NOTE: Be sure to install a new electrical harness grommet every time a new injector is installed.**

**To install:**

9. To install, use new O-rings and push the injectors into the throttle body until the O-rings are fully seated. Invert the throttle body and look to make sure the injector tips are properly seated.

10. Using silicone sealant, apply it to the injector harness grommet. An airtight seal is essential to ensure a stable idling condition.

11. Apply a thread locking compound to the injector cover screw threads and install the injector cover. Torque the injector cover screws in a criss-cross pattern to 2.5 ft. lbs. (3 Nm). Do not over tighten or the O-rings will be damaged.

12. Using silicone sealant, coat the top of the throttle body and install the air cleaner rubber seal.

**NOTE: Do not install the air cleaner until the air cleaner seal (silicone sealant) has hardened.**

13. Install the throttle body and torque the throttle body-to-intake manifold nuts to 13 ft. lbs. (18 Nm).

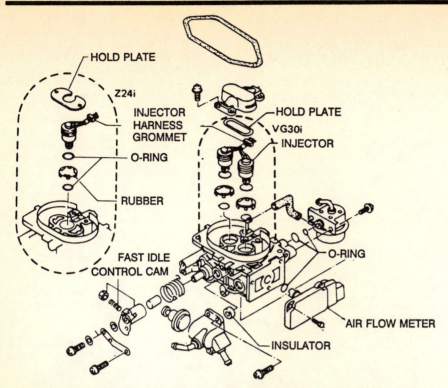

The injectors are pushed out of the throttle body from below the throttle plates

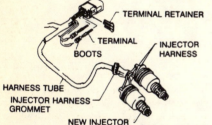

When replacing throttle body injectors, feed the wires through the tube and attach the terminal

14. To complete the installation, connect the wiring, hoses and cables and refill the cooling system.

15. Start the engine, check for leaks and check and adjust idle speed as required. Stop the engine and check to make sure the injector is fully closed; check for dripping fuel on the throttle valve.

### 1990

**2.4L ENGINE**

The engine is equipped 4 fuel injectors, with one located at each cylinder.
1. Relieve the fuel pressure.
2. Label and disconnect the electrical connectors from the fuel injectors.
3. Disconnect the fuel hoses from the rail.
4. Remove the fuel rail with injectors attached from the intake manifold.
5. Separate the fuel injectors from the fuel rail.

**To install:**
6. Replace the fuel injector O-rings.
7. Install the fuel injectors to the fuel rail.
8. Lubricate the fuel injector O-rings with automatic transmission fluid and press them, with the fuel rail, into the intake manifold.
9. Install the fuel rail-to-intake manifold bolts.
10. Connect the fuel hoses to the rail.
11. Connect the electrical connectors to the fuel injectors.
12. Turn the ignition switch **ON** and check for fuel leaks at the fuel rail.

**3.0L ENGINE**

The engine is equipped 6 fuel injectors, with one located at each cylinder.
1. Relieve the fuel pressure.
2. Remove the air cleaner from the throttle body.
3. Label and disconnect the vacuum hoses, electrical connectors and throttle cable from the throttle body/upper intake manifold assembly.
4. Remove the upper intake manifold.
5. Disconnect the electrical connectors from the fuel injectors.
6. Disconnect the supply and return hoses from the fuel rail.
7. The injectors can be removed separately or as an assembly with the rail. Do not use the old O-rings or insulators when installing the injectors.

**To install:**
8. Replace the fuel injector O-rings.

9. Lubricate the fuel injector O-rings with automatic transmission fluid and press them into the fuel rail assembly.
10. Connect the electrical connectors to the fuel injectors.
11. Using a new gasket, install the upper intake manifold and torque the bolts to 16 ft. lbs. (22 Nm).
12. Connect the electrical connectors, the vacuum lines and the accelerator cable.
13. Install the air cleaner to the throttle body.
14. Turn the ignition switch **ON** and check for fuel leaks at the fuel rail.

---

# DRIVE AXLE

## Halfshaft

### REMOVAL & INSTALLATION

#### *Pick-Up and Pathfinder With 4WD*

The front steering knuckle must be removed to remove the halfshaft.
1. Raise and safely support the vehicle.
2. Have an assistant depress the brake pedal and remove the halfshaft-to-differential flange bolts.
3. Remove the locking hub and front drive clutch assemblies.
4. Remove the steering knuckle with the halfshaft and clamp the knuckle in a vise.
5. Using a hammer and a block of wood, tap the halfshaft from the steering knuckle.
6. Installation is the reverse of removal. Torque the inner halfshaft drive flange bolts to 33 ft. lbs. (44 Nm).
7. Measure halfshaft end-play with a dial indicator against the end of the shaft; it should be 0.004–0.012 in. (0.1–0.3mm). Endplay can be adjusted with different thickness snaprings available at the dealer.

#### *Axxess*

**FRONT HALFSHAFTS**

1. With the hub cap and grease cap removed, have an assistant hold the brake pedal. Remove the front axle cotter pin, adjusting cap and washer and loosen the axle nut. The torque is very high, if possible this nut should be tightened and loosened with the wheels installed and the vehicle on the ground.
2. Raise and safely support the vehicle.
3. Without disconnecting the hydraulic hose, remove the brake cali-

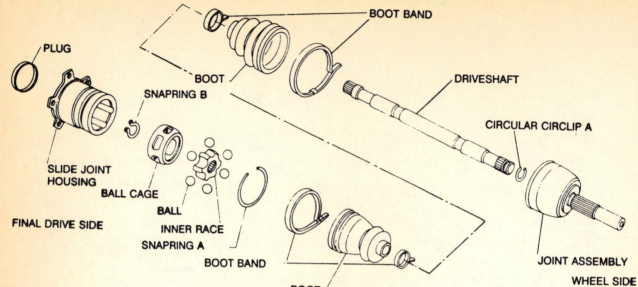

**Front halfshaft on 4WD Pick-Up and Pathfinder with 3.0L engine**

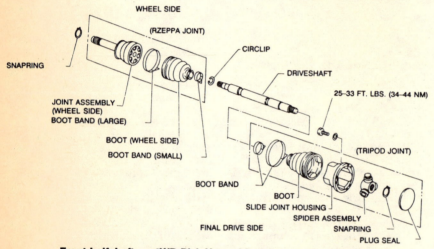

**Front halfshaft on 4WD Pick-Up and Pathfinder with 2.4L engine**

circlip into place. Pull out on the halfshaft to make sure the clip is seated.

10. When installing the right side extension shaft on 2WD models, torque the support bearing bracket bolts to 26 ft. lbs. (35 Nm).

11. When installing the left side halfshaft on 4WD models, torque the inner CV-joint bolts to 36 ft. lbs. (45 Nm).

12. Make sure the outer axle splines are clean and insert the axle into the hub. Connect the tie rod end to the steering knuckle and torque the nut to 29 ft. lbs. (39 Nm) and tighten as required to install a new cotter pin.

13. Install the washer and nut onto the axle but do not torque the nut yet.

14. Install the brake calipers and

pers and hang them from the body. Do not let the caliper hang by the hose.

4. Disconnect the tie rod end from the steering knuckle. Turn the knuckle all the way out at the front and use a soft hammer to tap the axle out of the hub.

5. Carefully pry the right inner CV-joint from the transaxle or transfer case.

6. On 2WD with automatic transaxle, insert a thin drift pin through the right side of differential and tap the left inner CV-joint out. Be carefull not to damage the mate pinion shaft or side gear inside the differential.

7. On all other models, pry the left CV-joint out the same way as the right.

**To install:**

8. Carefully insert the inner CV-joint into the differential gear to make sure the splines engage properly.

9. Push the shaft in to click the

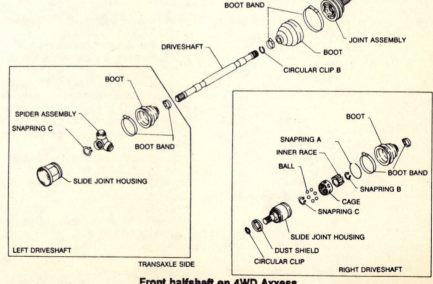

**Front halfshaft on 4WD Axxess**

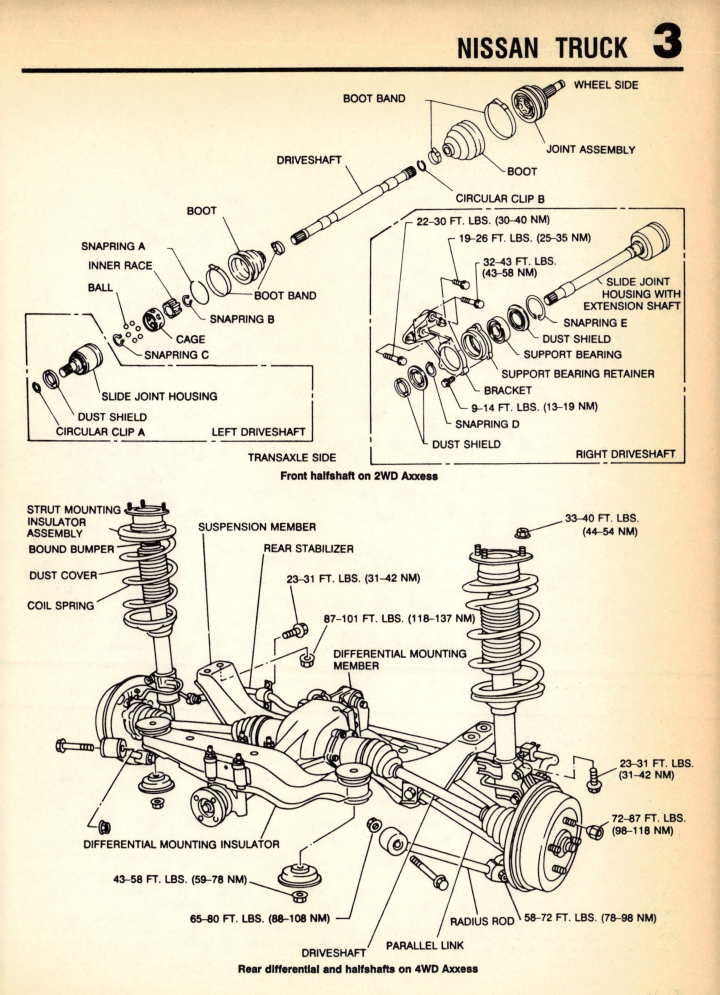

BOOT BAND

WHEEL SIDE

DRIVESHAFT

JOINT ASSEMBLY

BOOT

CIRCULAR CLIP B

BOOT

22–30 FT. LBS. (30–40 NM)

19–26 FT. LBS. (25–35 NM)

SNAPRING A

32–43 FT. LBS. (43–58 NM)

INNER RACE

BALL

SLIDE JOINT HOUSING WITH EXTENSION SHAFT

BOOT BAND

SNAPRING E

SNAPRING B

DUST SHIELD

CAGE

SUPPORT BEARING

SNAPRING C

SUPPORT BEARING RETAINER

BRACKET

SLIDE JOINT HOUSING

9–14 FT. LBS. (13–19 NM)

DUST SHIELD

SNAPRING D

CIRCULAR CLIP A

LEFT DRIVESHAFT

DUST SHIELD

TRANSAXLE SIDE

RIGHT DRIVESHAFT

**Front halfshaft on 2WD Axxess**

STRUT MOUNTING INSULATOR ASSEMBLY

SUSPENSION MEMBER

33–40 FT. LBS. (44–54 NM)

BOUND BUMPER

REAR STABILIZER

DUST COVER

23–31 FT. LBS. (31–42 NM)

COIL SPRING

87–101 FT. LBS. (118–137 NM)

DIFFERENTIAL MOUNTING MEMBER

23–31 FT. LBS. (31–42 NM)

DIFFERENTIAL MOUNTING INSULATOR

72–87 FT. LBS. (98–118 NM)

43–58 FT. LBS. (59–78 NM)

65–80 FT. LBS. (88–108 NM)

RADIUS ROD

58–72 FT. LBS. (78–98 NM)

DRIVESHAFT

PARALLEL LINK

**Rear differential and halfshafts on 4WD Axxess**

torque the carrier bolts to 72 ft. lbs. (97 Nm).

15. With all 4 wheels on the ground, torque the axle nuts to 231 ft. lbs. (314 Nm). Install the cap and cotter pin and install the grease cap.

## REAR HALFSHAFT

1. Remove the grease cap, the cotter pin and loosen the wheel bearing locknut.
2. Raise and safely support the vehicle.
3. Using a drift and a hammer, lightly separate the halfshaft from the knuckle; be sure to drive it inward.
4. Using shop cloths, cover the halfshaft boots to prevent damaging them.
5. Remove the parallel link-to-knuckle bolt and the radius rods-to-knuckle bolts.
6. Pull the knuckle outward and remove the halfshaft from it.
7. While supporting the halfshaft, use a prybar to separate the halfshaft from the differential.

**To install:**

8. To install, insert the halfshaft into the differential until the circlip snaps into position.
9. Position the halfshaft into the hub and assemble the rear suspension. Torque the radius rods-to-knuckle bolts to 72 ft. lbs. (98 Nm), the parallel link-to-knuckle bolt to 72 ft. lbs. (98 Nm) and the hub nut to 231 ft. lbs. (314 Nm).

# Driveshaft and U-Joints

## REMOVAL & INSTALLATION

### Pick-Up and Pathfinder

#### ONE PIECE REAR DRIVESHAFT

1. Raise and safely support the vehicle.
2. Matchmark the driveshaft flange to the pinion flange on the differential.
3. Remove the flange bolts, lower the driveshaft and pull it from the transmission.
4. Using a clean rag, plug the rear of the transmission to keep the oil from leaking out.
5. To install, insert the sleeve yoke into the transmission, align the matchmarks and fit the driveshaft into place. Torque the driveshaft flange nuts/bolts to 65 ft. lbs. (88 Nm).

#### TWO PIECE REAR DRIVESHAFT

1. Raise and safely support the vehicle.
2. Matchmark the driveshaft flange to the pinion flange on the differential and to the transmission drive flange.
3. Remove the bolts from both

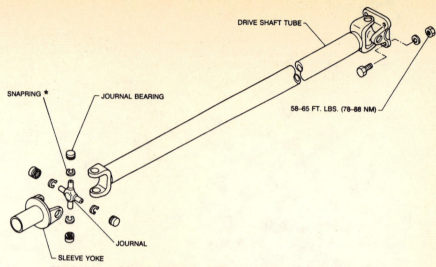

**Single piece driveshaft used on Pick-Up and Pathfinder, Van similar**

flanges, then remove the bolts from the center bearing flange-to-chassis bracket and lower the driveshaft out of the vehicle.
4. Using a clean rag, plug the rear of the transmission to keep the oil from leaking out.
5. If necessary, separate the front section of the driveshaft from the rear section.
6. To install, align the matchmarks and reverse the removal procedures. Torque as follows:
    Center bearing-to-chassis bolts to 16 ft. lbs. (22 Nm)
    Driveshaft-to-differential flange nuts/bolts
        Model 3S63 — 33 ft. lbs. (44 Nm)
        Model 3S80 — 65 ft. lbs. (88 Nm)
7. If the center bearing was separated from the front driveshaft, torque as follows:
    Companion flange-to-front drive-shaft nut — 174–203 ft. lbs. (235–275 Nm)
    Rear driveshaft-to-center bearing flange nuts/bolts
        Model 3S63 — 17–24 ft. lbs. (24–32 Nm)
        Model 3S71H — 29–33 ft. lbs. (39–44 Nm)
        Model 3S80 — 58–65 ft. lbs. (78–88 Nm)

#### 4WD FRONT DRIVESHAFT

1. Raise and safely support the vehicle.
2. Matchmark the driveshaft flange to the pinion flange on the differential and to the transfer case drive flange.
3. Remove the nuts and bolts and remove the front driveshaft.
4. To install, align the matchmarks and reverse the removal procedures. Torque the all the flange nuts and bolts to 33 ft. lbs. (44 Nm).

### Van

1. Raise and safely support the vehicle.
2. Matchmark the driveshaft flange to the pinion flange on the differential.
3. Remove the flange bolts, lower the driveshaft and pull it from the transmission.
4. Using a clean rag, plug the rear of the transmission to keep the oil from leaking out.
5. To install, insert the sleeve yoke into the transmission, align the matchmarks and fit the driveshaft into place. Torque the driveshaft flange nuts/bolts to 33 ft. lbs. (44 Nm).

### Axxess

#### WITH 4WD

1. Raise and safely support the vehicle.
2. Matchmark the driveshaft flange to the pinion flange on the differential and to the transmission drive flange.
3. Remove the bolts from both flanges, then remove the bolts from the center bearing flange-to-chassis brackets and lower the driveshaft out of the vehicle. Take care to not damage the center CV-joints by bending them too far.
4. Using a clean rag, plug the rear of the transmission to keep the oil from leaking out.
5. If necessary, separate the drive-shaft sections for repair or replacement.
6. To install, align the matchmarks and reverse the removal procedures. Torque the flange nuts and bolts to 33 ft. lbs. (44 Nm) and the center bearing bracket bolts to 30 ft. lbs. (41 Nm).

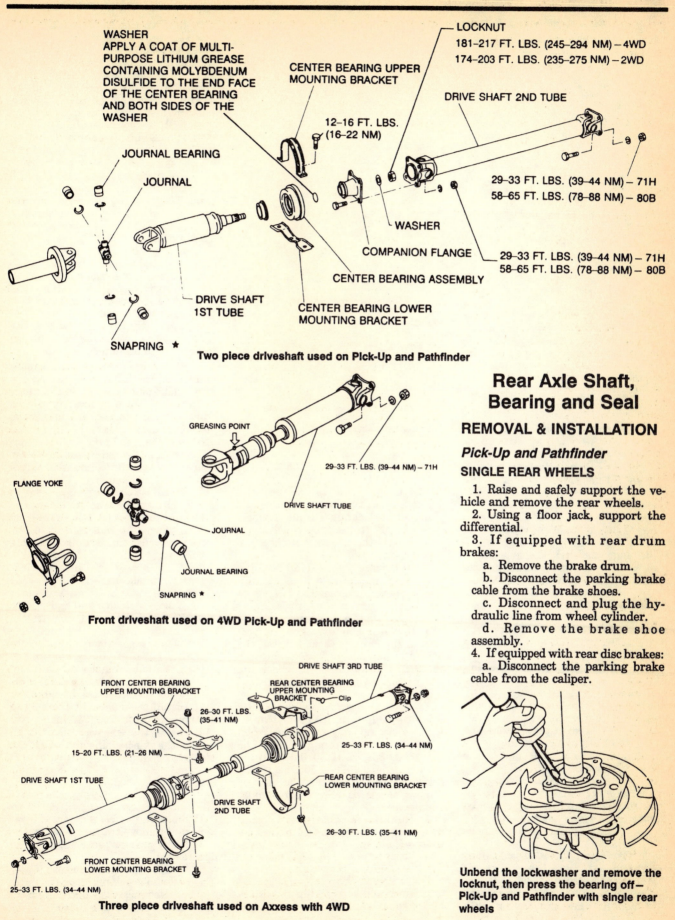

WASHER
APPLY A COAT OF MULTI-PURPOSE LITHIUM GREASE CONTAINING MOLYBDENUM DISULFIDE TO THE END FACE OF THE CENTER BEARING AND BOTH SIDES OF THE WASHER

CENTER BEARING UPPER MOUNTING BRACKET

LOCKNUT
181–217 FT. LBS. (245–294 NM) – 4WD
174–203 FT. LBS. (235–275 NM) – 2WD

DRIVE SHAFT 2ND TUBE

JOURNAL BEARING

JOURNAL

12–16 FT. LBS. (16–22 NM)

29–33 FT. LBS. (39–44 NM) – 71H
58–65 FT. LBS. (78–88 NM) – 80B

WASHER

COMPANION FLANGE

29–33 FT. LBS. (39–44 NM) – 71H
58–65 FT. LBS. (78–88 NM) – 80B

CENTER BEARING ASSEMBLY

DRIVE SHAFT 1ST TUBE

CENTER BEARING LOWER MOUNTING BRACKET

SNAPRING ★

**Two piece driveshaft used on Pick-Up and Pathfinder**

GREASING POINT

FLANGE YOKE

29–33 FT. LBS. (39–44 NM) – 71H

DRIVE SHAFT TUBE

JOURNAL

JOURNAL BEARING

SNAPRING ★

**Front driveshaft used on 4WD Pick-Up and Pathfinder**

FRONT CENTER BEARING UPPER MOUNTING BRACKET

DRIVE SHAFT 3RD TUBE

REAR CENTER BEARING UPPER MOUNTING BRACKET

Clip

26–30 FT. LBS. (35–41 NM)

25–33 FT. LBS. (34–44 NM)

15–20 FT. LBS. (21–26 NM)

DRIVE SHAFT 1ST TUBE

REAR CENTER BEARING LOWER MOUNTING BRACKET

DRIVE SHAFT 2ND TUBE

26–30 FT. LBS. (35–41 NM)

FRONT CENTER BEARING LOWER MOUNTING BRACKET

25–33 FT. LBS. (34–44 NM)

**Three piece driveshaft used on Axxess with 4WD**

## Rear Axle Shaft, Bearing and Seal

### REMOVAL & INSTALLATION

*Pick-Up and Pathfinder*

**SINGLE REAR WHEELS**

1. Raise and safely support the vehicle and remove the rear wheels.

2. Using a floor jack, support the differential.

3. If equipped with rear drum brakes:

   a. Remove the brake drum.

   b. Disconnect the parking brake cable from the brake shoes.

   c. Disconnect and plug the hydraulic line from wheel cylinder.

   d. Remove the brake shoe assembly.

4. If equipped with rear disc brakes:

   a. Disconnect the parking brake cable from the caliper.

**Unbend the lockwasher and remove the locknut, then press the bearing off— Pick-Up and Pathfinder with single rear wheels**

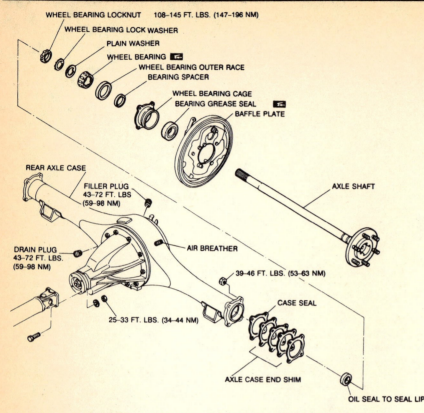

WHEEL BEARING LOCKNUT    108–145 FT. LBS. (147–196 NM)
WHEEL BEARING LOCK WASHER
PLAIN WASHER
WHEEL BEARING
WHEEL BEARING OUTER RACE
BEARING SPACER
WHEEL BEARING CAGE
BEARING GREASE SEAL
BAFFLE PLATE

REAR AXLE CASE

FILLER PLUG
43–72 FT. LBS
(59–98 NM)

DRAIN PLUG
43–72 FT. LBS.
(59–98 NM)

AIR BREATHER

AXLE SHAFT

39–46 FT. LBS. (53–63 NM)

25–33 FT. LBS. (34–44 NM)

CASE SEAL

AXLE CASE END SHIM

OIL SEAL TO SEAL LIP

**Rear axle assembly on Pick-Up and Pathfinder with single rear wheels**

b. Remove the caliper-to-knuckle bolts and hang the caliper from the body on a piece of wire. Do not disconnect the hydraulic line.

c. Remove the rotor disc.

5. Remove the backing plate nuts.

6. Attach a slide hammer to the wheel lugs and pull the axle shaft/backing plate assembly from the axle housing. Whenever the axle shaft is removed, the oil seal should be replaced.

**To install:**

7. To replace the wheel bearing, leave the slide hammer attached to the lugs and secure it in a vise with the axle pointing up.

a. At the rear of the backing plate, unbend and discard the lockwasher.

b. Using a brass drift and a hammer, loosen and remove the locknut.

c. Using a shop press, press the axle shaft out of the bearing.

d. Press the bearing out of the bearing housing.

8. To install the wheel bearing:

a. Press the new bearing into the housing. Be sure to press only on the outer race of the bearing.

b. Grease the inside of the bearing housing.

c. To install a new oil seal, lubricate the seal lips and carefully press it into the bearing housing.

d. Position the back plate on the bearing housing, support the inner

bearing race and press the axle into the bearing.

e. Grease the flat washer and lockwasher, lay them into place and install the locknut. Torque the locknut to 217 ft. lbs. (294 Nm).

f. Bend the lockwasher tabs into place.

9. Lubricate the bearing housing and recess in the axle housing with wheel bearing grease. Coat the axle splines with gear oil. Coat the seal surface of the shaft with grease.

10. Install a new axle housing seal behind the shim pack and install the axle into the housing. Torque the nuts to 46 ft. lbs. (63 Nm) and check the endplay of the axle with a dial indicator.

11. The axle endplay should be 0.0008–0.0059 in. (0.02–0.15mm) when servicing only one axle. When servicing both sides, endplay should be 0.0118–0.0354 in. (0.30–0.90mm) for the first axle, 0.0008–0.0059 in. (0.02–0.15mm) for the second axle. Add or remove shims as required to adjust endplay.

12. Install the remaining components and adjust the brakes as required.

**DUAL REAR WHEELS**

1. Raise and safely support the vehicle and remove the rear wheels.

2. Remove the bolts and slide the axle shaft out of the housing. Be prepared to catch the oil that leaks out.

3. Remove the screw to remove the lockwasher and use a pin wrench to remove the locknut. The torque on the locknut is very high, do not use a hammer and drift pin to remove it.

4. With the locknut off, the brake drum/wheel hub assembly will pull off easily with both bearings inside. Be careful not to drop the outer bearing.

5. Pry the grease seal out of the hub to remove the inner bearing for inspection. The bearing races can be removed from the hub with a hammer and a soft drift pin.

**To install:**

6. To replace the oil seal, pry the old seal out of the axle housing. Lubricate and carefully install the new seal with an appropriate seal installation tool. Make sure it goes in evenly and bottoms against the seat.

7. Carefully install new bearing races into the hub. Make sure they go in evenly and bottom against the seat.

8. Pack both bearings with grease and install the inner bearing into the hub. Pack some grease into the hub.

9. Lubricate and press the new wheel bearing seal into the hub. Wipe away the excess grease.

10. Slip the hub/brake drum assembly onto the axle and install the outer bearing. Grease the locknut and install it onto the axle housing.

11. To adjust the bearing preload:

a. Use a pin wrench to torque the locknut to 125–145 ft. lbs. (167–196 Nm). Turn the hub in both directions several times while torquing the nut.

b. The new grease may make it stiff but make sure the hub turns smoothly without catching or roughness. Attach a pull scale to one of the wheel studs and measure the pull required to turn the hub.

c. If it is not smooth or if more than 4.7 lbs. of pull is required to turn the hub, remove the hub and look for improperly installed bearing races or dirt in the bearings.

12. Install the axle shaft and torque the bolts to 55 ft. lbs. (75 Nm).

13. Install the wheels, check the oil level in the axle housing and adjust the brakes as required.

*Van*

1. Raise and safely support the vehicle and remove the rear wheels.

2. Using a floor jack, support the differential.

3. Remove the rear brakes:

a. Remove the brake drum.

b. Disconnect the parking brake cable from the brake shoes.

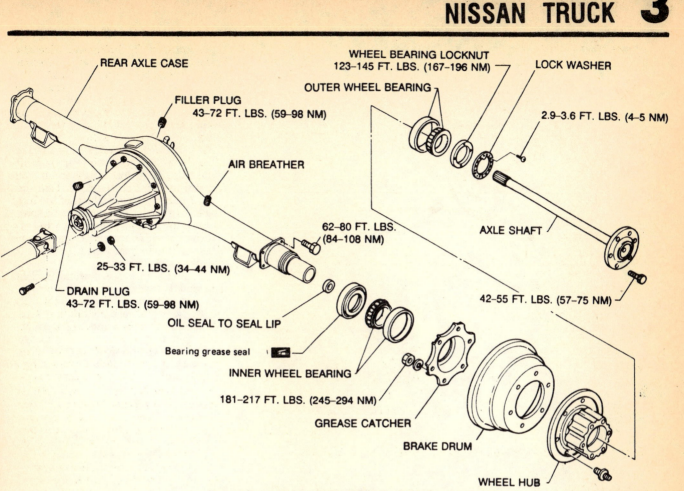

REAR AXLE CASE

FILLER PLUG
43–72 FT. LBS. (59–98 NM)

WHEEL BEARING LOCKNUT
123–145 FT. LBS. (167–196 NM)

OUTER WHEEL BEARING

LOCK WASHER

2.9–3.6 FT. LBS. (4–5 NM)

AIR BREATHER

62–80 FT. LBS.
(84–108 NM)

AXLE SHAFT

25–33 FT. LBS. (34–44 NM)

DRAIN PLUG
43–72 FT. LBS. (59–98 NM)

OIL SEAL TO SEAL LIP

42–55 FT. LBS. (57–75 NM)

Bearing grease seal

INNER WHEEL BEARING

181–217 FT. LBS. (245–294 NM)

GREASE CATCHER

BRAKE DRUM

WHEEL HUB

**Rear axle assembly on Pick-Up with dual rear wheels**

c. Disconnect and plug the hydraulic line from wheel cylinder.

d. Remove the brake shoe assembly.

4. Remove the backing plate nuts.

5. Attach a slide hammer to the wheel lugs and pull the axle shaft/backing plate assembly from the axle housing. Whenever the axle shaft is removed, the oil seal should be replaced.

6. To remove the rear bearing, the bearing collar must be cut off the axle shaft with a cold chisel. Be careful not to damage the axle shaft.

7. Use a press or a bearing puller to pull the bearing housing and bearing off the axle shaft.

**To install:**

8. Install the bearing spacer with the chamfer facing the axle flange (facing out). Make sure there is no oil or grease on the axle shaft or the other parts.

9. Install the bearing, collar and housing in the correct order and press them onto the axle shaft. Be sure to support the proper bearing race when pressing or the bearing will be damaged.

10. To set the correct bearing clearance:

a. Use a depth caliper to measure the depth of the outer bearing race in the bearing housing, Dimension A.

b. Remove the shim pack and clean the axle housing flange. Measure the distance between the flange and the end of the axle housing, Dimension B.

c. Subtract A from B. The difference must be 0–0.004 in. (0–0.1mm). If A is larger than B, the bearing outer race will be squeezed between the axle housing and the bearing housing and the bearing will wear quickly. Measure the shims and adjust the shim pack as required.

11. Pry the old oil seal out of the axle housing. Lubricate the new oil seal and use an appropriate seal installation tool to make sure it is evenly seated in the housing.

12. Install the axle shaft and torque the bearing housing bolts to 40 ft. lbs. (54 Nm).

13. Install the brakes and bleed and adjust as required.

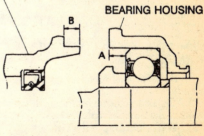

REAR AXLE HOUSING

BEARING HOUSING

**To remove the rear axle bearing on Van, the bearing collar must be cut**

**Measure the bearing clearance when installing Van rear axle shaft**

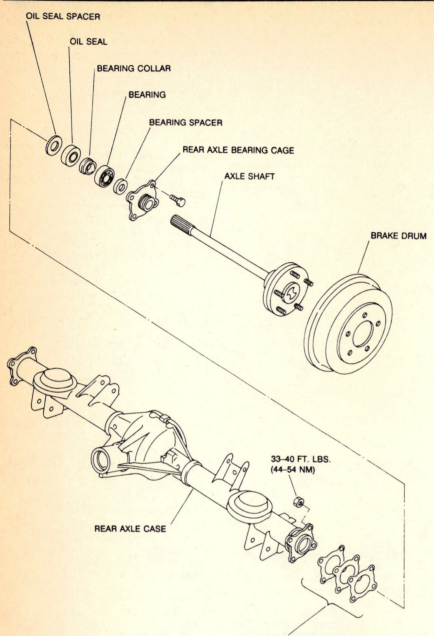

**Rear axle assembly on Van**

pension arm. The arm is connected to the torsion bar and will spring down if not supported.

9. Use a ball joint press and disconnect the tie rod end and upper and lower ball joints. Remove the front spindle.

**To install:**

10. Install the spindle and start all the nuts. Torque the lower ball joint nuts to 141 ft. lbs. (191 Nm) and the upper ball joint nuts to 108 ft. lbs. (147 Nm). Install new cotter pins.

11. Make sure the bearings are clean and in good condition. Pack the bearings and the hub with new grease and install the bearings into the hub. Install a new grease seal.

12. Make sure the spindle is clean. Install the spacer with the chamfer facing in on the spindle.

13. Lightly grease the lips on the seal and slide the hub and bearings onto the spindle. Install the washer and nut and adjust the pre-load on the bearing. Check and adjust front wheel alignment.

### 1989–92 Pathfinder and All 4WD

With the exception of the front locking hubs, the front wheel bearings are the same on 1989–92 Pathfinder as on all 4WD models.

1. Raise and safely support the vehicle and remove the front wheels.

2. Have an assistant hold the brake pedal and loosen the locking front hub housing bolts. Remove the hub assembly housing, the snapring and the hub assembly.

3. Without disconnecting the hydraulic line, remove the brake caliper and hang it from the body with wire. Do not allow the caliper to hang by the hose.

4. Remove the locking screw and remove the lock washer. Use a pin wrench to loosen the wheel bearing locknut. The torque may be fairly high, do not use a hammer and drift pin.

5. Remove the locknut and pull the hub off with the bearings. Pry the inner grease seal out to remove the inner bearing. Discard the seal.

6. Use a block of wood and hammer to tap on the end of the halfshaft to break it loose from the hub spline.

7. To remove the knuckle, remove the cotter pins from the upper and lower ball joint nuts and the tie rod nut. Remove the tie rod nut and loosen the ball joint nuts but do not remove them yet.

8. Place a jack under the lower suspension arm. The arm is connected to the torsion bar and will spring down if not supported.

9. Use a ball joint press and discon-

## Front Wheel Hub, Knuckle and Bearings

### REMOVAL & INSTALLATION

#### Pick-Up and 1988 Pathfinder With 2WD

1. Raise and safely support the vehicle and remove the front wheels.

2. Disconnect the brake hose from the bracket on the knuckle.

3. Without disconnecting the hydraulic line, remove the brake caliper and hang it from the body on a wire.

Do not let it hang by the hose.

4. Remove the wheel hub cup, the cotter pin, the adjusting cap and hub nut.

5. Remove the wheel hub and brake disc assembly. Be careful not to drop the outer wheel bearing.

6. To remove the inner bearing, pry out the grease seal. Discard the seal.

7. To remove the knuckle, remove the cotter pins from the upper and lower ball joint nuts and the tie rod nut. Remove the tie rod nut and loosen the ball joint nuts but do not remove them yet.

8. Place a jack under the lower sus-

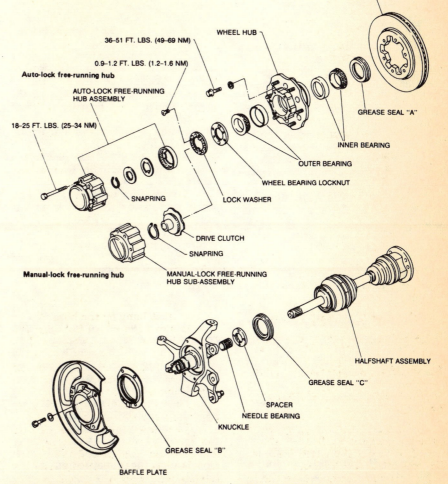

**Front wheel bearing on Pick-Up and 1988 Pathfinder with 2WD**

nect the tie rod end and upper and lower ball joints. Remove the front spindle.

**To install:**

10. Clean all parts of grease and check the condition of the bearings. If bearings are to be replaced, the inner races can be removed from the hub with a hammer and soft drift pin. Be careful not to damage the hub.

11. Install the spindle and start all the nuts. Torque the lower ball joint nuts to 141 ft. lbs. (191 Nm) and the upper ball joint nuts to 108 ft. lbs. (147 Nm). Install new cotter pins.

12. Connect the tie rods and torque the nuts to 72 ft. lbs. (98 Nm). Install new cotter pins.

13. Carefully install the new inner races with the drift pin, making sure they seat in the hub.

14. Pack the bearings with new grease and pack grease into the hub. Install the inner bearing and press a new inner seal into the hub.

15. Slip the hub assembly onto the spindle and install the outer bearing. Grease the locknut, thread it into place and set the bearing pre-load. Check and adjust front wheel alignment.

## BEARING PRE-LOAD ADJUSTMENT

### Pick-Up and 1988 Pathfinder With 2WD

1. With the bearings and hub properly cleaned and lubricated, install the nut and torque it to 25 ft. lbs. (34 Nm).

2. Spin the hub several times in both directions, then torque the nut to 29 ft. lbs. (39 Nm).

3. Loosen the nut 45 degrees. Install the locknut cap and a new cotter pin.

### 1989–92 Pathfinder and All 4WD

1. Use a pin wrench to torque the locknut to 58–72 ft. lbs. (78–98 Nm). Turn the hub in both directions several times while torquing the nut.

2. Loosen the locknut, then torque again to 13 inch lbs. (1.5 Nm).

3. Turn the hub several times and check the nut torque again.

4. Install the lock washer. When installing the screw, make sure the locknut turns no more than 30 degrees in either direction.

5. When bearing pre-load is properly set, there will be no endplay in the hub and it will require no more than 4.7 lbs. of pull at the wheel stud to turn the hub.

6. Install the locking hub and the brake caliper. Torque the caliper carri-

**Front wheel bearing and hub assembly on 1989–92 Pathfinder and all Pick-Up and Pathfinder with 4WD**

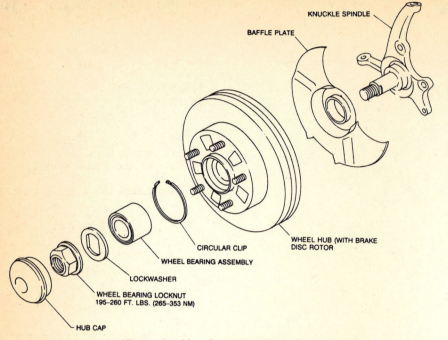

**Front wheel bearing assembly on Van**

er bolts to 72 ft. lbs. (98 Nm) and the hub bolts to 25 ft. lbs. (34 Nm).

## Van

1. With the vehicle on the ground, remove the hub cap and loosen the wheel bearing locknut. The torque on this nut is high enough to cause the vehicle to fall off the supports.

2. Raise and safely support the vehicle and remove the wheels.

3. Without disconnecting the hydraulic line, remove the brake caliper and hang it from the body with wire. Do not allow the caliper to hang by the hose.

4. Remove the locknut and lock washer and pull the hub and disc assembly off.

5. To remove the bearing, remove the circlip and press the bearing out of the hub. Discard the bearing.

6. To remove the knuckle, remove the cotter pins and disconnect the tie rod ends.

7. Place a jack under the lower suspension arm, remove the cotter pins and loosen the ball joint nuts.

8. Press the upper ball joint out of the knuckle first, reinstall the nut finger tight to hold the knuckle in place, then press out the lower ball joint. Remove the nut and remove the knuckle.

**To install:**

9. Make sure the ball joint tapered studs are clean and dry. Use a floor jack to hold the lower suspension arm up and fit the knuckle to the ball joints. Install both nuts.

10. Torque the upper ball joint nut to 72 ft. lbs. (98 Nm), then torque the

lower ball joint nut to 141 ft. lbs. (191 Nm). Install new cotter pins.

11. Connect the tie rod end and torque the nut to 72 ft. lbs. (98 Nm). Install new cotter pins.

12. When pressing the new bearing into the hub, be sure to press only on the outer race or the bearing will be damaged. Make sure the lips of the grease seal on the bearing face the circlip.

13. Install a new circlip and lightly grease the lips of the seal.

14. Install the hub, lock washer and locknut onto the spindle. Do not fully tighten the locknut yet.

15. Install the brake caliper and wheel and lower the vehicle to the ground.

16. With the vehicle on all 4 wheels, torque the locknut to 260 ft. lbs. (353 Nm). Install the hub cap. Check and adjust front wheel alignment.

## Axxess

1. With the vehicle on the ground, remove the hub cap, cotter pin, adjusting cap and insulator and loosen the wheel bearing locknut. The torque on this nut is high enough to cause the vehicle to fall off the supports.

2. Raise and safely support the vehicle and remove the wheels.

3. Without disconnecting the hydraulic line, remove the brake caliper and hang it from the body with wire. Do not allow the caliper to hang by the hose.

4. Remove the wheel bearing locknut and washer and hold a piece of

wood against the axle. Tap the wood with a hammer to loosen the axle spline in the hub.

5. To remove the knuckle, remove the cotter pin and disconnect the tie rod end. Matchmark the adjusting pin to the strut and remove the knuckle-to-strut bolt and the lower ball joint nut. Use a ball joint press to separate the joint.

6. To remove the bearing from the knuckle:

   a. Pry out the seal and press the hub out of the bearing with a hydraulic press. The inner bearing race will probably stay on the hub.

   b. Remove the snaprings and press the bearing out towards the halfshaft side of the knuckle. Be careful not to bend the brake backing plate. Discard the bearing.

**To install:**

7. Carefully inspect the hub for signs of wear or cracks. If the bearing has been replaced before and seems to have failed early, the hub is distorted and should be replaced.

8. With all parts clean and dry, install the inner snapring and press the new bearing into the knuckle. Be sure to press only on the outer race or the bearing will be damaged.

9. Install the outer snapring. Pack the new grease seals with clean grease and install them.

10. Press the hub into the inner race. Be sure the inner race is properly supported or the bearing will be damaged. While the hub and bearing are still clamped in the press, turn the knuckle to make sure it turns smoothly on the bearing.

11. Make sure the halfshaft splines are clean and install the knuckle. With the adjusting pin matchmarks aligned, torque the knuckle-to-strut bolt to 91 ft. lbs. (124 Nm) and the lower ball joint nut to 64 ft. lbs. (86 Nm). Tighten as required to install a new cotter pin.

12. Connect the tie rod end, torque the nut to 29 ft. lbs. (39 Nm) and tighten as required to install a new cotter pin.

13. Install the brake caliper and torque the carrier bolts to 72 ft. lbs. (97 Nm). Install the wheel and lower the vehicle. Do not roll the vehicle before tightening the wheel bearing locknut.

14. With the vehicle on all 4 wheels, install the washer and wheel bearing locknut and torque the nut to 231 ft. lbs. (314 Nm). Install the adjusting cap and a new cotter pin. Check and adjust front wheel alignment.

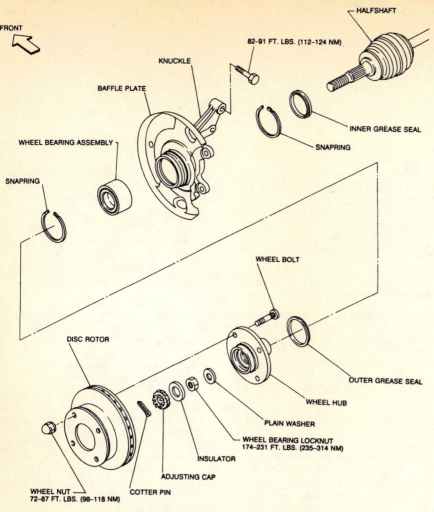

FRONT

HALFSHAFT

82-91 FT. LBS. (112-124 NM)

KNUCKLE

BAFFLE PLATE

INNER GREASE SEAL

WHEEL BEARING ASSEMBLY

SNAPRING

SNAPRING

WHEEL BOLT

DISC ROTOR

OUTER GREASE SEAL

WHEEL HUB

PLAIN WASHER

WHEEL BEARING LOCKNUT
174-231 FT. LBS. (235-314 NM)

INSULATOR

ADJUSTING CAP

COTTER PIN

WHEEL NUT
72-87 FT. LBS. (98-118 NM)

**Front wheel bearing and knuckle on Axxess**

# Rear Wheel Hub, Knuckle and Bearings

## REMOVAL & INSTALLATION

### Axxess

**2WD MODELS**

The rear knuckle and wheel spindle are a part of the rear strut and must be replaced as an assembly. The wheel bearing locknut torque is very high; loosen and tighten this nut with the vehicle on the ground.

1. Remove the hub cap and cotter pin.
2. Apply the brakes and loosen the wheel bearing locknut.
3. Raise and safely support the vehicle, remove the wheel.
4. Remove the wheel bearing nut, washer and wheel hub. The bearing is part of the hub and cannot be replaced separately.
**To install:**
5. Install the hub, washer and lock-

nut. Do not fully tighten the locknut yet.
6. With the vehicle on all 4 wheels,

torque the bearing locknut to 188 ft. lbs. (255 Nm). Install a new cotter pin.

**4WD MODELS**

1. The wheel bearing locknut torque is very high; loosen and tighten this nut with the vehicle on the ground. Remove the hub cap, cotter pin, the adjusting cap and insulator.
2. Apply the brakes and loosen the wheel bearing locknut.
3. Raise and safely support the vehicle and remove the wheel.
4. Remove the wheel bearing nut and washer.
5. Disconnect the hydraulic line from the wheel cylinder and parking brake cable from the brake shoes.
6. Using shop cloths, cover the halfshaft boots.
7. Using a mallet, tap in on the halfshaft to loosen it from the wheel hub.
8. Remove the radius rods-to-knuckle bolts and the parallel link-to-knuckle bolt.
9. Support the knuckle and remove the strut-to-knuckle nuts and bolts. Remove the knuckle assembly from the vehicle and position the assembly in a vise.
10. Using a piece of pipe and a hammer, drive the wheel hub from the knuckle. The inner bearing race will probably stay on the hub. Use a press and a bearing puller to remove it.
11. Remove the inner and outer snaprings and use the press to remove the bearing.
**To install:**
12. Carefully inspect the hub for signs of wear or cracks. If the bearing has been replaced before and seems to have failed early, the hub is distorted and should be replaced.
13. With all parts clean and dry, install the inner snapring and press the

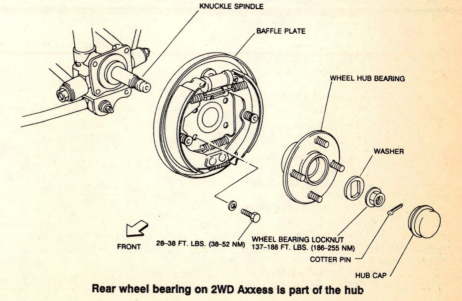

KNUCKLE SPINDLE

BAFFLE PLATE

WHEEL HUB BEARING

WASHER

FRONT

28-38 FT. LBS. (38-52 NM)

WHEEL BEARING LOCKNUT
137-188 FT. LBS. (186-255 NM)

COTTER PIN

HUB CAP

**Rear wheel bearing on 2WD Axxess is part of the hub**

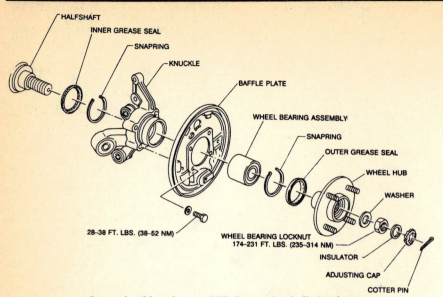

Rear wheel bearing on 4WD Axxess is similar to front

new bearing into the knuckle. Be sure to press only on the outer race or the bearing will be damaged.

14. Install the outer snapring. Pack the new grease seals with clean grease and install them. Install the brake backing plate.

15. Press the hub into the inner race, do not exceed 3 tons pressure. Be sure the inner race is properly supported or the bearing will be damaged. While the hub and bearing are still clamped in the press, turn the knuckle to make sure it turns smoothly on the bearing.

16. When installing the knuckle, be sure the halfshaft spline is clean and insert it into the wheel hub. Torque the knuckle–to–strut bolts to 91 ft. lbs. (124 Nm) and the remaining knuckle mounting bolts to 72 ft. lbs. (98 Nm).

17. Install the parking brake cable and the pressure line to the wheel cylinder. Install the wheel bearing locknut but do not fully tighten it yet.

18. With all 4 wheels on the ground, torque the wheel hub locknut to 231 ft. lbs. (314 Nm).

19. Check and adjust rear wheel alignment and bleed and adjust the rear brakes.

## Manual Locking Hubs

### REMOVAL & INSTALLATION

1. Raise and safely support the vehicle and remove the wheels.
2. Set the knob of the manual lock to the **FREE** position.
3. Have an assistant hold the brake pedal and use a Torx® wrench to remove the locking hub housing bolts.
4. Remove the snapring to disassemble the drive clutch.
5. Installation is the reverse of removal. Make sure the parts are clean

and lubricated with new grease. With the hub in the **FREE** position, torque the bolts to 25 ft. lbs. (34 Nm).

## Automatic Locking Hubs

### REMOVAL & INSTALLATION

1. Raise and safely support the vehicle and remove the wheels.
2. Set the knob of the manual lock to the **FREE** position.
3. Have an assistant hold the brake

pedal and use a Torx® wrench to remove the locking hub housing bolts.
4. Remove the snapring to disassemble the drive clutch.
5. Installation is the reverse of removal. Make sure the parts are clean and lubricated with new grease. With the hub in the **FREE** position, torque the bolts to 25 ft. lbs. (34 Nm).

## Pinion Seal

### REMOVAL & INSTALLATION

#### Pick-Up and Pathfinder

The pinion oil seal on Models H190A, H233B and C200 differentials can not be replaced without disassembling the differential. A collapsible spacer is used to set pinion bearing pre-load.

1. Raise and safely support the vehicle.
2. Remove the driveshaft.
3. Using a socket wrench and the differential flange holding tool, hold the differential flange and the remove the differential pinion nut.
4. Using a wheel puller tool, pull the pinion flange from the differential.
5. Using a small prybar, pry the oil seal from the differential.
6. Using the oil seal driver tool (Model R180A and H190A differentials), lubricate the new oil seal lips with multi-purpose grease and drive the new seal into the differential housing until it is flush with the end of the housing.

Manual locking hubs used on 4WD Pick-Up and Pathfinder

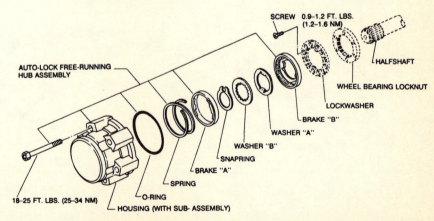

Automatic locking hubs used on 4WD Pick-Up and Pathfinder

7. Using a soft hammer, tap the pinion flange onto the pinion shaft.

8. Using a socket wrench and the differential flange holding tool (Model H233B), hold the differential flange and torque the pinion flange nut as follows:

Model R180 — 123–145 ft. lbs. (166–196 Nm)

Model R190A — 94–217 ft. lbs. (127–294 Nm)

Model H233B — 145–181 ft. lbs. (196–245 Nm)

9. Check the oil level in the differential and install the driveshaft and wheels.

### Van

1. Raise and safely support the vehicle. Remove the driveshaft.

2. Using a socket wrench and the differential flange holding tool, hold the differential flange and the remove the differential pinion nut.

3. Using a wheel puller tool, pull the pinion flange from the differential.

4. Using a small prybar, pry the oil seal from the differential.

5. Using the oil seal driver tool, lubricate the new oil seal lips with multipurpose grease and drive the new seal into the differential housing until it is flush with the end of the housing.

6. Using a soft hammer, tap the pinion flange onto the pinion shaft.

7. Using a socket wrench and the differential flange holding tool, hold the differential flange and torque the pinion flange nut to 94 ft. lbs.

8. Turn the pinion flange, in both directions, several times to set the bearings. Using a small torque wrench, measure the pinion preload; it should be 9.5–14.8 inch lbs. (1–1.7 Nm). If the preload value is not obtained, repeat the pinion torquing procedure.

9. Check the oil level in the differential and install the driveshaft and wheels.

### Axxess

#### 4WD MODELS

1. Raise and safely support the vehicle.

2. Remove the driveshaft.

3. Using a spanner wrench and a socket wrench, remove the drive pinion nut.

4. Using a wheel puller tool, press the companion flange from the differential.

5. Using an oil seal remover tool, press the oil seal from the differential.

**To install:**

6. Using a new oil seal, lubricate it with multi-purpose grease.

7. Using an oil seal installation tool, drive the new oil seal into the differential.

8. Install the companion flange and torque the drive pinion nut to 123–145 ft. lbs. (167–196 Nm).

9. Install the driveshaft and lower the vehicle.

## Differential Carrier

### REMOVAL & INSTALLATION

#### Pick-Up and Pathfinder (4WD)

#### FRONT

1. Raise and safely support the vehicle. Drain the differential.

2. Matchmark and disconnect the front halfshafts from the front differential.

3. Matchmark the front driveshaft to the flanges and remove the driveshaft.

4. Attach a chain hoist to the engine, remove the front engine mount bolts and raise the engine slightly.

5. Remove the differential crossmember-to-chassis bolts and lower the differential with the crossmember as an assembly.

**To install:**

6. Fit the differential without the crossmember into place and start all the bolts. Torque all nuts and bolts to 64 ft. lbs. (87 Nm) in the following sequence to avoid excess vibration:

a. First tighten the differential mounts to the frame.

b. Tighten the 2 long differential mount bolts.

c. Install the crossmember and tighten the differential mount bolts.

d. Tighten the crossmember mount bolts.

7. Install the front driveshaft and halfshafts, making sure to align the matchmarks.

#### REAR

#### Except Models C200 Differential

1. Raise and safely support the vehicle.

2. Matchmark the driveshaft to the differential flange and remove the driveshaft.

3. Drain all fluid from the differential carrier and remove the axle shafts.

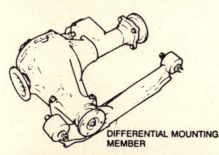

**DIFFERENTIAL MOUNTING MEMBER**

**When removing the front differential from 4WD Pick-Up and Pathfinder, remove the crossmember**

4. Remove the differential carrier-to-axle housing bolts and remove the carrier.

5. Installation is the reverse of removal. Be sure the gasket is correctly installed and torque the bolts to 18 ft. lbs. (25 Nm).

6. Install the remaining components and fill the differential with oil.

### Axxess

A differential carrier is used only with 4WD models.

1. Raise and safely support the vehicle.

2. Matchmark and disconnect the driveshaft. Remove the halfshafts.

3. Disconnect the breather hose from the differential carrier.

4. Using a floor jack, support the differential carrier.

5. Remove the all differential mounting bolts, move it forward to clear the rear mount, then lower it and move it back to clear the crossmember.

**To install:**

6. Installation is the reverse of removal. Torque the mounting bolts to 58 ft. lbs. (78 Nm).

7. Install the halfshafts, connect the driveshaft and fill the differential with oil.

## Axle Housing

### REMOVAL & INSTALLATION

#### Pick-Up

1. Block the front wheels.

2. Raise and safely support the vehicle. Using a floor jack, position it under the differential and support its weight.

3. Remove the rear wheel/tire assemblies.

4. Matchmark the driveshaft to the differential flange and remove the driveshaft.

5. If equipped with drum brakes, remove the brake drum and disconnect the parking brake cable from the brake assembly. If equipped with disc brakes, disconnect the parking brake cable from the caliper.

6. Disconnect and plug the brake hydraulic lines from the wheel cylinders or calipers. Disconnect the brake line from the retaining clips.

7. Disconnect the shock absorber from the lower mount.

8. On vehicles with 2WD, remove all 4 leaf spring mount bolts and remove the axle housing and leaf springs together. Remove the U-bolts to remove the springs from the axle housing.

9. On vehicles with 4WD, remove the nuts from the U-bolts and lower the axle housing away from the leaf springs.

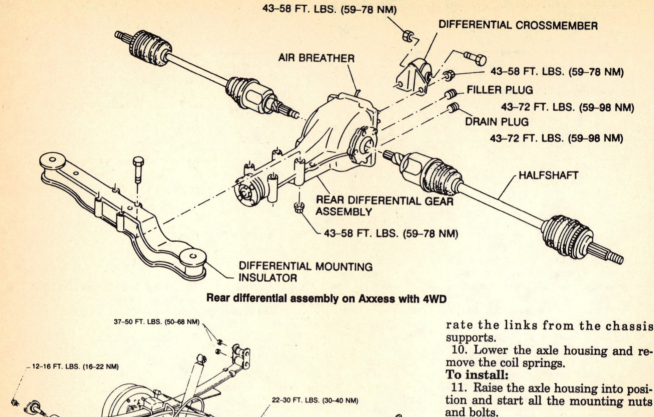

43–58 FT. LBS. (59–78 NM)

DIFFERENTIAL CROSSMEMBER

AIR BREATHER

43–58 FT. LBS. (59–78 NM)

FILLER PLUG

43–72 FT. LBS. (59–98 NM)

DRAIN PLUG

43–72 FT. LBS. (59–98 NM)

HALFSHAFT

REAR DIFFERENTIAL GEAR ASSEMBLY

43–58 FT. LBS. (59–78 NM)

DIFFERENTIAL MOUNTING INSULATOR

**Rear differential assembly on Axxess with 4WD**

37–50 FT. LBS. (50–68 NM)

12–16 FT. LBS. (16–22 NM)

22–30 FT. LBS. (30–40 NM)

37–50 FT. LBS. (50–68 NM)

FRONT

**Rear axle housing on Pick-Up with 4WD; with 2WD, the leaf springs must be removed to remove the axle housing**

### To install:

10. Raise the axle housing into position and start all the mounting bolts and nuts.

11. On 2WD vehicles, torque the rear leaf spring mount nuts to 50 ft. lbs. (68 Nm), then the front mount nuts to 72 ft. lbs. (98 Nm).

12. On 4WD vehicles, torque the U-bolt nuts to 72 ft. lbs. (98 Nm).

13. Connect the shock absorbers to the lower mounts and torque the nut to 30 ft. lbs. (40 Nm).

14. Connect the brake parking cable and hydraulic line and bleed and adjust the brakes.

15. Install the driveshaft with the matchmarks aligned.

### Pathfinder and Van

1. Raise and safely support the vehicle and remove the rear wheels.

2. Using a floor jack, position it under the differential and support its weight.

3. Matchmark the driveshaft to the differential flange and remove the driveshaft.

4. Remove the brake drum and disconnect the parking brake cable from the brake assembly.

5. Disconnect and plug the main brake line from the differential junction block.

6. Disconnect the stabilizer bar from the axle housing and from the body and remove the stabilizer bar.

7. Disconnect the shock absorber from its upper mount. On Van, the mounting nuts are inside the vehicle.

8. Remove the panhard rod-to-chassis nut/bolt and lower the rod.

9. Remove the upper and lower links-to-chassis nuts/bolts, then separate the links from the chassis supports.

10. Lower the axle housing and remove the coil springs.

### To install:

11. Raise the axle housing into position and start all the mounting nuts and bolts.

12. Lower the vehicle to the ground, bounce the vehicle several times and torque all nuts and bolts as shown.

13. Connect the brake cable and hydraulic line and bleed and adjust the brakes.

14. Install the driveshaft.

# MANUAL TRANSMISSION

For further information on transmissions/transaxles, please refer to "Chilton's Guide to Transmission Repair".

## Transmission Assembly

### REMOVAL & INSTALLATION

#### Pick-Up and Pathfinder

1. Disconnect the negative battery cable.

2. Remove the shifter knob and boot and remove the snapring to lift the shift lever out of the transmission. Stuff a rag in the opening to keep dirt out of the transmission.

3. Raise and safely support the vehicle. If equipped, remove the splash pan or skid plate.

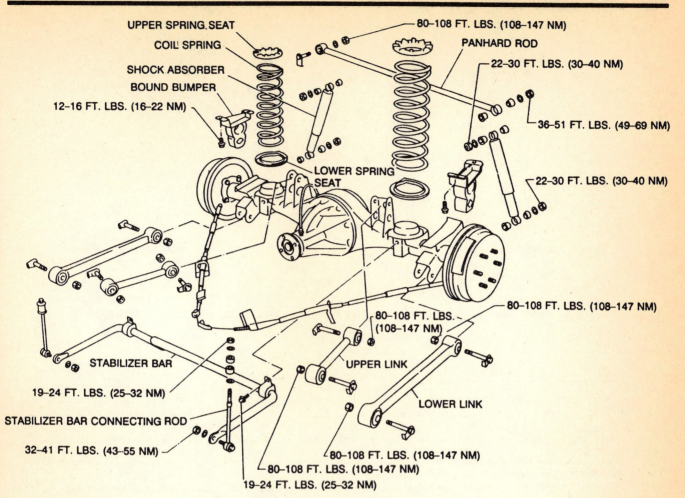

UPPER SPRING SEAT
COIL SPRING
SHOCK ABSORBER
BOUND BUMPER
12–16 FT. LBS. (16–22 NM)
80–108 FT. LBS. (108–147 NM)
PANHARD ROD
22–30 FT. LBS. (30–40 NM)
36–51 FT. LBS. (49–69 NM)
22–30 FT. LBS. (30–40 NM)
LOWER SPRING SEAT
80–108 FT. LBS. (108–147 NM)
80–108 FT. LBS. (108–147 NM)
UPPER LINK
LOWER LINK
STABILIZER BAR
19–24 FT. LBS. (25–32 NM)
STABILIZER BAR CONNECTING ROD
32–41 FT. LBS. (43–55 NM)
80–108 FT. LBS. (108–147 NM)
80–108 FT. LBS. (108–147 NM)
19–24 FT. LBS. (25–32 NM)

**Rear axle housing removal on Van, Pathfinder similar**

4. Remove the starter and drain the oil from the transmission.

5. Matchmark the driveshaft flange at the rear pinion flange and remove the driveshaft. Plug the extension housing opening to prevent dirt from getting in.

6. If equipped with 4WD, matchmark both front driveshaft flanges so the shaft can be installed in the same position. Remove the driveshaft.

7. Disconnect the exhaust pipe from the manifolds and from the catalytic converter and remove the pipe.

8. Disconnect the speedometer cable and the wiring from the transmission.

9. Without disconnecting the hydraulic hose, remove the clutch slave cylinder from the transmission and secure it aside.

10. If equipped with 4WD, the torsion bars must be removed.

a. Working under the vehicle, measure and record the length of the threads on the torsion bar adjustment. At the front of the bar, pull the boot back and matchmark the bar to the mounting plate. The

spline on the bar must be re-installed in the same position on the plate.

b. Remove the locknut and adjustment nut from both torsion bars. Remove the 3 nuts at the mounting plate and remove the bars. Mark the bars left and right side for proper installation.

c. Remove the transfer case shift lever assembly from the transfer case.

d. If necessary, the transfer case can be removed at this point so the jack will be available to remove the transmission.

e. If equipped with a 3.0L engine, remove the gusset securing the engine to the transmission.

11. Using a chain hoist, attach it to the engine and lift the engine slightly to take the weight off the mounts. Using an appropriate transmission jack, properly support the transmission and remove the transmission mount and crossmember.

12. Remove the transmission-to-engine bolts and move the transmission back away from the engine. Lower the

transmission carefully from the vehicle.

**To install:**

13. Lightly grease the input shaft splines. On 4WD, apply a silicone sealant to the engine block or rear plate to seal the engine to the transmission.

14. Fit the transmission into place and start all the engine–to–transmission bolts. Make sure the input shaft fits properly into the clutch disc and pilot bearing.

15. Torque the 2.36 in. (60mm) and 2.56 in. (65mm) engine-to-transmission bolts to 36 ft. lbs. (49 Nm).

16. Torque the remaining bolts to 18 ft. lbs. (25 Nm) on the 2.4L engine or 29 ft. lbs. (39 Nm) on the 3.0L engine.

17. Install the crossmember and torque the crossmember-to-chassis bolts to 38 ft. lbs. (52 Nm) on 2WD or 31 ft. lbs. (42 Nm) on 4WD.

18. Install the rear transmission mount bolts, loosen the engine mount bolts, then torque all the mount bolts to 31 ft. lbs. (42 Nm), starting at the rear.

19. If the torsion bars were removed, install them in their original location.

Make sure the splines are in their original position and set the adjustment to its original position.

20. If the transfer case was removed, apply silicone sealant to seal the case to the transmission. Install the transfer case and torque the bolts to 30 ft. lbs. (41 Nm). Install the shift lever.

21. When installing the driveshafts, be sure to align the matchmarks. Torque the bolts on the front driveshaft (4WD) to 33 ft. lbs. (44 Nm). On single piece rear driveshafts, torque the bolts to 65 ft. lbs. (88 Nm). On 2 piece driveshafts, torque the bolts to 33 ft. lbs. (44 Nm). Torque the center bearing bracket bolts to 16 ft. lbs. (22 Nm).

22. When installing the exhaust system, use new gaskets and torque the flange bolts to 27 ft. lbs. (36 Nm).

23. Install the remaining components in order of removal and connect the wiring and speedometer cable. Refill the transmission with oil.

### Van

1. Disconnect the negative battery cable.

2. Raise and safely support the vehicle and remove the starter.

3. Disconnect the speedometer cable and all wiring from the transmission.

4. Without disconnecting the hydraulic line, remove the clutch release cylinder from the transmission and secure it out of the way.

5. To disconnect the transmission shift linkage without disturbing the adjustments, remove the pin clips and slide the levers off the shafts. Remove the cables and the mounting bracket from the transmission.

6. Matchmark the driveshaft to the differential flange and remove the driveshaft. Plug the transmission opening to prevent oil leakage.

7. Disconnect the exhaust pipe from the manifold and remove the pipe from the catalytic converter.

8. Support the transmission with a jack and support the engine with a second jack and wood under the oil pan.

9. Remove the long rear transmission mount bolt or, if they are easier to reach, remove the bolts that hold the rear transmission mount to the body.

10. Remove the transmission-to-engine bolts, pull the transmission rearward until the pilot shaft is free of the engine and lower the transmission from the vehicle.

**To install:**

11. Lightly grease the input shaft spline and fit the transmission into place. Make sure the shaft engages the clutch disc properly and that the transmission fits up against the engine evenly.

12. Start all the bolts, then torque the long bolts to 36 ft. lbs. (49 Nm) and the short bolts to 29 ft. lbs. (39 Nm).

13. Install the rear mount. Torque the long bolt to 72 ft. lbs. (98 Nm) and the mount–to–body bolts to 20 ft. lbs. (26 Nm).

14. Install the driveshaft with the matchmarks aligned and torque the bolts to 33 ft. lbs. (44 Nm).

15. Attach the shift cable brackets to the transmission and connect the cables.

16. Use new gaskets to install the exhaust pipe.

17. Install the remaining components and check for proper operation of the shift linkage. Refill the transmission with oil.

## LINKAGE ADJUSTMENT

### Van

1. To adjust the selector cable:

   a. Remove the console cover and loosen the adjuster locknut.

   b. Raise and support the vehicle safely.

   c. Working under the vehicle, put the transmission into **3rd** or **4th** gear by moving the shift change lever on the transmission.

   d. From inside the vehicle, adjust the selector cable length using the adjuster.

   e. After adjustment, tighten the locknut and make sure the shifter lever moves smoothly between the 1st–2nd and 3rd–4th gates (side to side).

2. To adjust the shifter cable:

   a. From under the vehicle, loosen the trunnion-to-shift cable locknut.

   b. Remove the shift cable trunnion from the cross shaft.

   c. Make sure the transmission is out of gear.

   d. At the shift lever, insert a 0.160 in. (4mm) pin into the adjustment index hole. This will align the shift lever vertically.

   e. Adjust the shifter cable to align the trunnion with the cross shaft and connect the trunnion. Tighten the locknut.

# MANUAL TRANSAXLE

## Transaxle Assembly

### REMOVAL & INSTALLATION

#### Axxess

On 4WD models, the left suspension arm and gusset plate must be removed. On all models, the halfshafts must be removed. The torque on the front axle nut is very high and an assistant is required to hold the brake pedal when tightening or loosening it.

1. Disconnect the negative battery cable. Remove the battery and bracket.

2. Remove the air cleaner with the air flow meter.

3. Remove the air duct.

4. Remove the air injection vent (AIR) unit.

5. Remove the slave cylinder-to-transaxle bolts and move the cylinder aside.

6. Remove the clutch hose clamp.

7. Disconnect the speedometer pinion and the position switch connectors.

8. Remove the breather hose clamp.

9. Disconnect the electrical connectors from the starter. Remove the starter-to-transaxle bolts and the starter.

10. Remove the shift control rod and support rod from the transaxle.

11. Raise and safely support the vehicle and drain the transaxle.

12. On 4WD models, matchmark the drive flanges and disconnect the driveshaft from the transfer case. If it is decided that the driveshaft is in the way of engine removal, matchmark the rear flange and remove the entire driveshaft. Do not disassemble the driveshaft and protect the CV-joint boot when moving the driveshaft.

13. On 4WD models, remove the front exhaust pipe and disconnect the transfer case shift linkage.

14. Make sure the vehicle is securely supported and have an assistant hold the brake pedal. Remove the front axle cotter pin, adjusting cap and washer and loosen the axle nut. The torque is very high: if possible, loosen and tighten this nut with the wheels installed and the vehicle on the ground.

15. Without disconnecting the hydraulic hose, remove the brake calipers and hang them from the body. Do not let the caliper hang by the hose. Be sure to remove the caliper, pads and carrier as an assembly. Do not remove the sliding pin bolts.

16. Disconnect the tie rod end from the steering knuckle. Turn the knuckle all the way out at the front and use a soft hammer to tap the axle out of the hub.

17. Carefully pry the inner CV-joints from the transaxle and remove the halfshafts. On the right side of 2WD models, remove the intermediate shaft bearing and the shaft.

18. On 4WD models, remove the left side lower suspension arm and the gusset.

19. Position a jack under the engine

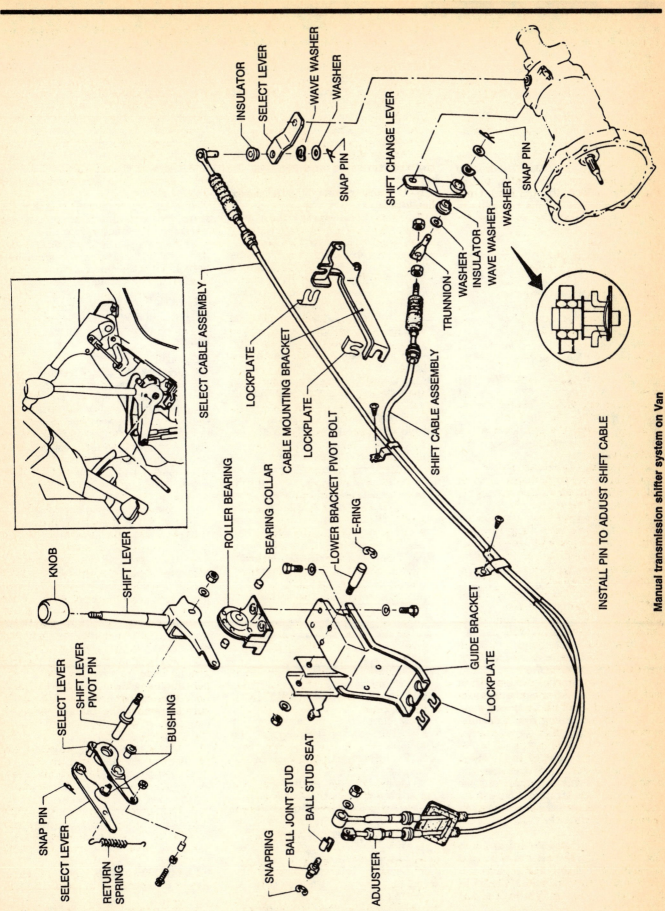

INSULATOR
SELECT LEVER
WAVE WASHER
WASHER
SNAP PIN
SHIFT CHANGE LEVER
SNAP PIN
WASHER
INSULATOR
WAVE WASHER
WASHER
TRUNNION
SHIFT CABLE ASSEMBLY
SELECT CABLE ASSEMBLY
LOCKPLATE
CABLE MOUNTING BRACKET
LOCKPLATE
LOWER BRACKET PIVOT BOLT
E-RING
GUIDE BRACKET
LOCKPLATE
ROLLER BEARING
BEARING COLLAR
KNOB
SHIFT LEVER
SELECT LEVER
SHIFT LEVER PIVOT PIN
BUSHING
SNAP PIN
SELECT LEVER
RETURN SPRING
SNAPRING
BALL JOINT STUD
BALL STUD SEAT
ADJUSTER

INSTALL PIN TO ADJUST SHIFT CABLE

**Manual transmission shifter system on Van**

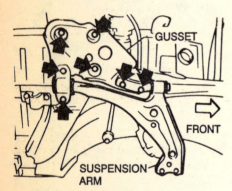

● M/T TO ENGINE (GUSSET)
◎ ENGINE (GUSSET)
○ M/T TO STARTER MOTOR

**Transaxle–to–engine bolt torque sequence on Axxess with 2WD**

● M/T TO ENGINE (GUSSET)
● ENGINE (GUSSET) TO M/T
○ TRANSFER TO M/T
● M/T TO TRANSFER
● M/T TO STARTER MOTOR
⊕ END PLATE TO ENGINE

**Transaxle–to–engine bolt torque sequence on Axxess with 4WD**

GUSSET

FRONT

SUSPENSION ARM

**Remove the suspension arm and the gusset to remove transaxle — Axxess with 4WD**

oil pan and another jack under the transaxle. Do not position the jack under the oil pan drain plug.

20. Remove the transaxle mount–to–body bolt or the transfer case mount and lower the transaxle jack enough to clear the mount. Remove the transaxle-to-engine bolts and move the transaxle away from the engine. Carefully lower it from the vehicle.

**To install:**

21. Lightly grease the input shaft spline before joining the engine and transaxle. Carefully fit the transaxle into place and start all the bolts.

22. With the transaxle flush against the engine, torque the bolts in the sequence shown.

On 2WD, torque bolts 1, 5 and 6 to 36 ft. lbs. (49 Nm) and bolts 2, 3 and 4 to 30 ft. lbs. (40 Nm).

On 4WD, torque bolts 1, 3, 7 and 8 to 36 ft. lbs. (49 Nm) and bolts 2, 4, 5, 6 and 9 to 30 ft. lbs. (40 Nm).

23. If the mount was removed from the transaxle, install it and torque the bolts to 41 ft. lbs. (55 Nm). Install the transaxle mount bolt and torque it to 58 ft. lbs. (78 Nm).

24. On 4WD, install the suspension arm and gusset plate. Torque the bolts to 108 ft. lbs. (147 Nm).

25. To install the halfshafts:

a. Carefully insert the inner CV-joint into the differential gear to make sure the splines engage properly.

b. Push the shaft in to click the circlip into place. Pull out on the halfshaft to make sure the clip is seated.

c. On 2WD, when installing the right side extension shaft, torque the support bearing bracket bolts to 26 ft. lbs. (35 Nm).

d. Make sure the outer axle splines are clean and insert the axle into the hub. Connect the tie rod end to the steering knuckle, torque the nut to 29 ft. lbs. (39 Nm) and tighten as required to install a new cotter pin.

e. Install the washer and nut onto the axle but do not torque the nut yet.

26. Install the brake calipers and torque the carrier bolts to 72 ft. lbs. (97 Nm).

27. Complete the installation of the remaining components. When the vehicle is resting on at least 3 wheels, have an assistant hold the brake pedal and torque the front axle nuts to 231 ft. lbs. (314 Nm). Install the adjusting cap and a new cotter pin. Don't forget to refill the transaxle.

28. Check and/or adjust the front wheel alignment.

# CLUTCH

## Clutch Assembly

### REMOVAL & INSTALLATION

1. Disconnect the negative battery cable. Raise and safely support the vehicle.

2. Remove the transmission or the transaxle.

3. Using a piece of chalk, paint or a center punch, mark the clutch assembly-to-flywheel relationship so it can be reassembled in the same position from which it is removed.

4. Using a clutch aligning tool, insert it into the clutch disc hub.

5. Loosen the clutch cover-to-flywheel bolts, a turn at a time in an alternating sequence, until the spring tension is relieved to avoid distorting

or bending the clutch cover. Remove the clutch assembly.

6. Inspect the flywheel for scoring, roughness or signs of overheating. Light scoring may be cleaned up with emery cloth, but any deep grooves or overheating (blue marks) warrant replacement or refacing of the flywheel. If the clutch facings or flywheel are oily, inspect the transmission/transaxle front cover oil seal, the pilot bushing and engine rear seals, etc. for leakage; replace any leaking seals before replacing the clutch.

7. If the crankshaft pilot bushing is worn, replace it. Install it using a soft hammer. The factory supplied part does not have to be oiled, but check the procedure if using an aftermarket part. Inspect the clutch cover for wear or scoring and replace it, if necessary.

**NOTE: The pressure plate and spring cannot be disassembled; replace the clutch cover as an assembly.**

**To install:**

8. Inspect the clutch release bearing. If it is rough or noisy, it should be replaced. The bearing can be removed from the sleeve with a puller; this requires a press to install the new bearing. After installation, coat the sleeve groove, the release lever contact surfaces, the pivot pin/sleeve and the release bearing-to-transmission/transaxle contact surfaces with a light coat of grease. Be careful not to use too much grease, which will run at high temperatures and get onto the clutch facings. Reinstall the release bearing on the lever.

9. Apply a thin coat of grease to the pressure plate wire ring, diaphragm spring, clutch cover grooves and the pressure plate drive bosses.

10. Apply a thin coat of Lubriplate® to the splines in the driven plate. Slide the clutch disc onto the splines and move it back and forth several times. Remove the disc and wipe off the excess lubricant. Be very careful not to get any grease on the clutch facings.

11. Assemble the clutch cover and the clutch plate on the clutch alignment arbor.

12. To complete the installation, align the clutch assembly-to-flywheel alignment marks and install the bolts. Tighten the bolts 1 or 2 turns at a time in a crisscross pattern to avoid distorting the cover. Torque the bolts to 22 ft. lbs. (30 Nm).

13. Install the transmission/transaxle and adjust the pedal height as necessary.

### PEDAL HEIGHT/FREE-PLAY ADJUSTMENT

The pedal height is the distance from

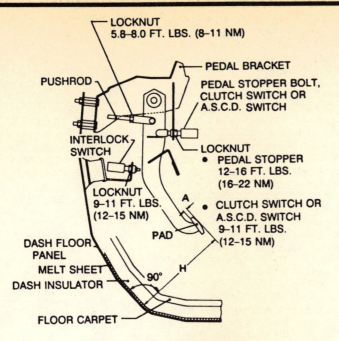

LOCKNUT
5.8–8.0 FT. LBS. (8–11 NM)

PUSHROD

PEDAL BRACKET

PEDAL STOPPER BOLT,
CLUTCH SWITCH OR
A.S.C.D. SWITCH

INTERLOCK
SWITCH

LOCKNUT
• PEDAL STOPPER
12–16 FT. LBS.
(16–22 NM)

LOCKNUT
9–11 FT. LBS.
(12–15 NM)

A

PAD

• CLUTCH SWITCH OR
A.S.C.D. SWITCH
9–11 FT. LBS.
(12–15 NM)

DASH FLOOR
PANEL

MELT SHEET

DASH INSULATOR

90°

H

FLOOR CARPET

**Clutch pedal on all except Van**

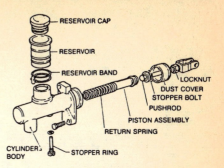

RESERVOIR CAP

RESERVOIR

RESERVOIR BAND

LOCKNUT
DUST COVER
STOPPER BOLT
PUSHROD
PISTON ASSEMBLY
RETURN SPRING

CYLINDER
BODY

STOPPER RING

**Clutch master cylinder assembly**

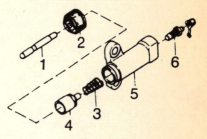

1. Pushrod
2. Dust cover
3. Piston spring
4. Piston
5. Operating cylinder
6. Bleeder screw

**Clutch slave cylinder**

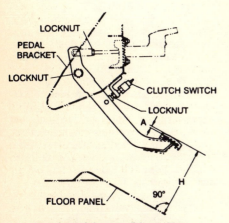

LOCKNUT

PEDAL
BRACKET

LOCKNUT

CLUTCH SWITCH

LOCKNUT

A

FLOOR PANEL

90°

H

**Clutch pedal assembly on Van**

the top of the clutch pedal to the floor board without the carpet.

The pedal free-play is the distance the clutch pedal pad moves from the released position to the point where resistance is felt.

1. To adjust the pedal height on Pick-Up and Pathfinder:

   a. From under the dash, loosen the pedal stopper locknut.

   b. Turn the pedal stopper until the specified pedal height is obtained: 9.29–9.69 in. (236–246mm) with the 2.4L engine or 8.94–9.33 in. (227–236mm) with the 3.0L engine.

   c. After adjustment, torque the pedal stopper locknut to 16 ft. lbs. (22 Nm).

2. To adjust the pedal height on Axxess:

   a. From under the dash, loosen the pedal stopper locknut.

   b. Turn the pedal stopper until

the specified pedal height is obtained: 6.97–7.36 in. (177–187mm).

   c. After adjustment, torque the pedal stopper locknut to 16 ft. lbs. (22 Nm).

3. To adjust the pedal height on the Van, perform the following procedure:

   a. From under the dash, loosen the clutch switch locknut.

   b. Turn the clutch switch until the specified pedal height is obtained: 6.97–7.36 in. (117–187mm).

   c. After adjustment, torque the clutch switch locknut to 11 ft. lbs. (15 Nm).

4. To adjust the pedal free-play, perform the following procedures:

   a. Loosen the clutch pedal, pushrod locknut.

   b. Using a ruler, measure the clutch pedal free-play.

   c. Turn the clutch pedal pushrod to set the free-play at 0.040–0.120 in. (1–3mm).

   d. After adjustment, torque the locknut to 9 ft. lbs. (12 Nm).

## Clutch Master Cylinder

### REMOVAL & INSTALLATION

The master cylinder is attached to a bracket located under the dash.

1. Disconnect the negative battery cable.

2. From under the dash, remove the clevis pin snap pin and pull the clevis pin from the clutch pedal.

3. Disconnect the clutch pedal arm from the pushrod clevis. Remove the dust cover (boot) from the master cylinder body and pushrod. It will not go through the cowl without tearing.

4. Disconnect and plug the hydraulic line from the clutch master cylinder.

**NOTE: Take precautions to keep brake fluid from coming in contact with any painted surfaces.**

5. Remove the clutch master cylinder.

**To install:**

6. Installation is the reverse of removal. Torque the clutch master cylinder-to-cowl bolts/nuts to 14 ft. lbs. (19 Nm) on Van or to 9 ft. lbs. 12 Nm) on all others.

7. Bleed the clutch hydraulic system.

## Clutch Slave Cylinder

### REMOVAL & INSTALLATION

1. If necessary, raise and safely support the vehicle.

2. Remove the slave cylinder-to-clutch housing bolts and the pushrod from the shift fork.

3. Disconnect and plug the hydraulic hose from the slave cylinder, then, remove the cylinder from the vehicle.

**To install:**

4. To install, reverse the removal procedures. Torque the slave cylinder-to-clutch housing bolts to 30 ft. lbs. (40 Nm).

5. Bleed the clutch hydraulic system.

## BLEEDING THE HYDRAULIC CLUTCH SYSTEM

1. Check and refill the clutch fluid reservoir to the full mark. During the bleeding process, continue to check and replenish the reservoir to prevent the fluid level from getting lower than ½ full.

2. Connect a clear vinyl hose to the bleeder screw on the slave cylinder. Immerse the other end of the hose in a clear jar ½ filled with brake fluid.

3. Have an assistant pump the clutch pedal several times and hold it down. Loosen the bleeder screw slowly.

4. Tighten the bleeder screw and release the clutch pedal gradually. Repeat this operation until the air bubbles disappear from the brake fluid being expelled out through the bleeder screw.

5. When the air is completely removed, securely tighten the bleeder screw and replace the dust cap.

6. Check and refill the master cylinder reservoir as necessary.

7. Depress the clutch pedal several times to check the operation of the clutch and check for leaks.

# AUTOMATIC TRANSMISSION

For further information on transmissions/transaxles, please refer to "Chilton's Guide to Transmission Repair".

## Transmission Assembly

### REMOVAL & INSTALLATION

*Pick-Up and Pathfinder*

1. Disconnect the negative battery cable.

2. Raise and safely support the vehicle. If equipped, remove the splash pan or skid plate.

3. Remove the starter.

4. Matchmark the driveshaft flange at the rear pinion flange and remove the driveshaft. Plug the extension housing opening to prevent fluid from leaking out.

5. If equipped with 4WD, matchmark both front driveshaft flanges so the shaft can be installed in the same position. Remove the driveshaft.

6. Disconnect the exhaust pipe from the manifolds and from the catalytic converter and remove the pipe.

7. Disconnect the speedometer cable and the wiring from the transmission.

8. Disconnect the selector lever and throttle cables from the transmission.

9. Remove the dipstick tube and disconnect the cooling lines from the transmission.

10. Remove the torque converter housing dust cover. Matchmark the torque converter with the driveplate for reassembly; these are balanced together at the factory. Remove the torque converter-to-driveplate (flywheel) bolts. Use a wrench on the crankshaft pulley bolt to rotate the crankshaft to expose the hidden torque converter bolts.

11. If equipped with 4WD, the torsion bars must be removed.

   a. Working under the vehicle, measure and record the length of the threads on the torsion bar adjustment. At the front of the bar, pull the boot back and matchmark the bar to the mounting plate. The spline on the bar must be re-installed in the same position on the plate.

   b. Remove the locknut and adjustment nut from both torsion bars. Remove the 3 nuts at the mounting plate and remove the bars. Mark the bars left and right side for proper installation.

   c. Remove the transfer case shift lever assembly from the transfer case.

   d. If necessary, the transfer case can be removed at this point.

   e. If equipped with a 3.0L engine, remove the gusset securing the engine to the transmission.

12. Using a chain hoist, attach it to the engine and lift the engine slightly to take the weight off the mounts. Using an appropriate transmission jack, properly support the transmission and remove the transmission mount and crossmember.

13. Remove the transmission-to-engine bolts and move the transmission back away from the engine. Lower the transmission carefully from the vehicle.

**To install:**

14. Use a dial indicator to check the driveplate runout while turning the crankshaft. Maximum allowable runout is 0.020 in. (0.5mm); if beyond specification, replace the driveplate.

15. Measure and adjust how far the torque converter is recessed into the transmission housing. The distance between the front mounting surface of the transmission and the torque converter-to-driveplate bolt boss should be at least 1.024 in. (26mm).

16. Install the transmission and torque the 4 upper transmission-to-engine bolts to 36 ft. lbs. (49 Nm). Torque to transmission-to-engine gusset bolts to 29 ft. lbs. (39 Nm). Torque the remaining bolts to 18 ft. lbs. (25 Nm) on the 2.4L engine or 29 ft. lbs. (39 Nm) on the 3.0L engine.

17. Install the crossmember and torque the crossmember-to-chassis bolts to 38 ft. lbs. (52 Nm) on 2WD or 31 ft. lbs. (42 Nm) on 4WD.

18. Install the rear transmission mount bolts, loosen the engine mount bolts, then torque all the mount bolts to 31 ft. lbs. (42 Nm), starting at the rear.

19. Align the matchmarks on the driveplate and torque converter, install the bolts and torque to 36 ft. lbs. (49 Nm). Turn the crankshaft after tightening the bolts to make sure there is no binding at the driveplate.

20. If the torsion bars were removed, install them in their original location. Make sure the splines are in their original position and set the adjustment to its original position.

21. If the transfer case was removed, apply silicone sealant to seal the case to the transmission. Install the transfer case and torque the bolts to 30 ft. lbs. (41 Nm). Install the shift lever.

22. When installing the driveshafts, be sure to align the matchmarks. Torque the bolts on the front driveshaft (4WD) to 33 ft. lbs. (44 Nm). On single piece rear driveshafts, torque the bolts to 65 ft. lbs. (88 Nm). On 2 piece driveshafts, torque the bolts to 33 ft. lbs. (44 Nm). Torque the center bearing bracket bolts to 16 ft. lbs. (22 Nm).

23. When installing the exhaust system, use new gaskets and torque the flange bolts to 27 ft. lbs. (36 Nm).

24. Install the remaining components in order of removal and connect the wiring, cooling lines and speedometer cable. Refill the transmission with fluid and adjust as required.

*Van*

1. Disconnect the negative battery cable and raise and safely support the vehicle.

2. Disconnect the speedometer cable and all wiring from the transmission. Disconnect the cooling lines. Disconnect the transmission shift linkage without disturbing the adjustments.

3. Matchmark the driveshaft to the differential flange and remove the driveshaft. Plug the transmission opening to prevent oil leakage.

4. Disconnect the exhaust pipe from the manifold and remove the pipe from the catalytic converter.

5. Matchmark the torque converter to the driveplate and remove the

torque converter–to–driveplate bolts. Push the torque converter back so it does not fall out.

6. Support the transmission with a jack and support the engine with a second jack and wood under the oil pan.

7. Remove the long rear transmission mount bolt or, if they are easier to reach, remove the bolts that hold the rear transmission mount to the body.

8. Remove the transmission-to-engine bolts, pull the transmission rearward until the pilot shaft is free of the engine and lower the transmission from the vehicle.

**To install:**

9. Before installing an automatic transmission:

   a. Use a dial indicator to check the driveplate runout while turning the crankshaft. Maximum allowable runout is 0.020 in. (0.5mm); if beyond specifications, replace the driveplate.

   b. Measure and adjust how far the torque converter is recessed into the transmission housing. The distance between the front mounting surface of the transmission and the torque converter–to–driveplate bolt boss should be at least 1.380 in. (35mm).

10. Fit the transmission into place and start all the transmission–to–engine bolts. Torque the long bolts to 36 ft. lbs. (49 Nm), the short bolts to 24 ft. lbs. (32 Nm).

11. Align the matchmarks on the torque converter and driveplate and install the bolts. Torque the bolts to 36 ft. lbs. (49 Nm). Turn the crankshaft to make sure there is no binding at the driveplate.

12. Install the rear mount. Torque the long bolt to 72 ft. lbs. (98 Nm) and the mount–to–body bolts to 20 ft. lbs. (26 Nm).

13. Install the driveshaft with the matchmarks aligned and torque the bolts to 33 ft. lbs. (44 Nm).

14. Attach the shift linkage and the dipstick tube. Connect the wiring and cooling lines.

15. Use new gaskets to install the exhaust pipe.

16. Install the remaining components and check for proper operation of the shift linkage. Refill the transmission with oil.

## SHIFT LINKAGE ADJUSTMENT

### Pick-Up and Pathfinder

#### 2WD FLOOR SHIFT MODELS

1. Place the shift selector in the **P** position.

2. Raise and safely support the vehicle.

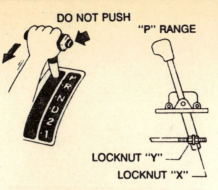

**Automatic Pick-Up and Pathfinder with 2WD and floor shift**

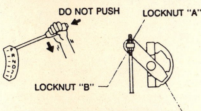

**Automatic Pick-Up and Pathfinder with 2WD and column shift adjustment**

3. From under the vehicle, loosen the shift lever locknuts.

4. Tighten the rear locknut **X** until it touches the trunnion.

5. Pull the selector lever toward the **R** position without pushing the button. Back off the rear locknut **X** a complete revolution, adjust the front locknut **Y** and torque the locknuts to 8.0 ft. lbs. (11 Nm).

6. After adjustment, move the selector lever through the gears to make sure it moves smoothly.

#### 2WD COLUMN SHIFT MODELS

1. Place the shift selector in the **P** position.

2. Raise and safely support the vehicle.

3. From under the vehicle, loosen the shift lever locknuts.

4. Tighten the front locknut **A** until it touches the trunnion.

5. Pull the selector lever toward the **R** position without pushing the button. Back off the front locknut **A** 2 complete revolutions, adjust the rear locknut **B** and torque the locknuts to 8.0 ft. lbs. (11 Nm).

6. After adjustment, move the selector lever through the gears to make sure it moves smoothly.

#### 4WD FLOOR SHIFT MODELS

1. Place the shift selector in the **P** position.

2. Raise and safely support the vehicle.

3. Remove the console cover.

4. Loosen the turn buckle locknuts.

5. Tighten the turn buckle until it aligns with the inner cable.

6. Pull the selector lever toward the **R** position without pushing the button. Back off the turn buckle a complete revolution, torque the locknuts to 48 inch lbs. (5 Nm).

7. After adjustment, move the selector lever through the gears to make sure it moves smoothly.

### Van

1. Place the shift selector in the **P** position.

2. Raise and safely support the vehicle.

3. From under the vehicle, loosen the shift lever locknuts.

4. Tighten the front locknut **X** until it touches the trunnion.

5. Pull the selector lever toward the **R** position without pushing the button. Back off the front locknut **X** a ¼ revolution, adjust the rear locknut **Y** and torque the locknuts to 9 ft. lbs. (12 Nm).

6. After adjustment, move the selector lever through the ranges to make sure it moves smoothly.

## KICKDOWN SWITCH ADJUSTMENT

### Pick-Up and Pathfinder With 71B Transmission

A kickdown switch is located inside the vehicle at the upper post of the accelerator pedal. Its purpose is to provide transmission downshifting when the accelerator pedal is fully depressed; a click can be heard just before the pedal bottoms out.

With the ignition switch in the **ON** position and the engine **OFF**, when

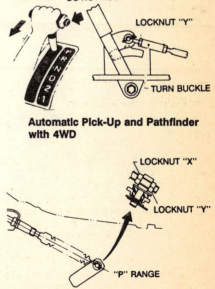

**Automatic Pick-Up and Pathfinder with 4WD**

**Automatic floor shifter adjustment on Van**

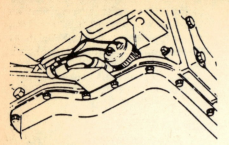

Downshift solenoid on Pick-Up and Pathfinder with 71B transmission

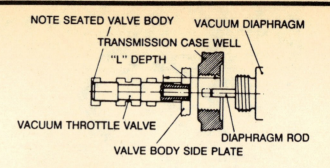

Vacuum diaphragm on Pick-Up and Pathfinder with 71B transmission

the accelerator pedal is depressed fully, the kick-down switch contacts should be closed and the downshift solenoid activated, emitting a clicking sound. If the components fail to operate in this manner, check for continuity at the switch and then at the solenoid. Replace either of the components as necessary.

## VACUUM MODULATOR ADJUSTMENT

### Pick-Up and Pathfinder

#### WITH 71B TRANSMISSION

1. Raise and safely support the vehicle.
2. Remove the vacuum modulator from the transmission.
3. Using a depth gauge, measure the **L** depth; be sure the vacuum throttle valve is pushed into the valve body as far as possible.
4. Select the correct length rod and install it into the vacuum modulator.
5. Using a new O-ring, install the modulator into the transmission.

## THROTTLE LINKAGE ADJUSTMENT

### Pick-Up and Pathfinder

#### WITH RL4R01A TRANSMISSION

1. Press the lock plate and move the adjusting tube in the direction **T**.
2. Release the lock plate.
3. Quickly move the throttle drum from $P_2$-to-$P_1$.
4. Ensure the throttle wire stroke **L** is within specified range between full throttle and idle; the throttle wire stroke **L** should be 1.50–1.65 in. (38–42mm).

**NOTE: Adjust the throttle wire stroke when the throttle wire/accelerator wire is installed. Place marks on the throttle wire to facilitate measuring the wire stroke.**

5. If the throttle wire stroke is not adjusted, the following problems may arise:
    a. When full-open position $P_1$ of the throttle drum is closer to the direction **T**, the kickdown range will greatly increase.
    b. When the full-open position $P_1$ of the throttle drum is closer to the direction **U**, the kickdown range will not occur.

## NEUTRAL SAFETY SWITCH ADJUSTMENT

The neutral safety switch is located on the transmission shift selector lever. The switch operates the back-up lights and controls the operation of the starter. The starter should only operate when the transmission is in **P** or **N**.

### Pick-Up and Pathfinder

#### WITH 71B TRANSMISSION

1. Unscrew the securing nut of the shift selector lever and the switch-to-transmission screws.
2. Position the shift selector to the **N** position (in vertical detent position). Move the switch slightly aside so the screw hole will be aligned with the pin hole of the shift selector lever.
3. Using a 0.080 in. (2mm) diameter alignment pin, place it in the alignment holes of the neutral start switch and the shift selector lever.

**NOTE: A No. 47 drill bit will substitute for the pin gauge.**

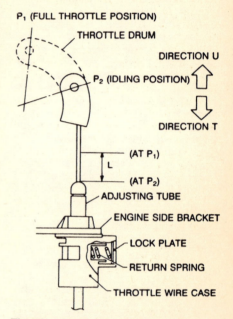

Throttle wire adjustment on 1990 Pick-Up and Pathfinder with RL4R10A transmission

4. Secure the switch body with the screws and pull out the pin.

**NOTE: If the neutral safety switch does not perform satisfactorily after adjustment, replace it with a new one.**

#### WITH "R" SERIES TRANSMISSION

1. Unscrew the securing nut of the

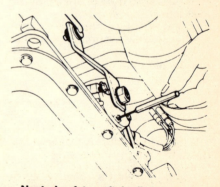

Neutral safety switch alignment—Pick-Up and Pathfinder with 71B transmission

| Measured depth "L" mm (in) | Rod length mm (in) | Part number |
|---|---|---|
| Under 25.55 (1.0059) | 29.0 (1.142) | 31932-X0103 |
| 25.65 - 26.05 (1.0098 - 1.0256) | 29.5 (1.161) | 31932-X0104 |
| 26.15 - 26.55 (1.0295 - 1.0453) | 30.0 (1.181) | 31932-X0100 |
| 26.65 - 27.05 (1.0492 - 1.0650) | 30.5 (1.201) | 31932-X0102 |
| Over 27.15 (1.0689) | 31.0 (1.220) | 31932-X0101 |

Vacuum diaphragm rod selection chart—71B transmission

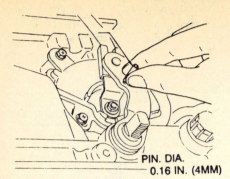

PIN. DIA.
0.16 IN. (4MM)

**Neutral safety switch alignment—
Pick-Up and Pathfinder with "R"
series transmission**

shift selector lever and the switch-to-transmission screws.

2. Position the shift selector to the N position (in vertical detent).

3. Using a 0.16 in. (4mm) diameter alignment pin, place it in the alignment holes of the neutral start switch and the shift selector lever.

4. Secure the switch body with the screws and pull out the pin.

**NOTE: If the neutral safety switch does not perform satisfactorily after adjustment, replace it with a new one.**

# AUTOMATIC TRANSAXLE

For further information on transmissions/transaxles, please refer to "Chilton's Guide to Transmission Repair".

## Transaxle Assembly

### REMOVAL & INSTALLATION
*Axxess*

On all models, the halfshafts must be removed. The torque on the front axle nut is very high and an assistant is required to hold the brake pedal when tightening or loosening it.

1. Disconnect the negative battery cable. Remove the battery and bracket.

2. Remove the air cleaner with the air flow meter.

3. Remove the air duct.

4. Disconnect the heater hose from the dash panel.

5. Remove the starter.

6. Disconnect the transaxle–throttle control cable from the throttle. The nut towards the cable end is the locknut; mark the position of the adjusting nut and loosen the locknut to disconnect the cable. Disconnect the shifter cable from the transaxle.

7. Disconnect the speedometer cable and all wiring from the transaxle.

8. Raise and safely support the vehicle.

9. Disconnect the exhaust pipe from the manifold and remove the pipe from the catalytic converter.

10. On 4WD models, matchmark the drive flanges and disconnect the driveshaft from the transfer case. If it is decided that the driveshaft is in the way of engine removal, matchmark the rear flange and remove the entire driveshaft. Do not disassemble the driveshaft and protect the CV-joint boot when moving the driveshaft.

11. On 4WD models, remove the transfer case gusset under the intake manifold. Use a long socket extension and work from above the manifold.

12. Make sure the vehicle is securely supported and have an assistant hold the brake pedal. Remove the front axle cotter pin, adjusting cap and washer and loosen the axle nut. The torque is very high, if possible; tighten this nut with the wheels installed and the vehicle on the ground.

13. Without disconnecting the hydraulic hose, remove the brake calipers and hang them from the body. Do not let the caliper hang by the hose. Be sure to remove the caliper, pads and carrier as an assembly. Do not remove the sliding pin bolts.

14. Disconnect the tie rod end from the steering knuckle. Turn the knuckle all the way out at the front and use a soft hammer to tap the axle out of the hub.

15. Carefully pry the right inner CV-joint from the transaxle or transfer case. On the right side of 2WD models, remove the intermediate shaft bearing and the shaft.

16. On 2WD, insert a thin drift pin through the right side of differential and tap the left inner CV-joint out. Be careful not to damage the mate pinion shaft or side gear inside the differential.

17. On 4WD, pry the left CV-joint out the same way as the right.

18. On 4WD models, remove the left side lower suspension arm and the gusset.

19. On 2WD, remove the center frame member and remove the transaxle mount. Reinstall the center member and support the engine with a wood block under the oil pan.

20. Matchmark the torque converter to the driveplate for re-assembly and remove the torque converter-to-driveplate bolts. When separating the engine and transaxle, be careful that the torque converter does not fall out.

21. Position a jack under the transaxle, remove the transaxle mount-to-body mount bolts or the transfer case mounts and lower the transaxle jack

enough to clear the mount. Remove the transaxle-to-engine bolts and move the transaxle away from the engine. Carefully lower it from the vehicle.

**To install:**

22. Check the driveplate and mount the torque converter:

a. Use a dial indicator to check the driveplate runout while turning the crankshaft. Maximum allowable runout is 0.020 in. (0.5mm); if beyond specifications, replace the driveplate.

b. Measure and adjust how far the torque converter is recessed into the transaxle housing. The distance between the front mounting surface of the transaxle and the torque converter–to–driveplate bolt boss should be at least ¾ in. (19mm).

23. Fit the transaxle into place and start all the engine bolts, then torque them to 33 ft. lbs. (44 Nm).

24. Raise the transaxle to engage the mounts. On 2WD models, remove the center member and install the mounts. When all the mounts and support members are in place, tighten the bolts starting at the rear and working forward. Torque all mount–to–transaxle bolts to 41 ft. lbs. (55 Nm), the mount–to–body bolts to 58 ft. lbs. (78 Nm) and the long mounting bolts to 58 ft. lbs. (78 Nm).

25. Align the matchmarks on the torque converter and driveplate and install the bolts. Torque the bolts to 43 ft. lbs. (59 Nm). Turn the crankshaft to make sure there is no binding at the driveplate.

26. Install the halfshafts:

a. Carefully insert the inner CV-joint into the differential gear to make sure the splines engage properly.

b. Push the shaft in to click the circlip into place. Pull out on the halfshaft to make sure the clip is seated.

c. When installing the right side extension shaft on 2WD models, torque the support bearing bracket bolts to 26 ft. lbs. (35 Nm).

d. When installing the left side halfshaft on 4WD models, torque the inner CV-joint bolts to 36 ft. lbs. (45 Nm).

e. Make sure the outer axle splines are clean and insert the axle into the hub. Connect the tie rod end to the steering knuckle and torque the nut to 29 ft. lbs. (39 Nm) and tighten as required to install a new cotter pin.

f. Install the washer and nut onto the axle but do not torque the nut yet.

27. Install the brake calipers and torque the carrier bolts to 72 ft. lbs (97 Nm).

28. On 4WD models, connect the driveshaft and torque the bolts to 33 ft. lbs. (44 Nm). If the driveshaft was removed, torque the center bearing support bolts to 30 ft. lbs. (41 Nm).

29. When installing the exhaust pipe, use new gaskets and torque the manifold flange nuts to 37 ft. lbs. (50 Nm), the catalytic converter flange bolts to 31 ft. lbs. (42 Nm).

30. Complete the installation of the remaining components. When the vehicle is resting on at least 3 wheels, have an assistant hold the brake pedal and torque the front axle nuts to 231 ft. lbs. (314 Nm). Install the adjusting cap and an new cotter pin.

## SHIFT LINKAGE ADJUSTMENT

1. Remove the center console.
2. Move the selector lever from P-to-1 range and return to P; make sure the lever can move smoothly and without sliding noise. Leave the lever in P.
3. At the bottom of the shift lever, loosen both locknuts.
4. Make sure the manual lever on the transaxle is locked into the P position.
5. Adjust the rear locknut until it touches the trunnion and tighten both locknuts to 16 ft. lbs. (22 Nm).
6. Move the selector lever from P to 1 range; make sure the lever can move smoothly and without sliding noise.
7. Using grease, apply to the contact areas of the selector lever and the select rod.
8. Install the center console.

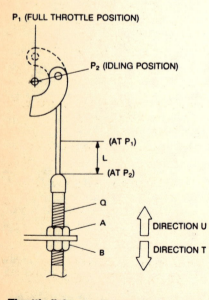

Throttle linkage adjustment on Axxess with automatic transaxle

PIN. DIA.
0.16 IN. (4MM)

Neutral safety switch on Axxess is on the cylinder head

## THROTTLE LINKAGE ADJUSTMENT

1. Loosen the throttle wire locknuts A and B.
2. With the throttle drum set at $P_1$ (fully open), move the fitting Q fully in the T direction and tighten the nut B in the U direction.
3. Loosen the B 2¾–3¼ turns in the T direction and tighten the A nut, securely.
4. Make sure the throttle wire stroke L is 1.54–1.69 in. (39–43mm) between full throttle and idle.

**NOTE: Adjust the throttle wire stroke when the throttle wire/accelerator wire is installed. Place marks on the throttle wire to facilitate measuring the wire stroke.**

5. If the throttle wire stroke is not adjusted, the following problems may arise:
   a. When full-open position $P_1$ of the throttle drum is closer to the direction T, the kickdown range will greatly increase.
   b. When the full-open position $P_1$ of the throttle drum is closer to the direction U, the kickdown range will not occur.

## NEUTRAL SAFETY SWITCH ADJUSTMENT

The neutral safety switch is attached to the right, rear side of the cylinder head. The switch operates the back-up lights and controls the operation of the starter. The starter should only operate when the transaxle is in P or N.

1. Loosen the neutral safely switch-to-engine bolts.
2. Position the shift selector to the N position, in the vertical detent.
3. Using a 0.16 in. (4mm) diameter alignment pin, place it in the alignment holes of the neutral start switch and the shift selector lever.
4. Secure the switch body with the screws and pull out the pin.

**NOTE: If the neutral safety switch does not perform satisfactorily after adjustment, replace it with a new one.**

# TRANSFER CASE

## Transfer Case Assembly

### REMOVAL & INSTALLATION

*Except Axxess*

1. Disconnect the negative battery cable.
2. Raise and safely support the vehicle. If equipped, remove the splash pan or skid plate.
3. Remove the starter. Drain the oil from both the transmission and the transfer case.
4. Matchmark the driveshaft flange at the rear differential pinion flange and at both front driveshaft flanges. Remove both driveshafts.
5. Disconnect the selector lever assembly from the transfer case.
6. The torsion bars must be removed:
   a. Working under the vehicle, measure and record the length of the threads on the torsion bar adjustment.
   b. At the front of the bar, pull the boot back and matchmark the bar to the mounting plate. The spline on the bar must be re-installed in the same position on the plate.
   c. Remove the locknut and adjustment nut and remove the 3 nuts at the mounting plate to remove each bar. Mark the bars left and right side for proper installation.
7. Using an appropriate transmission jack, properly support the transmission and remove the transmission mount and crossmember.
8. Remove the transfer case-to-transmission bolts and move the unit back away from the transmission.
**To install:**
9. Clean the mating surfaces and apply a bead of silicone sealant to the transfer case mounting flange.
10. Carfully fit the case into place and start all the mounting bolts. Torque the bolts to 30 ft. lbs. (41 Nm).
11. Install the crossmember and torque the bolts to 58 ft. lbs. (78 Nm). Install the mount bolts and torque to 38 ft. lbs. (52 Nm).
12. Install the driveshafts and make sure to align the matchmarks:
   a. On the front driveshaft, torque the bolts to 33 ft. lbs. (44 Nm).

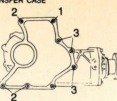

⊕ TRANSFER CASE TO TRANSAXLE
⊗ TRANSAXLE TO TRANSFER CASE

**Bolt torque sequence for Installing transfer case on Axxess**

b. On 2 piece rear driveshafts, torque the flange bolts to 33 ft. lbs. (44 Nm) and the center bearing bracket bolts to 16 ft. lbs. (22 Nm).

c. On single piece rear driveshafts, torque the flange bolts to 65 ft. lbs. (88 Nm).

13. Install the selector lever assembly.

14. Install the torsion bars in their original location. Make sure the splines are in their original position and set the adjustment to its original position.

15. Install the remaining components and fill the transfer case and transmission with oil. Check and adjust front suspension height.

### Axxess

The transaxle must be removed to remove the transfer case.

1. Disconnect the negative battery cable.

2. If equipped with a manual transaxle, remove the breather clamp from the transfer case.

3. Remove the transaxle/transfer case assembly from the vehicle.

4. Remove the transfer case-to-transaxle bolts and the transfer case.

**To install:**

5. Using multi-purpose grease, lubricate the transaxle's oil seal on the transfer case side.

6. Using sealant, apply it around the ring gear oil seal on the transfer case.

**NOTE: Be careful not to damage the transaxle oil seal when inserting the spline portion of the transfer ring gear and placing the shaft into the transaxle.**

7. Torque the transfer case-to-transaxle bolts in the correct sequence to 30 ft. lbs. (40 Nm).

8. Install the transaxle and fill the transfer case with oil.

9. Test the vehicle by performing the following procedures:

a. Position the vehicle so all 4 wheels are not touching the ground and are free to turn.

b. Position the transfer case into the 4WD position.

c. Make sure the rear wheels are turning.

**NOTE: Never test drive the vehicle with the transfer case in the 2WD position.**

# FRONT SUSPENSION

## Shock Absorbers

### REMOVAL & INSTALLATION

#### Except Axxess

1. Raise and safely support the vehicle. Remove the wheel assembly.

2. While holding the upper stem of the shock absorber, remove the shock absorber-to-chassis nut and/or bolt, washer and rubber bushing.

3. Remove the lower shock absorber-to-lower control arm nut and/or bolt and remove the shock absorber from the vehicle.

4. To install, use new rubber bushings and reverse the removal procedures. Torque the shock absorber-to-lower control arm nut/bolt to 58 ft. lbs. (78 Nm) and the shock absorber-to-chassis nut to 16 ft. lbs. (22 Nm) on Pick-Up and Pathfinder or nut/bolt to 30 ft. lbs. (41 Nm) on Van.

## MacPherson Strut

### REMOVAL & INSTALLATION

#### Axxess

1. Raise and safely support the vehicle; position support under the front of the frame.

2. Remove the wheel assembly.

3. Matchmark the strut-to-steering knuckle position.

4. Remove the strut-to-steering knuckle nut/bolts.

5. Remove the strut-to-chassis nuts and the strut from the vehicle.

6. To install, reverse the removal procedures. Align the strut-to-steering knuckle matchmarks. Torque the strut-to-chassis nuts to 40 ft. lbs. (54 Nm) and the strut-to-steering knuckle nuts/bolts to 91 ft. lbs. (124 Nm).

7. Check and/or adjust the front end alignment.

## Leaf Springs

### REMOVAL & INSTALLATION

#### Van

1. Raise and safely support the vehicle; position supports under the frame.

2. Remove the wheel assembly.

3. Remove the lower control arm from one side.

4. From the opposite side, loosen the leaf spring-to-lower control arm bolt.

5. Remove the leaf spring by sliding it from the opposite lower control arm.

6. Inspect the spring for wear and/or cracks; if necessary, replace the spring.

7. To install, reverse the removal procedures.

## Torsion Bars

### REMOVAL & INSTALLATION

#### Pick-Up and Pathfinder

1. Raise and safely support the vehicle with supports placed under the frame. Remove the wheel assemblies.

2. Remove the torsion bar spring adjusting nut.

3. Remove the dust cover and the snapring from the anchor arm.

4. Pull the anchor arm off rearward and remove the torsion bar spring. Keep them separated left and right, they are not interchangable.

5. Remove the torque arm.

**To install:**

6. Check the torsion bars for wear, cracks or other damage; replace them if necessary.

7. Install the torque arm on the lower link (control arm) and torque the bolts to 50 ft. lbs. (68 Nm).

8. Install the snapring and dust cove on the torsion bar.

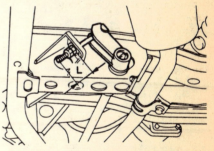

**Adjusting torsion bar anchor arm bolt length L on 2WD Pick-Up and Pathfinder**

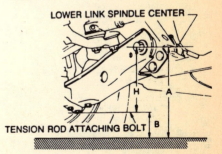

**Adjust dimension H with vehicle on the ground; 2WD Pick-Up and Pathfinder**

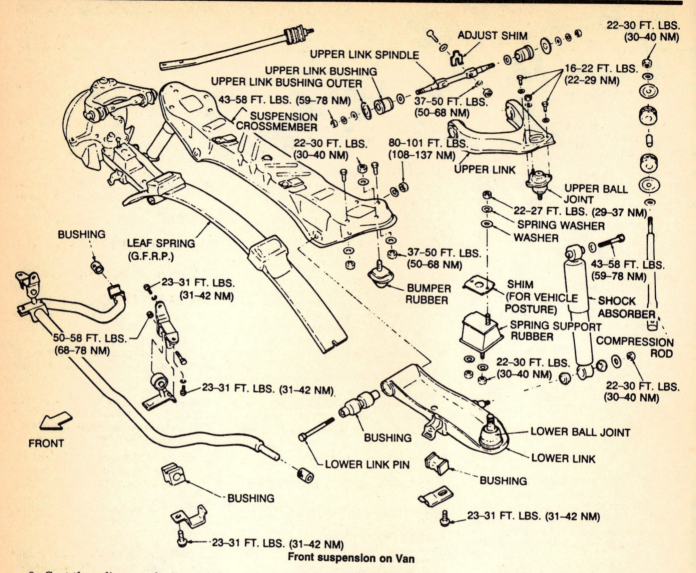

**Front suspension on Van**

9. Coat the splines on the inner end of the torsion bar with chassis lube and install it into the torque arm. The torsion bars are marked **L** and **R** and are not interchangeable. Adjust the torsion bars.

## ADJUSTMENT

### 2WD Models

1. Position a floor jack under the lower suspension arm and raise it so the clearance between the arm and the rebound bumper is 0.

2. Install the anchor arm so the dimension **L** is 0.24–0.71 in. (6–18mm).

3. Install the snapring to the anchor arm and dust cover. Make sure the snapring is properly installed in the groove of the anchor arm.

4. Tighten the anchor arm adjusting nut until dimension **L** is 1.38 in. (35mm) for heavy duty, cab/chassis and std models or 1.93 in. (49mm) for all other models.

5. Lower the vehicle so it is resting on the wheels and bounce it several times to set the suspension. Turn the anchor bolt adjusting nut so dimension **H** is 4.25–4.65 in. (108–118mm).

### 4WD Models

1. Position a floor jack under the lower suspension arm and raise it so the clearance between the arm and the rebound bumper is 0.

2. Install the anchor arm so the dimension **G** is 01.97–2.36 in. (50–60mm).

3. Install the snapring to the anchor arm and dust cover. Make sure the snapring is properly installed in the groove of the anchor arm.

4. Tighten the anchor arm adjusting nut until dimension **L** is 3.03 in. (77mm).

5. Lower the vehicle so it is resting on the wheels and bounce it several times to set the suspension. Turn the anchor bolt adjusting nut so dimension **H** is 1.61–2.01 in. (41–51mm).

## Upper Ball Joints

### INSPECTION

#### Except Axxess

The ball joint(s) should be replaced when play becomes excessive. The manufacturer does not publish specifications on just what constitutes excessive play, relying instead on a method of determining the force (in inch lbs.) required to keep the ball joint turning. An effective way to determine ball joint play is to raise the vehicle until the wheel is just a few inches off the ground and the ball joint is unloaded, which means not to jack directly under the ball joint. Place a long bar under the tire and move the wheel and tire assembly up and down; place one hand on top of the tire while you are doing this. If there is over ¼ in. of play at the top of the tire, the ball joint is probably bad. This assuming that the wheel bearings are in good shape and proper-

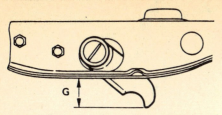

**Anchor arm length G on 4WD Pick-Up and Pathfinder**

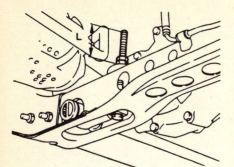

**Torsion bar adjusting bolt length L on 4WD Pick-Up and Pathfinder**

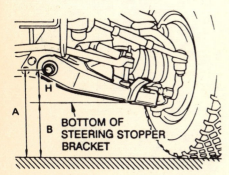

**Adjust dimension H with vehicle on the ground; 4WD Pick-Up and Pathfinder**

ly adjusted. As a double check, have someone watch the ball joint while you move the tire up and down with the bar. If considerable play is seen, besides feeling play at the top of the wheel, the ball joints need to be replaced.

## REMOVAL & INSTALLATION

### Except Axxess

1. Raise and safely support the vehicle.
2. Remove the wheel/tire assembly.

**NOTE: On the Pick-Up and Pathfinder, it may be necessary to loosen the torsion bar anchor lock and adjusting nuts to relieve spring tension.**

3. Place a floor jack under the steering knuckle and support it.
4. Remove and discard the cotter pin from the ball joint stud, then loosen the nut. Using the ball joint removal tool, press the upper ball joint from

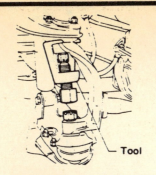

**Use a ball joint press to disconnect the ball joints and tie rod ends -- Pick-Up and Pathfinder**

the lower control arm. Remove the upper ball joint nut.
5. Remove the upper ball joint-to-upper control arm bolts and the ball joint from the vehicle.
6. To install, use a new ball joint, a new cotter pin and reverse the removal procedures. Torque as follows:
  Upper ball joint-to-upper control arm bolts — 16 ft. lbs. (22 Nm)
  Upper ball-to-steering knuckle nut
    Pick-Up and Pathfinder — 108 ft. lbs. (146 Nm)
    Van — 72 ft. lbs. (98 Nm)
7. Check and/or adjust the ride height and the front end alignment.

## Lower Ball Joints

### REMOVAL & INSTALLATION

The lower control arm ball joint on the 2WD Pick-Up and 2WD Pathfinder models are not removable; if the ball joint is defective, replace the lower control arm.

1. Raise and safely support the vehicle.
2. Remove the wheel/tire assembly.

**NOTE: On the Pick-Up and Pathfinder, loosen the torsion bar spring anchor lock and adjusting nuts and remove the anchor arm bolt from the anchor arm. Remove the snapring, then move the anchor arm and torsion bar fully rearward. This procedure is to relieve the spring pressure on the lower control arm.**

3. If equipped, it may be necessary to disconnect the sway bar from the lower arm.
4. Disconnect the tension rod from the lower arm.
5. Remove the cotter pin from the ball joint stud and loosen the nut.
6. Using the ball joint separator tool, press the ball joint from the steering knuckle.
7. Remove the lower ball joint-to-

lower control arm bolts and the ball joint.
8. To install, use a new cotter pin and reverse the removal procedures. Torque as follows:
  Ball joint-to-control arm bolts
    4WD Pick-Up and 4WD Pathfinder — 45 ft. lbs. (61 Nm)
    Axxess — 80 ft. lbs. (108 Nm)
  Ball joint-to-steering knuckle nut
    Pick-Up and Pathfinder — 141 ft. lbs. (190 Nm)
    Axxess — 64 ft. lbs. (87 Nm)
    Van — 141 ft. lbs. (190 Nm)
9. Check and/or adjust the torsion bar ride height assembly and the front end alignment.

## Upper Control Arms

### REMOVAL & INSTALLATION

#### Pick-Up and Pathfinder

1. Raise and safely support the vehicle.
2. Remove the wheels.
3. Remove the upper shock absorber-to-chassis nut and compress the shock absorber.

**NOTE: If may be necessary to loosen the torsion bar anchor lock and adjusting nuts to relieve the torsion bar tension.**

4. Remove the upper ball joint-to-upper control arm bolts.
5. Using a floor jack, raise the lower control arm.
6. Remove the upper control arm-to-chassis bolts and the upper control arm from the vehicle.

**NOTE: If shims are used, be sure to keep them in order for reinstallation purposes.**

7. Inspect the ball joint, replace as required.
8. To install, replace the shims, if used, in their original locations and reverse the removal procedures. Torque the upper control arm-to-chassis bolts to 108 ft. lbs. (146 Nm), the ball joint-to-upper control arm bolts to 15 ft. lbs. (20 Nm) and the upper shock absorber-to-chassis nut to 16 ft. lbs. (21 Nm).
9. Lower the vehicle and adjust the ride height. Check and/or adjust the front end alignment.

#### Van

1. Raise and safely support the vehicle. Remove the wheel assembly.
2. Using a floor jack, support the lower control arm.
3. Remove the upper ball joint-to-upper control arm bolts and separate the ball joint from the upper control arm.
4. Remove the trupper control arm-

to-chassis bolts and the control arm from the vehicle.

**NOTE: If shims are used, be sure to keep them in order for reinstallation purposes.**

5. To install, replace the shims, if used, in their original locations and reverse the removal procedures. Torque the upper control arm-to-chassis bolts to 50 ft. lbs. (68 Nm) and the upper ball joint-to-upper control arm bolts to 22 ft. lbs. (30 Nm).

6. Check and/or adjust the front end alignment.

## Lower Control Arms

### REMOVAL & INSTALLATION

#### 2WD Pick-Up

1. Raise and safely support the vehicle and remove the front wheels.
2. Remove the shock absorber.
3. Remove the torsion bar.
4. Disconnect the stabilizer bar linkage from the lower control arm.
5. Disconnect the tension rod-to-lower control arm bolts.
6. Remove the cotter pin from the ball joint and use a ball joint press to separate the ball joints from the control arm.
7. Remove the lower control arm-to-chassis nut/bolt, tap the pivot shaft from the bushing. Push down on the tension rod and remove the lower control arm.

**To install:**

8. Install the control arm and the pivot bolt and torque the bolt to 108 ft. lbs. (147 Nm).
9. Connect the lower ball joint and sway bar. Torque the ball joint nut to 141 ft. lbs. (191 Nm) and tighten as required to install a new cotter pin.
10. Connect the tension rod and torque the bolts to 47 ft. lbs. (64 Nm). Install the stabilizer bar linkage and torque to 16 ft. lbs. (22 Nm).
11. Install the torsion bar and shock absorber. Adjust the torsion bar height and front wheel alignment.

#### 4WD and Pathfinder

1. Raise and safely support the vehicle and remove the front wheels.
2. Remove the torsion bar.
3. Remove the shock absorber.
4. Disconnect the stabilizer bar linkage.
5. Remove the cotter pin and lower ball joint nut and use a ball joint press to separate the ball joint from the lower control arm.
6. Remove the lower arm spindle bolt and the bushing nut and remove the lower control arm.

**To install:**

7. Fit the arm into place and start the bushing nut. Torque this nut when the vehicle is on the wheels. Torque the spindle bolt to 108 ft. lbs. (147 Nm).
8. Connect the lower ball joint and torque the nut to 141 ft. lbs. (191 Nm) and tighten as required to install a new cotter pin.
9. Connect the stabilizer bar linkage and install the shock absorber. Torque the stabilizer bar linkage when the vehicle is on the wheels to 16 ft. lbs. (22 Nm).
10. Install the torsion bar and adjust the bar and front wheel alignment.

#### Van

1. Raise and safely support the vehicle and remove the wheels.
2. Remove the brackets to remove the stabilizer bar.
3. Support the lower control arm with a floor jack. Disconnect the shock absorber from the control arm.
4. Disconnect the compression rod from the lower control arm.
5. Use wire or rope to support the upper control arm and steering knuckle assembly to the body so it does not fall when the lower arm is removed.
6. Remove the nut from the lower ball joint and use a ball joint press to separate the lower ball joint from the control arm.
7. Carefully lower the floor jack to release the leaf spring tension. Remove the nuts securing the spring to the bump stop.
8. Remove the lower control arm pivot bolt and remove the arm.

**To install:**

9. Install the lower control arm and temporarily tighten the pivot bolt.
10. Raise the arm into position to engage the leaf spring with the bump stop bolt. Make sure the washer is fully on the spring and torque the nut to 27 ft. lbs. (37 Nm).
11. Connect the ball joint and torque the nut to 141 ft. lbs. (191 Nm). Install a new cotter pin.
12. Connect the compression rod and torque the bolts to 30 ft. lbs. (41 Nm).
13. Connect the shock absorber and stabilizer bar. Torque the nuts and bolts to 31 ft. lbs. (42 Nm).
14. With all of the suspension pieces connected, set the vehicle on the wheels and torque the control arm pivot bolt to 101 ft. lbs. (137 Nm). Check and adjust the front wheel alignment.

#### Axxess

1. Raise and safely support the vehicle and remove the front wheels.
2. Remove the stabilizer bar.
3. Remove the bolts securing the control arm to the lower ball joint. Remove the bolts securing the control arm to the frame and remove the arm.

**To install:**

4. Install the control arm and temporarily tighten the bolts.

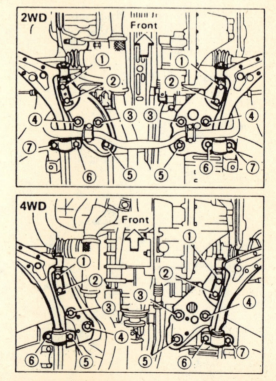

Bolt tightening sequence for installing lower control arm on Axxess with 2WD and 4WD

5. Torque the ball joint nuts to 80 ft. lbs. (109 Nm).

6. Install the stabilizer bar.

7. With the vehicle resting on all 4 wheels, torque the numbered bolts in the sequence shown to 108 ft. lbs. (147 Nm). Torque the front bushing nut to 87 ft. lbs. (118 Nm).

8. Check and adjust front wheel alignment.

## Stabilizer Bar

### REMOVAL & INSTALLATION

#### Pick-Up and Pathfinder

1. Raise and safely support the vehicle.

2. From both sides of the vehicle, remove the stabilizer bar-to-lower control arm connecting rod nut, bushings and tube.

3. Remove the bracket bolts and brackets and remove the stabilizer bar.

4. Installation is the reverse of removal. Make sure the brackets are to the outside of the white painted marks on the stabilizer bar. Torque the bracket bolts to 16 ft. lbs. (22 Nm) and the connecting rod nut to 22 ft. lbs. (30 Nm).

#### Van

1. Raise and safely support the front of the vehicle.

2. From both sides of the vehicle, remove the stabilizer bar-to-lower control arm bracket bolts and brackets. Note the orientation of the bushings so they can be installed the same way.

3. Remove the stabilizer bar-to-chassis bracket bolts and remove the bar. Note the orientation of the bushings so they can be installed the same way.

4. When installing the stabilizer bar, make sure the bushings are installed correctly. With the vehicle on all 4 wheels, torque the bolts to 31 ft. lbs. (42 Nm).

#### Axxess

A stabilizer bar is used on the 2WD models only.

1. Raise and safely support the front of the vehicle.

2. Remove the stabilizer bar-to-connecting rod nut.

3. Remove the stabilizer bar clamp-to-chassis bolts and the stabilizer bar from the vehicle.

4. To install, reverse the removal procedures. Torque the stabilizer bar clamp-to-chassis bolts to 31 ft. lbs. (42 Nm). and the stabilizer bar-to-connecting rod nuts to 38 ft. lbs. (51 Nm).

## Front Wheel Bearings

For the FWD Axxess, the 4WD Pick-Up and 4WD Pathfinder models, please refer to the Drive Axle section.

### REMOVAL & INSTALLATION

#### 2WD Pick-Up

1. Raise and safely support the vehicle and remove the front wheels.

2. Disconnect the brake hose from the bracket on the knuckle.

3. Without disconnecting the hydraulic line, remove the brake caliper and hang it from the body on a wire. Do not let it hang by the hose.

4. Remove the wheel hub cup, the cotter pin, the adjusting cap and hub nut.

5. Remove the wheel hub and brake disc assembly. Be careful not to drop the outer wheel bearing.

6. To remove the inner bearing, pry out the grease seal. Discard the seal.

**To install:**

7. Make sure the bearings are clean and in good condition. Replace as required. Pack the bearings and the hub with new grease and install the bearings into the hub. Install a new grease seal.

8. Make sure the spindle is clean. Install the spacer with the chamfer facing in on the spindle.

9. Lightly grease the lips on the seal and slide the hub and bearings onto the spindle. Install the washer and nut.

10. To adjust the pre-load on the bearing:

   a. Torque the wheel bearing nut to 25 ft. lbs. (34 Nm).

   b. Spin the hub several times in both directions, then torque the nut to 29 ft. lbs. (39 Nm).

   c. Loosen the nut 45 degrees. Install the locknut cap and a new cotter pin.

11. Install the brake caliper and torque the caliper carrier bolts to 72 ft. lbs. (98 Nm).

#### 2WD Pathfinder

1. Raise and safely support the vehicle and remove the front wheels.

2. Without disconnecting the hydraulic line, remove the brake caliper and hang it from the body with wire. Do not allow the caliper to hang by the hose.

3. Remove the hub cap and locking screw and remove the lock washer. Use a pin wrench to loosen the wheel bearing locknut. The torque may be fairly high, do not use a hammer and drift pin.

4. Remove the locknut and pull the hub off with the bearings. Pry the in-

ner grease seal out to remove the inner bearing. Discard the seal.

**To install:**

5. Clean all parts of grease and check the condition of the bearings. If bearings are to be replaced, the inner races can be removed from the hub with a hammer and soft drift pin. Be careful not to damage the hub.

6. Carefully install the new inner races with the drift pin, making sure they seat in the hub.

7. Pack the bearings with new grease and pack grease into the hub. Install the inner bearing and press a new inner seal into the hub.

8. Slip the hub assembly onto the spindle and install the outer bearing. Grease the locknut and thread it into place.

9. To adjust bearing pre-load:

   a. Use a pin wrench to torque the locknut to 58–72 ft. lbs. (78–98 Nm). Turn the hub in both directions several times while torquing the nut.

   b. Loosen the locknut, then torque again to 13 inch lbs. (1.5 Nm).

   c. Turn the hub several times and check the nut torque again.

   d. Install the lock washer. When installing the screw, make sure the locknut turns no more than 30 degrees in either direction.

   e. When bearing pre-load is properly set, there will be no endplay in the hub and it will require no more than 4.7 lbs. of pull at the wheel stud to turn the hub.

10. Install the brake caliper and torque the caliper carrier bolts to 72 ft. lbs. (98 Nm).

#### Van

1. Loosen the wheel lug nuts. Raise and safely support the vehicle. Remove the wheel/tire assembly.

2. Remove the caliper-to-steering knuckle bolts and the caliper. Using a wire, suspend the caliper from the vehicle; do not disconnect the brake hose from the caliper.

3. Remove the grease cap from the wheel hub.

4. Remove the wheel bearing nut and the lockwasher. Pull the rotor/wheel hub from the spindle.

5. Remove the lock ring from the rotor/wheel hub.

6. Using a hydraulic press, press the wheel bearing and grease seal from the rotor/wheel hub assembly.

7. Using a new bearing, press it into the rotor/wheel hub assembly until it seats; use no more than 3 tons pressure. Install a new lock ring into the rotor/wheel hub.

8. To complete the installation, reverse the removal procedures. Torque the wheel bearing nut to 195–260 ft. lbs.

# REAR SUSPENSION

## Shock Absorbers

### REMOVAL & INSTALLATION

1. Raise and safely support the vehicle.
2. Remove the upper shock-to-vehicle nut, the lower shock-to-vehicle nut and the shock from the vehicle.

**NOTE: The weight of the vehicle must be on the rear wheels before tightening the shock absorber attaching nuts.**

3. To install, reverse the removal procedures. Torque as follows:
Upper shock-to-vehicle nut
Pick-Up and Pathfinder—22–30 ft. lbs.
Van—12–18 ft. lbs.
Lower shock absorber-to-axle nut
2WD Pick-Up and 2WD Pathfinder—12–16 ft. lbs.
4WD Pick-Up and 4WD Pathfinder—22–30 ft. lbs.
Van—53–72 ft. lbs.

## MacPherson Strut

### REMOVAL & INSTALLATION

*Axxess*

**2WD MODEL**

On the 2WD models, the wheel spindle and knuckle are a part of the strut.
1. Remove the hub cap and cotter pin.
2. Apply the brakes and loosen the wheel bearing locknut.
3. Raise and safely support the vehicle. Remove the wheel assembly.
4. Remove the wheel bearing nut, washer and wheel hub bearing.

**NOTE: The wheel hub bearing must be replaced as an assembly if the bearing is defective.**

5. Disconnect and plug the brake line from the wheel cylinder.
6. Remove radius rod-to-knuckle nut/bolt, the stabilizer rod-to-knuckle nut/bolt and the parallel rods-to-knuckle nut/bolt.
7. From inside the vehicle, remove the strut cover.
8. Remove the strut-to-chassis nuts and the strut.
**To install:**
9. Install strut and the strut-to-chassis nuts and torque to 58 ft. lbs. (78 Nm).
10. Install the parallel rods-to-

knuckle nut/bolt and torque to 87 ft. lbs. (118 Nm).
11. Install the stabilizer rod-to-knuckle nut/bolt and torque to 58 ft. lbs. (78 Nm).
12. Install the radius rod-to-knuckle nut/bolt and torque to 87 ft. lbs. (118 Nm).
13. Complete the installation of the remaining components. Torque the wheel hub bearing assembly to 137–188 ft. lbs. (186–255 Nm). Bleed the rear brakes and inspect the rear wheel alignment.
14. Using a dial indicator, measure the bearing axial endplay; it should be 0.0020 in. (0.05mm) or less.

**4WD MODELS**

1. Raise and safely support the vehicle. Remove the wheel assembly.
2. Matchmark the strut-to-knuckle location.
3. Support the knuckle and remove the strut-to-knuckle nuts and bolts.
4. From inside the vehicle, remove the strut-to-chassis nuts.
5. Remove the strut from the vehicle.
6. To install, reverse the removal procedures. Torque the strut-to-chassis nuts to 51 ft. lbs. (69 Nm) and the strut-to-knuckle nuts/bolts to 91 ft. lbs. (124 Nm).
7. To complete the installation, reverse the removal procedures. Inspect the rear wheel alignment.

## Coil Springs

### REMOVAL & INSTALLATION

*Van*

1. Raise and safely support the vehicle.
2. Lower the axle housing and remove the coil spring(s).
3. To install, reverse the removal procedures.

## Leaf Springs

### REMOVAL & INSTALLATION

*Pick-Up and Pathfinder*

——— CAUTION ———
*The leaf springs are under a considerable amount of tension. Be very careful when removing or installing them; they can exert enough force to cause serious injuries.*

1. Raise and safely support the vehicle. Using a floor jack, support the axle housing.
2. Disconnect the shock absorbers at their lower end.
3. Remove the axle housing-to-spring pad U-bolt nuts and the spring pad.

4. Raise the axle housing to remove the weight off the springs.
5. Remove the spring shackle nuts, drive out the shackle pins and remove the spring from the vehicle.

**NOTE: The weight of the vehicle must be on the rear wheels before torquing the front pin, shackle and shock absorber nuts.**

6. To install, reverse the removal procedures. Torque as follows:
Front pin and shackle nuts—94 ft. lbs. (127 Nm)
U-bolt nuts—72 ft. lbs. (98 Nm)
Shock absorber lower end nut
2WD—16 ft. lbs. (22 Nm)
4WD—30 ft. lbs. (41 Nm)

## Rear Control Arms

### REMOVAL & INSTALLATION

*Van*

**LOWER LINK**

1. Raise and safely support the vehicle.
2. Remove the lower link-to-axle housing nut/bolt and the lower link-to-chassis nut/bolt.
3. Remove the lower link from the vehicle.
4. To install, reverse the removal procedures. Torque the lower link-to-chassis nut/bolt and the lower link-to-axle housing nut/bolt to 94 ft. lbs. (127 Nm).

**UPPER LINK**

1. Raise and safely support the vehicle.
2. Remove the upper link-to-axle housing nut/bolt and the upper link-to-chassis nut/bolt.
3. Remove the upper link from the vehicle.
4. To install, reverse the removal procedures. Torque the upper link-to-chassis nut/bolt and the upper link-to-axle housing nut/bolt to 94 ft. lbs. (127 Nm).

**PANHARD ROD**

1. Raise and safely support the vehicle.
2. Remove the panhard rod-to-axle housing nut and the panhard rod-to-chassis nut/bolt.
3. Remove the panhard rod from the vehicle.
4. To install, reverse the removal procedures. Torque the panhard rod-to-chassis nut/bolt to 94 ft. lbs. (127 Nm) and the panhard rod-to-axle housing nut to 50 ft. lbs. (68 Nm).

*Axxess*

### 2WD MODELS WITH RADIUS ROD

1. Raise and safely support the vehicle.
2. Remove the wheel assembly.
3. Remove the radius rod-to-knuckle nut and bolt.
4. Remove the radius rod-to-chassis nut/bolt and the rod.
5. To install, reverse the removal procedures. Torque the radius rod-to-chassis nut/bolt to 80 ft. lbs. (108 Nm) and the radius rod-to-knuckle nut/bolt to 80 ft. lbs. (108 Nm).

### 2WD MODELS WITH PARALLEL RODS

Dual rods are connected from the chassis to the knuckle.
1. Raise and safely support the vehicle.
2. Remove the wheel assembly.
3. Remove the parallel rods-to-knuckle nut and bolt.
4. Remove the parallel rods-to-chassis nut/bolt and the rods.
5. To install, reverse the removal procedures. Torque the parallel rods-to-chassis nut/bolt and the parallel rods-to-knuckle nut/bolt to 87 ft. lbs. (118 Nm).

### 4WD MODELS WITH RADIUS ROD

1. Raise and safely support the vehicle.
2. Remove the wheel assembly.
3. Remove the radius rod-to-knuckle nut and bolt.
4. Remove the radius rod-to-chassis nut/bolt and the rod.
5. To install, reverse the removal procedures. Torque the radius rod-to-chassis nut/bolt to 80 ft. lbs. (108 Nm) and the radius rod-to-knuckle nut/bolt to 72 ft. lbs. (98 Nm).

### 4WD WITH PARALLEL RODS

Dual rods are connected from the chassis to the knuckle.
1. Raise and safely support the vehicle.
2. Remove the wheel assembly.
3. Remove the parallel rods-to-knuckle nut and bolt.
4. Remove the parallel rods-to-chassis nut/bolt and the rods.
5. To install, reverse the removal procedures. Torque the parallel rods-to-chassis nut/bolt and the parallel rods-to-knuckle nut/bolt to 72 ft. lbs. (98 Nm).

## Rear Wheel Bearings

For RWD models, refer to the drive axle section.

## REMOVAL & INSTALLATION

*Axxess*

1. Remove the hub cap, the grease cap and the cotter pin.
2. Loosen the wheel hub nut; do not remove it.
3. Raise and safely support the vehicle.
4. Remove the wheel assembly and the brake drum.
5. Remove the hub nut, the washer and the wheel hub assembly.

**NOTE: If the wheel bearings are defective, replace the entire wheel hub bearing assembly.**

6. To install, reverse the removal procedures. With the vehicle on all 4 wheels, torque the wheel hub nut to 137–188 ft. lbs. (186–255 Nm).

---

# STEERING

## Steering Wheel

### REMOVAL & INSTALLATION

1. Position the steering wheel in the straight-ahead position.
2. Disconnect the negative battery cable.
3. Remove the horn pad by removing the screws from the rear of the steering wheel crossbar.
4. Matchmark the top of the steering column shaft and the steering wheel flange.
5. Remove the attaching nut and remove the steering wheel with a puller.

**NOTE: Do not strike the shaft with a hammer, the steering column may collapse.**

To install:
6. Install the steering wheel so the punchmarks are aligned. Torque the steering wheel nut to 22–29 ft. lbs. (29–39 Nm).
7. Install the horn pad and connect the negative battery cable.

## Manual Steering Gear

### REMOVAL & INSTALLATION

*Except Axxess*

1. Raise and safely support the vehicle.
2. Remove the steering gear-to-rubber coupling bolt.
3. Matchmark the pitman arm and sector shaft and with the wheels in a straight-ahead position, remove the idler arm-to-sector shaft nut.

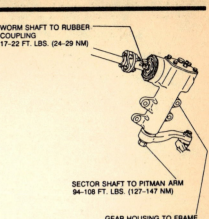

Steering gear box used on all except Axxess

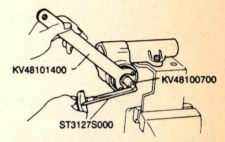

Use the special wrench to adjust worm gear preload—Pick-Up, Pathfinder and Van

4. Using the steering gear arm puller tool, press the arm from the steering gear.
5. Remove the steering gear-to-chassis bolts and the steering gear from the vehicle.
6. To install, reverse the removal procedures. Torque as follows:
 Steering gear-to-coupling bolt—17–22 ft. lbs. (24–29 Nm)
 Steering gear-to-pitman arm nut—94–108 ft. lbs. (127–147 Nm)
 Steering gear-to-frame bolts—62–71 ft. lbs. (84–96 Nm)

### ADJUSTMENT

*Worm Gear Preload*

For this procedure, the steering gear must be removed from the vehicle and placed in a vise.
1. Using the locknut wrench tool, loosen the locknut.
2. Rotate the worm shaft a few times, in both directions, to settle the worm bearing and check the preload.
3. Using the adjusting plug wrench, the torque wrench and an adapter socket, check the worm bearing preload; it should be 1.7–5.2 inch lbs. (0.20–0.59 Nm).
4. To adjust the worm gear preload, turn the adjusting plug with the special pin wrench and recheck the preload.
5. With the worm gear preload set,

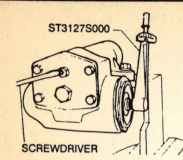

**Adjusting steering gear preload on Pick-Up, Pathfinder and Van**

hold the adjusting plug and tighten the locknut. Check preload again.

### Steering Gear Preload

1. Loosen the adjusting screw locknut.
2. Rotate the worm shaft a few times in both directions to settle the worm bearing and check the preload.
3. Set the worm gear in the straight ahead position.
4. Using the torque wrench tool and an adapter socket, check the worm gear preload; it should be 7.4–10.9 inch lbs. (0.83–1.23 Nm) for new parts or 5.2–8.7 inch lbs. (0.59–0.98 Nm) for used parts.
5. If necessary, loosen the locknut and turn the adjusting screw to obtain the correct preload.
6. With the preload set, tighten the locknut.

## Power Steering Gear

### REMOVAL & INSTALLATION

1. Raise and safely support the vehicle.
2. Remove the wormshaft-to-rubber coupling bolt.
3. Matchmark the idler arm and sector shaft and with the wheels in a straight-ahead position, remove the idler arm-to-sector shaft nut.
4. Disconnect the fluid lines from the gear and cap the lines and openings in the gear.
5. Using the steering gear arm puller, press the gear arm from the steering knuckle.
6. Remove the steering gear-to-chassis bolts and the steering gear from the vehicle.
7. To install, reverse the removal procedures. Torque as follows:
   Steering gear coupling bolt—17–22 ft. lbs. (49–51 Nm)
   Steering gear-to-pitman arm nut—101–130 ft. lbs. (137–177 Nm)
   Steering gear-to-frame bolts—62–71 ft. lbs. (84–96 Nm).
8. Refill the power steering pump reservoir and bleed the system.

## ADJUSTMENT

1. Remove the power steering gear and position it in a vise.
2. Loosen the adjusting screw locknut.
3. Set the worm gear in the straight-ahead position.
4. Using the torque wrench and an adapter socket, check the turning torque; it should be 0.9–3.5 inch lbs. (0.1–0.4 Nm).
5. If necessary, use a screwdriver, then, turn the adjusting screw to obtain the correct preload.
6. With the preload set, tighten the adjusting screw nut.

## Power Steering Rack

### REMOVAL & INSTALLATION

1. Raise and safely support the vehicle and remove the front wheels.
2. Remove the cotter pins and nuts and use a ball joint press to separate the tie rod ends from the steering knuckles.
3. Remove the rubber coupling pinch bolt.
4. Disconnect and plug the hydraulic lines coming from the pump.
5. Remove the bracket bolts and remove the rack from the chassis.
6. Installation is the reverse of removal. Torque the bracket bolts to 72 ft. lbs. (98 Nm). Torque the coupling pinch bolt to 22 ft. lbs. (29 Nm).
7. Connect the tie rod ends and torque the nuts to 29 ft. lbs. (39 Nm). Tighten as required to install new cotter pins.
8. Use new O-rings to connect the hydraulic lines. Fill and bleed the system.

### ADJUSTMENT

#### On Vehicle

1. Drive the vehicle on a flat road and turn the steering wheel about 20 degrees. If the wheel returns to center when released, no adjustment is required.
2. If the wheel does not self-center from a slight turn, loosen the locknut and loosen the adjusting screw.
3. If there is excessive play in the steering that is definitely in the rack, loosen the locknut and tighten the adjusting screw.
4. Road test the vehicle again. All adjustments should be made in very small increments. Under normal use, the steering rack should not require any adjustment. If adjustment does not cure the symptom, look for other problems in the steering system such as contaminated fluid, pump or sus-

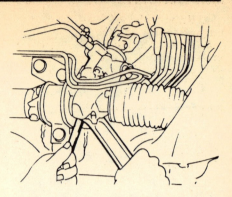

**Minor steering rack adjustment on Axxess can be made on the vehicle**

pension failure or incorrect wheel alignment.

#### Off Vehicle

For a complete adjustment, the power steering rack must be removed from the vehicle and positioned in a vise.

1. Without fluid in the rack, set the gears in the neutral position (wheels straight-ahead).
2. Lubricate the adjusting screw with locking sealant and screw it in.
3. Lightly, tighten the locknut.
4. Torque the adjusting screw to 43–52 inch lbs. (4.9–5.9 Nm).
5. Loosen the adjusting screw and retorque it to 0.43–1.74 inch lbs. (0.05–0.20 Nm).
6. Move the rack over its entire stroke several times.
7. Using an inch lb. torque wrench, measure the pinion rotating torque within the range of 180 degrees from the neutral position.
8. Loosen the adjusting screw and retorque it to 43–52 inch lbs. (4.9–5.9 Nm).
9. Loosen the adjusting screw 40–60 degrees.
10. While securing the adjusting screw in position, torque the locknut to 29–43 ft. lbs. (39–59 Nm).
11. Using a spring gauge, connect it to the tie rod end, pull the tie rod to check the frictional sliding force; it should be 27.6–37.5 lbs. (122.6–166.7 N) at neutral point or 27.6–41.9 lbs. (122.6–186.3 N) other than neutral point.

## Power Steering Pump

### REMOVAL & INSTALLATION

1. Disconnect the negative battery cable.
2. Remove the drive belt from the power steering pump.
3. Place a container under the power steering pump, disconnect and plug the pressure lines and drain the fluid into the container.

4. Remove the bolts to remove the pump from the vehicle.

5. To install, reverse the removal procedures. Adjust the drive belt tension. Bleed the power steering system.

## BELT ADJUSTMENT

1. To check belt deflection, press on the belt at a point mid-way between the pulleys with a force of 22 lbs. (98 N) and measure how far the belt moves.

2. Loosen the adjuster locking bolt and turn the adjuster bolt as required. Be careful not to make the belts too tight or bearings will fail. Check belt deflection specifications.

3. Torque the adjuster locking bolt to 12 ft. lbs. (17 Nm).

Axxess
Used belt – 0.24–28 in. (6–7mm)
New belt – 0.20–0.24 in. (5–6mm)
Pick-Up and Pathfinder
2.4L Engine
Used belt – 0.35–0.43 in. (9–11mm)
New belt – 0.28–0.35 in. (7–9mm)
3.0L Engine
Used belt – 0.43–0.51 in. (11–13mm)

New belt – 0.35–0.43 in. (9–11mm)
Van
Used belt – 0.35–0.39 in. (9–10mm)
New belt – 0.28–0.35 in. (7–9mm)

## SYSTEM BLEEDING

1. Raise and support the vehicle safely.

2. Check and add fluid to the reservoir, if necessary.

3. Start the engine. Turn the steering wheel quickly (all the way), right and left, just touching the stops; turn the steering wheel at least 10 times.

**NOTE: When bleeding the system, make sure the temperature of the fluid reaches 140–176°F (60–80°C).**

4. Stop the engine, check the fluid level, add as required.

5. Start and run the engine for 3–5 seconds.

6. Stop the engine, check the fluid level, add as required.

7. Start the engine. Turn the steering wheel (all the way) right and left, just touching the stops; turn the steering wheel at least 10 times.

8. Stop the engine, check the fluid level, add as required.

9. Repeat the steps until all of the air is bled from the system.

10. If the air cannot be bleed from the system, turn and hold the steering wheel at each stop for at least 5 seconds but never more than 15 seconds.

## Tie Rod Ends

### REMOVAL & INSTALLATION

*Except Axxess*

1. Raise and safely support the vehicle. Remove the wheel/tire assembly.

2. If removing the tie rod as an assembly:

  a. Remove the tie rod-to-cross rod cotter pin and nut.

  b. Remove the tie rods-to-steering knuckle cotter pin and nut.

  c. Using the ball joint remover tool, press the tie rod from the steering knuckle and the tie rod from the cross rod.

3. If removing a defective tie rod end:

  a. Remove the cotter pin and nut from the end being removed.

  b. Loosen the tie rod clamp or locknut.

  c. Using the ball joint remover tool, press the tie rod from the cross rod or steering knuckle and unscrew the tie rod end from the tie rod.

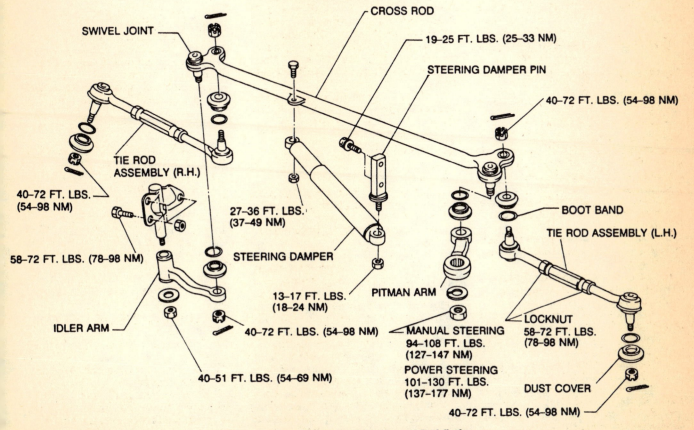

**Steering linkage on 4WD Pick-Up and Pathfinder**

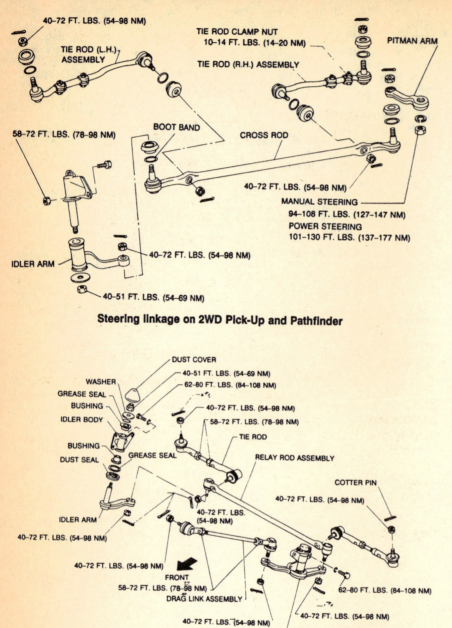

**Steering linkage on 2WD Pick-Up and Pathfinder**

**Steering linkage on Van**

6. To install, screw the tie rod end onto the tie rod the same number of turns necessary to remove it.

7. Install the tie rod end into the steering knuckle. Torque as follows:

Tie rod end-to-steering knuckle nut — 22–29 ft. lbs. (29–39 Nm)

Tie rod locknut

2WD — 27–34 ft. lbs. (37–46 Nm)

4WD — 58–72 ft. lbs. (78–98 Nm)

8. To complete the installation, reverse the removal procedures. Check and or adjust the front wheel alignment.

# BRAKES

For all brake system repair and service procedures not detailed below, please refer to "Brakes" in the Unit Repair section.

## Master Cylinder

**NOTE: Be careful not to spill brake fluid on the painted surfaces of the vehicle; it will damage the paint.**

### REMOVAL & INSTALLATION

1. Using a syringe, remove the brake fluid from the master cylinder.

2. Disconnect and plug the hydraulic lines at the master cylinder.

3. If equipped, disconnect the fluid level warning switch connector from the master cylinder.

4. Remove the clevis pin connecting the master cylinder to the pedal.

5. Remove the nuts or bolts securing the master cylinder to the firewall or power brake booster unit and pull the master cylinder out.

6. To install, reverse the removal procedures. Torque the master cylinder nuts to 8 ft. lbs. (11 Nm) and the brake lines-to-master cylinder to 13 ft. lbs. (18 Nm). Refill the master cylinder with new brake fluid and bleed the brake system.

**NOTE: Before tightening the master cylinder mounting nuts or bolts, screw the hydraulic line fitting into the cylinder body a few turns.**

## Load Sensing Proportioning Valve

The purpose of this valve is to control the fluid pressure applied to the brakes to prevent rear wheel lock-up

d. Measure the tie rod end-to-tie rod clamp distance.

e. Unscrew the tie rod end from the tie rod.

f. Using a new tie rod end, screw the new tie rod end into the tie rod clamp until the measured distance is the same, then, torque the tie rod clamp bolt to 10–14 ft. lbs. (14–20 Nm) or nut to 58–72 ft. lbs. (78–98 Nm).

4. Inspect the tie rod ball joint for wear; if necessary, replace it.

5. To install, use new cotter pins and reverse the removal procedures. Torque the tie rod-to-steering knuckle nut to 40–72 ft. lbs. (54–98 Nm) and

the tie rod-to-cross rod nut to 40–72 ft. lbs. (54–98 Nm). Check and/or adjust the front-end alignment.

### Axxess

1. Raise and safely support the vehicle.

2. Remove the wheel assembly.

3. Remove the tie rod end-to-steering knuckle cotter pin and nut. Using a tie rod removal tool, separate the tie rod end from the steering knuckle.

4. Loosen the tie rod end locknut.

5. While counting the number of turns, remove the tie rod end from the tie rod.

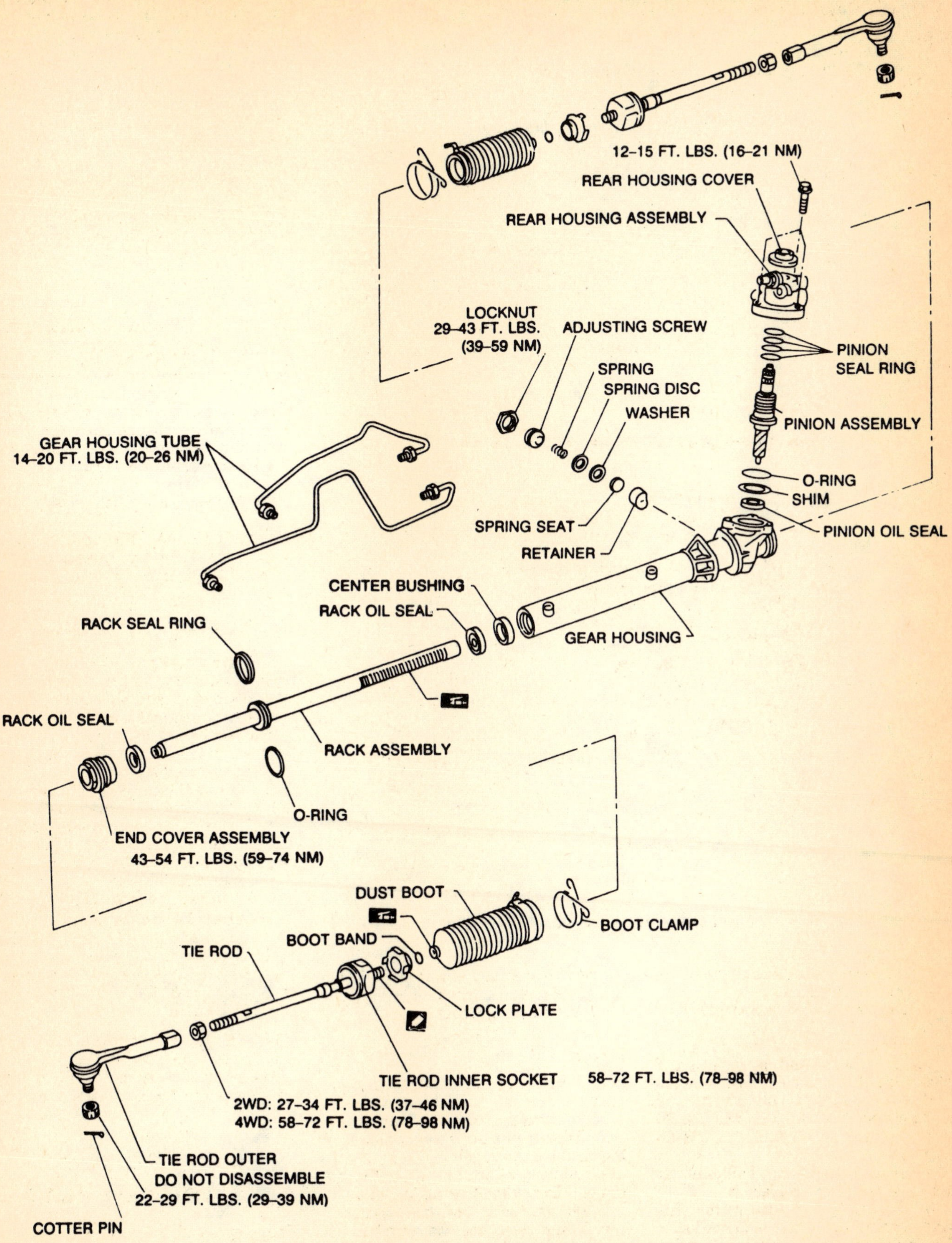

12–15 FT. LBS. (16–21 NM)

REAR HOUSING COVER

REAR HOUSING ASSEMBLY

LOCKNUT
29–43 FT. LBS.
(39–59 NM)

ADJUSTING SCREW

PINION
SEAL RING

SPRING

SPRING DISC

WASHER

PINION ASSEMBLY

GEAR HOUSING TUBE
14–20 FT. LBS. (20–26 NM)

O-RING

SHIM

SPRING SEAT

RETAINER

PINION OIL SEAL

CENTER BUSHING

RACK OIL SEAL

GEAR HOUSING

RACK SEAL RING

RACK OIL SEAL

RACK ASSEMBLY

O-RING

END COVER ASSEMBLY
43–54 FT. LBS. (59–74 NM)

DUST BOOT

BOOT CLAMP

BOOT BAND

TIE ROD

LOCK PLATE

TIE ROD INNER SOCKET
2WD: 27–34 FT. LBS. (37–46 NM)
4WD: 58–72 FT. LBS. (78–98 NM)

58–72 FT. LBS. (78–98 NM)

TIE ROD OUTER
DO NOT DISASSEMBLE
22–29 FT. LBS. (29–39 NM)

COTTER PIN

**Steering linkage on Axxess**

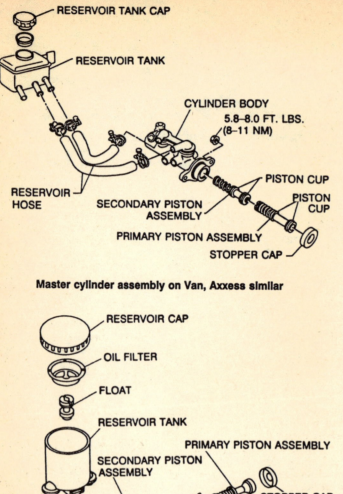

Master cylinder assembly on Van, Axxess similar

Master cylinder assembly on Pick-Up and Pathfinder

during weight transfer at high speed stops.

## REMOVAL & INSTALLATION

1. Raise and safely support the vehicle.
2. Disconnect and plug the lines going to the valve.
3. Remove the valve-to-chassis bolts and the valve.
4. To install, reverse the removal procedures.
5. Bleed the brake system.

## ADJUSTMENT

### Pick-Up and Pathfinder

**1989**

1. Position approximately 220 lbs. (100 kg) of weight over the rear axle.
2. Install pressure gauges at the front and rear brakes.
3. Depress the brake pedal until the front brake is approximately 711 psi (4900 KPa) Check that the rear brake pressure is 327–469 lbs. (2255–3234 KPa).
4. Depress the brake pedal until the

front brake pressure is approximately 1422 lbs. (1928 KPa). Check that the rear brake pressure is 455–654 lbs. (3137–4509 KPa).

5. If the rear brake pressure is not within specifications, move the spring bracket to the left if the pressure is high or to the right if the pressure is low. Repeat this process until the rear brake pressure is correct.

**1990–92**

1. Ensure the fuel tank, the cooling system and the engine crankcase are filled. Make sure the spare tire, the jack, the hand tools and the mats are installed.
2. Position a person in the driver's seat and one on the rear end;, then have the person on the rear end slowly get off.
3. Attach a lever to the stopper bolt and adjust the length **L** to approx. 7.44 in. (189mm).
4. Install pressure gauges at the front and rear brakes.
5. Depress the brake pedal until the front brake pressure is approximately 1422 psi (9805 KPa). Check that the

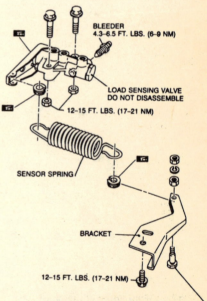

Load sensing brake valve—Pick-Up and Pathfinder

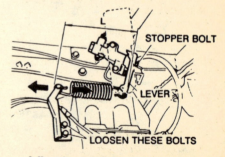

Adjust load sensing valve spring length—Pick-Up and Pathfinder

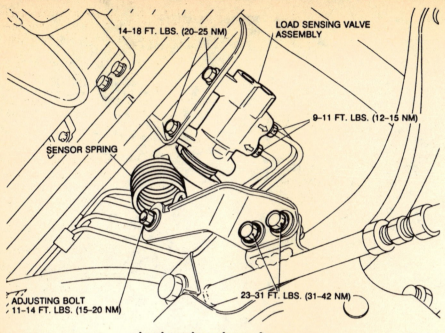

Load sensing valve on Axxess

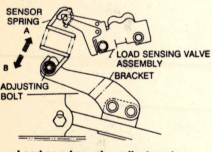

Load sensing valve adjustment on 2WD Axxess

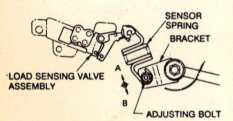

Load sensing valve adjustment on 4WD Axxess

rear brake pressure is 327–441 psi (2255–3041 KPa).

6. Slowly, set a 220 lbs. (100 kg) weight on the rear axle.

7. Depress the brake pedal until the front brake pressure is approximately 1422 psi. Check that the rear brake pressure is 711–995 psi (4902–6861 KPa) for all except heavy duty or 640–924 psi (4413–6371 KPa) for heavy duty.

8. If the rear brake pressure is above specification, adjust the bracket away from the valve.

9. If the rear brake pressure is be-

low specification, adjust the bracket towards the valve.

*Axxess*

1. Position a person in the driver's seat and position 1544 lbs. (702 kg) over the rear axle.

2. Install pressure gauges at the front and rear brakes.

3. Bleed the air from the front and rear brake lines.

4. Depress the brake pedal until the front brake is approximately 711 psi (4902 KPa). Check the rear brake pressure:

455–597 psi (3137–4116 KPa)— 2WD, 5-passenger model
412–555 psi (4909–3827 KPa)— 2WD, 7-passenger model
370–512 psi (2551–3530 KPa)— 4WD, 5-passenger model
341–483 psi (2351–3330 KPa)— 4WD, 7-passenger model

5. Depress the brake pedal until the front brake pressure is approximately 1422 psi. (9805 KPa). Check the rear brake pressure:

455–597 psi (3137–4116 KPa)— 2WD, 5-passenger model
412–555 psi (4909–3827 KPa)— 2WD, 7-passenger model
370–512 psi (2551–3530 KPa)— 4WD, 5-passenger model
341–483 psi (2351–3330 KPa)— 4WD, 7-passenger model

6. If the rear brake pressure is above specification, adjust the bracket in the **A** direction.

7. If the rear brake pressure is below specification, adjust the bracket in the **B** direction.

8. If necessary, repeat the pressure procedure.

9. If the pressure is outside the specified range after the spring length is adjusted, replace the load sensing valve assembly.

## Power Brake Booster

### REMOVAL & INSTALLATION

1. Remove the master cylinder from the power brake booster.

2. Remove the vacuum hose form the power brake booster.

3. Working under the instrument panel, remove the brake pedal-to-brake booster rod clevis pin. Remove the power brake booster mounting bolts and the booster from the vehicle.

4. To install, reverse the removal procedures. Torque the power brake booster-to-cowl nuts to 5.8–8 ft. lbs. (8–11 Nm). Check and/or adjust the brake pedal height.

**NOTE: When installing the power brake booster, make sure there is 0.40–0.41 in. (10–10.5mm) clearance between the pushrod end and the master cylinder piston.**

## Brake Caliper

### REMOVAL & INSTALLATION

1. Raise and safely support the vehicle. Remove the wheel assembly.

2. Remove the lower sliding pin bolt and swing the caliper up to remove disc brake pads from the caliper.

3. Disconnect and plug the brake hose from the brake caliper.

4. Remove the caliper torque member bolts and the caliper from the vehicle.

5. Make sure the caliper moves freely on the sliding pins. Clean, repair or replace as necessary. Use a small amount of light grease to lubricate the pins.

6. To install, reverse the removal procedures. Torque the sliding pin bolts to 31 ft. lbs. (42 Nm). If the torque member was removed, torque the bolts to 72 ft. lbs. (97 Nm) on front calipers, 38 ft. lbs. (52 Nm) on rear calipers.

7. Bleed the brake system.

## Disc Brake Pads

### REMOVAL & INSTALLATION

1. Raise and safely support the vehicle. Remove the wheels and the brake fluid reservoir cap.

2. Remove the bottom sliding pin bolt and swing the caliper upward.

3. Remove the pad retainers, the in-

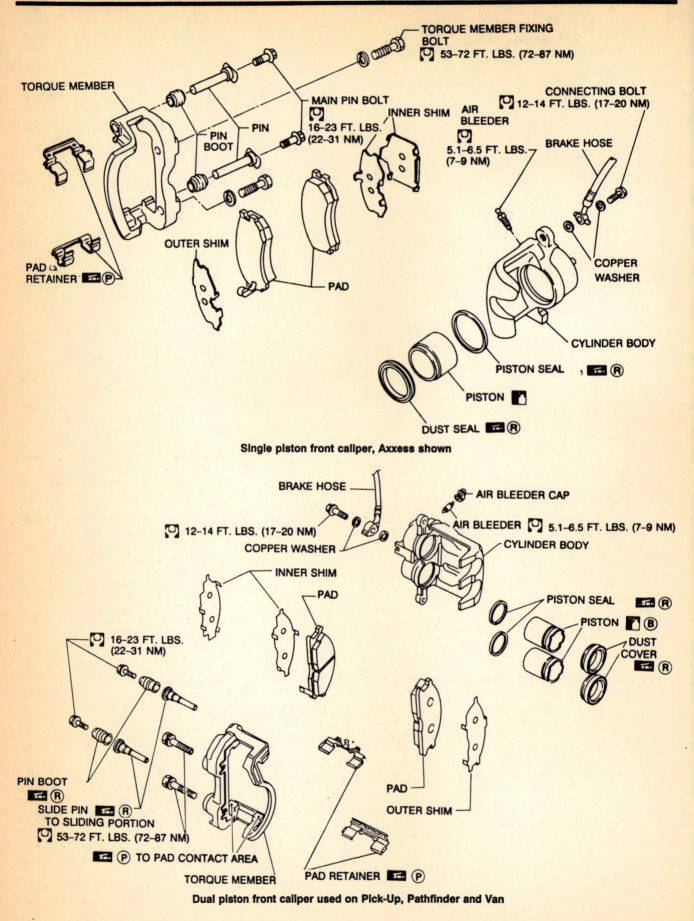

**TORQUE MEMBER FIXING BOLT** 🔧 53–72 FT. LBS. (72–87 NM)

**TORQUE MEMBER**

**PIN BOOT**

**PIN**

**MAIN PIN BOLT** 🔧 16–23 FT. LBS. (22–31 NM)

**INNER SHIM**

**AIR BLEEDER** 🔧 5.1–6.5 FT. LBS. (7–9 NM)

**CONNECTING BOLT** 🔧 12–14 FT. LBS. (17–20 NM)

**BRAKE HOSE**

**COPPER WASHER**

**CYLINDER BODY**

**PAD RETAINER** 🔧 P

**OUTER SHIM**

**PAD**

**PISTON SEAL** , 🔧 R

**PISTON** 🔧

**DUST SEAL** 🔧 R

**Single piston front caliper, Axxess shown**

**BRAKE HOSE**

**AIR BLEEDER CAP**

🔧 12–14 FT. LBS. (17–20 NM)

**COPPER WASHER**

**AIR BLEEDER** 🔧 5.1–6.5 FT. LBS. (7–9 NM)

**CYLINDER BODY**

**INNER SHIM**

**PAD**

**PISTON SEAL** 🔧 R

**PISTON** 🔧 B

🔧 16–23 FT. LBS. (22–31 NM)

**DUST COVER** 🔧 R

**PIN BOOT** 🔧 R

**SLIDE PIN** 🔧 R **TO SLIDING PORTION** 🔧 53–72 FT. LBS. (72–87 NM)

🔧 P **TO PAD CONTACT AREA**

**PAD**

**OUTER SHIM**

**TORQUE MEMBER**

**PAD RETAINER** 🔧 P

**Dual piston front caliper used on Pick-Up, Pathfinder and Van**

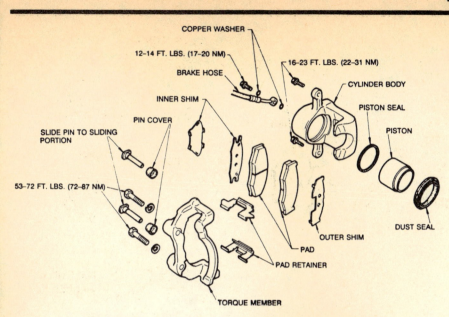

**Single piston front caliper used on Pick-Up and Pathfinder**

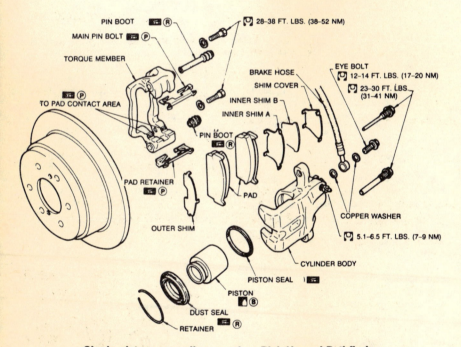

**Single piston rear caliper used on Pick-Up and Pathfinder**

ner/outer retainers and the brake pads.

4. Using a medium C-clamp and a block of wood, place the wood against the caliper piston(s) and use the C-clamp press the piston into the caliper. Some brake fluid may be expelled from the reservoir.

5. Inspect the caliper for signs of fluid leakage; if necessary, replace or rebuild the caliper.

6. Make sure the caliper moves freely on the sliding pins. Clean, repair or replace as necessary. Use a small amount of light grease to lubricate the pins.

7. To install, use new brake pads and reverse the removal procedures. Torque the sliding pin bolts to 31 ft. lbs. (42 Nm).

## Front Brake Rotor

### REMOVAL & INSTALLATION

#### Pick-Up and Pathfinder

#### 2WD

1. Raise and safely support the vehicle. Remove the wheel assembly.

2. Without disconnecting the hy-draulic hose, remove the and torque member bolts and hang the caliper from the body with wire. Do not let the caliper hang by the hose.

3. Remove the wheel bearing grease cup, cotter pin, adjusting nut cap, hub nut, thrust washer and wheel bearing.

4. Pull the wheel hub/brake rotor assembly from the wheel spindle.

5. From the rear of the brake rotor, remove the rotor-to-wheel hub bolts and the rotor.

6. Inspect the rotor for cracks, wear and/or other damage; if necessary, replace it.

**To install:**

7. Install the rotor to the hub and torque the bolts to 51 ft. lbs. (69 Nm).

8. Install the hub and wheel bearings and adjust the bearing pre-load according to the proper procedure.

9. Install the caliper and pump the brake pedal to adjust the brakes.

#### 4WD

1. Raise and support the vehicle safely under the axle case. Remove the wheels and brake calipers.

2. Block the wheels or hold the brake pedal and remove the Torx® screws to remove the locking hubs.

3. Remove the snapring from the end of the halfshaft and remove the locking hub parts.

4. From the halfshaft, remove the thrust washer, the snapring, the lockwasher screw and the lockwasher.

5. Use the proper pin wrench to loosen and remove the wheel bearing locknut.

6. Pull the wheel hub/rotor assembly from the spindle.

7. Remove the bolts to remove the rotor from the hub.

**To install:**

8. Install the rotor to the hub and torque the bolts to 51 ft. lbs. (69 Nm).

9. Install the hub and bearings and adjust the wheel bearing pre-load according to the proper procedure.

10. Install the brake caliper.

11. Install the locking hub assembly and torque the Torx® bolts to 25 ft. lbs. (34 Nm).

#### Van

1. With the vehicle on the ground, remove the hub cap and loosen the wheel bearing locknut. The torque on this nut is high enough to cause the vehicle to fall off the supports.

2. Raise and safely support the vehicle and remove the wheels.

3. Without disconnecting the hy-draulic line, remove the brake caliper and hang it from the body with wire. Do not allow the caliper to hang by the hose.

4. Remove the locknut and lock washer and pull the hub and rotor as-

sembly off. The brake rotor and the hub are all one piece and the bearing is pressed into the hub.

**To install:**

5. Install the hub, lock washer and locknut onto the spindle. Do not fully tighten the locknut yet.

6. Install the brake caliper and wheel and lower the vehicle to the ground.

7. With the vehicle on all 4 wheels, torque the locknut to 260 ft. lbs. (353 Nm). Install the hub cap. Check and adjust front wheel alignment.

### Axxess

1. Raise and safely support the vehicle and remove the front wheels.

2. Without disconnecting the hydraulic hose, remove the and torque member bolts and hang the caliper from the body with wire. Do not let the caliper hang by the hose.

3. The rotor can be pulled off the hub. If it sticks, use a penetrating lubricant and a soft mallet to break it free.

4. Installation is the reverse of removal.

## Rear Brake Rotor

### REMOVAL & INSTALLATION

#### Pick-Up and Pathfinder

1. Raise and safely support the vehicle.

2. Remove the wheel assembly.

3. Without disconnecting the hydraulic hose, remove the and torque member bolts and hang the caliper from the body with wire. Do not let the caliper hang by the hose.

4. Remove the rotor from the hub.

5. To install, reverse the removal procedures.

## Brake Drums

### REMOVAL & INSTALLATION

1. Raise and safely support the vehicle.

2. Remove the wheel assembly.

3. Pull the brake drum from the wheel hub. It may be necessary to back off the brake adjustment.

4. Inspect and/or replace the brake drum.

5. To install, reverse the removal procedures.

## Brake Shoes

### REMOVAL & INSTALLATION

1. Fully release the parking truke.

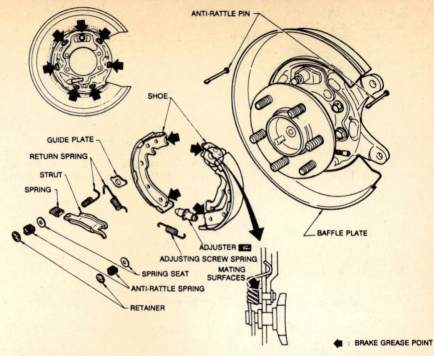

Rear brake shoe assembly on vehicles with rear disc brakes and drum parking brakes; lightly lubricate the backing plate in the areas indicated with arrows—Pick-Up and Pathfinder

2. Raise and safely support the vehicle. Remove the wheel assembly.

3. If equipped with rear disc brakes and drum type parking brakes, remove the brake caliper. Without disconnecting the hydraulic hose, remove the torque member bolts and hang the caliper from the body with wire. Do not let the caliper hang by the hose.

4. Remove the brake drum. If the drum is difficult to remove, insert 2–8mm × 1.25 screws in the disc/drum holes, tighten the screws to press the drum from the hub.

5. When removing the brake shoes and springs, be sure to remove only one side at a time so the other side is available as a reference. Remove the brake shoe retainers and the springs.

6. Separate the parking brake cable from the from the parking brake lever.

**To install:**

7. Using brake grease, lubricate the shoe adjuster and the backing plate contact points.

8. Turn the shoe adjuster all the way inward.

9. To install, reverse the removal procedures. Adjust the parking brakes by turning the adjuster wheel.

### ADJUSTMENT

1. Raise and safely support the vehicle. Make sure the parking brake lever is fully released.

2. From the rear of the backing plate, remove the adjuster hole plug.

3. Using a small prybar, rotate the adjuster wheel until the wheel will not turn.

4. Back off the adjuster wheel 7–8 notches. Make sure the wheel turns freely.

5. Install the adjuster hole plug.

## Wheel Cylinder

### REMOVAL & INSTALLATION

1. Raise and safely support the vehicle.

2. Remove the wheel, brake drum and brake shoes.

3. Disconnect the hydraulic line from the rear of the wheel cylinder.

4. Remove the wheel cylinder-to-backing plate bolts and the wheel cylinder from the backing plate.

5. To install, reverse the removal procedures. Torque the wheel cylinder-to-backing plate nuts to bolt to 65 inch lbs. (7 Nm). Bleed the brake hydraulic system.

## Parking Brake Cable

### REMOVAL & INSTALLATION

#### Rear Cable

1. Fully release the parking brake handle.

2. Raise and safely support the vehicle.

3. Loosen the adjusting nut at the adjuster cable lever.

4. Disconnect the cable from the balance lever or adjuster.

5. Disconnect the rear parking brake cable(s) from the parking brake toggle levers of the rear service brake assemblies.

6. Remove the rear parking brake cable brackets-to-chassis bracket screws.

7. Remove parking brake cable(s) from the vehicle.

8. To install, reverse the removal procedures. Apply a light coat of grease to the cables to make sure they slide properly. Adjust the parking brake cables.

### Front Cable

1. Fully release the parking brake control lever.

2. Raise and safely support the vehicle.

3. Loosen the adjusting nut at the adjuster cable lever.

4. Disconnect the cable from the balance lever or adjuster.

5. Remove the front cable bracket-to-chassis bolt(s) and the cable from the vehicle.

6. To install, reverse the removal procedures. Apply a light coat of grease to the cable to make sure it slides properly. Adjust the parking brake cables.

### ADJUSTMENT

1. Raise and safely support the vehicle.

2. Adjust the rear brakes.

3. From under the vehicle, adjust the parking brake cable locknut(s). Turn the adjusting nut until the parking brake control lever operating stroke is (using 44 lbs. force):

  10–12 clicks—console lever—Pick-Up and Pathfinder

  10–12 clicks—stick lever—2WD Pick-Up and 2WD Pathfinder

  9–11 clicks—stick lever—4WD Pick-Up and 4WD Pathfinder

  7–9 clicks—Van

  8–9 clicks—2WD Axxess

  10–11 clicks—4WD Axxess

4. Release the parking brake and make sure the rear wheels turn freely with no drag.

## Brake System Bleeding

1. Raise and safely support the vehicle.

2. Make sure the brake fluid reservoir is full. Keep checking the level during the procedure, do not allow the level to fall too low.

3. Have an assistant pump the brake pedal, then hold pressure on the pedal.

4. Connect a tube to the bleeder at the right rear wheel and put the other end in a container. Open the bleeder until the pressure is released, then close it before releasing pressure on the pedal.

5. Repeat the procedure until fluid flows from the bleeder with no air bubbles. If the bubbles do not stop, a problem is indicated in the master cylinder.

6. Repeat the procedure on the left rear, right front, then left front brakes in order.

7. Fill the fluid reservoir.

# CHASSIS ELECTRICAL

## Heater Blower Motor

### REMOVAL & INSTALLATION

#### Van

**FRONT UNIT**

1. Disconnect the negative battery cable.

2. Remove the package tray or glove box.

3. Disconnect the electrical connector from the blower motor.

4. Remove the blower motor-to-housing screws and the blower motor.

5. To install, reverse the removal procedures.

**REAR UNIT**

1. Disconnect the negative battery cable.

2. Remove the rear heater unit cover panel.

3. Disconnect the electrical connector from the blower motor.

4. Remove the blower motor-to-housing screws and the blower motor.

5. To install, reverse the removal procedures.

#### Except Van

The blower motor is accessible from under the right side of the instrument panel.

1. Disconnect the negative battery cable.

2. Disconnect the electrical connector from the blower motor.

3. Remove the blower motor-to-heater unit screws and the blower motor from the unit. It may be necessary to remove the glove box or package tray.

4. To install, reverse the removal procedures.

## Windshield Wiper Motor

### REMOVAL & INSTALLATION

#### Front Wiper

1. Disconnect the negative battery cable.

2. Remove the wiper blades and arms as an assembly from the pivots. The arms are retained to the pivots by nuts; remove the nuts and pull the arms straight off.

3. Remove the cowl top grille screws (from the front edge) and pull the grille forward to disengage the rear tabs.

4. Remove the wiper motor arm-to-connecting rod stop ring.

5. From under the instrument panel, disconnect the electrical connector from the wiper motor harness.

6. Remove the wiper motor-to-cowl screws and the wiper motor from the vehicle.

**To install:**

7. Install the motor and secure the bolts. Install the cowl grille.

8. Before installing the wiper arms, be sure the motor is in the PARK position. To do this, connect the battery and wiper motor wiring and turn the ignition switch ON. Turn the wiper switch ON and cycle the motor 3–4 times, then turn the wiper switch OFF. The motor should stop in the correct PARK position.

9. When installing the arms, the blades should be the correct distance above the lower windshield molding:

  Pick-Up and Pathfinder—0.98 in. (25mm)

  Axxess—1.62 in. (40mm)

  Van—1.12 in. (55mm) on the driver's side or 0.20 in. (5mm) on the passenger's side

#### Rear Wiper

1. Disconnect the negative battery cable.

2. From the rear door, remove the wiper blade/arm as an assembly from the pivot. The arm is retained to the pivots by a nut; remove the nut and pull the arm straight off.

3. From inside the rear door, remove wiper motor cover plate.

4. Remove the wiper motor arm-to-connecting rod stop ring.

5. Disconnect the wiring and remove the screws to remove the motor from the door.

6. Installation is the reverse of removal. Before installing the wiper arm, be sure the motor is in the PARK position. To do this, connect the battery and wiper motor wiring and turn the ignition switch ON. Turn the wiper switch ON and cycle the motor 3–4

times, then turn the wiper switch **OFF**. The motor should stop in the correct PARK position.

## Windshield Wiper Switch

The windshield wiper switch is a part of the combination switch located on the steering column. The switch can be removed without removing the steering wheel.

### REMOVAL & INSTALLATION

1. Disconnect the negative battery cable.
2. Remove the steering column covers.
3. Disconnect the windshield wiper switch electrical connector.
4. Remove the windshield wiper switch-to-combination switch screws and the windshield wiper switch from the steering column.
5. To install, reverse the removal procedures.

## Instrument Cluster

### REMOVAL & INSTALLATION

1. Disconnect the negative battery cable.
2. Remove the instrument cluster bezel screws and the bezel. Except on the Van, the bezel is also secured with clips; pull the bezel straight out after removing the screws.
3. Remove the instrument cluster-to-dash screws and pull the cluster assembly out far enough to disconnect the wiring and speedometer cable.
4. Installation is the reverse of removal.

## Headlight and Turn Signal Switch

The headlight, turn signal and dimmer switches make up the combination switch located on the steering column.

### REMOVAL & INSTALLATION

1. Disconnect the negative battery cable.
2. Remove the steering column covers.
3. Disconnect the switch electrical connector.
4. Remove the switch-to-combination switch screws and remove the switch from the steering column.
5. To install, reverse the removal procedures.

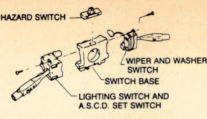

**Combination switch assembly—the steering wheel must be remove to remove the base**

## Combination Switch

The combination switch includes switches for headlights and dimmer, windshield washer and wiper, turn signal, horn contacts and cruise control, if equipped. The steering wheel must be removed to remove the combination switch as an assembly. The 2 switch stalks can be removed separately as described above.

### REMOVAL & INSTALLATION

1. Disconnect the negative battery cable. Remove the steering column covers.
2. Remove the horn pad and the steering wheel nut. Use a puller to remove the steering wheel.
3. Disconnect the wiring harness from the clip which retains it to the lower instrument panel.
4. Disconnect the electrical connectors from the combination switch.
5. Loosen the combination switch-to-steering column screw and remove the switch assembly.
6. To install, align the hole in the steering column with the protrusion on the switch base and reverse the removal procedures.

## Ignition Lock/Switch

### REMOVAL & INSTALLATION

1. Disconnect the negative battery cable.
2. From the upper steering column, remove the shell cover screws and the covers.
3. Disconnect the electrical connector from the rear of the ignition switch.
4. Drill out the 2 self shear screws from the ignition lock holder.
5. Remove the screws and the ignition switch.
6. To install, reverse the removal procedures. Torque the shear-type screws until the heads shear.

## Stoplight Switch

The stoplight switch is attached to a bracket at the top of the brake pedal.

## REMOVAL & INSTALLATION

1. Disconnect the negative battery cable.
2. From under the dash, disconnect the electrical connector from the stoplight switch.
3. Loosen and remove the locknut from the stoplight switch.
4. Unscrew the stoplight switch from the brake pedal bracket.
5. To install, reverse the removal procedures. Adjust the switch, torque the stoplight switch locknut to 11 ft. lbs. (15 Nm) and adjust the pedal height and free-play.

### ADJUSTMENT

1. Start the engine and press the brake pedal by hand until pushrod resistance is felt.
2. Use a feeler gauge to measure stoplight switch-to-brake pedal gap: it should be 0.012–0.039 in. (0.3–1.0mm).
3. If necessary, disconnect the electrical connector from the stoplight switch, loosen the switch locknut and adjust the gap. Torque the lock nut to 11 ft. lbs. (15 Nm).

## Clutch Cruise Control Switch

If equipped with cruise control, the clutch switch is attached to a bracket mounted to the upper portion of the clutch pedal bracket. This switch replaces the stopper bolt and is used to set pedal height.

### REMOVAL & INSTALLATION

1. Disconnect the negative battery cable.
2. Disconnect the electrical connector from the clutch switch.
3. Loosen the locknut and unscrew the switch from the bracket.
4. To install, screw the clutch switch into the bracket until the correct pedal height is established and torque the locknut to 11 ft. lbs. (15 Nm).

**Pick-Up and Pathfinder**
    2.4L engine—9.29–9.69 in. (236–246mm)
    3.0L engine—8.94–9.33 in. (227–237mm)
    **Van**—6.97–7.25 in. (177–184mm)
    **Axxess**—6.97–7.25 in. (177–184mm)

**NOTE: The pedal height is the distance from the floor board to the pedal pad with the carpet removed.**

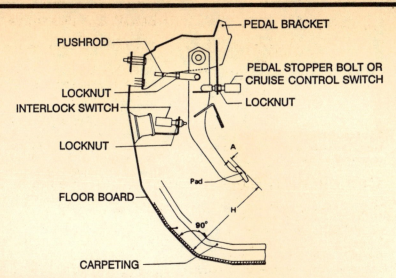

PEDAL BRACKET

PUSHROD

PEDAL STOPPER BOLT OR
CRUISE CONTROL SWITCH

LOCKNUT
INTERLOCK SWITCH

LOCKNUT

LOCKNUT

FLOOR BOARD

A

Pad

H

90°

CARPETING

**Clutch pedal switch adjustment; vehicles with cruise control use the switch to set pedal height**

# Clutch Interlock Switch

The clutch interlock switch is attached to a bracket mounted to the cowl.

## REMOVAL & INSTALLATION

1. Disconnect the negative battery cable.

2. Disconnect the electrical connector from the clutch interlock switch.

3. Loosen the locknut and unscrew the switch from the bracket.

4. To install, use a feeler gauge and screw the clutch interlock switch into the bracket.

5. Fully depress the clutch pedal and adjust the gap between the clutch pedal stopper bracket and the threaded end of the clutch interlock switch. The gap should be 0.012–0.039 in. (0.3–1.0mm) on Pick-Up, Pathfinder and Axxess or 0.059–0.138 in. (1.5–3.5mm) on Van.

6. Torque the locknut to 11 ft. lbs. (15 Nm), reconnect the wiring and make sure the started operates only when the clutch pedal is fully depressed.

# Fuses, Circuit Breakers and Relays

## LOCATION

### Axxess

The main fuse block is under the dashboard to the left of the steering column. Some of the relays are on the fuse block, the rest are on the secondary panel under the hood near the battery. All relays are color coded according to internal circuitry and should be replaced with relays of the same color.

### Van

The main fuse block is under the dashboard to the left of the steering column. The battery is under a panel in the floor behind the driver's seat. The turn signal flasher and all of the relays are in the right side dashboard behind the glove compartment.

### Pick-Up and Pathfinder

The main fuse block is behind a panel to the right or the steering column. The turn signal flasher is to the left of the brake pedal. A series relays in mounted under the hood on the right fender. All relays are color coded according to internal circuitry and should be replaced with relays of the same color.

# Computers

## LOCATION

### Axxess

The main engine ECU is under the dashboard immediately in front of the shift lever. The cruise control ECU is behind the driver's side kick panel and the power window amplifier is in the driver's door.

### Van

Most of the electronic control units are in the right side dashboard behind the glove compartment. The main engine ECU is behind the wall panel directly above the battery.

### Pick-Up and Pathfinder

The main engine ECU is under the passenger's seat along with the automatic transmission control unit. The power window amplifier is behind the passenger's side kick panel. The door lock timer and cruise control ECU are under the driver's seat.

# Turn Signal Flasher

## LOCATION

### Axxess

The turn signal flasher is next to the brake pedal.

### Van

The turn signal flasher is in the right side dashboard behind the glove compartment.

### Pick-Up and Pathfinder

The turn signal flasher is to the left of the brake pedal.

## SE MODEL

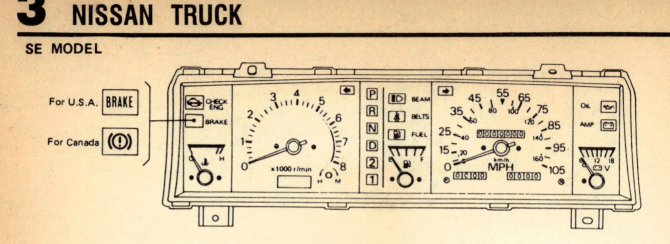

Voltage regulator

Instrument cluster   Pick-Up and Pathfinder